Controversy in American Education

Controversy in American Education

AN ANTHOLOGY OF CRUCIAL ISSUES / SECOND EDITION

Harold Full

QUEENS COLLEGE
OF THE CITY UNIVERSITY OF NEW YORK

THE MACMILLAN COMPANY, NEW YORK
COLLIER-MACMILLAN LIMITED, LONDON

Printed in the United States of America

The Macmillan Company
866 Third Avenue, New York, New York 10022

Collier-Macmillan Canada, Ltd., Toronto, Ontario

Library of Congress catalog card number: 75-165243

First Printing

Preface

Controversy is a part of the American educational tradition, a tradition that it shares with the total democratic society. In education controversy has played an influential role in the growth and development of formal training, from its meager beginnings in Colonial times to the present-day extensive network of public and private institutions encompassing prenursery schools through postdoctoral university programs. The role of controversy in education, however, has changed markedly in that long history. Earlier struggles—such as those represented by Horace Mann's movement for a free, public, nonsectarian common school—centered on a few issues which were debated over long periods of time.

Today's controversy in education has no single focus; conflicting and contradictory opinions are voiced on every aspect of education in an ever-changing pattern of emphases and degrees. One is easily tempted to regard controversy as a modern phenomenon. A more accurate observation is that current controversy to some degree represents an intensification of yesterday's conflicts, yet in larger measure it grows out of conflicts and challenges that are unique to a highly complex, technological society.

The readings in this anthology represent a sampling of the dissension, debates, and disputes that characterize controversy in American education today. The selections are designed specifically for students, teachers, administrators, and laymen who want to engage in the challenging intellectual task of objectively examining their own thoughts and feelings, of expanding their knowledge of current conflicts, of deepening their understanding both of education and of society, and of seeing an intimate relationship between them. Those who peruse these readings to find confirmation of previously held beliefs can discover the truly complex nature of current controversy and can be stimulated to seek more informed positions. Controversy itself is born when conflict arises, when challenges confront us, when doubt is expressed. An examination of controversy in American education can proceed productively only if inquiry begins not with a statement but with a question.

One of the modern-day myths that seriously interferes with intelligent discussion of crucial issues in education is the commonly heard expression, "There are two sides to every question." Presumably, the intent of this statement is to force the listener to be "objective," to examine a view opposed to his own. Unfortunately, the ultimate effect is the stifling of further inquiry. An individual exposed only to the extreme positions on any issue is prevented from observing the wide range of alternatives. John Dewey cautioned in his 1938 Kappa Delta Pi address that many of the crucial mistakes made in education stem from seeing problems in an either-or context, a position that recognizes no intermediate possibilities.[1]

In keeping with this point of view, no attempt has been made to select articles for and articles against a particular issue in order to achieve a "balanced" presentation. If the issues selected are indeed crucial ones, then the variety and diversity of current views represent a broad range of alternative positions, some varying subtly, yet importantly, from others, some representing a wider divergency of opinion. Obviously, because of the limitations of space, the readings contained herein cannot present all views on all issues. The scope of opinions included does give a representative sampling of the issues and permits an adequate presentation of the authors' points of view so that the reader can appreciate the authentic flavor of current controversies in education. It is obvious that the issues included are not of equal importance, nor should it be assumed that the amount of space given to any issue is an accurate reflection of its relative importance. In some instances it was necessary to include several selections about one issue so that a reasonably sufficient sampling of views could be presented; in other cases, a single article gives a thorough discussion of basic considerations and alternatives.

This anthology begins with an original essay by the editor on the nature of controversy designed to assist the reader in examining more carefully the issues and problems encountered throughout the remainder of the volume. In Part I the readings are focused on significant background information concerning the complex nature of change and conflict in contemporary society. The editor regards this knowledge as essential for any intelligent insight into the issues and problems of education and the schools. Frequently, the study of education proceeds in almost total disregard of the political, economic, social, or scientific mainstreams of the culture, even though some tacit recognition is made of the belief that the schools are a part of a larger society which affects them. Especially pertinent in the study of controversy is some conception of the nature of the society in which we live; controversies in education are often the reflections of the larger conflicts in society itself.

Part II deals with what some individuals might regard as the heart of current educational controversy: the manifold demands on the schools and the schools' efforts—some feeble, some effective—to meet them. In large measure these demands come from the consumers of education, the children and youth. Perhaps no greater challenge has ever been faced by American education than the current one to provide a vital educational program of quality and excellence that will engage the

[1] John Dewey, *Experience and Education* (New York: The Macmillan Company, 1938).

interest and intellect of *all* youth—the haves and have-nots, the advantaged and the disadvantaged, the urban and the rural, the difficult and those desirably motivated. Part III enlists the talents of a diverse group of respected writers who exhibit a sensitivity to the challenges that youth proclaim.

The readings in Part IV are organized around two mutually reinforcing themes: (1) the problems concerning the education profession, its organization, its qualifications, its autonomy; and (2) the problems concerning the teacher and his ever-changing role. One eye-opening essay in particular, "Will Teacher Be the New Drop-Out?" warns of the widening gap that appears to be developing between the profession and the consumers they serve.

Recently, it seems, everybody is in the education act. The educator is under attack from all kinds of controversial pressure groups. Understandably, much of this pressure originates with the very families whose children benefit most from the daily activities of the teacher. However, there is strong reason to believe that too often these groups are reacting to secondary or outside influences in pressing their demands. Part V of this anthology is intended as a brief introduction to some of the outside or secondary influences and pressures. Here we look at the relationship between education and industry. We study the interrelationships between teaching institutions and day-care centers. And we observe, ever so fleetingly, the disputed though obvious connection between television and teaching. From the limited space devoted to these outside influences, it will be obvious that this section should be regarded as an overview, but one which, it is hoped, will encourage readers to delve more deeply.

The editor is grateful for the generous permission of the authors and publishers to reprint their material in this anthology. Because these works are organized in a form that differs from their original presentation, the authors' divergent views gain new significance. Through their opinions a more meaningful understanding of the essential character of controversy in American education is seen, not in isolation but in relation to the thinking of other authors. These new dimensions, added to his own experience and background, should lead the reader to a deeper analysis of the issues and should prevent a premature crystallization of thought and attitude.

Miss Maureen Nasse gave valuable assistance in compiling this book of readings.

H. F.

Suggestions to Instructors

To engage students in a vital and meaningful understanding of the crucial problems of contemporary American education and to help them participate in the educationally valuable experience of discussing controversial issues are the purposes for which this anthology is designed. In order to achieve these important general objectives as well as specific aims tailored to individual classroom situations, many flexible arrangements for using this book are possible.

The readings meet the needs of both undergraduate and graduate levels of instruction and of both elementary and secondary specialization. The kinds of courses for which it can be adapted are also varied. Although ideally suited to a basic foundations course characteristic of many college undergraduate or graduate programs, these readings can also provide an important focus for courses in the history of education, educational sociology, educational administration, curriculum and methods (both general and special), and philosophy of education as well as for courses, such as current educational problems and issues and history of ideas in education, whose organizational structure cuts across conventional areas. Within each of these particular situations the book lends itself to a variety of approaches. The ideas here presented are intended not to proscribe or limit the uses of this book but to stimulate each instructor to create methods or activities that meet the specific requirements of his course. The following suggestions reflect the editor's experience in teaching a basic foundations course at Queens College for the past fifteen years.

1. Certain important philosophical questions in education should direct and guide the students' reading and thinking, regardless of the specific issue under discussion. These questions are implicit in all the readings, yet need to be referred to from time to time to provide an understanding of the assumptions on which each author's article is based. What does it mean to be "educated" in today's world? To what objectives should education be directed? What are the most desirable means or conditions for this education to take place? What is teaching? What is learning? What is knowledge? What knowledge is of the most worth? Who should be educated? For how long? Under what conditions? What is the role of the school in a democratic society? How does the school supplement, complement, or coincide

with other social agencies? What is the source for curriculum content? Since everything cannot be taught, how is intelligent selection to be made? What kind of organization is necessary to carry out the objectives? What is subject matter? This list is not exhaustive, but it suggests the kind of questions and concerns that are inherent in all the material in this volume.

2. A specific assignment that can be made for any article is a written paper or an oral report focused on these questions: What is the author's major thesis? What examples does he give to support this thesis? What are the implications of his views to problems in other fields or in the larger society? What questions would you raise with the author's point of view? In what ways does his position relate to other authors you have read? Did the author force you to examine your previously held ideas, values, or beliefs?

3. Students can prepare a short questionnaire to record the reactions of parents, neighbors, students, and teachers regarding the important aspects of any controversial questions raised by the articles. This assignment can be varied by using the technique of a personal interview.

4. A valuable supplementary resource for individual or group assignment that is not used widely is that of speeches recorded on tape. Most educational organizations and other groups record important speeches from their national conventions on tapes which are available for rent or purchase; college and public libraries and audiovisual departments are sources for such material. The instructor or student can also make tapes of important events from radio or television.

5. Germane to the subject matter of this book is an assignment tracing the historical development of one of the issues presented. Such an assignment is well adapted for a semester project or a term paper. Consider, for instance, the general topic of religion and the schools. Throughout the history of the United States, many problems and issues have centered around this theme, though never in the same manner. Every issue grew out of the political, social, and economic changes and conditions at the time and can be understood only in relation to those larger events. In fact, a large theme such as this has such a wealth of material that it could be undertaken by several students, each developing a particular phase of the historical background.

6. The instructor may wish to develop an approach almost the opposite of the historical by focusing on the contemporary. Around each issue in this volume, the student will be able to research in current professional journals or scholarly periodicals for material to update or expand the information presented herein. In our ever-changing world new aspects, new knowledge, and new developments spur authors into print with new ideas and reformulations of the old.

7. The format of this book groups articles around five vital centers of conflict and dispute—the society, the school, the youth, the profession and the teacher, and some outside influences on education. Another possible method of organizing the material might have been around the issues themselves. This approach was rejected in favor of the former for two primary reasons. In the first place, an organization around issues forces an editor to select either the superficial approach of using only the pro's and con's of the specific issue or the depth approach showing many

alternative points of view of a limited number of issues. Secondly, the present organization provides the instructor with greater opportunities to help the student assume more responsibility for his own learning. In the present format the student is forced not only to identify the issues but also to become more skillful in seeing differing points of view which may vary only subtly. Further, the instructor has the opportunity of making assignments from the selected references or from his own sources, to help the student obtain greater insight into and a fuller understanding of the complex nature of each issue.

8. Using the material in this book as a starting point, the instructor can tailor individual assignments for investigation and research in the student's subject specialization. What changes and new developments in his specialization have led to conflicts and disputes that give rise to controversial issues? This gives the student an opportunity to apply knowledge gained in one area to a different situation and to become more skillful in searching for crucial issues. Such an investigation can be made at any level—early childhood education, elementary education, or secondary education, with the secondary level further subdivided by subject fields.

9. Panel discussions are invaluable in helping the students become more directly involved in issues under study. Care must be taken, however, to see that the members of the panel understand that a panel discussion is not a debate, not an argument, not a formal presentation of prepared material. Advance preparation is indeed required, but the panel itself should be a forum for the *sharing* of ideas concerning, in this instance, a controversial issue. Whether the panel members are selected by the instructor or chosen by the students themselves, they need guidance from the instructor about their organization and presentation. With adequate preparation, no other method is so effective in helping students to become engaged in the process of identifying, examining, and evaluating controversial ideas.

10. The above suggestions, together with the instructor's own ideas for presentation and discussion, are all valuable means for evaluating the student's progress. Yet, within the context of these means, the formal examination plays an important role. Among the various types of examinations available, it seems almost a necessity that the essay form be used as the most appropriate for the subject matter of controversy. Such examinations, however, are extremely time consuming to evaluate. The editor has found that a variation of the essay form, which he calls an "essay-type" examination, can be at least as reliable, and in some respects more accurate, than the regular essay form. An "essay-type" examination requires the student to list the major ideas or points he would use to develop his answer without actually formulating his thoughts into a finished essay. Such procedure provides the student with more time to think about the problem and forces him to be more precise in setting down and organizing his ideas.

11. Two additional instructional aids are found at the conclusion of the editor's introductions to each of the five parts of this volume: (1) questions for further study, which focus on the specific material in each section; and (2) a bibliography of carefully screened, selected references which provide the instructor and the student with an important guide for further study in depth of the issues under discussion.

Contents

Controversy in American Education

The Nature of Controversy

Controversy, whether in education or in other areas of social life, has its basis in the contradictory yet interrelated needs, ideas, beliefs, and values of men. The intellectual expression of the conflicts, anxieties, and hostilities in society, controversy serves to ease tensions by permitting the peaceful processes of discussion and debate to minimize the danger of strife. Even though some form of conflict is a precondition for controversy, controversy itself can channel these continuing conflicts in desirable directions by creating an intellectual climate which, by moving beyond the immediate dispute, can permit opportunities to develop for reasoned evaluation or resolution. Such creative interaction can prepare the society for intelligent change and progress.[1]

Although controversy alone cannot account for all the myriad changes that take place in a society, it can and does set the stage for changes to occur. The United States, as the most open, most mobile, most dynamic society in the world, is a society that is characterized by the greatest frequency of controversies. Openness of a society is conducive to divergent ideas and beliefs. It creates an atmosphere for the acceptance of change. The society that resists change and controversy fails to realize the greater danger that confronts it, a danger arising from its inadaptability. In a society dominated by revolutionary changes taking place at an accelerating pace, as is characteristic of the United States today, it is essential to develop an intelligent understanding of the nature of controversy and its role in a contemporary democratic society.

Controversy is embedded in the tradition of American democracy. The freedoms embodied in the Constitution were not given to Americans; they were the result of a long series of struggles in which controversy played an important role. Controversy helped to resolve the enormous problems facing a growing nation: the settling of forty million new immigrants, the giant growth of industry, the tremendous expansion westward, the zealous movements for social and political reform, and the unique development of a system of free public schools open to all. The continuous give and take of conflicting points of view created levels of understanding that were more inclusive than those represented by the ideas or practices of the contending parties. Through this process new questions were raised and new alternatives were seen. Current pressing problems, some new and some reformulations of the old, are being tested in the fires of controversy. Through intelligent direction of controversy, new concepts and new modes of behavior can emerge to provide society with enough elasticity to meet changes.

When past and present controversies are examined, at least six basic phases can

[1] Some ideas in this essay have been freely adapted from Lewis A. Coser, *The Functions of Social Conflict* (Glencoe, Ill.: The Free Press, 1956), and Georg Simmel, *Conflict and the Web of Group Associations* (Glencoe, Ill.: The Free Press, 1955).

be identified. The term phases of controversy (stages of controversy would also be acceptable), rather than kinds or types of controversy, was deliberately selected to indicate the dynamic nature of controversy. The word phases suggests the movement that takes place in discussion of conflicting points of view. Even when a controversy becomes hardened into intransigent positions attracting few new participants or new ideas, it becomes static only temporarily and will appear again in new dress to meet current fashion. Once this quality of controversy is recognized, it should be understood that the following identified phases are not intended to make distinctions so sharp that rigid boundaries are established between them. Nor do controversies proceed precisely in the manner outlined. They can and do begin at any one of the phases, or at several phases simultaneously. Being aware of these qualifications, the student should find these classifications useful in stimulating him to closer examination of the conflicting points of view presented in the articles in this anthology and helpful in identifying the dominant phases in current disputes.

Phase One. *One phase is represented by oversimplification. Very complicated problems are reduced to a single cause. Statements such as "The way to prevent juvenile delinquency is to impose a curfew" are typical. Little effort is made to identify the issue under discussion or to evaluate it within the conditions that currently prevail. This leads to great fragmentation. What is seen are single units, individual parts, without any relationship to each other or to the whole.*

Phase Two. *A second phase is identified by polarization of thought. Arguments are put in forms of extremes; beliefs are formulated in an either-or context. The participants are so profoundly discontented that they are able to identify only the contrasts between opposites. Charges are often made which cannot be substantiated. This phase is further characterized by the introduction of irrelevant information. Frequently, too, proponents of opposing views are derided and belittled by personal attacks. The disputants will often take refuge in the past, producing "answers" for the contemporary problem in the views of traditional authority figures, often misquoted or quoted out of context to bolster a preconceived position.*

Phase Three. *As controversy proceeds, the discussion is sometimes directed against a secondary target instead of the original cause of the conflict. The danger here is twofold: it is possible to hurt or offend the secondary target, and it is possible, unless care is taken, to mistake the secondary target for the source of the problem. This practice makes repeated use of stereotype and exaggerated generalization as techniques to suppress discussion of fundamental issues. For example, some politicians who opposed the federal medical care program for the aged used the argument that this program was "socialized medicine," knowing that with many people the phrase would carry such a negative connotation that they would not even consider the alternatives of providing and financing medical care for the aged. These techniques used against controversial programs, however, are harmless compared with their destructive quality when employed against individuals or groups. A moment's reflection can recall numerous instances in which group stereotype has done immeasurable harm to the group and to individuals within the group and which in turn has effectively prevented further examination of the real problem.*

Phase Four. *A fourth phase involves controversy among individuals within the same group. It can best be characterized by attempts to impose conformity upon members of a group. Through discussions of controversial matters groups are assisted in becoming established and maintained. Controversy, in this instance, helps a group affirm its identity. Conformity to the views of the group under these conditions has a positive value; it serves to maintain unity. If groups are engaged in continued controversy with those outside the group, however, they can in time become intolerant to individuals within who deviate from the common ideas, values, or beliefs shared by most of the other members. Their conflicting positions are regarded as a threat both to the unity of the group and to its identity. The disturbances in Chicago during the 1968 presidential nomination convention illustrate such intragroup conflicts and controversies. Should the in-group hostility continue long enough, the group may restrict its membership only to those who conform to the will of the majority. The group then tends to assume the character of a sect. In order to maintain cohesion, it may even search for outside "threats" though none are actually present. Many extremist groups in the United States tend to fit this description.*

Phase Five. *Another phase can be identified as a search for common ground. Participants in the controversy explore ways and means to resolve the conflict. They seek alternatives that may exist between the most extreme positions represented; they seek views or ideas that parallel and could displace other values or beliefs. Even though their ultimate goals or beliefs remain widely separated, ground for compromise or for resolution of the controversy is sought on lesser values or interests which the participants may share. In fact, what is sought is some resolution of the controversy in terms that make possible the continuation of differences and even fundamental disagreements.*

Charles Frankel puts it this way:

> *The failure to see that men can work well together without the same ultimate goals leads to a failure to take account of the most distinctive technique of a liberal society for maintaining voluntary cooperation–the technique of compromise. For compromise does not only take place when men are bound by a common creed. It takes place at least as often for a much simpler reason–that men have other values besides those that are in dispute. As a result, they do not choose to risk everything on a single issue.*[2]

Phase Six. *As controversy continues, we can expect to discern a shifting of emphasis among participants. Positions change as new, more objective, ground is broken. New kinds of questions are asked, new alternatives sought. Entirely different views of the world and new images of man can be introduced. From these, new perspectives are gained on old problems and new ones are discerned. The participants and those on the sidelines are educated to new ideas.*

[2] Charles Frankel, *The Case for Modern Man* (New York: Harper and Brothers, 1956), p. 82.

It is evident from the description of this phase that it represents the most productive plane on which a controversy can be waged. Unfortunately, not all, perhaps only a few, controversies ever reach this stage. Often the participants are trapped or trap themselves at one of the beginning phases and fail to realize the potential of the issue under discussion or their own potential for intellectual growth. Yet the opposite is also true. Some controversies begin at this phase and descend to the level of oversimplification or polarization of thought where stereotypes are substituted for reason and logic. John Dewey's philosophy of education is a case in point. His theory of experience based on intellectual and moral standards for a scientific age offered a new vision of what education was all about, of what must be worthy of the name education. Soon, however, those who took up his banner, being either uninformed or misinformed, substituted catch phrases or slogans—"progressive" education versus "traditional" education—for the fundamental issue. They became more noted for what they opposed than for what they stood for.

Implicit in the six phases just described is a hierarchy through which controversy may move, proceeding from the least informed to the most informed. Implicit also in these descriptions are various levels at which controversy may be joined. The word levels, in this sense, implies the ability to see the issue under discussion from its simplest formulation to its most complex proportions or to see its immediate and practical as well as its theoretical dimensions. The more levels we are able to identify the greater is our understanding and the deeper our insight into the controversy.

An illustration of the levels of controversy is the famous Scopes trial in Tennessee in 1925, concerning the teaching of Darwin's theory of evolution in the public schools. What began as a controversy between science and religion later became a clash among various shades of opinion represented by the religious modernists and the religious fundamentalists. Still later, the controversy was focused in larger issues surrounding the relation of church and state in the control of education. Embedded within these central concerns was a range of opinion grouped around other conflicting themes—religion versus atheism, rural versus urban, old versus new, conservative versus liberal, censorship versus freedom. Because much of the discussion represented extreme positions, attention was diverted from some of the major, overriding issues implicit in a thorough understanding of the controversy—What is science? What is religion? Does a teacher have the right, in the name of truth, to indoctrinate children in what those children's parents profoundly believe to be wrong? Does a minority have the right to force its will upon the majority?

The negative and positive features of controversy are revealed from further examination of the six phases presented. At first glance the negative aspects seem to loom large. Frequently in controversy thought is polarized, issues are oversimplified, objects and groups are stereotyped, and pressures are exerted for conformity. In assessing the negative results of controversy, some individuals see these factors as paramount, leading them to the conclusion that controversy should be avoided.

This view seems rather widespread in the field of education. Some teachers and administrators in the public schools and some of those engaged in teacher education in the colleges become overly sensitive, hence defensive, when conflicting opinions are aired concerning important educational issues of our time. Part of this defensive posture might be accounted for by a lack of historical perspective. By being involved in the wealth of current educational controversy, some educators are led to believe that contemporary conflicts are the first, or at least the greatest, the schools have ever faced; they fail to realize not only that the disputes of the past were many and long and bitter but that much positive progress resulted from them.

Then, too, it is not uncommon that little distinction is made in the source of criticism. Most criticism of the schools comes from those who are dedicated in their support of public education; criticism is not the exclusive product of a minority who seek to subvert the goals of American education. Lack of discrimination in evaluating sources of criticism unfortunately is reflected in opposing arguments that often are a strong defense of the status quo—of not only the strengths of public education, but of its weaknesses. Quite naturally, this defensive stance can give the impression of weakness or infer that an apology is in order for the unsettled state of affairs in education today. Such reactions prevent professionals in education from providing informed leadership to the public and meeting their responsibility to develop with youth a mature, reasoned, and sophisticated approach to controversy.

The positive dimensions of controversy seem to outweigh the negative. Not all controversies are brought out into the open; some are suppressed by individuals or the group. The motivation for expressing a difference of opinion thus must be strong enough to overcome any doubts that a person or group may have. In this sense, then, conflicting points of view can have a counterbalancing effect on the pressures for conformity in society. The motivation for expressing differing views provides democracy with a vital spirit for self-renewal.

The act of entering into controversy serves to establish relations where none existed before and to provide the possibility that other relations will follow. Once these new relationships are created, the climate is ripe for additional interaction. Further, through the course of controversy, new situations develop that call for new rules, new norms, new ideas, and new values to be created while old rules, norms, ideas, and values are being revised, reformulated, or replaced. Thus, the very nature of controversy safeguards the society from becoming static and helps the participants to derive inner satisfaction. By reducing hostilities or by diminishing tensions the participants are able to view their problems more objectively.

Controversy assists in maintaining a balance in society. The pluralistic structure of American society provides stability for its social system through the interdependence of conflicting groups whose crisscrossing controversies provide opportunities for individuals and groups to test their relative strength and to reassess their relative power. By intelligent discussion of controversial issues individuals and groups are allowed to shift and choose among various values and beliefs. Through this process new forms of flexible social arrangements are brought about which create avenues for positive and desirable social action. Thus, controversy is a vital form of social interaction. Through this form of social interaction the area is widened for man to act by free choice and not by coercion. The free give and take of conflicting ideas, values, and beliefs forces man to go beyond the parochial point of view, to expand his horizons. This process maintains the vitality of the democratic open society and provides the means by which the society can continue to be open.

Conformity, in its various guises, is the enemy of the openness of society which controversy helps to sustain. The throttling of discussion by conformity closes many avenues of social communication and reduces opportunities for individuals to think, to criticize, and to evaluate for themselves. Further, in narrowing the choices available to the individual or the opportunities for making choices, conformity progressively restricts personal and social responsibilities. Conformity encourages the receptive mind; controversy develops the inquiring mind. The unsettling pace of modern change breeds doubt and uneasiness of mind on which conformity thrives by providing a false sense of security. Thus, man is robbed of his vision of an endless future with unlimited possibilities, and his awareness of belonging to a larger community of mankind is dulled.

There are moments in the lives of most men when we yearn to escape into a more simple past age when society and its problems were less complex, or to escape to some future utopia where common agreement and consent will banish problems and conflicts and bring continual happiness, comfort, and security. There are other moments when man feels resentful that problems he did not create are imposed upon him. Yet in these resentful moments, as in the moments of escape, he knows that he cannot evade the exceptional moment in which he is living with all its problems, crises, and controversies, nor can he ignore them. He knows that he must live in their full gravity under all conditions and with all consequences.

Selected References

Berlyne, D. E. *Conflict, Arousal, and Curiosity.* New York: McGraw-Hill Book Company, 1960.

Coser, Lewis A., and Bernard Rosenberg. *Sociological Theory: A Book of Readings* (3rd ed.). New York: The Macmillan Company, 1969.

________. *The Functions of Social Conflict.* Glencoe, Ill.: The Free Press, 1956.

Falk, W. D. "Symposium: Reasons." *The Journal of Philosophy* (November 1963), 702–718.

Henderson, Donald. "Minority Response and the Conflict Problem." *Phylon* (Spring 1964), 18–26.

Horowitz, Irving L. "Consensus, Conflict, and Cooperation: A Sociological Inventory." *Social Forces* (December 1962), 177–188.

Simmel, Georg. *Conflict and the Web of Group Associations.* Glencoe, Ill.: The Free Press, 1955.

PART I The Society: Change and Crisis

The forces of change have never been so busy as in recent years. And with these changes have come new problems and new crises for society. Man has been forced to continually adjust to new surroundings. No sooner did he learn to adapt to the amazing sophistication of advanced scientific intelligence and technological knowledge that allowed him to land astronauts on the moon, than was he forced to cope with widespread ecological and environmental problems and a revolution in human affairs.

Important areas of the vast changes continually going on in America include the increasing specialization of labor; the continued growth of great centers of population and their movement toward the coasts; the ever-increasing mobility of occupations, with a corresponding mobility of population; the development of new fields, such as cybernetics, to identify the processes of communication and control in men and machines; the growth of special interest groups and of government; the continued expansion of the concept of human rights; the fundamental transformation of the economy in which the production of services is now greater than the production of goods; the reversal in the classical conception of work and leisure, with the less educated having more time for leisure than those with more skill or knowledge; and the tremendous advances in biology and chemistry, with corresponding advances in allied fields such as medicine. These and an almost endless list of others represent an extraordinary explosion of knowledge in just the past twenty years which has affected practically every sphere of human endeavor.

Most of these changes are difficult to comprehend in depth. The focus is likely to be on such dramatic forms of change as the incredible ventures into space rather than on the changes constantly going on in the normal ways of living. Difficult as it is to grasp the significance of change, there is yet another important dimension to take into account—the rapidity of change. Alvin Toffler refers to the phenomenon of "too much change in too short a time" as "future shock."[1] *In times past, the rate of change was slow enough to permit a comfortable margin of acceptance over*

[1] Alvin Toffler, *Future Shock* (New York: Random House, 1970), p. 4.

a long period of time. Such luxury does not exist today. Current changes are hardly understood by the average individual before vast new transitions are in order. This accelerating pace of change has permeated the culture to such an extent that the basic values and beliefs characteristic of Western civilization are being challenged, revised, and reformulated. The quantitative effect of change is responsible for a qualitatively different society.

This radical transformation of the world in which we live, with the resultant conflicts, tensions, and anxieties, leaves man with few opportunities to reflect on what is happening and where all these changes may take him. His responses are many and varied, informed and uninformed. Some of the changes have been accepted and are already affecting the lives of most members of society at all levels; others, representing vastly different ideas or methods, are neither widely understood nor generally accepted. Some changes develop as alternative ways of production or of ideas and beliefs that parallel existing ideas or processes; others are more subtle, more fragmentary, involving only separate specialities that do not immediately affect the whole society.

Some people react to change by withdrawing and seeking security in the past where, it is thought, answers to most of the current problems exist. Katherine Kuh suggests that "as our world becomes larger our sights tend to shrink, in repudiation, perhaps, of a vastly expanded universe."[2] Others, overwhelmed by the change going on about them, try to ignore these events as if by their neglect the changes will disappear. A more arrogant variation of the same attitude is that expressed by a shrug of the shoulder and a "So what?" when we are reminded of the change in the world in which we live.

Those who have anything to do with education in America today have a solemn responsibility to reflect on the revolutionary changes going on about them and to help prepare the children and youth to meet an ever-changing future. Instead of becoming engulfed by what is happening around him, each individual must be helped to see that man's intelligence can govern the changes taking place, can shape their direction, and can create enlightened attitudes toward desirable changes that are necessary for the growth of a dynamic society.

The importance of studying change is the certainty that changes will increase in the future. It is especially pertinent to the study of controversy in education that we have some conception of the nature of society in which we live because many of the conflicts of the larger society are reflected in those that affect education. It is in this belief that this section of the readings is presented.

The great transition that man is currently making is perceptively viewed by Kenneth Boulding as being the stage of postcivilization. By comparing the extent of change brought about by past revolutions, Boulding makes it clear that the current transition greatly exceeds those that have gone before. It is a transition that affects not only science, technology, and forms of energy, but one that shapes social institutions, beliefs, and ideologies—both in Western society and in cultures around

[2] Katherine Kuh, "Art's Voyage of Discovery," *Saturday Review* (August 29, 1964), 150.

the world. Yet he sees four new horsemen of the apocalypse who can drastically alter either the transition or its direction—war, population, technology, and ennui. Although not dismissing their relevance, Emmanuel Mesthene, executive director of the Harvard University Program on Science and Technology, sees these four basically as a "failure of nerve," a lack of faith in the ability of man's intelligence to achieve almost anything man wants it to. The risk is great, but so is the reward—the wisdom for mastery over our technology.

While Boulding and Mesthene explore the changing dimensions of science and society, Barry Commoner concentrates on man's increasing reliance on the "balance of nature" and our "lack of achievement in solving social problems" despite "intruding technology." Commoner is supported in his argument that man must set new objectives for scientific accomplishments by Paul Ehrlich, Stanford University biologist and Center Associate, who underlines the fact that the mounting ecological consequences of technological breakthroughs have been widely ignored. His concern is no less real when he discusses the computer's "brainwashing" role and the dangers of developing increasingly better technology while ignoring the critical questions of changing human attitudes.

Concern with the ever-spreading pollution problem is also voiced by eminent British scientific author and United Nations science adviser Lord Ritchie-Calder, who views pollution as worldwide and requiring intergovernmental action. His observations bring into sharp focus population problems we will undoubtedly experience in the next ten to fifteen years, including an "Ecumenopolis—World City" like that suggested by Doxladis, where one urban area will "ooze into the next" with accompanying pollution and destruction of the biosphere. The American dreams of "escape" and "frontier freedoms" are contrasted with the ever-spreading decay and stifling traffic jams, smog, and pollution of modern society and its slums by C. W. Griffin, Jr.

Henry Steele Commager sees a different kind of environmental problem. Quoting from an 1838 address by young Abraham Lincoln, Commager discusses lawlessness and its effects on society. Endorsing Lincoln's statement, "If destruction be our lot, we must ourselves be its author and finisher," this educator, historian, and man of letters details the relevance of the statement today. Dr. Herbert Otto also calls for a better understanding of our "interpersonal environment" in a changing society where the lack of a "close and meaningful relationship" is presented as a key reason man may become increasingly irritated, ugly, and violent.

Robert L. Heilbroner discusses "immediate survival" and "ultimate salvation" in an address on national priorities. He details military versus civilian needs and private versus public interests and asks what should "be on top of the agenda." R. Freeman Butts also looks to a future of continuous change but suggests we "must keep both the future and past in mind" to accurately chart our present position on the way to a "truly ecumenical civilization embracing a world society and a world culture."

Questions for Discussion and Further Study

1. Do you agree with Emmanuel Mesthene's hypothesis that there will come a time when machines will put most people permanently out of work? What will man occupy himself with if that happens? Will we find better ways to employ leisure? Even if we do, will leisure be an adequate substitute for work? What does the author mean by "Social Heracliteanism?"

2. In addition to the views of Mesthene and Commoner concerning values in an age of science presented in this section, two essays listed in the selected references discuss this theme from the standpoint of scientists. The opinions are those of Rene Dubos of the Rockefeller Institute and Ludwig von Bertalanffy, Professor of Zoology and Psychology at the University of Alberta, Canada. In what respects do these views complement or contrast with those of Mesthene or Commoner? Which author seems to reflect the spirit of "The Great Transition" by Kenneth Boulding? In addition to reading these and other pertinent materials, what other kinds of experiences can be suggested for further study of the values-science discussion?

3. That voluminous flow of garbage and trash that is part of our everyday life can either destroy us or provide us with a valuable source of salvageable materials. Lord Ritchie-Calder's article on pollution in which he calls for an end to this crime compounded of ignorance and avarice is so appropriate today that it must be re-read by all. Calder and other conservationists and ecologists are concerned that we may have waited too long already. Are you in agreement with this observation? Are you aware of the tremendous dollar implications of a pollution control program? How much information do you have on recycling? Its costs? Its necessity? Have you devoted any real time and effort to the question of an informed citizenry, what you can do to help?

4. In the "Roots of Lawlessness," Henry Steele Commager repeats a long-standing American boast—there has never been a genuine "revolution" in this country. At the same time he warns us of the dangers of widespread lawlessness hinting that our past may yet catch up with us and plunge us into a true state of revolt. Do you share Commager's fears? What examples of lawlessness can you cite to support your arguments? Is there a way to head off this problem before it's too late? If you could appear before some of the dissident groups in America, what hope could you offer them that favorable and orderly change is in the wind? What constructive promises would you try to extract from them that would help the country achieve a new and better "normality"?

5. Human potential often remains latent for the better part of a lifetime, according to Herbert Otto. It oftens appears that too many teenagers seem to be "coasting" today, for example. Have you personally observed this problem among your associates? Is it a problem which originates with the family or must we blame education for failing to stimulate interest and initial drive? How would you prepare young people to develop and sustain initiative throughout the formative years?

6. In Donald Michael's book, *The Next Generation*, listed in the selected

references, a valuable appendix contains some provocative questions and pertinent actions for orienting youth-development programs that will meet the radical changes youth must face in the future. These are well worth examining if only to see the difficult process that must be undertaken to plan intelligently for the foreseeable future. Michael's suggestions are less important than the impetus they provide to stimulate your own thinking.

Selected References

"A Center Report: Priorities in an Affluent Society." *The Center Magazine* (January 1970), 72–83.

Allen, James E. Jr. "Education for Survival." *American Education* (March 1970), 19–23.

Aron, Raymond, George Keenan, Robert Oppenheimer, et al. *World Technology and Human Destiny*. Ann Arbor: University of Michigan Press, 1963.

Asbell, Bernard. *The New Improved American*. New York: McGraw-Hill, 1965.

Bertalanffy, Ludwig von. "The World of Science and the World of Value." *Teachers College Record* (March 1964), 496–507.

Bird, David. "Udall Says Nation Must Curb Growth to Spare Environment." *The New York Times* (January 15, 1970), 32.

Bowles, Chester. "America's Next Rendezvous with Destiny." *Saturday Review* (September 6, 1969), 17–19, 48.

Burck, Gilbert. "There'll Be Less Leisure Than You Think." *Fortune* (March 1970), 87–89, 162, 165–166.

Clark, Kenneth B. "Fifteen Years of Deliberate Speed." *Saturday Review* (December 20, 1969), 59–61, 70.

Cousins, Norman. "A Philosophy for the Environment." *Saturday Review* (March 7, 1970), 47.

Deloria, Vine Jr. "The War Between the Redskins and the Feds." *The New York Times Magazine* (December 7, 1969), 47, 82, 84, 86, 88, 92, 94, 96, 98, 102.

Drew, Elizabeth B. "Dam Outrage: The Story of the Army Engineers." *The Atlantic* (April 1970), 51–62.

Dubos, René. "Escape from the Land of the Lotus Eaters." *Teachers College Record* (May 1963), 660–670.

Farrell, Barry. "The View from the Year 2000." *Life* (February 26, 1971), 47–58.

Ferry, W. H. "The Unanswerable Questions." *The Center Magazine* (July 1969), 2–7.

"Fighting to Save the Earth from Man." *Time* (February 2, 1970), 56–63.

Greer, Colin. "Cultural Pluralism and Racism." *Change* (January 1969), 341–345.

Hechinger, Fred M. "Gardner's Prescription for the Sick Society." *The New York Times* (March 30, 1969), E9.

Isenberg, Barbara. "Red Man's Plight." *The Wall Street Journal* (March 9, 1970), 1, 19.

Jones, Howard Mumford. "History and the Contemporary." *Teachers College Record* (May 1963), 625–636.

Kelly, Frank K. "The Possibilities of Transformation, A Report on the State of Mankind: 1970." *Saturday Review* (March 7, 1970), 17–19, 66–67.

Krutch, Joseph Wood. "Can We Survive the Fun Explosion?" *Saturday Review* (January 16, 1965), 14–16.

La Piere, R. T. *Social Change*. New York: McGraw-Hill, 1965.

Lessing, Lawrence. "The Senseless War on Science." *Fortune* (March 1971), 88–91, 153–155.

Maruyana, Magorah. "Cybernetics." *NEA Journal* (December 1964), 51–54.

Mead, Margaret. "The Future as a Basis for Establishing a Shared Culture." *Daedalus* (Winter 1965), 135–155.

Melman, Seymour. *The Depleted Society.* New York: Holt, Rinehart, and Winston, 1965.

Michael, Donald N. *Cybernation: The Silent Conquest.* Santa Barbara, Calif.: Center for the Study of Democratic Institutions, 1962.

———. *The Next Generation: The Prospects Ahead for the Youth of Today and Tomorrow.* New York: Random House, 1965.

"Modern Man Is Obsolete." *Saturday Review* (August 1, 1970), 16–18, 53.

Murdoch, William, and Joseph Connell. "All About Ecology." *The Center Magazine* (January 1970), 56–63.

Nef, John U. "The Search for Civilization." *The Center Magazine* (May 1969), 2–6.

Potter, Frank M. Jr. "Everyone Wants to Save the Environment but No One Knows Quite What to Do." *The Center Magazine* (March 1970), 35–70.

Price, Don K. "Purists and Politicians," *Harvard Today* (Spring 1969), 2–6, 27–31.

Ritchie-Calder, Lord. "Polluting the Environment." *The Center Magazine* (May 1969), 7–12.

"Second Edition: Good Buildings and the Good Life." An Interview with Allan Temko. *The Center Magazine* (November 1969), 57–63.

Sisson, Daniel. "Toward a New Patriotism." *The Center Magazine* (May 1969), 31–36.

Tebel, John. "Forecasting the Seventies." *Saturday Review* (November 8, 1969), 80–81.

"The Next Decade: A Search for Goals." *Time* (December 19, 1969), 22–25.

"The Ravaged Environment." *Newsweek* (January 26, 1970), 31–40, 45–48.

"The Search for Intelligent Life." *Saturday Review* (August 9, 1969), 20.

"The Spectacular '70's." *U.S. News & World Report* (June 23, 1969), 42–45.

Ways, Max. "How to Think About the Environment." *Fortune* (February 1970), 98–101, 159–160, 162, 165–166.

Weaver, Warren. "Basic Research and the Common Good." *Saturday Review* (August 9, 1969), 17–18, 54.

Wheeler, Harvey. "The Politics of Ecology." *Saturday Review* (March 7, 1970), 51–52, 62–64.

The Great Transition

KENNETH E. BOULDING

The twentieth century marks the middle period of a great transition in the state of the human race. It may properly be called the second great transition in the history of mankind.

The first transition was that from precivilized to civilized society which began to take place about five (or ten) thousand years ago.[1] This is a transition that is still going on in some parts of the world, although it can be regarded as almost complete. Precivilized society can now be found only in small and rapidly diminishing pockets in remote areas. It is doubtful whether more than 5 per cent of the world's population could now be classified as living in a genuinely precivilized society.

Even as the first great transition is approaching completion, however, a second great transition is treading on its heels. It may be called the transition from civilized to postcivilized society. We are so accustomed to giving the word civilization a favorable overtone that the words postcivilized or postcivilization may strike us as implying something unfavorable. If, therefore, the word technological or the term developed society is preferred I would have no objection. The word postcivilized, however, does bring out the fact that civilization is an intermediate state of man dividing the million or so years of precivilized society from an equally long or longer period which we may expect to extend into the future postcivilization. It is furthermore a rather disagreeable state for most people living in it, and its disappearance need occasion few tears.

The origins of the first great transition from precivilized society are lost in the mists of prehistory except in so far as they can be reconstructed with the aid of archeology. The more we know the further these origins seem to recede in time, and it now seems clear that the beginning of agriculture and the domestication of animals can be traced back at least ten thousand years. Agriculture is a precondition of the development of civilization because it is not until man settles down and begins to cultivate crops and domesticate livestock that he is able to develop a surplus of food from the food producer above and beyond what the food producer

[1] The first transition falls into two parts, the transition from the paleolithic to the neolithic, following the invention of agriculture, and the subsequent transition from the neolithic village to urban civilization. I prefer to think of these two parts as parts of a single process, but some may prefer to regard them as two separate transitions, in which case the modern transition would be the "third."

and his family require themselves for their own maintenance. In hunting, fishing and pastoral societies it seems to have been hard for the food producer to produce much more than the immediate requirements of himself and his family. In these circumstances it is clear that no urban culture can possibly exist. If persons who do not produce food are to be fed, there must be surplus food available from the food producer. Some precivilized societies seem to have enjoyed such a surplus, but it was always precarious and temporary. There must be a continuous and reasonable stable excess of food production above the requirements of the food producer if civilization is to be established.

The mere existence of surplus food, while it is a prerequisite for the existence of civilization, does not necessarily produce it, for surplus may be "wasted" in leisure or unproductive activities. In order for towns and cities to exist there must be some machinery whereby the food surplus of the food producer is extracted from him and collected in one place so that the kings, priests, soldiers, builders, and artisans of civilization can subsist. I am assuming here that the prime mark of civilization is the city. This is indeed what the derivation of the word civilization suggests. In its earliest form the city seems to have been a product of some system of coercion. Agriculture provides the opportunity, but in the early stages at least it seems to take some form of coercion to take advantage of it. The earliest forms of coercion may well have been spiritual, for there is some evidence that the earliest cities were organized as theocracies. A priesthood arises which claims a monopoly on the supposedly supernatural forces which govern the affairs of man and the fertility of crops and livestock. The priest then is able to extract food from the food producer by threatening to deprive him of the assistance of these supernatural forces. The coercive system of the priest, however, is based to a large extent on bluff, for the priest does not really control the forces that make the crops grow. When the priest ceases to inspire belief in his imaginary powers the spiritual coercive system usually seems to be replaced by a more physical coercive system in the shape of a king and army. In isolation this is a fairly stable system because when the king has sufficient means of violence at his disposal he can threaten the food producer enough to make him give up his surplus. With this food surplus the king can feed his army and so reinforce the threat if necessary. With what is left over from feeding the army, the king can feed architects, builders, priests, philosophers, and other adornments of civilization. In this stage an alliance is frequently made between the king and the priest, and physical and spiritual threats reinforce each other. The economic basis on which classical civilization has been built, however, has universally been meager. Whether it was Sumeria, Egypt, Greece, Rome, Ancient China, the Incas, or the Mayans, all these were societies based on a food surplus from the food producer that rarely exceeded 20 or 25 per cent of the total product. In these circumstances three quarters to four fifths of the population must be in agriculture or other food production, and these people barely produce enough to feed the remaining quarter or fifth of the population in the towns and in the army. Almost all the cities of classical civilization were within a few weeks of starvation at any time, and a relatively small worsening in general conditions, in the means of transportation or in conditions of peace and war, was frequently enough to undermine the precarious foundation of civilized life. I have never seen any figure for the expectation of life of the city itself under conditions of classical civilization, but I would be surprised if this turned out to be more than about three hundred years.

The origins of the second great transition are perhaps not so obscure as the origins of the first, but there are many puzzling and unresolved questions connected with them. All through the history of civilization, indeed, one can detect a slowly rising stream of knowledge and organization that has a different quality from that of the civilized society around it. The astronomy of Babylonia, the geometry of the Greeks, and the algebra of the Arabs represent as it were foretastes of the great flood of knowledge and technological change to come. Some of the ancient empires, even the Roman Empire, seem to have been technologically stagnant and scientifically backward. If one is looking for the beginning of a continuous process of scientific and technological development, this might be traced to the monastic movement in the West of the sixth century A.D., especially the Benedictines. Here for almost the first time in history we had intellectuals who worked with their hands, and who belonged to a religion which regarded the physical world as in some sense sacred and capable of enshrining goodness. It is not surprising therefore that an interest in the economizing of labor and in extending its productive powers began in the monasteries, however slowly. From the sixth century on we can trace a slowly expanding technology. The water wheel comes in the sixth century, the stirrup in the eighth, the horse collar and the rudder in the ninth, the windmill in the twelfth, and so on. For Europe the invention of printing in the fifteenth century represents an irreversible take-off, because from this point on the dissemination of information increased with great rapidity. The seventeenth century saw the beginning of science, the eighteenth century an acceleration of technological change so great that it has been called, perhaps rather misleadingly, the Industrial Revolution. The nineteenth century saw the development of science as an ongoing social organization, and the twentieth century has seen research and development heavily institutionalized with an enormous increase in the rate of change both of knowledge and of technology as a result. It must be emphasized that the rate of change still seems to be accelerating. We may not even have reached the middle of whatever process we are passing through, and there are certainly no signs that the rate of change is slowing down. It seems clear for instance that we are now on the edge of a biological revolution which may have results for mankind just as dramatic as the nuclear revolution of a generation ago.

A few symptoms will indicate the magnitude of the change through which we are now passing. Consider for instance the position of agriculture in the most developed societies today. In all societies of classical civillization, as we have seen, at least 75 per cent of the population, and often a larger percentage, were engaged in agriculture and would merely produce enough to support themselves and the remaining urban 25 per cent. Even in the United States at the time of the American Revolution, it has been estimated that about 90 per cent of the people were in agriculture. Today in the United States only about 10 per cent of the population are so engaged, and if present trends continue it will not be long before we can produce all the food that we need with 5 per cent, or even less, of the population. This is because with modern techniques, a single farmer and his family can produce enough food to feed ten, twenty, or even thirty families. This releases more than 90 per cent of the population to work on other things, and to produce automobiles, houses, clothing, all the luxuries and conveniences of life as well as missiles and nuclear weapons.

Another indication of the magnitude of the present transition is the fact that, as far as many statistical series related to activities of mankind are concerned, the date that divides human history into two equal parts is well within living memory. For the volume and number of chemical publications, for instance, this date is now (*i.e.* 1964) about 1950. For many statistical series of quantities of metal or other materials extracted, this date is about 1910. That is, man took about as much out of mines before 1910 as he did after 1910. Another startling fact is that about 25 per cent of the human beings who have ever lived are now alive, and what is even more astonishing, something like 90 per cent of all the scientists who have ever lived are now alive. My eight-year-old son asked me the other day, "Daddy, were you born in the olden days?" It is the sort of question that makes a parent feel suddenly middle-aged. There is perhaps more truth in his remark than he knew. In a very real sense the changes in the state of mankind since the date of my birth have been greater than the changes that took place in many thousands of years before this date.

Another indication of the magnitude of the transition is the extraordinary ability of modern societies to recover from disaster. In 1945, for instance, many of the cities of Germany and Japan lay in almost total ruin. Today it is hard to tell that they were ever destroyed, for they have been completely rebuilt in a space of less than twenty years. It took Western Europe almost three hundred years to recover from the fall of the Roman Empire, and took Germany decades to recover from the Thirty Years War (1618–1648). It is perhaps an optimistic feature of the present time that as well as great powers of destruction, we also have greatly increased powers of recuperation and recovery.

The great transition is not only something that takes place in science, technology, the physical machinery of society, and in the utilization of physical energy. It is also a transition in social institutions. Changes in technology produce change in social institutions, and changes in institutions produce change in technology. In the enormously complex world of social interrelations we cannot say in any simple way that one change produces the other, only that they are enormously interrelated and both aspects of human life change together. For instance, it has been argued that the invention of the rudder and the improvement in the arts of navigation and shipbuilding which took place in Europe in the fifteenth century led inevitably to the discovery of America by Europeans. As a schoolboy is reported to have said, "How could Columbus miss it?" Once it was possible to navigate a course of three thousand miles in a straight line, the discovery of America by the Europeans was virtually inevitable, and of course this discovery enormously expanded the horizon and the opportunities of these European societies.

On the other hand, the societies which pioneered in the discovery of America did not ultimately profit very much from it. Spain and Portugal obtained a great empire and a sizable inflation but stagnated as a result, because of the failure of their social institutions to adapt.

It has likewise been argued that the discovery of the horse collar eventually led to the abolition of slavery, at least in its more extreme forms, because of the fact that with a horse collar the horse became a much more efficient source of mere animal power than a human, and the slave as a simple source of power could not compete with him. A horse collar seems to be such an obvious invention that one can hardly believe that it took until the ninth century for mankind to think of it. However, it seems to be clear that the Romans did not use it, and that the Roman horse pulled on rope that was something like a noose around its neck, which greatly reduced its efficiency. The horse collar, coupled with the development of the three-field system, led to a substantial improvement in the techniques of agriculture in Europe in the ninth, tenth, and eleventh centuries which was the foundation on which the cultural and architectural achievements of the later Middle Ages were built. Here again, however, the social institutions of its feudal and authoritarian societies led to a freezing of the technological situation, and further advance in agriculture did not come until the institutions of the Middle Ages had largely disintegrated or at least were weakened through the inflation which followed on the inflow of the Spanish gold from the New World. The rise of Protestantism and the breakup of the old transitional society produced a situation in Holland and in England in which innovation was once more possible, and the agricultural revolution of the seventeenth and early eighteenth centuries grew out of the developing of root crops, the use of intertilled crops on previously fallow ground, and the sowing of artificial grasses. This improvement in agriculture, at least in England and the Low Countries in the early eighteenth century, laid the foundation for a growing food surplus for the industrial cities to come.

The social invention of parliamentary democracy permitted societies to develop with much greater diversity and wider distribution of power than in the earlier absolute monarchies, and the rise of modern science is quite closely associated with the development of democratic and pluralistic institutions of this kind. It could not arise, for instance, in imperial China or feudal Japan. It is no accident that an acceleration in the growth of science took place in Western Europe following the French Revolution. It is clear that we must look at pure science, technological change, and social invention as parts of a single pattern of development in which each element supports the other. It may be argued indeed that social institutions play more of a negative than a positive role, in that they can inhibit scientific and technological change but cannot initiate it. Even this proposition, however, must now be called in question. Organized research and development is essentially a social invention which has resulted in an enormous increase in the pace of technological change.

As another example of the interrelation of technical and political change it can be argued, for instance, that it is the progress of technology, especially under the stimulus of organized research and development, that has effectively abolished imperialism. Ancient civilization, as we have seen, rested firmly on a basis of coercion. The food producer had to be coerced into giving up the surplus to king or priest because there was nothing much that either of them produced that could be exchanged for it. The ancient city is to a large extent an instrument of exploitation and must be regarded as parasitic on the food producer. In the modern world things are different. Since the development of industrial society, exchange has replaced coercion as the principal means of social organization even though coercion and the threat of violence still retain a great importance in the relations of national states. But with the coming of science and technology, it is fair to say that we can get ten dollars out of nature for every dollar that we can squeeze out of man. Under these circumstances imperial adventure or political coercion is simply an investment with a much lower rate of return than investment in applied science and technological progress at home. We see this very clearly, for instance, in the case of Portugal, which has probably the largest *per capita* empire and the lowest *per capita* income in Europe. By contrast, the Scandinavian countries and Switzerland, which have refrained from imperial adventures, have probably done better economically than their more imperial counterparts. The progressive abandonment of empire by the British, the French, the Dutch, and the Belgians reflects not so much a power shift on the part of these countries as their recognition that in terms of the values of a modern society, empire simply does not pay.

Social inventions often take place so softly and imperceptibly that they are hardly noticed, and the history of social invention as a result still largely remains to be written. Who for instance invented the handshake? How did we change from a society in which almost every man went armed to a society in which we have achieved almost complete personal disarmament, and in which human relations are governed by conventions of politeness, by disarming methods of communication, and by largely nonviolent techniques of conflict? Most of all, how do changes take place in child rearing? These perhaps are the most fundamental social inventions of all, for the personality structure of one generation depends mainly on the way children were brought up in the previous generation.

As part of the ongoing process of social invention the great transition involves changes in moral, religious, and aesthetic aspects of life just as much as it involves changes in our knowledge and use of the physical world. It involves, for instance, change in the nature of the family and in the patterns of child rearing. Civilized society on the whole is characterized by the extended family, and by strong loyalty to kinfolk and by methods of child rearing which generally involve a rough transition from an extremely permissive and protective early childhood to an authoritarian and unpleasant regime in later childhood. As we move to postcivilized society, we find an extension of loyalty from the kinship to larger areas such as the national state, or even to the world as a whole. The family structure and living arrangement tend to shift from the extended family group and large household to the small nuclear family of parents and children, and we find that the child-rearing practices which may be well adapted to a society in which the threat systems are important and aggression pays off, have become poorly adapted to a society in which the subtler arts of personal manipulation replace the more violent forms of aggression. We therefore find a shift in the methods of child rearing from those which produce the authoritarian personalities which are characteristic of civilized societies to those which produce more flexible, adaptable, and manipulative persons.

Drastic changes in the nature and behavior of the family are also implied by the health revolution which is also a part of the transition. In civilized society, mortality is high and there is a necessity therefore for a high birth rate. Civilized society can be in equilibrium with birth and death rates between thirty and forty per thousand and a corresponding expectation of life between thirty-three and twenty-five. It is a matter of simple arithmetic that in an equilibrium population in which birth rate and death rate are equal, the level of the birth and death rates is the simple reciprocal of the average age at death. In the advanced societies today the average age at death is about seventy, and for such a population to be in equilibrium the birth and death rate must be about fourteen. To put the matter in somewhat different terms, if all children live to maturity and if the whole population marries, then the average number of children in one family cannot exceed two, if population is to be stable. This also implies no more than an average of two births per family. This involves an enormous shift in attitude toward children and even perhaps toward sex. Yet this is an essential part of the transition. If this part of the transition is not made, all the rest cannot be made either, except as a temporary and unstable condition.

The great transition likewise involves a profound change in the nature of religion and ideology. In a society in which religion is associated with animistic views of the universe and with a belief in magic, the behavior changes which are necessary to the great transition can hardly take place. If man believes that natural objects like stones, wind, water, and crops are moved by essentially arbitrary wills, either he will despair of manipulating nature to his own advantage or he will attempt to do this in the same way that he would attempt to manipulate his fellow man—that is, by attempts at verbal or symbolic communication, in the form of incantation and ritual. It is not until animism is replaced by an attitude which regards will as essentially and solely a property of the minds and souls of men, rather than of inanimate natural objects, that a scientific and technological attitude toward the material world becomes possible. It is no accident therefore that the scientific transition originated in Western Europe, where the prevailing religion was an ethical monotheism, which either tended to concentrate the whole animistic enterprise in a single sacramental act of the Mass, as in Catholic Christianity, or which denied even this apparent remnant of animism by stressing that the operation of the will of God takes place principally in the souls of men, as in Protestant Christianity.

We may even attribute the success of atheistic communism in promoting economic development and the movement toward postcivilized society not so much to its specific dogmas as to the fact that it is an instrument for undermining primitive animism and for replacing a belief in the arbitrary and willful nature of the material world by a belief in its stability and orderliness. Whether this view can ultimately satisfy the spiritual needs of man is another question altogether. It is clear that the scientific and technological transition is consistent with many different views about the ultimate nature of the universe, provided that they all involve a faith in the orderliness of the natural world, faith in man's ability to perceive this order and manipulate it for his own benefit, and faith in processes of learning which involve direct experience rather than mere acceptance of the received tradition from the elders.

The various civilizations which resulted from the first great transition, even though they had much in common, nevertheless exhibited great differences. One needs merely to think of Ancient Egypt, Babylonia, Greece, Rome, medieval Europe, and China. Similarly it seems probable that the second great transition will not immediately at least result in a uniform world culture but will result in a considerable variety of cultural patterns, each of them however exhibiting very similar technologies and levels of income. But it is probable that postcivilized society, simply because of the fact that its techniques are much less bound either to geography or to past culture than are the techniques of civilized society, will turn out to be much more uniform than the civilized societies have been. We see this, for instance, in the airports of the world. Air travel is a distinct mark of postcivilized society, and airports are much the same whether we find them in Bangkok or in Chicago. Similarly, steel mills are much the same in Volta Redonda in Brazil, in Birmingham, Alabama, or in India. In so far as civilization was based on agriculture, the physical basis made for wide differences. The agriculture of the Nile delta is very different from the agriculture of wheat fields of the steppes and prairies, which again is different from that of the rice paddies of Asia. We should therefore expect that civilizations based on agriculture would exhibit markedly different technological as well as cultural forms. Professor Wittfogel[2] has suggested indeed that the political and social institutions of civilized society are closely related to the type of agriculture from which it draws its food supply, and in particular an agriculture which requires extensive public works and irrigation like that of Ancient Egypt and China is much more likely to develop hierarchical and authoritarian societies than an agriculture based on small peasant holdings in humid lands where no public organization of any great magnitude or large public works are needed in order to grow food. Even in postcivilized societies, of course, rice paddies are different from wheat fields and produce a different kind of culture. Nevertheless the tractor is much the same everywhere, just as the automobile and factories are much the same everywhere, and this imposes a uniformity at least on the technological culture of the world which it never possessed before.

Furthermore the rapid and easy transportation which postcivilization permits makes it much more difficult to maintain culture traits in isolation. Civilizations

[2] Karl A. Wittfogel, *Oriental Despotism* (New Haven: Yale University Press, 1957).

could flourish at the same time on the earth which had little or no contact one with another. The Mayan civilization certainly had no contact with Rome, and Rome had very little contact with China. The transition to civilization indeed may have been accomplished in at least three independent locations or perhaps even more, though these origins are so obscure that we cannot be sure of this. Now, however, it is as easy to go halfway around the world as it used to be to go to a neighboring town, and under these circumstances an enormous process of cultural mixture is taking place which can hardly halp producing much greater uniformity even in a few hundred years. It is doubtful whether a single world language will emerge in the near future, but certainly in styles of clothing, housing, mass entertainment, and transportation it is becoming increasingly hard to distinguish one part of the world from another.

An important difference which is likely to be maintained for a considerable time is that between societies which are making the transition under democratic and capitalistic institutions and those which are making the transition under institutions of totalitarian socialism. It certainly seems possible to make the technological transition under both sets of institutions. Nevertheless the societies which will emerge as a result might be quite different not only in the political and social institutions but in the value systems and the nature and quality of human life which they support. In the short run this raises many problems and unquestionably increases the danger of war and the probability that the transition will not be made. In the long perspective of history, however, this may turn out to have been a fortunate accident, if indeed it is an accident. It might well be that one of the greatest problems of postcivilized society will be how to preserve enough differentiation of human culture and how to prevent the universal spread of a drab uniformity. Cultural change and development at all times has frequently come about as a result of the interaction of cultures which previously have developed in isolation. This is a phenomenon somewhat analogous to the devolopment of hybrid varieties in plants and animals. If we are to have hybrid cultures, however, just as if we are to have hybrid animals, there must be pure stocks maintained to interbreed. The strength of the mule and the fertility of hybrid corn would be impossible if the pure stocks from which these hybrids are derived are not maintained. Similarly in the case of cultures if we are to have vigorous hybrid cultures, the pure cultures from which these are derived must be maintained, and in a world of easy travel and rapid communication the maintenance of the pure cultures may be difficult. It may therefore be possible that things which now we regard as unfortunate sources of conflict and separation may turn out to be blessings in disguise. If socialist culture and free-market culture can develop side by side without fatal conflict, their constant interaction may be beneficial to both parties. Similarly even the development of religious sects and subcultures which are isolated from the world by what may seem a nonrational ideology may turn out to be extremely useful devices for preserving the diversity of mankind.

Perhaps the most difficult of all these problems involving diversity and uniformity is the problem of the future of different races. The different races of mankind have a sufficient sexual attraction for each other so that in the absence of any geographical or cultural obstacles to genetic mixture it is highly probable that in the course of a few thousand years the human race would become racially uniform, and the existing differences between races will be largely eliminated. From some points of view this may be very desirable, and it will certainly eliminate certain problems of interhuman conflict, most of which however are defined culturally rather than biologically. We know so little about human genetics, however, especially on the positive side of the forces which lead to genetic excellence, that it is impossible now to prophesy what may be regarded as eugenic in the future. The eugenic movement of the nineteenth century was based on inadequate knowledge of human genetics and hence could not get very far. If we develop as we may well do more accurate knowledge of the genetic factors which made for human excellence both of mind and body, the consequences for ethics, for almost all social relations, and for political behavior might be immense. But this is a bridge which we have not yet come to, and it may be well to postpone worrying about it until we do. In the meantime knowledge of human genetics, apart from a few factors making for certain defects, is not developed enough so that from it we can justify either racial purity or racial admixture. It might well be indeed that we will end by classifying mankind genetically along quite different lines from the way in which the races are now classified by strictly superficial characteristics, and we may then be able to warn against dangerous genetic combinations, as we do already with the Rh factor, and perhaps even encourage desirable combinations. Much of this, however, is in the future, though at the rate at which the biological sciences are now developing it may not be in the very distant future.

The great question as to whether the transition from civilization to postcivilization is a "good" change is one that cannot be answered completely until we know the nature and quality of different postcivilized societies. We might well argue in contemplating the first great transition from precivilized to civilized societies that in many cases this was a transition from a better state of man to a worse. As we contemplate the innumerable wars of civilized societies, as we contemplate the hideous religion of human sacrifice and the bloody backs of innumerable slaves on which the great monuments of civilization have been built, it is sometimes hard to refrain from a certain romantic nostalgia for the "noble savage." Indeed, the *philosophes* of the eighteenth century indulged in this feeling at great length. Anthropologists have somewhat dispelled the romantic view of precivilized society, which was in many cases not only poor but cruel and disagreeable beyond even the excesses of civilization. Nevertheless it will not be difficult to contrast the best of precivilized societies and the worst of civilized societies and come out much in favor of the precivilized. Similarly a type of postcivilized society is possible as portrayed, for instance, in the anti-Utopias of George Orwell and Aldous Huxley in the middle of the twentieth century, in which the quality of human life and the dignity of man seem to be much inferior to that in the best of civilized societies.

There is clearly here a problem to be solved. We do not make men automatically good and virtuous by making them rich and powerful; indeed the truth frequently seems to be the opposite. Nevertheless we must not fall into the other trap of equating innocence with ignorance or of thinking that impotence is the same thing as virtue. An increase in power increases the potential both for good and for evil. A postcivilized society of unshakable tyranny, resting upon all the knowledge which we are going to gain in social sciences, and of unspeakable corruption resting on man's enormous power over nature, especially biological nature, is by no means inconceivable. On the other hand the techniques of postcivilization also offer us the possibility of a society in which the major sources of human misery have been eliminated, a society in which there will be no war, poverty, or disease, and in which a large majority of human beings will be able to live out their lives in relative freedom from most of the ills which now oppress a major part of mankind. This is a prize worth driving for even at the risk of tyranny and corruption. There is no real virtue in impotence, and the virtue to strive for is surely the combination of power with goodness.

In any case there is probably no way back. The growth of knowledge is one of the most irreversible forces known to mankind. It takes a catastrophe of very large dimensions to diminish the total stock of knowledge in the possession of man. Even in the rise and fall of great civilizations surprisingly little has been permanently lost, and much that was lost for a short time was easily regained. Hence there is no hope for ignorance or for a morality based on it. Once we have tasted the fruit of the tree of knowledge, as the Biblical story illustrates so well, Eden is closed to us. We cannot go back to the childhood of our race any more than we can go back to our own childhood without disaster. Eden has been lost to us forever and an angel with a flaming sword stands guard at its gates. Therefore either we must wander hopelessly in the world or we must press forward to Zion. We must learn to master ourselves as we are learning to master nature. There is no reason in the nature of things which says that ethical development is impossible, and indeed one would expect that the process of development, whether economic, political, or social, will go hand in hand with a similar process of ethical development which will enable us to use wisely the power that we have gained. This ethical development may take forms which will seem strange to us now, but just as we can trace development in the values and ethical standards of mankind as his economic and physical powers increased from precivilized society, so it is reasonable that new ethical standards will arise appropriate to the new technology of postcivilization.

We must emphasize that there is no inevitability and no determinism in making this great transition. There are a number of traps which lies along the way and which may either prevent man and his planet earth from making the transition altogether or delay it for many generations or even thousands of years. The first most obvious and immediate trap is the war trap. It is now theoretically possible for man to build a device which will eliminate all life from the earth. Even if this extreme event is highly improbable, less extreme disasters are at least within a range of probability that makes them a matter of serious concern. A major nuclear war would unquestionably set back the transition to a postcivilized world by many generations, and it might indeed eliminate the possibility of making this transition altogether. The effect of such war on the whole ecological system of the planet is so unpredictable that we cannot tell how large a disaster it will be, although we know it will be very large. It is possible that such a disaster will be irretrievable. It is also possible that even if we had a retrievable disaster we might not learn enough from it to retrieve ourselves. It is clear that what is desperately needed at the present time is to diminish the probability of such a disaster to the vanishing point.

Another possible trap which might delay the attainment of the transition for a long time is the population trap. This is perhaps the main reason for believing that the impact of a few postcivilized techniques on existing civilized societies might easily be disastrous in the next hundred years or so. One of the first impacts of postcivilized medicine and medical knowledge on civilized society is a large and immediate reduction in the death rate, especially in infant mortality. This is seldom if ever accompanied by a similar decrease in birth rate, and hence the first impact of postcivilized techniques on a previously stable civilized society is a tremendous upsurge in the rate of population increase. This increase may be so large that the society is incapable of adapting itself to it, and incapable in particular of devoting sufficient resources to the education of its unusually large cohorts of young people. We therefore have the tragic situation that the alleviation of much human misery and suffering in the short run may result in enormous insoluble problems in a longer period.

A third possible trap is the technological trap itself: that we may not be able to develop a genuinely stable high-level technology which is independent of exhaustible resources. Technology at the present time, even the highest technology, is largely dependent for its sources of energy and materials on accumulations in the earth which date from its geological past. In a few centuries, or at most a few thousand years, these are likely to be exhausted, and either man will fall back on a more primitive technology or he will have to advance to knowledge well beyond what he has now. Fortunately there are signs that this transition to a stable high-level technology may be accomplished, but we certainly cannot claim that it has been accomplished up to date.

A fourth possible trap may lie in the very nature of man itself. If the dangers and difficulties which now beset man are eliminated in postcivilized society and if he has no longer anything to fear but death itself, will not his creativity be diminished and may he not dissipate his energies in a vast ennui and boredom? This is a question which cannot be answered. But it lurks uneasily at the back of all optimistic statements about the long-run future of man.

Learning to Live with Science

EMMANUEL G. MESTHENE

It was Gilbert Murray who first used the celebrated phrase "the failure of nerve." Writing about ancient Greek religions, Murray characterized as a failure of nerve the change of temper that occurred in Hellenistic civilization around the turn of the era. The Greeks of the fifth and fourth centuries B.C. believed in the ultimate intelligibility of the universe. There was nothing in the nature of existence or of man that was inherently unknowable. They accordingly believed also in the power of the human intelligence to know all there was to know about the world, and to guide man's career in it.

The wars, increased commerce, and infiltration of Oriental cultures that marked the subsequent period brought with them vicissitude and uncertainty that shook this classic faith in the intelligibility of the world and in the capacity of men to know and to do. There was henceforth to be a realm of knowledge available only to God, not achievable by human reason. Men, in other words, more and more turned to God to do for them what they no longer felt confident to do for themselves. That was the failure of nerve.

I think things are changing. I doubt that there are many men today who would question that life will be produced in the laboratory, that psychologists and their personality drugs will soon reveal what really makes men tick, that scientific prediction is a far more promising guide to the future than divination, and that the heavens cannot long remain mysterious in the face of our ability to hit the moon today and the stars tomorrow. In a recent article, Daniel Bell characterized this new-found faith as follows: "Today we feel that there are no inherent secrets in the universe . . . and this is one of the significant changes in the modern moral temper." I would say, indeed, that this is a major implication of our new world of science and technology. We are witnessing a widespread recovery of nerve.

Paradoxically, this taking on of new courage is tending at the same time to produce an opposite reaction, vague but disturbingly widespread. At the same time that we admire the new machines we build—the ones that play chess, and translate Russian, and catch and correct their own mistakes, and tend each other—we also begin to fear them. We fear them in two ways—one that we talk about, and one that we joke about.

We talk quite openly about our fear that machines may take away jobs, deprive people of work. But we dare only to joke about our fear that machines will replace people, not only as workers, but as people. Already they do arithmetic better than any of us. How much longer can it be before they make people obsolete? This fear

From *Saturday Review*, XLVIII, 29 (July 17, 1965), 14–17.

is part of our technological world, but I see it only as derivative. I think it has its roots in a deeper, moral implication.

Some who have seen farthest and most clearly in recent decades have warned of a growing imbalance between man's capabilities in the physical and in the social realms. John Dewey, for example, said: "We have displayed enough intelligence in the physical field to create the new and powerful instrument of science and technology. We have not as yet had enough intelligence to use this instrument deliberately and systematically to control its social operations and consequences." Dewey said this more than thirty years ago, before television, before atomic power, before electronic computers, before space satellites. He had been saying it, moreover, for at least thirty years before that. He saw early the problems that would arise when man learned to do anything he wanted before he learned what he wanted.

I think the time Dewey warned about is here. My more thoughtful scientific friends tell me that we now have, or know how to acquire, the technical capability to do very nearly anything we want. Can we transplant human hearts, control personality, order the weather that suits us, travel to Mars or to Venus? Of course we can, if not now or in five to ten years, then certainly in twenty-five, or in fifty or a hundred. If each of us examined the extent of his own restored faith in the essential intelligibility of the world, we might find that we have recovered our nerve to the point that we are becoming almost nervy. (I think, incidentally, that this recovery of nerve largely explains the current crisis of the churches. After twenty centuries of doing man's work, they are now having to learn how to do God's. The Ecumenical Council is evidence that the long but false war between religion and science is ended, and that we are once more facing Augustine's problem, to distinguish what is God's and what is man's.)

If the answer to the question "What can we do?" is "Anything," then the emphasis shifts far more heavily than before onto the question "What should we do?" The commitment to universal intelligibility entails moral responsibility. Abandonment of the belief in intelligibility 2,000 years ago was justly described as a failure of nerve because it was the prelude to moral surrender. Men gave up the effort to be wise because they found it too hard. Renewed belief in intelligibility 2,000 years later means that men must take up again the hard work of becoming wise. And it is much harder work now, because we have so much more power than the Greeks. On the other hand, the benefits of wisdom are potentially greater, too, because we have the means at hand to *make* the good life, right here and now, rather than just to go on contemplating it in Plato's heaven.

The question "What should we do?" is thus no idle one but challenges each one of us. That, I think, is the principal moral implication of our new world. It is what all the shouting is about in the mounting concern about the relations of science and public policy, and about the impact of technology on society. Our almost total mastery of the physical world entails a challenge to the public intelligence of a degree heretofore unknown in history.

But how do we come to grips with the challenge? How do we pull together and learn to use the knowledge we already have, and in using it learn the other things we need to know? What do the implications of our great contemporary scientific and technical spurt forward add up to? I do not have the answers, but I should like to propose some hypotheses.

My first hypothesis is that the time will come when machines will put most people permanently out of work. What will happen to people when there is no longer work for them to do? Consider the foreman in a steel plant. He brings thirty years' experience to one of the half-dozen really crucial jobs in the mill. At the critical point in the process, it is his trained eye that tells him the molten metal is ready to pour, and it is his well-developed sense of timing and steady hand that tip the cauldron synchronously with the processes that precede and follow. For this he is well paid, and can provide for his family perhaps better than the average. For this, too, he is looked up to by his fellows. They seek him out as a friend. He has prestige at his work, status in the town, and the respect of his children. He belongs. He contributes. He is needed.

Then you move in a machine that takes his job away, and does it better. What happens to this man? What happens to his many juniors at the mill whose aspiration was to an achievement like his? One of the pervasive characteristics of our civilization has been the identification of life's meaning with life's work. The evidence is strong in the problem of the aged: how do they fight the conviction that their life is done, that the world could do very well, perhaps better, without them? Are we heading toward a time when society will be burdened with a problem of the aged beginning in most cases at age twenty, because there will no longer be work to enter upon, let alone retire from, at the age of sixty-five?

Among the suggestions for banishing this specter are two that do not impress me much. The first is essentially a cry of anguish. Stop automation! Stop making more and more complicated machines! What business have we going to the moon, or tampering with life and heredity? Life is difficult enough without going out of our way to make it more so.

All the odds are against the success of that kind of solution. The technologies of the atom bomb, the automobile, the industrial revolution, gunpowder, all provoked social dislocations accompanied by similar demands that they be stopped. But there is clearly no stopping. Aristotle said a long time ago that "man by nature desires to know." He will probe and learn all that his curiosity leads him to and his brain makes possible, until he is dead. The cry of "stop" is the fear reaction I talked about earlier. It comes from those who have not yet recovered their nerve.

A second suggestion, specifically aimed at the prospect of loss of work, is that we find better ways to employ leisure. There is a whole literature growing up on this theme, and I think it should be encouraged. Other things being equal, and given my own biases, it is better to read a good book than to watch television, or to play a Beethoven quartet than listen to the Beatles. But leisure activity, no matter how uplifting and educational, is not a substitute for work. The very concept loses meaning in the absence of the correlative concept of "work." No, I do not think that is the happiest solution.

But then that may not be the problem either. My second hypothesis is that my first hypothesis is wrong. Machines might not in fact put a significant number of people out of work permanently. It might just be that machines will simply take over the kinds of work that people have done up to now, and that people will then be freed, not to become problems to themselves and to society, but to do entirely new kinds of work that have hardly been thought about seriously because there has not yet been a serious possibility that they could be done.

It is often said, for example, that as work in agriculture and industry is progressively mechanized, job opportunities in the service sector of the economy will increase and absorb released manpower. I assume that production processes will not be mechanized except as machines prove more efficient than human labor. There should then follow a significant increment in wealth, which, adequately distributed, could buy more of the services already available, from baby-sitting to education and government and from better waiters to art and religion. The structure of the work force might thus be altered significantly.

Even more exciting is the possibility that the nature of service itself might be altered. I suggest a trivial, perhaps ridiculous example. Doubled police forces and quadrupled sanitation forces could give us, for the first time, really safe and really clean cities. Put 20,000 people into the streets every day to catch the cigarette butts before they even hit the ground, and you might have a clean city.

Inherently, there is nothing ridiculous about a clean city. If the suggestion makes one smile, it is rather because such use of people, by today's standards, is ridiculously uneconomical. People are more efficiently employed to produce the goods we consume. But if machines will be doing most of that, then maybe people can be employed to produce the services, such as street-cleaning or teaching, that we would like to have more of it we could.

Consider another example. One of the genuinely new and exciting ideas of the Kennedy Administration, I think, was the Peace Corps, the idea that young Americans in large numbers could, by example, help less favored peoples to help themselves. Imagine a Peace Corps 50,000,000 strong in Africa, released by machines to pour the kind of sweat that machines will never pour. This is the kind of service that can anticipate, peacefully and constructively, the ugly danger that the have-nots of the world will resort to uncontrollable violence as the gap between their expectations and reality widens. It is also the kind of service that might provide to individuals a satisfaction and a goal to life undreamed of by today's assembly-line worker in Detroit, however fully employed. From such a perspective, the new machines and the new technologies may spell, not the end of the world, but the beginning of a new one. We might begin to see, for the first time, what God meant when he said that the meek shall inherit the earth.

There has been a long tradition that divides work into creative and intellectual for the few, and routine and mechanical for the many. There has grown up around that distinction (although we are told that that was not yet true in the time of the Greeks) a moral judgment: that the first kind of work was for superior people, the second for inferior people. There then occurred, I think, one of those curious inversions of history whereby an effect is later seen as cause. The reason the majority of people did routine and mechanical work, we were told, was that that was the only kind of work they were fit to do, because they were inferior.

It seems to me much more plausible, however, that the reason the majority of people have done routine and mechanical work is that there has been a very great deal of routine and mechanical work to do. I am not denying that some people are more gifted than other people. But it seems to me that we have not yet been motivated to inquire sufficiently into how many people of what kinds can do what, because there has up to now been so much routine and mechanical work to do that most people have necessarily been impressed into doing it.

I suggest also that it is this same imperative of a great deal of routine and mechanical work to do that has led to the ivory-tower syndrome on the part of creative, intellectual workers. I doubt that artists and scientists have typically detached themselves from the world because they liked it that way. The cry for application of knowledge, at least since Francis Bacon, and the essential need of the artist to communicate preclude that view. I suspect, rather, that there may be another reversal of cause and effect here: that the ivory tower may be symptomatic of a world by necessity too preoccupied with the routine and mechanical to generate a real demand for the product of the artist and the scholar. It is no accident that art and philosophy were the exclusive province of the freemen, not the slaves, in Greece, or that science, even in our own age, has for most of its history been indulged in by the gifted amateur who was rich in fact or by philanthropy.

And now machines will do the routine and mechanical work of the world. Very large numbers of human resources will be released and available for services to mankind beyond those required for subsistence. The need to discover the nature of this new kind of work, to plan it and to do it, just might overcome the traditional gap between the creative and the routine. The many will be challenged as they have not been before, to rise to their maximum potentialities. The few—the scholars and the artists—may find that there is a new demand for them in the world, to muster, to shape, and to guide this new force. The two historical judgments that I have criticized as inverted, in other words, might become true from now on in: work could finally become the measure of man, and efficacy the measure of ideas.

What will be the nature of this new work? What goals will it serve? How will it be done? What talents will be needed for it? I do not know the answers to these questions, either. Each, I think, provides an opportunity for imaginative inquiry still to be done. I have undertaken only to state a hypothesis, or, more accurately, to indicate a hunch that precedes hypothesis. My hunch is that man may have finally expiated his original sin, and might now aspire to bliss. I think also that my hunch may hang together historically. Original sin was invented after, and to account for, the failure of nerve. With the recovery of nerve, we do not need the concept any more, and the advance of technology frees us from the drudgery it has imposed.

But freedom from drudgery, as I have suggested, entails a commitment to wisdom. Consider, as one example, the staggering implications for education.

Education (in foot-high letters on public billboards) has become a panacean word. But education for what? For whom? What kind of education? And when? There is very little small print on the billboards to answer those questions.

The response of education to the new world of science and technology up to now has taken the form of five principal proposals or goals: 1) more education for more people, 2) educational booster shots in some form of continuing adult education, 3) increased production of scientists and engineers, 4) expanded vocational training, and 5) mid-career refresher training or retraining for a different specialty.

It is hard to quarrel with more education, or with continuing education. With respect to the other three goals, however, one can raise the question "For how long?" To be sure, we need more scientists and engineers than we have now, but we already hear warnings that the demand will level off, and it is perhaps not too early to start thinking about a massive effort in the social sciences and the humanities.

Similarly with vocational education. Training in a trade is desirable and useful. But in which trade? Certainly not in those doomed to extinction in the next ten to twenty years. The informal experience of the young people who have recently been crusading in Mississippi and Alabama might prove a much more relevant vocational education for the future that lies ahead of us.

Today's best educational judgments, in other words, might turn into tomorrow's worst mistakes, because they depend on forecasting successfully the shape of what is coming. Of course, the judgments must still be made today, despite the risk, despite the increased uncertainties of a world that changes shape rapidly and radically. This is a measure of the difficulty of the modern educator's task. Yet in this very change may lie a relative certainty, with a particular further implication for the job of education. I add a word about that.

There were two ancient Greek philosophers, long before even Socrates haunted the streets of Athens, who had diametrically opposed views about reality. There was Parmenides, who argued that all change is illusory, transitory, imperfect, unreal. And later there was Heraclitus, who saw reality as a flowing river, apparently the same but never the same, to whom all was constant flux and change, and who dismissed the permanent as unreal, as evidence of human imperfection, as a distortion of reality.

I go back to those ancient thinkers, because each gave his name to a major and persistent theme in Western intellectual history. Parmenides, the apostle of the eternal, has had his emulators in Christian theology, in romantic idealism, and in twentieth-century mathematics and logic. The followers of Heraclitus, who saw the world as flux, include the medieval nominalists, the nineteenth-century evolutionary philosophers, and today's existentialists.

Are we Parmenidians or Heracliteans? In our social attitudes, we certainly lean to Parmenides. In our concept of work, the real is the career that holds together, makes sense, and lasts a lifetime. If a man changes jobs too often, we consider him a drifter, or, if we like him, we say he has not yet found his proper work. We see the change as unnatural, unreal, unwanted, and feel much more comfortable with the permanent, the stable.

Similarly with our social institutions. Democracy, capitalism, socialism, the organized faiths—these are the real, the cherished, and any change is transitional, accidental, to be avoided, or dealt with as quickly as possible, to return to the stable, the familiar, the true.

The evidence is becoming compelling that we are going to have to change these attitudes and comfortable habits. Careers are increasingly becoming shorter-lived than people. The complexities of national existence lead to an increasing and inevitable mixing-up of the public and the private. State's rights, that honored mark of eighteenth-century federalism, has become a slogan of those who would have us return to the eighteenth century. The profit motive is being introduced into the Soviet economy, and the world's religions are beginning to talk to each other. All our familiar institutions, in other words, are changing so rapidly and so constantly that the change is becoming more familiar now than the institutions that are changing. The change is the new reality. We are entering an era that might aptly be called Social Heracliteanism.

The challenge to education is indeed staggering. Teachers who have been brought up to cherish the stable must take the children of parents who have been brought up to cherish the stable, and try to teach them that the stable, the unchanging, is unreal, constraining, a false goal, and that they will survive in an age of change to the degree that they become familiar with change, feel comfortable with it, understand it, master and control it.

When that task is done, the recovery of nerve will be complete, because our new technical mastery will have been supplemented by the wisdom necessary to harness it to human ends. John Dewey's dream will have been realized. We will be the masters of our techniques instead of their slaves, and we might just become the first civilization since 500 B.C. to be able to look the Greeks in the face with pride, instead of just with wonder. I do not like to think of the alternative, which is that the people of a century from now will say of us: "Look at the trouble and woe they had with their technology, and look what ours has done for us."

The Dual Crisis in Science and Society

BARRY COMMONER

Our present achievements in science and technology appear to contrast vividly with our present lack of achievement in solving social problems. We can nourish a man in the supreme isolation of outer space—but we cannot adequately feed the children

From *Today's Education*, NEA Journal (October 1968), 11–15. Article, "The Dual Crisis in Science and Society." Copyright 1970, by Barry Commoner. Reprinted by permission of Barry Commoner.

of Calcutta or Harlem. We hope to analyze life on other planets—but we have not yet learned to understand our own neighbors. We are attempting to live on the moon—but we cannot yet live peacefully on our own planet.

The usual explanation of this frightening paradox is that we are competent in the realm of science because no value judgments are demanded and that we are tragically incompetent in dealing with each other because this requires adjustment between personal values and the social good—a capacity that frequently eludes us.

I should like to propose another explanation—that the contrast between our technological competence and our ethical ineptitude is only apparent. We are tragically blind, I believe, not only about our fellowmen but also about important aspects of nature; we are dangerously incompetent in our relations to the natural world as well as in our relations to each other.

Our society is threatened not only by a growing social crisis but also by a technological crisis. In our eager search for the benefits of modern science and technology, we have blundered unwittingly into serious hazards:

We used to be told that nuclear testing was perfectly harmless. Only now, long after the damage has been done, do we know differently.

We produced power plants and automobiles that enveloped our cities in smog—before anyone understood its harmful effects on health.

We synthesized and disseminated new insecticides. What scientific principle can tell us how to make the choice—which may be forced upon us by the insecticide problem—between the shade of the elm tree and the song of the robin?

Certainly, science can validly describe the hard facts about these issues. But the choice of the balance point between benefit and hazard is a value judgment; it is based on ideals of social good or morality or religion—not on science. And if this choice is a social and moral judgment, it ought to be made, not by scientists and technologists alone, but by all citizens.

How can a citizen make such judgments? Deciding these issues requires a confrontation between human values and rather complex scientific data that most citizens are poorly prepared to understand.

The solution demands a new duty of scientists. As the custodians of the technical knowledge relevant to these public issues, scientists have an obligation to bring this information before their fellow citizens in understandable terms.

But first, scientists themselves must determine the causes of our recent failures in the environment and learn from such a determination about the relationship between science and technology and human values. If we are to succeed as inhabitants of a world increasingly transformed by technology, we need to undertake a searching reassessment of our attitudes toward the natural world and the technology that intrudes on it.

Among primitive people, man is always seen as a dependent part of nature, a frail reed in a harsh world, governed by immutable processes that must be obeyed if he is to survive. And the knowledge of nature achieved by primitive peoples is remarkable.

The African bushman's habitat is one of the most stringent on earth: Food is scarce; water, even more so; and extremes of weather come rapidly. The bushman survives in this environment because his understanding of it is incredibly intimate. A bushman can, for example, return after many months and miles of travel to find a single underground tuber, noted in his previous wanderings, when he needs it for his water supply.

We claim to have escaped from such dependence on the environment. While the bushman must squeeze water from a searched-out tuber, we get ours by the turn of a tap. Instead of trackless wastes, we have the grid of city streets. Instead of seeking the sun's heat when we need it and shunning it when it is too strong, we warm ourselves or cool ourselves with man-made machines. And we have thus become enticed into the nearly fatal illusion that we can ignore the balance of nature.

The truth is tragically different. We have become not less dependent on the balance of nature but more dependent on it. Modern technology has so stressed the web of processes in the living environment that there is little leeway left in the system.

I would contend, therefore, that despite our vaunted mastery of nature, despite our brilliant success in managing those processes that can be confined to a laboratory or a factory, we in the "advanced" countries are far less competent inhabitants of our environment than bushmen are of theirs.

This reflects, I believe, a basic inadequacy in modern science—neglect of systems and processes that are intrinsically complex. The systems at risk in environmental pollution are natural, and because they are natural they are complex. Hence they are not readily approached by the atomistic methodology so characteristic of much of modern biological research.

Water pollutants stress the total ecological web that ties together the numerous organisms inhabiting lakes and rivers; their effects on the whole natural system are not adequately described by laboratory studies of pure cultures of separate organisms. Smog attacks the self-protective mechanism of the human lung; its noxious effects on man are not accountable by an influence on a single enzyme or even a single tissue.

If, for the sake of analytical detail, molecular constituents are isolated from the smashed remains of a cell or single organisms are separated from their natural neighbors, what is lost is the network of interrelationships that crucially determines the properties of the natural whole. And this suggests that any new basic knowledge, if it is to elucidate environmental biology and guide our efforts to understand and control pollution, must be relevant to the natural biological systems that are the arena in which these problems exist.

Nor is our neglect of complex systems limited to environmental biology. This is quickly revealed, for example, by a brief inquiry into the state of modern computer science. Shortly before he died, Norbert Wiener, the mathematician who did so much to develop cybernetics, the science that guides the design of computers, warned us about the problem. He cited, as a parable, experience with computers that had been programed to play checkers. Engineers built into the electronic circuits a correct understanding of the rules of checkers and also a way of judging (from a stored record of its opponents' moves) what moves were most likely to beat the human opponents.

Dr. Wiener described the results of the checker tournaments between the computer and its human programmers: The machine started out playing an accurate but uninspired game that was easy to beat; but after about 10 or 20 hours of practice, the machine got the hang of it, *and from then on the human player always lost and the machine won.*

Dr. Wiener concluded that it had become technically possible to build automatic machines able to carry out very complex activities that elude the comprehension of their operators and that "most definitely escape from the complete effective control of the man who has made them."

Recently this difficulty has become painfully evident to the specialists who are attempting to manage the operation of the current generation of electronic computers. They are extraordinarily frustrated men. They have at their disposal beautifully designed machines capable, in theory, of complex interdigitation of numerous mathematical operations. However, the operators have not yet learned how to operate these machines at their full capacity for complex computations without encountering inexplicable errors.

A spectacular example of a similar difficulty is the New England power blackout of November 1965, in which a complex powerline network designed to effect an even distribution of generating capacity over an 80,000-square-mile area failed. Instead of providing outside power to a local Canadian power system that had suffered a relay failure, the network acted in reverse, causing every connected power system to shut down. And a frightening potential catastrophe lies in the possibility that the complex, computer-guided missile systems—which can in minutes thrust us into the last World War—are equally susceptible to such failures.

It is not a coincidence, I believe, that the scientific and technological problems affecting the human condition involve inherently complex systems. Life, as we live it, is rarely encompassed by a single academic discipline. Real problems that touch our lives and impinge on what we value rarely fit into the neat categories of the college catalog: medeival history, nuclear physics, molecular biology.

For example, to encompass in our minds the terrifying deterioration of our cities we need to know not only the principles of economics, architecture, and social planning, but also the chemistry of air quality areas, the biology of water systems, and the ecology of the domestic rat and the cockroach. In a word, we need to understand science and technology that are relevant to the human condition.

However, we, in the university community, have been brought up in a different tradition. We have a justified pride in our intellectual independence and know—for we often have to battle to maintain it—how essential this independence is to the search for truth. But academic people may sometimes tend to translate intellectual independence into a kind of mandatory disinterest in all problems that do not arise in their own minds—an approach that may in some cases cut them off from their students and from the real and urgent needs of society.

I believe we university scientists have a clear obligation to the society that supports us. We have no right to retreat behind the walls of our laboratories; instead, we must use our knowledge to help improve the world.

If we accept this obligation, how can we make it jibe with the principle of academic freedom, which holds that every scholar should be free to pursue the studies that interest him and free to express whatever conclusions the evidence and the powers of his mind may generate?

There is no simple answer to this question, but Alexander Meiklejohn, who contributed much to the making of the modern American university, gave us a useful guide. According to Meiklejohn, academic freedom is not a special immunity from social responsibility but, on the contrary, a basic part of the duty that the university and the scholar owe to society.

The university, he believed, is an institution established by society to fill its own need for knowledge about the nature of the world and man. The scholar's search for the truth is thus not merely an obligation to himself, to his profession, or to the university, but to society. And in this search, open and unconstrained discourse is essential, for no scholar's work is complete or faultless.

Our duty, then, is not to truth for its own sake, but to truth for society's sake. In Meiklejohn's words: "Our final responsibility as scholars and teachers is not to the truth. It is to the people who need the truth." Hence, the scholar's duty inevitably becomes coupled with social issues. The scholar will become concerned not only with social needs, but with social goals as well. And if society expects the scholar to honor a duty toward the development of socially significant knowledge, society must equally honor his freedom openly to express a concern with social goals. Those whom we serve should see in our zeal for this freedom not the selfish exercise of privilege, but a response to these solemn obligations.

The academic world is now emerging from a long period of silence, a silence that has obscured the true purpose of the university and has weakened its service to society. We now hear many new voices in the universities. Some speak in the traditional well-modulated language of the scholar, some in the sharper tones of dissent, and some in a new language that is less concerned with transmitting ideas than feelings. But behind nearly all the voices is a mutual concern with the quality of life.

Among our students this concern is often reduced to its most elementary level—a demand for the right to life itself. And this is natural, for our students represent the first generation of human beings who have grown to adulthood under the constant threat of instant annihilation.

Our own generation is often criticized because we have, with our own minds and hands, created the weapon of total human destruction; we invented the first atomic bomb. But an even greater sin is that our generation has become numb to the frightful meaning of what we have done.

The newer generation has a different way of sensing things. If nuclear death threatens our generation with an earlier end to a life already in part fulfilled, it threatens our students with the total loss of a life yet to be fulfilled. They, far better than we, can sense the total inhumanity of the civilization that we share.

If they fail to suggest a reasonable way out, the more thoughtful of them have at least defined what it is that we must try to escape. We need the sharpness of their definition of the issue; they need from us the competence and steady purpose that is the gift of experience. Together we can, I believe, secure for all of us what is so gravely threatened by the dual crisis in science and in society—a technology that serves the life of man and a society that cherishes the right to life.

The Biological Revolution

PAUL R. EHRLICH

In the several billion years that life has existed on the earth no event has been as startling as the rise of the species *Homo sapiens* to its present position of prominence. A mere eight thousand years ago mankind—then numbering perhaps five million individuals, far fewer than the number of such a contemporary species as bison—was just one of many kinds of large mammals. But even then man's hunting and food-gathering way of life was causing substantial disturbance in the planetary ecology. There is substantial evidence that Pleistocene man in America brought about the extinction of seventy per cent of the land mammals of large size, such as mammoths, horses, and camels; in Africa, about a third of the megafauna of the land was wiped out. Furthermore, many ecologists attribute the great grasslands of the world to primitive man's use of fire.

About 6000 B.C. the first groups of men, living on the edge of the Fertile Crescent in western Asia, gave up the nomadic life and settled down to agriculture. This change in man's way of life may have been the most important single happening in the history of the earth. It started a trend toward security from hunger for mankind, and initiated an irregular but persistent decline in the death rate in the human population. It also marked the beginning of the potentially lethal disturbance by man of the ecological systems upon which his life depends. When man practices agriculture he arrests the natural processes of ecological change at an unstable midpoint. Much of the planetary environment has already been severely damaged. Now its utter destruction is threatened. In the last century alone the percentage of the earth's land surface classified as desert and wasteland has more than doubled, increasing from less than ten per cent to over twenty-five per cent, largely because of farming and grazing. Now mechanization and the use of pesticides, herbicides, and inorganic nitrogen fertilizers are rapidly accelerating the

From *The Center Magazine*, 2, no. 6: 28–31. Reprinted, by permission, from the November 1969 issue of *The Center Magazine*, a publication of the Center for the Study of Democratic Institutions in Santa Barbara, California.

destruction of the earth's ecosystems. Insecticides alone have the potential of destroying the planet as a habitat for civilized man.

The agricultural revolution has been going on for about eight thousand years now; until a few hundred years ago it was the major cause of decline in the death rate. Population growth is a result of the difference between the birth and death rates, and birth rates have remained relatively high. Agriculture, therefore, has been largely responsible for the spectacular growth of the human population. Virtually alone, it caused the hundred-fold increase from five million to five hundred million between 6000 B.C. and 1650 A.D. Since then other revolutions, industrial and biomedical, have been added to the agricultural revolution. They have all contributed to reducing death rates. The human condition has improved sufficiently since 1650 for a further increase in the population to more than seven hundred times its size at the start of the agricultural revolution. By the nineteen-sixties some 3.5 billion human beings were crowded onto "Spaceship Earth."

While man's population has been growing, his culture has been evolving. He has developed a vast array of techniques for modifying his environment and himself, but he has failed to develop ways of understanding, guiding, and controlling his new-found abilities. Indeed our growing ability to change ourselves and our environments is at the heart of what is being called the biological revolution. For instance:

1. Man has been extremely successful at lowering the human death rate, but has made no significant effort to lower the birth rate. As a result the human population is now growing at a rate which will double it in about thirty-five years, and the population growth continues to outstrip mankind's ability to produce and distribute food in proper quantities and of proper quality. We now have between 1.5 and two billion people living on inadequate diets. That is, there are now more hungry people on earth than the total world population in 1875. Although calories are in short supply, the most serious problem is probably the shortage of high-quality protein.

2. Agricultural technology has developed to the point where very high food yields per acre are attained under certain conditions, primarily in the temperate zone. But the ecological consequences of this technology are widely ignored. Furthermore, modern fishing technology and the escalation of pollution threaten to destroy the resources of the sea on which man depends heavily for the all-important protein component of his diet. These resources are not unlimited, contrary to what one often reads in the popular press. We may already have exceeded the annual sustainable yield, and even under the best possible conditions more than a few-fold increase would be difficult to obtain.

3. Molecular biologists have uncovered many of the basic chemical mechanisms of life and their work may be put to broad practical use in the near future. It should, for instance, soon be possible to predetermine the sex of a child and to correct certain inborn defects of metabolism. Indeed, the future potential for "genetic engineering" seems incredible. But then so does our lack of consideration of just what kinds of human beings we want to engineer, and to what purpose. The discoveries of molecular biology also pose a direct threat to human survival. Some

molecular biologists are at work in chemical and biological warfare laboratories, engineering ever-more-lethal strains of viruses and bacteria which could very well bring the population explosion to an end once and for all.

4. Medical scientists in the United States have followed the flow of federal money and, with varying degrees of success, put a great deal of effort into curing the kinds of disease suffered by middle-aged congressmen. Thus we have a spectacle of vast resources poured into programs leading to heart transplants for a very few individuals in a country where many millions are malnourished. The United States, furthermore, ranks only fifteenth in the world in infant mortality. It is, on the other hand, fortunate that the serious ethical problems associated with organ transplants and prostheses are being aired now while they are still a minor sideshow as far as the mass of humanity is concerned. For in the unlikely event that mankind should solve its pressing problems, reduce the size of the human population, and preserve a world in which medical science flourishes, these questions will become more serious than anything contemplated today. The most elemental questions will be: "what is an individual?" and "how long should an individual's life be preserved?" I can see no theoretical barrier standing in the way of our eventually achieving individual life spans of hundreds or even thousands of years, even though we have not yet made any significant progress in this direction. (We have increased the average life span, permitting more people to live out what is probably a genetically determined span. But there is no known reason why we should not discover how greatly to expand that span.) It is quite clear that in the near future the problem of rejection of transplanted foreign tissues will be more or less solved and substantial life extension by transplants will be possible. But where will the replacements come from, who will pay for them, and who will decide on the allocation of parts in short supply?

5. The most revolutionary of all man's prosthetic devices is probably the computer, which may be used as a replacement for, or an extension of, the human mind. Computers, in conjunction with modern communications systems, have already revolutionized the lives of people in the developed countries. They have done much more than facilitate the obvious breakthroughs in science, technology, and social science. Computers have changed the power structures of institutions from universities to governments; to some degree they have taken decision-making away from human beings. Indeed, there is now talk that technological advances in armaments may require such rapid reaction times that computers will have to make the decisions about whether we will or will not go to war.

6. Man has begun, for the first time, to turn systematically toward the frontiers of the mind. At a strictly empirical level, so-called "brainwashing" has demonstrated the kinds of horrors possible. Holistic experiments on the mind, using drugs, hypnotism, and electrical and surgical intervention, are being made increasingly in order to "change minds." Computers enter the picture here also. They have, for instance, been used successfully to teach children to read and write. Slowly but surely, biologists are beginning to unravel the secrets of the nervous system and learning the bases of perception and memory. It seems a safe assump-

tion that various kinds of controlled biochemical manipulation of the mind eventually will be possible. Such manipulation could, of course, be used for what almost everyone considers an obvious "good"—for example, the cure of mental illness or retardation. However, the potential for misuse of this power, whether accidental or intentional, needs no elaboration.

From these few examples, we can see that because of biological revolutions we are confronted with a set of extraordinarily difficult social and political problems. Such problems are growing at an incredible rate. At the root of all of them is an increasingly efficacious biological technology, which had its origins in agriculture. (If man had never practiced agriculture it is unlikely that he would ever have practiced molecular biology.)

There is a tendency, in meeting new challenges, to solve the problems accompanying biological technology by encouraging the further growth of biological technology, without any careful consideration of the consequences of such a growth. Thus we see the further development of ecologically naive agriculture technology as a "solution" to the population-food crisis. How do we solve the problem of too many people? Develop a better contraceptive technology, but neglect critical questions of human attitudes toward reproduction. Shortage of organs for transplant? Grow them in tissue culture or develop artificial organs. Information overload? Build bigger and better computers and communications networks.

The questions that need asking are all too rarely raised: What for? What kind of life are those additional people we feed going to live? What will the composite men of the Age of Transplants do with their extra years of life? When we can "improve" our minds genetically or biochemically, what kind of world will we have to think about? What kind of information will flow through our improved communications networks, and be processed by future generations of computers? Is Western cultural evolution taking us where we want to go—and taking the rest of humanity where it wants to go? These are some of the fundamental questions raised by the biological revolutions of the last eight thousand years. As the pace of change accelerates, our chances of answering them satisfactorily and modifying our behavior are diminishing rapidly. It is possible that the rapid growth of technology will lead to that common end of runaway evolutionary trends—extinction. The signs now point that way.

Mortgaging the Old Homestead

LORD RITCHIE-CALDER

Past civilizations are buried in the graveyards of their own mistakes, but as each died of its greed, its carelessness or its effeteness another took its place. That was because such civilizations took their character from a locality or region. Today ours is a global civilization; it is not bounded by the Tigris and the Euphrates nor even the Hellespont and the Indus; it is the whole world. Its planet has shrunk to a neighborhood round which a man-made satellite can patrol sixteen times a day, riding the gravitational fences of Man's family estate. It is a community so interdependent that our mistakes are exaggerated on a world scale.

For the first time in history, Man has the power of veto over the evolution of his own species through a nuclear holocaust. The overkill is enough to wipe out every man, woman and child on earth, together with our fellow lodgers, the animals, the birds and the insects, and to reduce our planet to a radioactive wilderness. Or the Doomsday Machine could be replaced by the Doomsday Bug. By gene-manipulation and man-made mutations, it is possible to produce, or generate, a disease against which there would be no natural immunity; by "generate" is meant that even if the perpetrators inoculated themselves protectively, the disease in spreading round the world could assume a virulence of its own and involve them too. When a British bacteriologist died of the bug he had invented, a distinguished scientist said, "Thank God he didn't sneeze; he could have started a pandemic against which there would have been no immunity."

Modern Man can outboast the Ancients, who in the arrogance of their material achievements built pyramids as the gravestones of their civilizations. We can blast our pyramids into space to orbit through all eternity round a planet which perished by our neglect.

A hundred years ago Claude Bernard, the famous French physiologist, enjoined his colleagues, "True science teaches us to doubt and in ignorance to refrain." What he meant was that the scientist must proceed from one tested foothold to the next (like going into a mine-field with a mine-detector). Today we are using the biosphere, the living space, as an experimental laboratory. When the mad scientist of fiction blows himself and his laboratory skyhigh, that is all right, but when scientists and decision-makers act out of ignorance and pretend that it is knowledge, they are putting the whole world in hazard. Anyway, science at best is not wisdom; it is knowledge, while wisdom is knowledge tempered with judgment. Because of overspecialization, most scientists are disabled from exercising judgments beyond their own sphere.

From *Foreign Affairs* (January 1970).

A classic example was the atomic bomb. It was the Physicists' Bomb. When the device exploded at Alamogordo on July 16, 1945, and made a notch-mark in history from which Man's future would be dated, the safe-breakers had cracked the lock of the nucleus before the locksmiths knew how it worked. (The evidence of this is the billions of dollars which have been spent since 1945 on gargantuan machines to study the fundamental particles, the components of the nucleus; and they still do not know how they interrelate.)

Prime Minister Clement Attlee, who concurred with President Truman's decision to drop the bomb on Hiroshima, later said: "We knew nothing whatever at that time about the genetic effects of an atomic explosion. I knew nothing about fall-out and all the rest of what emerged after Hiroshima. As far as I know, President Truman and Winston Churchill knew nothing of those things either, nor did Sir John Anderson who coordinated research on our side. Whether the scientists directly concerned knew or guessed, I do not know. But if they did, then so far as I am aware, they said nothing of it to those who had to make the decision."[1]

That sounds absurd, since as long before as 1927, Herman J. Muller had been studying the genetic effects of radiation, work for which he was awarded the Nobel Prize in 1946. But it is true that in the whole documentation of the British effort, before it merged in the Manhattan Project, there is only one reference to genetic effects—a Medical Research Council minute which was not connected with the bomb they were intending to make; it concerned the possibility that the Germans might, short of the bomb, produce radioactive isotopes as a form of biological warfare. In the Franck Report, the most statesmanlike document ever produced by scientists, with its percipience of the military and political consequences of unilateral use of the bomb (presented to Secretary of War Henry L. Stimson even before the test bomb exploded), no reference is made to the biological effects, although one would have supposed that to have been a very powerful argument. The explanation, of course, was that it was the Physicists' Bomb and military security restricted information and discussion to the bomb-makers, which excluded the biologists.

The same kind of breakdown in interdisciplinary consultation was manifest in the subsequent testing of fission and fusion bombs. Categorical assurances were given that the fallout would be confined to the testing area, but the Japanese fishing-boat *Lucky Dragon* was "dusted" well outside the predicted range. Then we got the story of radiostrontium. Radiostrontium is an analogue of calcium. Therefore in bone-formation an atom of natural strontium can take the place of calcium and the radioactive version can do likewise. Radiostrontium did not exist in the world before 1945; it is a man-made element. Today every young person, anywhere in the world, whose bones were forming during the massive bomb-testing in the atmosphere, carries this brandmark of the Atomic Age. The radiostrontium in their bones is medically insignificant, but, if the test ban (belated recognition) had not prevented the escalation of atmospheric testing, it might not have been.

[1] "Twilight of Empire," by Clement Attlee with Francis Williams (New York: Barnes, 1961), p. 74.

Every young person everywhere was affected, and why? Because those responsible for H-bomb testing miscalculated. They assumed that the upthrust of the H-bomb would punch a hole in the stratosphere and that the gaseous radioactivity would dissipate itself. One of those gases was radioactive krypton, which quickly decays into radiostrontium, which is a particulate. The technicians had been wrongly briefed about the nature of the troposphere, the climatic ceiling which would, they maintained, prevent the fall-back. But between the equatorial troposphere and the polar troposphere there is a gap, and the radiostrontium came back through this fanlight into the climatic jet-streams. It was swept all round the world to come to earth as radioactive rain, to be deposited on foodcrops and pastures, to be ingested by animals and to get into milk and into babies and children and adolescents whose growing bones were hungry for calcium or its equivalent strontium, in this case radioactive. Incidentally, radio-strontium was known to the biologists before it "hit the headlines." They had found it in the skin burns of animals exposed on the Nevada testing ranges and they knew its sinister nature as a "bone-seeker." But the authorities clapped security on their work, classified it as "Operation Sunshine" and cynically called the units of radiostrontium "Sunshine Units"—an instance not of ignorance but of deliberate non-communication.

One beneficial effect of the alarm caused by all this has been that the atoms industry is, bar none, the safest in the world for those working in it. Precautions, now universal, were built into the code of practice from the beginning. Indeed it can be admitted that the safety margins in health and in working conditions are perhaps excessive in the light of experience, but no one would dare to modify them. There can, however, be accidents in which the public assumes the risk. At Windscale, the British atomic center in Cumberland, a reactor burned out. Radioactive fumes escaped from the stacks in spite of the filters. They drifted over the country. Milk was dumped into the sea because radioactive iodine had covered the dairy pastures.

There is the problem of atomic waste disposal, which persists in the peaceful uses as well as in the making of nuclear explosives. Low energy wastes, carefully monitored, can be safely disposed of. Trash, irradiated metals and laboratory waste can be embedded in concrete and dumped in the ocean deeps—although this practice raises some misgivings. But high-level wastes, some with elements the radioactivity of which can persist for *hundreds of thousands* of years, present prodigious difficulties. There must be "burial grounds" (or euphemistically "farms"), the biggest of which is at Hanford, Washington. It encloses a stretch of the Columbia River in a tract covering 575 square miles, where no one is allowed to live or to trespass.

There, in the twentieth century Giza, it has cost more, much more, to bury live atoms than it cost to entomb the sun-god Kings of Egypt. The capital outlay runs into hundreds of millions of dollars and the maintenance of the U.S. sepulchres is over $6 million a year. (Add to that the buried waste of the U.S.S.R., Britain, Canada, France and China, and one can see what it costs to bury live atoms.) And they are very much alive. At Hanford they are kept in million-gallon carbon-steel tanks. Their radioactive vitality keeps the accompanying acids boiling like a witches' cauldron. A cooling system has to be maintained continuously. The vapors from the self-boiling tanks have to be condensed and "scrubbed" (radioactive atoms removed); otherwise a radioactive miasma would escape from the vents. The tanks will not endure as long as the pyramids and certainly not for the hundreds of thousands of years of the long-lived atoms. The acids and the atomic ferments erode the toughest metal, so the tanks have to be periodically decanted. Another method is to entomb them in disused salt mines. Another is to embed them in ceramics, lock them up in glass beads. Another is what is known as "hydraulic fraction": a hole is drilled into a shale formation (below the subsoil water); liquid is piped down under pressure and causes the shale to split laterally. Hence the atoms in liquid cement can be injected under enormous pressure and spread into the fissures to set like a radioactive sandwich.

This accumulating waste from fission plants will persist until the promise, still far from fulfilled, of peaceful thermonuclear power comes about. With the multiplication of power reactors, the wastes will increase. It is calculated that by the year 2000, the number of six-ton nuclear "hearses" in transit to "burial grounds" at any given time on the highways of the United States will be well over 3,000 and the amount of radioactive products will be about a billion curies, which is a mighty lot of curies to be roaming around a populated country.

The alarming possibilities were well illustrated by the incident at Palomares, on the coast of Spain, when there occurred a collision of a refueling aircraft with a U.S. nuclear bomber on "live" mission. The bombs were scattered. There was no explosion, but radioactive materials broke loose and the contaminated beaches and farm soil had to be scooped up and taken to the United States for burial.

Imagine what would have happened if the *Torrey Canyon,* the giant tanker which was wrecked off the Scilly Isles, had been nuclear-powered. Some experts make comforting noises and say that the reactors would have "closed down," but the *Torrey Canyon* was a wreck and the Palomares incident showed what happens when radioactive materials break loose. All those oil-polluted beaches of southwest England and the coasts of Brittany would have had to be scooped up for nuclear burial.

II

The *Torrey Canyon* is a nightmarish example of progress for its own sake. The bigger the tanker the cheaper the freightage, which is supposed to be progress. This ship was built at Newport News, Virginia, in 1959 for the Union Oil Company; it was a giant for the time–810 feet long and 104 feet beam–but, five years later, that was not big enough. She was taken to Japan to be "stretched." The ship was cut in half amidship and a mid-body section inserted. With a new bow, this made her 974 feet long, and her beam was extended 21 feet. She could carry 850,000 barrels of oil, twice her original capacity.

Built for Union Oil, she was "owned" by the Barracuda Tanker Corporation, the head office of which is a filing cabinet in Hamilton, Bermuda. She was registered under the Liberian flag of convenience and her captain and crew were Italians, recruited in Genoa. Just to complicate the international triangle, she was under charter to the British Petroleum Tanker Company to bring 118,000 tons of crude oil from Kuwait to Milford Haven in Wales, via the Cape of Good Hope. Approaching Lands End, the Italian captain was informed that if he did not reach Milford Haven by 11 p.m. Saturday night, he would miss highwater and would not be able to enter the harbor for another five days, which would have annoyed his employers. He took a shortcut, setting course between Seven Stones rocks and the Scilly Isles, and he finished up on Pollard Rock, in an area where no ship of that size should ever have been.

Her ruptured tanks began to vomit oil and great slicks spread over the sea in the direction of the Cornish holiday beaches. A Dutch tug made a dash for the stranded ship, gambling on the salvage money. (Where the salvaged ship could have been taken one cannot imagine, since no place would offer harborage to a leaking tanker). After delays and a death in the futile salvage effort, the British Government moved in with the navy, the air force and, on the beaches, the army. They tried to set fire to the floating oil which, of course, would not volatilize. They covered the slicks with detergents (supplied at a price by the oil companies), and then the bombers moved in to try to cut open the deck and, with incendiaries, to set fire to the remaining oil in the tanks. Finally the ship foundered and divers confirmed that the oil had been effectively consumed.

Nevertheless the result was havoc. All measures had had to be improvised. Twelve thousand tons of detergent went into the sea. Later marine biologists found that the cure had been worse than the complaint. The oil was disastrous for seabirds, but marine organic life was destroyed by the detergents. By arduous physical efforts, with bulldozers and flame-throwers and, again, more detergents, the beaches were cleaned up for the holiday-makers. Northerly winds swept the oil slicks down Channel to the French coast with even more serious consequences, particularly to the valuable shellfish industry. With even bigger tankers being launched, this affair is a portentous warning.

Two years after *Torrey Canyon* an offshore oil rig erupted in the Santa Barbara Channel. The disaster to wildlife in this area, which has island nature reserves and is on the migratory route of whales, seals and seabirds, was a repetition of the *Torrey Canyon* oil-spill. And the operator of the lethal oil rig was Union Oil.

III

Another piece of stupidity shows how much we are at the mercy of ignorant men pretending to be knowledgeable. During the International Geophysical Year, 1957–58, the Van Allen Belt was discovered. This is an area of magnetic phenomena. Immediately it was decided to explode a nuclear bomb in the Belt to see whether an artificial aurora could be produced. The colorful draperies and luminous skirts of the aurora borealis are caused by the drawing in of cosmic particles through the rare bases of the upper atmosphere—ionization it is called; it is like passing electrons through the vacuum tubes of our familiar florescent lighting. The name Rainbow Bomb was given it in anticipation of the display it was expected to produce. Every eminent scientist in the field of cosmology, radio-astronomy or physics of the atmosphere protested at this irresponsible tampering with a system which we did not understand. And typical of the casual attitude toward this kind of thing, the Prime Minister of the day, answering protests in the House of Commons that called on him to intervene with the Americans, asked what all the fuss was about. After all, they hadn't known that the Van Allen Belt even existed a year before. This was the cosmic equivalent of Chamberlain's remark about Czechoslovakia, at the time of Munich, about that distant country of which we knew so little. They exploded the bomb. They got their pyrotechnics and we still do not know the cost we may have to pay for this artificial magnetic disturbance.

In the same way we can look with misgivings on those tracks—the white tails of the jets, which are introducing into our climatic system new factors, the effects of which are immensurable. Formation of rain clouds depends upon water vapor having a nucleus on which to form. That is how artificial precipitation is introduced—the so-called rain-making. So the jets, criss-crossing the weather system, playing noughts and crosses with it, can produce a man-made change.

In the longer term we can foresee even more drastic effects from Man's unthinking operations. At the United Nations' Science and Technology Conference in Geneva in 1963 we took stock of the effects of industrialization on our total environment thus far. The atmosphere is not only the air which humans, animals and plants breathe; it is also the envelope which protects living things from harmful radiation from the sun and outer space. It is also the medium of climate, the winds and the rain. Those are inseparable from the hydrosphere—the oceans, covering seven-tenths of the globe, with their currents and extraordinary rates of evaporation; the biosphere, with its trees and their transpiration; and, in terms of human activities, the minerals mined from the lithosphere, the rock crust. Millions of years ago the sun encouraged the growth of the primeval forests, which became our coal, and the plant growth of the seas, which became our oil. Those fossil fuels, locked away for æons of time, are extracted by man and put back into the atmosphere from the chimney stacks and the exhaust pipes of modern engineering. About 6 billion tons of carbon are mixed with the atmosphere annually. During the past century, in the process of industrialization, with its release of carbon by the burning of fossil fuels, more than 400 billion tons of carbon have been artificially introduced into the atmosphere. The concentration in the air we breathe has been increased by approximately 10 percent, and if all the known reserves of coal and oil were burnt at once, the concentration would be ten times greater.

This is something more than a public health problem, more than a question of what goes into the lungs of an individual, more than a question of smog. The carbon cycle in nature is a self-adjusting mechanism. Carbon dioxide is, of course, indispensable for plants and is, therefore, a source of life, but there is a balance which is maintained by excess carbon being absorbed by the seas. The excess is now taxing this absorption and it can seriously disturb the heat balance of the earth because of what is known as the "greenhouse effect." A greenhouse lets in the sun's rays but retains the heat. Carbon dioxide, as a transparent diffusion, does likewise. It keeps the heat at the surface of the earth and in excess modifies the climate.

It has been estimated that, at the present rate of increase, the mean annual temperature all over the world might increase by 3.6 degrees centigrade in the next forty to fifty years. The experts may argue about the time factor and even about the effects, but certain things are apparent, not only in the industrialized Northern Hemisphere but in the Southern Hemisphere also. The North-polar icecap is thinning and shrinking. The seas, with their blanket of carbon dioxide, are changing their temperature, with the result that marine plant life is increasing and is transpiring more carbon dioxide. As a result of the combination, fish are migrating, changing even their latitudes. On land the snow line is retreating and glaciers are melting. In Scandinavia, land which was perennially under snow and ice is thawing, and arrowheads of over 1,000 years ago, when the black soils were last exposed, have been found. The melting of sea ice will not affect the sea level, because the volume of floating ice is the same as the water it displaces, but the melting of icecaps or glaciers, in which the water is locked up, will introduce additional water to the sea and raise the level. Rivers originating in glaciers and permanent snow fields will increase their flow; and if ice dams, such as those in the Himalayas, break, the results in flooding may be catastrophic. In this process the patterns of rainfall will change, with increased precipitation in some areas and the possibility of aridity in now fertile regions. One would be well advised not to take ninety-nine year leases on properties at present sea level.

IV

At the same conference, there was a sobering reminder of mistakes which can be writ large, from the very best intentions. In the Indus Valley in West Pakistan, the population is increasing at the rate of ten more mouths to be fed every five minutes. In that same five minutes in that same place, an acre of land is being lost through water-logging and salinity. This is the largest irrigated region in the world. Twenty-three million acres are artificially watered by canals. The Indus and its tributaries, the Jhelum, the Chenab, the Ravi, the Beas and the Sutlej, created the alluvial plains of the Punjab and the Sind. In the nineteenth century, the British began a big program of farm development in lands which were fertile but had low rainfall. Barrages and distribution canals were constructed. One thing which, for economy's sake, was not done was to line the canals. In the early days, this genuinely did not matter. The water was being spread from the Indus into a thirsty plain and if it soaked in so much the better. The system also depended on what is called "inland delta drainage," that is to say, the water spreads out like a delta and then drains itself back into the river. After independence, Pakistan, with external aid, started vigorously to extend the Indus irrigation. The experts all said the soil was good and would produce abundantly once it got the distributed water. There were plenty of experts, but they all overlooked one thing—the hydrological imperatives. The incline from Lahore to the Rann of Kutch—700 miles—is a foot a mile, a quite inadequate drainage gradient. So as more and more barrages and more and more lateral canals were built, the water was not draining back into the Indus. Some 40 percent of the water in the unlined canals seeped underground, and in a network of 40,000 miles of canals that is a lot of water. The result was that the watertable rose. Low-lying areas became waterlogged, drowning the roots of the crops. In other areas the water crept upwards, leaching salts which accumulated in the surface layers, poisoning the crops. At the same time the irrigation régime, which used just 1½ inches of water a year in the fields, did not sluice out those salts but added, through evaporation, its own salts. The result was tragically spectacular. In flying over large tracts of this area one would imagine that it was an Arctic landscape because the white crust of salt glistens like snow.

The situation was deteriorating so rapidly that President Ayub appealed in person to President Kennedy, who sent out a high-powered mission which encompassed twenty disciplines. This was backed by the computers at Harvard. The answers were pretty grim. It would take twenty years and $2 billion to repair the damage—more than it cost to create the installations that did the damage. It would mean using vertical drainage to bring up the water and use it for irrigation, and also to sluice out the salt in the surface soil. If those twenty scientific disciplines had been brought together in the first instance it would not have happened.

One more instance of the far-flung consequences of men's localized mistakes: No insecticides or pesticides have ever been allowed into the continent of Antarctica. Yet they have been found in the fauna along the northern coasts. They have come almost certainly from the Northern Hemisphere, carried from the rivers of the farm-states into the currents sweeping south. In November 1969, the U.S. Government decided to "phase out" the use of DDT.

Pollution is a crime compounded of ignorance and avarice. The great achievements of *Homo sapiens* become the disaster-ridden blunders of Unthinking Man—poisoned rivers and dead lakes, polluted with the effluents of industries which give something called "prosperity" at the expense of posterity. Rivers are treated like sewers and lakes like cesspools. These natural systems—and they are living systems—have struggled hard. The benevolent microorganisms which cope with reasonable amounts of organic matter have been destroyed by mineral detergents. Witness our foaming streams. Lake Erie did its best to provide the oxygen to neutralize the pickling acids of the great steel works. But it could not contend. It lost its oxygen in the battle. Its once rich commercial fishing industry died and its revitalizing microorganic life gave place to anaerobic organisms which do not need oxygen but give off foul smells, the mortuary smells of dead water. As one Erie industrialist retorted, "It's not our effluent; it's those damned dead fish."

We have had the Freedom from Hunger Campaign; presently we shall need a Freedom from Thirst Campaign. If the International Hydrological Decade does not bring us to our senses we will face a desperate situation. Of course it is bound up with the increasing population but also with the extravagances of the technologies which claim that they are serving that population. There is a competition between the water needs of the land which has to feed the increasing population and the domestic and industrial needs of that population. The theoretical minimum to sustain living standards is about 300 gallons a day per person. This is the approximate amount of water needed to produce grain for 2½ pounds of bread, but a diet of 2 pounds of bread and 1 pound of beef would require about 2,500 gallons. And that is nothing compared with the gluttonous requirements of steel-making, paper-making and the chemical industry.

Water—just H_2O—is as indispensable as food. To die of hunger one needs more than fifteen days. To die of thirst one needs only three. Yet we are squandering, polluting and destroying water. In Los Angeles and neighboring Southern California, a thousand times more water is being consumed than is being precipitated in the locality. They have preëmpted the water of neighboring states. They are piping it from Northern California and there is a plan to pipe it all the way from Canada's Northwest Territories, from the Mackenzie and the Liard which flow northwards to the Arctic Ocean, to turn them back into deserts.

V

Always and everywhere we come back to the problem of population—more people to make more mistakes, more people to be the victims of the mistakes of others, more people to suffer Hell upon Earth. It is appalling to hear people complacently talking about the population explosion as though it belonged to the future, or world hunger as though it were threatening, when hundreds of millions can testify that it is already here—swear it with panting breath.

We know to the exact countdown second when the nuclear explosion took place—5:30 a.m., July 16, 1945, when the first device went off in the desert of Alamogordo, New Mexico. The fuse of the population explosion had been lit ten years earlier—February 1935. On that day a girl called Hildegarde was dying of generalized septicaemia. She had pricked her finger with a sewing needle and the infection had run amok. The doctors could not save her. Her desperate father injected a red dye into her body. Her father was Gerhard Domagk. The red dye was prontosil which he, a pharmaceutical chemist, had produced and had successfully used on mice lethally infected with streptococci, but never before on a human. Prontosil was the first of the sulfa drugs—chemotherapeutics, which could attack the germ within the living body. Thus was prepared the way for the rediscovery of penicillin—rediscovery because although Fleming had discovered it in 1928, it had been ignored because neither he nor anybody else had seen its supreme virtue of attacking germs within the living body. That is the operative phrase, for while medical science and the medical profession had used antiseptics for surface wounds and sores, they were always labeled "Poison, not to be taken internally." The sulfa drugs had shown that it was possible to attack specific germs within the living body and had changed this attitude. So when Chain and Florey looked again at Fleming's penicillin in 1938, they were seeing it in the light of the experience of the sulphas.

A new era of disease-fighting had begun—the sulfas, the antibiotics, DDT insecticides. Doctors could now attack a whole range of invisible enemies. They could master the old killer diseases. They proved it during the war, and when the war ended there were not only stockpiles of the drugs, there were tooled up factories to produce them. So to prevent the spread of the deadly epidemics which follow wars, the supplies were made available to the war-ravaged countries with their displaced persons, and then to the developing countries. Their indigenous infections and contagions and insect-borne diseases were checked.

Almost symbolically, the first great clinical use of prontosil had been in dealing with puerperal sepsis, childbed fever. It had spectacularly saved mothers' lives in Queen Charlotte's Hospital, London. Now its successors took up the story. Fewer mothers died in childbirth, to live and have more babies. Fewer infants died, fewer toddlers, fewer adolescents. They lived to marry and have children. Older people were not killed off by, for instance, malaria. The average life-span increased.

Professor Kingsley Davis of the University of California at Berkeley, the authority on urban development, has presented a hair-raising picture from his survey of the world's cities. He has shown that 38 percent of the world's population is already living in what are defined as urban places. Over one-fifth of the world's population is living in cities of 100,000 or more. And over one-tenth of the world's population is now living in cities of a million or more inhabitants. In 1968, 375 million people were living in million-and-over cities. The proportions are changing so quickly that on present trends it would take only 16 years for half the world's population to be living in cities and only 55 years for it to reach 100 percent.

Within the lifetime of a child born today, Kingsley Davis foresees, on present trends of population-increase, 15 billion people to be fed and housed—nearly five times as many as now. The whole human species would be living in cities of a million-and-over inhabitants, and—wait for it!—the biggest city would have 1.3 billion inhabitants. That means 186 times as many as there are in Greater London.

For years the Greek architect Doxiadis has been warning us about such prospects. In his Ecumenopolis—World City—one urban area like confluent ulcers would ooze into the next. The East Side of World City would have as its High Street the Eurasian Highway stretching from Glasgow to Bangkok, with the Channel Tunnel as its subway and a built-up area all the way. On the West Side of World City, divided not by the tracks but by the Atlantic, the pattern is already emerging, or rather, merging. Americans already talk about Boswash, the urban development of a built-up area stretching from Boston to Washington; and on the West Coast, apart from Los Angeles, sprawling into the desert, the realtors are already slurring one city into another all along the Pacific Coast from the Mexican Border to San Francisco. We don't need a crystal ball to foresee what Davis and Doxiadis are predicting; we can already see it through smog-covered spectacles; a blind man can smell what is coming.

The danger of prediction is that experts and men of affairs are likely to plan for the predicted trends and confirm these trends. "Prognosis" is something different from "prediction." An intelligent doctor having diagnosed your symptoms and examined your condition does not say (except in novelettes), "You have six months to live." An intelligent doctor says, "Frankly, your condition is serious. Unless you do so-and-so, and I do so-and-so, it is bound to deteriorate." The operative phrase is "do so-and-so." We don't have to plan for trends; if they are socially undesirable our duty is to plan away from them; to treat the symptoms before they become malignant.

We have to do this on the local, the national and the international scale, through intergovernmental action, because there are no frontiers in present-day pollution and destruction of the biosphere. Mankind shares a common habitat. We have mortgaged the old homestead and nature is liable to foreclose.

Frontier Freedoms and Space Age Cities

C. W. GRIFFIN, JR.

Several years ago, in a magazine article ominously entitled "Is Your Right to Drive in Danger?" former Secretary of Commerce Luther Hodges denounced the mass-transit boosters who want frontier Americans to stop driving their motorized steeds to work and ride the stagecoach with the dudes. "Fuzzy-minded theorists" reacting to spreading traffic jams, warned Mr. Hodges, have proposed imposition of rush-hour tolls to reduce traffic volume on major urban highways and a cutback in the urban freeway-building program. Such proposals, he said, threaten "our right to come and go as we please . . . a heritage from frontier days."

Nostalgia for frontier freedoms is manifest in almost every facet of American life—from the popularity of Wild West paperbacks, screenplays, and television shows to the economic "rugged individualism" extolled by businessmen living off cost-plus government contracts. The vicarious reliving of frontier days is both psychological escape and protest against the increasing frictions and collisions accompanying urban growth.

Many public issues reveal the depth of the pioneer strain. Obscured by campus protests and civil rights battles, less dramatic struggles to retain pioneer freedoms vent the irritations of urban Americans. In 1963, the citizens of Phoenix, Arizona, repealed a "socialistic" housing code that required slum landlords to provide toilets, running water, and other decadent luxuries for tenants. Blissfully oblivious of their downstream neighbors, the citizens of frontier-fabled St. Joseph, Missouri, fought for the right to discharge raw sewage into the Missouri River. After voting down two sewage-treatment bond issues, they abandoned their struggle only after the federal government instituted court action against their city. In June 1955, against the orders of the Los Angeles County Air Pollution Control District, citizens fought to retain their forefathers' right to burn trash in backyard incinerators rather than accept the imposition of a municipal trash collection system. The exercise of this right released some 500 tons of contaminants into Los Angeles's smog-polluted atmosphere every day. But that fact meant little compared with the historic freedom to burn trash.

Even more passionate in defending frontier freedoms are the gun buffs parroting the propaganda of the National Rifle Association and others who profit from gun traffic. At the primitive level of frontier civilization, vigilantism and widespread gun ownership were perhaps a partially rational adaptation to that lawless society. But today, in the tension-filled, crowded cities of modern America, resurgence of the gun mentality is a dangerous, infantile regression. Atavistic frontier outposts, such as Dallas, produce proportionately 100 to 200 times as many gun killings as civilized, gun-controlled nations such as Great Britain.

Instancing frontier freedoms in a less lethal but more visible way, the trash-littered streets of American cities immediately differentiate them from European cities. This still potent American talent for fouling the urban environment is merely a pallid vestige of the frontiersmen's talent. Everett Dick's book *The Sodhouse Frontier: 1854-1890* depicts the stark historical facts. In Wichita, Kansas, a typical frontier town, the ground at the hitching post was a stinking, fly-infested cesspool. Superimposed on this heady odor was the stench of outhouses, pigpens, and garbage tossed into the street or left at the doorstep by these pristine rugged individualists. The artfully blended aroma inspired the Wichita *Eagle's* fastidious editor, a nineteenth-century precursor of the "fuzzy-minded theorists and wild-eyed planners" denounced by latter-day frontiersmen, to advocate controls that must have seemed socialistic: "heavy fines should be imposed on those who will throw slops, old meats, and decaying vegetable matter at their doors or on the street."

The price paid for these filthy freedoms only began with the stench. Spread by disease-bearing flies that fed on the filth of outhouses and streets, typhoid epidemics sometimes swept through entire towns. Cholera, smallpox, and diphtheria were also epidemic. Primitive frontier technology made adequate sanitation difficult, and frontier medicine was just this side of witchcraft. But the mentally musclebound individualism of the frontier, with its contempt for public sanitation, extorted a graver price than was necessary. Even the almost instinctively visualized picture of vigorous, ruddy-faced pioneers was largely a myth. Disembarking from trains arriving in these frontier towns, visiting Easterners were often struck by the natives' sallow complexions, a consequence of the prairie's most common disease, the ague.

Town-building in frontier America often entailed an incredibly crude combination of greed and chicanery. Federal policy encouraged the mischievous work of land speculators (as it still does in subtler ways). To qualify for purchase of a 160-acre quarter section at a bargain price, a frontier land preemptor merely had to produce a witness to swear that the land was cultivated and improved with a "habitable dwelling" twelve feet square in plan. Among the ruses used to circumvent the law was a house on wheels (the archetypal trailer), rented for $5 a day and moved from claim to claim. Another was a house erected by railroad agents at the intersection of four lots, with one corner in each of the four 160-acre plots.

Railroad towns exhibited the "impatience, the speculative greed, and the lack of taste which characterized the founders," according to planner John W. Reps. Existing towns, hoping to become important cities, fought fiercely for the railroads' favor. But the railroads sometimes by-passed towns that refused to pay the required tribute and built their own. Railroad town-building was often ludicrous. Seeking access to newly opened markets west of the Mississippi, some railroad towns literally moved as track construction proceeded westward. One such town moved westward to exploit the location of Cheyenne, Wyoming, terminal depot for a rail line. According to a witness, a train arrived laden with framehouse lumber, furniture, paling, old tents, and other paraphernalia. A train guard called out, "Gentlemen, here's Julesburg."

In a letter dated March 13, 1878, preserved by the State Historical Society of Colorado, a commentator on the impending move of a town on the Denver and Rio Grande Railroad, wrote: "Soon Garland will be a thing of the past, and only battered oyster cans, cast-off clothing, old shoes, and debris generally will mark the site of where once stood a flourishing city, with its hotels, its stores, its theater comique."

Even under the normal conditions of frontier town development, the transience of population worked against the cultivation of the civic spirit that inspires the stable populations of old European cities to preserve and enhance the beauty and amenity of their urban environment. Migration became a way of life for many Midwesterners. In his essay *The Significance of the Frontier in American History*, historian Frederick Jackson Turner tells of hundreds of men, less than fifty years old, who had resettled five or six times.

Capitalists instituted a civilizing process when they bought out the original settlers of small villages. Following traders, ranchers, miners, and farmers, this last wave of settlers transformed the frontier from villages of roughhewn loghouses to towns of respectable brick structures.

But the farmers' practice of depleting the soil and moving on to exhaust new virgin tracts of prairie land nourished the frontier attitude of anarchic, antisocial individualism. With El Dorado always beckoning from beyond the western horizon, the migrant frontiersmen cared little for their present surroundings. Their attitude survives in today's mobile Americans who have learned well their forefathers' lesson to value private goods higher than public goods.

What little justification was retained by the frontier ethic disappeared with the advent of the Industrial Revolution and the accelerated growth of American cities. The U.S. was not alone in creating hellish urban landscapes. The Coketowns of Dickens's day, with their soot-blackened buildings, crowded tenements, smoke-poisoned air, and foul, gray rivers, were models for their American counterparts. But America's frontier ethic, reinforcing the warped, utilitarian philosophy of the new industrialists, produced more uniformly desolate cities than those in Europe. The older European cities generally had a form and a tradition that resisted the depredations of the capitalists. But nineteenth-century Americans lacked the architectural splendors of Venice's Piazza San Marco or London's magnificent system of parks to inspire and educate them. They had no tradition of city planning or land-use control. And they were burdened with a city-hating intellectual history expressed most violently by Thomas Jefferson: "The mobs of great cities add just so much to the support of pure government as sores do to the strength of the human body."

Flaunting the national contempt for urban values, we designed our cities as sensitively as barnyards. Riverfronts were sacrificed to factories, warehouses, and wharves, with no concession to the citizens' need for recreational park sites. Sprawling railroad yards blighted vast areas adjacent to the central business districts. Soot-belching engines chugged through the densest urban districts, in contrast to the European example of banning railroads from the urban core. In New York's most thickly settled slums, people were packed into six-story tenements at insect-scale densities unequaled in the Western world.

Yet, despite the tedious horror of these bleak monuments to greed, urban growth continued for decades without major breakdowns. White immigrants, sustained by the American dream, accepted their start in the urban slums. Successful urbanites, retreating before the advancing immigrants throughout most of our history, deserted the Commons in Boston, the Independence Hall area in Philadelphia, and Astor Place in New York. In Henry James's novel *Washington Square* (published in 1881), a character described the strategy: "At the end of three or four years we'll move. That's the way to live in New York. . . .Then you always get the last thing." Fueled by the immigrants' hope of upward economic mobility and the middle class's hope of outward physical mobility, the industrializing-urbanizing process kept going, despite the increasing frictions of accelerated growth.

Today, however, as hostility supplants hope in the central city ghettos, the old urbanizing mechanism threatens to break down. The earlier Italian, German, Irish, and Jewish newcomers never had to contend with the race prejudice that helps keep Negro migrants trapped in the ghettos. Like the earlier immigrants, urban Negroes occupy the lowest rung of the ladder to success. But for them the higher rungs have been sawed off, and the old American dream inspired by hope has yielded to escapist delusions inspired by dope.

Prosperous Americans' dreams of continual escape, if not shattered, are fading. Slums, with their accompanying crime and other social ills, are spreading outward through the old suburbs and even into newer ones, continuing the historic trend. Current housing policies offer no hope of eliminating the slum racket. It remains the last pure vestige of primitive nineteenth-century capitalism, subsidized by ludicrously generous federal depreciation formulas, archaic local tax-assessing policies, and slumlord-favoring condemnation pricing procedures. So long as they are profitable (and possibly even after they aren't), slums will endure. Unlike the more civilized European nations that have eradicated slums, the United States has no national commitment to do so.

The white retreat from the spreading blight, through suburbia and exurbia, can't continue indefinitely. The rising costs of land and public services and the ordeal of intra-urban transportation are curtailing the sprawling development that has spread recklessly over the countryside throughout the past two decades. The carving of white commuters' freeways through black neighborhoods is meeting stronger resistance. Decaying central cities, spreading traffic jams, smog, polluted water, and vanishing recreational space have become the norm. Intensive planning and control on a regional basis, a subjugation of anarchic individual and local prerogatives to overall community interests offer the only hope of creating a decent urban environment, or even halting the deterioration of our present environment.

The idea of planning and conservation hits American traditions broadside. The successive waves of pioneers and farmers who rolled westward across the continent were as oblivious to their impact as the breakers that crash on the beach, shift the sands, and bend the coastline. Less innocent but more destructive, the industrial pirates who followed the pioneers plundered the resources and fouled the natural beauty of this continent, often to the applause of Congress. Not until the timber raiders had left trails of blackened woods and stripped hillsides, demonstrating to all but the willfully blind that our resources were not inexhaustible, did Congress reluctantly enact conservation legislation.

The most zealous nineteenth-century preachers of the frontier ethic glorified timber thieves as public benefactors persecuted by an oppressive government. In a speech delivered in 1852 to the U.S. House of Representatives, Henry Hastings Sibley, delegate from the Wisconsin Territory, denounced the federal trespass laws as "a disgrace to the country and to the nineteenth century." In ringing phrases, Delegate Sibley extolled the virtuous victims of the law:

> Especially is he pursued with unrelenting severity, who has dared to break the silence of the primeval forest by the blows of the American ax. The hardy lumberman who has penetrated to the remotest wilds of the North-west, to drag from their recesses the materials for building up towns and cities in the great valley of the Mississippi, has been particularly marked out as a victim. After enduring all the privations and subjecting himself to all the perils incident to his vocation—when he has toiled for months to add by his honest labor to the comfort of his fellow men, and to the aggregate wealth of the nation, he finds himself suddenly in the clutches of the law for trespassing on the public domain. The proceeds of his long winter's work are reft from him, and exposed to public sale for the benefit of his paternal government . . . and the object of this oppression and wrong is further harassed by vexatious law proceedings against him.

As evidence that praise for timber thieves was eminently respectable, Frederick Jackson Turner cites the lack of protest from other Congressmen and the subsequent success of Delegate Sibley. He became Minnesota's first governor, a regent of its university, president of its historical society, and a doctor of laws from

Princeton University—an exquisitely polished pillar of society. Commenting, Turner concludes, "Thus many of the pioneers, following the ideal of the right of the individual to rise, subordinated the rights of the nation and posterity to the desire that the country should be 'developed' and that the individual should advance with as little interference as possible. Squatter doctrines and individualism have left deep traces upon American conceptions."

Today, well over half a century since Turner wrote this passage, those "traces" remain disgracefully deep. Contemporary industrial polluters, who recklessly poison the nation's air and water, secretly agree with Delegate Sibley, but they can no longer openly defend lawbreaking without staining their image. The contemptuous, plundering spirit of nineteenth-century capitalism lives on today in industrial polluters, highway-building lobbyists, land speculators, slumlords, and investment builders. Unlike the Swedes, who have accepted city planning and public land controls for centuries, we subsidize the destruction of our urban environment. That is why our disordered, traffic-plagued metropolises are such a contrast to Stockholm's well-planned open spaces and its coordinated rapid transit system.

More than any major American city, Los Angeles illustrates the ludicrous conflict between frontier mythology and contemporary reality. The frontier mystique survives in almost pristine purity in America's Southwest. As described by the late Christopher Rand in his book *Los Angeles: The Ultimate City*, the "short-range jet set," shuttling between the southern California beaches and the Texas oil fields, lives a luxurious imitation of frontier life—camping, hunting, fishing, and ranching. Inspired by such political heroes as Governor Ronald Reagan and Arizona Senator Barry Goldwater, Los Angeles's make-believe frontiersmen still preach laissez-faire, rugged individualism, despite their city's desperate economic dependence on federal arms contracts.

More ominous for their city's future, these latter-day Babbitts cheer growth while still preaching the provincial frontier virtues that obstruct Los Angeles's orderly transition into a supermetropolis. Before the year 2000, the Los Angeles region's projected thirty-two-million population should overtake New York as the nation's largest urbanized area. Yet, the transplanted, small-town Midwesterners who have dominated Los Angeles's stream of immigrants have never really accepted their new home as a city.

Los Angeles's physical form conveys the paradox of small-town people congregating in a big city. Its sprawling, unplanned development, a product of the city's extreme laissez-faire frontier tradition, has spawned a host of social ills. Unlike New York police, patrolling beats on foot, Los Angeles's officers patrol the city's sprawling precincts in radio cars, remote and alienated from its citizens. With its characteristic contempt for public services, Los Angeles long ago taxed rail transit service to death to build competing highways. Having abandoned the rail network, which could have promoted orderly development and conserved open space, the city delivered itself almost totally to the cult of the automobile, thereby encouraging sprawl. Commuters forced to drive in the frenzied traffic made Los Angeles the photochemical smog capital of the world. The lack of public transportation also aggravates the isolation of the Watts ghetto, severely limiting access to the city's widely scattered centers of employment.

Los Angeles's obsession with the private side of life is expressed in other ways. Its zoning ordinances favor the single-family house as the most morally exalted form of human habitation, isolated from corrupting contact with residential apartments or commercial development. This policy promotes a more rigorous racial segregation than could possibly be achieved in a city such as New York, with its greater mingling of land uses and its greater reliance on public facilities.

The City of the Angels has squandered countless opportunities to build public parks and preserve open space; despite the unequaled resource of twenty-five square miles of wild land within its city limits, Los Angeles has no counterpart to New York's Central Park or San Francisco's equally remarkable Golden Gate Park.

The private developers' bulldozed desecration of the Santa Monica Mountains recalls the depredations of the nineteenth-century miners, who washed away hillsides, silted streams, and ruined fertile valleys in their frantic search for gold. The conservationists' failure to preserve these mountains for public use is another reminder of Los Angeles's frontier ethos. Los Angeles land speculators pursue their frantic quest for private wealth in a desert of public poverty.

The throat-catching rhetoric of frontier freedom still stirs Americans, but at best the frontier ethic was only a partially valid response to the challenge of the wilderness. It has lasted at least a century past its time, and, viewed in retrospect, many of its values appear corrupt. Our nineteenth-century tradition of destroying our own natural environment doubtless helps anesthetize us to American atrocities against nature in Vietnam, where massive jungle defoliation and crop poisoning may inflict permanent ecological damage. And our casual slaughter of Vietnamese villagers may be a contemporary version of frontier barbarism, which viewed the annihilation of animal herds and Indians as totally just sacrifices to the white man's superior power.

Today, even in its less objectionable aspects, the anarchic individualism of the frontier is as outmoded as the prairie schooner. What has survived is not true rugged individualism, but its ugly residue—the obsession with private over public goods. To accommodate 100 million additional Americans destined to descend on our cities and suburbs over the next three decades, we must reject the insipid dream of a tamed frontier transformed into a semirural, suburban Arcadia. There is no place to hide from the stark realities of our crowded, city-centered society with its inevitable frictions, conflict, and turmoil. As pioneers on the urban frontier, can we outgrow the values of our rural ancestors and adapt to civilized urban life?

The Roots of Lawlessness

HENRY STEELE COMMAGER

It was in 1838 that the young Abraham Lincoln—he was not yet twenty-nine—delivered an address at Springfield, Illinois, on "The Perpetuation of Our Political Institutions." What he had to say is curiously relevant today. Like many of us, Lincoln was by no means sure that our institutions could be perpetuated; unlike some of us, he was convinced that they should be.

What, after all, threatened American political institutions? There was no threat from outside, for "all the armies of Europe, Asia, and Africa combined could not by force take a drink from the Ohio or make a track on the Blue Ridge in a thousand years." No, the danger was from within. "If destruction be our lot, we must ourselves be its author and finisher. As a nation of freemen, we must live through all time or die by suicide."

This, Lincoln asserted, was not outside the realm of possibility; as he looked about him, he saw everywhere a lawlessness that, if persisted in, would surely destroy both law and Constitution and eventually the nation itself. In the end, lawlessness *did* do that—lawlessness in official guise that refused to abide by the Constitutional processes of election or by the will of the Constitutional majority. It was to be Lincoln's fate to be called upon to frustrate that lawless attack on the nation, and to be remembered as the savior of the Union. And it has been our fate to be so bemused by that particular threat to unity—the threat of sectional fragmentation—that we have failed to appreciate the danger that so deeply disturbed Lincoln at the threshold of his political career.

The explanation of our confusion is rooted in history. The United States invented, or developed, a new kind of nationalism, one that differed in important ways from the nationalism that flourished in the Old World. One difference was the enormous emphasis that Americans, from the beginning, put on territory and the extent to which American nationalism came to be bound up with the acquisition of all the territory west to the Pacific and with the notion of territorial integrity on a continental scale. The idea that a nation should "round out" its territory, or take over all unoccupied territory, was not prominent in the nationalism of the Old World. Territory there, after all, was pretty well pre-empted, and there was no compelling urge to acquire neighboring land for its own sake.

In the Old World, threats to unity had been, for the most part, dynastic or religious rather than territorial. As proximity did not dictate assimilation, distance did not require separation. But in America space and distance appeared to pose threats to the Union from the beginning. Some of the Founding Fathers, to be sure, continued to think of unity and disunion in Old World terms of interests and factions, rather than in terms of territory. This was perhaps because they had little choice in the matter or none that they could publicly acknowledge, for the United States was born the largest nation in the Western world, and the Framers had to put a good face on the matter. But Europeans generally, and some Americans, long familiar with Montesquieu's dictum that, while a republic could flourish in a small territory, a large territory required a despotism, assumed that the new United States, with boundaries so extensive, could not survive.

Jefferson and his associates were determined to prove Montesquieu mistaken. From the beginning, they formulated a counter-argument that size would strengthen rather than weaken the nation. Brushing aside the warnings of such men as Gouverneur Morris, they boldly added new states west of the Alleghenies. They made the Louisiana Purchase, seized West Florida, and looked with confidence to acquiring all the territory west to the Pacific; thus, the Lewis and Clark expedition into foreign territory, something we would not tolerate today in our territory. Territorial expansion and integrity became a prime test of the American experiment, and within a few years what had been a test became, no less, a providential command: Manifest Destiny. From this flowed naturally the principle that the proof of union was territorial, and the threat to union territorial.

A second American contribution to the ideology of nationalism was, in time, to become its most prominent characteristic; the notion that national unity required not merely territorial unity but social and cultural. In the Old World, the only cultural unity that had any meaning was religious: The principle *Cuius regio eius religio* was dictated by the fact that the ruler's religion determined the religion of the state. But class distinctions were taken for granted, as were profound differences in cultural and social habits—in speech, for example, or in such simple things as food and drink and dress and games.

Americans changed this pattern around. They rejected the principle of religious unity—doubtless in large part because they had no alternative—and then substituted cultural for religious unity. Americans were not expected to pray alike, but they were expected to talk alike, dress alike, work alike, profess the same moral code, and subscribe to the same legal code. Eventually, as we know, they were expected to eat the same food, drink the same liquors, play the same games, read the same journals, watch the same television programs, and even have the same political ideas—expectations never seriously entertained by, say, German or Italian nationalists.

American nationalism thus became, at a very early stage, a self-conscious affair of imposing unity upon a vast territory, a heterogeneous population, and a miscellaneous culture. Because there was indeed land enough to absorb some forty million immigrants, because those immigrants were so heterogeneous that (with the exception of the Germans and, in modern times, the Negroes) they were unable to maintain a cultural identity counter to the prevailing American culture, and because, in provisions for naturalization and opportunities for active participation, the political system was the most hospitable of any in the world, an artificial unity became, in time, a real unity. Americans managed to achieve a single language with fewer deviations than were to be found in England, Germany, or Italy; to achieve a common education—not universal, to be sure, but more nearly universal than elsewhere in the nineteenth-century world; to create a common political system, each state like every other state; and, *mirabile dictu*, to conjure up a common history and a common past.

The threat to union, as Lincoln saw it in 1838, was not sectional or economic or social or even moral; it was quite simply the "spirit of lawlessness." As early as *Notes on Virginia* (1782), Thomas Jefferson had confessed that he trembled for his country when he reflected that "God is just and his justice cannot sleep forever," and throughout his life Jefferson saw slavery as a moral threat, but in this he was more farsighted than most. The threat to union posed by slavery was unprecedented; it was a product of that elementary fact by now so familiar that we take it for granted: that deep economic, social, and moral differences assumed a geographical pattern, and that the American Constitutional system, namely federalism, permitted them to take a political pattern as well. As it happened, the sectional pattern of slavery was in mortal conflict with a very different sectional pattern, and it was this conflict that proved in the end fatal to the thrust for Southern independence: the sectionalism created by the Mississippi River and its tributaries. That, as it turned out, was the decisive fact that preserved the Union; when, in the summer of 1863, Lincoln wrote that "the signs look better," what he noted first was that "the Father of Waters goes again unvexed to the sea."

Suppose slavery had rooted itself vertically in the Mississippi Valley rather than horizontally across the South from the Atlantic to Texas. That would have given sectionalism a more rational base than it had in the South—a base that in all likelihood would have been impregnable.

Here we have one of the assumptions about American history that gets in the way of an appreciation of our distinctive characteristics. Because thirteen American states, hugging the Atlantic seaboard, became a single nation spanning a continent, we either take American unity for granted or consider fragmentation only in terms of the experiment in Southern nationalism, which misfired. But there was nothing foreordained about the triumph of unity. Why did not the vast American territory between Canada and the Gulf of Mexico go the way of Latin America, which, with a common religion, language, and territory, nevertheless fragmented into numerous independent states?

The spectacular nature of the American achievement has bemused almost all students of American nationalism and dictated most interpretations of the problem of American unity. The transcendent fact of slavery and of the Negro—so largely responsible for creating a sectionalism that did not yield to the ameliorating influences of economy, social mobility, cultural uniformity, and political compromise—has distracted our attention from other threats, if not to union then to unity. Because we had a civil war, precipitated by secional fragmentation, we did not imagine that we could have a revolution based on social fragmentation.

We are tempted to say of Lincoln's Springfield address that it was shortsighted of him not to have seen that the threats to union were slavery and sectionalism—

something he learned, in time. We should say rather that he was farsighted in imagining the possibility of a very different threat to union: an internal dissension and lawlessness that bespoke a breakdown in cultural and moral unity. This is what confronts us today: blacks against whites, old against young, skinheads against eggheads, militarists against doves, the cities against the suburbs and the countryside—hostilities that more and more frequently erupt into open violence.

Two considerations warrant attention. First, that what Lincoln described was in fact normal—we have always been a lawless and a violent people. Thus, our almost unbroken record of violence against the Indians and all others who got in our way—the Spaniards in the Floridas, the Mexicans in Texas; the violence of the vigilantes on a hundred frontiers; the pervasive violence of slavery (a "perpetual exercise," Jefferson called it, "of the most boisterous passions"); the lawlessness of the Ku Klux Klan during Reconstruction and after; and of scores of race riots from those of New Orleans in the 1860s to those of Chicago in 1919. Yet, all this violence, shocking as it doubtless was, no more threatened the fabric of our society or the integrity of the Union than did the lawlessness of Prohibition back in the Twenties. The explanation for this is to be found in the embarrassing fact that most of it was official, quasi-official, or countenanced by public opinion: exterminating the Indian; flogging the slave; lynching the outlaw; exploiting women and children in textile mills and sweatshops; hiring Pinkertons to shoot down strikers; condemning immigrants to fetid ghettos; punishing Negroes who tried to exercise their civil or political rights. Most of this was socially acceptable—or at least not wholly unacceptable—just as so much of our current violence is socially acceptable: the 50,000 automobile deaths every year; the mortality rate for Negro babies twice that for white; the deaths from cancer induced by cigarettes or by air pollution; the sadism of our penal system and the horrors of our prisons; the violence of the police against what Theodore Parker called the "perishing and dangerous classes of society."

What we have now is the emergence of violence that is not acceptable either to the Establishment, which is frightened and alarmed, or to the victims of the Establishment, who are no longer submissive and who are numerous and powerful. This is the now familiar "crime in the streets," or it is the revolt of the young against the economy, the politics, and the wars of the established order, or it is the convulsive reaction of the blacks to a century of injustice. But now, too, official violence is no longer acceptable to its victims—or to their ever more numerous sympathizers: the violence of great corporations and of government itself against the natural resources of the nation; the long drawn-out violence of the white majority against Negroes and other minorities; the violence of the police and the National Guard against the young; the massive and never-ending violence of the military against the peoples of Vietnam and Cambodia. These acts can no longer be absorbed by large segments of our society. It is this new polarization that threatens the body politic and the social fabric much as religious dissent threatened them in the Europe of the sixteenth and seventeenth centuries.

A second consideration is this: The center of gravity has shifted from "obedience" to "enforcement." This shift in vocabulary is doubtless unconscious but nonetheless revealing. Obedience is the vocabulary of democracy, for it recognizes that the responsibility for the commonwealth is in the people and appeals to the people to recognize and fulfill their responsibility. Enforcement is the language of authority prepared to impose its will on the people. Lincoln knew instinctively that a democracy flourishes when men obey and revere the law; he did not invoke the language of authority. We are no longer confident of the virtue or good will of the people; so it is natural that we fall back on force. The resort to lawless force—by the Weathermen, the Black Panthers, the Ku Klux Klan, the hardhats; by the police in Chicago; by the National Guard at Orangeburg, South Carolina, and Kent, Ohio; or by highway police at Jackson, Mississippi—is a confession that both the people and their government have lost faith in the law, and that the political and social fabric that has held our society together is unraveling: "By such examples," said Lincoln at Springfield, "the lawless in spirit are encouraged to become lawless in practice."

It has long been our boast—repeated by the President's Commission on Violence—that notwithstanding our lengthy history of violence we have never had a "revolution," and that our political system appears to be more stable than those of other nations. Our only real revolution took a sectional pattern and was not called revolution but rebellion; since it was rationalized by high-minded rhetoric, led by honorable men, and fought with gallantry, it speedily took on an aura of respectability, and to this day Southerners who would be outraged by the display of the red flag of rebellion proudly wave the Stars and Bars of rebellion.

Thus, like most of our violence, violence against the Constitution and the Union, and by implication against the blacks who were to be kept in slavery, is socially approved. Where such violence has been dramatic (as in lynching or industrial warfare), it has not been widespread or prolonged; where it has been widespread and prolonged (as in slavery and the persistent humiliation of the Negro), it has not been dramatic. Where its victims were desperate, they were not numerous enough or strong enough to revolt; where they were numerous (never strong), they did not *appear* to be desperate, and it was easy to ignore their despair. Now this situation is changing. Lawlessness is more pervasive than ever; the sense of outrage against the malpractices of those in power is more widespread and articulate; and the divisions in society are both deeper and more diverse, and the response to them more intractable.

One explanation of our current malaise is that it seems to belong to the Old World pattern rather than that of the New. Much of the rhetoric of the conflict between generations is that of class or religious wars—class war on the part of, let us say, Vice President Agnew; religious protest on the part of Professor Charles Reich and those involved in what he calls "the greening of America." If this is so, it goes far toward explaining some of our current confusion and blundering: the almost convulsive efforts to distract attention from the genuine problems of environment, social injustice, and war, and to fasten it on such phony issues as campus unrest or social permissiveness or pornography. What this implies is ominous: Our society is not prepared, either by history or philosophy, for the kind of lawlessness and violence and alienation that now afflict us.

Why is this so ominous?

Traditionally, our federal system could and did absorb regionalism and particularism, or channel these into political conduits. More accurately than in any other political system, our representatives represent geographical places—a specific Congressional district or a state—and our parties, too, are organized atop and through states. Our system is not designed to absorb or to dissipate such internal animosities as those of class against class, race against race, or generation against generation.

A people confident of progress, with a social philosophy that assumed that what counted most was children and that took for granted that each new generation would be bigger, stronger, brighter, and better educated than its predecessor, could afford to indulge the young. "Permissiveness" is not an invention of Dr. Spock but of the first settlers in America. Today, a people that has lost faith in progress and in the future, and that has lost confidence in the ameliorating influence of education, indulges instead in convulsive counter-attacks upon the young.

A nation with, in Jefferson's glowing words, "land enough for our descendants to the thousandth and thousandth generation" could indulge itself in reckless exploitation of that land—the mining of natural resources, the destruction of deer and bison and beavers, of the birds in the skies and the fish in the streams, and could even (this was a risky business from the beginning) afford to ignore its fiduciary obligations to coming generations without exciting dangerous resentment. But a nation of more than two hundred million, working through giant corporations and giant governments that ravage, pollute, and destroy on a scale heretofore unimagined, cannot afford such self-indulgence. Nor can it persist in its habit of violating its fiduciary obligations without outraging those who are its legal and moral legatees.

A nation that had more and better land available for its people than any other in history and that, for the first time, equated civilization with the pastoral life and exalted the farmer over the denizen of the city could take urban development in its stride, confident that the city would never get the upper hand, as it were. Modern America seems wholly unable to adapt its institutions or its psychology to massive urbanization, but proceeds instead to the fateful policy of reducing its farm population to a fraction and, at the same time, destroying its cities and turning them into ghettos that are breeding places for crime and violence.

A system that maintained and respected the principle of the superiority of the civil power over that of the military could afford to fight even such great conflicts as the Civil War, the First World War, and the Second World War without danger to its Constitution or its moral character. It cannot absorb the kind of war we are now fighting in Southeast Asia without irreparable damage to its moral values, nor can it exercise power on a world scale without moving the military to the center of power.

No nation could afford slavery, certainly not one that thought itself dedicated to equality and justice. The issue of slavery tore the nation asunder and left wounds still unhealed. Here is our greatest failure: that we destroyed slavery but not racism, promised legal equality but retained a dual citizenship, did away with legal exploitation of a whole race but substituted for it an economic exploitation almost as cruel. And this political and legal failure reflects a deeper psychological and moral failure.

Unlike some of our contemporary politicians, Lincoln was not content with decrying lawlessness. He inquired into its causes and, less perspicaciously, into its cure. In this inquiry, he identified two explanations that illuminated the problem. These—translated into modern vocabulary—are the decline of the sense of fiduciary obligation and the evaporation of political resourcefulness and creativity. Both are still with us.

No one who immerses himself in the writings of the Revolutionary generation—a generation still in command when Lincoln was born—can doubt that the sense of obligation to posterity was pervasive and lively. Recall Tom Paine's plea for independence: "'Tis not the concern of a day, a year, or an age; *Posterity* are virtually involved in the contest and will be . . . affected to the end of time." Or John Adam's moving letter to his beloved Abigail when he had signed the Declaration of Independence: "Through all the gloom I can see the rays of ravishing light and glory. *Posterity* will triumph in this day's transaction." Or Dr. Benjamin Rush's confession, after his signing, that "I was animated constantly by a belief that I was acting for the benefit of the whole world and of future ages." So were they all.

The decline of the awareness of posterity and of the fiduciary principle is a complex phenomenon not unconnected with the hostility to the young that animates many older Americans today. It is to be explained, in part, by the concept of an equality that had to be vindicated by each individual; in part, by the fragmentation of the Old World concepts of family and community relationships, which was an almost inevitable consequence of the uprooting from the Old World and the transplanting to the New; in part, by the seeming infinity of resources and the seeming advantages of rapid exploitation and rapid aggrandizement; in part, by the weakness of governmental and institutional controls; in part, by the ostentatious potentialities of industry and technology, the advent of which coincided with the emergence of nationalism in the United States; and, in part, by the triumph of private enterprise over public.

However complex the explanation, the fact is simple enough: We have wasted our natural resources more recklessly than has any other people in modern history and are persisting in this waste and destruction even though we are fully aware that our children will pay for our folly and our greed.

Lincoln's second explanation—if it can be called that—was that we had suffered a decline of the creativity and resourcefulness that had been the special distinction of the Founding Fathers. "The field of glory is harvested," he said, "the crop is already appropriated." Other leaders would emerge, no doubt, and would "seek regions hitherto unexplored." At a time when Martin Van Buren was in the White House, to be succeeded by Harrison, Tyler, Polk, Taylor, Fillmore, Pierce, and Buchanan, that expectation doubtless represented the triumph of hope over history. But the decline of political creativity and leadership was not confined to this somewhat dismal period of our history; it has persisted into our own day. We can no more afford it than could Lincoln's generation. At a time when the white population of English America was less than three million, it produced Franklin and Washington, Jefferson and Madison, John Adams and Hamilton, John Jay and James Wilson, George Wythe and John Marshall, and Tom Paine, who emerged, first, in America. We have not done that well since.

Even more arresting is the undeniable fact that this Revolutionary generation produced not only many of our major leaders but all of our major political institutions, among them federalism, the Constitutional convention, the Bill of Rights, the effective separation of powers, judicial review, the new colonial system, the political party. It is no exaggeration to say that we have been living on that political capital ever since.

Here again the explanation is obscure. There is the consoling consideration that the Founding Fathers did the job so well that it did not need to be done over; the depressing consideration that American talent has gone, for the past century or so, more into private than into public enterprise; and the sobering consideration that at a time when our chief preoccupation appears to be with extension of power rather than with wise application of resources, those "regions hitherto unexplored" appear to be in the global arena rather than the domestic. Whatever the explanation, lack of leadership is the most prominent feature on our political landscape, and lack of creativity the most striking characteristic of our political life.

It is still true that, "if destruction be our lot, we must ourselves be its author"—that the danger is not from without but from within. But

> . . . passions spin the plot;
> We are betrayed by what is false within.

For, paradoxically, the danger from within is rooted in and precipitated by foreign adventures that we seem unable either to understand or to control. We have not been attacked from Latin America or from Asia; we have attacked ourselves by our own ventures into these areas.

The problem Lincoln faced in 1838 is with us once again: the breakdown of the social fabric and its overt expression in the breakdown of the law. Lincoln's solution, if greatly oversimplified, is still valid: reverence for the law. A people will revere the law when it is just and is seen to be just. But no matter how many litanies we intone, we will not induce our people to obey laws that those in authority do not themselves obey. The most striking feature of lawlessness in America today is that it is encouraged by public examples. It is no use telling a Mississippi Negro to revere the law that is palpably an instrument of injustice to him and his race. It is no use exhorting the young to obey the law when most of the major institutions of our society—the great corporations, the powerful trade unions, the very instruments of government—flout the law whenever it gets in their way. It is of little use to admonish a young man about to be drafted to revere the law when he knows that he is to be an instrument for the violation of international law on a massive scale by his own government. It is futile to celebrate the rule of law and the sanctity of life when our own armies engage in ghoulish "body counts," burn unoffending villages, and massacre civilians. While governments, corporations, and respectable elements in our society not only countenance lawlessness and violence but actively engage in it, violence will spread and lawlessness will flourish. We are betrayed by what is false within.

New Light on the Human Potential

HERBERT A. OTTO

William James once estimated that the healthy human being is functioning at less than 10 per cent of his capacity. It took more than half a century before this idea found acceptance among a small proportion of behavioral scientists. In 1954, the highly respected and widely known psychologist Gardner Murphy published his pioneering volume *Human Potentialities.* The early Sixties saw the beginnings of the human potentialities research project at the University of Utah and the organization of Esalen Institute in California, the first of a series of "Growth Centers" that were later to be referred to as the Human Potentialities Movement.

Today, many well-known scientists such as Abraham Maslow, Margaret Mead, Gardner Murphy, O. Spurgeon English, and Carl Rogers subscribe to the hypothesis that man is using a very small fraction of his capacities. Margaret Mead quotes a 6 per cent figure, and my own estimate is 5 per cent or less. Commitment to the hypothesis is not restricted to the United States. Scientists in the U.S.S.R. and other countries are also at work. Surprisingly, the so-called human potentialities hypothesis is still largely unknown.

What are the dimensions of the human potential? The knowledge we do have about man is minimal and has not as yet been brought together with the human potentialities hypothesis as an organizing force and synthesizing element. Of course, we know more about man today than we did fifty years ago, but this is like the very small part of the iceberg we see above the water. Man essentially remains a mystery. From the depths of this mystery there are numerous indicators of the human potential.

Certain indicators of man's potential are revealed to us in childhood. They become "lost" or submerged as we succumb to the imprinting of the cultural mold

From *Saturday Review* (December 20, 1969). Copyright 1969 Saturday Review, Inc., 14–17. Reprinted by permission.

in the "growing up" process. Do you remember when you were a child and it rained after a dry spell and there was a very particular, intensive earthy smell in the air? Do you remember how people smelled when they hugged you? Do you recall the brilliant colors of leaves, flowers, grass, and even brick surfaces and lighted signs that you experienced as a child? Furthermore, do you recall that when father and mother stepped into the room you *knew* how they felt about themselves, about life, and about you—at that moment.

Today we know that man's sense of smell, one of the most powerful and primitive senses, is highly developed. In the average man this capacity has been suppressed except for very occasional use. Some scientists claim that man's sense of smell is almost as keen as a hunting dog's. Some connoisseurs of wines, for example, can tell by the bouquet not only the type of grape and locality where they were grown but even the vintage year and vineyard. Perfume mixers can often detect fantastically minute amounts in mixed essences; finally there are considerable data on odor discrimination from the laboratory. It is also clear that, since the air has become an overcrowded garbage dump for industrial wastes and the internal combustion engine, it is easier to turn off our sense of smell than to keep it functioning. The capacity to experience the environment more fully through our olfactory organs remains a potential.

It is possible to regain these capacities through training. In a similar manner, sensory and other capacities, including visual, kinesthetic, and tactile abilities, have become stunted and dulled. We perceive less clearly, and as a result we feel less—we use our dulled senses to close ourselves off from both our physical and interpersonal environments. Today we also dull our perceptions of how other people feel and we consistently shut off awareness of our own feelings. For many who put their senses to sleep it is a sleep that lasts unto death. Again, through sensory and other training the doors of perception can be cleansed (to use Blake's words) and our capacities reawakened. Anthropological research abounds with reports of primitive tribes that have developed exceptional sensory and perceptive abilities as a result of training. Utilization of these capacities by modern man for life-enrichment purposes awaits the future.

Neurological research has shed new light on man's potential. Work at the UCLA Brain Research Institute points to enormous abilities latent in everyone by suggesting an incredible hypothesis: The ultimate creative capacity of the human brain may be, for all practical purposes, infinite. To use the computer analogy, man is a vast storehouse of data, but we have not learned how to program ourselves to utilize these data for problem-solving purposes. Recall of experiential data is extremely spotty and selective for most adults. My own research has convinced me that the recall of experiences can be vastly improved by use of certain simple training techniques, provided sufficient motivation is present.

Under emergency conditions, man is capable of prodigious feats of physical strength. For example, a middle-aged California woman with various ailments lifted a car just enough to let her son roll out from under it after it had collapsed on him. According to newspaper reports the car weighed in excess of 2,000 pounds. There are numerous similar accounts indicating that every person has vast physical reserve capacities that can be tapped. Similarly, the extraordinary feats of athletes and acrobats—involving the conscious and specialized development of certain parts of the human organism as a result of consistent application and a high degree of motivation—point to the fantastic plasticity and capabilities of the human being.

Until World War II, the field of hypnosis was not regarded as respectable by many scientists and was associated with stage performances and charlatanism. Since that time hypnosis has attained a measure of scientific respectability. Medical and therapeutic applications of hypnosis include the use of this technique in surgery and anesthesiology (hypnoanesthesia for major and minor surgery), gynecology (infertility, frigidity, menopausal conditions), pediatrics (enuresis, tics, asthma in children, etc.), and in dentistry. Scores of texts on medical and dental hypnosis are available. Dr. William S. Kroger, one of the specialists in the field and author of the well-known text *Clinical and Experimental Hypnosis,* writes that hypnotherapy is "directed to the patient's needs and is a methodology to tap the 'forgotten assets' of the *hidden potentials* of behavior and response that so often lead to new learnings and understanding." (My italics.) As far as we know now, the possibilities opened by hypnosis for the potential functioning of the human organism are not brought about by the hypnotist. Changes are induced by the subject, utilizing his belief-structure, with the hypnotist operating as an "enabler," making it possible for the subject to tap some of his unrealized potential.

The whole area of parapsychology that deals with extrasensory perception (ESP), "mental telepathy," and other paranormal phenomena, and that owes much of its development to the work of Dr. J. B. Rhine and others is still regarded by much of the scientific establishment with the same measure of suspicion accorded hypnosis in the pre-World War II days. It is of interest that a number of laboratories in the U.S.S.R. are devoted to the study of telepathy as a physical phenomenon, with research conducted under the heading "cerebral radiocommunication" and "bioelectronics." The work is supported by the Soviet government. The reluctance to accept findings from this field of research is perhaps best summarized by an observation of Carl C. Jung's in 1958:

> [Some] people deny the findings of parapsychology outright, either for philosophical reasons or from intellectual laziness. This can hardly be considered a scientifically responsible attitude, even though it is a popular way out of quite extraordinary intellectual difficulty.

Although the intensive study of creativity had its beginnings in fairly recent times, much of value has been discovered about man's creative potential. There is evidence that every person has creative abilities that can be developed. A considerable number of studies indicate that much in our educational system—including conformity pressures exerted by teachers, emphasis on memory development, and rote learning, plus the overcrowding of classrooms—militates against the development of creative capacities. Research has established that children between the ages of two and three can learn to read, tape record a story, and type it as it is played back. Hundreds of children between the ages of four and six have been taught by the Japanese pedagogue Suzuki to play violin concertos. Japanese research with infants and small children also suggests the value of early "maximum input" (music, color, verbal, tactile stimuli) in the personality development of infants. My own observations tend to confirm this. We have consistently underestimated the child's capacity to learn and his ability to realize his potential while *enjoying* both the play elements and the discipline involved in this process.

In contrast to the Japanese work, much recent Russian research appears to be concentrated in the area of mentation, with special emphasis on extending and enlarging man's mental processes and his capacity for learning. As early as 1964 the following appeared in *Soviet Life Today*, a U.S.S.R. English language magazine:

> The latest findings in anthropology, psychology, logic, and physiology show that the potential of the human mind is very great indeed. "As soon as modern science gave us some understanding of the structure and work of the human brain, we were struck with its enormous reserve capacity," writes Yefremov (Ivan Yefremov, eminent Soviet scholar and writer). "Man, under average conditions of work and life, uses only a small part of his thinking equipment....If we were able to force our brain to work at only half its capacity, we could, without any difficulty whatever, learn forty languages, memorize the large Soviet Encyclopedia from cover to cover, and complete the required courses of dozens of colleges."
>
> The statement is hardly an exaggeration. It is the generally accepted theoretical view of man's mental potentialities.
>
> How can we tap this gigantic potential? It is a big and very complex problem with many ramifications.

Another signpost of man's potential is what I have come to call the "Grandma Moses effect." This artist's experience indicates that artistic talents can be discovered and brought to full flowering in the latter part of the life cycle. In every retirement community there can be found similar examples of residents who did not use latent artistic abilities or other talents until after retirement. In many instances the presence of a talent is suspected or known but allowed to remain fallow for the best part of a lifetime.

Reasons why well-functioning mature adults do not use specific abilities are complex. Studies conducted at the University of Utah as a part of the Human Potentialities Research Project revealed that unconscious blocks are often present. In a number of instances a person with definite evidence that he has a specific talent (let's say he won a state-wide contest in sculpture while in high school) may not wish to realize this talent at a later time because he fears this would introduce a change in life-style. Sometimes fear of the passion of creation is another roadblock in self-actualization. On the basis of work at Utah it became clear that persons who live close to their capacity, who continue to activate their potential, have a pronounced sense of well-being and considerable energy and see themselves as leading purposeful and creative lives.

Most people are unaware of their strengths and potentialities. If a person with some college background is handed a form and asked to write out his personality strengths, he will list, on an average, five or six strengths. Asked to do the same thing for his weaknesses, the list will be two to three times as long. There are a number of reasons for this low self-assessment. Many participants in my classes and marathon group weekends have pointed out that "listing your strengths feels like bragging about yourself. It's something that just isn't done." Paradoxically, in a group, people feel more comfortable about sharing problem areas and hang-ups than they do about personality resources and latent abilities. This is traceable to the fact that we are members of a pathology-oriented culture. Psychological and psychiatric jargon dealing with emotional dysfunction and mental illness has become the parlance of the man in the street. In addition, from early childhood in our educational system we learn largely by our mistakes—by having them pointed out to us repeatedly. All this results in early "negative conditioning" and influences our attitude and perception of ourselves and other people. An attitudinal climate has become established which is continually fed and reinforced.

As a part of this negative conditioning there is the heavy emphasis by communications media on violence in television programs and motion pictures. The current American news format of radio, television, and newspapers—the widely prevalent idea of what constitutes news—results from a narrow, brutalizing concept thirty or forty years behind the times and is inimical to the development of human potential.

The news media give much time and prominent space to violence and consistently underplay "good" news. This gives the consumer the impression that important things that happen are various types of destructive activities. Consistent and repeated emphasis on bad news not only creates anxiety and tension but instills the belief that there is little except violence, disasters, accidents, and mayhem abroad in the world. As a consequence, the consumer of such news gradually experiences a shift in his outlook about the world leading to the formation of feelings of alienation and separation. The world is increasingly perceived as a threat, as the viewer becomes anxious that violence and mayhem may be perpetrated on him from somewhere out of the strange and unpredictable environment in which he lives. There slowly grows a conviction that it is safer to withdraw from such a world, to isolate himself from its struggles, and to let others make the decisions and become involved.

As a result of the steady diet of violence in the media, an even more fundamental and insidious erosion in man's self-system takes place. The erosion affects what I call the "trust factor." If we have been given a certain amount of affection, love, and understanding in our formative years, we are able to place a certain amount of trust in our fellow man. Trust is one of the most important elements in today's society although we tend to minimize its importance. *We basically trust people.* For example, we place an enormous amount of trust in our fellow man when driving on a freeway or in an express lane. We trust those with whom we are associated to fulfill their obligations and responsibilities. The element of trust is the basic rule in human relations. When we distrust people, they usually sense our attitude and reciprocate in kind.

The consistent emphasis in the news on criminal violence, burglarizing, and assault makes slow but pervasive inroads into our reservoir of trust. As we hear and read much about the acts of violence and injury men perpetrate upon one another, year after year, with so little emphasis placed on the loving, caring, and humanitarian acts of man, we begin to trust our fellow man less, and we thereby diminish ourselves. It is my conclusion the media's excessive emphasis on violence, like the drop of water on the stone, erodes and wears away the trust factor in man. By undermining the trust factor in man, media contribute to man's estrangement from man and prevent the full flourishing and deeper development of a sense of community and communion with all men.

Our self-concept, how we feel about ourselves and our fellow man and the world, is determined to a considerable extent by the inputs from the physical and interpersonal environment to which we are exposed. In the physical environment, there are the irritants in the air, i.e., air pollution plus the ugliness and noise of megapolis. Our interpersonal environment is characterized by estrangement and distance from others (and self), and by the artificiality and superficiality of our social encounters and the resultant violation of authenticity. Existing in a setting that provides as consistent inputs multiple irritants, ugliness and violence, and lack of close and meaningful relationships, man is in danger of becoming increasingly irritated, ugly, and violent.

As work in the area of human potentialities progressed, it has become ever clearer that personality, to a much greater degree than previously suspected, functions in response to the environment. This is additional confirmation of what field theorists and proponents of the holistic approach to the study of man have long suspected.

Perhaps the most important task facing us today is the regeneration of our environment and institutional structures such as school, government, church, etc. With increasing sophistication has come the recognition that institutions are not sacrosanct and that they have but one purpose and function—to serve as a framework for the actualization of human potential. It is possible to evaluate both the institution and the contribution of the institution by asking this question: "To what extent does the function of the institution foster the realization of human potential?"

Experimental groups consistently have found that the more a person's environment can be involved in the process of realizing potential, the greater the gains. It is understandable why scientists concerned with the study of personality have been reluctant to consider the importance of here-and-now inputs in relation to personality functioning. To do so would open a Pandora's box of possibilities and complex forces that until fairly recently were considered to be the exclusive domain of the social scientist. Many scientists and professionals, particularly psychotherapists, feel they have acquired a certain familiarity with the topography of "intra-psychic forces" and are reluctant to admit the reality of additional complex factors in the functioning of the personality.

It is significant that an increasing number of psychologists, psychiatrists, and social workers now realize that over and beyond keeping up with developments in their respective fields, the best way to acquire additional professional competence is through group experiences designed for personal growth and that focus on the unfolding of individual possibilities. From this group of aware professionals and others came much of the initial support and interest in Esalen Institute and similar "Growth Centers" later referred to as the Human Potentialities Movement.

Esalen Institute in Big Sur, California, was organized in 1962 by Michael Murphy and his partner, Dick Price. Under their imaginative management the institute experienced a phenomenal growth, established a branch in San Francisco, and is now famous for its seminars and weekend experiences offered by pioneering professionals. Since 1962 more than 100,000 persons have enrolled for one of these activities.

The past three years have seen a rapid mushrooming of Growth Centers. There are more than fifty such organizations ranging from Esalen and Kairos Institutes in California to Oasis in Chicago and Aureon Institute in New York. The experiences offered at these Growth Centers are based on several hypotheses: 1) that the average healthy person functions at a fraction of his capacity; 2) that man's most exciting life-long adventure is actualizing his potential; 3) that the group environment is one of the best settings in which to achieve growth; and 4) that personality growth can be achieved by anyone willing to invest himself in this process.

Human potentialities is rapidly emerging as a discrete field of scientific inquiry. Exploring the human potential can become the meeting ground for a wide range of disciplines, offering a dynamic synthesis for seemingly divergent areas of research. It is possible that the field of human potentialities offers an answer to the long search for a synthesizing and organizing principle which will unify the sciences. The explosive growth of the Human Potentialities Movement is indicative of a growing public interest. Although there exist a considerable number of methods—all designed to tap human potential—work on assessment or evaluation of these methods has in most instances not progressed beyond field testing and informal feedback of results. The need for research in the area of human potentialities has never been more pressing. The National Center for the Exploration of Human Potential in La Jolla, California, has recently been organized for this purpose. A nonprofit organization, the center will act as a clearing house of information for current and past approaches that have been successful in fostering personal growth. One of the main purposes of the center will be to conduct and coordinate basic and applied research concerning the expansion of human potential.

Among the many fascinating questions posed by researchers are some of the following: What is the relationship of body-rhythms, biorhythms, and the expansion of sensory awareness to the uncovering of human potential? What are the applications of methods and approaches from other cultures such as yoga techniques, Sufi methods, types of meditation, etc.? What is the role of ecstasy and play vis-á-vis the realizing of human possibilities? The exploration of these and similar questions can help us create a society truly devoted to the full development of human capacities—particularly the capacities for love, joy, creativity, spiritual experiencing. This is the challenge and promise of our lifetime.

Priorities for the Seventies

ROBERT L. HEILBRONER

To talk about national priorities is to talk about precedence, the order in which things are ranked. It is not difficult to establish what that order is in America today. Military needs rank above civilian needs. Private interests rank above public interests. The claims of the affluent take precedence over those of the poor. This is all so familiar that it no longer even has the power to rouse us to indignation. There is no shock value left in saying that we are a militaristic nation, or a people uninterested in the elimination of poverty, or a citizenry whose only response to the decay of the cities is a decision to move to the suburbs. To get a rise out of people, these days, one has to say something really outrageous, such as that the main cultural effect of advertising on television is to teach our children that grown-ups tell lies for money.

But I do not want to expatiate on the present order of things. For I presume that to talk of priorities is to determine what they *should* be. What should come first? What ought to be on top of the agenda?

To ask such questions is to invite pious answers. I shall try to avoid the pieties by grouping my priorities into three categories. The first has to do with our immediate survival—not as a nation-state, but as a *decent* nation-state. The second has to do with our ultimate salvation. The third with our moving from survival to salvation.

The initial set of priorities is simple to specify. It consists of three courses of action necessary to restore American society to life. The first of these is the demilitarization of the national budget. That budget now calls for the expenditure of $80-billion a year for military purposes. Its rationale is that it will permit us to fight simultaneously two "major" (though, of course, non-nuclear) wars and one "minor" or "brushfire" war. This requires the maintenance of eighteen army divisions, as against eleven in 1961; of 11,000 deliverable nuclear warheads, compared with 1,100 in 1961; of a naval force far larger than that of any other nation in the world.

Politically, economically—even militarily—this budget is a disaster for America. It has sucked into the service of fear and death the energies and resources desperately needed for hope and life. Until and unless that budget is significantly cut, there will be little chance of restoring vitality to American society.

By how much can it be cut? The Nixon administration proposes to reduce it by $4- to $6-billion by June 1971, and by an equivalent amount each year for another four years. *Fortune* magazine claims it can be cut faster—$17.6-billion less by June 1972. Seymour Melman, professor of industrial engineering at Columbia University, has stated that it can be slashed by over $50-billion—and his reduced budget would still leave 2,300,000 men under arms, an obliterative power aimed at 156 Soviet cities, and an air and naval armada of staggering dimensions.

This conflicting testimony suggests that the question of how much the budget can be cut depends not on expertise alone, but on outlook—on how much one wants to reassign into other channels the resources absorbed by the military. Here let us make a first approximation as to how much the military budget can be cut by determining how large are the life-giving aims to which we must now give priority. I see two of these as being essential for the attainment of decency in American society. One is the long overdue relief of poverty. In 1967, 10 per cent of all white families, 35 per cent of all black families, and 58 per cent of all black families over age sixty-five, lived in poverty—a condition that we define by the expenditure for food of $4.90 per person per week. *Per week.* To raise these families to levels of minimum adequacy will require annual transfer payments of approximately $10- to $15- billion. This is half the annual cost of the Vietnam war. I would make this conversion of death into life a first guide to the demilitarization of the budget.

A second guide is provided by the remaining essential priority for American decency. This is the need to rebuild the cities before they collapse on us. This means not only replacing the hideous tenements and junkyards and prison-like schools of the slums, but providing the services needed to make urban living tolerable—regular garbage collection, dependable police protection, and adequate recreational facilities.

It has been estimated that New York City alone would need $4.3-billion per year for ten years to replace its slums. To provide proper levels of health and educational services would add another billion. And then there are Chicago and Newark and Washington and Los Angeles. It would take at least $20- to $25-billion a year for at least a decade to begin to make the American city viable.

These objectives are minimal requirements for America. Fortunately, they are easy to accomplish—at least in a technical sense. There will be no problem in cutting the military budget by the necessary $30- to $40-billion once that task is entrusted to men who are not prisoners of the military-industrial superiority complex. There are no great problems in the alleviation of poverty that the direct disbursement of money to the poor will not tolerably remedy. And whereas I do not doubt that it will be hard to build new cities handsomely and well, I do not think it will be difficult to tear down the rotten hulks that now constitute the slums, and to replace them with something that is unmistakably better.

Thus the essential priorities have the virtue of being as simple as they are compelling. This does not mean, however, that we will therefore attend to them. On the contrary, the chances are good that we will not do what must be done, or at best will act halfheartedly, in token fashion. The power of the vested interests of business and politics and labor in the preservation of military spending is enormous. The unwillingness of the American upper and middle classes to assist the less fortunate is a clear matter of record. The resistance to the repair of the cities is too well documented to require exposition here. Hence, we may never rise to the simple challenge of making America viable. In that case it is easy to make a prognosis for this country. It will be even more than it is today a dangerous, dirty, and depressing place in which to live. There will be an America, but it will not be a civilized America.

There is, however, at least a fighting chance that we *will* cut the military budget, that we *will* declare poverty to be an anachronistic social disease, that we *will* begin to halt the process of urban deterioration. Let me therefore speak of another set of priorities—one that many people would place even higher on the list than my initial three. They are, first, the elimination of racism in the United States, and second, the enlistment of the enthusiasm—or at least the tolerance—of the younger generation.

I have said that these priorities have to do with our salvation rather than with our survival. This is because their achievement would lift the spirit of America as if a great shadow had been removed from its soul. But like all salvations, this one is not near at hand. For unlike the first set of priorities, which is well within our power to accomplish, this second set lies beyond our present capabilities. Even if we manage to cut the military budget, to end poverty, to rebuild the cities, the bitter fact remains that we do not know how to change the deep conviction within the hearts of millions of Americans that blackness spells inferiority. Neither do we know how to win the enthusiasm of young people—and I mean the best and soberest of them, not the drop-outs and the do-nothings—for a society that is technocratic, bureaucratic, and depersonalized.

Thus the second set of priorities is considerably different from the first. It constitutes a distant goal, not an immediate target. Any projection of what America should try to become that does not include the goals of racial equality and youthful enlistment is seriously deficient, but any projection that does not expect that we will be a racist and alienated society for a long while is simply unrealistic.

What then are we to do in the meantime? How are we to set for ourselves a course that is within the bounds of realism and that will yet move us toward the long-term goals we seek? This brings me to my third set of priorities—a set of tasks neither so simple as the first, nor so difficult as the second. I shall offer four such tasks—not in any particular order of urgency—as exemplifying the *kinds* of priorities we need in order to move from mere survival toward ultimate salvation.

I begin with a proposal that will seem small by comparison with the large-scale goals discussed so far. Yet, it is important for a society that seeks to lessen racial tensions and to win the approbation of the young. It consists of a full-scale effort to improve the treatment of criminality in the United States.

No one knows exactly how large is the criminal population of the United States, but certainly it is very large. Two million persons a year pass through the major prisons and "reformatories," some 300,000 residing in them at any given time. Another 800,000 are on probation or parole; a still larger number lurk on the fringes of serious misbehavior, but have so far escaped the law. Our response to this core of seriously disturbed and dangerous persons is to send a certain number, who are unfortunate enough to get caught, to prison. These prisons include among them the foulest places in America—charnel houses comparable to Nazi concentration camps. At Tucker State Farm in Arkansas, inmates have been reported to be forty to sixty pounds underweight, and have been subjected to acts of unspeakable cruelty, and even to murder. The sadistic practices in military stockades have become notorious. But even the more humane institutions largely fail in their purposes. In New York State the rate of recidivism for crimes of comparable importance is 50 per cent. A recent FBI study of 18,000 federal offenders released in 1963 showed that 63 per cent had been arrested again five years later.

Indeed, as every criminologist will testify, prisons mainly serve not to deter, but to confirm and train the inmate for a career in criminality. These institutions exist not for the humanization but for the brutalization of their charges.

What is to be done? One inkling of the course to be followed is provided by reflecting on the statistics of prison care. In federal adult institutions we average one custodial person per seven inmates; one educational person per 121 inmates; one treatment person per 179 inmates. In local institutions and jails the ratio of educational or treatment personnel to inmates broadens to one to 550. In some state correctional institutions the ratio is as high as one to 2,400.

Another clue is suggested by the fact that work-release camps, widely used abroad to bridge the gap between prison and normal life, are available here in only four states. Still another is the clear need for the early detection of asocial behavior among school children, and for the application of therapy before, not after, criminality has become a way of life.

It must be obvious that an all-out effort to lessen criminality is not nearly so simple to achieve as slicing the military budget or tearing down the slums. But neither is it so difficult to achieve as racial tolerance. I suggest it is an objective well worth being placed high on the list of those "middle" priorities for which we are now seeking examples.

Recently, the Administration has declared the reform of prisons to be a major objective. Let us now see if this rhetoric will be translated into action.

My second suggestion is not unrelated to the first. Only it concerns not criminals, but those who represent the other end of the spectrum—the symbols of law and order, the police forces of America. I propose that an important item on the agenda must be an effort to contain and control a police arm that is already a principal reason for black anger and youthful disgust.

First, a few words to spell out the problem. In New York City, the Patrolmen's Benevolent Association, itself a potent force for reaction (as witness its key role in the defeat of the Civilian Review Board), is now outflanked on the right by "law enforcement" groups of super-patriot vigilantes who on several occasions have taken the law into their own hands. The actions of the Chicago police force as seen on national television during the Democratic convention do not require further comment here. In Detroit the United Press reports "open hostility" between the city's mainly white police force and the city's 40 per cent black population. At Berkeley, Harvard, and Columbia we have witnessed the dreadful spectacle of policemen smashing indiscriminately at students and using tear gas and Mace.

There is no simple cure for this ugly situation. Police forces are recruited largely from the lower middle class; they bring with them deeply ingrained attitudes of racial contempt and envious hostility to privileged youth. But there are at least a few measures that can be taken to prevent what is already a dangerous rift from widening further. To begin with, one way to minimize police abuse of Negroes is to minimize occasions for contact with them. The obvious conclusion is that black ghettos must be given the funds and the authorization to form their own police forces. Another necessary step is to lessen the contact of police forces with college youth; the legalization of marijuana would help in this regard. So would the training of special, highly paid, *unarmed*, elite police forces who would be used to direct all police actions having to do with civil demonstrations.

I do not doubt that there are many other ways to attack the problem. What is essential is to take measures now that will prevent the police from driving a permanent wedge between white and black, between student and government. Mace, tear gas, and billy clubs are weapons of repression, not of order. Few steps would contribute more to the return of American self-respect than those that would assist the growth of law and order among the forces of law and order.

Here, too, the report of the Eisenhower Commission signals an overdue awakening of public consciousness. But here again we shall have to see whether this awareness will be translated into action.

My third suggestion seemingly departs markedly from the first two. It concerns a wider problem than criminality or police misbehavior, but not a less pressing problem. It is how to rescue the environment from the devastating impact of an unregulated technology.

I need mention only a few well-known results of this ferocious process of destruction. Lake Erie is dead. The beaches at Santa Barbara are deserted. The air in New York is dangerous to breathe. We are drowning in a sea of swill; in a normal year the United States "produces" 142 million tons of smoke and fumes, seven million junked cars, twenty million tons of waste paper, forty-eight billion used cans, and fifty trillion gallons of industrial sewage. And presiding over this rampant process of environmental overloading is the most fearsome reality of all—a population that is still increasing like an uncontrollable cancer on the surface of the globe. I know of no more sobering statistic in this regard than that between now and 1980 the number of women in the most fertile age brackets, eighteen to thirty-two, will double.

Aghast at this terrific imbalance between the power of technology and the capacity of society to control and order the effects of technology, some people are calling for a moratorium on technology, for a kind of national breathing space while we decide how to deal with such problems as the sonic boom and the new supertankers. But this approach ignores the fact that it is not new technology alone that breeds trouble, but the cumulative effect of our existing technology; perhaps no single cause is more responsible for air pollution than the familiar combustion engine.

Hence, I call for a different priority in dealing with this crucial question—not for less technology, but for more technology *of a different kind*. For clearly what we need are technological answers to technological problems. We need a reliable method of birth control suitable for application among illiterate and superstitious peoples. We need an exhaustless automobile, a noiseless and versatile airplane. We need new methods of reducing and coping with wastes—radioactive, sewage, gaseous, and liquid. We need new modes of transporting goods and people, within cities and between them.

The priority then is technological research—research aimed at devising the techniques needed to live in a place that we have just begun to recognize as (in Kenneth Boulding's phrase) our Spaceship Earth. There is a further consideration here, as well. Many people wonder where we can direct the energies of the engineers, draftsmen, scientists, and skilled workmen who are now employed in building weapons systems, once we cut our military budget. I suggest that the design of a technology for our planetary spaceship will provide challenge enough to occupy their attention for a long time. We have not hesitated to support private enterprise for years while it devoted its organizational talents to producing instruments of war. We must now begin to apply equally lavish support while private enterprise perfects the instruments of peace. There would be an important side effect to such a civilian-industrial complex. It is that young people who are bored or repelled by the prospect of joining an industrial establishment, one of whose most spectacular accomplishments has been the rape of the environment, will, I believe, feel differently if they are offered an opportunity to work in research and development that has as its aim the renewal and reconstitution of this planet as a human habitat.

The items I have suggested as middle priorities could be extended into a long list. But what I am suggesting, after all, are only the *kinds* of tasks that cry out for attention, not each and every one of them.

But to speak of priorities without mentioning education seems wrong, especially for someone in education. The question is, what is there to say? What is there left to declare about the process of schooling that has not been said again and again? Perhaps I can suggest just one thing, aimed specifically at the upper echelons of the educational apparatus. It is a proposal that the universities add a new orientation to their traditional goals and programs. I urge that they deliberately set out to become the laboratories of applied research into the future. I urge that they direct a major portion of their efforts toward research into, training for, and advocacy of programs for social change.

It may be said that there is no precedent for such an orientation of education toward action, and that the pursuit of such a course will endanger the traditional purity and aloofness of the academic community. The reply would be more convincing did not the precedent already exist and were not the purity already sullied. Scientists of all kinds, in the social as well as in the physical disciplines, have not hesitated to work on programs for social change—financed by the Department of Defense, the Office of Naval Research, NASA, etc.—programs designed to alter the world by high explosives in some cases, by cooptation or skillful propaganda in others.

Some members of the academic community, aware of the destruction they have helped to commit, have now begun to withdraw from contact with the war machine. That is to their credit. But what is needed now is for them to redirect their energies to the peace machine. We live in a time during which social experimentation—in the factory, in the office, in the city; in economic policy, in political institutions, in life-styles—is essential if a technologically dominated future is not simply to mold us willy-nilly to its requirements. The forces of change in our time render obsolete many of the institutions of managerial capitalism and centrally planned socialism alike; new institutions, new modes of social control and social cohesion now have to be invented and tried.

In part the university must continue its traditional role, studying this period of historic transformation with all the detachment and objectivity it can muster. But that is not enough. As Marx wrote: "The philosophers have only *interpreted* the world; the thing, however, is to change it." As the last item on my agenda, I would like to make the university the focus of action for the initiation of such change.

Charting Our Position on the Way to...

R. FREEMAN BUTTS

I find it both sobering and exhilarating to realize that my students who are now in their twenties will be about as old as I am now when the clocks strike midnight on December 31, 1999. I do not expect to be able to join them, whether sober or exhilarated, on that particular New Year's Eve which will usher in the year 2000, but my point is surely obvious. Today we are literally preparing our students to be teachers in the 21st century. And the children already born who will be *their* students will spend half or more of their lives in the third millenium A.D., or, if you please, they will spend their lives roughly in the sixth millenium since human civilization itself took form around 3000 B.C.

I have started this paper by looking to the future, and in four sentences I have brought in the remote past. I have done this deliberately, because (especially in our

From *Teachers College Record* (March 1969), 479–493. Reprinted by permission.

more sober moments) we must keep both the future and the past in mind if we wish to chart accurately our present position on the course of the human career. I call your attention to the way this point is put by my colleague at Columbia, Daniel Bell, in his introduction to the symposium on The Year 2000 which was reported in last summer's issue of *Daedalus,* the Journal of the American Academy of Arts and Sciences:

> Time, said St. Augustine, is a three-fold present: the present as we experience it, the past as a present memory, and the future as a present expectation. By that criterion, the world of The year 2000 has already arrived, for in the decisions we make now, in the way we design our environment and thus sketch the lines of constaint, the future is committed. . . . The future is not an overarching leap into the distance; it begins in the present.[1]

Now Daniel Bell and his associates on the Commission on the Year 2000 are quite right in their insistence that the future begins in the present, and I take it this is a basic assumption of this project and this conference. But I take it, too, that we recognize equally well that the present began in the past. And while the future may be more intriguing or dramatic to talk about than the past, the linkage is undeniable. Where then are we on the course from the past to the future?

I would like to divide my answer into two parts, first taking a very long view and then taking a more contemporary view; both must necessarily be extremely sketchy and staccato in form.

We are, of course, accustomed to thinking of our times as "modern" in contrast to "ancient" and "medieval." This is perhaps the most common periodization assigned to Western history by Western historians. But our age is often referred to by social scientists as dominantly "modern," or industrial, or technological, or scientific in contrast to "traditional," pre-industrial, pre-technological, or pre-scientific societies. In addition, Peter Drucker talks about "post-modern" society. Daniel Bell and Bertram Gross speak of "post-industrial" society, and Kenneth Boulding of a "post-civilized" period in human history.[2] Now these are intriguing, and I believe important, terms. They illustrate that the human career can be defined in different ways depending on what theme or problem is uppermost for study.

Historical Transformations

My own preference, having the role of education in mind, is to think of three major transformations in the history of mankind: The first is the civilizing process

[1] Daniel Bell, "The Year 2000—The Trajectory of an Idea" in *Daedalus,* Vol. 96, No. 3, the Proceedings of the American Academy of Arts and Sciences, Summer 1967, p. 639.

[2] See, for example, Daniel Bell, *et al., ibid.*; Peter F. Drucker. *Landmarks of Tomorrow: a Report on the New "Post Modern" World.* New York: Harper & Row, 1957; Kenneth E. Boulding. *The Meaning of the Twentieth Century.* New York: Harper & Row, 1965; Bertram M. Gross. *The Managing of Organizations,* 2 vols. New York: Free Press, 1964.

by which folk societies adopt an urban way of life which we call civilization; the second is the modernizing process by which traditional civilizations become modern; and the third is the ecumenicizing process by which modern civilization is becoming world-wide.[3] I refer to these as historical transformations, but I use the present tense to emphasize that they are all still going on today in various parts of the world.

In the process of developing a literate urban way of life, beginning some 5,000 years ago in Southwest Asia, the social institutions of small, homogeneous and intimate folk societies gradually became larger in scale, more differentiated, and more specialized as farmers, herdsmen, and warrior bands became city-builders. Integral to this process was the invention of writing and the appearance of organized educational institutions based on written language and literacy and designed for small elites in the urban centers.

A second great transformation began some 500 years ago in Western Europe when traditional urban societies began to become "modern" as they developed new modes of production and distribution of goods based on the use of inanimate power and more efficient tools. Underlying the technological developments were new social institutions still more highly differentiated and specialized than in traditional civilization, and, above all, new bodies of knowledge which were more scientific and rational in content and method, and new forms of widespread education made possible by the invention of printing.

Joseph Elder even goes so far as to define the essence of modernity itself as corresponding to "secular education" by which he means that type of education which endorses the establishment of objectifiable evidence as the basis for proof of phenomena in opposition to the type of education which endorses tradition or faith as the basis for proof of phenomena.[4]

The United States, as much of the West, and some parts of the East are well launched into the stage of Modern Civilization. Many other parts of the world, and even some parts or sub-cultures of the United States and Europe, are still largely in the stage of Traditional Civilization. This gap between tradition and modernity, between societies that are at different stages in social development, accounts for some of the most critical problems facing the United States and the world.

To complicate matters still more, we are now on the threshold of a third great transformation in the human career, a social process that is becoming world-wide as a result of the organizational and technological revolutions of the past 50 years. These revolutions are associated with universal education, electronic forms of information gathering, storing, and retrieval as well as electric and nuclear power, and the enormous increase in the speed and transmission of energy and the transportation of material things and people. Bertram M. Gross of Syracuse has a lively term for this enormous speed-up in the movement over space of information,

[3]For elaboration of this theme see R. Freeman Butts, "Civilization-Building and the Modernization Process" in *History of Education Quarterly*, Summer 1967; and "Civilization as Historical Process" in *Comparative Education*, Vol. 3, No. 3, June 1967.

[4]William B. Hamilton, Ed. *The Transfer of Institutions.* Durham, N.C.: Duke University Press, 1964.

energy, and things; he calls it the "Mobiletic Revolution,"[5] a process already familiar to most of us but still largely incomprehensible to many.

And Recent Trends

In the long view then, our position is one that brings us to the brink of a world-embracing modern civilization. What of the shorter view, say the last 50 years? I should like to mention four trends which I believe are enormously important for education and for the education of teachers.

The first is an increasing recognition that knowledge and education are themselves the basic sources of social change. This in itself is a drastic change from earlier and more simplistic assumptions that social or cultural development depended principally upon a favored class, whether merchant, industrial, proletarian, military, or a superior race or nation or religion, on a special accumulation of land, capital, labor, technology, or natural resources. The elevation of the role of knowledge and of education in the hierarchy of importance as creators and maintainers of civilization carries the seed of a shift which is of incalculable value for the educational profession. Mr. Chips now holds several trump cards to back up his growing stock of blue chips.

Let me mention a few examples of this trend. In a felicitous phrase John Kenneth Galbraith refers to the recent emergence of the "educational and scientific estate" as a key group in modern industrial society.[6] He argues that the rapidly growing body of educators and scientists in the schools, colleges, universities, and research institutions provide the decisive factor in modern production, namely, qualified talent and highly trained manpower, much as the banking and financial community provided the decisive factor of wealth for the earlier industrial system. What was once an inferior and tolerated caste has now become a large and increasingly powerful estate. The size of the educational community in the United States in 1900 was approximately 450,000, of whom the vast majority were elementary school teachers, and less than 25,000 were in higher education. Today, the educational estate approaches 3 million of whom slightly less than half are in elementary schools, and a half million are in colleges and universities.

This growth in teaching staff reflects, of course, the tremendous growth in school and university attendance in the past few decades. The greatest percentage increases have been in secondary and higher education: from less than 200,000 in high school in 1900 to nearly 15 million today; and from a quarter of a million in college to nearly seven million today. And the still more important thing is that the prospects are for continued rapid growth especially at the lower and the upper ends. The expectation is that in a decade the preschool enrollments will double

[5] Bertram M. Gross, *Space-Time and Post-Industrial Society*, Occasional Paper of the Comparative Administration Group, American Society for Public Administration, May 1966 (mimeographed).

[6] J. K. Galbraith. *The New Industrial State.* Boston: Houghton Mifflin, 1967.

(from 3 million to 6 million) and the higher education enrollments will nearly double (from 7 million to 12 million). Both of these increases will have fundamental meaning for the relatively more stable elementary and secondary schools: an increasing number of children will have a longer period of "schooling" before they enter the first grade, and an increasing number of high school graduates will go on to further formal education. The high school that was largely a college preparatory institution in 1900 is becoming once again principally a college preparatory institution. But there is now a fundamental difference. Whereas the high school in 1900 dealt with about 10 percent of youth of high school age and sent 75 percent of them on to college, it now deals with some 90 percent of high school age youth, and it may well be that it will soon again be sending 75 percent of them on to college.

This is not simply an extraordinary quantitative expansion. It may well amount to a qualitative difference, for it is something new in all human history: the prospect of nearly universal secondary education leading to virtually universal post-secondary education. The term "educational civilization" which had such a visionary sound a few years ago is almost upon us.

But the expansion of the formal school and university system is not all. In another striking phrase Bertram Gross has coined the term "learning force" to embrace all of the people engaged in some form of group-learning process. He defines the term as follows: "the total number of people developing their capacities through systematic education—that is, where learning is aided by teaching and there are formal, organized efforts to impart knowledge through instruction."[7] So if we add to the 60 million now in school and university, those 30 million who are engaged in vocational, technical, and professional training outside the regular educational structure, and those 20 million who take part in some form of adult education, we get a total of some 110 million people in the "learning force." This amounts to more than half of all Americans and considerably more than the total labor force in the country (some 80 million). Projections are even more startling with the estimate that the learning force in 1975 will be half again as large as the labor force, approximately 150 million to 100 million.

But this is *still* not all. We now hear of the "knowledge industry" (a term that happens to grate on me) which includes not only organized education but the rapidly expanding fields of research and development, publishing and printing, entertainment, communication media, and information machines. It is estimated that close to $200 billion are being spent annually in the knowledge industry. This amounts to approximately one-fourth of our Gross National Product. Expenditure for education alone has surpassed $50 billion and thus totals nearly 7 percent of the GNP. So education is not only Big Business itself. It is needed by Big Business, and it is a lucrative market and target for Big Business. All this requires that we look again at the kind of life our students are likely to lead in a society in which teaching

[7] See, for example, Wilbur Cohen, "Education and Learning" in *Annals of the American Academy of Political and Social Science,* Vol. 373, September 1967, an issue entitled "Social Goals and Indicators for American Society," Vol. II, p. 83, Note 3.

is a major occupation and in which learning is a major preoccupation of the vast majority of the people for a large part of their lives.

The Educational Estate

This is a society in which the *production* of goods will require fewer and fewer people with higher and higher training, and the *service* occupations and professions (with as much as 70 percent of the labor force) will require more and more people with higher and higher training. In such a society the role of formal education becomes more important than ever. I am not one who believes or implies that because the "knowledge industry" is so active that the role of the formal school can be lessened or can be narrowed. I believe just the contrary. The more the predominantly non-educational agencies of society get into the business of education the more active and effective the predominantly educational institutions must become, and the more socially responsible professional autonomy they must demand and exert. What is good for the "knowledge industry" is not necessarily good for education. If the educational estate is to assume the mantle of moral, political, and social authority which has been worn in the past by the clergy, the statesman, and the wealthy, it may find that it must add to its rightly claimed freedom the social responsibility that goes with moral and social authority. Whereas education has been the tool of other classes throughout much of history, it may well now be in a position, as Clark Kerr has put it, to write its own independent chapter in history. It is a fearsome but exhilarating prospect. The education of teachers in this event must temper its transmission of knowledge and its development of skills with social vision and commitment.

By dwelling on the emergence of the educational estate as a major factor in social change I assume that there will be a closer relationship between all "levels" of the educational system, but I do not mean to imply that therefore the only function of lower schools is to prepare children for higher education. I look upon the "higher" and "lower" as genuine partners. The universities will inevitably become more and more specialized as they train for the increasingly complex range of intellectual, professional, and technical activities required by a post-industrial society, and the schools will need to make ready large numbers of their students for this training, but the schools will also have their own function of providing a common culture and common medium of discourse that will enable the individual as well as the society to function together in ways that perhaps cannot now even be anticipated. The schools have as much right to exert their claims for participation in the educational estate as do the universities and the research institutes. Neither can exist without the other in the educational civilization of the future.

The Speed of Knowledge Accumulation

A second trend, closely related to the first, is the increasing *speed* with which knowledge is accumulating and the accompanying expectation that social change will be continuous as well as rapid. This takes the form most spectacularly of technological development and innovation, but what is often overlooked is that innovation and technology now rest heavily upon the deliberate partnership of academic organization, industrial organization, and governmental organization. This is part of the overall "organizational revolution"—which has been going on for 200 years as large scale formal organizations have appeared in nearly all phases of modern society: Big Business, Big Government, Big Military, Big Labor, Big Science, Big Religion, Big Education.

Education must somehow reckon with the speed of the accumulation of "cultural content" of our civilization and the massive impact this ever-growing cultural content will have upon the individual. We are all familiar with the predictions concerning what we are in for in the coming years—some dire, some enthusiastic. These range from the now astounding but familiar developments in moon landings and heart transplants to such no-less astounding but still unfamiliar developments as automated language translators, drugs to increase intelligence and learning, direct electromagnetic interaction between the human brain and the computer, education by recording on the brain, et cetera.

General Sarnoff in the *Saturday Review* of July 1966 predicted that the 1,000 computers of 1956 in the United States would become 100,000 in 1976 and the 12 billion computations per hour they could do ten years ago will become in the next ten years 400 trillion per hour—or about 2 billion computations per hour for every man, woman, and child. Not only will every school have a computer but possibly every home. Your first reaction of course may be: "I don't want that much computation, I'll stick to reading." But then a billion books are being published every year, and they will soon be published electronically so that hundreds of lines of text can be set in a minute; and 2,000 pages of scientific knowledge are *now* being published every 60 seconds; and the whole Bible can be contained on a "2" by "2" piece of film by micro-imagery, and . . . et cetera, et cetera, et cetera.

Now, the usual conclusion to such a recital as this is that the speaker or writer urges that educators "get with it," beef up their educational technology, and start using computer-assisted instruction, teaching machines, programed instruction, audio-visual aids, closed circuit television, team teaching, and teacher aides. And the usual reaction of the professional audience is to express alarm that the teacher will be ousted from the educational process or that the individual child will be lost or that personal contact in teaching will be destroyed. Or it may simply be a weary or wary suspicion that the exhorter really has some "hardware" to sell.

I do not have this conclusion in mind. I *assume* that we shall be concerned about the impact of technology on learning. I assume that we must consider what kind of thinking and what kind of personality development will best enable an individual to cope with the constant bombardment of information and the multi-sensory multi-media saturation of our lives that Marshall McLuhan talks more or less lucidly about. But I have another purpose in mind. I believe that we must try to recognize that the rapid accumulation of knowledge poses fundamental *social* problems for education that are basically different from any ever faced before. Universal literacy and universal elementary schooling were in their time revolutionary social developments having great impact upon the very structure of modern social organization, the rise of nation states, participant forms of political organization, economic and industrial development, and the like. Now, I am interested in the similar impact upon social organization that universal "information technology" will or may have in a post-industrial society. In other words, what kind of *society* shall we educate for?

Organized Innovation

What is even more important than the present speed of communication of knowledge, of energy, and of transportation is the cumulative mobilization of men and ideas designed not only to promote deliberate innovation in the technological field but to assure that continuing and constant innovating will continue indefinitely into the future. Now I know that "innovation" has nearly become a catchword or a slogan used by the newest educational reformers and their followers to prove that they are *not* stodgy members of the Educational Establishment, which is, of course, opposed to all innovation. But I do not have in mind here an injunction for teachers "to innovate," which often means "Stop whatever you are doing, and do something else—especially do what *I* think is important."

What I have in mind is the fact that the present day mobilization of scientific knowledge woven together with large scale social organization is now so effective that it seems destined to mean a constant transformation of society and of culture as far as we can see into the future. Scientific invention may be the business of university and industrial laboratories, but social invention to *cope* with technology as well as to promote it is surely the business of the entire educational estate.

The challenge to education is not merely to learn how to use the new technological hardware to make the instructional process more efficient, but how to enable the learners to live in and deal with a constantly and rapidly changing technological society. My emphasis here is upon how to cope with constant transformation in *society*, not technology alone. My colleague, Dankwart Rustow, in a stunning new book, defines the modernization process as man's "rapidly widening control over nature *through closer cooperation among men.* It transforms both man and society, but most of all man's mind."[8] *This* is the fundamental locus of the problem posed for education by technological innovation: "cooperation among men" and "man's mind." Let us remind the educational technology salesman that the real business of education is not "hardware"; it is ideas, knowledge, teaching, learning, *and* their inter-relationship with social organization and cultural development, i.e., man and his developing civilization.

[8] Dankwart A. Rustow. *A World of Nations: Problems of Political Modernization.* Washington, D.C.: The Brookings Institution, 1967. (Italics added.)

Empirics, Policies and Concepts

My third trend is closely related to the second; it has to do with a three-pronged development that has been taking place in the social sciences during the past 50 years and the gradual linking together of the three prongs in the last decade. The three prongs may be denoted as empirical investigation, policy orientation, and conceptual schematizations.

In the 1920's and 1930's American historians and social scientists, deeply affected by the horrors of World War I, were disillusioned with the prevailing theories of inevitable progress of Western civilization, with the nationalistic tone of the theories of social evolution which had come out of the 19th century and which seemed to find all peoples except Westerners as backward in the scale of social evolution, and with the individualistic, capitalistic bias of a Social Darwinism which somehow favored the well-to-do and the upper classes of privilege. As the disillusion was reenforced by the depression some social scientists and educational spokesmen turned to social theories that were heavily oriented to social reform, social crusading, and even social revolution. A policy orientation was paramount in their objectives, and conceptual schemes of a political and economic nature were popular, ranging from capitalism to socialism.

Empirical investigation was not in the forefront of the thinking of the reformist wing of social scientists and educators, but it was in the minds of a large contingent of behavioral psychologists, testers, anthropologists, and sociologists who assumed a neutralist stance as far as social reform in the U. S. A. was concerned and a position of cultural relativism with regard to the relations of one society to another. Cultural relativism said in effect that standards of moral, intellectual, and aesthetic value which grow out of one society are reflections of that society alone and are not properly subject to judgment or criticism or change from outside the society. So, outsiders should not try to change another culture. Many empiricists virtually took the stance, "I am a scientist describing society; social change is not my business except as an observer."

So, in over-simplified terms, the policy-oriented social scientists and educators employed ideological conceptual schema but neglected empirical investigation; and the empirically-oriented social scientists and educators neglected both policy matters *and* conceptual schema in favor of simply gathering hard data or "teaching facts."

Following World War II and especially in the 1950's many social scientists and educators alike found it convenient to soft-pedal the reformist character of social science (remember the other Senator McCarthy?). They played down controversy and class struggle in their studies and teaching and generally reflected the Eisenhower period of social accommodation and conservatism at home or they reflected the Cold War abroad. In any case, an attachment to empirical investigation and to intellectual conceptualization as method of thought within the separate disciplines of knowledge (rather than as social ideology) came to the fore. This was also the period of widespread attack on progressive education for being reform-minded instead of discipline-minded. You remember the roster—Hutchins, Bestor, Lynd, Rickover, Koerner, Rafferty, and the rest.

Our response to these attacks and then to Sputnik was to reform science instruction in the schools and universities and then turn to the other subject matter fields, but these efforts have not been matched in importance in the schools by a renewed attention to policy-oriented research that has appeared in the social sciences. In the late 1950's and 1960's a growing number of social scientists (but fewer educators) began to focus attention upon conceptual schema that would be not only tools of thought within the disciplines but also would aid understanding of the most critical policy problems facing the nation and the world. The problems of war and peace, military strategy, political, economic, and social development of the new nations, world-wide modernization, world-wide urbanization and the development of megalopolis, rural transformation and migration, the confrontation of the super-powers, the population crisis, and a host of others.

These social scientists began to find that they could not divorce themselves from the portentous policy questions posed by problems like these. They turned to social systems analysis, organization theory, games theory, model building, ideal types, typology, and I do not know what all. But I do know that extremely significant work is going on in anthropology, sociology, political science, economics, and history in the effort to meld rigorous empirical investigation with policy-oriented studies which can be illuminated by conceptual schema that will give policy makers a handle on the regularities and uniformities in social behavior, on social change, and on social development. In some part of the 19th century theories of historical social evolution have been substantiated by archeological digging; the idea of progress has been found to have a kind of empirical though not a moral justification; and cultural relativism sounds a little dated in the face of massive efforts by a hundred underdeveloped nations to borrow from and to emulate the already modernized nations as they attempt to move from traditional forms to modern forms of society.

Towards a Three-Pronged Education

My conclusion is that education and teacher education must somehow blend an empirical regard for hard facts with conceptual frameworks that will organize and generalize relevant knowledge in such a way as to be useful for helping to solve the critical problems that face the civilization of the world. A research institute may confine itself to empirical investigation; a think-tank may devote itself exclusively to conceptual schema; a political party or government may focus its energies on policy decisions, but an educational institution has the hardest job of all. It has to prepare people who can act in all three capacities with a sense of reason and a strong commitment to the improvement of public and world affairs. I see no lesser way in which education can perform its legitimate task of leadership in civilization-building. Otherwise it will be buffeted and perhaps even swamped by the rising winds of alienation, unrest, militancy, and violence, whether symbolized by Black Power, or White Power, or Red Power, or Poor Power, or Rich Power, or Student Power, or Teacher Power. I know it is trite but I can find no other way to say it: The only antidote within reason for these Powers is Educational Power.

My fourth trend has two prongs which I devoutly hope will come together and support each other. They are the trend toward comparative study in the social sciences and education and the trend toward international engagement of the United States in the affairs of the world. Both subjects are of enormous importance, but only a few words can be given by the way of outline for each.[9]

The first generation of American historians in the late 19th and early 20th century had an international outlook; they saw American history as part of European or imperial history. But Progressive historians like Turner, Beard, and Parrington began to look within the United States for its own distinctive characteristics; and a generation of American historians followed suit. Who can say what influence they had in building the generally ethnocentric if not isolationist view that Americans have of themselves? In any case, the trend has been reversing since World War II with a rapidly growing interest in world history, Western civilization, world civilizations, area studies, non-Western studies, and comparative historical studies.

Somewhat parallel experience can be cited for the other social sciences. The great sociologists of late 19th century Europe (Durkheim, Toennies, Weber) worked cross-nationally and comparatively, and the first generation of American sociologists (Sumner, Thomas, Ross, Park) were deeply interested in comparative studies. But the empirical trend in sociology prompted the second generation of American sociologists to "study the small," as Immanuel Wallerstein puts it. So when you study the small, you study yourself, your local community, or possibly the U.S.A. But after World War II, some sociologists turned again to comparative analysis, to cross cultural studies, to the study of whole nations, whole societies, and whole regions—or the comparative study of such major institutions as bureaucracy, empires, organization, family, elites, and the like. In fact, this interest of sociologists in comparative analysis was preceded by developmentalist and comparative political scientists who began to adopt sociological techniques and conceptual schema in their comparative political studies and their studies of political development around the world.

Anthropology showed a similar trend although it has always been more comparative than the other social disciplines. The giant anthropological synthesizers of the 19th century (men like Tylor and Morgan) tried to conceptualize the stages

[9]For elaboration of my view and supporting bibliographies, see my articles cited in footnote 3; also *American Education in International Development.* New York: Harper & Row, 1963; a task force paper on the International Education Act and Professional Education; chapters in the Oxford University Press publication of papers of the Williamsburg Conference on the World Crisis in Education, *Essays on World Education,* 1969; and in the 1969 Yearbook of the National Society for the Study of Education.

of human evolution that would encompass all human societies both past and present, but their work was often speculative, for they were handicapped by the lack of world-wide empirical evidence for their schema. Then the anthropologists of the early 20th century took a narrower view, stressed the study of small cultures, especially primitive cultures, gave up much of the earlier historical and synthesizing interest, took on a heavy psychological orientation, and stressed the differences, the variations, and thus the relativity of cultures. But, of late, some anthropologists have become concerned again with the broad developmental sweep of cultures, with civilized as well as pre-civilized societies, the influence of one culture upon another, and the uniformities and regularities as well as the differences among cultures.

What all this adds up to is that strong elements in the American intellectual endeavor are now more conscious of the rest of the world and of the problems of the world than they have been for 50 years. But I believe our schools still largely reflect the ethnocentric views as well as the socially neutral stance of the university scholars of the between-the-wars generation who were, and perhaps still are, preoccupied with looking inward instead of outward.

However, I have hopes that the second prong, i.e., the international involvement of the United States in the economic, social, political, and educational development of the rest of the world, will prompt the educational estate to make this the object of urgent, prolonged, and continuing study for that enormous "learning force" that promises to grow larger and larger. This should be at the top of the educational agenda as it is on the national agenda. But I am very much afraid that it is not very high on the priority list of many educators or of many learners.

Planning for a World Civilization

And, finally, still less do we educators study, plan for, or work for what *has* to come—what *is* coming—a recognizable and viable world civilization. The ingredients of an emerging world society are described thus by Bertram M. Gross:

> Today, unheralded and uncelebrated, a world society is slowly and painfully coming into being. It is characterized by the growth of increasingly interdependent nations, both industrializing and post-industrializing, of world-spanning organizations, of urban world centers, and of world-oriented elites. This growing interdependence is facilitated by communication-transportation systems that, for some activities, are continuously decreasing the space-time distance between Washington and Moscow more rapidly than that between Washington and Wichita or Moscow and Mintz.
>
> The emerging "One World" hardly conforms to the visions of the utopians—any more than does the giant organization to "classical" ideas of administration, the megalopolis to the models of city planners or the "great societies" to Keynesian theory. The world society includes a bewildering variety of subsystems increasingly locked together in conflict-

> cooperation relationships. The world polity is characterized by polycentric conflict, intersecting coalitions, continuing outbreaks of localized violence, many possibilities of "escalation," and spreading capacities for nuclear destruction. The political instrumentalities of conflict resolution and regional and world integration operate—as in nations, states and cities—in an atmosphere of pressure and power politics, behind-the-scene lobbying, rotten borough representation, moralistic double-talk, deception and self-deception. The world economy tends to be disorderly—neither free nor planned. The world culture, on the one hand, tends to submerge national characteristics and values in a homogenizing flood of material goods and international styles. On the other hand, it includes vast value differences and sharp value conflicts. Like Megalopolis, the world society is a territorial entity without government. It is an all-inclusive complex macro-system with remarkably complicated and unpredictable—although increasingly structured—mechanisms of mutual adjustment.[10]

I believe that study of the concept of a world society is of the first importance for American education. And yet I was appalled a few weeks ago when some of my younger colleagues at Teachers College argued that the concept of world society was so complicated that it could not be dealt with fruitfully at all by teachers or students in the schools.

I am convinced that the two overriding problems facing the United States today are: (1) How to create and learn to live in decent urban centers and (2) how to create and learn to live in a decent world civilization. And the two problems are closely related, for urbanization and the urban way of life are now encircling the globe. Not only does the world-wide urban revolution pose enormous threats to human dignity and serious dangers to peace and security, but it also holds out great hope. Today the educational nucleus of the world's cities are beginning to form what Kenneth Boulding calls an "invisible college" of persons devoted to bringing into existence and spreading a world culture.

The world culture as the essence of modern life has, according to Lucian Pye, a degree of inner coherence:

> It is based upon a secular rather than a sacred view of human relations, a rational outlook, an acceptance of the substance and spirit of the scientific approach, a vigorous application of an expanding technology, an industralized organization of production, and a generally humanistic and popularistic set of values for political life.[11]

What American education must do is to play its role in building and strengthening the incipient world society described by Gross and the recognizable world culture described by Pye. Taken together, world society and world culture in their

[10] Bertram M. Gross, *op.cit.,* pp. 45–46.

[11] Lucian W. Pye. *Aspects of Political Development.* Boston: Little, Brown & Co., 1966.

interactions can constitute world civilization. For five thousand years formal education has been a formative force, sometimes conservative, sometimes innovative, in the building of civilization. The school itself as an organized institution arose as one of the building blocks of the first civilization as it emerged in the cities of the Middle East and as civilization later appeared in and related to the cities of India, China, Greece, and the West. As the school played its role in the building of the major civilizations of the world, it must now play its role in the building of a genuinely world civilization.

Building the Ecumenopolis

And the Greeks, bless them, had the words for it. The *polis* was the city, the creative center and focus of the civilized man's life. And the *ecumene* was their word for the entire civilized or settled region of the world. Outside the cities were the barbarians. In their ethnocentric view the ecumene of their day radiated out from Athens. We know now that great urban centers nourished the spread of civilization not only in the Middle East and Europe but in East Asia, South Asia, Africa, and finally the Americas. The polis which became metropolis, the mother city for colonies; or the cosmopolis to which people from the world came; or the megalopolis as it spreads along the United States East Coast (Boswash), or the Mid-West (Chippits) or the West Coast (Sansan) are only points along the way. The genuine world city or the city of a world-wide civilization is still to be created—the ecumenopolis.

That is an awkward word to say. The Greeks would have known better than to garble their beautiful language in that way. But the word "ecumene" should become better known. The churches have acquired a near monopoly on the word "ecumenical" because they have thought for so long in world-wide terms, but the modern world and modern civilization can no longer be wholly encompassed by The City of God or the City of Man as viewed by St. Augustine. The scientific and humanistic and religious reformations in the West since the 16th century irrevocably set the world on a new course toward modern civilization. And now we are on a still speedier and more inclusive course—not just toward post-industrial society, or post-modern society, or post-civilized society, but a truly ecumenical civilization embracing a world society and a world culture.

Building the ecumenopolis is the overriding task before the world's educators. This is what the educational estate should be doing, this is what educational innovation and technology are for, this is the goal of the social sciences in education, and this is the purpose of comparative study and international education. Some progress toward this end is what I would like to think my students and your students and their students will be celebrating on New Year's Eve in 1999.

PART II The School: Conflicts and Challenges

If ever there were a time for the school to perform a vital, dynamic role in society, the time is now. It is the one social institution, outside the family, that comes into significant relationship with practically the entire population. Its effect for good or ill is found not only in the present generation, but in succeeding ones. The school is under tremendous pressures from an ever-changing society to become a more meaningful influence in the lives of today's youth. World events force the school to ask what kind of knowledge, understanding, and awareness it can develop about the newly emerging nations, about the growing imbalance among the developed and underdeveloped nations, about the problems centered around the world's exploding population, a problem unique in its dimension in the history of mankind, about the sophistication and phenomenal growth of man's knowledge, about the revolutionary technology that has spurred man's never-ending exploration from the depths of the oceans to the infinite reaches of space, and about the problems of nuclear energy which can bring a new era in man's control of his environment—or man's destruction.

What kind of knowledge and understanding can the school hope to develop in those it is charged to induct into the highly complex technological society that the United States represents today? What understanding and guidance can it bring to the anticipated upheavals in the work force resulting from the increasingly widespread use of the techniques of cybernation, to the continued expansion of huge corporations and centralized federal government, to the vital health problems arising from the wholesale pollution of the air and water and the wasteful destruction of plant and animal life? Is the school able to help youth understand the nature of the urban trends toward megalopolis when by 1980, it is estimated, 75 per cent of the population of the United States will be living in great population centers, and where, unless care is taken, the present huge areas of urban blight may be vastly expanded and expanding? Can it help youth to understand that many of these problems transcend the presently organized units of government at the state and local levels and must be attacked by long-range regional planning on a scale not yet envisioned? Can the school, then, prepare youth to be adults flexible enough to deal effectively with problems of continuing change that they must face as part of their everyday lives?

Pressured by the problems of society and by the problems of youth growing up in that society, the schools are caught in a classic struggle to free themselves from the inertia of the past and to strike boldly for a more dynamic conception of their role in society. To complicate an already difficult situation, the schools are faced with conflicting demands from within and without. At a time when there is increased demand to extend the system of mass education there also is a renewed emphasis on individual instruction. The demand for more discipline is opposed by the emphasis on greater freedom. The demand for earlier specialization is opposed by the emphasis on general education. The demand for conformity and uniformity is opposed by the growing stress on creativity, individuality, and diversity. The demand for more effective vocational preparation is opposed by the emphasis on a liberal arts background. The demand for greater emphasis on mathematics and science is opposed by an insistence on a balanced curriculum.

Such concerns give an indication of the demands and pressures which, however unrealistic, are nevertheless forced upon the school. No one social institution could possibly cope with all these pressures, but an alternative is not found in inaction or apathy. What are the chances that the schools of today will respond with the bold thinking and bold planning that seem to be called for? If we are to gauge our response from a look at the historical development of the school in our society, the answer will not be at all reassuring.

The school has always been haunted by the question of where we go from here—a question asked more often with a note of despair than one of hope. In its past history, the school has shared resistance to change with other social institutions, yet the school is the one social agency whose basic purpose has been to effect change in the lives of those who come under its direction. Either by resisting change or ignoring it, the school seldom really resolved its problems. When changes were made, they were additive by nature—the schools retained everything they were presently engaged in and added a few new ideas, usually in the form of new courses. Admittedly this was the safest way to proceed; it deeply offended nobody, if it deeply stimulated nobody. In this manner the schools subdued real forms of controversy and disputes that might have enlivened or enriched their active role in society.

There were, of course, the Horace Manns, the Henry Barnards, the John Deweys, who formulated, each in his own way, visions of the school that were bold and dynamic, and which at least for the moment, stirred fundamental questions about the nature of the school in society. In the discussions that ensued, however, proponents and adversaries all too quickly adopted stereotyped versions of the original ideas. In the case of Dewey, for instance, his ideas were soon translated into catch phrases such as "learning by doing" and "teach the child, not the subject." His challenge to education was interpreted as a clash between "progressivism" and "traditionalism." The real matter, as Dewey pointed out, was "of what anything whatever must be to be worthy of the name education."[1]

[1] John Dewey. *Experience and Education* (New York: The Macmillan Company, 1937), p. 90.

If the schools are to achieve positive direction and play a significant role in society today and tomorrow, they must begin again with the challenge Dewey issued—What is it that is worthy of the name education? This was no rigid standard that he was proposing, but one flexible enough to meet changing conditions and situations. His ideas regarding the worthiness of education may or may not be the ones that hold greatest relevance today. That search must go on in every age. The schools are challenged today to prepare students for an unknown future, yet even in a future that is not known, it is still possible to sense likely developments, to anticipate, to plan, to look for alternatives, and to continue an intelligent discussion of conflicting views. Those who have responsibility for the schools should refrain from actions based on narrow assumptions as well as from reacting to crises with merely expedient changes.

The next twenty to thirty years in education will be filled with critical needs that must be met. Decisions regarding what must be done will affect all facets of the school—curriculum, organization, instruction, school design, and so on: even the conception of formal education itself. Indications are that education in schools and colleges will be so different in degree as to be profoundly different in kind. Such challenges will demand the intellectual endeavors of scholars in every field.

In contemplating the current controversies in education we need to look backward into the past as a vantage point to see old problems and conflicts in new perspective, to look to the present to clearly define today's issues and see how they relate to previous conflicts, and to look forward to the future to anticipate newly emerging issues and how they will affect and be affected by current problems.

The articles selected for Part II present conflicting views concerning the schools' responses to the pressures from within the profession and those from the larger society. Not every view is represented; it would be impossible to do so. An important criterion for the selection was to choose those views that are not widely held or those that have not yet gained wide circulation as a background to provoke lively discussion.

When radical changes occur in a culture its educational system must adapt to and in fact lead those changes. Philip H. Phenix observes such changes in our culture and proposes a new moral theory in education that is more responsive, current, and relevant. Phenix calls for action by the educative enterprise—action that is more directly related to the needs of today's students.

In "Education and the Clarifying Experience," Norman Cousins is concerned with oral communications and the profession's inability to prepare students with "vocabulary control." He cites "sequence" and "clarity" as absolute musts if students are to make themselves understood, rather than concern with developing "ability to absorb knowledge."

John Martin Rich writes about an "erosion of traditional values" and diluted standards in America. He suggests that our educational system has contributed to a "rise of the meritocracy" as he discusses the role of specialists and generalists in our society. James L. Fenner questions the relevance of the high school curriculum, if young people are going to make sense of the real world. Fenner proposes both traditional studies and elective courses that will relate the school to out-of-school interests.

James S. Coleman sees several different problems for American education in the 1970's, each demanding different solutions. Most pressing of these, according to Coleman, are basic reading and numerical skills for the deprived. He is concerned that the educational resources outside schools have not been tapped and that we will continue to fail to make use of these institutions in future years. Such "insulation" leaves society with an "action void" that can only be partially filled by the school.

Several alternate organizational structures for secondary schools are examined by Lloyd S. Michael which he believes will afford youth a better opportunity for "self-fulfillment and self-growth." Michael presents a case for the "building principal" as the primary motivator and leader if the school is to produce "optimum learning." Calling on schools to "build learning expectations in youth," Michael asks for more interaction and participation by students in school life.

Using a traveling seminar on the subject of computer-assisted instruction as a jumping-off point, Elizabeth C. Wilson explores the "educational Utopia" visualized by Marshall McLuhan and George B. Leonard as a result of technological advances. Miss Wilson's excellent article, "The Knowledge Machine," concludes that although studies and research and programs related to the school and the computer are important, first priority should go to the establishment and maintenance of dialogues about education in every forum in America.

Pills that make children "behave better in school" are the focal point of Edward T. Ladd's contribution to this part of the anthology. Ladd reviews the use of drugs aimed at improving student performance, discussing them from both a medical standpoint and from the point of view of whether they infringe upon individual liberty. Ladd prescribes "eternal vigilance" by each state in the use it permits of such medication.

Edgar Z. Friedenberg adapts a paper he first delivered at the 1969 Invitational Conference on Testing Problems for an article entitled "The Real Functions of Educational Testing," in which he explores the present social functions of educational measurement.

The problems of education in megalopolis are outlined in detail by Edward Joseph Shoben, Jr., as he reminds us of H. G. Wells' characterization of civilization as a "race between education and catastrophe." Shoben believes megalopolitan education must continue throughout our life span, concentrating less on subject matter than on learning how to learn. He proposes further emphasis on independent inquiry and postsecondary study.

The public school has been forced to review its role as a "melting pot" as minority groups become more and more aware of their ethnic identities. Marjorie S. Friedman reviews these changes and calls for a new approach to pluralism and a shaping of an uncommon school system attractive to both middle-class families and the minority communities.

The final article in Part II is by Christopher Jencks. It is a reappraisal of

"Equality of Educational Opportunity," the Coleman Report. Jencks concludes with a suggestion that the reader follow his own review of the report with a visit to a slum school to see what the schools actually are doing to prepare students for life in the real world.

Questions for Discussion and Further Study

1. Philip Phenix uses the popular term "relevant" in describing the type of education that concerned students are demanding today. He defines *relevant* to mean an education that will enable students to transform a world that their consciences bid them reject in its present form. Is this the way you would define "relevant" teaching? What criteria can be set up for the selection of a "relevant" curriculum? Who should determine what is "relevant"? Should students participate in the selection of a "relevant" curriculum?

2. James Coleman touches one of the current hot spots in education in a brief review of educational vouchers in "Schools Look to Society as a Resource." Do you think this method of financing outside assistance will become widespread in the years to come? How will the distribution of such funds be allocated and controlled? Is there a better and more efficient way to finance a program aimed at improving or augmenting the basic skills of children?

3. A crucial problem is the selection of content to be included in the curriculum. James L. Fenner's new "elective" curriculum was designed to "turn people on." He suggests 40 courses for high school students that would be intrinsically interesting enough to make students want to take them. What did you think of Fenner's curriculum? Would you supplement it with other courses? What would you drop from his list? Why? Do you agree with his conclusions about out-of-school learning?

4. Do you agree with Lloyd Michael that every principal should spend three fourths of his time on the instructional program as a facilitator of learning? If so, how will the myriad of jobs that fall under his jurisdiction be accomplished? Can these be delegated to other personnel? Who should perform them? Can the students participate in these jobs and take some of the burden off the teacher and principal?

5. Should drugs be used on school children? Under what circumstances would you be in favor of behavior modification medicine? Should these be given at home prior to classroom attendance or should they be left to the school to administer? Do you believe such practices would contribute to illicit drug use in the school as children reach junior high and high school ages? Why or why not?

6. Edgar Friedenberg outlines the two recognized functions of educational testing as (1) an assessment of individual competence, and (2) a resultant assignment of the person receiving the score to an ideologically acceptable social category in line with his test results. Do you share Friedenberg's views on testing? Are there better ways to measure performance? Does testing judge performance or merely measure it? What alternative methods could you propose for "measuring" the accomplishments of large groups of students? Are they feasible?

7. Which of the issues discussed in this section did you find most important? Which authors stimulated the greatest number of new questions, ideas, thoughts? What suggestions can you offer for the inclusion of additional issues?

Selected References

Atkins, Neil P. "Rethinking Education in the Middle." *Theory into Practice* (June 1968), 118–119.

Aubrey, Roger F. "Drug Education: Can Teachers Really Do the Job?" *Teachers College Record* (February 1971), 417–422.

Berlin, Irving N. "Education for What?" *Teachers College Record* (March 1969), 505–511.

Bettelheim, Bruno. "Children Must Learn to Fear." *The New York Times Magazine* (April 13, 1969), 125, 135–136, 140, 143, 145.

Cass, James. "Hot Spots in Education." *New York State Education* (December 1969), 11–15.

Ellena, William J. "Extending the School Year." *Today's Education* (May 1969), 48–49.

Empey, Donald W. "What Is Independent Study All About?" *Journal of Secondary Education* (March 1968), 104–108.

Fantini, Mario D. "Schools for the Seventies: Institutional Reform." *Today's Education* (April 1970), 43–44, 60–61.

Fischer, John H. "Education for All an Unkept Promise." *The New York Times* (Special Education Supplement) (January 12, 1970), 66.

Fuchs, Estelle. "American Indian Education: Time to Redeem an Old Promise." *Saturday Review* (January 24, 1970), 54–57, 74–75.

Glatthorn, Allan A. "What Makes an Effective High School?" *Parents' Magazine* (September 1969), 64–65, 116, 120–121.

Hampton, Alfred P. "Discipline and the Disadvantaged Child." *New York State Education* (April 1969), 19–21, 50

Hansen, Carl E. "When Courts Try to Run the Public Schools." *U.S. News & World Report* (April 21, 1969), 94–96.

Harding, Vincent. "Fighting the 'Mainstream' Seen for 'Black Decade.' " *The New York Times* (Special Education Supplement) (January 12, 1970), C50.

Holt, John. "The Tyranny of Testing." *Parents' Magazine* (September 1969), 60–61, 122, 124–125.

Kerber, August, and Barbara Bommarito (eds.). *The Schools and the Urban Crisis.* New York: Holt, Rinehart and Winston, 1965.

Kimball, Solon T., and James E. McClellan, Jr. *Education in the New America.* New York: Random House, 1962.

Leonard, George B. "How School Stunts Your Child." *Look* (September 17, 1968), 31–32, 34, 39–42.

_______. "The Future Now." *Look* (October 15, 1968), 57, 59–60, 65–68.

_______. "Visiting Day 2001 A.D." *Look* (October 1, 1968), 37, 39–40, 45–48.

Loretan, Joseph O. "The Decline and Fall of Intelligence Testing." *Teachers College Record* (October 1965), 10–17.

Paske, Gerald H. "Violence, Value, and Education." *Teachers College Record* (September 1969), 51–63.

Pickard, H. Stuart. "Outward Bound." *Today's Education* (November 1968), 21–22.

Rustin, Bayard. "The Failure of Black Separatism." *Harper's Magazine* (January 1970), 25–34.

_______. "The Myths of the Black Revolt," in *Three Essays by Bayard Rustin.* New York: A. Philip Randolph Institute, September 1969.

Schneir, Walter and Miriam Schneir. "The Joy of Learning–In the Open Corridor." *The New York Times Magazine* (April 4, 1971), 30–31, 72, 75–78, 80, 92–93, 96–98.

Shaplin, Judson T., and Henry F. Olds, Jr. (eds.). *Team Teaching.* New York: Harper and Row, 1964.

Smith, Robert. "Educating Youth in a Revolutionary Society." *Educational Leadership* (January 1966), 279–284.

"Symposium: Technology's Challenge to Education." *Saturday Review* (December 12, 1964), 21–25, 77–79.

Tanner, Daniel. *Schools for Youth: Change and Challenge in Secondary Education.* New York: The Macmillan Company, 1965.

________. *Secondary Curriculum: Theory and Development.* New York: The Macmillan Company, 1970.

Westby-Gibson, Dorothy. *Social Perspectives on Education: The Society, the Student, the School.* New York: John Wiley and Sons, 1965.

"What the Courts Are Saying About Student Rights." *NEA Research Bulletin* (October 1969), 86–89.

"What's Really Wrong with Colleges." *U.S. News & World Report* (June 16, 1969), 36–38.

Williams, Lloyd P. "The Struggle for Balance—Vocational Education in the Western World." *Phi Delta Kappan* (April 1965), 335–359.

Wolfbein, Seymour L. "Automation, Education, and Individual Liberty," *Teachers College Record* (October 1964), 27–32.

The Moral Imperative in Contemporary American Education

PHILIP H. PHENIX

Within the past three or four years there has occurred one of those sea changes in the American scene that radically alters the entire climate of common presuppositions and expectations. While in previous periods the central issues might be characterized as ideological, technical, political, and the like, I think the most apt term for what is new in the present atmosphere is moral concern.

By moral I do not mean moralistic. Few contemporary Americans are moved by the kind of self-assured reforming zeal that, for example, made possible the Eighteenth Amendment. When I say the dominant atmosphere is one of moral concern I mean that questions of conscience have now moved into the foreground of the American cultural scene. The immediate stimulus is, of course, Vietnam, but Vietnam only symbolizes the conflicts of conscience in a wide range of social and personal issues, including those of race, poverty, sex, drugs, and politics, both national and international.

Americans are becoming increasingly aware that material and technical approaches to these issues do not suffice, that without a moral basis and the morale that flows from it, typical American practicalism and activism prove impractical and stultifying.

American schools and colleges are, naturally enough, deeply involved in these recent transformations in the cultural climate. It is in the young that the probings of conscience are most evident. Their lives and their futures are most at stake in the various social, political, economic, racial, and personal struggles of our time. Hence it is not surprising that the universities, inhabited by large numbers of young people with abundant resources of intelligence, imagination, and energy, should now be in the midst of a period of ferment unparalleled in the history of American education. The present student discontent is in large measure animated by a powerful undercurrent of profoundly moral concern.

What the morally concerned students are asking is nothing less than a thorough moral reconstruction of education itself. Most of them would not couch their protest and their aspiration in those terms; they would rather use a term like "relevant," meaning an education that will enable them to transform a world that their consciences bid them reject in its present form.

What are the prospects for such a transformation? What can teachers, students,

From *Perspectives on Education* (Winter 1969), 6–13. Reprinted by permission of *Perspectives on Education,* Teachers College, Columbia University.

and administrators do together to contribute constructively to the moral imperatives that are grasping the present generation? I am convinced that the present unrest offers signal opportunities for the educative enterprise and that we would do well to think carefully and to act resolutely to avail ourselves of the creative moment presented to us.

I wish to sketch in broad strokes a theory of moral education that aims to speak to the contemporary cultural and educational situation. One might argue that not theory but resolute practical action is what the current crisis and opportunity call for. To this I respond that just now nothing is more urgently needed than a moral theory—a vision that justifies and animates the educator's and the student's active moral endeavor. In this context, as in so many others, it turns out that nothing is so practical as theory.

If one presumes to engage in moral instruction, the basic question that arises concerns the value standards or norms that are to be used and the sources and justification for those norms. In this regard there are four possible orientations that one can take, each defining a practice-controlling theoretical outlook.

First, one can assume an essentially nihilistic position *vis a vis* values. Such a position of normlessness can be called *anomic*. It is a denial that there are really any standards of right or wrong, of better or worse, because the whole human endeavor appears to be meaningless and without purpose.

The anomic outlook is common in a time of widespread cultural change. When traditional values disintegrate because of altered social and material conditions, many persons become deeply anxious and disoriented. In the modern world the disintegration of norms caused by social and technical change is greatly accentuated by the meeting and mixing of many different cultural traditions. Travel and communication have brought about a situation of world-wide cultural pluralism which presents each individual with such a bewildering array of possible value-orientations that he is tempted to deny the meaning of any of them.

The practical consequence of the anomic position is an attitude of frustration and cynicism which leads one to drift aimlessly with the current and to react passively to internal impulses and external compulsions. In extreme cases it results in suicide, the culminating expression of the sense of meaninglessness. Many who adopt one or another of the forms of social deviance do so as an expression of their inability to find any meaning in the established orders of human life.

Obviously, the anomic outlook cannot provide a basis for moral education, if, indeed, for any kind of education. If life is essentially meaningless, there is no point in trying to promote it or to improve it. An anomic theory of values is fatal to education, as it is to any sustained cultural pursuit. Unfortunately, it is a theory all too widely held, either explicitly or tacitly, and it should be recognized as an enemy of human morale and of educational effectiveness.

A more constructive position, and one that its adherents are generally more willing to acknowledge and disseminate, may be termed the *autonomic*. The autonomist believes that there are norms or values, and that their source and justification are in the persons who make them. Every individual invests existence with meaning, and its significance is nothing more nor less than the meaning he gives it.

The autonomic theory of values, like the anomic, constitutes a response to the dissolution of traditional value systems and the confrontation of divergent cultural norms. Powerful impetus for it comes from the scientific studies of cultures that indicate the boundless varieties of institutions and customs that human ingenuity has devised. A common result of such investigations is the theoretical conviction that values are nothing but human artefacts and that all standards are relative to the persons and societies that make them.

The value theory of most contemporary philosophies including existentialism is essentially autonomic. The dominant empirical and naturalistic systems of thought, denying transcendent realms of being, admit of no normative reality beyond the observable natural and social orders. Human beings are creative agents who make their own world and who can depend on no objective moral order to guide their choices. The only moral truth for man is in the passionate subjectivity of his own creative value-projections.

The educational consequences of the autonomic theory of value are far-reaching. If norms are simply what people posit them to be—if human beings make values—then it is inadmissible to teach people how they *ought* to behave. All one can teach is how this person or that group of persons have decided they will behave. The key educational problem is to impart skill in adjusting the varieties of values that people have so as to create a reasonably congruent social scheme. Moral decision is thus defined by (or perhaps better, replaced by) political strategy. It is not a question of learning what is right or wrong, but what is socially expedient.

The prevalence of the autonomic theory of values is plainly seen in the fact that the most crucial present-day value issues are being dealt with mainly in political, not moral, terms. The most dramatic case in point is the rapid transfer of the racial question from the moral to the political arena. What was only a few years ago argued in terms of right is now often treated primarily as a matter of power, with scant reference to the moral ends to be served. From the autonomic standpoint, why should the black man want to become integrated into the value structures of the white man, from whom he has suffered such humiliation and deprivation? If people make their own values, is it not high time black people claim their freedom to create their own culture and to set their own norms, which are neither better nor worse, but simply different from those of white people? The result of such an argument is strong educational emphasis on the integrity and distinctive cultural identity of black people and insistence on full treatment of the norms of the black community in education as valuable in their own terms, simply by virtue of their being the standards by which blacks have defined the meaning of their existence.

The same autonomic value theory is operative in the movement to politicize the institutions of education. The question increasingly being asked by those who hold school and college buildings under seige, and by strikers and pressure groups, whether of students, of teachers, or of parents, is not what is good and right but who has the power—whose will is to prevail. I believe that one fundamental reason for this politicization is that the various parties to the conflict over policy do not believe there are any norms of judgment beyond the interests and prescriptions of the people and groups involved. Educational institutions, recognized as important agencies for the sorting and grading of persons for positions within the power structure of society, thus become key factors in the political struggle. The curriculum is judged in terms of "relevance" (a basic idea in current reform movements) which in political terms means effectiveness in promoting autonomous interests and demands.

In contrast to both of the foregoing value-orientations, a third theory, the *heteronomic*, asserts that there are objective standards of value that are known, that can be taught, and that provide clear and unambiguous norms of judgment for human conduct. According to this theory, people do not make values, they discover them. Right and wrong are just as real as the laws of physical nature, only they take the form of moral obligation not of physical necessity. These moral laws are sometimes regarded as divine commands, promulgated by an all-wise sovereign deity, and sometimes as rationally intuitable demands apprehended by the moral sensibility.

The heteronomic standpoint is operative in those who look with alarm and disapproval on the disintegration of traditional values, who decry the anomic and autonomic responses so widespread today, and who urge the adoption of strong programs of explicit religious and ethical instruction in order to restore the lost values to the coming generation. The heteronomists also stress law and order and the taking of all necessary enforcement measures to prevent deviance from established standards of belief and conduct.

Of many different persuasions, the heteronomists may be staunch conservatives, orthodox communists, or doctrinaire liberals of the middle way. What makes them heteronomic is their ideological certainty and their consequent pedagogical commitment to transmit and inculcate values they are convinced are right.

All three of the foregoing value theories fail to do justice to the realities of moral conscience and fail to provide a basis for moral education. It seems to me that heteronomy is unsatisfactory because of the perennial conflict of value systems. Each ideology is regarded by its adherents as the ultimate standard of value, by which all others must be criticized. It does not take a great deal of historical or anthropological perspective to see how untenable such ethnocentrism is. In the face of the staggering multiplicity of norms by which people have actually lived and do live, it is hard to justify an exclusivist ideological position. That is why so many adopt an anomic or an autonomic view. But these latter positions are unsatisfactory for a different reason, namely, that they cut the nerve of moral inquiry and effectively negate moral conscience. The anomist is not morally concerned because he regards the whole human enterprise as meaningless, while the autonomist substitutes political strategy for morality. If values are human creations, then there is no objective basis for judging their worth, analogous, for example, to the objective observational norms used in judging the truth of statements in natural science.

What serious moral education in the modern age requires is a theoretical persuasion that moral inquiry has some objective referent. Thus I propose that a fourth theory which I shall call *teleonomic* is required. By *teleonomic* I refer to the theory that the moral demand is grounded in a comprehensive purpose or "telos" that is objective and normative, but that forever transcends concrete institutional embodiment or ideological formulation.

Teleonomy, in short, is an interpretation of the persistent commitment of persons of conscience to the progressive *discovery* of what they ought to do. Just as the commitment to truth is a common presupposition of all scientific inquiry, expressing acknowledgement of an objective order of perceptual relationships in a world of great variety and complexity, so the commitment to right is a common presupposition of all moral inquiry, expressing dedication to an objective order of values in the domain of human choices, equally various and complex. Teleonomy interprets the moral enterprise as a venture of faith, not in the sense of blind adherence to a set of precepts that cannot be rationally justified, but in the sense of willingness to believe in and to pursue the right through the partial and imperfect embodiments of it in the concrete historical institutions of society, confident that these are always subject to criticism from the standpoint of an ideal order forever beyond specification and finite embodiment.

The practical operational consequence of the teleonomic outlook is to foster dialogue and to make moral inquiry a life-long practice. The person who believes that moral conscience is an essential concommitant of being human above all wants to do right. He is not satisfied with getting his own way and promoting his own demands. Furthermore, he readily sees that what is right is a very complicated matter and that the judgments he makes on the basis of his own limited experience are extremely partial and unreliable. Therefore he needs to associate with other persons who can complement and correct his understandings through bringing to bear other perspectives on the issues requiring decision. Furthermore, he has the grace to perceive that every value-determination is subject to further scrutiny and to continuing revision in the light of new understandings.

If we are convinced by the evidence of conscience in ourselves and by the deep and pervasive moral concern on the part of many Americans as they grapple with our critical social issues, then we will agree that there is a moral imperative in education that needs to be responded to by educational means both consonant with genuinely moral ends and not governed either by political or doctrinaire ideological considerations. The contemporary educational responses to the moral issues of our time tend to polarize into two opposing forces: the absolutists, who seek to inculcate some orthodoxy of law and order, whether of right, left, or middle; and the relativists, who aim to transform educational institutions into essentially political instrumentalities. What the moral imperative in education requires is the practice of teaching and learning in response to an absolute commitment to the good, 'by means of the relativities of concrete historical institutions to which humans as finite and fallible creatures are inescapably limited.

What, then, are the appropriate terms of the educative response to this imperative? I have already suggested that they should be dialogic. But who should participate in the dialogue, and according to what procedures? That is to say, what is the indicated methodology of moral instruction?

The distinctive office of the school, as I see it, in the domain of moral education, is to develop skills in moral deliberation through bringing to bear on concrete personal and social problems the relevant perspectives drawn from a variety of specialized disciplines. The premise on which moral instruction depends is that choices can be improved by widening and deepening one's understanding, both cognitive and affective, in particualar decision-situations. Unwise choices result from partiality and narrowness of view, both of which can be overcome by exhibiting, through dialogue, the bearings of various specialized studies.

A dialogue whose participants are merely other concerned persons, without specialized competences directed toward the issue at hand, can provide alternative insights that may enlarge the chooser's perspective. But any improvement thus achieved is uncontrolled, accidental, and likely to be superficial. The use in the dialogue of relevant specialists allows for a far more profound transformation of understanding. Even a single specialized inquiry may afford a radically fresh outlook on a given problem. However, each such unitary modification of view by itself distorts the moral outlook, and therefore must be complemented and corrected by perspectives from other specialized studies.

I shall illustrate these general methodological recommendations by referring to the specific case of sex education. Let us assume that we do not adopt the heteronomic stand that we already know the absolute right about sexual conduct. Let us assume further that we do not regard sexual behavior as a matter of moral indifference, and as subject to no judgment beyond one's autonomous preferences. Let us assume, then, that we regard sex as a subject for conscientious moral decision.

Clearly, common sense and hear-say about sex are quite inadequate. Specialized knowledge must be brought to bear in sex education. Obviously relevant are the biologist's and the physician's knowledge of human physiology, of the reproductive process, of the means available for preventing conception, of abortion, and of the various pathologies associated with sex, and their treatment. Yet important as such specialized knowledge is, by itself it does not constitute a basis for guiding responsible sexual conduct. It is necessary but not sufficient. I would hazard the judgment that the transformation of perspective effected by such studies offered in isolation from complementary disciplines may do more harm than good to the student. A genuinely moral decision depends on an outlook that is both deeply informed and comprehensively integrated.

Hence the physiology of sex needs to be complemented by psychological insights, including understanding of the role of affect in human personality, of the various motivations for sexual relations, and of how sexuality is sublimated or expressed in other human pursuits. To these insights should be added the important findings of social scientists concerning the family, the diverse patterns of sexual behavior actually practiced in various cultures, and the ways in which such patterns fit into the total complex of practices constituting these alternative ways of life.

Still the picture of what sexuality means is far from complete if based only on the inquiries of specialists in the natural and social sciences and psychology. These must be supplemented by humanistic perspectives. For example, literature contains profound expressions of the subjective meanings of sex. Sex is a central theme in much poetry, in the novel, and in drama. In these sources are articulated a great variety of attitudes of persons confronted with specific moral choices in the realm of sex, and one can imaginatively observe the outworkings of the various decisions made. Likewise, it is important to view sexuality in historical perspective in order to be freed from the provinciality of present preoccupations.

These scientific, aesthetic, and historical perspectives finally must be considered in the light of a comprehensive coordinating vision stemming from philosophical and theological inquiry. Such questions as the creation, nature, and destiny of the human person, the meaning of human relatedness, the uniqueness and sanctity of the person, and the significance of loyalty and promise-making are obviously fundamental to the question of sexual relations.

The insights provided by the various specialized studies do not, of course, yield any clear and conclusive answer to the moral inquirer. They do not simplify the problem of moral decision, they make it more complicated. In the end, each person must respond in conscience to the persuasion of the right that best commends itself to him. From an educational standpoint what matters is that the persuasion emerge from a mind deeply and widely informed and not from a congeries of chance impressions, haphazard impulses, and accidents of personal history.

In short, the moral imperative in education requires the nurture of intelligence in concrete decision-making. "Intelligent" choice, as I have indicated, includes not only scientific, but also affective, aesthetic, religious, and metaphysical elements.

The process of moral inquiry sketched above is designed to suggest justifiable principles of conduct in an area such as sex. Beyond such general principles of moral orientation, of course, lie matters of individual decision in particular contexts. Circumstances determine just how the general principles apply in a given case. Instruction might thus profitably include both multi-disciplinary critical elaboration of general rules and the use of case studies to illustrate the particular deployment of these rules.

I see the moral imperative requiring a substantial restructuring of the curriculum so as to institutionalize the requisite moral inquiry. This would not be done by creating separate courses in ethics taught by specialists. Instead, major, continuing study would be required in the basic personal and social issues, with instruction organized on a multi-disciplinary basis. At the same time, faculty and students should continue to pursue specialized diciplinary studies, which are the prime sources of significant and useful knowledge. This duality of specialized studies and multi-disciplinary moral investigations would be carefully guarded. Disciplinary studies alone tend toward academic fragmentation and a sense of academic irrelevance. Education organized exclusively on a problem basis, on the other hand, tends to degenerate into an insipid exchange of prejudices among the mutually uninformed.

The contemporary American scene provides a fertile field for the deployment of moral imagination. There are abundant signs that conscience is very much alive in many Americans, especially of the younger generation. The problems that confront us as a nation and world are enormous but so also are our personal and material resources. It is a time of magnificent prospects for an education reconstituted in response to the moral imperative that is presented in these stirrings of conscience. To counteract both static moralistic traditionalsim and moral nihilism and subjectivism, I believe that we require a renewed conviction of the objective though ultimately transcendent reality of the moral realm, together with institutionalized procedures for moral instruction, procedures based on the dialogic interpenetration of the various academic specializations within dedicated communities of inquiry.

Education and the Clarifying Experience

NORMAN COUSINS

In the present scratchy and undiscriminating national mood, education is an easy target. I deplore the tendency but would like to get into the act nonetheless. One of the prime weaknesses of education, it seems to me, is that it doesn't give enough attention to the need for developing the individual's communications skills. It is concerned with his ability to absorb knowledge but it assigns somewhat lesser importance to his need to make himself clear. This is less a matter of vocabulary range than of vocabulary control. It has to do with the entire process by which an individual organizes his thoughts for purposes of transmission.

The prime element in this process is sequence. Ideas have to be fitted together. The movement of a concept or an image from the mind of the speaker to the mind of the listener is retarded when words become random chunks rather than sequential parts of an ordered whole. This doesn't rule out unhurried allusions; these can give color to an account and help to make a claim on the imagination and memory. But it does rule out ungoverned circling and droning, reminiscent of buzzards hovering and swooping over a victim until he drops.

From *Perspectives on Education* (Winter 1969), 1–5. Reprinted by permission of *Perspectives on Education*, Teachers College, Columbia University.

It contributes nothing to a conversation to have an individual interrupt himself in order to insert sudden thoughts. The abuse is compounded when these obtrusive thoughts are invaded by yet others so that nothing is complete, neither the sentence, nor the paragraph, nor any of the vagrant incidents or ideas that are strewn around like fragments of an automobile wreck.

The following quotation is a fair approximation drawn from a recent conversation:

"This book I want to talk to you about," a visitor told me, "is one of the finest novels that I—well, let me put it this way, when I first heard about it I said to myself—actually, I told my wife who asked me if we were publishing anything exciting, you know, my wife is one of the finest assets I have in my job. She doesn't come to the office or anything like that you know, but—well, she does have a reputation in the shop for being a good critic and she—well, first let me tell you that she did disagree with me about two manuscripts I turned down and they were published by another house and of course they became best sellers. First let me tell you I once had a manuscript reader who was working for me and, well, she was two years out of Radcliffe but she had taken Levin's course in writing at Yale. I don't agree that writing can't be taught. I remember my own lit course with Jenney who told me—well, you know, he had the highest standards and I was very pleased to see him published last month in *Saturday Review.* What I meant was, someone always publishes the manuscript that everyone considers unpublishable, and this is what one always hears about and it is what always comes up in conversation. One always hears about *A Tree Grows in Brooklyn*—it was rejected by a dozen publishers—or *The Naked and the Dead*—it must have been turned down by ten publishers. Of course, Norman Mailer has turned out quite differently from what everyone expected him to be. His report on the Chicago convention was one of the finest—I don't know whether you saw it in *Harper's*—it was better, you know, than his piece on the Pentagon riots in *Commentary* which—well, let me put it this way, the best writing is being done by—I mean the best reporting—no one has come close, you know, to Truman Capote and this is where we go, you know, when we want to find out what is really— you know, nothing in any of the newspapers can tell us what it is like, especially if you want to know what the real facts were...."

He was at least two hundred words and three minutes beyond his topic sentence and I had yet to hear the title of the book. The quotation is not a parody. If you want its equivalent, I suggest you take a tape recording of a cross-section of an average day's office interviews or serious conversations. Chances are you will be appalled by the sprawling and fragmented character of the transcript. Complete sentences will be largely nonexistent; central ideas will emerge as from a deep mist. The surprise will not be that the meaning should be as obscured as it is by the unrelated turnings and self-interruptions but that there should be any meaning at all. Oral communication in our society comes close to being a complete bust.

Let me be a little crotchety at this point. During the course of an average work week, it is necessary for me to see perhaps forty or fifty people. Most of them come on matters related to the business of the magazine. Some may have ideas for articles or have projects for which they seek *Saturday Review's* sponsorship. I value these meetings; they bring a rich supply of information and opinions. They widen our editorial options.

Having said this, I must also confess that not all our callers know how pressing and persistent magazine deadlines can be. Nothing is more fatiguing than to be pinned down in a chair on a busy day while a visitor seeks through sheer volume of words to get a message across. There is the raging desire to terminate a "conversation" with a man who has talked for forty minutes without making his purpose known—or, what is even worse, who has talked for forty minutes *after* he has made his purpose known. But the compulsion to walk away is downed. Such things just aren't done.

I see that recent medical research indicates that a wide variety of maladies, including rheumatoid arthritis and adrenal exhaustion, are sometimes directly related to the intense frustration and restlessness a man suffers when subjected to mindless and predatory assaults on his time by people who don't know how to come to the point. It is astounding that otherwise well-educated men should have so little awareness of their obligation to make themselves clear and to stay within reasonable time limits. My heart sinks whenever a caller takes out a note pad on which he has listed a dozen or more separate items for our conversation. When, fifteen minutes later, he is still in the middle of item one, I make a hasty calculation and realize that at this rate we won't be through for a couple of days. That is when the corticoids and all the other stress chemicals in the body begin to race up and down.

Not long ago a man arrived at the *Saturday Review*, identified himself as a Charter subscriber, and asked to see the editor for a few minutes. He came into my office and proceeded to talk volubly and obscurely. Finally, I perceived he was telling me about his daughter's book, published by a firm unknown to me. As a father who likes to think his own daughters are bursting with literary ability, I was impressed by my visitor's determination to do everything he could to help herald his child's talents. Unfortunately, he continued to herald long past the point of reasonable persuasion. Finally, I broke in and told him we would be glad to look at the book in order to determine whether it could be sent out for review.

"I don't want you to review it," he said. "I want you to buy it. It costs only $4.95 and...."

I gave him the $4.95. It was an inexpensive way to terminate a conversation, considering the price I would otherwise have to pay in suppressed anguish over the delay in getting back to my desk.

If there is no excuse for blurring and meandering in conversation, there is even less excuse for it in written forms of communication. The memo and correspondence baskets are greater sources of fatigue than anything that has been invented to harass a man whose work requires him to be in almost constant communication. I have a vivid picture in my mind of Dr. Albert Schweitzer at the age of 84 spending most of his time struggling with his correspondence. Every day two sacks of mail would arrive at the hospital at Lambaréné—letters from people who wanted to visit the hospital or work there; letters from Schweitzer Fellowship members all over the world; letters from admirers and readers of his books; letters from doctors and theologians, musicologists and scientists, all of them writing on matters within his professional competence.

Late at night, long after the hospital was put to bed, Schweitzer would be bent over his desk, working on his correspondence. One night, during my visit in 1958, I was unable to sleep. I left my bunk and walked towards the river. I saw a light in Dr. Schweitzer's quarters and peeked in. There was Le Grand Docteur, struggling with his correspondence at 2:00 a.m.

We discussed the matter the next day.

"My correspondence is killing me," he said. "I try to answer all my letters, but I keep falling further and further behind. I get great joy out of reading my letters. It keeps me in touch with the outside world. I like to hear from people. But most of the time I don't really know what my letters are trying to tell me. They wander so, ach!"

Is it unreasonable to expect education to attach primary importance to the techniques of clarity, either oral or written? Is it unreasonable to suggest that respect for the next man's time is one of the most essential and useful lessons a person can learn? Time is capital. Time is finite. Clarity is a coefficient of time.

I should like to think that the school provides an environment conducive to the development of habits of clarity. But I am troubled by what I know. A recent high school test in English composition that came to my attention called upon the student to write descriptive material of 1,000 words or more in ninety minutes. If the school allowed (or even required) the student to spend half a day thinking about such a writing assignment, and a full day for the actual writing, the time would not be excessive. A writer like Thomas Mann felt he had put in a productive day if he had been able to write five hundred words. Good writing, most of all, is clear writing. This is painstaking work. It requires time. It requires sustained and sequential thought.

But the school itself is not yet a model of organization, either in its internal structure or in its relationship to the student. I see very little evidence of total time-management in the demands made by the school on the student. Each course of study has its own claim. Unable to get it all in, the student is often under pressure to cut corners. He finds himself forced into a strategy of intellectual merchandising and packaging; he becomes more concerned with the voluminous trappings and the appurtenances of surface scholarship than with genuine achievement. He learns the tricks of glibness.

It is difficult to understand why the school should foster habits of juggling and fragmentation rather than of concentration. Why is so little consideration given to the coordination of work assignments for students? Why is it considered good educational practice to compel a student to work on more than one major paper at a time? It is the full mobilization of an individual's intelligence, rather than its pyrotechnics, that should engage the aims of the school. Some of the greatest feats of the human intelligence have proceeded out of total focus on a single problem. Charles Darwin was riding on a London bus top when some key thoughts on his theory of evolution burst upon him. This doesn't mean that there is something about the topside of a London omnibus that triggers profound ideas on the origin of the species. What it does mean is that Darwin had allowed his mind to fill up with a complex problem until it spilled over to the subconscious; the result was that, even when he did not consciously direct his thoughts, his mind kept working away at the problem, sorting all the factors that were being accumulated, weighing them, making correlations, and engaging in all the operations leading to a deduction or a discovery. It was the gestative process of ideas, rather than the environment of a bus top, that was responsible for the flash that electrified Darwin. Socrates had no particular liking for the term "teacher" when applied to himself; he preferred to think of himself as an intellectual midwife who helped bring ideas to birth out of laboring minds. What is most valuable in the Socratic method is the painstaking and systematic development of a thought from its earliest beginnings to its full-bodied state. The mind was fully engaged; this was what was most vital to the process.

What I am trying to suggest is that the natural requirements of thought are the essential and prior business of education. No teacher I knew had a better understanding of this basic purpose than Harold Rugg. He never wavered in his confidence in the ability of the mind to create its own optimum environment. His belief in the importance of integrative education was directly related to this concept.

My apprehension about modern education is that it tends to diffusion, even as it promotes over-specialization. That is, it lacks a philosophy of education to go along with the education it provides. It has yet to come to terms with the constant accretion of new knowledge. The result is that we are producing a generation of idea-hoppers. It is not necessarily true that the school is helpless to cope with the onrush of increasing specialization. Major emphasis can be given to the interrelationships of knowledge and to the points of contact and convergence. It may not be possible to keep the student up to date in the accumulation of new knowledge—or even to instruct him fully in the old. But what is possible is to define the significance of what is happening and to identify the juncture at which different areas of knowledge come together.

All this has to do with the student's ability to organize his time, to give his total attention to a difficult problem or objective, and to make himself clear. The school is not the only conditioning agent in the thought patterns and habits of the student, but it is possibly the dominant one.

Meanwhile, there is the ongoing problem of all those who are beyond the reach of the school. It is churlish and absurd to take the postition that a poor communicator is locked into his low-level condition. For a man whose professional life depends ultimately on having people know what he is talking about, a few suggestions may be in order.

Effective communications, oral or written, depend absolutely on a clear understanding of one's purpose. That purpose should be clearly identified. It should not be cluttered with extensive comment or side excursions. It should be developed point by point, with the rigorous attention to sequence and gradations of a professional bead-stringer at work.

In verbal communication, the prime requisite is to anticipate the circumstances of a meeting or encounter. If it seems likely that the available time for the meeting will be limited, then it is obviously suicidal to use up most of the time in clearing one's throat. Nor does it seem especially perspicacious to have an overly long agenda, saving the most important items for last, when there is every likelihood that time will run out long before the main event.

In written communication, no better advice can be offered than to cite the favorite six-word question of Harold Ross, late editor of the *New Yorker:* "What the hell do you mean?" Ross was a great editor because he was death on ambiguities. Though he edited one of the most sophisticated magazines in the nation, he cherished the simplicities. He insisted on identifications for all names and places. And he hated extraneous words or observations. Under his rule, the *New Yorker* became a model of clear, effective writing.

My purpose here is not to drum up business for the *New Yorker* (I have a drum of my own), but to point out that institutions have been built on clarity. Also, that clarity is one of the truly distinguishing characteristics of the educated man.

Mass Man, Popular Education, and the Meritocracy

JOHN MARTIN RICH

It was Friedrich Nietzsche, more than any of his contemporaries and philosophical predecessors, who had the prescience to envisage the plight of twentieth-century man. For Nietzsche, a vision of the shattering of traditional morality with the death of God created a dissolution of the normative social fabric that only the overman, the higher man of culture, could reconstruct through a radical transvaluation of values. Yet the specific measures which would bring about a needed reconstruction Nietzsche left for those who would come later.

Marx did not foresee capitalistic systems offering industrial workers the enjoyment of a moderately high level of goods and services;[1] but he was not mistaken

From *The Educational Forum* (May 1967), 495–499. Reprinted by permission of Kappa Delta Pi, An Honor Society in Education, owners of the copyright.

[1] Actually, capitalism is an ideal construct. The American economic system is a mixed system: what Galbraith would call an "oligopoly." Cf.: John Kenneth Galbraith, *American Capitalism* (Boston: Houghton Mifflin Company, 1952).

about the alienation of workers, even though the forms that alienation would take were difficult to divine. With the later developments of the Industrial Revolution and machine technology, increasing urbanization and centralization, the weakening of the family, the breakdown of primary group relations, and the proliferated uses of mass production, consumption, and the increasing homogeneity of tastes promoted by the mass media, alienation grew as these trends accentuated themselves. Durkheim called it "anomie," the breakdown of what formerly were common values and the growing isolation of the members of a society.

The "mass man"[2] is the creation of the aforementioned social trends. Such a person becomes the unwitting servant of industrial machinery that aims for greater levels of efficiency and higher profits. This has lead to bureaucratic organizations, both in industry and education.[3] Max Weber, the German sociologist, established a formal model of a bureaucracy, organizations designed to operate on the principle of efficiency in order to accomplish large-scale administrative tasks.[4] By eliminating irrationality, subordinating personnel to the administrative hierarchy, and elevating precision, speed, and continuity, efficiency, theoretically, is maximized. Given the type of technology and economy that we have today, bureaucratic organizations would seem to follow inevitably from the goals set by management. And whenever education adopts the management model, teachers are likely to be viewed as obedient servants of administrative authority.[5]

Satisfactions once derived from some form of work and the warmth of face-to-face relationships have been replaced by materialistic strivings and the frenetic search for status. The plight of the masses has been created by, on the one hand, the loss of traditional values and the inability to find a new set of values equally as compelling and, on the other hand, increased opportunity to enjoy the fruits of an education and, with it, the ability to envision a better life. Coupling the loss of traditional values with the rising expectations of those who have enjoyed educational and material advantages not experienced by their parents, dissatisfaction, drift, and blind striving have set in.

The incessant search for pleasure and materialistic satisfactions are manifestations not of immorality but the lack of a reasoned set of values which could afford some direction to one's life. The inherent danger for the masses, who have not as yet fully acclimated themselves to existing technology, is that they are moving rapidly into a cybernated age which promises to generate far greater dislocations and value conflicts. The danger lies for the masses, in their search for direction, in turning to a charismatic leader who could usher in a new era of fascism. Mannheim, for instance, sees that the worker's lack of personal gratification in large-scale

[2] A term we will use tentatively and later criticize.

[3] For an analysis of the development of bureaucracies in education see Raymond E. Callahan, *The Cult of Efficiency* (Chicago: University of Chicago Press, 1962).

[4] Cf.: *From Max Weber: Essays in Sociology*, trans. and edited by E. Gerth and C. Wright Mills (New York: Oxford University Press, 1958); *Max Weber: The Theory of Social and Economic Organization*, trans. by A. M. Henderson and Talcott Parsons (New York: The Free Press, 1947).

[5] William Chandler Bagley, *Classroom Management* (New York: Macmillan, 1907).

organizations and his inability to locate the source of his frustrations when confronting an impersonal bureaucratic structure, leads him, as his helplessness increases, to seek scapegoats and, thereby, become a willing subject for fascism.[6]

What has American education done to help alleviate the growing sense of helplessness, drift, and alienation stemming from a loss of tradional values? It has, first of all, extended the age of formal schooling and served as an agency of socialization during a period when the influence of the family has diminished. And it has disseminated to the masses, on a wider scale than in the past, the rudiments of culture and, to a certain extent, the means for its enjoyment. Education, in order to meet the demands of a highly specialized technology, has sought to prepare specialists in sufficient numbers. Heading the list of specialists needed by society is the scientist, whom Ortega y Gasset in *The Revolt of the Masses* claims to be the prototype of mass man. The scientist, for Ortega, is a mass man for he, too, is uncultured.

Those who write in the conservative vein, as did Ortega, frequently use the term "mass" as a synonym for "modern." It becomes a lament that the "masses" have learned to read well enough to dilute standards. Their fear that the masses have taken the reins of power may not reflect the realities of Western political systems, but their great concern that the older aristocratic order may not be able to maintain its position and advantage has been warranted by events in a number of Western countries.

But the fear of the masses is not original with Ortega. We can find in Aristotle's *Politics* the conception of the masses who are violent, excessive, and easily swayed by demagogues who usher in states of tyranny. In the Roman republic, in the early Christian theory of Augustine and extending through theories of many writers up to T. S. Eliot, we find, in divergent forms, a distrust of the masses. Even in Tocqueville and Acton there is the fear that democratic forms have the tendency to offer equality without genuine liberty—a leveling of the social structure coupled with an oppressive conformity. The picture that we get frequently overlooks constitutionalism, universal sufferage, and the rule of law found in democracies. Such criticisms tend also to ignore in democracies free public school systems which provide, even though imperfectly, an opportunity for advancement in society on the basis of achievement rather than through an exclusive system of ascribed characteristics.

"The masses" is not a clear-cut, functional term; seldom do we know what criteria are to be used in identifying the people who constitute the masses. The term is employed by conservatives to denote all those who are not aristocrats; yet, in a society in which there is a modicum of social mobility, these are not fixed divisions. It would appear that the term "social class," as used by sociologists who study social stratification, would more effectively differentiate groups. But perhaps the reference to "the masses" by certain individuals is tenaciously protected because it is a pejorative term used to denigrate those for whom a distaste has been

[6] Karl Mannheim, *Man and Society in an Age of Reconstruction* (London, 1940).

cultivated, and as a summons to others of similar social standing as themselves to combat dangers, real or imagined, posed by the masses.

The real problem, whether we speak of masses and aristocracy, social classes, is the erosion of traditional values in our times. Since the schools, according to several contemporary writers, have increasingly exacerbated the alienation of youth and heightened the manipulative level of the environment, there is a call, at times, for a simpler type of relationship nostalgically reminiscent of the past wherein an imagined pristine purity devoid of exploitation constituted the fabric of human relations. Yet, it does not seem that either those who would safeguard the aristocracy from the invasion of the *hoi polloi,* or the romantics can provide needed guidance for the crisis which we confront.

First of all, it is not likely that there will be an abatement of the crisis; rather, it will surely intensify if present trends continue. As America enters the cybernated age our values surrounding work, personal responsibility, the relation of government to people, and the control that science exercises over our lives is likely to be dramatically altered.

The most salient feature of this revolution will, in all likelihood, be the rise of the "meritocracy."[7] The life-blood of the revolution is an army of highly trained specialists. Thus, where the high-school drop-out and the unskilled and semi-skilled workers were unable to find gainful employment, cybernation will shortly take its toll in the skilled ranks and among white-collar workers. In a meritocracy awards, recognition, and the apportionment of the goods and services would be based upon demonstrated ability rather than seniority, race, religion, nationality, family background, and other artificial distinctions that are used to mete out the perquisites and positions in life. One can imagine the severity of the problems confronting society as meritocracy grows and expands its influence in various areas of the economy. That an absolute meritocracy could never exist is insufficient reason to deny the trends which indicate we are moving increasingly in that direction. With a growing need for specialized intelligence and barring a nuclear holocaust, the importance of schooling, especially higher education, will be vastly greater.

As the barriers to equality of educational opportunity are progressively removed, the inability to measure up educationally in a brave new world will be traumatic indeed. For the first time in our history artificial impediments–race, religion, and nationality–erected to suffocate opportunity will be removed. And as means are devised to provide financial resources for all those who are academically deserving, the last psychological support will be destroyed–rationalization. Today some can legitimately claim discrimination as the reason for their failure to advance; while others conjure up elaborate rationalizations having little basis in fact to explain away why they are the kind of person they are. It will be a stunning blow to persons who fail to demonstrate the requisite levels of achievement in a meritocracy system that has removed these artificial barriers. The whole system of fabricating rationalizations will resoundingly collapse, leaving the individual's

[7] Michael Young was probably the first to coin this term in his imaginative essay: *The Rise of the Meritocracy, 1870–2033* (Baltimore: Penguin Books, 1961).

psyche and self-respect in a particularly vulnerable position. A humane society will have to devise ways to protect such persons.

The problem of the erosion of traditional values will be further precipitated by the move toward a meritocracy. The school will have a role to play in this crisis. The process of socialization will continue but will be directed to new and different ends.

Uppermost in the educational program should be the reflective examination of value issues and conflicts. Noting the present disenchantment with the use of reason and the scientific method, some may demur that the present sorry state of mankind is a result of the awesome destructiveness that science and various uses of reason have wrought. Of course, the faulty uses to which new discoveries are put may very well be a deficiency in the use of "humane" reason, not a superfluity. But in any case, although we may not agree today with Plato that knowing the Good will lead to doing the Good if we conceive of knowing as some form of knowledge–action, it would seem that reflective inquiry into values is at least a necessary, though not a sufficient, condition for dealing with the value crisis.

To delineate the other conditions necessary for value decisions would involve exploration beyond the scope of this paper.[8] There is, however, a critical problem confronting a meritocracy that should be mentioned. With the rapid rate by which specialization will proceed, the need of the specialists to communicate will become increasingly acute–not only with those who do not have the ability to gain an advanced education–but even with those in their own discipline.

A society based on meritocracy will be in dire need of generalists, highly talented persons who can keep the communications network open and promote understanding of public policy. But what would such a generalist be like in view of the vastness of extant knowledge at the time? He will not be a classical scholar, although the classics will not be denigrated; he will be more like those men in our own time of vast talent and imagination, who have pursued the unification of all knowledge. A meritocracy must save its most talented minds for the role of the generalist. He must, however, have an additional quality or the meritocracy will surely flounder. He must, above all, be a "humanistic generalist." His *raison d'être* will be the promotion of human good and his love for mankind and human values should be exemplary and unusual in its scope and depth. This is much to ask, but without it a meritocracy can not survive.

[8] For a further exploration, see the author's *Education and Human Values* (Reading, Mass.: Addison-Wesley Publishing Company, Inc., 1968). Chap. III.

Schools Look to Society as a Resource

JAMES S. COLEMAN

The first point that must be recognized in discussing the future of American education is that there are several different problems that demand different solutions.

Most immediately pressing is the need for basic reading and numerical skills by lower class blacks, Puerto Ricans, and other groups who come into industrial society with a heritage of deprivation. Existing educational practice has not shown itself equal to this task of reducing racial and class inequalities of opportunity through education, and these groups are demanding that it begin to do so.

At the same time middle-class adolescents, to whom the combination of school and background has given a high level of these academic skills, are demanding that the schools address themselves less to the classical tasks of education, and more to questions that are relevant to present social changes.

These diverse needs and interests derive from the simple fact that our society contains in it a number of strata of history: It contains the legacy of rural isolation and of servitude along with the beginnings of post-industrial affluence.

The problems posed by the first of these strata—that of imparting basic skills to students from disadvantaged backgrounds—have shown a high degree of intransigence to usual methods. Compensatory programs have not shown great success in developing cognitive skills, nor have summertime and short-term interventions like Head Start.

Two points, however, do indicate avenues of promise.

One is that it appears clear that any programs to be successful must modify a larger portion of the child's environment than schools currently do. This can occur in three ways: environmental changes that begin at an earlier age, such as early childhood educational centers; modification of a larger portion of the child's day, through extended day programs; or finally through intensification of the environmental modifications that occur during the school day, through integration with children who have greater cognitive skills, or through a more intense involvement with reading and numerical tasks.

A second point that shows avenues of promise is the fact that in our society today, these skills, and some ability to transmit these skills are widespread outside the confines of school walls. In societies of the past, where information and knowledge were scarce, the school was a repository and transmitter of this scarce commodity. Now we are an information-rich society, with many more educational resources outside the school than within.

From *The New York Times* (Special Education Supplement) January 12, 1970, C66.

There are numerous groups outside school, from groups of volunteer tutors to storefront schools to large corporations that offer educational services. There is television and radio, newspapers, magazines, books, and there is a larger number of educated adults than in any previous society.

It becomes possible, in these circumstances, to augment the school's goals through these agencies outside the school.

Television is a remarkable educative aid; but only in the recently begun "Sesame Street" has explicit use been made of it for augmenting the aims of the school. There is much discussion now in the Federal Government and in some state governments of educational vouchers that parents could use outside school to augment their child's reading or numerical skills.

Even without such vouchers, some of these educational resources outside the schools have been put to use, in volunteer tutorial groups, street academies and contract schools. But in the absence of some means of regular public financing, they are ordinarily short-lived.

This general avenue, the use of educational resources from the information-rich environment outside schools, appears a very promising means of solving the basic-skills task of education. By relegating education solely to the school, we have failed, until now, to make use of these resources. They abound in American society and require only a means of public funding, such as vouchers, public expenditures on educational TV, and other devices, in order to be activated.

The opposite end of the historical continuum, the academically skilled youth of a post-industrial society, suffers from a fault of modern society that has accompanied its information-richness. Modern society is information-rich and action-poor for the young.

The school comprises a larger part of the life of the young, for an ever-longer period of time. For this period, they are forced to be students without the opportunity for responsible action affecting their lives and those of others. The role of student, which was once only a part of a young person's life, now comes to encompass it, as he is more and more shut off from responsible action.

In this context, what is necessary, of course, is not a greater pursuit of the classical goals by educational institutions, but addition of activities that allow responsible productive action. In the high schools, this means a closer link to the community, and a shift of activities: away from being taught, toward teaching of those younger; away from services for adolescents by the community, toward services for the community by adolescents; away from individual-centered activities, toward school-centered and community-centered ones.

New models of a high school will undoubtedly be tried. Three that seem most likely are a self-sufficient school-community along the lines of the George Junior Republic, a self-contained but more academic community along the lines of the English public schools (both models which, however, imply residential settings, and are thus not likely to soon be widespread), and an integration of secondary schools with companies in the economy (in which the teen-ager would have a daily schedule like anyone else, but would have a portion of his day devoted to learning).

In colleges, a fundamental problem arises. Universities have classically held a position insulated from society and some such insulated institutions are necessary to perform the classical role of universities as a leavening for society. However, colleges and universities have come to perform mass education, and for this function, the classical role of insulated student is inappropriate. The action-poverty of the outside society for the young is thereby exacerbated by the college, which is equally action-poor.

If the college is to provide for the young the opportunities for responsible action which are now missing outside the school, it must forgo its insulation from society, and become in some part an institution for action. This implies active, productive roles for the young who are currently only "students," in teaching, in social services, in producing things. The young will not passively sit by in their roles as students, but will rebel against the action-poverty of their environment—unless the action void left by the society itself is filled by the school.

The prospects for such change in the 1970's at the high school and college level are not bright. There are some movements in this direction at the level of colleges, mostly at the insistence of radical students, and thus often misled by the rhetoric of these students. I see, however, little systematic planning of community colleges and other new institutions to create an environment that includes as high a component of action as of classroom learning.

Altogether, then, the problems of the sixties demand diverse educational solutions in the seventies. The continuum of history contained in present-day America has created diverse problems ranging from the development of basic cognitive skills in children with information-poor environments to the development of no less basic skills of a productive life among those children with action-poor environments.

Reconnection for Relevance: A Proposed New High School Curriculum

JAMES L. FENNER

Before high school can make real sense to teenagers, we have to change it in important ways. We have to find administrators who will be more responsive to students than to bureaucratic higherups. We have to decompartmentalize course work, not by dismantling traditional departments of English, secretarial studies, science, and so forth, but instead by offering additional nondepartmental and interdisciplinary courses as electives. We have to tune the high school experience in on the real concerns of young people: self-realization, money, power, the future, sex. And most important, we have to try to relate what we teach in high school to the other things adolescents are learning and to those other sources of experience, information, and understanding that teach them so much so indelibly today.

Any meaningful proposed connection between high school studies and out-of-school learning taking place in our society must presuppose an analysis of just what this out-of-school learning really consists of, what it means to young people, what changes can be made in the schools to relate it to the curriculum, and what effects can be expected to flow from these changes. Fearing [1] has described the great impact and power of the mass media, and Gans [2] has explored the similarities and differences between school and the media as regards their structure, functions, problems, content, and policies. And Newcomb [3] has indicated how tenaciously attitudes formed out of school stick with us (where favorable reinforcements exist) long after their formation.

Extra-School Learnings

TV is certainly the most productive non-school source of learning today. Even though, as Maccoby [4] reveals, high school students watch less TV than younger kids do, they still spend more time in front of the bug-box than they do in school and pay closer attention to what it offers than to the school's intellectual menu. Unlike school, TV gives them a sense of involvement which McLuhan [5] has shown to be all the more intense because it is so sketchy, so "cool." It brings them the most expensive and fashionable entertainment talent in the world, "live" from wherever. Witty [6] insists that TV has value: it brings youngsters open-ended talk programs which, with seeming authority, touch upon the most important issues of the day; and it brings documentaries more informative—and certainly more stylish—than anything in their textbooks. With TV, it seems, they live; by comparison, their textbooks seem dead.

Radio is far from dead in the world of today's teenagers. Rock 'n Roll and folk-rock are adolescent-aimed industries now, and they add up to a vast segment of our economy. The "love now" and "student power" action fashions of the day are fed and fertilized by the fare radio purveys: protest lyrics, psychedelic songs,

From *Teachers College Record* (February 1970), 423–438. Reprinted by permission.

[1] Franklin Fearing, "Social Impact of the Mass Media of Communication," in N. B. Henry, Ed., *Mass Media and Education.* NSSE Yearbook. Chicago: University of Chicago Press, 1954.

[2] Herbert Gans, "The Mass Media as an Educational Institution," *The Urban Review,* February, 1967.

[3] Theodore M. Newcomb, "Persistence and Regression of Changed Attitudes: Long-Range Studies," *Journal of Social Issues,* Vol. 19, 1963.

[4] Eleanor Maccoby, "Effects of Mass Media," in M. C. Hoffman and Lois W. Hoffman, Eds., *Review of Child Development Research.* New York: Russell Sage Foundation, 1964.

[5] Marshall McLuhan. *Understanding Media.* New York: McGraw-Hill, Inc., 1965.

[6] Paul Witty, "Effects of TV on Attitudes and Behavior," *Education* October, 1964.

red-hot news, uninhibited talk, and millions of commercial messages that do for the transistorized corner boys what the bugbox does for the stay-at-homes. Rock groups like the Beatles, the Jefferson Airplane, the Mamas and the Papas, and Vanilla Fudge; oddballs like Tiny Tim; folk artists like Odetta and Joan Baez; and folk-rock performers like Bob Dylan and Simon and Garfunkel are true folk heroes among young Americans from 13 to 30.

Film is a rich world for teen-agers, and not just because of its role as a medium of individual and social recreation. It is contemporary, style-setting, camp, kitsch, social comment, sex education, philosophical orientation, and escape, all rolled into one, and its appeal is as intense as it is multifarious. Sitting back in the welcoming dark of the movie theater, the youngster learns about love, country, heroism, alienation, politics, business, adulthood, and tragedy. And in the realms of personal appearance, manner, talk, action, gesture, and (especially) motivation, he learns about style.

Students learn more than we sometimes realize from non-verbal sources. Interpersonal distance and the meaning of spatial and kinesthetic relationships between individuals have been explored by Hall[7] and shown to convey important meanings. The symbolism of static visual messages is equally important,[8] especially in such areas as advertising, architecture, and interior decoration. High school teachers have long known the strength of latent messages that seating arrangements convey, and how much more conducive to free discussion some such set-ups are than others. Human spaces and non-verbal communication are consciously and unconsciously used, abused, and learned from, everywhere.

World events teach a youngster much. It hardly matters whether he gets his information from a newspaper, radio, TV, newsweekly, or hearsay: ultimately it comes from the media one way or another. Ellul[9] has shown how much propaganda affects the attitudes of citizens—even young citizens—in a technological society, and how pervasive and powerful they must of necessity be. And today's teenager knows, as perhaps his father never knew, the extent to which events concern him directly: the war, the riots, the black power movement, the draft, the campus protests, the peace marches, the French general strike, the assassinations—everything.

The job market teaches adolescents a great deal. If they work, they learn how the great world works. They learn how to present themselves, how to "make it" with the company, how to play adult, how to save and spend money. If they don't work, they learn about unemployment, about leisure, about discouragement, about job requirements, screening practices, interviews, and questionnaires. They learn about taxes, budgets, the cost of self-support, the difficulty of saving something extra. Or if they don't learn these things, then they learn about poverty, indignity, idleness, despair, impotence, and futility.

[7] Edward T. Hall. *The Hidden Dimension.* New York: Doubleday and Co., 1966.

[8] Jurgen Ruesch and Weldon Kees. *Non-Verbal Communication.* Berkeley: University of California Press, 1956.

[9] Jacques Ellul. *Propaganda.* New York: Alfred A. Knopf, 1965.

Personal enjoyments teach kids tremendously important learnings. Social and physical relationships with the opposite sex teach them the meaning of love, pleasure, commitment, manipulation, cynicism, and faith in their dealings with others. Cars and drugs provide vehicles for literal and figurative trips away from the confines of home, family, school, neighborhood, or boss, and into a world of adventure and self-discovery. Fashion is a universe of self-expression, originality, conformity, timeliness, self-image-adjustment, consumership, and self-acceptance.

Finally, society's formal, hierarchical structure of power and influence reinforce much that school teaches and provide learnings that go far beyond what school attempts. The changes that Pearl [10] and Bundy [11] propose are intended to be as beneficial to the kids as they are for the adult poor. On the other hand, student power is one thing; civil disorders in the streets are another. Deans of discipline are one thing; police with nightsticks are another. The cop who doesn't see the pusher, the cop who uses tear gas, the cop who accepts a small bribe not to give a ticket for a moving violation, the window clerk at the Bureau of Motor Vehicles who won't lift a finger to help, the bureaucratic supervisor who won't do anything about it—all these represent evils of a credential-ridden and bureaucratic society that a young person finds particularly insufferable. And to him, the flag-wavers that brag about America and seem blind to its emptiness seem contemptible.

What Do Non-School Learnings Mean?

School learnings connect students with the world of the past, with the textbook world of the received wisdom and knowledge of the ages. Non-school learnings connect them with the present and future world around them. Where school shows them how they must see each new emphemeral and maybe "tastless" fad in the perspective of a stable tradition, the media show them how necessary it is to change with the changing world in order to be with it, to be in, to swing. Where the former teaches them how to live in the status-ridden world of the "real" power structure, the latter teaches them how to live in whatever enticing dream-world they desire. Where school teaches them required roles, out-of-school experience shows them congenial new ones to try. Where the one gives them information about set subjects, about set authority, about set regulations, etc., the other gives information about new politics, new style, new entertainment, and new issues. Where the one provides inculcation in traditional values, in conservatism, in playing the game, the other propagandizes for current values.

The middle class has found, both in and out of school, an array of indispensable guides of self-realization. The media have given them consumer expertise, a feel for making it, a style for advancement, a fistful of job skills: reading, writing, accounting, organization, and so on. Goodman [12] and Friedenberg [13] demonstrate

[10] Arthur Pearl, "New Careers and the Manpower Crisis in Education." Mimeo, 1968.

[11] McGeorge Bundy, *et al. Reconnection for Learning.* Mayor's Advisory Panel on Decentralization of the New York City Schools. New York, 1967.

[12] Paul Goodman. *Compulsory Mis-education.* New York: Horizon Press, 1964.

[13] Edgar Z. Friedenberg. *The Vanishing Adolescent.* Boston: Beacon Press, 1964.

the extent to which the schools and the media have neglected the potentially-fulfilling road to honest spiritual development in favor of the emptier and more convenient middle-class personal-management skills of thrift, investment, diligence, respect, gratification-postponement, and other forms of hoop-jumping.

For the poor, both school and the media have been powerful inducements to self-hatred and self-contempt. The advertising media have made them hunger for consumer goodies they can never legitimately afford. While Nat Hentoff [14] and Jonathan Kozol [15] on the one hand have shown vividly how they have suffered alienation from self, from middle-class values they don't espouse, from school routines, regulations, and, worst of all, irrelevancies, Martin Deutsch [16] and Frank Riessman [17] have outlined not only their deprivations but their resources as well. The schools have yet to institutionalize ways of capitalizing on these.

Roads to Relevancy

There is, of course, more than one road to relevancy in schooling. What is relevant to one aspect of our many-faceted civilization is unrelated to another. What helps one person get a job or get into this or that college prevents someone else from getting anything at all worth knowing out of school. The first attempt to solve this question came in the 1930's after it became apparent that the compulsory education laws were filling up the high schools with students to whom the traditional "academic" course of study—classical and modern languages, mathematics, science, literature, and history—meant little, and who weren't willing or able to get all that stuff into their heads. When these "new" high-school youngsters arrived on the scene and proceded to fail the traditional courses in droves, to express their hostility at great cost to their teachers' peace of mind, to prevent the "good" students from learning by their disruptions, and to wreak havoc upon the schools' educational statistics, the "general" course was created for them. Because these students were the dumb ones, or "slow" or "disadvantaged," or whatever fashionable euphemism you choose, the "general" course was simply designed as a reduction of the standard course. If the dumb ones couldn't learn as much, then give them less. If some subjects were too hard, then substitute easier ones. So they got—and are getting—a simplified curriculum. However inadequate the traditional courses were in dealing with the problems of the twentieth century, the "general" courses were worse. The high schools had one inadequate (difficult, but outdated) curriculum for the "good" students, and another worse one (empty and outdated) for the "dumb" ones.

In as varied a society as ours, it would be just plain silly to condemn every traditional subject as irrelevant. Some of the old academic and commercial standbys have great value for certain students. One need not be either an adherent of the

[14] Nat Hentoff. *Our Children Are Dying.* New York: Viking Press, 1966.
[15] Jonathan Kozol. *Death at an Early Age.* Boston: Houghton Mifflin, Inc., 1967.
[16] Martin Deutsch, Ed. *The Disadvantaged Child.* New York: Basic Books, 1967.
[17] Frank Riessman. *The Culturally Deprived Child.* New York: Harper and Row, 1962.

Bestor-Rickover[18] thesis or an enemy of John Holt[19] to see value in foreign languages, mathematics, science, social studies, literature, music, shop, bookkeeping, stenography, typing, and many other job-oriented, or college-oriented or recreation-oriented or broadening or "skill" subjects—*for some students.* Certainly these should be retained in the high schools, whether as required courses for specialized curricula or as electives for anyone who might be interested. But one need not hark back to the days of Jane Addams and yearn to see the school as a glorified settlement house to know that these old standard tradional courses are not enough today. They are not enough for the college-bound youngster, and they are not enough for the job-bound. They are not enough for the middle class, and they are not enough for the poor. Other subjects—ones that deal with contemporary life and that make use of contemporary issues and media—are required if any youngster is to gain from high school some sense of what his world is like and where it's at and how it hangs together. Probably the naive faith expressed in George S. Counts' *Dare the Schools Build a New Social Order?*[20] is out of place among today's complexities, but certainly reality and reconnection (to borrow a term current in another context) cannot hurt.

The following proposed elective courses for high school are intended to fulfill this requirement. They are intended as electives because I believe students—at least *some* students—would find them—at least *some* of them—intrinsically interesting enough to make them want to take them. This alone would relate them, as far as the nature of their appeal went, to out-of-school interests. They are intended as courses for everybody; and that means a heterogeneous student body. This too would relate them, if only superficially on an organizational basis, to life outside the school. And, most important, they are intended to cut across interdisciplinary boundaries, to bridge some of the gaps between subject and subject or between school and the "real" world, to combine and recombine the world, the media, the person, and the school in new and significant configurations, so that adolescence need not be the nightmare that Jules Henry,[21] John Holt, Paul Goodman, and Edgar Z. Friedenberg assert it to be. It is this feature of the proposals that, I hope, would make these courses valuable for the society (because its youngsters would be able to experience some sense of synthesis), for the school (because students might not feel so hostile to an institution that is giving them an education with a little life in it), and for the young people themselves (because they would be able to see some purpose, some pattern of interrelationships, some relevance to reality, in what the school is offering them). Here are the proposed electives, with brief descriptions of each:

1. *Entertainment.* This course would deal with current films, with TV, with radio (very much a source of adolescent entertainment today: "We're portable!" as

[18] See Arthur Bestor. *Educational Wastelands.* Urbana: University of Illinois Press, 1953; and Hyman G. Rickover. *Education and Freedom.* New York: Dutton and Co., 1960.

[19] John Holt. *How Children Fail.* New York: Pitman and Co., 1964.

[20] George S. Counts. *Dare the Schools Build a New Social Order?* New York: John Day, 1932.

[21] Jules Henry. *Culture Against Man.* New York: Vintage Books, 1963.

the "good guys" put it), records, with the theater, and with the entertainment aspects of the mass-circulation magazines. Sebastian De Grazia[22] underlines the hollowness of our leisure. A course like this one wouldn't cure the malaise he describes, but it might be a start, and it would surely be popular. Its purpose would not be primarily to entertain the students; it would be aimed at helping them to understand and assess and respond knowingly to what the entertainment media offer. Materials would be plentiful; they constitute a major part of the out-of-school life of youngsters already, and in class they could be analyzed as to their methods, their craftmanship, their social implications, their psychological impact, and their visual, verbal, rhetorical, sensory, and kinesthetic structures.

2. *Personal Relationships*. This subject would explore the many levels and values in personal relationships. Carl Rogers[23] insists upon the essential importance of self-discovery. "Psychology" would have been the traditional name for a course like this, and there would still be that aspect to it, but in addition it would deal with the style and content of relationships within the family and the peer-group, and with personal concerns such as love, sex, friendship, ambition, the draft, and perhaps it would touch upon the philosophical as well as the psychological aspects of such matters. Here too, the content of the course would be life as students actually and personally live it outside of school. Although it would deal with these situations in general and in principle instead of attempting to guide pupils in their personal lives directly, it most certainly would bear a direct and magnetic relationship to the reality with which they are in daily contact.

3. *Moral Issues*. This would be a study of ethics as exemplified by the personal relationships of the previous course, or by political questions, or by school or business problems. The course would aim to present issues and analyze them with penetration and clarity rather than to present solutions. Any kind of written or other material could provide the basis for a sequence of discussions: magazine articles, news items, TV, radio, or film shows, excerpts from philosophical writings, the Bible—whatever. These would be grouped into "topics" representing different *kinds* of ethical issues, and presented in discussion as they relate to adolescent concerns both immediate and future. Here the ethics of business, politics, international affairs, child-rearing, sex, and school could be subjected to the kind of analysis that might make even school look relevant.

4. *Washington Politics Today*. This would combine the current events that the media inundate us with, the national aspects of what used to be called "Civics," political theory, debates on national programs and/or bills before Congress, biographical and/or political studies of national figures, a little history as the need for it arose in discussion of the day's issues, and perhaps some class predictions of future political developments. The text for the course would be the daily paper, the newsweeklies, the radio, TV, and perhaps some traditional textbook material on the structure of the Federal government.

5. *Local Politics Today*. The emphasis here would be on state and municipal

[22] Sebastian De Grazia. *Of Time, Work, and Leisure.* Twentieth Century Fund, 1962.
[23] Carl Rogers. *On Becoming a Person.* Boston: Houghton Mifflin, Inc., 1961.

politics, including education, the police, welfare, the courts, and the tax structure. City and neighborhood newspapers would provide the texts. TV and radio coverage of local events would be monitored daily. Local politicians might be asked to address the students. Jury duty would be discussed, possibly in connection with the film *Twelve Angry Men.* Magazine articles on such topics as corruption in politics would certainly be of value and interest. An aspect of such a course that would capture the interest of young people and seem relevant to their real concerns and out-of-school experience is the discovery and discussion of ways of "fighting city hall" effectively: how to mount an effective campaign, when to write letters, when to obstruct, when to visit whom—how, in other words, to make one's weight felt as a citizen.

6. *International Affairs Today.* All the media would provide material for this course. Propaganda analysis would form a considerable part of the subject-matter, as would the metaphors of international discourse. The foreign press could be studied for alternative points of view. WNYC has an interesting suppertime "Foreign Press Review" several times a week. The course would not try merely to acquaint students with international events; it would seek to help them understand the rivalries, pressures, aspirations, and other motivations that they reflect. And it would undertake some evaluation of the thoroughness, effectiveness, objectivity, and reliability of the media's presentations of international news.

7. *How to Think Straight.* The traditional name for this course is "Logic," but here a commonsense rather than a technical approach would be stressed. Books like Stuart Chase's *Guides to Straight Thinking*[24] or Robert Thouless' *How to Think Straight*[25] could be used as texts, and issues and examples for analysis could be found in every news presentation or public document, whether political, social, religious, or whatever, published in America. The popularizers of Korzybski[26] have provided interesting case studies in straight and crooked thinking. In this kind of course, the "purely" intellectual enterprise of thinking accurately could be given a contemporary applicability to social and personal issues that vitally concern young people, thus serving to help integrate in-school and out-of-school learning and experience.

8. *The Future.* Nothing concerns teenagers more than the future; probably not even the present. This course, cutting across many subject-matter boundaries, would explore and speculate about the future of technology, or politics, or school, of personal relationships, of sports, of communications, of America, or the Negro, of practically everything. It would draw upon the present as depicted in the media, upon the past as researched out of books for this or that investigation, upon logic, experience, and intention. It might help pupils to feel that they have some realistic

[24] Stuart Chase. *Guides to Straight Thinking.* New York: Harper and Row, 1956.

[25] Robert H. Thouless. *How to Think Straight.* New York: Hart Publishing Company, 1939.

[26] See Alfred Korzybski. *Science and Sanity.* Lakeville, Conn.: Institute of General Semantics, 1958; and the following: Wendell Johnson. *People in Quandaries.* New York: Harper and Row, 1946; Stuart Chase. *The Power of Words.* New York: Harcourt, Brace and World, 1954; Hugh R. Walpole. *Semantics.* New York: W. W. Norton and Co., 1942; S. I. Hayakawa. *Language in Thought and Action.* New York: Harcourt, Brace, and World, 1964.

possibility of contributing to the shaping of their own futures if they understood more fully the processes and probabilities in accordance with which the future tends to unfold.

9. *Outer and Inner Space: A Science Survey.* In descriptive rather than technical terms, the principles, discoveries, and chief theories of the social and natural sciences would be presented and discussed here. The course, while relying to a degree on historical material about previous discoveries and innovations in the sciences, would be kept rigorously up-to-the-minute via regular scrutiny of current material presented in the media. Thus, new advances in the technology of space exploration, communications, computerization, automation, or even recent re-evaluations of theoretical systems could be made a part of the course. Biology, psychology, sociology, and anthropology might justify the "inner" part of the title; mechanics, chemistry, sub-atomic physics, and astronomy would be the "outer" space. The point of the course would be not to introduce the technical aspects of the sciences, but to give some pupils some familiarity with underlying concepts of scientific understanding, such as the "reflective thinking" of Dewey [27], so that they will be better able to follow and comprehend the technological society in which they live.

10. *How to Use Figures.* The computational problems of everyday existence stump many pupils because they have learned in school to fear and hate quantitative subject-matter. But computational math and useful arithmetic, if presented afresh in the guise of "tricks" or "speed math" or "mental arithmetic" or "short cuts to accuracy," might grab youngsters and sustain their interest. The Trachtenberg System and other computational devices could be made the basis of a truly useful arithmetic course that would be of value to academic, commercial, vocational, and "general" students. For some, its value would be vocational; for others, academic; for still others, perhaps just recreational or curiosity-satisfying. Certainly it would help relate school to actual student needs.

11. *Local Resources: Information, Recreation, Service.* The aim here would be to engage directly in the task of acquainting students with what is real in their surroundings. Particularly among the poor, many students have had limited experiences outside their immediate neighborhoods. In this class, they would have a chance to take the trips their elementary-school teachers never took them on: walking tours through their city's neighborhoods, to the underground cinema, night court, domestic court, the Chinese New Year celebration (if there are such), and scores of others. It would acquaint them with where and what the tourist attractions are; it would take them to the airport; it would show them how to file for services when they need them; it would give them a sense of their city. Here they would find out how to call an ambulance, how to get psychiatric emergency service, how to apply for these or those benefits, whom to complain to about this or that: the Better Business Bureau, the Rent Control Office, the District Attorney's office, and so on. It would acquaint them with the services offered by the Housing Authority, the Board of Health, adult education programs, the Legal Aid Society,

[27] John Dewey. *How We Think.* Boston: D. C. Heath, 1933.

private and public family service organizations, the Department of Hospitals, the Civil Liberties Union, out-patient clinics, the Visiting Nurses' Association.

12. *Advertising and Propaganda.* Here students would practice analyzing and interpreting the political and economic persuasions that flow around them incessantly. They would deal with local and international propaganda pitches, with the relationship, as Ellul[28] describes it, between technological progress and propaganda, with advertising's protean forms: radio and TV commercials, printed ads, direct mail, billboards, packaging and point-of-sale promotions. They would practice reading between the lines, understanding what is *not* said, understanding the *purposes* of the message-originator, understanding the weaknesses of the receiver. Students would consider the interrelationships inherent in the multiple appeals of advertising: visual, verbal, auditory, etc. A course like this is bound to have practical value and intense interest for adolescents. Chase's *The Power of Words* and Hayakawa's *Language in Thought and Action* might be used as texts with average classes. Even as demanding a work as Ellul's *Propaganda* might be used with superior groups.

13. *Child Development and Family Psychology.* Here girls would study family resources, sources of outside help on personal and family problems (medical and psychiatric clinics, marriage counseling, etc.), principles of child development, cause of family friction, etc. As texts, the class could use not only popular books like Spock's *Baby and Child Care*[29] and Gesell and Ilg's *Child Development*,[30] and the U.S. Government pamphlets, but they could also study popular presentations in the magazines, papers, and on TV to evaluate their worth and seriousness.

14. *Do-It-Yourself Household Repairs and Improvements.* This would deal with strictly practical matters that any boy who's going to be a tenant or home-owner would want to know: wiring and rewiring, fuses, circuits, over-loading, circuit-breakers, types of cables and their uses, plumbing, changing washers, fixing valves, carpentry, plastering, painting various types of surfaces for various purposes with various types of paint, waterproofing, insulating, weather-stripping, caulking, air conditioning, fans, circulation, ventilation, floors and their care, fire-hazards and how to prevent them, and appliance repairs. Especially now that the so-called "comprehensive high school" looks as though it is to become a reality in most places, a course like this could well satisfy the requirements of a quite heterogeneous group of boys, including many who might not be interested in any of the regular vocational shop courses.

15. *Car Repairs and Improvements.* This would not be a course in auto mechanics. Instead it would provide theory and practice in "little" jobs like polishing, washing, tuneups, tires, minor adjustments, gasolines, oils, checking and replacement of parts, customizing, accessories and their usefulness, sources of supply and advice, how not to get cheated at the service station, how to check things for yourself, and how to judge a used car. Texts might include repair

[28] Jacques Ellul. *The Technological Society.* New York: Alfred A. Knopf, 1964.

[29] Benjamin Spock. *Baby and Child Care.* New York: Pocket Books, 1946.

[30] Arnold Gesell and Frances L. Ilg. *Child Development.* New York: Harper and Row, 1949.

manuals, *Consumer Reports* (the annual car issue), and hot rod and custom car magazines. Or all this material might be incorporated into an expanded "driver education" course.

16. *Medical Science.* This would be designed to acquaint the layman with modern principles and concepts related to medicine and human health. It might include discussion of matters such as sex: its psychology, physiology, and mores; medical hygiene; preventive medicine; medical practices (what to expect your doctor to do for you); sanitation; medical research and recent discoveries; health emergencies and what to do about them; danger signals and symptoms; where and how to get help and treatment. In addition to current medical columns purveyed by the various periodicals, students might study a popular medical "encyclopedia" or the Consumer's Union manual, *The Medicine Show.* Here again, an elective course in school would capitalize on a significant out-of-school interest and use it to convey a useful body of integrated and current information and a sensible set of attitudes.

17. *Consumer and Leisure English.* Students would discuss and practice how to read labels and other "fine print" intelligently; how to read and understand applications for loans, charge accounts, subscriptions, book clubs, and similar promotional programs; writing letters of inquiry and complaint; reading advertisements between the lines; understanding and appraising TV and radio commercials; getting reliable information on quality and prices; entering promotional "contests": writing last lines for jingles, figuring out rebuses, or telling "Why I like Gloppo in 25 words or less"; doing crossword puzzles; learning teenage etiquette. As texts, the class could use magazines, catalogs, newspapers, and similar materials.

18. *Getting Your Money's Worth.* The emphasis here would be on such concerns as comparing supermarket prices (on a cost-per-unit basis, for example); family and personal budgeting; home rents and purchases; charge accounts and their "real" cost; installment purchases and their costs; insurance of various kinds, liability, health, straight life, term, hospitalization, etc.; savings and investment media; where to get reliable information on products and prices; how to save on taxes and compute returns. The thesis expressed by David K. Gast in his article, "Consumer Education and the Madison Avenue Morality,"[31] would be part of the course; major materials would include *Consumer Reports, Changing Times,* advertisements, and application blanks.

19. *How to Get a Job and Get Ahead.* This course would survey job resources and requirements in service, communications, manufacturing, white-collar, retail, professional, armed-forces, civil-service, and other lines of work. As a career survey, it could be adapted to the "level" and needs of any class. It would acquaint students with job resource manuals available in the library, with job-getting services like the commercial employment agencies and the state employment service, and other similar matters.

20. *Everyday Law.* This would be a little like the conventional "business law"

[31] David K. Gast, "Consumer Education and the Madison Avenue Morality," *Phi Delta Kappan,* June 1967.

courses widely offered in commercial curricula today, but it would not be restricted to commercial applications. In addition to these, it would familiarize students with the ins and outs of negligence suits, leases, contracts, citizens' rights and duties both in court and vis-a-vis the police, and it would acquaint them with the nature of civil suits, family court, small claims court, etc. Trips to the various types of courts would supplement a simple law text. Class discussions would be based on hypothetical and even actual cases representing real situations.

21. *Part-time and Summer Employment Opportunities Workshop.* This would be an exploration of job possibilities; instruction in job requirements and duties; a survey of retail, camp, resort, civil-service, library, diningroom, Park Department, ice-cream, post-office, even baby-sitting opportunities, and how to get and make the most of them. The mechanics and legalities of working papers and other school and governmental requirements would be touched upon. Students would be acquainted with school programs such as STEP (School To Employment Program), the Job Corps, co-op educational programs, and others.

22. *Home Decoration.* This would combine features of traditional courses touching upon this area that are currently offered by art, home economics, shop, and merchandising departments. For interior decoration, it would cover color, texture, shape, size, line, pattern, fabric, furniture, accessories, utility, quality, sources, costs. For exterior decoration, topics would include painting, gardening, outdoor design, patios, porches, grills, houseplants, flower-cutting and arranging, landscaping, and bug and pest control.

23. *Design Crafts.* This would correlate art and shop and perhaps even sewing in providing introduction to and practice in the creative crafts of jewelry-making, block printing, ceramics, fabric printing, weaving, knitting, crocheting, gros-point and petit-point embroidery, rug braiding and hooking, quilt-making, sculpture, wall decoration, gift wrapping, toy making, and making ornaments and artificial flowers.

24. *Movie, TV, and Still Photography.* Going beyond the typical art department course in still photography, this would include color, black and white, film types, film speeds, camera types, shutter speeds and lens openings, camera accessories, filters, darkroom chemicals, processing, and manipulations. In addition, using movie and TV equipment (cameras, sound equipment, monitoring screens, TV tape recorder, etc.) it would correlate the arts of improvisation, acting, dramatic writing, continuity, sound background, advertising psychology, and others, in providing students with an opportunity to create commercial and artistic work of all kinds for film and TV. Kohl in *36 Children* [32] has written of how successful ordinary creative writing can be in capable and imaginative hands. A course in creative photography might be even more exciting to adolescents.

25. *Nutrition, Diet, and Partymaking.* This course would cover nutrients and what they do, calorie counting and special diets, expensive vs. inexpensive foods, economy in shopping, planning ahead for meals, budgeting food purchases. In addition, it would deal with problems of entertaining, such as providing hors d'oeuvres, beverages, dinners, after-dinner noshes, table settings, etc.

[32] Herbert Kohl. *36 Children.* New York: New American Library, 1967.

26. *The Stock Market.* Any student, rich or poor, might experience an interest in mediums of investment and speculation. This course could introduce such matters as the mechanics of financial transactions, the stock exchanges, round-lot and odd-lot trading, commissions, margin, analysis of individual companies and industries, sources of information and advice, "technical" (chart) analysis, fundamental economic influences, and other investment and speculative vehicles like bonds, puts and calls, mutual funds, rights, and commodities. Popular and technical publications that could supplement the *Times* and the *Wall Street Journal* as test materials are plentiful.

27. *Songwriting.* This course would be taught jointly by a music teacher and an English teacher and would be open to would-be lyricists, tunesmiths, and arrangers. As an elective, it would have appeal for many youngsters because of its concern with the here-and-now world of fads and fashions in popular music. As education, it would make sense because it would help transform a largely passive interest into something approaching craftmanship and creativity.

28. *Intermedia.* Here students interested in creative enterprises like the theater, film, dance, "happenings," painting, sculpture, or just plain self-expression could experiment with new kinds and combinations of art productions. Some of this material could be developed and polished for public presentation in auditorium or library, or coordinated with the school's regular extracurricular activities, such as the school play or "sing." Combinations of media, like lighting, color, sound, shape, depth, movement, and texture would be organized into new and experimental artforms.

29. *Choreography.* Open to students interested in dance, this elective would give them an opportunity for creative self-expression, for coping with the problems of organizing movement interestingly and effectively, of filling the stage, of achieving audience involvement, of building a climax, of coordinating and unifying diverse kinds of movement into a viable whole, etc. The class would involve itself in public performance within and outside the school, both at recital form and as participants in many school theatrical presentations.

30. *Protest Literature.* Taught by an English-Social Studies team, this elective would acquaint students with major works of protest literature, from Aristophanes through Swift to the present day. Masterpieces, as well as current ephemera, would be studied both as metaphors of the human condition and as effective reflections of their times and places of origin.

31. *Speed Reading.* Open to any student who wants to increase his reading power, this course would appeal, I believe, primarily to the college-bound or commercial student. The many books available today on better and faster reading, along with tachistoscopic exercises, would provide ample materials for a truly challenging and effective course.

32. *Speedwriting.* As an alternative to standard courses in stenography, an elective in speedwriting might have appeal for students who want a system of fast note-taking for personal use rather than a commercially salable skill. Students might well be attracted by the possibility of mastering a high-speed writing method based

on the familiar longhand symbols and therefore more accessible from the start and easier to practice at any time, even when incompletely learned.

33. *Memory Training.* Self-help books on this subject are numerous and interesting, but they cannot provide the stimulus or supervisions that a teacher and a course can give. Aside from the trivial and superficial appeals that may inhere in this kind of skill-subject, in today's increasingly non-"linear" world it may be more and more important for students to develop methods (even gimmicky ones) for remembering what they see and hear.

34. *Rock and Folk Survey.* The history and current state of the rock'n'roll and folk music industries would be the subject matter here. Recordings and dittoed lyrics would be the text. Student research, presentations, symposia, TV tapes, audio tapes, visits to recording and broadcasting studios, and many other activities could form the methodology.

35. *Independent Study.* With the approval of the appropriate faculty member, a student wanting to pursue studies along lines dictated by his own interests would have the opportunity to consult on the preparation of a study program consisting, perhaps, of suggested readings and an appropriate time schedule. Whether the subject were statistics or psychological novels, the student could proceed at his own pace, consult when necessary with his advisor, and reap the private benefit of having explored a subject himself.

36. *World Religions.* Comparative study of religious beliefs and practices would acquaint students with the traditions, rituals, and dogmas of the great religions of the East and West. In an age of ecumenism, this kind of factual study would be of interest and of value to students. Parents would approve of it and religious organizations would cooperate in planning and executing it.

37. *The Arts Today.* A study of the avant-garde in painting, sculpture, film, architecture, multimedia, happenings, dance, theater, poetry, the novel, etc., would capitalize on everything that is happening in the world of the creative arts concurrently with the course. Students would see actual productions and exhibitions throughout the semester and read current materials such as exhibition catalogs, magazines and newspaper criticism, and the Sunday *Times.* Interrelationships between the various art forms and the milieux in which they occur, taboos and conventions observed and broken, and the implications of what a medium is *not* attempting would comprise the substance of the course.

38. *Variety in American Society.* This survey of American sociology would explore varying traditions and customs among segments of America's population drawn from diverse ethnic groups, national origins, ages, socioeconomic classes, and parts of the country. Emphasis would be not on a mere anecdotal account of other groups' funny customs, but on how traditions interact with social, political, ethnic, economic, and geographical background factors as well as with the future. One possible text resource for such a course would be the magazine *Transaction.*

39. *Emceeing, Newscasting and Diskjockeying.* This speech elective would give showbiz-minded students a chance to study and practice the techniques required in the entertainment industry: gagwriting, timing, introducing guests, interviewing, introducing songs, reading commercials, newscasting. Video tape and audio tape

would be the standard performance media for classroom sessions. These could culminate in weekly or monthly assembly or P-A system entertainment and public service programs featuring the work of the class.

40. *Computer Technology*. As an elective course this could appeal to a heterogeneous group including those with a philosophical interest in works such as those by Ellul and Weiner, those with a mathematical bent and a possible career interest in programming, and those commercial students who want to learn key punch operation in a realistic setting.

Conclusion: So What?

The foregoing has dealt almost exclusively with the content—as opposed to the methods and hardware—of the relevant high school curriculum. Naturally, much must be done to make the manner as strongly integrative as the matter. TV tapes, programed texts, team-teaching arrangements, individual language-lab style modules, multimedia materials, and the actual commercial media of newspapers, magazines, radio, TV, and film all would play a more prominent role in the new curriculum than they typically do today. The reason for this would be partly that such a school would probably be more interested in relevant methodology by virtue of its commitment to relevant content, and partly because many of the above courses would necessitate the use of out-of-school learnings, both as to substance and as to vehicle. The point here is that although this paper has stressed substance, there can be no doubt that an immensely important feature of the relevant high school will be its style.

A panacea? Hardly, because the out-of-school learnings will stem from the same society that supports the schools, with all its weakness, contradiction, corruption, vulgarity, and short-sightedness. But at least the school will stand a chance of playing an integrative rather than an alienating role. At least it may help students, not to ignore the realities around them while they are in school, but actually to deal with them. At least it may acquaint them with ways in which their surroundings can be useful, threatening, amusing, significant. At least it may help them to find resources within themselves that they can exercise with pride and pleasure. At least it will help them feel that school is for real, that school is "with it," that school is aware that electronic and social revolutions are transforming America. At least it will give them an awareness that controversy can be a source of revelation and illumination, not just repression and discomfort. At least the pupils—even the poor—can feel that school is giving them experiences that count, that they want, that they value, and that connect them with the world instead of isolating them from it. And at least there would be less reason to think of the dropouts as being the smart ones.

How to overcome the inertia and conservatism that paralyze big-system schools, or the local pressures that hound decentralized systems, remains unsolved. But if the problem can be solved, and if the above courses and others like them can be instituted as the elective half of a youngster's high school experience, then adolescence might finally make more sense to kids.

Alternative Modes of Organizing Secondary Schools

LLOYD S. MICHAEL

The primary question in this chapter is: How do we organize secondary schools to educate youth for self-fulfillment, for self-growth? To individualize our purpose, how do we organize and function to allow the individual student to grow, to become actualized, to avoid alienation, to enlarge his self? Raymond Houghton clearly identifies the focus of humanism and the teacher in these statements. He says:

> Everyone is an intellectual when provided with the opportunities for involvement. . . . As students find the teacher relevant and the school relevant, they will fight to become involved. It is to be suggested that children drop out of school, not because they wish to avoid involvement, but because they seek it and the schools deny it to them.[1]

The School Administrator

The uniqueness of school administration, as compared with the executive functions in other organizations, is its primary emphasis on teaching and learning. All administrative decisions in schools have as their highest value the facilitation of learning of boys and girls. All administrators are instructional officers, directly or indirectly. Some administrators, however, are more actively involved with instruction than are others. The underlying rationale for all administrative assignments is learning.

The superintendent is the crucial person on a district basis. The importance of his position is derived in large measure from his authority to allocate resources, people, and time which can serve to maintain the status quo or to effect improvement in the self-realization of students in the school system.

It is the building principal who has the strategic and vital role of leadership in teaching and learning. He has the opportunity to create a climate that nurtures or

From "Alternative Modes of Organizing Secondary Schools," in *Humanizing the Secondary School.* Norman K. Hamilton and J. Galen Saylor, editors. (Washington, D.C.: Association for Supervision and Curriculum Development, 1969), 90–99. Reprinted with permission of the Association for Supervision and Curriculum Development.

[1] Raymond W. Houghton. "The Focus of Humanism and the Teacher." In: *Humanizing Education: The Person in the Process.* Robert R. Leeper, editor. Washington, D.C.: Association for Supervision and Curriculum Development, 1967. pp. 60–61.

discourages improvement and change, but, more important, he has the opportunity to affect the commitment and involvement of students for their self-direction and responsible behavior.

A basic question is, how can a principal organize the school day, the school year, the staff, both professional and nonprofessional, the curriculum, instruction, and the facilities to produce optimum learning on the part of boys and girls? It is my assumption that unless the building principal assumes this responsibility and works diligently in its realization, the job will not be done. The emphasis here is on his role as an organizer. Other administrative functions, that is, planning, management, supervision, and evaluation, also have their place in the improvement of the teaching-learning process. Arthur Moehlman[2] many years ago stressed a principle that should underlie effective organization. His concept of a dynamic organization emphasized the structure of organization as a facilitating agency through which the purpose of the school might more effectively be achieved. He affirmed also that there was no final validity either in the mechanics or the form of organization. Structure or organization, therefore, is a means, never an end, in the realization of the objectives and functions of a secondary school.

How does the principal see himself? Does he act as an instructional leader who continues to perform those functions which have depersonalizing and alienating effects because of the overemphasis upon the informational phase of learning? Or does he see his role as one of emphasizing the human side of learning wherein commitment and involvement of students lead to responsibility and self-direction for learning?

For the past several years I have held the chairmanship of the National Association of Secondary-School Principals' Committee on the Administrative Internship in Secondary-School Improvement. During this time the Committee has sponsored several hundred interns in what we hoped were innovative high schools. Because the NASSP and the principals themselves all assert that the highest priority among the principal's professional tasks is the improvement of education, the Committee has given major attention to this most important responsibility.

The principal has many demands upon his time other than the responsibility for the improvement of teaching and learning. These demands include discipline, student activities, plant management, guidance and testing, public relations, and many other duties. The superintendent, teachers, and parents expect him to do these tasks. The Committee recognized that these jobs had to be done, but agreed that the principal need not do them. We concluded that:

1. The principal's first job is to separate what he needs to do himself from those duties that can be assigned to others.

2. Every principal, regardless of whether his school is large or small, should spend three-fourths of his time on the instructional program as a facilitator of learning.

3. In a large school, this means that a variety of specially trained assistants

[2] Arthur B. Moehlman. *School Administration.* Boston: Houghton Mifflin Company, 1951.

who are directly concerned with attendance, discipline, student activities, public relations, clerical services, plant management, cafeteria operation, and transportation should be appointed.

The Internship Program has emphasized that if the principal is to create a climate which leads to instructional improvement, a plan for teacher participation and student involvement is a necessary requisite.

School Size

The internal structure of a secondary school can contribute to humanizing the education of students. There is much debate about the optimum size of a high school because of our concern for the individual student and his welfare, and our awareness of the need for personal identification and close relationship between teacher and pupil. Many parents, teachers, and administrators have a sincere distrust of a large high school. It is felt that many of the unique advantages of the small school are lost in public secondary schools of over 1,000 enrollment unless the schools are organized to protect individual pupil interests and needs. On the other hand, there are definite disadvantages in a small school. Some of these limitations have been stated as:

1. Many important subjects either cannot be offered or must be offered at considerable cost to very few students.
2. The expense of maintaining a staff of good teachers may be extremely high.
3. Important educational services such as special education, instructional centers, specialized vocational and college guidance are not available.
4. Costly special facilities, such as shops, laboratories, and resource centers are not provided.

Some educators will claim excellence for their school on the sole criterion of numbers in the student body, regardless of the extent to which size contributes to the quantity and quality of the educational services available to the individual student and his identification with the school. There is the interesting paradox where, largely through consolidation or single community population growth, small schools are hopeful of attaining better status by becoming large schools, and large schools are organizing into several subunits to attain the advantages peculiar to small schools. In either situation, the purpose should be to introduce those changes and innovations which will facilitate improvement in learning and will give pupils the opportunity to experience self-direction and assume more responsibility for their behavior and learning.

Evanston Township High School since 1924 has been developing and refining a different model for the organization structure of a large secondary school. The focus of the school's concern for the past half century has been to effect an organization that will solve many of the problems characteristic of a large complex school. This is done by capitalizing on the resources and strengths of a large school and at the same time gaining the advantages that may be associated with a small school. The schools-within-a-school concept seeks to ensure the personal understanding of and attention to each student within a small school setting while utilizing fully the assets of diversity and specialization possible only in a very large high school. Thus it is believed that the opportunities for each student to become personally involved in the life of the school and to receive an education most appropriate for him will be greatly increased.

Evanston Township High School is organized as four semi-independent schools, each with its own identity, student body of 1,200, faculty, and physical facilities. The organization seeks to make the best possible use of staff, facilities, and instructional resources in a harmonious and effective relationship among the several autonomous units and the total school. The measure of the success of this organization will be the degree to which the excellence of teaching and learning is improved, the educational experiences of students are humanized, and the individual student experiences an education of high quality.

The school is certain that there are ways of dealing creatively with the large complex institution. The best organization for the students may not be the simple, cozy educational environment, but the truly complex one in which students, for example, can be professionals in the performing arts, amateurs in appreciation of the performing arts, or simply nonparticipants if they wish. While the small school, with its undermanned program, may allow or, indeed, require each student to participate, there is a tyranny in this demand and a kind of forced "togetherness" that makes psychologists happy, but may not really represent a superior environment for all students.

This high school, by creating significant subgroups, or schools that have identity and meaning, apparently succeeds in freeing students and faculty so that greater emphasis is placed on the ability of students to attack and solve problems of interest and meaning to them and in moving toward the position where students accept greater responsibility for their own learning. As Evanston Township High School succeeds in this objective, it will have moved to another and higher level of accomplishment and other school districts may have an alternate and perhaps better model for the organization of a secondary school.

The idea of the educational park is another model that is receiving much attention by some educators and the public. This plan provides for an organization with up to 30,000 pupils at various levels of schooling. It seeks to provide much better person-to-person contacts between teachers and students and to attain equality of educational opportunity at a new high level for many thousands of young people. The advocates of such parks claim that, if properly planned and organized, these approaches can help rather than hinder the humanizing of students and teachers.

Staffing

A third approach to humanizing the secondary school is a more flexible and efficient use of personnel, time, and facilities.

First as to personnel. Currently there are no acceptable standards for defining the "best" staffing pattern for a school. Staffing allocations are too frequently not influenced by the needs and interests of a particular student population. How many professional staff members in relation to a given number of students are needed and how shall they be deployed and for what instructional purposes? What is the desirable ratio between classroom teachers and specialists with supportive and evaluative functions? Can the number of professional personnel be significantly reduced as a result of the reorganization of staffing patterns through the use of large-group instruction and technological aids when the purpose of instruction is essentially to impart information?

This is a critical area in the improvement of teaching and learning. The present concept in most schools is still that almost everything done in a school outside the maintenance and administrative functions must be done by fully certified teachers. Until very recently there was little or no differentiation in staff responsibilities in most secondary schools. Teachers are commonly interchangeable. A teacher is a teacher is a teacher. Promotions are away from students. It is a strange kind of profession in which all promotions are away from the clients that are served.

If we are to humanize the high school we must rethink and redefine the role of teachers. Schools should be organized so that teachers can make optimum use of their individual abilities and receive optimum satisfaction. In most schools, because of the omnibus role of teachers and the prevalent standards of teaching load, it is difficult for teachers to find the time and energy to do those tasks that should be characteristic of professional workers. Organizational changes must be effected that provide teachers with more time during the school day to prepare better, to keep up-to-date in their subject field, to confer with colleagues, to work as needed with individual students, and to improve student evaluation techniques when reporting. Dwight Allen asserts that the educational system must be reanalyzed to allow new alternatives to staff use, alternatives which technology can enhance, and alternatives which lead to a more humane use of staff resources and their interaction with and use by students.

If the quality of teaching for meaning is to be materially improved in our schools, traditional staffing patterns must change and many innovations in the better utilization of both professional and nonprofessional persons introduced. The principal must be the key person in this effort at focusing teachers' attention and effort not only on the *what* but on the *how* of teaching.

Scheduling

A few schools are greatly extending scheduling procedures which permit flexibility and effectiveness of the time element by both teachers and students. We make at least two false assumptions about time in most of our secondary schools: (a) the same uniform period, usually 45 to 50 minutes, is equally appropriate for a wide variety of learning activities, and (b) all learners in a class are capable of mastering the same subject matter in the same length of time. Today many good ideas and innovations in secondary schools are barred because they cannot be scheduled. The restrictive manually constructed schedule is still the determiner of the allocation and use of time in most high schools, but more schools are adopting a computer-generated flexible schedule. For what purposes?

Time should not be the end but the means through which greater flexibility and efficiency in its use can contribute to improved teaching and learning. The main objective is to be achieved by flexible scheduling should be the individualization of the learning process. This individualization can be related to all the elements in instruction: the pupil, the teacher, the subject, and spaces. New time arrangements for students and teachers are viable. Possibilities may range from the present 30 students for 50 minutes, five days each week, to virtually any time and size variations of a basic structural model of five or more students and 15 or more minutes. Nearly any desired teaching configuration can be scheduled. A reasonable and usable amount of unscheduled time for independent study by students can be provided. After careful professional deliberation and planning, many new modes for teaching and learning can be developed.

A decreasing amount of factual transmission from teacher to student will provide more time to individualize instruction. Variation in interest and ability on the part of individual learners will be less controlled by the pattern of time uniformity. Greater provision for independent and individual study can be made. Lloyd Trump and Delmas Miller[3] define independent study as "the activities in which pupils engage when their teachers stop talking." New emphasis on inquiry, creative and critical thinking, self-direction, and responsibility for learning can result if students are permitted to spend less time on listening and more time on being human.

Facilities for Learning

Good facilities are important factors in the improvement of the learning environment. A school building is not just a shelter, it is a tool for teaching and learning. Learning resources centers for students and instructional materials centers for teachers should be essential spaces in new and renovated school plants. Adequate, functional facilities with a high degree of flexibility can create an open, adaptable kind of environment that lends itself to new concepts in the organization of teaching and learning. The limitations at present of "egg crate" allocation of space are well known. Viewing the curriculum and instruction as a function of space has provided the opportunity for the development of new, imaginative course structures, for large-group presentations, small-group discussions in small spaces, and independent and individual study in a resource center or at a carrel in many places throughout the building.

[3] J. Lloyd Trump and Delmas F. Miller. *Secondary School Curriculum Improvement.* Boston: Allyn and Bacon, Inc., 1968. p. 265.

The Teacher

The teacher is the most important person in any effort to humanize the school and to lessen the forces of alienation and depersonalization. I sense many situations that do not point in this direction. Today a spirit of aggressiveness, militancy, and dissatisfaction has swept across the ranks of the teaching profession. Don Davies summarizes one of their chief demands: "We want to have a more important part in managing our own affairs, in making decisions about what shall be taught, how, when, by whom, and under what conditions."[4]

Professional negotiations in an increasing number of school districts, without any involvement of principals and only occasionally of superintendents, include much more than requests for increased salaries, fringe benefits, and grievance procedures. Leslee J. Bishop,[5] has effectively identified the trend toward collective negotiations in curriculum and instruction.

Many agreements state that teachers have the right and responsibility to participate and share in the development of educational policy and procedures that influence the program of the school system and their classrooms. A recently adopted negotiation agreement in a New York school district, and there are many other examples, clearly establishes a new role for the teacher. The agreement states:

> Teacher Association shall discuss, participate in, and/or negotiate on the following matters of material concern: recruitment of teachers, teacher turnover, in-service training, teaching assignments, teaching conditions, class size, curriculum, district planning, budget preparation, school calendar, salaries, communications, protection of teachers, leaves of absence, general absence provisions, sabbatical leave or other fringe benefits, dues deductions, grievance procedures, and other matters which affect the quality of the education program and morale of the teaching staff.

This particular board of education (and many more are falling in line) agreed that their teachers were qualified to make significant contributions to educational problems in the district and should assist in the development of policy and program.

Teacher demands, with or without negotiation agreements, are tending to bypass, to blitz the building principal and his leadership role and to support a traditional and less useful model of the school. Strong pressures in many school districts are being exercised to narrow and to regiment the tasks of teachers, compensation, class size, teacher load, and other working conditions. The effect of these demands, already present in many school systems, may seriously deter staff involvement in curriculum and instructional improvement, and the diffusion of

[4] Don Davies. "EPDA—What's in It for Us?" Speech delivered at one of the informal meetings at the NEA Convention in Dallas, July 1–6, 1968.

[5] Leslee J. Bishop. *Collective Negotiation in Curriculum and Instruction: Questions and Concerns.* Washington, D.C.: Association for Supervision and Curriculum Development, 1967.

promising practices in the allocation and utilization of time and personnel in school betterment.

What are the alternatives if the teacher organization is to have major responsibility for curriculum development and instructional improvement? It seems evident that the roles of teachers, principals, supervisors, and curriculum workers might change dramatically if, when teachers enter the decision-making process, they also assume a commitment for implementation. Some of us have believed that it is essential that the principal, in his leadership role, assisted by central office specialists, work continuously with teachers to help them identify, prepare, and evaluate new approaches to curriculum and instruction. I can find less of this professional activity being done by principals and much more evidence of written agreements which write the principal off as an educational leader and leave a serious void in the leadership function.

The Student in the Organization

Finally, the individual student is the focus of our concern as we consider alternate ways of organizing our secondary schools and their instructional programs. New concepts of independent study and individualized instruction emphasize the critical need for the continuous development of responsibility on the part of the individual learner rather than what Dwight W. Allen terms "a demanded metamorphosis at the time of college entrance or vocational employment." The goal of education must be self-direction and self-realization. Young people in high school must become more active in learning, more involved intellectually, more independent of teachers.

Schools must encourage students to believe that they come to school to learn rather than to be taught. Today's society is a learning society. Learning is essential not only to enter the society but to maintain one's position in it. The inculcation of the desire to learn and the teaching of effective methods of inquiry and decision making are probably the most important outcomes that students can learn from their experiences in high school. The school must improve its role as a contributor to the student's lifelong learning process. It must build learning expectations in youth that have deep meaning and personal significance and that transcend their current roles as students and emphasize the need for learning throughout adult life.

The implications for organization and administration are obvious. There must be much more interaction and participation by students in school life. Many more opportunities for self-direction and responsibility must be afforded students. The innovative secondary school must guarantee commitment and involvement of students in every phase of the educational endeavor. This is a new dimension in our commitment to a higher quality of secondary education for all youth.

The Knowledge Machine

ELIZABETH C. WILSON

Marshall McLuhan and George B. Leonard (in a recent issue of *Look* magazine)[1] visualize an educational Utopia as a result of technological advances. According to these prophets, "schooling as we now know it may be only a memory." They foresee computers with the capacity to understand both speech and writing, making "all of mankind's factual knowledge available to students everywhere in a matter of minutes or seconds." Computers as part of electronic learning systems containing television and sophisticated programed materials will help tomorrow's student become "an explorer, a researcher, a huntsman who ranges through the new educational world of electronic circuitry and heightened human interaction just as the tribal huntsman ranged the wilds."

The McLuhan-Leonard vision assumes that standarized mass education will be a thing of the past, discarded along with the material mass-production line with which it has run parallel. It takes for granted that tomorrow's teachers will have adjusted to a new role in a schoolroom which is literally the world. It expects that "fragmentation, specialization and sameness will be replaced by wholeness, diversity and, above all, a deep involvement." Mankind can then truly be "educated by possibility . . . in accordance with his infinity," as Soren Kierkegaard had hoped.[2]

But Kierkegaard, we remember, linked educational possibility with dread. And dread is the mood we tend to associate with other distinguished contemporary prophets like Aldous Huxley, George Orwell, and more recently Leo Szilard.[3] These men were equally fascinated by the future and, if not by computers per se, at least by technology and by communication. They were, however, painfully aware of the sombre possibilities of the political control of education and of the slow death of the humane values we now cherish. They had a healthy fear of man's lack of self control and ability to misuse his technological advances.

The predictions of these two sets of prophets are poles apart. Which of them has more validity for the future? Which is more probable?

I would like to believe that McLuhan and Leonard are *not* dealing with dreams—that future educational patterns can break out of old molds—that the school of tomorrow can in fact be "more concerned with training the senses and perceptions than with stuffing brains."[4] But I have lived a long time with educa-

From *Teachers College Record* (November 1968), 109–119. Reprinted by permission.

[1] Marshall McLuhan and George B. Leonard, "The Future of Education: The Class of 1989," *Look*, February 21, 1967.

[2] Soren Kierkegaard, *The Concept of Dread.* Translated by Walter Lowrie. Princeton University Press.

[3] Leo Szilard, *The Voice of the Dolphins.* New York: Simon and Schuster, 1961.

[4] McLuhan and Leonard, *op. cit.*

tion, both in its formal existence in places called schools, and in its informal manifestations in the socialization process. This experience documents the layers of conservatism which exist within the educative establishment, within the local communities whose values the schools reflect, and within the local and national political structure. Conventional wisdom regarding the task of the school dies hard.

The Making of the Mold

We must remember that the function of the school has evolved slowly over literally thousands of years. In simple societies, where learning to become adult members of the society was relatively uncomplicated, educational arrangements tended to be informal. They were handled by the family, by elders and chief priests, and by peer groups, through ceremonies, rituals, and participation in the economic work of the groups. When a society became more complex, and especially when there grew up a heritage of written symbols, specialized agencies or schools appeared. A particular group of people known as teachers were given the task of transmitting the more complicated, symbolic, and abstract aspects of the culture. Thus the schools became the formal institutions which augmented and supplemented the educational function of the family and of the religious and economic institutions of the society. As I. L. Kandel once wrote:

> When a formal system of education is organized, society selects from all those cultural experiences to which the child is exposed those aspects of its culture which it regards as most valuable for its own coherence and survival.[5]

In our society, the conscious task of the schools has traditionally been an intellectual one. The "major" subjects of the curriculum have been related to the learning of symbols, i.e. language (native and foreign, written and spoken) and mathematics, and to "factual," data-collecting subjects, i.e., history and the social sciences and science. By and large, these subjects were taught and learned by rote. The progressive education movement of the twenties and thirties abortively attempted to bring higher levels of cognition into the process. The current Curriculum Reform Movement with its emphasis upon the "structure of the disciplines" and the "scholar's method of inquiry" is the second thrust of this century to help the schools breed inquiring minds and to help students learn how to learn.

The idea that the primary function of the school is to teach the basic skills and to acquaint the student with the funded knowledge of mankind has a long history both in theory and in practice. It is one which I have espoused since the beginning of my career and one which I will abandon with reluctance. But if McLuhan and

[5] I. L. Kandel, "The Transmission of Culture: Education as an Instrument of National Policy," in *Conflicts of Power in Modern Culture*, Symposium of the Conference on Science, Philosophy and Religion. New York: Harpers, 1948.

other experts[6] are correct about the scope and speed of the electronic revolution already on our doorsteps, then the whole concept of the function of the school in our society needs massive reexamination.

Reexaminations

According to my best judgment, the first section of the "standard" curriculum to be absorbed by electronic multi-media will be the skills of language and mathematics–those subjects which can be logically and sequentially programed. Next will come what one scholar has called the "empirics," that is, science and the social sciences.

When that curricular absorption happens, what then will be the function of the school? To prepare students for vocations? To concentrate on the "soft" subjects like the fine arts, recreation, social and moral education? To use the knowledge acquired? To become a baby sitter?

The vocational function of the school seems less and less likely to be prominent in the year 1985. The first reason for this phenomenon has to do with swift and wide-spread change in the world of work. Specific vocational preparation will need to be done on the job, if at all. Actually, this situation already obtains. A second reason relates to the need of tomorrow's worker to be flexible, and hence to concentrate on the basic skills and concepts which will help him learn how to learn. A third reason suggests a revolutionary change in attitudes toward work–the death of the Protestant work ethic, if you will, and concurrently a shift from concentration on products to a concentration on services and leisure time activities.

If vocational and professional training are increasingly accomplished through internships in the "real" world, the "school," if it continues to exist at all, is left with what are now considered "minor subjects" in the explicit curriculum, and with a great deal of what we educators call the implicit and affective curriculum. By implicit curriculum here we mean the social system of the institution–those potent and seldom conscious factors by which institutions mold the young. For example, look at the Americanization of hordes of first and second generation immigrant children, or more recently, at the enhancement of adolescent peer culture by the schools. By the affective curriculum, we mean the values and attitudes that are absorbed from the climate and the person-to-person contacts created by an institution. And we also mean the "soft" and controversial elements of curriculum which historically were assumed by the family or by religious and social agencies. Examples of this kind of "soft" curriculum are sex education, driver training, race relations, and guidance in self understanding.

Another possibility is that the school as an institution will cease to exist. If its primary intellectual functions can be performed by electronic media, then there is little need for the institution in its traditional sense. Rather, other social agencies

[6] See "The Electronic Revolution," a special issue of *The American Scholar*, Spring 1966, Vol. 35, No. 2.

could divide up the "frill" curricula left, and the schools as we know them could be dissolved.

This possibility, however, seems unlikely. In the first place, despite the press of the basic education movement for the schools to go back to the three R's and cut out frills, and despite the return to the scholarly disciplines characterized by this decade's Curriculum Reform Movement, the public has more and more looked to the schools to solve its social as well as its intellectual problems. Thus the schools have been asked to take on the race and poverty problems of Inner City and the sex and delinquency problems of Suburbia. The school is seen more and more *in loco parentis*—a place that is really responsible for the socialization process of the young and for the transmission of middle class morality.

New Models

It is probably time that the public faced up to what it has been asking of the schools. Perhaps the school of tomorrow should model itself upon the Israeli kibbutz, assuming the basic affective educative function of the family, when that does not exist, and assisting parents in a modern version of the extended family of simple times and cultures. The school might also serve as the coordinator and integrator of a variety of educational agencies outside the school like fine arts centers, or laboratory-work centers sponsored and manned by industry and the professions, or recreational centers and camps, or multi-media centers where the "knowledge machine" would be available.

This version of the school of 1985 has elements in common with that of McLuhan and Leonard, with that of two young Harvard professors Fred Newmann and Donald Oliver,[7] and with that of Peter Peterson, President of Bell and Howell Company.[8] There are many others. The point is not how many versions but how radical. For radical the future schools will need to be if they are to absorb rather than be absorbed by the computer.

Any of these projections are light years ahead of present day conventional wisdom about the education process, whether that wisdom is housed within the educational establishment or within the public-political domain. The projections, furthermore, are based not only upon the electronic revolution, but also upon some educated guesses about the effects of such phenomena as the "pill," megalopolis, and growing leisure time upon institutions like the family, the church, and the government. All these subjects are emotional dynamite. The public would prefer not to examine them too closely. Yet, they are all part of the whole, as is an embryonic new morality which is now only a small cloud on the horizon. The task ahead will be far more simple. We will do well to keep in mind Toynbee's comment that:

[7] Fred Newmann and Donald Oliver, "Education and Community," *Harvard Educational Review*, Volume 37, Number 1, 1967.

[8] Peter G. Peterson, "The Class of 1984 . . . Where Is It Going?" Keynote Address National Conference of State Legislators, December 4, 1966.

> every historical-culture pattern is an organic whole in which all the parts are interdependent, so that if any part is prised out of its setting, both the isolated part and the mutilated whole behave differently from their behavior when the pattern is intact.[9]

Policy-Making and Planning

The electronic revolution is hard on us. If its social accomplishment is to move without major disasters, particularly in the moral and political realms, policy planning of the first order of magnitude is required. The impact of the knowledge machine may well be greater than that of the atomic bomb upon warfare. Task-forces of the best minds in the country should open continuing debates upon the issues involved. Long range studies must be mounted to conceptualize and document the problems and issues. The five new research centers just announced by the United States Office of Education are a step in the right direction.[10] Let us hope they will consider at length the privacy and the control issues—in my mind the most serious of the moral and political questions raised by computer technology. They should also consider the changing role of the school in the total educative process.

These tasks will require Renaissance men—mature, humane philosophers of a kind not much in demand earlier this century. These wise men must not permit themselves to be seduced by big money or by the cyberneticians—a self-confident group with a private in-group language. Rather, they need to address themselves to the problem stated in the following paragraph:

> In the field of computer design the most severe lack of knowledge is not how to design and build bigger and faster machines, but how to make them function, how to integrate them into the human world, and how to make them do what we want them to do. Norbert Wiener's later writing harped upon the danger we risk by building machines to perform functions that we do not adequately understand. The dangers are real because our ability to design machines is more fully developed than is our ability to understand the purposes to which they might be put; and we could end by putting electronic machines to uses we would not want to put them if we really understood what the uses were.[11]

Further, these task forces and scholars need to think long and hard about the kinds of people and the kinds of society seen as desired and desirable by the end of the century, and about how computer technology can help and how it can hinder such growth and development. Value questions will be paramount.

These discussions and arguments should not be held within ivied walls. They

[9] Arnold Toynbee, *The World and the West.* London: Oxford University Press, 1963.

[10] *Education USA: Washington Monitor*, June 19, 1967.

[11] Robert McClintock, "Machines and Vitalists: Reflections on the Ideology of Cybernetics," *American Scholar*, Spring, 1966, Vol. 35, Number 2, pp. 254–255.

need wide dissemination and involvement by every imaginable variety of citizen, business, government, and professional groups. The continuing dialogue should become part of the atmosphere, just as is continuing discussion about the control and use of the atomic bomb.

Such thrashing out of direction needs to be based upon scientific and technological literacy on the part of participants—a cross-fertilization of C. P. Snow's two cultures. Such literacy presupposes adult education—for teachers as well as for interested citizens. Indeed, the impact of technology upon society should be a persistent theme which pervades the entire curriculum at all levels from the kindergarten through graduate school. An immediate step in this direction could well be the sponsoring of a well-planned curriculum project of this nature. Then, at the least, we might start to build a reservoir of informed citizenry, who have more than a nodding acquaintance with the space age, and with the astonishing new developments in the biological sciences, as well as with the computer. Designed for both young people and their elders, such a curriculum might help to narrow an otherwise ever widening generation gap.

Curriculum Development

Consideration of the need for building substantive curriculum on the effect of technology on society initiates the whole subject of future curricular imperatives. They are multiple. Let us start from the premise that tomorrow's educated citizen will need more liberal education in the Greek sense of the word liberal than ever before. The reasons are obvious. In the first place, the Greek citizen's education will soon be a possibility for every man. Secondly, every man will have the leisure to cultivate grace and beauty, to contemplate the good life, and to wonder about the unknown. Thirdly, tomorrow's citizen will need more direct sensory contact with reality than ever before to counteract the potent artificial environment created by electronic media systems.

Increasingly important, therefore, are the arts—particularly the performing and the applied arts. Physical education should regain the place it had in the Greek curriculum. Outdoor education, camping, and home arts take on new meaning in this context. (Even today we are recognizing that "roughing it" in natural surroundings is now only possible for the privileged few.) Much of tomorrow's curriculum must take place in studios, in laboratories, on trips. Thus children may cultivate their perceptions and delight in the singular—in the concreteness of everyday contact with the natural world—in the stuff which makes artists out of people.

Similarly, deep and lasting personal contacts must be an integral part of this new educative process. The warmth of individual for individual and the intimacy of a stable caring community must offset the cool objectivity and impersonality of the machine, as well as provide an important motivational base for further learning. As Gerald Johnson puts it:

> The knower and the known are not a pair. They are two thirds of a trio.

> There remains the relation between them, a third factor as important as either of the others.[12]

This relationship must be as much a part of the new curriculum as the direct aesthetic experience itself. Indeed this new curriculum should be concerned equally with process and with product.

This person-to-person contact needs also to be an essential ingredient of the part of curriculum which deals with application and synthesis of knowledge. The community seminar described by Fred Newmann and Donald Oliver[13] suggests this kind of affective background for the probing of intellectual issues. But until such natural forums become part of ordinary practice, the task can be done by the schools, providing they can be backed up with curriculum and instructional materials centering around such vital issues as urban slums, the generation gap, and pollution. The new courses on technology and society mentioned earlier could provide some of the substance for these dialogues.

This call for non-computerized sections of an increasingly humane curriculum does not imply lack of attention to the crying need for more curriculum software for computers. What exists now is pathetically thin. I suspect, however that we have put the cart before the horse. Surely, except for experimental purposes, we don't want to develop curriculum simply because it lends itself to computer programing. Good curriculum comes first. Then the job is to see what subject matter and approaches can be best handled by the computer. For example, as stated earlier, logical sequences of symbolic learning seem particularly well suited to computer programing. So also are all kinds of informational retrieval systems in all subjects from science to histories of art and music. Games and simulation schemes also seem easily adapted for computer use. But in all curriculum building, the first question to ask is why? Unimportant or mediocre ends will produce unimportant and mediocre means whether the teacher is alive or is a mechanical monster.

To summarize, policy makers need to provide for the full-range of a rich and varied curriculum for all sorts and conditions of learners, modes of learning, and subject matters. Whether or not it is to be computerized is a second order of priority. Let us, of course, continue to experiment with computer programs which treat the logical, the symbolic, and the empirical. But let us remember that the better these programs deal adequately with the funded knowledge of mankind, the more important will be the "soft-soft" sides of the present day curriculum, i.e., philosophy, the humanities, and the arts, both fine and practical.

Studying Institutional Change

Dreaming about the educational process of tomorrow and developing new curriculum tailored to the future can be empty exercises if these ideas and materials

[12] Gerald Johnson, "Some Cold Comfort," *American Scholar*, Spring 1966, Vol. 35, Number 2, p. 194.

[13] Fred Newmann and Donald Oliver, *op. cit.*

are not accepted and used. And to date, the schools have been the despair of innovators. During the last decade a brave new world in the schools was to have been ushered in by the Curriculum Reform Movement, with the advent of new organizational patterns like team teaching and nongraded schools, and with the development and promotion of new instructional media like television, language laboratories, and programed materials, including computers. Yet despite the amount of publicity given to these innovations and to the examples of a few schools and school districts given national visibility, not much basic change has occurred in the rank and file of classrooms in the nation. Very little has happened of an organic nature or of the proportions required by projections for 1985.

Given this background of experience, what strategies are in order? Is it hopeless to attempt to move the Leviathan that is the public school? Or should the government continue the strategy it has employed within the last few years, namely, to by-pass the educational establishment?

Probably both strategies will be needed for some time to come, particularly if the policy makers feel any responsibility toward the current generation of students and teachers now in the schools. In this connection we note that the great mass of public school teachers and admininstrators and the faculties of teacher-training institutions have not been involved in the excitement of the sixties. Nor will they be in the seventies and eighties if the problems of massive change of a conservative social institution are not faced head on. Attempts to get at this problem have been flying blind much of the time. This blind spot has several causes. One has to do with the lack of real school knowledge and experience on the part of the innovators of the last decade. Another relates to the lack of articulate non-defensive leadership within the schools. A third suggests that the major energies of the Great Society leaders have been more directed toward social problems than toward educational ones. But, for whatever reasons, the fact remains that the task is huge, that a bits-and-pieces approach has been singularly unproductive, and that the full complexities of institutional change have been to date ignored.

At the same time, there *are* some attacks which hold promise, even though far from fool-proof. One of these relates to applications of systems analysis to the complex problems faced by school systems. Such applications will require conceptualization of the relationships of administrative and managerial decision-making with models of rational planning for curriculum and instruction. Field testing of such models and conceptual schemes is essential to their development and use, and there is a body of theory and experience upon which to build. Furthermore, school systems, whatever their fate, could profit from the self study and long-range planning required by full scale adaptation of systems analysis to their problems. Computers, incidentally, could greatly enhance the proper study of a school system either by itself or by outsiders.

Systems Approaches

Similarly, a systems approach to the computer as one of many instructional tools is badly needed. Such studies would place the computer in a multimedia context and would examine what learning modes, media, and material seem to work best with what curriculum and with what learners. We suspect, for instance, that there are many less sophisticated devices for enhancing learning (such as the book) which will continue on occasion to be an effective means to an educational end. Systems approach studies could give perspective to the potential of the computer as an instructional aid, refine its contributions, and speed its acceptance by the profession and by the public.

Another complex which requires long-range study is the whole teacher-education-leadership-training continuum. This is an arena which must be entered if change in the school system is a desired aim. Again there is need for conceptualization of the problem and for a systems approach to its administration and management. This approach hopefully would be intimately related both to the multimedia materials approach and to the curriculum and institutional schemes discussed earlier. Only as all the dimensions of the problems are defined can the issue be attacked in any rational fashion. Only against such a background can predictions about changes in the role of the teacher make much sense. Thus action research into such issues as the effects of computer-assisted instruction upon teacher percepts of their roles or as the impact of various staffing and organizational patterns somehow must tie into a larger whole. Only under such conditions can we take into account Toynbee's observation that the "isolated part and the mutilated whole behave differently" when they are removed from their natural setting.

Other obvious large long-range studies relate to the school and community structure, to the political decision-making process outside the school system, to the whole psychology of learning and child-rearing, as well as to the future functions of the family. These studies are undoubtedly under way now in several universities. They need continued governmental or foundation support. Equally important, however, is the building of a cadre of educational engineers or change agents who can translate the results of such studies into ongoing operational school programs.

Circumventing Establishments

In addition to all these studies of change within the school system, strategies which circumvent the school establishment need to be explored and their consequences studied. There seems little doubt that some products of this strategy, for example, the Head Start program, promise to have remarkable impacts and staying powers. There is much to be said for the generation of ideas and practice *outside* the body politic and for the creation of new institutions or agencies designed to assume functions traditionally belonging to the older institutions. These strategies, however, are only successful part of the time. The federal government, we know, has buried countless numbers of task force reports and has often built new agencies on new agencies in the vain hope of breathing life into important governmental functions. Despite this history, it would be interesting to follow experiments with the studio-workshop-laboratory idea outside of the school, or with local adaptations of the kibbutz, or with computer or multimedia learning centers, community based and separated from the school. And surely business enterprises should be encouraged to be partners in the process, providing authorities recognize that they are not infallible either, despite their sophisticated talk and smooth exterior charisma.

Of note is the fact that I have omitted any references to research and development in computer hardware. This omission is on purpose. I have confidence that the hardware will continue to be developed and be adapted to instructional uses without outside assistance. Rather, my plea is for software, software, and more software. Perhaps this is an incorrect use of this term, but my definition relates to the *messages* the computers will carry, such as sequential skill development in mathematics or retrieval systems for topics in the social sciences. My definition of software also includes the promotion of programs, like the development of small, family-like, outdoor camps, designed to offset the environment created by the computer and to balance the "new" curriculum. In addition, my "soft-ware" encompasses public examination of the emerging new roles for schools in our society, and searching appraisals of the political and moral issues relating to control of the knowledge machine.

Conclusion

All the studies and researches and programs related to the school and the computer are important. Were I a maker of policy, however, I would give first priority to the establishment and maintenance of dialogues about education in every forum and market place in the land. The major topics would be:

1. What should be the role of the school in tomorrow's society?
2. What authorities are to have the responsibility for control and regulation of education, in or out of school?
3. Who will control the knowledge machine?

Again, were I a policy maker, I would approach the task with fear and trembling. Tampering with the functions of a major social institution is a risky business. Yet the electronic revolution leaves us very little choice. Either we consciously take on the job or the knowledge machine will do it for us.

Pills for Classroom Peace?

EDWARD T. LADD

Last Fourth of July, after a day of celebrating their inalienable rights to liberty and the pursuit of happiness, Americans were jolted to learn from the Huntley-Brinkley program that doctors in Omaha, Nebraska, are giving hundreds of school children so-called behavior modification drugs, to "make them behave better in school." This report drew the nation's attention to a practice first reported in a Washington *Post* scoop five days before. Already a violent controversy was under way. Does giving hyperactive children drugs to improve their classroom behavior free them for the better pursuit of happiness? Or does it infringe on their liberty?

The Omaha story brought to the public's attention that for well over a decade physicians increasingly have been using drugs to treat children for certain difficulties they have in school. Why and how the practice started helps to explain the issues in the controversy over it.

Originally, psychiatrists and psychologists had become interested in the study of learning difficulties through their work with children who were institutionalized or were visiting clinics because of emotional disturbance or delinquency, most of whom have trouble with learning of one kind or another. Later they broadened out to work with learning difficulties as such. They established that many learning disabilities—which may involve from 5 per cent to 20 per cent of our children—can't be attributed to low intelligence, emotional disturbance, or overt physical handicaps, but seem to reflect something abnormal about the workings of the children's central nervous systems (CNS), the parts of their brains where, so to speak, messages come in and get sorted out. The intensive work of first-rate investigators in several academic disciplines has still failed to reveal just what is wrong with these children's CNS, whether its cause is genetic, a result of injury, or both, and what is best to do about it. If the new terms—specific learning disability, dyslexia, cerebral dysfunction, minimum brain damage, neurological handicaps, and perceptual handicaps—have confused laymen who follow educational developments, the confusion reflects in part this continuing lack of agreement among the experts themselves.

Soon, concern with learning troubles came to be intertwined with concern with "behavior disorders"—a term that is unhappily ambiguous. The intertwining was natural, since learning and behavior themselves are closely related, not only in the obvious ways, but through their common source in the CNS. The way a child's CNS works, it was concluded, can interfere with both his learning and the conduct of the class he is in, by making him compulsively responsive to stimuli from within or without, and hence compulsively hyperactive. Apparently, what happens in such a case is that the instructions the child sends his CNS more or less deliberately are

From *Saturday Review* (November 21, 1970), 66–68, 81–83.

superseded or swamped by other messages coming in from elsewhere in his brain, his body, or his environment, and, as a Canadian researcher has put it, "the child tries to react to everything at once." Fidgety Phil cannot sit still, however much he may want to. This phenomenon has the medical name hyperkinesis, but is often simply called hyperactivity, the latter being another ambiguous term, the use of which has helped to confuse the issue.

As physicians have known for years, hyperkinesis can be controlled by amphetamine and amphetamine-like drugs. These drugs are not tranquilizers; in fact, for a person whose CNS functions normally, they are the opposite: By blocking out messages about fatigue, discomfort, or hunger that would normally interfere with his concentrating on an activity, they pep him up. In the case of the medically hyperactive child, it seems, the blocking-out of messages that make him fidgety enables him to be quieter and to do better work. Incidentally, the effect they have of speeding up some persons and quieting down others, often called paradoxical, provides a pretty good guarantee that they will make children more subdued only if the hyperactivity is organic. Such hyperactivity has been helpfully treated with a number of drugs in this category, including three reported as being used in Omaha: dextroamphetamine, Ritalin, and Deaner.

A more familiar group of drugs that also control hyperactivity and "behavior disorders" but are given less frequently is the tranquilizers. One of these, Raudixin, a strong drug derived from the *Rauwolfia serpentina* root, was mentioned in one Omaha report. Tranquilizers, as is commonly known, can dilute the strength of a child's emotions, and they can thus combat temper tantrums, destructiveness, and boisterousness.

Tofranil and Aventyl, the other two drugs mentioned as being given in Omaha, are mood-changing drugs of a third kind: anti-depressants. Their main use is for treating neurotic depression, which may make children irritable and restless. It is drugs of these different kinds that in laymen's language are called behavior modification drugs. Both the American Medical Association's Council on Drugs and a panel of the National Academy of Science have evaluated the use of drugs for this purpose, and, while caution is still recommended, the medical support for it is impressive.

The use of drugs to improve school performance by controlling hyperactivity and disabling emotions is now so well established it is not surprising that, even in the face of violent criticism, Omaha physicians and school officials stood their ground. The pediatrician in the middle of the controversy said he felt like a Ping-pong ball, but insisted that he and other physicians were circumspect about what they were doing and were following good medical practice. Apparently, most parents of children being treated were behind it. An article on the science page of *The New York Times* entitled "Drugs That Help Control the Unruly Child" cited distinguished support, as did a major story on the Omaha affair in the AMA's *American Medical News.* The latter journal, interviewing pediatricians and child psychiatrists across the nation, summed up their attitude as being "What's all the fuss about?"

School officials appeared equally unperturbed. To them, it seems, the use of drugs for modifying behavior was strictly a medical matter. Quite apart from the fact that for teachers to administer drugs to children would have been illegal, by Board of Education policy educators were not to be involved in behavior control through medication "in any manner whatsoever." Officials apparently saw no reason for concern about the school system's efforts to build communication between parents and physicians, the presence of school personnel at meetings addressed by representatives of drug companies, the reported practice of having teachers identify children they think can benefit from drugs, the screening of children for referral to private physicians by the school system's health and psychological services, teachers' holding drugs in safe-keeping for children and on occasion probably reminding children to take them, or the convincing evidence that some teachers have approached parents about getting their children put on drugs in a way that made the parents feel they were being badgered.

These practices are not unique to Omaha but are common throughout the United States and, indeed, abroad. Most educators believe that such practices give no grounds for concern. They seem pleased, in fact, to be working alongside physicians as fellow professionals. They share with physicians a devotion to helping children and know they are in a particularly good position to spot those who have special medical needs, refer them for help, and then observe them intensively. What *is* all the fuss about?

The real fuss is about the fact that using drugs to influence classroom behavior entails at least five serious risks, four of which the professionals take far too lightly, even though parents and politicians, in their intuitive and sometimes inarticulate way, have recognized them with some dismay.

Two of the five risks are medical, the most dramatic being that of producing undesirable physiological side effects, known or as yet unknown, possibly including addiction–in the physiological sense. Although some of the drugs mentioned can have bad side effects, the danger of such effects is one the physicians in question are well aware of, have studied, and keep very much in mind. The drugs being used are prescription drugs, they are not physiologically addictive for children, and the pediatricians who prescribe them no doubt feel that if they give them to children only with the informed consent of their parents, and then with care, the safeguards are adequate. Since pediatricians are conscientious, dedicated people, and there is fairly good reason to accept their assurances on this score, and since, anyway, the Food and Drug Administration polices their behavior, this risk need not concern us further.

The other medical risk to be considered is that of faulty diagnoses. While physicians seem to feel that they have avoided this risk, too, it is probable that they have not. When the drug is Ritalin or another of the amphetamine types, as it most often is, an error may correct itself: If the child isn't suffering from clinical hyperactivity, his pills will probably make him livelier. This is not true, however, for the tranquilizers.

The real reason why physicians are confident of their diagnoses seems to lie in the cooperation they have from school people who observe their patients' behavior day in, day out. The physicians working in this area lean on teachers very heavily, frequently giving as a reason for doing so their belief that teachers' judgments about children are objective.

In their great desire to help, however, physicians are inclined to trust teachers' judgments too much. One distinguished physician who has done a great deal of research in this area has used a check list for identifying children with an "emo-onal disturbance," which defines "deviancy" as doing anything disapproved by the teacher; it lists as abnormal behavior a child's dismantling his ballpoint pen, propping up his desk with his pencil, or stopping on the way back from the pencil sharpener to talk with someone or to look at things on the teacher's desk. When teachers' evaluations of children's behavior are that questionable (the reasons for this will be explained below), diagnoses based on their reports are questionable, too.

The three non-medical risks, though less tangible, are at least as serious. The first of these is the risk of contributing to the drug culture. As one Omaha parent remarked, "I don't want my child to grow up believing that as soon as things aren't going right, they can take a pill to make it better." The risk of disposing children psychologically toward drugs in general is in a sense an educational one. Since no one yet knows how to deal with it, and since at the same time medical people might be a bit overinclined to resort to medication, it would make sense for physicians themselves, parents, and school people who might influence a decision to put an overactive child on drugs, to keep this risk very much in mind.

The other two risks arise when the purpose of the drug is specifically the modifying of classroom behavior. The first has directly to do with education, one aim of which is to help children learn to regulate their behavior for themselves. For them to do this requires that they come to grips with their natural dispositions and learn to use in a certain way what Philip Jackson at the University of Chicago has nicely called their own "executive powers." Any form of intervention that relieves a restless or unruly child of the need, or deprives him of the opportunity, to use his executive powers deprives him to that extent of the chance to develop insight and skill in self-control. True, this is a price we constantly pay and have to pay so that school and life can go on. Still, for each child these opportunities are finite, and beyond a certain point interfering with his governing his own behavior jeopardizes his growth in independence.

The fifth risk is that of infringing on children's legal rights or their civil liberties. Recent court cases have brought to light a number of things school children do that teachers and principals think disruptive, but that the children are legally entitled to do, such as refusing to pledge allegiance to the flag, distributing political pamphlets, and, in many cases, wearing long hair and saying nasty things in school newspapers. There are no doubt other kinds of behavior that children have a right to engage in, and that are just as repugnant to teachers and principals, but on which the courts haven't yet ruled. Actually, according to legal theory, the only objectionable behavior the school has a right to control is that which it *must* control in order to accomplish its job and protect persons and the institution.

Going still further, civil libertarians and some educators hold that over and above behavior protected by law, there are many other things a child should be free to do, however objectionable they may be. For legal reasons, then, and perhaps educational and moral ones, too, the kinds of behavior the school tries to bring under control should be limited. Whether the school's effort along this line is aimed directly at the student or channeled through his parent or doctor, there is always the risk of its pushing beyond that limit.

Neither school people nor physicians concerned with "children with special problems" show much concern about any of these non-medical risks. Why? Since they have to do with learning and the conduct of schools, it seems fair to attribute the physicians' obliviousness of them to the educators' not having pointed them out. Who could be expected to know as much as educators do about ways of helping children develop mental health, about the classroom conditions under which children can best learn self-control, and about the proper extent of their rights and liberties? Who should be more able to gauge the extent to which a child's behavior in school is productive, legitimate, disruptive, or dangerous?

Unfortunately, while educators are aware of the issues in a general way, most are themselves as oblivious of the practical risks as physicians. This is why they are satisfied that control of classroom hyperactivity through drugs is strictly a medical matter. The root of the trouble is that they have no rationally thought-out criteria for disciplinary practice in general, so that their decisions about it can only be intuitive and subjective. Thus, behavior that some teachers regard as healthy, constructive, and within children's rights causes others great concern.

As long as this remains so, physicians, parents, and teachers themselves should not look upon teachers' negative assessments of children's behavior as informed professional judgments but take them with a grain of salt. Several grains, indeed, because of a number of factors tending to distort those assessments in the direction of repressiveness. These factors have been studied so little that most people are hardly aware of them. Four are particularly important to understand.

First, a special ideology about discipline holds sway in most American schools. One aspect of it is the idea that children will not only behave best but learn best how to regulate their behavior later on if they are kept under tight control; control produces self-control. This is a view inherited from Puritan days, cultivated by school boards, and enshrined for decades in American school law, a view that contrary findings of psychology have weakened only in part. Another aspect, paradoxically, is a very optimistic idea derived indirectly from Rousseau, Dewey, and the mental hygienists, and promoted by schools of education: Children's behavior is naturally good, a good teacher shouldn't have to be concerned with regulating it, and any behavior the teacher finds objectionable is an abnormal phenomenon, a "discipline problem," a form of pathology having some specific cause. Hence the belief—the third aspect of the ideology—that any misbehavior can be stopped if one can just pinpoint its cause and find the right cure. Taken together, these notions lead teachers and principals to believe that objectionable behavior must never be countenanced, and that if it occurs something is seriously wrong; so, since it always does occur, "classroom control" may come to be an obsession. (European educators are often surprised to find American school children very orderly, yet American teachers greatly concerned nonetheless about disorder.) More often than not, obviously, a teacher looks for the presumed cause of a conflict between the child and the school, not in a disturbing school setting or an inappropriate demand made on the child, but inside the child himself.

Second, public school systems in America are monopolistic, classical, government bureaucracies, in which the students, for most purposes, compose the bottom echelon. Although some children are glad to attend school, and it wouldn't be right to call their membership in this bureaucracy unwilling, they can hardly ever forget that it is compulsory. When it comes to children's behavior, these facts are important in two ways. For one thing, the form of organization cannot but greatly restrict children's freedom: The superintendent is responsible for *everything* that goes on in the system, the principal for *everything* that goes on in the school, and the teacher for *everything* that goes on in his classroom, and responsibility must, of course, be accompanied by control. Then, too, when teachers or other professional school personnel are caught in conflicts between their professional standards and the preferences of their administrators, they tend to follow the latter. So, because principals, for several reasons, usually insist on a high degree of order, teachers are forced to do the same. Administrators' pressure on teachers to sit on children is described by a team of Yale psychologists as "most intolerant."

Ironically, however, our public schools provide teachers quite inadequate means for performing the task. Organizations characteristically regulate behavior through rewards and punishments, and most provide supervisors with persuasive repertoires of both. The one great power the school gives the teacher, his say over children's academic futures, is too remote to have much effect on most children's behavior. Otherwise the typical school affords the teacher practically no rewards to dispense and arms him with at most five kinds of punishment—extra work, physical hitting and beating, detention, referral to the principal or the parent, and barring from extracurricular activities—each of which may be so disadvantageous to the teacher or the child that its usefulness is limited. The contrast is stark between the disciplinary situations in ordinary public schools and in schools where researchers or private entrepreneurs are allowed to reward children with money, trading stamps, transistor radios, field trips, or free time.

Lacking resources supplied by the school, teachers are forced to try to regulate children's behavior almost exclusively with more personal ones, their skill in manipulating, their smiles and frowns, encouragement and praise, expressions of disapproval, reproaches, humiliation, and the like. Up to a point, a personal approach to children is normal and proper. But when it is almost the only one a teacher can use, and the pressure to keep the class under tight control is great, any obstreperous child is likely to become a personal threat. In this situation the idea that there is something wrong with the child that someone might fix up by doctoring his internal mechanisms, whether through psychotherapy or chemotherapy, may become irresistible. And, because misbehavior is defined as abnormal anyway, changing the child so that he will behave is easily justified as being in the child's own interest.

Fourth, teachers have unrecognized power over parents, stemming from the strong position they are in to favor or harass children day by day, as well as to influence their futures. This power teachers themselves overlook, probably because the parents who catch their special attention are those who are intransigent. Parents who are uneducated or poor or lack political clout are particularly vulnerable to pressure. So when teachers make suggestions, many parents take them as recommendations, while recommendations, in turn, are often taken as witting or unwitting threats.

It is because these aspects of the typical public school teacher's ideology and role are likely to color his judgment that his judgment is no adequate protection against the risks. At least until teachers' situations and their thinking change, then, other protections must be established. If the dedicated Omaha people who were battered by controversy last summer have been the vehicles for educating us on this score, they have served us well.

What might be realistic safeguards? Following are a few suggestions:

1. It would be useful for school officials, pediatricians, and parents of children with behavior difficulties to explore *all* the risks in behavior modification through drugs openly, thoroughly, and continuously.

2. School systems would do well to draw up policies to guide teachers' and administrators' activities in educational associations that concern themselves with influencing classroom behavior and that include parents and physicians. These policies should take account of the conflict of interest that may arise between a teacher's personal desire to help an individual child and his obligation as a functionary of the state's school system to enforce that system's policies.

3. When a teacher or someone else in a school system finds a child's behavior intolerable and suspects a medical cause, the school system might well follow a different procedure from that for ordinary medical cases and allow only school personnel whose relationship with the child is a strictly professional, confidential one; and who are not in a position to reward or penalize him directly or indirectly, to approach a parent about possible medical treatment. (This sort of safeguard might well apply to psychotherapeutic treatment, too.)

4. It would be a good policy to allow school personnel to do nothing in regard to the referring of a child with behavior problems to a physician or clinic or the treating of such a child, except as requested in writing by the parent.

5. When physicians receive reports that children behave badly in school, they should remain skeptical until they have obtained independent evidence.

It is important that the state make its proper contributions to the health and the education of the young. Drugs have a part to play in both. But it is important, too, that the state be restrained in the limits it sets on deviancy. Drugs, perhaps more than any other instrument for controlling children's behavior, may endanger both of these ideals. Eternal vigilance has no substitute.

The Real Functions of Educational Testing

EDGAR Z. FRIEDENBERG

Educational measurement, though its manifold unplanned consequences are probably more important, has two generally recognized functions. In a society as hung-up on competitive achievement as ours, testing first of all emphasizes the assessment of individual competence. Then it assigns test scores, and with them the persons who made them, to ideologically acceptable social categories.

The second of these functions is much more important, since individual competence is not generally esteemed in our society—nor is it over the long haul demonstrably and consistently the major factor determining relative success. Educational testing is, of course, crucial for every individual on certain occasions; but it is not very helpful in assigning particular individuals to particular social roles, because the norms on the basis of which their scores might be interpreted are grossly contaminated by factors that operate to keep competence from obstructing the social process. We can measure performance much more accurately than we can judge it, for we have established few applicable standards for determininng what makes for good performance. Thus, in medicine and several other professions, the esteem in which a practitioner is held by his colleagues, and the consistency with which he follows what he himself regards as sound professional practice, have been shown to be quite unrelated to his class rank or record in professional school. Similarly, employers, rather than risk their corporate welfare on grades and test scores earned in school or college, test and train on the job. Meanwhile, modern production methods depend increasingly on systems of quality control instead of individual competence and conscientiousness to maintain acceptable standards, while individuals depend on their socially-defined identity rather than on a sharp awareness of themselves and their skills for self-esteem. You have to be really good in America to make it for long as a physicist, a rock musician or a parent; but for the rest, Spiro T. Agnew is probably good enough.

Preoccupation with individual test scores, though understandable in the individuals being tested, today serves chiefly the ideological function of convincing the young that the American social system recognizes and rewards individual competitive achievement. This induces them to cooperate in testing because they expect it to serve as the gateway to opportunity by providing a precise assessment of their individual merits. But for the managers of the social system, testing has a contrary function: it is the means of stocking the various manpower pools with compatible varieties matched in predacity and adaptive characteristics. They do not want to be troubled later by conflict or random variation; greater precision and subtlety, in the interests of a just appraisal, do not concern them.

From *Change Magazine*—the magazine of higher education (January/February 1970), 43–47. Reprinted by permission.

Paradoxically, as the ideological impact of testing on students declines, the real rewards of successful test performance may increase. As higher-status, more sophisticated students reject the social system the schools serve, and the concept of testable success that prevails within it, they will be replaced by lower-status youth who are still hungry for the rewards the system offers, and who are willing to agree that they *are* rewards. It thus may well be that the ends of social mobility and equality of opportunity are best served by a system of rewards so sickening that the successful are ultimately forced to hasten, tight-lipped and intoxicated, from the arena to make way for those of lesser endowments who press upon their heels. Certainly educators are fortunate in having still available a pool of some twenty million black people, most of whom remain more firmly convinced than their oppressors of the value of such rewards. It is therefore understandable that beleaguered college presidents find the angry demands of blacks less threatening and humiliating than the derision of radical whites who treat them like a bad joke that has run on too long.

But it is frustrating that just when blacks are desperately needed as the last available untapped pool of candidates for socialization into the American middle class, a serious question should be raised as to whether they are as capable, on the average, of "making it." In an article called "How Much Can We Boost I.Q. and Scholastic Achievement?" published last winter in the *Harvard Educational Review*, the psychologist Arthur R. Jensen argued strongly, on the basis of evidence culled from a variety of previously published studies, that black children have a cognitive style qualitatively different from that of whites, and that blacks are less suited to the performance-demands both of the educational system and of life in the middle or upper ranges of industrial society. Jensen perceives black children as inherently less adept at abstract reasoning and requiring instruction by techniques that emphasize drill and rote learning if they are to develop marketable skills and a life-style suited to prevailing American custom.

Jensen's article was perceived as a threat by educational liberals from the moment it was distributed in the form of galley proofs; and surely the education industry has a great deal to be concerned about from the issues he raises. But the threat is not, exactly, what it thinks it is. The Jensen argument is not really very startling. The chromosome being what it is, there are certainly clusters of genetic characteristics that come to be socially defined as racial; and it is surely plausible that certain of these characteristics should be related to cognitive functioning. The proposition is rendered more plausible, moreover, by the fact that ideological inhibition has impeded scrutiny of this possibility by American social scientists. Kurt Vonnegut, Jr., is not really being funny when he says in *Slaughterhouse-Five:*

> I think about my education sometimes. I went to the University of Chicago for a while after the Second World War. I was a student in the Department of Anthropology. At that time, they were teaching that there was absolutely no difference between anybody. They may be teaching that still.

They may, indeed; but if they are, Jensen is not the only scholar to think they might be wrong. In a study reported in the *Harvard Educational Review* about two years ago, Gerald Lesser and Susan S. Stodolsky found consistent differences in patterns of mental ability among Chinese, Jewish, Negro and Puerto Rican first-graders in New York, differences quite independent of social class. Their finding that Jewish children ranked significantly higher than the other groups in verbal ability, though as damaging in view of the prevailing social stereotype to the Jewish image as anything Jensen says about Negroes, caused neither astonishment nor consternation.

Where Jensen is on weakest ground—and ground onto which Lesser and Stodolsky were never tempted to precede him—is in inferring that the differences he cites are not merely ethnic but genetic in origin. In a society as permeated by discriminatory practice and perception as ours, this is hardly an empirically testable proposition, since the effects of racism probably penetrate every situation—certainly, in the form of health and nutritional factors, the womb—and color every parameter that might be observed. Being black today is like Abe Martin said being poor was forty years ago: it ain't a crime but it might as well be.

The experience of stigmatization is so pervasive that even conscientious attempts to factor-out its effects remain unconvincing. Jensen, for example, cites evidence that American Indian children, though more disadvantaged than black children on all available environmental indices, still do significantly better in school; but surely this is a classic example of empiricists' folly: the assumption that if you measure something on a scale, and if you get consistent results, then somehow it must be important, even if it isn't exactly relevant. The Indian children on whom such comparisons are based are precisely those who live in communities that, though squalid and poor, still retain some supportive sense of tribal tradition, which now is romanticized, not denigrated. To be denigrated today, you have to be a nigra; the difference is qualitative, and there is no use mucking about with scales to measure it.

The fact is neither Jensen nor his opponents can escape the ethnocentrism implicit in their respective positions by the purifying rituals of science; for those rituals are themselves central to their common ideological pattern. Both start with the assumption that our society, with its dominant values, is the given—the reality with which one must come to terms, and those who do not accept its terms or meet its demands have no just basis for making demands on it. In this context, Jensen is of course threatening, because he infers that blacks are systematically less able, on the average, to meet those demands than whites; and that efforts to compensate for this difference by education cannot be wholly successful, even if racial discrimination were eliminated. Since both informal observation, like Jonathan Kozol's and James Herndon's, and formal studies, like that of Eleanor Leacock and the Bundy Report, suggest that racial discrimination could be eliminated from our urban school systems only by genocide, the policy implications of Jensen's work seem rather remote.

But if success, as society defines it, is what black people want—and most doubtless do—then the implications represent bad, though hardly tragic, news. Jensen specifically insists that his conclusions cannot justifiably be applied, pejoratively or otherwise, to the cognitive possibilities of any *individual.* Most people, regardless of ethnic differences, have far more potential ability of every kind than they ever get to use; wherever the mean may be there is room to stand erect under almost any part of the curve. Only a very bad, or disingenuously racist, statistician would infer from Jensen's argument that any *particular* black student would be incompetent to meet the demands of the educational system, though one might quite properly conclude that those demands, if consistently inappropriate to the cognitive style most comfortable for black students, do indeed constitute a form of *de facto* discrimination. But the more relevant question concerns the *nature* of those demands.

Jensen implies that in any large random group of blacks one would likely find fewer persons than in a comparable group of whites—for purely ethnic reasons—capable of developing the abilities of, say, Robert McNamara or John McCone or John Gardner or Theodore Sorensen or Roger Heyns—to name five men whose excellence and consistent devotion to rational cognition, undistracted by excessive passion or subjectivity, have become a matter of public record and brought them both international distinction and groovy positions of public trust (if that is quite the right phrase for a director of the Central Intelligence Agency or a president of the World Bank). This may be true; I fear it is. There may *never* be a black man with the kind of mind needed to produce a report like that produced by the McCone Commission on the disorders in Watts a few years ago. But the more fundamental question is whether and to what degree any person, white or black, must possess such a mind in order to live in this society with a reasonable guarantee against insult and a reasonable prospect of satisfaction. Must one master the techniques of affect-free cognition in order to succeed? Must one succeed to retain any shred of self-esteem? Must success be defined as the power to dominate and manipulate the life-styles of others, masked in the rhetoric of pluralism and equality of opportunity? Poverty, brutality and exclusion are hard to bear; and no race can be so different—or so irrational—as to choose them. Jensen, however, suggests that there may be groups of human beings who cannot become quite like the dominant class in America, even if their lives, or more precisely their life-chances, depend on it.

If this is true, the process of educational measurement cannot have much relevance to their aspirations. Educational measurement is an inherently conservative function. It depends on the application of established norms to the selection of candidates for positions in the existing social structure, and on the terms and for the purposes set by that structure. The testing process usually cannot muster either the imagination or the sponsorship needed to search out and legitimate new conceptions of excellence which might threaten the hegemony of existing elites. On the contrary, educational measurement is at present wholly committed to the assumption that legitimate forms of learning are rational and cognitive, and that such learning is the proper goal of the academic process. This is an ideological, not a technical, difficulty. It is perfectly possible to detect and appraise, in critical though not scalar terms, poetic skill, humane sensitivity, the breadth and subtlety of human compassion, and the like. In experimental revisions of testing programs in the humanities and in personality assessment, some of this has been done; it is at least enough to prove that the technology of testing *could* serve humane goals in a more humane society.

But a more humane society might have little use for large-scale educational measurement, because such a society would perforce be less competitive and universalistic, and more generous and genuinely pluralistic, than ours. Educational measurement is technically capable of as great or greater service in helping people find out what kinds of knowledge, or what kind of job, or what college, or even what life would suit them best as it is in serving the competitive ends of society. (For a people already ankledeep in moon-shit and happy-ever-after in the market-place, even those computer-arranged courtships are a form of salvation, or at least no joke.) But society is not about to buy such a diagnostic use of testing on anything like the scale it buys a competitive use. For under our current ideology only competitive testing can assign youthful subjects to ideologically defensible categories for social action.

The major premise of the American system of social morality is that every individual should have an equal opportunity to compete for the prizes offered. The less frequently stated but probably more crucial minor premise is that if he does, he has no legitimate basis for complaint. The contest may be destructive or banal, the prizes worthless, the victory empty or Pyrrhic, but to complain of that is to be a bad sport, perhaps even an elitist; and such complaints are not honored in our system. What is most important is that every contest be objectively judged, as impersonally as possible, with no favoritism, nepotism or any other kind of ism. And to make this objectivity evident, access to preferred categories should wherever possible be granted on the basis of scaled scores that a machine could handle.

This is a crucial dynamic in maintaining the American illusion of objectivity because it permits the biases that are useful in maintaining our status-structure and our institutions to be hidden beneath several levels of abstraction. Beneficiaries of the system, like middle-class, college-bound students and their parents, or even its naive victims, like the more old-fashioned students in "general" or "commercial" tracks, may assume there is no bias in the tests (since there can be none in the scoring). Educators and more sophisticated students and parents, including a growing number of those of lower status, aware of the problem of bias in the tests themselves, may demand a "culture-free" test, or the use of different norms in grading "disadvantaged" groups, or the suspension of testing altogether. But even they are unlikely to recognize the bias—quite apart from the content of the test itself—which is inherent in the very practice of basing judgments that may determine the entire life of a student (and in view of our Selective Service policy, his death as well) on the display of a narrow range of cognitive behavior. And virtually no one recognizes the value judgment built into the monstrous notion that the welfare of any individual in a society with the means to nurture all its members should depend on any test score at all.

The widespread use of educational measurement reinforces our commitment to universalism and our conviction that equality is the core of justice, and the value of this set of assumptions to the process of domestic counterinsurgency can hardly be overestimated. Every high school principal, college admissions officer, fellowship selection board and employment recruiter lives under continual menace from losers ready to accuse him of favoritism. And he is impeded, of course, by an egalitarian ideology from making the obvious rejoinder that favoritism, in the sense of allowing himself to be guided by his human and subjective perception of the needs and qualities of others, is a part of his professional responsibility. Partly for this reason, testing has proliferated far beyond any expectation that the data it yields are needed to make any rational decisions. The data are needed, rather, to *justify* decisions for which no data were needed at all, by showing that however insensitive, uptight and uncritical the institution and the educational process might have been, and however willing the administrators to serve a corrupt master in a dubious cause, they are nevertheless fair and impartial and play by the rules, and have really nothing to answer for.

The reason Jensen is so disturbing to liberals, fundamentally, is because his analysis threatens this basic stabilizing function of educational measurement and, with it, universalism itself. For if he is right, no amount of fairness and psychometric ingenuity can afford equality of treatment. Instead, one must choose between fairness and justice; and if a commitment to justice is to be preserved and finally implemented, the educational system must manage, against the pressure of so-called backlash, the difficult political decision to be generous and, as they say in the South, partial.

There is no reason to suppose that we find ourselves on this earth for the purpose of performing well on tasks involving abstract cognition or, indeed, for any purpose at all except our own. Educational measurement can serve those who want help in making a more precise estimate than they could unassisted of what purposes might be realistic for them in view of their actual characteristics and the scenes they might make. It can also help them in legitimating their demands that they be permitted to make these scenes against possible social opposition; the test-makers could, for example, provide College Board and achievement test scores in support of applications for college admission by high school dropouts, pushouts and troublemakers who have poor recommendations and possibly no diplomas. They can do all this and more quite as proficiently as they can continue to assist in the grand process of channeling by which our society meets its manpower needs, sustains its status system and brings peace of a kind to Southeast Asia. What they cannot do is get our society to authorize the process, and pay for it.

Education in Megalopolis

EDWARD JOSEPH SHOBEN, JR.

Between 1880 and 1890, the United States committed itself irrevocably to a shift from an agricultural to an industrial economy and from a rural to an urban society. It was not until the decade of the 'fifties, however, that we committed ourselves to the megalopolis. Before this second change, there tended to be a sharp break between the city, with its blocks of houses and shops and its gridiron of streets, and the surrounding countryside, with its fields and woods and farms. Now, in place of the compact, ordered, and intensively used space within the clear boundaries of the city, there is a vastly larger, more diffuse, and more disorderly appearing community. For want of a better term, we call it a metropolitan area, comprising a core city and its abutting suburbs and exurban satellites. And the metropolitan areas themselves are beginning to fuse and grow into each other, forming the great megalopolitan[1] regions of the near future. The American northeast is already a functional example—in effect, one great supercity stretching from Boston to Washington. The California coastal belt from San Francisco to San Diego is not far behind in its process of urbanization. The Great Lakes industrial strip, centered in Chicago and reaching from Cleveland to Milwaukee, is another illustration. The Gulf Coast complex that extends from New Orleans through Houston into Dallas is still another. As our modes of transportation become faster and more efficient, it seems virtually inevitable that these nebulous megalopolitan agglomerates will provide the social and economic bases of life for almost all of us.

What makes megalopolis possible, of course, is applied science under the regulation of conventional economics. Medical advances and improved public health measures contribute to the huge populations of the urbanized world. The mechanical and chemical revolutions in agriculture allow us to set ever more sumptuous

From *The Educational Forum* (May 1967), 431–439. Reprinted by permission of Kappa Delta Pi, An Honor Society in Education, owners of the copyright.

[1] The classic study here—and the one giving currency to the term "megalopolis"—is Jean Gottman, *Megalopolis: The Urbanized Northeastern Seaboard of the United States* (Cambridge, Mass.: M.I.T. Press, 1961).

tables although fewer than ten percent of America's people now live on farms. The radio, telephone, and teletype, together with the jet plane, the fast car, and the superhighway, shrink great spans of space into manageable packages. Because new techniques of production make it more efficient for a manufacturer to organize work on a single floor rather than in multi-storied buildings, he moves from the core city to the urban periphery, where he constructs a plant that rambles like a country club through huge parking lots for employees and customers. Similarly, good roads, automobiles, and extended public utilities permit individual families, striving for always higher standards of living, to search for a balance between the richer offerings of cosmopolitan centers and the more open *Lebensraum* that lies on their fringes. Both retail business and many forms of industry, anticipating new foci of buying power and adjusting to new cost factors in a constantly changing technology, also migrate out of quite comparable motives. Megalopolis, then, is not a static state but a dynamic and gigantic pattern of growth, stimulated by technologized science and by an expansionist economy.

If megalopolis is to be understood not as a thing but a process, not as an end product but as an extremely rapid flowing of people and enterprises, then our urban problems take on a new cast. Our way of life is profoundly in flux; and our difficulties are those of instability, a constant confrontation by novelty, and a perpetual confusion because the immediate past no longer predicts more than the barest lineaments of the immediate future. We are always on the edge of an unfamiliar tomorrow; and this state of affairs, exciting and challenging though it may be, is disquieting to the human heart and mind. One of the central responses this disquiet has evoked has been a major, if somewhat ambivalent, investment of faith in education.

But if education is to prepare children for responsible adulthood in a world of change, for a tomorrow that has less and less in common with yesterday—in short, for the megalopolis—then it cannot simply transmit to a new generation the traditional culture. It is by no means true that the traditional culture has entirely lost its viability and worth. But it is profoundly true that the conditions have radically altered that once made the passing on of our cultural heritage the fundament of effective schooling.

In the last ten years, the family of man has increased by over 600 million people. The entire history of flight, from the first minutes aloft over the sand dunes of North Carolina to the latest traffic in outer space, comprises only sixty-four years, less than the lifetime of a man not yet ready for retirement. The television set was invented only in 1928 and did not become commercially feasible until after the end of World War II. We have not yet lived a quarter of a century with atomic energy; automated industry is an awesome novelty; and the cardiac pacemaker, the electronic gadget that can be surgically inserted into human hearts that otherwise would cease to beat, may indeed be the harbinger of a new race of androids, beings who are part organism and part machine but far more clever and efficient than *homo sapiens*, as we now know him. Given our new computers and cybernetic mechanisms, can we really say with confidence that the day will never come when men not only control but actually *become* a spaceship, a submarine, or a communications network? Irrespective of the answer, that such a question can be seriously asked defines the enormous difference between the world of our fathers and the world of our children and the reduced (which is *not* a synonym for "eliminated") relevance of our traditional heritage for the megalopolitan society.

It is within this framework, then, that the structure of a genuinely modern education must be developed. The issues here are numerous and complex, and if education is truly to contribute to the humanization of megalopolitan life, then they need to be thought about and debated. One illustrative problem has to do with how schools shall be supported in megalopolis.

As we have seen, megalopolis is characterized by a high degree of mobility; people and businesses move with considerable frequency as they attempt to alter their economic and social position. When, in favor of a new plant in a new location, a long-established industry closes down, it tends to draw away with it (a) certain of its employees and (b) some of the auxiliary enterprises—restaurants and bars, supermarkets and neighborhood shops, etc.—that it supported. Typically, the result is a decline in the tax base that finances schools, and the people who remain are usually those whose cultural experiences least disposes them to regard education as a capital investment rather than as a current expense.[2] Large enclaves of our metropolitan areas therefore are more concerned with tax bills than with the quality of educational services. Ironically, these enclaves are not infrequently places where educational services are most urgently needed and the sources from which ignorance, irresponsibility, and violence creep into the more privileged segments of the city. Such problems are compounded when one remembers that a large proportion of the housing in these areas, both residential and commercial, is owned by absentee landlords whose local interest is essentially economic and who understandably but shortsightedly resent increased property levies. When communities were relatively small and stable, when people tended to remain in the same areas in which they grew up, and when property owners tended to live in close proximity to their real estate, then the property tax as the chief source of educational revenues was sound and sensible. If our faith in education is to be realized under megalopolitan conditions, however, we need to think hard about how wise it is to continue to rely on property taxes as the primary basis for school support.

But vitally important as problems such as those of school finance are, they are likely to be resolved wisely only as we achieve a viable concept of education in megalopolis. What must we do if we are to serve our youngsters and our changing society well? Any attempt to cope with this question may be an instance of a fool's rushing in where angels fear to tread. Yet H. G. Wells's old characterization of civilization as a race between education and catastrophe was never more on target.

The basis for one answer to our question is the concept of megalopolitan

[2] The conception of education as a form of capital investment is a centrally important one. The basic discussion is that by T. W. Schultz, *The Economic Value of Education* (New York: Columbia University Press, 1963). A comparable, British-based view is developed by John Vaizey, *The Economics of Education* (New York: Free Press, 1962). Another important analysis is that by B. A. Weisbrod, *External Benefits of Public Education* (Princeton, N.J.: Industrial Relations Section, Dept. of Economics, 1964).

education as being lifelong. A modern education can have no terminal point, marked by a high school diploma or a university degree; it must be continued systematically throughout the rapidly changing circumstances with which one must deal in the course of his life span. In the current educational stratosphere, the half-life of scientific knowledge is roughly ten years.[3] That is, only about half of what a new scientist knows at the time he receives his Ph.D. degree will probably be regarded as true ten years later. As a result, many universities and even more industries are finding it both desirable and necessary to send their scientists and engineers back to school to prevent their becoming walking analogues of the hour glass or abacus. The establishment of the new University of California at La Jolla from the top down—beginning with doctoral and postdoctoral work in the sciences, leaving to later the founding of less advanced programs of study—is only one large-scale response to this situation.

But one need not fly so high to make the point about the necessity of lifelong education. In the spring of 1962, President Kennedy was wrestling with the problem of whether to stop atomic testing in the atmosphere. James Reston, the *New York Times* columnist, pointed out that the President's scientific advisers were split into two camps.[4] Some were arguing that nuclear fallout would make genetic monsters out of untold numbers of unborn children for many generations to come. Others, equally illustrious and equally well qualified, were arguing that such claims grossly and luridly overstated the case. On Kennedy's shoulders sat the heavy burden of making a decision, and many of us were not unsympathetic to the lonely load he carried. But sooner or later, Reston reminded us, the average American citizens would have to make some judgment about the wisdom of that presidential decision. The faith on which any democracy rests is compactly summarized in that little drama. That faith holds that any man, properly educated, can indeed judge wisely in such circumstances. With applied science at the very base of megalopolis, there can be no doubt that comparable issues will frequently recur, and if the understanding of citizens is not constantly renewed at the fount of education, then they will surrender their power and their rights to oligarchs or despots whose benevolence can never be trusted.

Nor need we stay with science. Ours is a world in which place-names like Viet Nam, Tibet, Cuba, Egypt, and the Congo have a familiarity once reserved for Kansas and California. No spot on the globe is more than a day's journey by jet from any other, and the supersonic missiles now trained on us from Russia are soon to be duplicated in China and, regardless of how they may be aimed, other parts of the planet's surface. Because events in Africa or central Asia can quite literally mean life or death for us in North America, they can hardly be of merely exotic interest. The same factors that have given rise to megalopolis have shrunk the earth. But if the earth has shrunk, it has become more complex rather than less. If we are to survive and prosper, we must understand the backgrounds and aspirations of Tanzanians, Japanese, Pakistanis, Argentinians, Laotians, Israelis, Algerians, and

[3] For one useful discussion of the rate and character of scientific expansion, see Derek J. de S. Price, *Science since Babylon* (New Haven: Yale University Press, 1961).

[4] *The New York Times*, 7 March, 1962, p. 34.

many others, as well as Chinese, Russians, Spanish, Scandinavians, the incomprehensible French, and the too often forgotten Canadians! If less theatrical, the requirements of meaningful citizenship are more pervasive with respect to world politics and social development than with respect to the control of atomic energy. Influential debate and informed judgment about world affairs have never been so urgently called for, and their achievement makes it impossible to specify a point in our education at which we "completed" our study of international relations.

What has been said about science and technical knowledge, the public policies regulating weaponry (or space programs or automation), and international politics can be modified to fit a host of other important topics: economics and the operations of the business establishment, population growth and the thorny questions associated with its control, conservation and recreational resources, race relations and the embarrassment of grinding poverty in the context of affluence, etc. The range of vital topics is huge, and in the world of the megalopolis it is virtually endless. Obviously, no one can become a master of such a diversity of complex problems, so our principle of lifelong education must be elaborated in two directions.

In the first place, modern education must concentrate less on subject matter and more on learning how to learn and on cultivating the habit of independent inquiry. This notion puts a heavy premium on increasing individual sensitivity to human issues, on the techniques for acquiring reliable information, and on the processes of thinking about the moral and political, as well as the scientific questions that cut through the affairs of citizenship. Part of the apparatus for further learning is a background of knowledge against which new data and new ideas can be assimilated. But a great deal of our schooling has been built on a curious sequence: Facts and principles, defined as appropriate to particular grades by curriculum committees, have been learned by teachers, who then poured their own learning into pupils; tests were then administered to determine the degree to which youngsters had soaked up this material, not as a background for further learning, but as a kind of end in itself and a ticket to the next grade level.

The point is not to carp about past procedures, but to indicate that films and kinescopes, taped lectures, programed materials, and a rich array of inexpensive and easily accessible books make the amassing of background easy for an individual to manage on his own. What he needs from classroom and teacher is help in the perception of significant problems, a chance to organize his thoughts on paper and to have them rigorously criticized, and the discipline of responsible discussion in which he learns that one of his most crucial auditors is himself. Under these conditions, he is consistently pressed to check his sources, attend to his reasoning, and re-examine his ideas in order both to clarify them in his own mind and to give them some more articulate and public shape. When these circumstances obtain, the student is not preparing for his role of citizen; he is playing it. The teacher, while centrally important, is no longer the source of information and principles. Rather, he is another citizen collaborating in the designing of relevant learning opportunities and serving as a critic of a student's responses to them.

That this conception of education as a systematic and continuing dialogue among citizens is more appropriate to the older ages is, of course, correct. Two qualifiers, however, must be entered into the record. First, as any attentive parent knows, the capacity for meaningful if limited discussion on the part of quite small children is considerable. In our haste to give youngsters the "right" answers to their questions, and in our tendency to regard them as passive receptacles for information and moral values, we have done far too little toward encouraging their becoming self-propelling learners and toward converting their inherent curiosity into the blend of informed criticism and commitment that defines thoughtful citizenship in a world of change. Active dialogue should certainly increase and become more disciplined by logic and knowledge as the educational process continues, but it can be begun much earlier than we have characteristically believed.[5]

Our second qualifier is of a somewhat different order. Megalopolis teems with information. The urban world is flooded with news and commentary, material on science and international affairs, statements by public officials, and a thousand varieties of similar stimuli. For this reason, today's generation is demonstrably better informed than yesterday's for all the worries and disappointments of its older compatriots. And it is for this reason that one can travel from Baltimore to Seattle, from Duluth to Biloxi, and never have trouble recognizing one's fellow Americans. Formed and informed by a national press, national radio and television networks, and national movies, all of us share in a common culture whatever the particular wrinkles we bring to it from family or region. This commonality, born of *Time* and the *Saturday Evening Post* (including their highly persuasive advertising) and of TV and the film, is a major source of our sense of community and our unapologetic patriotism. The term "mass civilization," part of the vocabulary of megalopolis, is by no means entirely an insult, implying as it does a body of knowledge and a set of values which are deeply shared and which serve to bind large numbers of people together in mutual loyalties and reasonable respect if not in friendliness.[6]

On the other hand, our common culture is also marked by a worrisome tenuousness. Despite the obvious lessons of American history, mistrust and tension still run high, for example, among our various ethnic and racial groups.[7] The current crimes and disruptions associated with the too long delayed inclusion of

[5] Useful technical discussions of this point can be found in the chapter on "Research on Teaching in the Nursery School" by Pauline S. Sears and Edith Dowley (and in their useful bibliography) in N. L. Gage (ed.), *Handbook of Research in Teaching.* (Chicago: Rand McNally, 1963), pp. 814–864. A representative and responsible popular treatment is by Maya Pines, "How Three-Year-Olds Teach Themselves to Read—and Love It," *Harper's Magazine,* May, 1963. Jerome Bruner's influential *The Process of Education* (Cambridge, Mass.: Harvard University Press, 1960), is also relevant here.

[6] The problem of a common culture that is unifying but not stultifying is discussed provocatively by a number of the essayists in Philip Olson's anthology, *America as a Mass Society* (New York: Free Press, 1963). See also L. A. Cremin, *The Transformation of the School* (New York: Alfred A. Knopf, 1961).

[7] Perhaps the most comprehensive and authoritative analysis is Nathan Glazer's and Daniel Moynihan's *Beyond the Melting Pot* (Cambridge, Mass.: M.I.T. Press and Harvard University Press, 1963).

Negroes into full citizenship are only virulent symptoms of a long illness in our basic pattern of social life. In spite of these tears in our cultural fabric, the mass civilization of megalopolis threatens the individuality and pluralism that are our historic and fundamental values. As a prominent economist[8] has noted, "It is in the very nature of a scientific technology (the basis of megalopolis) that it steadily contracts the boundaries of the self-sufficient person while expanding those of the public particle." "Conformity," another term in megalopolis' lexicon of danger, means precisely this debasing of the person into the public particle.

And it is here that education finds its greatest significance. Schools have traditionally meant the enhancement of individual lives, the encouragement of intellectual, moral, and aesthetic growth in *persons,* not "public particles." For this reason lifelong education for citizenship in megalopolis must put a new stress on expression, criticism, and the discipline of dialogue. It is worth repeating that expression, criticism, and dialogue are worthless unless they are informed and rational. But our technology now bombards us with information; the wise use of that technology makes much of it easier than ever to acquire; and rationality for most of us is an endless quest, best pursued through honest interaction with one's fellows in important issues. For the foreseeable future, the extension of our educational establishment (with a small "e") represents the best device for insuring the individuality that we rightfully prize, as well as for making it possible for men to stay responsibly and zestfully abreast of the changes that are the megalopolitan hallmark.

But it is time to return to our second elaboration of the theme of lifelong education. If education must reach up in the age-scale, it must also reach down. Universal and compulsory education has been well established for children between the ages of six and sixteen. It is now being extended in a preliminary and *de facto* sort of way, into the post-secondary years through community colleges and technical schools. It seems odd that the most plastic and formative period of life has been exempted from formal educational influences.[9] Until very recently, our official doctrine was that the child from birth to six belonged at home. Aside from a few nursery schools, sometimes regarded as baby-sitting operations, we have seldom considered openly the possibility that this policy may be inappropriate to our times.

With the beginnings of Project Head Start, we have learned that, in the case of the culturally underprivileged, waiting until a child is of kindergarten or first-grade age to begin his systematic education may entirely vitiate the opportunity for personal growth that the school represents. Such a youngster tends to bring with him a strong pattern of attitudes toward language and communication, toward print and film, and toward relationships with both adults and other children that are

[8] Robert L. Heilbroner. See his *The Making of Economic Society* (Englewood Cliffs, N.J.: Prentice-Hall, 1962). The issue is also dealt with provocatively by David Riesman in *Abundance for What?* (Garden City, N.Y.: Doubleday, 1964), and it is analyzed in depth by Jacques Ellul, *The Technological Society* (New York: Alfred Knopf, 1964).

[9] The balance of this discussion leans heavily on the important study by Benjamin Bloom, *Stability and Change in Human Characteristics* (New York: John Wiley & Sons, 1964).

inimical to his launching himself successfully toward the role of citizen-learner. A great deal of such a boy's or girl's school experience for a long time must be remedial, an arrangement that is both less effective and less economical than we can afford. Head Start is fundamentally an effort to draw children into the orbit of critical citizenship before they have developed serious inhibitions against it.

To the extent that Head Start and comparable programs prove useful for disadvantaged children, they may also be highly desirable for those from other segments of our society. It has become evident that children can learn a great deal more at earlier ages than we have previously thought. Even good parents are not necessarily skillful teachers. If we can make the distinction between parenthood and the role of the teacher for the first six years of life, just as we have learned to make it for the elementary-school years, then we may be able to register exciting gains, otherwise unobtainable, in the quality of American personhood and citizenship. Rapid reading and good comprehension, for instance, require not only the mastery of some basic skills, but also a friendly and curious attitude toward print as a source of interesting and useful information. Further, growth in reading is broadly linked to growth in written expression. Recent work strongly suggests that the pencil point has been a clumsy obstruction to a child's discovery of how to put his thoughts and observations on paper; a typewriter, on the other hand, is much more manipulable for young hands, more fun, and a greater facilitator of interest and pride in learning to write. An earlier introduction to language functions, using the pedagogical techniques relevant to three- to five-year-olds, could markedly raise the level of cognitive competence in our society in a single generation.[10]

Similarly, we know that early childhood is far freer from the ravages of prejudice than are later ages. [11] An earlier school experience, where youngsters become familiar with each other directly, could materially reduce the fear, the disrespect, and the feelings of hierarchy—of inferiority and superiority—that are not irrelevant to urban violence and vandalism.

In any case, we now know that not only arithmetic and language ability, but aggression and personal autonomy are much more amenable to change at earlier ages than later. The longer one waits to develop these traits along socially constructive lines, the more difficult it is to do so. In the static society before the urban revolution, ignorance and eccentricity were not major causes for concern. One of the humane features of megalopolis is that it makes aberrant development an object of shared worry. The school dropout, the delinquent, and the poisonously prejudiced can be neither hidden nor tolerated. If education is indeed the hinge on which a democratic civilization swings, then its effectiveness as a pivot depends in large part on its accessibility to children during their most responsive and pliable years.

Megalopolis means more than big cities. It means a way of life for dense

[10] A great deal of useful material here has been collected by Alfred de Grazia and D. A Sohn (eds.), *Revolution in Teaching: New Theory, Technology, and Curricula* (New York: Bantam Books, 1964). Despite its technicalities, an invaluable paper is Eleanor J. Gibson's "Learning to Read," *Science* (May 21, 1965), 148:1066–1072.

[11] A sound and nontechnical discussion can be found in Boyd McCandless, *Children and Adolescents: Behavior and Development* (New York: Holt, Rinehart, & Winston, 1961), pp. 355–404.

populations. That way of life will remain marked by an increasing rate of change; change not only in our gadgets, but change in our habits, institutions, relationships, and understandings. The megalopolitan way of life is not without its extensive and expensive strains; but it also implies opportunities for humane and gracious living that have never before been imagined for such a vast proportion of society's members. If those opportunities are to be realized, then education, beginning early in childhood, must play a lifelong part in the creation and maintenance of megalopolitan citizens, capable of both enjoying and directing the rapid currents of contemporary culture.

Public School: Melting Pot or What?

MARJORIE S. FRIEDMAN

America's educational system has been thrust into a nation-wide battle that involves not only the demands of American Negroes for "equal education" but, by extension, the aspiration of all minority groups as they pit their demands for justice against the power structures. Minority groups have become conscious of themselves as distinctive and identify with people in other nations and societies. Actions taken by what is viewed as the Establishment (conceived as either acquiescent or castrating) have wide repercussions; and American responses to ostensibly domestic challenges take on international significance.

The American public school system has responded to the demands made on it in two important ways. Educators have accepted Federal funds for pre-kindergarten programs, experiments in ungraded schooling, etc.; and, by implication, they have accepted Federal directives and control. Decentralization has taken place, allowing for increasing community control and opening the way to increased accountability for local groups. Although these and other efforts by northern schools to meet the more insistent demands of minority groups have been widely supported and well publicized, and although some steps towards integration have been taken, what has not occurred is a genuine re-evaluation of the fundamental rationale of the American public school.

The Melting Pot Approach

The schools' major assumption is that every newcomer to this society desires to adapt to the dominant culture, if not ultimately to be assimilated by it.

From *Teachers College Record* (January 1969), 347–351. Reprinted by permission.

> The common school, started in Massachusetts in the early 19th century, was apparently conceived as a deliberate instrument to reduce cultural and religious differences . . . The schools have attempted to file down or erase distinctive cultural traits, denying that important cultural diversity ever existed; the procedures of the school reflect a mandate to persuade youth that all groups share a common language, common political and economic institutions, and common standards of right and wrong behavior.[1]

The educational cliché having to do with respect for individual differences has had psychological rather than cultural implications. The emphasis continues to be placed on cultural deficiencies, cultural negatives; the cultural positives have yet to be recognized.

In the nineteenth century, the problems created by immigration and the advent of new minority groups were defined as largely economic. Was a rising population desirable? Did immigrants lower the standards of living? What was the effect of immigration upon industrialization, the business cycle, and labor conditions? Europeans and Americans both believed that acculturation was a simple process. The experience of living in a new environment, it was believed, could be depended upon to alter the nature of the immigrant and bring him into conformity with the cultural patterns of his adopted country.

In the twentieth century, the professional community has enlarged this configuration. Immigration—and related acculturation problems—now include ethical, social, familial, and psychological factors. The new environment's impact on the inner life of man has been subjected to scientific scrutiny. "Through the normal socialization and learning process within the family, during childhood, the migrant has internalized the culture of his origin."[2] Cultural inscriptions cannot, it is admitted, be easily erased. Family, cultural heritage, and the broad social context itself leave deep marks upon individual character, culture, and personality—marks that do not simply disappear with a change in residence.

The Inequality of Assimilation

"Acculturation" means a variety of things: the result of somewhat close contact between peoples, resulting in a give-and-take of their cultures; a process whereby a specific trait is ingested by a recipient culture; or initiation in the patterns of an individual's own culture. There is implied in the term a relative degree of equality between the giving and receiving cultures. "Assimilation" is quite different. It means the process of transforming aspects of a conquered or engulfed culture into a version of the ruling culture.[3] The tendency is for the ruling cultural group to

[1] Fred M. Newmann and Donald W. Oliver, "Education and Community," *Harvard Educational Review,* Vol. 37, Winter, 1967.

[2] Philip M. Hauser, Ed. *Handbook for Social Research in Urban Areas.* Paris: UNESCO, 1965.

[3] International Sociological Association, *Population and Culture: The Positive Contribution of Immigrants,* a Symposium. Paris: UNESCO, 1955.

enforce the adoption of certain externals, in terms of which a superficial "adjustment" is secured. The adopting culture, it must be emphasized, is not in a position to choose.

Although oversimplified, the distinction remains significant. The concept of assimilation involves a relationship between a dominant and a submissive group. Basic to the "melting pot" orientation of the American school system, it pervades that system with inequalities.

Noting the mounting unrest, the drop-out statistics, and the fight for power among American minority groups, can we still insist on this assimilationist philosophy? Or can we afford to permit separate and distinct cultures to exist within society? Can we insist that our educational institutions find, foster, and forward a multiplicity of *different* cultures?

Toward Cultural Pluralism

Pluralism means that minority groups are accepted as distinct and separate elements in the nation at large. Is this nation unified enough to take such a risk? Psychologically, pluralism demands an acceptance of the idea that individual differences are partially cultural, that it is *culture*, which forms the unity of the self, to be destroyed at an intolerable cost to the very essence of the individual. Instead of suppressing, eliminating, and filing down to a sterile and monotonous mass image, educators might well make an effort to identify the diverse elements that do exist in our culture. The next step would be to preserve those aspects of each foreign culture considered significant for the growth of identity, pride, and personality in individual cases. The problem of assimilation of "out" groups then disappears; and something quite new and rich is added to the nation's culture.

An example of what is being proposed can be found in the work done at the Institute of American Indian Arts in New Mexico. Here, Indian boys and girls of many different tribes (each of whom has introjected the sense of shame and rejection imposed by white culture) are relearning the arts of their Indian culture as a means of achieving identity and pride, and as a way of building potential bridges to the adult world.

The concept of cultural pluralism is surely not new. Horace Kallen, well-known pragmatic philosopher,[4] became a spokesman half a century ago for the idea that each nationality should maintain its own dialect or speech, its own emotional and involuntary life style. Envisioning an America revitalized by the cultures of many peoples, he asked–in 1915–that each incoming group be permitted to preserve its own individual, aesthetic, and intellectual forms. But many were fearful–*are* fearful today.

The common school experience has been considered crucial in the development of an informed public, necessary for the inculcation of American values and for the

[4]Professor Kallen, a founder of the New School of Social Research, has written–among many other works–*Culture and Democracy in the United States.* His latest book is *Liberty, Laughter, and Tears.* De Kalb: Northern Illinois University, 1968.

maintenance of democracy. Intense, perhaps naive emotion has often been aroused by the idea of a "melting pot":

> There she lies, the great Melting Pot—listen! Can't you hear the roaring and the bubbling? There gapes her mouth—the harbour where a thousand mammoth feeders come from the ends of the world to pour in their human freight. Ah, what a stirring and a seething! Celt and Latin, Slav and Teuton, Greek and Syrian,—black and yellow— . . . East and West, and North and South . . . the crescent and the cross—how the great Alchemist melts and fuses them . . . what is the glory of Rome and Jerusalem where all nations and races come to worship and look back, compared with the glory of America, where all races and nations come to labour and look forward?[5]

Our schools will reflect the society's dominant values and are dedicated to the sustenance of the white middle class, which still equates schooling with success, upward and outward mobility, and money. It has been the policy of the educational establishment to keep the assimilative philosophy nonexplicit, "grey area," so that vocal or highly organized minority groups would not be able to see that *their* values were being erased rather than taught. This "hiding" has been passed off as muddling-through, allowing discretion to local boards, freedom for teachers, etc. Close examination makes it possible to see that power has been the decisive factor: the values which can be enforced will prevail, and a teacher will be safe and free if he stays within this area. But power shifts. In communities where it has shifted, we see reversals. White teachers are forced to resign; principals are ousted. But the "assimilative" stuff of the schools is still being demanded, as the Negroes ask for the traditional middle-class benefits—success, mobility, money.

Yesterday's Success Today's Failure

Minorities have always composed an important part of the American social structure. The original immigrants (the "old" minorities) accepted the assimilative conditions in the school; and, pragmatically speaking, the system worked for a long time. Thousands of European immigrants went through primary schools in the late 19th and early 20th centuries. The second generation of Jewish, Italian, and Irish immigrants tended to accept the traditional success values, whether or not they held to the pluralistic traditions of their parents. They entered universities in large numbers; and many went on to professional and business careers. Judging by appearances, the system seemed indeed to work.

But it is becoming increasingly obvious that the "new" minorities do not fare this well. Color prejudice clouds the future of many of them; and acculturation is easier for them than assimilation. The language and culture ties which provide

[5] Israel Zangwill. *The Melting Pot.* New York: Macmillan Company, 1916.

security for particular groups cause difficulties in a school system which has not even acceded to the need for dual-language teaching. The invisibility of the poor, the passivity and occasional withdrawals of some minority groups, all militate against assimilation. Ugly inequities, in consequence, characterize schools with large minority populations. Some Negro communities militantly demand desegregation in order to achieve "equality"; others demand separation from the system. The Puerto Rican community campaigns politically for dual-language teaching, more meaningful vocational education, increased attention to English language teaching. The Mexican-American community is beginning to test its strength in the west and southwest. What do all these minority groups want?

The social theorist, Louis Wirth,[6] once constructed a "schema" helpful for viewing minority aspirations and, it may be, predicting minority pressures. As he saw it, minorities may be typed as pluralistic, assimilationist, secessionist, and militant. Each one calls for different strategies; but the aims of the first two types are most relevant here. The Wirth typology permits us to describe Spanish-speaking minority groups as pluralistic, verging on the assimilative; the Negro minority as assimilative, verging on the militant. Also, it offers us a life-cycle view of minority movements:

> The initial goal of an emerging minority group as it becomes aware of ethnic identity is to seek toleration for its cultural differences. By virtue of this striving it constitutes a pluralistic minority. If sufficient toleration and autonomy are attained, the pluralistic minority advances to the assimilationist stage, characterized by the desire for acceptance by and incorporation into the dominant group. Frustration of this desire for full participation is likely to produce (1) secessionist tendencies . . . (2) the drive to become incorporated into another state with which there exists close cultural or historical identification. Progress in either of these directions may in turn lead to the goal of domination over others and the resort to militant methods of achieving the objective. If this goal is actually reached, the group sheds the distinctive characteristic of a minority.[6]

The pushing and shoving described do not occur on an uninhabited island. Minority progress is made against resistance, hostility, and prejudice. The number of minorities in an area, however, seems to have a significant effect upon minority-dominant group relations. According to Wirth, if dominant group attitudes are directed towards a number of minorities, one can be played against the other. Also, he says, in a secular society the perpetuation of any group in a minority status requires that the dominant group resort to sanctions of custom, to law, or to violence, whenever the controls of public opinion, persuasion, and economic pressure fail.

Some educators, feeling morally incapable of taking any of the above positions, cite the "right of withdrawal" and simply cop out. This often means support of the

[6] Louis Wirth. *On Cities and Social Life.* Chicago: University of Chicago Press, 1964.

white middle class's right to flee from the urban schools when they lose control over them. Many middle class people, as is well known, transfer their children to private and suburban schools which they can dominate. Others, impressed by the studies indicating that segregation reinforces hostility, plead for re-integration of the suburb and the city. Certain teachers, too, see new hope in giving responsibility to community representatives and breaking up the bureaucratic structures which dominate the system. They talk of using para-professionals, drawn from various communities to serve as bridges between the professional (but white middle class) teacher and the minority community he serves. Obviously, there is a crisis in the urban centers. Can public education survive at all?

Toward a New Pluralism

We need a new pluralism and the shaping of an *uncommon* school system attractive to both middle-class families and the minority communities, predicated on the notion that knowledge of the minority cultures may be made valid educational stuff. There are the advantages of depth, breadth, and (often) a touch of needed exoticism to freshen the stale air hanging over conformist schools. There are possibilities of creating enriched, world-touching curricula, of widening language teaching and the scope of what is called "American history." Pride might well result for the adults of a suppressed minority group—at last given recognition in the school.

Educators and communities would have to cooperate to bring this about. There would have to be significant commitment on the part of professionals and, as well, on the part of individual minority groups. As assimilative techniques, based on dominant-minority thinking, continue to cause frustration, hostility, and repeated crises, we may have no alternative but to experiment with a new approach to pluralism.

A Reappraisal of the Most Controversial Educational Document of Our Time

CHRISTOPHER JENCKS

Three years have passed since James Coleman and his colleagues issued their now famous report on "Equality of Educational Opportunity." Virtually unnoticed at

From *The New York Times Magazine* (August 10, 1969), 12, 13, 34, 36, 38, 42, 44. ©1969 by The New York Times Company. Reprinted by permission.

the time of its publication, this 737-page monograph has since become the best-known and most controversial piece of educational research of our time.

Like a veritable Bible, the "Coleman Report" is cited today on almost every side of every major educational controversy, usually by people who have not read it and almost always by people who have not understood what the authors meant when they wrote it. It has been used to support arguments for increasing integration in the schools—and to buttress the position of those who would accept segregated schools with community control. It has been cited as evidence that what black children need is good teachers—and as proof that such increases in per pupil expenditure will not close the educational gap between black and white.

The report has also inspired a growing body of scholarly exegesis, interpretation and criticism, so that anyone who wants to know what the report "really" proves must now plow through not only the baffling charts and tables of the original document but dozens of subsequent critiques and reanalyses, most of which are available only in mimeographed form to the cognoscenti. The time has clearly come for a reappraisal.

The Coleman Report was a political football from its very inception. Like much American social science, it was initiated in order to avoid confronting a difficult political problem. In the summer of 1964 Congress had decided to pass a civil-rights law which was expected to end *de jure* school segregation in the South by cutting off Federal funds from segregated systems. The question inevitably arose: what about *de facto* segregation in the North? The expedient answer was that the Commissioner of Education should investigate the problem and report back in two years.

After nearly a year of bureaucratic squabbling and indecision in the U.S. Office of Education, Commissioner Frank Keppel decided to conduct an "Equality of Educational Opportunity" survey. The survey, theoretically covering nearly a million pupils in 6,000 different schools across the nation, was carried out in the fall of 1965. Prime responsibility for planning and analyzing it fell on James Coleman, a distinguished sociologist from Johns Hopkins University with a long record of interest in both education and survey research.

Coleman expected the survey to demonstrate three rather conventional propositions:

1. Nonwhite pupils, North and South, usually attend different schools from white pupils.

2. Nonwhite schools usually have less adequate facilities, inferior curriculums and worse teachers, as well as less affluent and academically adept student bodies.

3. Because they attend those inferior schools, nonwhite pupils learn less than white pupils.

The survey confirmed the first proposition. Black and white pupils are seldom in the same schools, even in the North. Not only that, but the black pupils do learn much less than the white pupils, at least judging by standardized tests of verbal and nonverbal skill, reading comprehension, arithmetic skill and general information.

The typical black first grader scores below about 85 per cent of white first graders. This relative disparity persists throughout elementary and secondary school, and thus the absolute difference between black and white children grows wider as they grow older. A 6-year-old who scores below 85 per cent of his classmates is about one year behind, while a 16-year-old is more than two years behind.

The survey did *not* support the second proposition, that black schools spend significantly less money per pupil than white ones, have substantially larger classes, get worse trained and less experienced teachers, operate in more antiquated and crowded facilities, rely on less adequate textbooks and equipment and so forth. On the contrary, the survey uncovered only one major measurable difference in these items between black and white schools: the black schools had more black teachers. This means that the black children's teachers also come from poorer homes and do worse on tests of academic ability. Black schools in the urban North also tended to have somewhat older buildings and smaller play areas. In other respects, however, black and white schools proved surprisingly similar. Later analyses, while largely confined to Northern urban elementary schools, have shown that schools which serve rich and poor children also have quite similar facilities, curriculums and teachers.

How could the conventional wisdom have been so wrong? The apparent answer is that claims of discrimination have usually been based on the obvious contrast between Northern ghetto schools and white schools in a few affluent nearby suburbs or in the city itself. In most (but not all) cities, the black schools get short-changed. What all such comparisons evidently ignore, however, is the fact that most white Americans live in smaller (and poorer) cities and towns, where the school facilities, curriculum and teachers evidently leave almost as much to be desired as they do in the big-city ghettos, where most blacks live.

More important, even, was the report's conclusion on the third proposition, the expected cause-and-effect relationship between inadequate school resources and low student achievement. In fact, neither black nor white children of a given family background did significantly better in schools with high expenditures, large libraries, accelerated curriculums and so forth. Coleman and his colleagues believed that pupils did slightly better in schools with experienced and articulate teachers, but even this difference was surprisingly small—and the evidence supporting their belief has subsequently proved to be rather shaky.

The report suggests—though it does not state in so many words—that black children clearly get less satisfactory schooling than white children in only one major respect. If a child happens to have a black skin, the odds are very strong that he or she will end up with classmates from impoverished homes and a plethora of learning and behavior problems. A child who attends such a school may be short-changed even if it has first-rate facilities and teachers. Most black sixth-graders, for example, attend schools in which the majority of their classmates are reading at the fourth- or fifth-grade level. This means that even if a black child has the ability to read at sixth-grade level, he will probably not be pushed to do so. The instruction in his classroom will be aimed not at him but at the laggard majority. Furthermore, there is reason to believe that children learn more from one another than from their teachers. If black children attend schools where this "informal curriculum" is based on a vocabulary half as large and on concepts far less abstract than in a white school, their chance of developing academic skills is reduced.

Coleman and his colleagues were extremely anxious to determine whether individual achievement was dependent on a school's social composition. After analyzing their data, they concluded that it was, but that a child was influenced by his classmates' social class background and aspirations rather than by their race. This implied that a poor black child would *not* benefit from attending school with poor white children, but that he *would* benefit from attending with middle-class children, black or white. Coleman and his colleagues also tentatively concluded that black children were more sensitive to peer influences than white children. This implied that a black child would benefit substantially from integration, while a white child would suffer very little. The apparent effects of integration were always small, however, relative to over-all differences in achievement between races, socio-economic groups and individuals.

If differences between schools do not account for most of the observed differences in achievement, what does? By far the most important factor measured in the survey was the ethnic and socio-economic background of the individual child. In addition, there is a strong association between children's achievement levels and their attitudes. Among black children in particular, there is a marked relationship between their achievement and their personal sense of control over their own destinies. Yet even when family background and attitudes are taken into account, more than half the variations in individual achievement remain completely unexplained. Whether this reflects unmeasured genetic differences in aptitude or unmeasured differences in environmental influence is a matter for speculation. One thing it did not seem to represent, however, was unmeasured effects of differences between school environments. The survey showed that the differences between the best and the worst pupils in the same school are invariably far larger than the differences between the best and the worst schools. Indeed, eliminating all school-to-school differences would only reduce the total variation in achievement by about 20 per cent. This does not definitely prove that schools have no role in generating inequality, since there could theoretically be systematic discrimination against certain kinds of pupils within most schools. Still, it is hard to believe that within-school differences play a large role in inequality when between-school differences play such a small role. Coleman and his colleagues therefore concluded that the major reasons for unequal academic achievement must lie outside the school.

This brief summary of the Coleman Report's major findings hardly does justice to the voluminous text, but it does suggest why the report became a major focus of political debate. The report was published at a time when America was vacillating between two different strategies for helping the disadvantaged. Some people advocated racial and socio-economic integration of the schools—and of the larger society. Others argued that integration was unattainable, undesirable or both; the only realistic strategy was to accept segregation and make black schools as good as white ones. The Coleman Report implied—though it did not say explicitly—that *neither* strategy would help achievement much. But insofar as anything was likely to work, the report seemed to indicate that integration was a better bet than what had come to be called "compensatory" education. Yet at the same time the finding that parental interest and pupil attitudes were strongly associated with achievement seemed to give oblique support to those who believed that parental participation and/or control over all-black schools might make a critical difference to student achievement.

The report's conclusions were inevitably subjected to stringent and sometimes extravagant criticism. The report had been prepared in great haste to meet the Congressional deadline, and the authors had had no time to examine many obvious objections to their tentative conclusions. Skeptics have been able to offer a variety of speculative reasons why the report's conclusions might be wrong, and those who have political reasons for wanting to discredit or ignore the report have naturally found such speculations very persuasive. For the past two years I have been part of a group of Harvard social scientists trying to determine whether any of the hypothetical objections to the report's conclusions are actually correct. My judgment is that the report's broad conclusions were sound, even though many of its specific methods and findings were wrong.

One common criticism of the survey has been that more than 10 per cent of the school districts in the original sample refused to cooperate, including such major cities as Chicago and Los Angeles. Some districts evidently feared that the Federal Government would use the survey to prove they were discriminating against minority groups. Other districts—especially those being sued for *de facto* segregation—feared that minority groups would get hold of the survey results and use them in court or in the press. Some districts also feared that simply asking questions about sensitive racial issues might stir up trouble in the schools. In addition, many schools in nominally cooperative districts failed to return data because it was too much bother or perhaps—a more serious matter—because they had something to hide. As a result, complete returns were received from only about 60 per cent of the schools in the original sample.

There were clearly some small differences between participating and nonparticipating schools, and selective participation may well have led to a slight underestimate of the qualitative differences between black and white schools. But there is no reason to suppose that nonparticipation led to an underestimate of the relationship between school quality and student achievement. It hardly seems likely, for example, that the dynamics of education in Chicago and Los Angeles, which refused to participate, differ significantly from Detroit and San Francisco, which agreed to do so. On the contrary, the dynamics of education are probably much the same in one big city as in another. The problem of nonparticipation is therefore probably a nonproblem.

A second criticism of the survey has been that the information provided by the superintendents, principals, teachers and pupils in the sample schools may not have been accurate. This criticism arose largely because of doubt that black children's teachers and facilities could really be the equal of those given white children. Since the Office of Education made no site visits to check up on the accuracy of replies given by principals and teachers, no definite answer to this charge is possible. Data supplied by state departments of education suggest, however, that the principals' replies about facilities were probably fairly accurate. Direct interviewing of parents in two communities likewise showed that most (though not all) of the pupils' responses were reasonably accurate. And the replies of principals, teachers and students to similar questions show a fairly high level of internal consistency for most "objective" items. On the other hand, questions which involved subjective judgment of any kind did *not* elicit internally consistent answers. The results of such subjective "attitude" questions must therefore be treated with great caution.

A third criticism of the report has been that the authors should not have concentrated on the determinants of verbal ability to the exclusion of reading, mathematics and general information. Those who believe that black people are peculiarly "nonverbal" have even argued that the decision to stress verbal ability was fundamentally racist. Unfortunately, black children did as badly on the tests of other abilities as on the verbal tests. Furthermore, while some individual children did well on one test and badly on another, schools as a whole either did well on them all or badly on them all. A Northern urban elementary school's mean verbal score, for example, correlated almost perfectly with its mean reading and math scores. Under these circumstances it hardly matters which test we use to measure over-all school achievement.

A fourth line of attack on the report has been more technical. The authors of the report employed a number of dubious statistical techniques and made a variety of mechanical errors in handling and labeling their data. But they also recognized that such errors were likely, given the extreme haste with which they worked, and they were generous in helping others reanalyze the data more meticulously. These analyses have shown that while the report's broadest conclusions were correct, many important details were wrong. In particular, and contrary to what some critics have argued, the net effect of the report's various errors was to *under*-estimate the importance of family background and *over*-estimate the importance of school in determining achievement.

A fifth criticism of the report has been that the authors made unwarranted causal inferences from their one-shot survey, which by its very nature could reveal only patterns of association rather than prove causation. Two examples illustrate the problem.

The report uncovered a strong association between teacher verbal ability and student achievement in secondary schools. Though they listed a number of qualifications, the authors concluded that able high school teachers probably boosted student achievement. Yet the report's data could equally well lead to the conclusion that school systems were assigning able students to schools with able teachers, or that they were assigning able teachers to schools with able pupils. Since we know from experience that both practices are widespread at the secondary level, it seems rash to assume that there need be any direct causal link between teacher ability and student achievement to explain the observed association between the two.

Fortunately, these problems are far less serious at the elementary level. Students are allocated to elementary schools largely on the basis of residence, race and social status, all of which were measured in the survey. With luck and ingenuity the effects of such allocation can be discounted and the effects of various school characteristics can then be estimated. Since there is little evidence that student transfers at the elementary school level are based on ability (as distinct from family background), the mean achievement of first graders entering a given elementary school can also be used to estimate the mean initial ability of sixth graders in the same school. With these precautions, causal inferences are considerably safer than at the secondary level; and when these precautions are taken, it turns out that facilities, curriculum and teacher characteristics are even less important than Coleman and his colleagues supposed. A student's peers may, however, have a modest effect on his achievement.

Another instance of ambiguous causation was the association between attitudes and achievement. The survey showed, for example, that students who did well on achievement tests were more likely to say that their parents expected them to go to college. The authors concluded that parental expectations probably had an important influence on children's achievement. Yet it would be equally reasonable to conclude that children's achievement had an important influence on their parents' expectations. Most parents know that if their child cannot read competently, he is unlikely to attend college, and the child is likely to be aware of this attitude and report it when asked. This same difficulty arises with all the report's inferences about the effects of attitudes on achievement.

What, then, is the present consensus about the policy implications of Coleman's survey? The answer is that no consensus exists, even among experts. My own judgments are as follows:

1. The resources—both fiscal and human—devoted to black and white children's schooling are not dramatically different, except perhaps in certain parts of the South. Nor do we devote substantially greater resources to educating middle-class children than to educating lower-class children.

2. Variations in schools' fiscal and human resources have very little effect on student achievement—probably even less than the Coleman Report originally implied.

3. The report's assertion that peers have a consistent effect on achievement may or may not be correct. My guess, based on available data, is that peers *do* have an effect, but that it is relatively small.

None of this denies that unusually dedicated and talented individuals can create schools in which initially disadvantaged children learn a remarkable amount. But it does deny that the achievement levels of large numbers of disadvantaged children can be appreciably enhanced by spending more money, hiring better teachers, buying new textbooks or making any of the other changes that reformers normally advocate.

If improved student achievement is our goal, the Coleman Report's implication is obvious: we must alter the whole social system rather than just tinker with the schools. There is plenty of evidence that major changes in a child's social and cultural environment will affect his intellectual development, often dramatically. Bruno Bettelheim and others have chronicled the impact of the Israeli kibbutz on hitherto deprived North African and Yemenite Jews. Here in America we know that children raised on Long Island do far better, even in first grade, than those raised in Appalachia. Similarly, children raised in Jewish homes do better than those raised in Christian homes, even in the same city. And the World War II draftees who grew up in the America of 1917-1941 did far better on standard tests than the World War I draftees who grew up in the America of 1900-1917. Intellectual skills are, therefore, not just a function of genetic differences. But neither are they a function of school differences. If the Coleman survey convinces us of that basic truth, it will have served its purpose.

Does this mean that we should simply let inferior schools rot? I think not. Good schools *can* make a difference—if we know what kind of a difference we want them to make.

Underlying the comments of most people who discuss the Coleman Report is the assumption that academic achievement is the most important objective of schooling, and that if school reform does not affect achievement, it is worthless. Yet despite much popular rhetoric, there is little evidence that academic competence is critically important to adults in most walks of life. If you ask employers why they won't hire dropouts, for example, or why they promote certain kinds of people and not others, they seldom complain that dropouts can't read. Instead, they complain that dropouts don't get to work on time, can't be counted on to do a careful job, don't get along with others in the plant or office, can't be trusted to keep their hands out of the till and so on. Nor do the available survey data suggest that the adult success of people from disadvantaged backgrounds depends primarily on their intellectual skills. If you compare black men who do well on the Armed Forces Qualifications Test to those who do badly, for example, you find that a black man who scores as high as the average white still earns only about two-thirds what the average white earns. Not only that, he hardly earns more than the average black. Even for whites, the mental abilities measured by the A.F.Q.T. account for less than a tenth of the variation in earnings.

With these observations in mind, go visit a slum school and ask yourself what the school is actually doing. You will usually find that it seems to share the employers' priorities. It devotes very little time to academic skills. Instead, the teachers spend their days in a vain effort to teach the children to behave in what they (and probably most employers) regard as the proper way. The teachers' ideas about proper behavior are silly in some respects. Nonetheless, they are probably right in feeling that what their children need first and foremost is not academic skill but such "middle-class" virtues as self-discipline and self-respect. It is the school's failure to develop these personal characteristics, not its failure to teach history or physics or verbal skill, that lies behind the present upheavals in the schools. And it is this failure to which reformers should be addressing themselves.

From this perspective the best index of a school's success or failure may not be reading scores but the number of rocks thrown through its windows in an average month. The Coleman survey does not speak to this question.

PART

III The Youth: Commitment and Confrontation

Many labels have been used to characterize the present generation of American youth—"the tense generation," "the cool generation," "the fun-oriented" and "the violence-oriented generation," "the conforming generation," "the new breed," "the alienated," "the uncommitted." As labels, they serve the function of all such terms when used for a subdivision of the population: they serve to stereotype whole groups with characteristics that in fact may be attributed only to a portion of them; they serve to fragment and divide a large problem or central concern by viewing it in a narrow context, so narrow, in fact, that the whole is obscured. Yet, the real danger in the use of such labels is that they are not totally untrue. Because they do express a partial truth, their acceptance without further examination prevents any real understanding. In the case of youth, the labels inhibit their achieving a more positive orientation.

If they are the tense generation, can it not be said that the age itself is a tense one to live in, for youth and adults alike? Their "coolness" is one way of responding to baffling situations over which they may have little control. If they feel alienated from the rest of society, particularly the adult world, can this not be accepted as a response to the triviality of life that often characterizes adult society and creates in youth a desire for thrills, excitement, and "kicks"? Or is it because certain youths see earlier and more clearly than others the "phoniness" of adults—the wide divergence that exists between their professed beliefs and values and their actions? Is this alienation not accentuated by the "cult of youth" developing rapidly in adult society itself? The adult members of this cult, who lack the ability or the willingness to provide direction, models, or guidance for the young, adopt in an indiscriminate fashion the ideas and values (or lack of them) of youth themselves. This adult worship at the shrine of youth is expressed in many patterns—in the commercial exploitation of the adolescent market, in a misunderstood "permissiveness" that caters to youthful desires, in attempts of adults to re-live their youth or to realize their ambitions in the lives of their children, or in a simple belief that "if you can't beat them, join them."

This adult fawning is interpreted by youth as a sign of weakness (a feeling they themselves are experiencing), which breeds distrust of the adult society as a whole. Alienation is further increased. What most youth want and what they want adult society to assist them in achieving is not exploitation, but the development of some sense of their own worth; not worship, but the achievement of some measure of self-esteem; not adult imitation of youth's society, but adult guidance in creating some conception of their own identity. Although it must be admitted that schools alone cannot be charged with the full responsibility of these tasks, they should not shrink from providing a large measure of assistance to youth in making a better transition into adulthood. Too often the schools are perpetuating adolescence into adult life.

The schools are also frequently guilty of instilling into the young a mere willingness to accept things as they are. The competition, the system of rewards and punishments, and the preference given to the "well-adjusted" student all force a conformity that soon dulls feelings and intellect. Students become trained in accepting at face value whatever is said and soon they are responding automatically to the world around them. Each new idea presented, each new fad to come along is accepted without real discrimination. Before long, students are not engaged in any worthwhile endeavor, nor vitally concerned in anything. They are uncommitted, alienated, cool. In this state youth not only reject adult values, but are not even concerned with their existence.

Real growth in children and youth comes about through struggles and conflicts. It comes about when realistic opportunities are provided to develop an awareness to alternatives, to examine, to analyze, to discuss, to refine, to discriminate, and to evaluate all areas of life including their own. When these opportunities are made available by the adult society and when positive guidance is given, most youth respond eagerly. Such experiences among youth and adults would aid tremendously in establishing or re-establishing a needed rapport based on mutual regard and respect between the young and old.

These and other concerns are discussed by a distinguished group of authors whose positions vary widely because they approach their tasks from differing perspectives. They represent a spectrum of views ranging from the cautious to the radical, and each in his own manner presents challenging ideas and stimulating thoughts. Their positions regarding youth in contemporary society should be viewed against the background of material read in the first two parts of this anthology.

In reviewing the articles in Part III, the reader should also consider their application in understanding the special problems of a large portion of youth in America. "There may even be something more than paranoid truth in the thought that today the most vehement complaint of the young against us can be made with greater justice against them, that it is they who are now manipulating us . . . forcing us to conform to their authoritarian and bureaucratic plans for the renovation of the modern world."[1] These are the words of John W. Aldridge writing in Harper's Magazine as he examines the "power" the young have achieved in the past twenty-five years. In an article aimed at understanding the reasons behind the

[1]John W. Aldridge, "In the Country of the Young," *Harper's Magazine* (October 1969), 49–64.

youth power play, Daniel Sisson calls on students to re-establish "constructive dialogue" between themselves and the community.

Sociologist Lewis Feuer examines the complex psychological origins of human idealism exemplified by various student movements. Feuer believes participants in such movements, as bearers of a higher ethic than the surrounding society, must be at odds with the "social system." They serve as the searching agents of social change and prevent society itself from becoming static.

Paul Goodman compares today's student protests with the religious crisis of the Reformation in the fifteen-hundreds. Goodman's writings begin with an assumption that young people doubt that there is "a nature of things," and he studies this "religious crisis" in detail in his article, "The New Reformation."

Two authors take opposing positions on the question of a "generation gap." Roger Rapoport explains why we need one. Joseph Adelson asks, "What gap?" Rapoport predicts it will widen so by 1980 that a "new national fault line" will rock the entire country. Adelson believes we may yield to the idea that there is a gap too easily. We oversimplify. He urges a genuine examination of the question.

In a summary of a series of exhaustive interviews with student "revolutionaries" at Barnard and Columbia, Herbert Hendin urges us to delve into the problems which drove these radicals to their particular form of protest. He offers some explanations of his own but opens up the subject for objective analysis. John D. Rockefeller 3rd updates an article that he first published in Saturday Review (December 14, 1968), as he joins Hendin in analyzing young revolutionaries. Rockefeller calls for "youth-Establishment collaboration on the pressing social problems of our time."

The final article in Part III is by Eric Hoffer. Reviewing the role of the young in our society, Hoffer dismisses "age" in favor of the "common" man as the more meaningful influence that we must reckon with in understanding "Whose Country Is America?"

Questions for Discussion and Further Study

1. In "The Youth Dialogue," Daniel Sisson outlines several plans for bringing the young and old together in meaningful communication. What are the basic differences in the Rustin idea and the student-community dialogue approach? Are these valid plans? What other approacher could you suggest to accomplish Sisson's objectives?

2. Lewis Feuer offers a thesis that every student movement of consequence attaches itself to a major "carrier" movement, such as a peasant, labor, nationalist, racial, or anti-colonial movement. What are your reactions to Feuer's arguments? If you are inclined to agree with him, develop a detailed case for his argument using one current movement with which you are familiar. If you disagree, what questions would you want to ask him in an interview?

3. In "The New Reformation," Paul Goodman charges that young dissidents

never offer a constructive program. Herbert Hendin also reviews this question. Did the two authors agree in their conclusions? Goodman presents arguments which indicated that most of the issues of protest have been immediate gut issues; the tactics have been mostly disruptive, without coherent proposals for a better society. What was Hendin's position? What are your reactions to Goodman's charges? If you agree with Goodman, what alternative "positive" protest methods would you propose? If you believe Goodman oversimplified the problems, what arguments would you present to try to convince him to change his mind? Did Hendin provide you with any additional arguments to support your postition?

4. Two authors discuss the generation gap. An interesting contrast is presented in the view of Roger Rapoport as opposed to that of Joseph Adelson. Both are essentially sympathetic with youth, yet they disagree about a number of things especially youth's purposes and motivations. From your own experience, with which author are you more inclined to agree? Do you see your generation in the manner in which it has been characterized? What additional ideas need to be presented for a more adequate presentation?

5. In "Whose Country Is America?" Eric Hoffer proposes a "ritual of work" whereby every boy and girl reaching age 17 or on graduation from high school, would be given an opportunity to spend two years earning a living at good pay. Hoffer believes that federal, state, and local government support of such a program would provide for the "positive" passage from boyhood to manhood and contribute to a solution of many of our pressing problems. What is your reaction to Hoffer's proposal? Would it really be an opportunity for youth to learn, earn, and mature? Is there a better way to implement a plan similar to Hoffer's?

Selected References

Aldridge, John W. "In the Country of the Young." *Harper's Magazine* (October 1969), 49–64.

"An Embattled Hypothesis: An Interview with Arthur P. Jensen." *The Center Magazine* (September 1969), 77–80.

Berger, Bennett M. "The New Stage of American Man—Almost Endless Adolescence." *The New York Times Magazine* (November 2, 1969), 32–33, 131–136.

Bettelheim, Bruno. "The Anatomy of Academic Discontent." *Change* (May–June 1969), 18–26.

"Class of '69: The Violent Years." *Newsweek* (June 23, 1969), 68–73.

Cottle, Thomas J. "Parents and Child—The Hazards of Equality." *Saturday Review* (February 1, 1969), 16–19, 46–48.

Dempsey, David. "Bruno Bettelheim Is Dr. No." *The New York Times Magazine* (January 11, 1970), 22–23, 107–111.

Dunbar, Ernest. "Vanguard of the Campus Revolt." *Look* (October 1, 1968), 23, 25, 26, 28–29.

Ford, Franklin L. "To Live with Complexity." *Harvard Today* (Autumn 1968), 4–12.

Gardner, John W. "Message for a Revolutionary Generation: You Can Remake This Society." *Look* (July 17, 1969), 85–86.

Goldberg, Arthur. "Juvenatrics: A Study of Prolonged Adolescence." *Clearing House* (April 1964), 488–492.

Goodman, Paul. *Compulsory Mis-Education.* New York: Horizon Press, 1964.

Gordon, Edmund W. "Relevance or Revolt." *Perspectives on Education* (Fall 1969), 10–11, 13–16.
Gussow, Mel. "Arlo: 'Kids Want to Be Free'." *The New York Times*(January 11, 1970), D1, D23.
Harris, Dale B. "Changing Values 1." *Young Children* (March 1965), 230–248.
Hechinger, Grace, and Fred M. *Teen-Age Tyranny.* New York: William Morrow, 1963.
Jaffa, Neubert. "The Disadvantaged Child." *The Instructor* (May 1965), 15–18.
Keats, John. "We Must Be Doing Something Right." *Quest* (December 1969), 14–15.
———, "Youth Is Always Revolting." *Quest* (September 1969), 28–29, 33.
Kelman, Steven. "These Are Three of the Alienated." *The New York Times Magazine* (October 22, 1967), 39, 140, 142, 143–148.
Keniston, Kenneth. "Notes on Young Radicals." *Change* (November–December 1969), 25–33.
———. "Youth: Changes and Violence." *HGSEA Bulletin* (Winter–Spring 1968), 2–9.
———. "You Have to Grow Up in Scarsdale to Know How Bad Things Really Are." *The New York Times Magazine* (April 27, 1969), 27–28, 122, 124, 126, 128–130.
Kennan, George F. "Rebels Without a Program." *The New York Times Magazine* (January 21, 1968), 22–23, 60, 62, 69, 71.
Kukla, David A. "Protest in Black and White: Student Radicals in High Schools." *The Bulletin of the National Association of Secondary School Principals* (January 1970), 72–86.
Main, Jeremy. "A Special Report on Youth." *Fortune* (June 1969), 73–74.
Marin, Peter. "Adolescence and the Apocalypse." *This Magazine Is About Schools* (Spring 1969), 41–63.
Mayer, Milton. "The Children's Crusade." *The Center Magazine* (September 1969), 2–7.
Mayer, Henry. "No Peace in Our Time." *Change* (January–February 1969), 22–25.
Menninger, Walter, M.D. "Student Demonstrations and Confrontations." *Menninger Quarterly* (Spring 1969), 1–14.
———. "Youth and Violence." *Menninger Quarterly* (Winter 1969-1970), 22, 24–30.
Nowlis, Helen H. "Youth and the Drug Problem." *New York State Education* (December 1968), 11–13, 28–29.
Nyquist, Ewald B. "Heed the Voices of Youth." *New York State Education* (October 1969), 11–12.
Postman, Neil. "Once Upon a Time–A Fable of Student Power." *The New York Times Magazine* (June 14, 1970), 10–11.
Roberts, Steven V. "The Children's Crusade–What Now?" *Change* (January–February 1969), 19–21.
Roberts, Wallace. "The Young Protestants." *Saturday Review* (December 27, 1969), 22.
Swados, Harvey. "The Joys and Terrors of Sending the Kids to College." *The New York Times Magazine* (February 14, 1971), 13, 28–32.
Toole, K. Ross. "I Am Tired of the Tyrany of Spoiled Brats." *U.S. News & World Report* (April 13, 1970), 76–78.
"The Student Revolt: Where It Is Headed." *U.S. News & World Report* (October 13, 1969), 38–40.
Tyrmand, Leopold. "Revolutionaries: European Vs. American." *The New York Times Magazine* (February 15, 1970), 25, 41–43.
"Why Students Act That Way–A Gallup Study." *U.S. News & World Report* (June 2, 1969), 34–35.
Winthrop, Henry. "The Sheltered Generation: Its Present and Future in American Education." *The Educational Forum* (January 1969), 231–240.

The Youth Dialogue

DANIEL SISSON

The classical model of dialogue established by Plato meant more than simply a series of conversations. It required tolerance of another's opinion and willingness to submit one's own to scrutiny. It encompassed the entire society, bringing the community together through a constant exchange of ideas. It transmitted knowledge from generation to generation and thus became the vehicle of communication for the society. In essence, the dialogue *was* the *polis*; it *was* Greek civilization.

It is important for youth today to recall that the Greeks were especially fond of using the dialogue to expose the foibles of their institutions and the pseudo-opinions of their artists, be they politicians, educators, merchants, or even poets. Equally significant, Socrates lived during a period of turmoil in Athens roughly parallel to the unrest gripping twentieth-century America.

In this twentieth-century America communication between youth and the adults has become tenuous indeed. For millions of young people the dialogue has already broken down in what they regard as a society gone mad. The turbulence indicates, among other things, that adult society has failed to communicate its ideals to the young, especially in the ghetto areas. For them dialogue has long since ceased. For many more of today's young people who still feel a bond with society, the trinity of peace, justice, and freedom seems no more than the cant of adult apologists. Told that all three exist in American society, the young see instead almost daily occurrences of massive violence, injustice, and tyranny. Equality is becoming synonymous with class warfare, its original meaning lost, its denial ringing forth in the bitter assertion of a bitter young man: "Violence is as American as cherry pie!"

More subtle contradictions reveal a growing gap between the generations. Hypocrisy reigns supreme in a social system that tells young people to discipline themselves while their elders do as they please, to fight for their country's "freedom" when what they really believe is threatened is their economic system. Meanwhile, disfranchised youth, held incommunicado because they cannot vote, vainly ask the government to change its policies. Communication proceeds in a straight line from adults to children. There is no feedback and hence no dialogue.

Education, politics, religion, the economic system, all calculate to bring the young into "the fold." Yet, something has gone wrong. The young, in many cases are not falling into the "bag." We are witnessing a strange phenomenon among youth, perhaps a prelude to full-scale rebellion: youth pitted against their elders. Ordinarily, open rebellion would suggest chaos in the society, and its ultimate

From the *Center Occasional Paper* (1968), 17–18. Reprinted by permission, from the Center Occasional Paper, "The Civilization of The Dialogue," a publication of the Center for the Study of Democratic Institutions in Santa Barbara, California.

disintegration. In this instance, I do not feel that we have reached the nadir of our civilization as much as we have descended to the lowest level of communication. Many young people have simply turned the adults off.

With their peers, on the other hand, they are communicating in new and more significant ways. They are more open, more trusting, more able to converse uninhibitedly together. The rejection of the gray-flannel suit may herald the beginning of a new and vital dialogue as the conventional barriers drop away. Into a culture long characterized by suspicion and alienation, youth, with its emphasis on love and "flower power," is injecting a disarming freshness. When people trust in one another, or even pretend to love one another, they will at the least communicate, and at best they will teach each other. Force inhibits the dialogue and makes constructive conversation impossible; love and respect promote it.

The young people most successful in articulating their problems are the students. It is probably upon them that the success or failure of future dialogue rests. Since they are highly critical, they must develop a sense of the dialectic. They must carry the dialogue to those in power who will listen. In short, they must set the tone of the dialogue. To those students who think in terms of community, the need to involve all parts of young society will be immediately apparent, for the possibility of engaging the adult world in a constructive dialogue will require the participation of more than an intellectual handful. Radical action will perhaps provide the cohesive element, but radical within the context of the dialogue. All theory, strategy, programs, and solutions must be subjected to the reality of the dialectic—and always with the good of society in mind. What is needed is a plan of action, political in nature, that will capture the imagination of the entire society. The prerequisites are a commitment to reason and truth, respect for human dignity, and perseverance.

One plan might be Bayard Rustin's suggestion that all students who attend high school and college be guaranteed an annual income by the federal government. Economic independence would enable students to devote their free time to educating the Negro in the ghetto. Dialogue between the student community and the uneducated minorities has the potential of changing the political climate of the entire society. The concept of students using their talents and minds during their training years for constructive work has major implications in terms of future political responsibility. Their elders, realizing the political significance of such a coalition, might be drawn into the dialogue. So too might those among the young who up until now have been largely apolitical.

Another plan perhaps more practical than Rustin's might be the setting up of small institutions at colleges and universities, the specific function of which would be to stimulate a dialogue between the students and the community. Within ten years there will be a college and a university built in this country every ten days. By 1985, there will be more than 3,000 colleges and universities in the United States. The student population is on the verge of an explosion, with the potential almost overnight to reshape society. Students who are in a position of leadership today will not, at least in the formal sense, remain enrolled forever at their college or university. New leaders will arise, and their ideas may be as radically different from ours as ours are from those of the generations that came before us. It seems only sensible to begin a process—a dialogue, if you will—that might enable us to communicate with those who will follow. It will be a lifelong job.

The Conflict of Generations

LEWIS S. FEUER

The distinctive character of student movements arises from the union in them of motives of youthful love, on the one hand, and those springing from the conflict of generations on the other. We shall thus be inquiring into the complex psychological origins of human idealism, for we cannot understand the destructive pole of student movements until we have brought to light the obscure unconscious workings of generational conflict. Then perhaps we shall know why student movements have been fated to tragedy.

To their own consciousness, students in student movements have been the bearers of a higher ethic than the surrounding society. Certainly in their essential character student movements are historical forces which are at odds with the "social system." A society is never altogether a social system precisely because such contra-systemic "unsocialized" agencies such as student movements arise. As Walter Weyl said: "Adolescence is the true day for revolt, the day when obscure forces, as mysterious as growth, push us, trembling, out of our narrow lives into the wide throbbing life beyond self." No society ever altogether succeeds in molding the various psychological types which comprise it to conform to its material, economic requirements. If there were a genuine correspondence between the material, economic base and the psychological superstructure, then societies would be static social systems, and basic social change would not take place. In every society, however, those psychological types and motivations which the society suppresses become the searching agents of social change. Thus psycho-ethical motives, which are not only independent of the socio-economic base but actually contrary to the economic ethics that the social system requires, become primary historical forces.

The Russian revolutionary student movement is the classic case of the historic workings of the ethical consciousness. When in the 1860s and 1870s several thousand student youth, inspired by feelings of guilt and responsibility for the

Excerpted from *The Conflict of Generations: The Character and Significance of Student Movements*, by Lewis S. Feuer (New York: Basic Books, 1969), pp. 3–27, 529–531.

backward people, embarked on their "back-to-the-people" movement, it was an unparalleled collective act of selfless idealism . . .

The students' ethical consciousness was utterly independent of class interests and class position. The largest single group among those who were arrested in the back-to-the-people movement from 1873 to 1877 were children of the nobility. They could have availed themselves of the ample openings in the governmental bureaucracy. Instead, many of them chose a path of self-sacrifice and suffering. Rebuffed by the peasants, the revolutionary student youth later gave themselves to the most extreme self-immolation of individual terrorism. And when terrorism failed to produce the desired social change, circles of student intellectuals provided the first nuclei of the Social Democratic party. Lenin aptly said that the intellectuals brought a socialist consciousness to the workers, who by themselves would not have gone beyond trade union aspirations. The intellectuals Lenin referred to were indeed largely the self-sacrificing revolutionary students.

The ethic of the Russian student generations was not shaped by the institutional requirements of the society. The universal theme of generational revolt, which cuts across all societies, produced in Russia a "conflict of generations" of unparalleled intensity because of special social circumstances. The Russian students lived their external lives in a social reality which was absolutist, politically tyrannical, and culturally backward; internally, on the other hand, they lived in a milieu imbued with Western cultural values. Their philosophical and idealistic aims transcended the social system, and were out of keeping with it; the philosophical culture and the social system were at odds with each other, in "contradiction." The revolutionists, we might say, were historical transcendentalists, not historical materialists. The government opened universities to provide recruits for its bureaucracy. Some students followed the appointed path, but the universities became the centers not only for bureaucratic education but for revolutionary dedication. The idealistic student as a psychological type was recalcitrant to the specifications of the social system.

The civil rights movement in the United States has likewise owed much to students as the bearers of an ethical vocation in history. A wave of sit-ins which spread through Negro college towns began on February 1, 1960, when four freshmen from the all-Negro Agricultural and Technical College at Greensboro, North Carolina, sat down at the lunch counter of the local Woolworth dime store. The surrounding community was puzzled that it was precisely "the best educated, the most disciplined and cultured—and essentially middle class—Negro students" who took the self-sacrificing initiative. Moreover, it was recognized generally, to use one writer's words, that "for the time being it is the students who have given a lift to the established civil rights organizations rather than the other way around." Then in the next years came movements which resembled even more the "back to the people" movement of the Russian studentry. The Freedom Riders of 1961, the several hundred white students in the Mississippi Summer Project of 1964 risking their lives to establish Freedom Schools among the Negroes, were descendants in spirit of the Russian students of the preceding century.

Nonetheless, the duality of motivation which has spurred student movements has always borne its duality of consequence. On the one hand, student movements during the past hundred and fifty years have been the bearers of a higher ethic for social reconstruction, of altruism, and of generous emotion. On the other hand, with all the uniformity of a sociological law, they have imposed on the political process a choice of means destructive both of self and of the goals which presumably were sought. Suicidalism and terrorism have both been invariably present in student movements. A youth-weighted rate of suicide is indeed characteristic of all countries in which large-scale revolutionary student movements are found. In what we might call a "normal" country, or one in which there is a "generational equilibrium," "suicide," as Louis Dublin said, "is much more prevalent in advanced years than during youth." But a "normal" country is one without a revolutionary student movement. Where such movements have existed, where countries are thus characterized by a severe conflict of generations, the rate of suicide has been highest precisely for the youthful group. Nihilism has tended to become the philosophy of student movements not only because it constitutes a negative critique of society; it is also a self-critique that is moved by an impulse toward self-annihilation . . . .

. . . Every student movement tries to attach itself to a "carrier" movement of more major proportions—such as a peasant, labor, nationalist, racial, or anti-colonial movement. We may call the latter the "carrier" movements by way of analogy with the harmonic waves superimposed on the carrier wave in physics. But the superimposition of waves of social movements differs in one basic respect from that of physical movements. The student movement gives a new qualitative character and direction to social change. It imparts to the carrier movement a quality of emotion, dualities of feeling, which would otherwise have been lacking. Emotions issuing from the students' unconscious, and deriving from the conflict of generations, impose or attach themselves to the underlying political carrier movement, and deflect it in irrational directions. Given a set of alternative paths—rational or irrational—for realizing a social goal—the influence of a student movement will be toward the use of the most irrational means to achieve the end. Student movements are thus what one would least expect—among the most irrationalist in history . . . .

In the case of the Russian student movement, it was the opinion of the most distinguished anarchist, Peter Kropotkin, that "the promulgation of a constitution was extremely near at hand during the last few months of the life of Alexander II." Kropotkin greatly admired the idealism of the Russian students, yet he felt their intervention had been part of an almost accidental chain of circumstances that had defeated Russia's hopes. Bernard Pares, the historian, who also witnessed the masochist-terrorist characteristics of the Russian students at first hand, wrote, "The bomb that killed Alexander II put an end to the faint beginnings of Russian constitutionalism." A half-hour before the Czar set out on his last journey on March 1, 1881, he approved the text of a decree announcing the establishment of a commission likely to lead to the writing of a constitution. "I have consented to this measure," said Alexander II, "although I do not conceal from myself the fact that this is the first step toward a constitution." Instead, the students' acts of Czar-killing and self-killing brought into Russian politics all the psychological overtones of sons destroying their fathers; their dramatic idealism projected on a national political scale the emotional pattern of "totem and taboo," the revolt and guilt of the primal sons Freud described. People turned in shock from the sick, self-destructive students; the liberals felt as if they had had the ground pulled out from under them . . . .

The history of civilization bears witness to certain universal themes. They assert themselves in every era, and they issue from the deepest universals in human nature. Every age sees its class struggles and imperialistic drives, just as every age sees its ethical aspirations transcend economic interest. Every society has among its members examples of all the varieties of motivation and temperament; it has its scientists and warriors, its entrepreneurs and withdrawers. Thus, too, generational conflict, generational struggle, has been a universal theme of history.

Unlike class struggle, however, the struggle of generations has been little studied and little understood. Class conflicts are easy to document. Labor movements have a continuous and intelligible history. Student movements, by contrast, have a fitful and transient character, and even seem lacking in the substantial dignity which a subject for political sociology should have. Indeed the student status, to begin with, unlike that of the workingman, is temporary; a few brief years, and the quantum-like experience in the student movement is over. Nevertheless, the history of our contemporary world has been basically affected by student movements. Social revolutions in Russia, China, and Burma sprang from student movements, while governments in Korea, Japan, and the Sudan have fallen in recent years largely because of massive student protest. Here, then, is a recurrent phenomenon of modern times which challenges our understanding.

Generational struggle demands categories of understanding unlike those which enable us to understand the class struggle. Student movements, unlike those of workingmen, are born of vague, undefined emotions which seek for some issue, some cause, to which to attach themselves. A complex of urges—altruism, idealism, revolt, self-sacrifice and self-destruction—searches the social order for a strategic avenue of expression. Labor movements have never had to search for issues in the way in which student movements do. A trade union, for instance, calls a strike because the workingmen want higher wages, better conditions of labor, shorter hours, more safety measures, more security. A trade union is a rational organization in the sense that its conscious aims are based on grievances which are well understood and on ambitions which are clearly defined. The wage demands and the specific grievances of workingmen are born directly of their conditions of life. Their existence determines their consciousness, and in this sense the historical materialism of Karl Marx is indeed the best theoretical framework for explaining the labor movement. The conflict of generations, on the other hand, derives from deep, unconscious sources, and the outlook and philosophy of student movements are rarely materialistic. If labor seeks to better its living conditions as directly as possible, student movements sacrifice their own economic interests for the sake of a vision of a nobler life for the lowliest. If historical materialism is the ideology of the working class, then historical idealism is the ideology of student movements. If "exploitation" is the master term for defining class conflict, then "alienation" does similar service for the conflict of generations . . . .

. . . We may define a student movement as a combination of students inspired by aims which they try to explicate in a political ideology, and moved by an emotional rebellion in which there is always present a disillusionment with and rejection of the values of the older generation; moreover, the members of a student movement have the conviction that their generation has a special historical mission to fulfill where the older generation, other elites, and other classes have failed . . . .

A student movement thus is founded upon a coalescence of several themes and conditions. It tends to arise in societies which are gerontocratic—that is, where the older generation possesses a disproportionate amount of economic and political power and social status. Where the influences of religion, ideology, and the family are especially designed to strengthen the rule of the old, there a student movement, as an uprising of the young, will be most apt to occur. As against the gerontocracy, a student movement in protest is moved by a spirit of what we may call *juvenocracy.* If an element of patriarchy prevails in most governments, the student movement by contrast is inspired by a will to *filiarchy.* Gerontocratic societies, however, have often existed without experiencing a revolt of the younger generation. A gerontocratic order is not a sufficient condition for the rise of a student movement. Among other factors, there must also be present a feeling that the older generation has failed. We may call this experience the process of the "de-authoritization" of the old. A student movement will not arise unless there is a sense that the older generation has discredited itself and lost its moral standing. The Chinese student movement which was born in May 1919 thus issued from a tremendous disillusionment with the elder statesmen who, in the students' eyes, had capitulated with shameful unmanliness to the Japanese demands at Versailles. The Japanese student movement which arose after the Second World War was based on the emotional trauma which the young students had experienced in the defeat of their country. Traditional authority was de-authoritized as it never had been before; their fathers, elders, teachers, and rulers were revealed as having deceived and misled them. Japan in 1960 was far more technologically advanced than it had been in the twenties, and also far more democratic. Yet because in 1960 the psychological hegemony of the older generation was undermined, there arose a large student movement, whereas there had been little unrest among students in earlier and more difficult years.

A student movement, moreover, tends to arise where political apathy or a sense of helplessness prevails among the people. Especially where the people are illiterate will the feeling exist among the young that the political initiative is theirs. The educated man has an inordinate prestige in a society of illiterates. He is a master of the arts of reading and writing, and a whole world of knowledge and the powers of expression are at his command. Throughout human history, whenever people of a society have been overwhelmingly illiterate and voiceless, the intellectual elite has been the sole rival for political power with the military elite . . . .

From the combination of youth, intellectuality, and altruistic emotion, there arise certain further basic traits of student movements. In the first place, a student movement, unlike a labor movement, has at its inception only a vague sense of its immediate goals; indeed, its "ultimate aims" are usually equally inchoate. A trade union, as we have mentioned, comes into being because a group of workers have certain specific grievances relating to wages, hours and conditions of work, seniority rights, safety precautions. It is only with difficulty that political propagandists can get workers to think in generic terms of opposing the "system." A student movement, on the other hand, arises from a diffused feeling of opposition to things as they are. It is revolutionary in emotion to begin with, and because its driving energy stems largely from unconscious sources, it has trouble defining what it wants. It tries to go from the general to the particular, and to find a justifying bill of grievances; what moves it at the outset, however, is less an idea than an emotion, vague, restless, ill-defined, stemming from the unconscious. A Japanese student leader of many years' standing, Shigeo Shima, remarked, "One cannot understand the student movement if one tries to understand it in terms of the labor movement. The strength of the student movement lies in its energy of consciousness trying to determine existence, instead of the other way around." An intellectual has been defined as a person whose consciousness determines his existence, in the case of the young intellectuals of a student movement we might add further that their ideological consciousness is founded on the emotional unconscious of generational revolt . . . .

A student movement thus tends to take its stand as the pure conscience of the society; it is concerned with ideal issues, not, like an economic movement, with the material, bread-and-butter ones. Every student movement, however, also has a populist ingredient. A student movement always looks for some lowly oppressed class with which it can psychologically identify itself. Whether it be to the peasantry, the proletariat, or the Negro, the students have a tremendous need to offer themselves in a self-sacrificial way, to seek out an exploited group on whose behalf their sacrifices will be made. Conceiving of themselves as deceived, exploited sons, they feel a kinship with the deceived and exploited of society as a whole. The back-to-the-people spirit is at once the most distinctive, noblest, and most self-destructive trait within student movements. The populist ingredient separates the student movement sharply from what we might call student syndicalism . . . .

The populist and elitist moods in student movements can merge into a morbid self-destructive masochism, as they did, for instance, among the Russian students. The burden of guilt which a generation in revolt takes upon itself is immense, and it issues in perverse and grotesque ways. Nevertheless, something would be lost in our understanding of student movements if we were to see in them solely a chapter of history written on an abnormal theme. For student movements, let us remember, are the most sincerely selfless and altruistic which the world has seen. A student is a person who, midway between childhood and maturity, is imbibing the highest ideals and hopes of the human cultural heritage; moreover, he lives in comradeship with his fellow-students. The comradeship of students is usually the last communal fellowship he will experience. The student feels that he will then enter into a maelstrom of competitive and bureaucratic pseudo-existence; he has a foreboding that he will become alienated from the self he now is. Articulate by education, he voices his protest. No edict in the world can control a classroom. It is everywhere the last free forum of mankind. Students meet together necessarily, think together, laugh together, and share a common animus against the authorities. The conditions of student existence remain optimal for spontaneous rebellion. When the absolutism of the Czar stifled the nascent democratic strivings in a culturally backward people, the universities stood as isolated fortresses of relatively free expression. As Lenin wrote in 1903, "The actual conditions of social life in Russia render (soon we shall have to be saying: rendered) extremely difficult any manifestation of political discontent except through the universities."...

The more backward a people is with respect to its culture and intellect, the greater is the likelihood that it will have a student movement of an elitist and revolutionary character. Where the "cultural distance" between the students and the surrounding population is great, the chances for the rise of a student movement are increased. One whole class of student movements is born of "uneven development," from the unbalanced situation in which advanced ideas are combined with material backwardness. In such cases the "cultural strain," the cultural alienation, which arises between the students and the masses, is most poignant and intense, for it involves a de-authoritization of the elder generation as cultural inferiors, as persons of whom one is ashamed. The students then are in part motivated to overcome the cultural distance between their people and themselves, and in part by an acceptance of the elitist status which their cultural superiority confers. What is most important to bear in mind is that the culture of the student movements, of the intellectual elite, is the one genuinely international culture. Students at any given time throughout the world tend to read the same books. We might call this the law of the universality of ideas, or the law of universal intellectual fashions, or the maximum rate of diffusion for intellectual culture. At any rate, the Chinese students of 1917, like their counterparts in Americaa and Britain, were reading Bertrand Russell, John Dewey, and later Lenin and Marx; earlier they had read Ibsen, Tolstoy, and Spencer. Kwame Nkrumah as a university student in America and Britain studied Marx and logical positivism, Jomo Kenyatta sank himself in the writings of Marx and Malinowski. Today in Africa the young students, like their fellows in France, the United States, and Japan, read Marx, Camus, and the existentialist writers. In the Soviet Union young university students try to find copies of Camus and Freud, and overcoming the obstacles interposed by the government against the free flow of books and ideas, succeed in maintaining a bond with the world intellectual community . . . .

. . . A generation in the sociological sense consists of persons in a common age group who in their formative years have known the same historical experiences, shared the same hopes and disappointments, and experienced a common disillusionment with respect to the elder age groups, toward whom their sense of opposition is defined.

Often a generation's consciousness is shaped by the experience of what we might call the "generational event." To the Chinese Communist students of the early thirties, for instance, it was the "Long March" with Mao Tse-tung; that was what one writer called their "unifying event." More than class origin, such an historical experience impresses itself on the consciousness of a student movement. The depression, the struggle against fascism, the ordeals of the civil rights agitation —all these were generational events; they demarcated a generation in its coming of age. . . .

What keeps generational consciousness most intense is the sense of generational martyrdom, the actual experience of one's fellow-students assaulted, killed, imprisoned, by armed deputies of the elder generation. Whether in Russian, Chinese or Latin American universities, or at Berkeley, the actual physical clash made students frenzied with indignation. The youthful adolescent resents the elders' violence especially for its assault upon his new manhood. Student movements make of their martyrs the high symbols of a common identity. The Iranian Students' Association, for example, published a leaflet in their exile to commemorate "Student Day" for three of their comrades. Its language was that of the martyrology of generational consciousness:

> STUDENTS MASSACRED
>
> On December 7th, 1953, the armed forces of the post-coup d'etat government invaded the Tehran University. Some soldiers entered a classroom and threatened to kill the professor . . . As the terrified students started to run away the soldiers opened fire with their machine guns in the hallway and wounded many students and killed three.
>
> . . . The students were going to demonstrate against the government on December 9th, 1953, the day that Vice-President Richard M. Nixon was going to visit Iran and its "free" people . . . .
>
> The three students, GHANDCHI, BOZORGNIA and SHARIATRAZAVI, died, but their memory and their heroic sacrifice will forever remain with us to guide the student movement of Iran. To honor their memories and to rededicate ourselves to the cause for which they gave their lives, this day will always be honored. . . .

Every student movement has cherished similar memories of brothers whom their fathers destroyed . . . .

We have tried to unravel the nature of political idealism, the complex of emotions of love, destruction, self-sacrifice, and nihilism on which it is founded. The unconscious ingredient of generational revolt in the students' idealism has tended to shape decisively their political expression. We have tried to bring to consciousness what otherwise are unconscious processes of history. That has been the whole purpose in our use of the psycho-historical method—to help defeat the cunning of history which has so often misused the idealistic emotions. With a melancholy uniformity, the historical record shows plainly how time and again the students' most idealistic movement has converted itself into a blind, irrational power hostile to liberal democratic values. Yet we refuse to accept a sociological determinism which would make this pattern into the fatality of all student idealism. Our working hypothesis is that knowledge can contribute to wisdom. When students perceive the historical defeat which has dogged their youthful hubris, they may perhaps be the more enabled to cope with irrational demonry; they may then make their political idealism into an even nobler historical force.

For student movements have thus far been too largely an example of what we might call *projective politics,* in the sense that they have been largely dominated by unconscious drives; the will to revolt against the de-authoritized father has evolved into a variety of patterns of political action. This hegemony of the unconscious has differentiated student movements from the more familiar ones of class and interest groups. The latter are usually conscious of their psychological sources and aims, whether they be material economic interests or enhanced prestige and power. Student movements, on the other hand, manifest a deep resistance to the psychological analysis of their emotional mainspring; they wish to keep unconscious the origins of their generational revolt. A politics of the unconscious carries with it untold dangers for the future of civilization. We have seen the students Karl Sand and Gavrilo Princip adding their irrational vector to deflect the peaceful evolution of a liberal Europe; we have seen the Russian students helping to stifle the first possibilities of a liberal constitution; we have seen the American student movement in its blind alley of the Oxford Pledge and its later pro-Soviet immolation. All these were fruits of the politics of the unconscious. It is only by persisting in the understanding of these unconscious determinants that we can hope to see a higher wisdom in human affairs.

Guilt feelings fused with altruistic emotions have led students to seek a "back to the people" identification. In Joseph Conrad's novel, the guilt-tormented Lord Jim could conquer his guilt only by merging his self in the most romantic dedication to an alien, impoverished, exploited people. The aged ex-revolutionist Stein saw Jim's salvation rendered possible only by his immersing himself in the "destructive element"; thereby, guilt was assuaged. And since it is guilt which assails the sense of one's existence with the reproaches of one's conscience, it is by the conquest of guilt in a higher self-sacrifice that one recovers the conviction of one's existence. In a sense, every student seeking to merge himself with peasant, proletarian, the Negro, the poor, the alien race has had something of the Lord Jim psychology. His guilt is that of his generational revolt, his would-be parricide. He can conquer this guilt only with the demonstration that he is selfless and by winning the comforting maternal love of the oppressed; they bring him the assurance of his needed place in the universe. To reduce this determinism of unconscious guilt has been one purpose of this study. For only thus can we isolate and counteract the ingredient of self-destruction.

When generational struggle grows most intense, it gives rise to generational theories of truth. Protagorean relativism is translated into generational terms; only youth, uncorrupted, is held to perceive the truth, and the generation becomes the measure of all things. This generational relativism in the sixties is the counterpart of the class relativism which flourished in the thirties; where once it was said that only the proletariat had an instinctive grasp of sociological truth, now it is said that only those under thirty, or twenty-five, or twenty, are thus privileged. It would be pointless to repeat the philosophical criticisms of relativist ideology. This generational doctrine is an ideology insofar as it expresses a "false consciousness"; it issues from unconscious motives of generational uprising, projects its youthful longings onto the nature of the cosmos, sociological reality, and sociological knowledge, but represses precisely those facts of self-destruction and self-defeat which we have documented. Moreover, the majority of studentries have usually been at odds with the student activists, whose emotional compulsions to generational revolt they do not share. The engineering and working-class students, who so often have been immune to the revolt-ardor of middle-class humanistic students, stand as dissenters to the doctrine of generational privilege. They have held more fast their sense of reality, whereas the literary-minded have seen reality through a mist of fantasy and wish-fulfillment.

The reactionary is also a generational relativist, for he believes that the old have a privileged perspective upon reality, that only the old have learned in experience the recalcitrance of facts to human desire. But the philosophical truth is that no generation has a privileged access to reality; each has its projective unconscious, its inner resentments, its repressions and exaggerations. Each generation will have to learn to look at itself with the same sincerity it demands of the other. The alternative is generational conflict, with its searing, sick emotions, and an unconscious which is a subterranean house of hatred.

The substance of history is psychological—the way human beings have felt, thought, and acted in varying circumstances—and the concept of generational struggle which we have used is a psychological one. There are those who see the dangers of "reductionism" in our psycho-historical method; they feel that the genesis of student movements in generational conflict has no bearing on the validity of their programs, goals, objectives. Of what import, they ask, is the psychology of student movements so long as they work for freedom, for liberating workers and peasants and colored races, for university reform, and the end of alienation? To such critics we reply that the psychological origin of student movements puts its impress on both their choice of political means and underlying ends. Wherever a set of alternative possible routes toward achieving a given end presents itself, a student movement will usually tend to choose the one which involves a higher measure of violence or humiliation directed against the older generation. The latent aim of generational revolt never surrenders its paramountcy to the avowed patent aims. The assassination of an archduke, for instance, may be justified by an appeal to nationalistic ideals which are said to have a sanctity overriding all other consequences; actually the sacred cause, the nationalistic ideal, becomes too easily a pseudo-end, a rationalization, a "cause" which affords the chance to express in a more socially admired way one's desire to murder an authority figure.

When all our analysis is done, however, what endures is the promise and hope of a purified idealism. I recall one evening in 1963 when I met with a secret circle of Russian students at Moscow University. There were twelve or thirteen of them drawn from various fields but moved by a common aspiration toward freedom. Among them were young physicists, philosophers, economists, students of languages. Their teachers had been apologists for the Stalinist repression, and the students were groping for truthful ideas, for an honest philosophy rather than an official ideology. Clandestine papers and books circulated among them—a copy of Boris Pasternak's *Dr. Zhivago,* of George Orwell's *1984*—reprints of Western articles on Soviet literature, a revelation of the fate of the poet Osip Mandelstamm. The social system had failed to "socialize" them, had failed to stifle their longing for freedom. The elder generation was de-authoritized in their eyes for its pusillanimous involvement in the "cult of personality." Here on a cold March night in a Moscow academic office I was encountering what gave hope to the future of the Soviet Union. The conflict of generations, disenthralled of its demonry, becomes a drama of sustenance and renewal which remains the historical bearer of humanity's highest hopes.

The New Reformation

PAUL GOODMAN

For a long time modern societies have been operating as if religion were a minor and moribund part of the scheme of things. But this is unlikely. Men do not do without a system of "meanings" that everybody believes and puts his hope in even if, or especially if, he doesn't know anything about it; what Freud called a "shared psychosis," meaningful because shared, and with the power that resides in deep fantasy and longing. In advanced countries, indeed, it is science and technology themselves that have gradually, and finally triumphantly, become the system of mass faith, not disputed by various political ideologies and nationalisms that have also had religious uses.

Now this basic faith is threatened. Dissident young people are saying that science is antilife, it is a Calvinist obsession, it has been a weapon of white Europe to subjugate colored races, and scientific technology has manifestly become diabolical. Along with science, the young discredit the professions in general, and the whole notion of "disciplines" and academic learning. If these views take hold, it adds up to a crisis of belief, and the effects are incalculable. Every status and

From *The New York Times Magazine* (September 14, 1969), 32–33, 142–47, 154–55.

institution would be affected. Present political troubles could become endless religious wars. Here again, as in politics and morals, the worldwide youth disturbance may indicate a turning point in history and we must listen to it carefully.

In 1967 I gave a course on "Professionalism" at the New School for Social Research in New York, attended by about 25 graduate students from all departments. My bias was the traditional one: professionals are autonomous individuals beholden to the nature of things and the judgment of their peers, and bound by an explicit or implicit oath to benefit their clients and the community. To teach this, I invited seasoned professionals whom I esteemed—a physician, engineer, journalist, architect, etc. These explained to the students the obstacles that increasingly stood in the way of honest practice, and their own life experience in circumventing them.

To my surprise, the class unanimously rejected them. Heatedly and rudely they called my guests liars, finks, mystifiers, or deluded. They showed that every professional was co-opted and corrupted by the System, all decisions were made top-down by the power structure and bureaucracy, professional peer-groups were conspiracies to make more money. All this was importantly true and had, of course, been said by the visitors. Why had the students not heard? As we explored further, we came to the deeper truth, that they did not believe in the existence of real professions at all; professions were concepts of repressive society and "linear thinking." I asked them to envisage any social order they pleased—Mao's, Castro's, some anarchist utopia—and wouldn't there be engineers who know about materials and stresses and strains? Wouldn't people get sick and need to be treated? Wouldn't there be problems of communication? No, they insisted; it was important only to be human, and all else would follow.

Suddenly I realized that they did not really believe that there was a nature of things. Somehow all functions could be reduced to interpersonal relations and power. There was no knowledge, but only the sociology of knowledge. They had so well learned that physical and sociological research is subsidized and conducted for the benefit of the ruling class that they did not believe there was such a thing as simple truth. To be required to learn something was a trap by which the young were put down and co-opted. Then I knew that I could not get through to them. I had imagined that the worldwide student protest had to do with changing political and moral institutions, to which I was sympathetic, but I now saw that we had to do with a religious crisis of the magnitude of the Reformation in the fifteen-hundreds, when not only all institutions but all learning had been corrupted by the Whore of Babylon.

The irony was that I myself had said 10 years ago, in "Growing Up Absurd," that these young were growing up without a world *for* them, and therefore they were "alienated," estranged from nature and other people. But I had then been thinking of juvenile delinquents and a few Beats; and a few years later I had been heartened by the Movement in Mississippi, the Free Speech protest in Berkeley, the Port Huron statement of S.D.S., the resistance to the Vietnam war, all of which made human sense and were not absurd at all. But the alienating circumstances had proved too strong after all; here were absurd graduate students, most of them political "activists."

Alienation is a Lutheran concept: "God has turned His face away, things have no meaning, I am estranged in the world." By the time of Hegel the term was applied to the general condition of rational man, with his "objective" sciences and institutions divorced from his "subjectivity," which was therefore irrational and impulsive. In his revision of Hegel, Marx explained this as the effect of man's losing his essential nature as a cooperative producer, because centuries of exploitation, culminating in capitalism, had fragmented the community and robbed the workman of the means of production. Comte and Durkheim pointed to the weakening of social solidarity and the contradiction between law and morality, so that people lost their bearings—this was anomie, an acute form of alienation that could lead to suicide or aimless riot. By the end of the 19th century, alienation came to be used as the term for insanity, derangement of perceived reality, and psychiatrists were called alienists.

Contemporary conditions of life have certainly deprived people, and especially young people, of a meaningful world in which they can act and find themselves. Many writers and the dissenting students themselves have spelled it out. For instance, in both schools and corporations, people cannot pursue their own interests or exercise initiative. Administrators are hypocrites who sell people out for the smooth operation of the system. The budget for war has grotesquely distorted reasonable social priorities. Worst of all, the authorities who make the decisions are incompetent to cope with modern times: we are in danger of extinction, the biosphere is being destroyed, two-thirds of mankind are starving. Let me here go on to some other factors that demand a religious response.

There is a lapse of faith in science. Science has not produced the general happiness that people expected, and now it has fallen under the sway of greed and power; whatever its beneficent past, people fear that its further progress will do more harm than good. And rationality itself is discredited. Probably it is more significant than we like to think that intelligent young people dabble in astrology, witchcraft, psychedelic dreams, and whatever else is despised by science; in some sense they are not kidding. They need to control their fate, but they hate scientific explanations.

Every one of these young grew up since Hiroshima. They do not talk about atom bombs—not nearly so much as we who campaigned against the shelters and fall-out—but the bombs explode in their dreams, as Otto Butz found in his study of collegians at San Francisco State, and now George Dennison, in "The Lives of Children," shows that it was the same with small slum children whom he taught at the First Street School in New York. Again and again students have told me that they take it for granted they will not survive the next 10 years. This is not an attitude with which to prepare for a career or to bring up a family.

Whether or not the bombs go off, human beings are becoming useless. Old people are shunted out of sight at an increasingly earlier age, young people are kept on ice till an increasingly later age. Small farmers and other technologically unemployed are dispossessed or left to rot. Large numbers are put away as incompetent or deviant. Racial minorities that cannot shape up are treated as a nuisance. Together, these groups are a large majority of the population. Since labor will not be needed much longer, there is vague talk of a future society of "leisure," but there is no thought of a kind of community in which all human beings would be necessary and valued.

The institutions, technology and communications have infected even the "biological core," so that people's sexual desires are no longer genuine. This was powerfully argued by Wilhelm Reich a generation ago and it is now repeated by Herbert Marcuse. When I spoke for it in the nineteen-forties, I was condemned by the radicals, for example, C. Wright Mills, as a "bedroom revisionist."

A special aspect of biological corruption is the spreading ugliness, filth, and tension of the environment in which the young grow up. If Wordsworth was right—I think he was—that children must grow up in an environment of beauty and simple affections in order to become trusting, open, and magnanimous citizens, then the offspring of our ghettos, suburbs, and complicated homes have been disadvantaged, no matter how much money there is. This lack cannot be remedied by art in the curriculum, nor by vest-pocket playgrounds, nor by banning billboards from bigger highways. Cleaning the river might help, but that will be the day.

If we start from the premise that the young are in a religious crisis, that they doubt there is really a nature of things, and they are sure there is not a world for themselves, many details of their present behavior become clearer. Alienation is a powerful motivation, of unrest, fantasy and reckless action. It leads, as we shall see, to religious innovation, new sacraments to give life meaning. But it is a poor basis for politics, including revolutionary politics.

It is said that the young dissidents never offer a constructive program. And apart from the special cases of Czechoslovakia and Poland, where they confront an unusually outdated system, this is largely true. In France, China, Germany, Egypt, England, the United States, etc., most of the issues of protest have been immediate gut issues, and the tactics have been mainly disruptive, without coherent proposals for a better society. But this makes for bad politics. Unless one has a program, there is no way to persuade the other citizens, who do not have one's gut complaints, to come along. Instead one confronts them hostilely and they are turned off, even when they might be sympathetic. But the confrontation is inept too, for the alienated young cannot take other people seriously as having needs of their own; a spectacular instance was the inability of the French youth to communicate with the French working class, in May 1968. In Gandhian theory, the confronter aims at future community with the confronted; he will not let him continue a course that is bad for *him*, and so he appeals to his deeper reason. But instead of this *Satyagraha*, soul force, we have seen plenty of hate. The confronted are *not* taken as human beings, but as pigs, etc. But how can the young people think of a future community when they themselves have no present world, no profession or other job in it, and no trust in other human beings? Instead, some young radicals seem to entertain the disastrous illusion that other people can be compelled by fear. This can lead only to crushing reaction.

All the "political" activity makes sense, however, if it is understood that it is not aimed at social reconstruction at all, but is a way of desperately affirming that they are alive and want a place in the sun. "I am a revolutionary," said Cohn-Bendit, leader of the French students in 1968, "because it is the best way of living." And young Americans pathetically and truly say that there is no other way to be taken seriously. Then it is not necessary to have a program; the right method is to act, against any vulnerable point and wherever one can rally support. The purpose is not politics but to have a movement and form a community. This is exactly what Saul Alinsky prescribed to rally outcast blacks.

And such conflictful action has indeed caused social changes. In France it was conceded by the Gaullists that "nothing would ever be the same." In the United States, the changes in social attitude during the last 10 years are unthinkable without the youth action, with regard to war, the military-industrial, corporate organization and administration, the police, the blacks. When the actors have been in touch with the underlying causes of things, issues have deepened and the Movement has grown. But for the alienated, again, action easily slips into activism, and conflict is often spite and stubbornness. There is excitement and notoriety, much human suffering, and the world no better off. (New Left Notes runs a column wryly called, "We Made the News Today, O Boy!") Instead of deepening awareness and a sharpening political conflict, there occurs the polarization of mere exasperation. It often seems that the aim is just to have a shambles. Impatiently the ante of tactics is raised beyond what the "issue" warrants, and support melts away. Out on a limb, the leaders become desperate and fanatical, intolerant of criticism, dictatorial. The Movement falls to pieces.

Yet it is noteworthy that when older people like myself are critical of the wrongheaded activism, we nevertheless almost invariably concede that the young are *morally* justified. For what is the use of patience and reason when meantime millions are being killed and starved, and when bombs and nerve gas are being stockpiled? Against the entrenched power responsible for these things, it might be better to do something idiotic now than something perhaps more practical in the long run. I don't know which is less demoralizing.

Maybe the truth is revealed in the following conversation I had with a young hippie at a college in Massachusetts. He was dressed like an (American) Indian —buckskin fringes and a headband, red paint on his face. All his life, he said, he had tried to escape the encompassing, evil of our society that was trying to destroy his soul. "But if you're always escaping," I said, "and never attentively study it, how can you make a wise judgment about society or act effectively to change it?" "You see, you don't dig!" he cried. "It's just ideas like 'wise' and 'acting effectively' that we can't stand." He was right. He was in the religious dilemma of Faith vs. Works. Where I sat, Works had some reality; but in the reign of the Devil, as he felt it, all Works are corrupted, they are part of the System; only Faith can avail. But he didn't have Faith either.

Inevitably, the alienated seem to be inconsistent in how they take the present world. Hippies attack technology and are scornful of rationality, but they buy up electronic equipment and motorcycles, and with them the whole infrastructure.

Activists say that civil liberties are bourgeois and they shout down their opponents; but they clamor in court for their civil liberties. Those who say that the university is an agent of the powers that be, do not mean thereby to reassert the ideal role of the university, but to use the university for their own propaganda. Yet if I point out these apparent inconsistencies, it does not arouse shame or guilt. How is this? It is simply that they do not really understand that technology, civil law, and the university are *human* institutions, for which they too are responsible; they take them as brute given, just what's there, to be manipulated as convenient. But convenient for whom? The trouble with this attitude is that these institutions, works of spirit in history, are how Man has made himself and is. If they treat them as mere things, rather than being vigilant for them, they themselves become nothing. And nothing comes from nothing.

In general, their lack of a sense of history is bewildering. It is impossible to convey to them that the deeds were done by human beings, that John Hampden confronted the King and wouldn't pay the war tax just like us, or that Beethoven too, just like a rock 'n' roll band, made up his music as he went along, from odds and ends, with energy, spontaneity and passion—how else do they think he made music? And they no longer remember their own history. A few years ago there was a commonly accepted story of mankind, beginning with the Beats, going on to the Chessman case, the HUAC bust, the Freedom Rides, and climaxing in the Berkeley Victory—"The first human event in 40,000 years," Mike Rossman, one of the innumerable spokesmen, told me. But this year I find that nothing antedates Chicago '68. Elder statesmen, like Sidney Lens and especially Staughton Lynd, have been trying with heroic effort to recall the American antecedents of present radical and libertarian slogans and tactics, but it doesn't rub off. I am often hectored to my face with formulations that I myself put in their mouths, that have become part of the oral tradition two years old, author prehistoric. Most significant of all, it has been whispered to me—but I can't check up, because I don't speak the language—that among the junior high school students, aged 12 and 13, that's really where it's at! Quite different from what goes on in the colleges that I visit.

What I do notice, however, is that dozens of Underground newspapers have a noisy style. Though each one is doing his thing, there is not much idiosyncracy in the spontaneous variety. The political radicals are, as if mesmerized, repeating the power plays, factionalism, random abuse, and tactical lies that aborted the movement in the thirties. And I have learned, to my disgust, that a major reason why the young don't trust people over 30 is that they don't understand them and are too conceited to try. Having grown up in a world too meaningless to learn anything, they know very little and are quick to resent it.

This is an unpleasant picture. Even so, the alienated young have no vital alternative except to confront the Evil, and to try to make a new way of life out of their own innards and suffering. As they are doing. It is irrelevant to point out that the System is not the monolith that they think and that the majority of people are not corrupt, just brow-beaten and confused. What is relevant is that they cannot see this, because they do not have an operable world for themselves. In such a case, the only advice I would dare to give them is that which Krishna gave Arjuna: to confront with nonattachment, to be brave and firm without hatred. (I don't here want to discuss the question of "violence," the hatred and disdain are far more important.) Also, when they are seeking a new way of life, for example when they are making a "journey inward," as Ronald Laing calls it, I find that I urge them occasionally to write a letter home.

As a citizen and father I have a right to try to prevent a shambles and to diminish the number of wrecked lives. But it is improper for us elders to keep saying, as we do, that their activity is "counterproductive." It's our business to do something more productive.

Religiously, the young have been inventive, much more than the God-is-dead theologians. They have hit on new sacraments, physical actions to get them out of their estrangement and (momentarily) break through into meaning. The terribly loud music is used sacramentally. The claim for the hallucinogenic drugs is almost never the paradisal pleasure of opium culture nor the escape from distress of heroin, but tuning in to the cosmos and communing with one another. They seem to have had flashes of success in bringing ritual participation back into theater, which for a hundred years playwrights and directors have tried to do in vain. And whatever the political purposes and results of activism, there is no doubt that shared danger for the sake of righteousness is used sacramentally as baptism of fire. Fearful moments of provocation and the poignant release of the bust bring unconscious contents to the surface, create a bond of solidarity, are "commitment."

But the most powerful magic, working in all these sacraments, is the close presence of other human beings, without competition or one-upping. The original sin is to be on an ego trip that isolates; and angry political factionalism has now also become a bad thing. What a drastic comment on the dehumanization and fragmentation of modern times that salvation can be attained simply by the "warmth of assembled animal bodies," as Kafka called it, describing his mice. At the 1967 Easter Be-In in New York's Central Park, when about 10,000 were crowded on the Sheep Meadow, a young man with a quite radiant face said to me, "Gee, human beings are legal!"–it was sufficient, to be saved, to be exempted from continual harassment by officious rules and Law and Order.

The extraordinary rock festivals at Bethel and on the Isle of Wight are evidently pilgrimages. Joan Baez, one of the hierophants, ecstatically described Bethel to me, and the gist of it was that people were nice to one another. A small group passing a joint of marijuana often behaves like a Quaker meeting waiting for the spirit, and the cigarette may be a placebo. Group therapy and sensitivity training, with Mecca at Esalen, have the same purpose. And I think this is the sense of the sexuality, which is certainly not hedonistic, nor mystical in the genre of D. H.Lawrence; nor does it have much to do with personal love, that is too threatening for these anxious youths. But it is human touch, without conquest or domination, and it obviates self-consciousness and embarrassed speech.

Around the rather pure faith there has inevitably collected a mess of eclectic liturgy and paraphernalia. Mandalas, beggars in saffron, (American) Indian beads, lectures in Zen. Obviously the exotic is desirable because it is not what they have grown up with. And it is true that fundamental facts of life are more acceptable if they come in fancy dress, e.g. it is good to breathe from the diaphragm and one can learn this by humming "OM," as Allen Ginsberg did for seven hours at Grant Park in Chicago. But college chaplains are also pretty busy, and they are now more likely to see the adventurous and off-beat than, as used to be the case, the staid and square. Flowers and strobe lights are indigenous talismans.

It is hard to describe this (or any) religiosity without lapsing into condescending humor. Yet it is genuine and it will, I am convinced, survive and develop—I don't know into what. In the end it is religion that constitutes the strength of this generation, and not, as I used to think, their morality, political will, and common sense. Except for a few, like the young people of the Resistance, I am not impressed by their moral courage or even honesty. For all their eccentricity they are singularly lacking in personality. They do not have enough world to have much character. And they are not especially attractive as animals. But they keep pouring out a kind of metaphysical vitality.

Let me try to account for it. On the one hand, these young have an unusual amount of available psychic energy. They were brought up on antibiotics that minimized depressing chronic childhood diseases, and with post-Freudian freedom to act out early drives. Up to age 6 or 7, television nourished them with masses of strange images and sometimes true information—McLuhan makes a lot of sense for the kindergarten years. Long schooling would tend to make them stupid, but it has been compensated by providing the vast isolated cities of youth that the high schools and colleges essentially are, where they can incubate their own thoughts. They are sexually precocious and not inhibited by taboos. They are superficially knowledgeable. On the other hand, all this psychic energy has had little practical use. The social environment is dehumanized. It discourages romantic love and lasting friendship. They are desperately bored because the world does not promise any fulfillment. Their knowledge gives no intellectual or poetic satisfaction. In this impasse, we can expect a ferment of new religion. As in Greek plays, impasse produces gods from the machine. For a long time we did not hear of the symptoms of adolescent religious conversion, once as common in the United States as in all other places and ages. Now it seems to be recurring as a mass phenomenon.

Without doubt the religious young are in touch with something historical, but I don't think they understand what it is. Let me quote from an editorial in New Seminary News, the newsletter of dissident seminarians of the Pacific School of Religion in Berkeley: "What we confront (willingly or not we are thrust into it) is a time of disintegration of a dying civilization and the emergence of a new one." This seems to envisage something like the instant decline of the Roman Empire and they, presumably, are like the Christians about to build, rapidly, another era. But there are no signs that this is the actual situation. It would mean, for instance, that our scientific technology, civil law, professions, universities, etc., are about to vanish from the earth and be replaced by something entirely different. This is a fantasy of alienated minds. Nobody behaves as if civilization would vanish, and nobody acts as if there were a new dispensation. Nobody is waiting patiently in the catacombs and the faithful have not withdrawn into the desert. Neither the Yippies nor the New Seminarians nor any other exalted group have produced anything that is the least bit miraculous. Our civilization may well destroy itself with its atom bombs or something else, but then we do not care what will emerge, if anything.

But the actual situation *is* very like 1510, when Luther went to Rome, the eve of the Reformation. There is everywhere protest, revaluation, attack on the Establishment. The protest is international. There is a generation gap. (Luther himself was all of 34 when he posted his 95 theses in 1517, but Melanchthon was 20, Bucer 26, Münzer 28, Jonas 24; the Movement consisted of undergraduates and junior faculty.) And the thrust of protest is not to give up science, technology, and civil institutions, but to purge them, humanize them, decentralize them, change the priorities, and stop the drain of wealth.

These were, of course, exactly the demands of the March 4 nationwide teach-in on science, initiated by the dissenting professors of the Massachusetts Institute of Technology. This and the waves of other teach-ins, ads and demonstrations have been the voices not of the alienated, of people who have no world, but of protestants, people deep in the world who will soon refuse to continue under the present auspices because they are not viable. It is populism permeated by moral and professional unease. What the young have done is to make it finally religious, to force the grown-ups to recognize that they too are threatened with meaninglessness.

The analogy to the Reformation is even closer if we notice that the bloated universities, and the expanded school systems under them, constitute the biggest collection of monks since the time of Henry VIII. And most of this mandarinism is hocus pocus, a mass superstition. In my opinion, much of the student dissent in the colleges and especially the high schools has little to do with the excellent political and social demands that are made, but is boredom and resentment because of the phoniness of the whole academic enterprise.

Viewed as incidents of a Reformation, as attempts to purge themselves and recover a lost integrity, the various movements of the alienated young are easily recognizable as characteristic protestant sects, intensely self-conscious. The dissenting seminarians of the Pacific School of Religion do not intend to go off to primitive love feasts in a new heaven and new earth, but to form their own Free University; that is, they are Congregationalists. The shaggy hippies are not nature children as they claim, but self-conscious Adamites trying to naturalize Sausalito and the East Village. Heads are Pentecostals or Children of Light. Those who spindle IBM cards and throw the dean down the stairs are Iconoclasts. Those who want Student Power, a say in the rules and curriculum, mean to deny infant baptism; they want to make up their own minds, like Henry Dunster, the first president of Harvard. Radicals who live among the poor and try to organize them are certainly intent on social change, but they are also trying to find themselves again. The support of the black revolt by white middle-class students is desperately like Anabaptism, but God grant that we can do better than the Peasants' War. These analogies are not fanciful; when authority is discredited, there is a pattern in the return of the repressed. A better scholar could make a longer list; but the reason I here spell it out is that, perhaps, some young person will suddenly remember that history was about something.

Naturally, traditional churches are themselves in transition. On college campuses and in bohemian neighborhoods, existentialist Protestants and Jews and updating Catholics have gone along with the political and social activism and, what is probably more important, they have changed their own moral, esthetic and personal tone. On many campuses, the chaplains provide the only official forum for discussion of sex, drugs and burning draft cards. Yet it seems to me that, in their zeal or relevance, they are badly failing in their chief duty to the religious young: to be professors of theology. They cannot really perform pastoral services, like giving consolation or advice, since the young believe they have the sacraments to do this for themselves. Chaplains say that the young are uninterested in dogma and untractable on this level, but I think this is simply a projection of their own distaste for the conventional theology that has gone dead for them. The young are hotly metaphysical—but alas, boringly so, because they don't know much, have no language to express their intuitions, and repeat every old fallacy. If the chaplains would stop looking in the conventional places where God is dead, and would explore the actualities where perhaps He is alive, they might learn something and have something to teach.

Why We Need a Generation Gap

ROGER RAPOPORT

Recently, I spoke with a man twice my age who expressed great faith in the future of American youth: "There's nothing wrong with them that ten years, a family, mortgage and car payments won't be able to cure." He, of course, envisions millions of young troublemakers shaving their beards, dropping their hems, marching across the generation gap and acculturating in a sea of baby food, weed killer and convertible debentures.

Such wishful thinking arises from the preconception that maturity will force the young to stop fighting for a future they want and begin to accept a future they can get. It is precisely this cynicism that has divided fathers and sons during the 1960's. For example, youths repeatedly risk the clubs and the courts to force an end to the Vietnam war while, to some, the President seems willing to end the

From *Look* Magazine (January 13, 1970), T 1/13/70.

fighting only when it doesn't cost him any percentage points on the latest Gallup poll.

But the conflict will widen, and, by 1980 when I am 33, I suspect that the gap between my generation and the generation now in power will have widened into a new national fault line rocking the entire country. It is one thing to smash powerless children on the picket line, it is a new game when the children begin assuming control of the country.

Young dissidents have been widely berated for lacking an alternative to the present system. But the fact is we have many goals for tomorrow. The first priority, of course, will be to reincarnate the political system. "Planned obsolescents" can no longer run the country. We can't continue institutionalizing yesterday's leaders; Richard M. Nixon, circa 1940; Gen. Lewis Hershey, circa 1930; J. Edgar Hoover, circa 1920, plus the extra added attraction of congressmen and generals trying to bomb their way back to the Stone Age with a Vietnam war circa 1890.

When 200 million Americans sign a Sunday *New York Times* ad opposed to the Vietnam war, the Pentagon will retreat. Likewise, we must call off the debate on the phantom political issues that have supposedly divided us in the past. We will no longer waste our time debating whether or not the internal combustion engine should be allowed to asphyxiate us, whether we should have a useless antimissile system to protect us from imaginary enemies, whether our children should be conscripted to fight and die in the name of leaders who enjoy handing out medals to widows. This senseless, futile debate between the obstetrician and the mortician will end.

For this is not the *Titanic*, where a lucky few can climb into lifeboats and survive. This is Air Force One, where there are no parachutes. All of us—President, pilot, stewardesses, first- and second-class passengers—must resuscitate a physically and morally depleted environment or go down together.

The United States should lead the world in taming technology. We will become a human sanctuary where SST's are neither built nor flown because we believe in the sanctity of the human eardrum. Instead of building synthetic alligators for amusement parks, we will save the real ones in the Everglades. We will stop offshore oil drilling so children can swim again off Santa Barbara and stop driving until we can see Los Angeles.

But once we have begun draining the novocaine out of our politicians and technocrats, installed Ralph Nader as the president of General Motors and Tommy Smothers as the head of CBS we will have to start looking inward. We will need to free ourselves of the stereotypes, the greed, the anxieties and vapid status symbols that propel our society. Tomorrow we must crown a Miss America who has buck teeth, cash in Las Vegas, abandon our calling cards and list everyone in *Who's Who.*

Aging can no longer be an excuse for stagnation. We cannot continue to stunt the growth of adults as if they were bonsai trees, intentionally kept in a precarious biological environment where it is impossible to grow, change, mature or expand, where it is impossible to do anything except vegetate or die. Man can no longer allow color television to suck his intellect down to the lowest common denominator. He cannot continue to find his highs and lows on the New York Stock Exchange, his diet in the frozen-food case, his sex in the centerfold.

He can't continue fighting his way up the corporate ladder. For on top he will find himself only one more executive unable to quit because he would lose the fringe benefit of free psychiatric care needed because the job is driving him crazy. He must smash his shock-proof gold watch, shed the corporate tattoo and come out of mental retirement.

When the scales start falling from their eyes, I suspect that many of today's adults will eventually join with their children in the fight against the men with goiters for cerebrums who want to do us in. I suspect that, like Dr. Spock, many of our parents are as troubled as we are. They know reckless leaders are on the loose in America. They know the soaring rhetoric of our verbose government officials is only so much thermal pollution, that the present course is only leading to an eternal human blackout. Eventually they will join forces with their children or simply move over and let us pass.

But when we find a governor for California who does not believe that when you have seen one redwood you have seen them all; when big business gives up trying to turn college radicals into square roots; when Spiro Agnew fires his speechwriter, turns off his teleprompter and throws away his cue cards; when the new FBI director catches Eldridge Cleaver and takes him out to dinner, then we will have only begun.

For there is another generation gap in the works, between us and our forthcoming children. For if my generation has seen through the political and technical sophistry of the times, we still have not come to understand ourselves. From the day in sixth grade when our Sputnik-obsessed teachers began clobbering us with homework, we have been too nervous, too anxious, too guilt-ridden to really know what we are all about. I suspect it will take my generation many years to recover from our education. We will continue to be awakened by nightmares about accidental smudges costing us points on our electrostatically graded answer sheets, of losing a gold star because we failed to finish our milk and cookies.

I suspect our children will find us a bit stiff from all those confining years in the classroom. They will probably find us too cerebral, better at thinking than feeling, better at seeing than sensing, better at listening than touching. Caught mind-tripping, we will be accused of absorbing too much and seeking too little. They may need our help in algebra, but I'm sure we're going to need their help in freeing us of our inhibitions.

There will be conflict between us because they will not be bound by all the constraints of the mind that bind us. They will know instinctively what freedom is all about, and no one will be able to take it away from them. Chronological age will become less important; perhaps they will force us to even stop using age as an excuse for obstinacy. Maybe we will stop declaring birthdays for awhile and all lie about our age.

I suspect they might demand with Kurt Vonnegut that we forget our linear concept of time, that we become "unstuck in time" and abandon the "illusion we have here on Earth that one moment follows another one, like beads on a string, and that once a moment is gone it is gone forever . . . . All moments, past, present, and future, always have existed, always will exist."

Perhaps we will reach 1984 and find we are in 2001.

In the end, I am sure that many of us who began this pervasive generational rebellion will have second thoughts when we see what our children do to us. But I hope that instead of meeting them with Mace, we will have the good sense to meet them with love, help them on their way and perhaps even join them. For any generation could go wrong. Even our own.

What Generation Gap?

JOSEPH ADELSON

Can the truth prevail against a false idea whose time has come?

The idea that there is a generation gap is not totally false, perhaps. But it is false enough, false in the sense of being overblown, oversimplified, sentimentalized. This may be too strong a way of putting it. Let us say, then, that the idea of a generation gap is at the least unexamined, one of those notions that seems so self-evident that we yield to it without taking thought, and without qualms about not taking thought.

Once we examine the idea, we find it is almost too slippery to hold. What *do* we mean by a generation gap? Do we mean widespread alienation between adolescents and their parents? Do we mean that the young have a different and distinctive political outlook? Are we speaking of differences in styles of pleasure-seeking: greater sexual freedom, or the marijuana culture? Or do we simply mean that the young and the old share the belief that there is a significant difference between them, whether or not there is?

These questions—and many others one might reasonably ask—are by no means easy to answer. Few of them can in fact be answered decisively. Nevertheless, enough information has been accumulated during the last few years to offer us some new understanding of the young. As we will see, this evidence contains some surprises; and persuades us to cast a very cold eye on the more simple-minded views about this young generation and its place in our society.

From *The New York Times Magazine* (January 18, 1970), 10–11, 34–36, 45.

Parents and Children

One definition of generational conflict locates it in rebellion against parental authority, or in the failure of parents and their adolescent youngsters to understand and communicate with each other. (In short, "The Graduate.") On this particular issue, there is, as it happens, abundant evidence, and all of it suggests strongly that there is no extensive degree of alienation between parents and their children. Vern Bengtson, one of the most careful scholars in this area, has collected data from more than 500 students enrolled in three Southern California colleges. About 80 per cent of them report generally close and friendly relationships with their parents; specifically, 79 per cent feel somewhat close or very close, 81 per cent regard communication as good, and 78 per cent feel that their parents understand them all or most of the time.

Essentially similar findings have emerged from Samuel Lubell's perceptive studies of college youth. He reports that only about 10 per cent of the students he interviewed were in serious discord with their parents, and there was in most of these cases a long history of family tension. Any clinician working with college-age students would agree; among the rebellious or alienated, we find that their troubles with their families go back a long way and surfaced well before the college years.

In some respects the findings of Bengtson and Lubell are not really surprising. What they do is bring us up to date, and tell us that a long-established line of findings on adolescence continues to be true. A few years ago my colleague Elizabeth Douvan and I studied 3,000 youngsters of 12 to 18, from all regions of the country and all socio-economic levels. We concluded that there were few signs of serious conflict between American adolescents and their parents; on the contrary, we found that it was more usual for their relationships to be amiable.

The recently published study by psychiatrist Daniel Offer—of a smaller group, but using more intensive methods of scrutiny—arrives at much the same conclusion. Incidentally, there is no support for the common belief that the adolescent is hostage to the influence of his friends and turns away from parental guidance. A number of studies, here and abroad, tell us that while peer opinion may carry some weight on trivial issues—taste, clothing and the like—on more central matters, such as career and college choice, it is parental opinion that counts.

Whatever the supposed generation gap may involve, it does not seem to include deep strains between the young and their parents. The idea of the adolescent's family milieu as a kind of *Götterdämmerung*, as the scene of a cataclysmic struggle between the forces of authority and rebellion, is exaggerated. As Lubell put it: "we found both much less authority and much less rebellion than popularly imagined."

Politics

Those who are convinced that there is a generation gap also tend to identify youth in general with radical or militantly liberal beliefs. Thus, the young are sometimes seen as a New Breed, impatient with the political pieties of the past, less subject to that fatigue and corruption of spirit characteristic of the older generation of voters.

There is indeed a generational element in politics; there always has been. But to identify the young with liberal or left militancy makes sense only from the perspective of the elite university campus. Once we look at the total population of the young a decidedly different picture emerges. We have, for example, a brilliant and revealing analysis of the 1968 election by the University of Michigan's Survey Research Center, based upon 1,600 interviews with a representative national sample of voters. Perhaps the most interesting finding was that the under-30 voter was distinctly over-represented in the Wallace constituency, and that the Wallace movement outside the South drew proportionately more of its strength from younger than from older voters.

Some of the center's commentary on generational influences is worth quoting at length. "One of the most important yet hidden lines of cleavage split the younger generation itself. Although privileged young college students angry at Vietnam and shabby treatment of the Negro saw themselves as sallying forth to do battle against a corrupted and cynical older generation, a more head-on confrontation at the polls, if a less apparent one, was with their own age mates who had gone from high school off to the factory instead of college, and who were appalled by the collapse of patriotism and respect for the law that they saw about them. Outside of the election period, when verbal articulateness and leisure for political activism count most heavily, it was the college share of the younger generation—or at least is politicized vanguard—that was most prominent as a political force. At the polls, however, the game shifts to 'one man, one vote,' and this vanguard is numerically swamped even within its own generation."

To overemphasize the role of generational conflict in politics is to ignore or dismiss what we have learned over the years about the transmission of political sentiments in the great majority of cases—it seems to average about 75 per cent in most studies—children vote the same party their parents do; it has often been noted that party preference is transmitted to about the same degree as religious affiliation. Political attitudes are also acquired within the family, though generally less strongly than party affiliation; among studies on this matter there is hardly one which reports a negative relationship between parental attitudes and those of their children.

My own research during the last few years has dealt with the acquisition of political values during adolescence, and it is patently clear that the political outlook of the parents, particularly when it is strongly felt, tends to impress itself firmly on the politics of the child. Thus, the most conservative youngster we interviewed was the daughter of a leader of the John Birch Society; the most radical was the daughter of a man who had—in 1965—ceased paying income taxes to the Federal Government in protest against our involvement in Vietnam.

The strongest recent evidence on this subject seems to come from studies of the student radical. These studies make it evident that the "rebellious" student is, for the most part, not rebelling against the politics he learned at home. Radical activists are for the most part children of radical or liberal-left parents; in many instances, their parents are—overtly or tacitly—sympathetic to what their children are doing. (This is shown in the letters written to the press by parents of the students expelled by Columbia and Chicago; the rhetoric of these letters reveals how strong the bond of political sympathy is between the parents and their children. For instance, a letter from a group of Columbia parents states: "We are, of course, concerned about the individual fates of our sons and daughters, but more so with resisting such pressures against a student movement which has done so much to arouse the nation to the gross horrors and injustices prevalent in our country.")

Values

Are the young abandoning traditional convictions and moving toward new moral and ideological frameworks? We hear it said that the old emphasis on personal achievement is giving way to a greater concern with self-realization or with leisure and consumption; that a selfish materialism is being succeeded by a more humanistic outlook; that authority and hierarchy are no longer automatically accepted, and are replaced by more democratic forms of participation; that rationalism is under attack by proponents of sensual or mystical perspectives, and so on.

The most ambitious recent survey on this topic was sponsored by Fortune magazine. Fortune seems to believe that its findings demonstrate a generation gap and a departure from "traditional moral values" on the part of many of the educated young. A careful look at the survey suggests that it proves neither of these propositions, but only how badly statistics can deceive in a murky area.

The Fortune pollsters interviewed a representative sample of 18-to-24-year-olds, dividing them into a non-college group (largely upward-mobile youngsters interested in education for its vocational advantages), and a so-called "forerunner" group (largely students interested in education as self-discovery and majoring in the humanities and social sciences). Some substantial, though not surprising, differences are found among these groups—the "forerunners" are more liberal politically, less traditional in values, less enchanted about business careers (naturally) than the two other groups. But the findings tell us nothing about a *generation* gap, since the opinions of older people were not surveyed. Nor do they tell us anything about changes in values, since we do not have equivalent findings on earlier generations of the young.

What the findings do tell us (and this is concealed in the way the data are presented, so much so that I have had to recompute the statistics) is, first, that an overwhelming majority of the young—as many as 80 per cent—tend to be traditionalist in values; and, second, that there is a sharp division within the younger generation between, on the one hand, that distinct minority that chooses a liberal education and, on the other, both those who do not go to college and the majority of college students who are vocationally oriented. In brief, the prevailing pattern (of intra-generational cleavage) is quite similar to that which we find in politics.

The Fortune poll brings out one interesting thing: many of those interviewed—well over 80 per cent—report that they do not believe that there are great differences in values between themselves and their parents. This is supported by other investigations. Bengtson's direct comparison of college students demonstrates that they "shared the same general value orientations and personal life goals." He concludes that "both students and parents in this sample are overwhelmingly oriented toward the traditional middle-class values of family and career." From his careful study of normal middle-class high-school boys, Daniel Offer states flatly, "Our evidence indicates that both generations *share the same basic values*" (his italics).

Despite the impressive unanimity of these appraisals, the question of value change should remain an open one. It is hard to imagine that some changes are not taking place, in view of the vast social, economic and technological changes occurring in industrialized countries: the growth of large organizations, shifts in the occupational structure, the rapid diffusion of information, etc., etc. Yet the nature of these changes in values, if any, is by no means evident, and our understanding remains extremely limited.

We simply do not know which areas of values are changing, how rapidly the changes are taking place, which segments of the population they involve, how deeply they run, how stable any of the new values will turn out to be. Many apparent changes in "values" seem to be no more than changes in manners, or in rhetoric.

All in all, the most prudent assessment we can make, on the basis of the evidence we now have, is that no "value revolution" or anything remotely like it is taking place or is in prospect; and that if changes are occurring, they will do so through the gradual erosion, building and shifting of values.

Pleasure

Let us limit ourselves to the two areas of pleasure where generational differences are often held to be present: sex and drugs. Is there a sexual revolution among the young? And has a drug culture established itself as a significant part of youth culture?

Announced about 10 or 15 years ago, the sexual revolution has yet to take place. Like the generation gap itself, it may be more apparent than real. Support for this statement is provided by the Institute for Sex Research at Indiana University, which has just completed a new study, begun in 1967, in the course of which 1,200 randomly selected college students were interviewed. Comparing the findings with those obtained in its study of 20 years ago, the institute reports increasing liberalism in sexual practices but stresses that these changes have been gradual. One of the study's authors states, "There remains a substantial commitment to what can only be called traditional values." Most close students of the sexual scene seem to agree that the trend toward greater permissiveness in the United States probably began back in the nineteen-twenties, and has been continuing since. Sexual attitudes and habits are becoming more liberal—slowly. We are becoming Scandinavians—gradually.

The sexual changes one notes on the advanced campuses are of two kinds. First, there is a greater readiness to establish quasi-marital pairings, many of which end in marriage; these are without question far more common than in the past, and are more often taken for granted. Second, there is a trend, among a very small but conspicuous number of students, toward extremely casual sexuality, sometimes undertaken in the name of sexual liberation. To the clinician, these casual relationships seem to be more miserable than not—compulsive, driven, shallow, often entered into in order to ward off depression or emotional isolation. The middle-class inhibitions persist, and the attempt at sexual freedom seems a desperate maneuver to overcome them. We have a long way to go before the sexually free are sexually free.

As to drugs, specifically marijuana: Here we have, without much question, a sharp difference between the generations. It is a rare citizen over 30 who has had any experience with marijuana, and it is not nearly so rare among the young, particularly those in college. Still, the great majority of youngsters—almost 90 per cent—have had no experience with marijuana, not even to the degree of having tried it once, and, of course, far fewer use it regularly. Furthermore, a strong majority of the young do not believe marijuana should be legalized. What we have here, then, is both a generation gap and (as we have had before) a gap in attitude and experience within the younger generation.

It would be nice if we could keep our wits about us when we contemplate the implications of marijuana for our society. That is hard to do in the presence of hysteria on one side, among those who hold it to be an instrument of the devil, and transcendent rapture on the other, among those who see it as the vehicle and expression of a revolution in values and consciousness. In any case, the drug scene is too new and too fluid a phenomenon for us to foretell its ultimate place in the lives of the young. Drug use has grown rapidly. Will it continue to grow? Has it reached a plateau? Will it subside?

A more interesting question concerns the sociological and ideological factors involved in marijuana use. As marijuana has become more familiar, it has become less of a symbol of defiance and alienation. Lubell points out that just a few years ago the use of marijuana among college students was associated with a liberal or left political outlook; now it has become acceptable and even popular among the politically conservative. From what I have been able to learn, on some campuses and in some suburban high schools drug use is now most conspicuous among the *Jeunesse dorée*—fraternity members and the like—where it succeeds or complements booze, and coexists quite easily with political indifference or reaction and Philistine values. To put it another way, marijuana has not so much generated a new life style—as Timothy Leary and others had hoped—as it has accommodated itself to existing life styles.

Is there a generation gap? Yes, no, maybe. Quite clearly, the answer depends upon the specific issue we are talking about. But if we are talking about a fundamental lack of articulation between the generations, then the answer is—decisively—no. From one perspective, the notion of a generation gap is a form of pop sociology, one of those appealing and facile ideas which sweep through a self-conscious culture from time to time. The quickness with which the idea has taken hold in the popular culture—in advertising, television game shows and semi-serious potboilers—should be sufficient to warn us that its appeal lies in its superficiality. From another perspective, we might say that the generation gap is an illusion, somewhat like flying saucers. Note: not a delusion, an illusion. There *is* something there, but we err in our interpretation of what it is. There *is* something going on among the young, but we have misunderstood it. Let us turn now to the errors of interpretation which bedevil us when we ponder youth.

Parts and Wholes

The most obvious conceptual error, and yet the most common, is to generalize from a narrow segment of the young to the entire younger generation. With some remarkable consistency, those who hold that there is a generation gap simply ignore the statements, beliefs and activities of the noncollege young, and indeed of the ordinary, straight, unturned-on, nonactivist collegian. And the error goes even beyond this: on the university scene, the elite campus is taken to stand for all campuses; within the elite university, the politically engaged are taken to reflect student sentiment in general; and among the politically active, the radical fraction is thought to speak for activists as a whole.

It is not surprising to come across these confusions in the mass media, given their understandable passion for simplification of the complex, and their search for vivid spokesmen of strong positions. Thus, the typical TV special on the theme, "What Is Happening to Our Youth?", is likely to feature a panel consisting of (1) a ferocious black militant, (2) a feverish member of S.D.S., (3) a supercilious leader of the Young Americans for Freedom (busily imitating William Buckley), and (4), presumably to represent the remaining 90 per cent, a hopelessly muddled moderate. But we have much the same state of affairs in the quality magazines, where the essays on youth are given to sober yet essentially apocalyptic ruminations on the spirit of the young and the consequent imminent decline (or rebirth) of Western civilization.

Not too surprisingly, perhaps, the most likely writer of these essays is an academic intellectual, teaching humanities or the social sciences at an elite university. Hence he is exposed, in his office, in his classes, to far more than the usual number of radical or hippyesque students. (And he will live in a neighborhood where many of the young adolescents are preparing themselves for such roles.)

On top of this, he is, like the rest of us, subject to the common errors of social perception, one of which is to overestimate the size of crowds, another to be attracted by and linger upon the colorful and deviant. So he looks out of his office window and sees what seems to be a crowd of thousands engaging in a demonstration; or he walks along the campus, noting that every second male face is bearded. If we were to count—and he is not likely to count, since his mind is teeming with insights—he might find that the demonstration is in hundreds rather than thousands, or that the proportion of beards is nearer one in 10 than one in two. It is through these and similar processes that some of our most alert and penetrating minds have been led astray on the actualities of the young; that is why we have a leading intellectual writing, in a recent issue of a good magazine, that there are "millions" of activist students.

It is not surprising, then, that both the mass media and the intellectual essayists have been misled (and misleading) on the infinite variety of the young: the first are focused upon the glittering surface of social reality, the second upon the darker meanings behind that surface (an art brought to its highest state, and its highest pitch, by Norman Mailer). What *is* surprising, and most discouraging, is that a similar incompleteness of perception dominates the professional literature—that is, technical psychological and sociological accounts of adolescence and youth.

Having attended, to my sorrow, many convocations of experts on the young, I can attest that most of us are experts on atypical fractions of the young: on heavy drug users, or delinquents, or hippies, or the alienated, or dropouts, or the dissident—and, above all, on the more sprightly and articulate youngsters of the upper middle class. By and large, our discourse at these meetings, when it is not clinical, is a kind of gossip: the upper middle class talking to itself about itself. The examples run: my son, my colleague's daughter, my psychoanalytic patient, my neighbor's drug-using son, my Ivy League students. Most of us have never had a serious and extended conversation with a youngster from the working or lower-middle classes. In our knowledge of the young we are, to use Isaiah Berlin's phrase, hedgehogs, in that we know one thing, and know it well, know it deeply, when we also need to be foxes, who know many things less deeply.

What we know deeply are the visibly disturbed, and the more volatile, more conspicuous segments of the upper middle class. These are the youngsters with problems, or with *panache*—makers and shakers, shakers of the present, makers of the future. Their discontents and their creativity, we hear it said, produce the new forms and the new dynamics of our social system. Thus they allow us to imagine the contours of a hopeful new order of things or, contrariwise, permit us visions of Armageddon.

Perhaps so, but before judging this matter, we would do well to recognize that our narrowness of vision has led us to a distorted view of adolescence and youth. We have become habituated to a conflict model of adolescence—the youngster at odds with the milieu and divided within himself. Now, adolescence is far from being a serene period of life. It is dominated by significant transitions, and like all transitional periods—from early childhood to middle age—it produces more than its share of inner and outer discord. Yet, we have become so committed to a view of the young based upon conflict, pathology and volatility—a view appropriate for some adolescents most of the time and for most some of the time—that we have no language or framework for handling conceptually either the sluggish conformity or the effectiveness of adaptation or the generational continuity which characterizes most youngsters most of the time.

Young and Old, New and Old

Another common error is to exaggerate the differences between the younger and older generations. Differences there are, and always have been. But the current tendency is to assume that anything new, any change in beliefs or habits, belongs to or derives from the country of the young.

This tendency is particularly evident in the realm of politics, especially on the left, where "young" and "new" are often taken to be synonymous. Is this really so? To be sure, the young serve as the shock troops of New Left action. But consider how much of the leadership is of an older generation; as one example, most of the leaders of the New Mobilization—Lens, Dellinger, Dowd and others—are in their forties and fifties. It is even more significant that the key ideologues of radical politics—such men as Marcuse, Chomsky, Paul Goodman—are of secure middle age and beyond. The young have, in fact, contributed little to radical thought, except perhaps to vulgarize it to a degree painful for those of us who can remember a time when that body of thought was intellectually subtle, rich and demanding.

For that matter, is New Left thought really new—that is, a product of the nineteen-sixties? I was dumfounded several weeks ago when I stumbled across a book review I had written in the nineteen-fifties, a commentary on books by Erich Fromm, Lionel Trilling and the then unknown Herbert Marcuse. My review suggested that these otherwise disparate authors were united in that they sensed and were responding to a crisis of liberalism. The optimistic, melioristic assumptions of liberalism seemed to be failing, unable to cope with the alienation and the atavistic revivals produced by technological civilization.

Thus, even in the sunny, sleepy nineteen-fifties a now-familiar critique of American society was already well-established. The seminal ideas, political and cultural, of current radical thought had been set down, in the writings of C. Wright Mills, Marcuse, Goodman and others, and from another flank, in the work of Norman O. Brown, Mailer and Allen Ginsberg. That sense of life out of control, of bureaucratic and technological things in the saddle, of malaise and restlessness were, in the nineteen-fifties, felt only dimly, as a kind of low-grade infection. In the middle and late nineteen-sixties, with the racial explosion in the cities and our involvement in Vietnam, our political and cultural crisis became, or seemed to become, acute.

What I am getting at is that there is no party of the young, no politics indigenous to or specific to the young, even on the radical left. The febrile politics of the day do not align the young against the old, not in any significant way. Rather, they reflect the ideological differences in a polarized nation.

What we have done is to misplace the emphasis, translating ideological conflict into generational conflict. We have done so, I believe, because it suits our various psychological purposes. On the left, one's weakness in numbers and political potency is masked by imagining hordes of radicalized youth, a wave of the future that will transform society. On the right, one can minimize the intense strains in the American polity by viewing it, and thus dismissing it, as merely a youth phenomenon—kid stuff. And for the troubled middle, it may be easier to contemplate a rift between the generations than to confront the depth and degree of our current social discord.

A third error we make is to see the mood of the young—as we imagine that to be—as a forecast of long-term national tendencies. In our anxious scrutiny of youth, we attempt to divine the future, much as the ancients did in their perusal of the entrails of birds. Yet consider how radically the image of the American young has changed within as brief a period as a decade.

Ten years ago, we were distressed by the apparent apathy and conformism of the young, their seeming willingness, even eagerness, to be absorbed into suburban complacency. We were dismayed by the loss of that idealism, that amplitude of impulse we felt to be the proper mood of the young. By the early nineteen-sixties we were ready to believe that that lost idealism had been regained; the prevailing image then was of the Peace Corps volunteer, whose spirit of generous activism seemed so much in the American grain. And for the last few years we have been held by a view of youth fixed in despair and anger.

It should be evident that these rapid shifts in our idea of the young run parallel to changes in the American mood. As we moved from the quietude of the Eisenhower years, to the brief period of quickened hope in the Kennedy years, to our current era of bitter internal conflict dominated by a hateful war and a fateful racial crisis, so have our images of youth moved and changed. Yet, we were in each of these earlier periods as willing as we are today to view the then current mood of youth, as we saw it, as a precursor of the social future.

The young have always haunted the American imagination, and never more so than in the past two decades. The young have emerged as the dominant projective figures of our culture. Holden Caulfield, Franny Glass, the delinquents of the Blackboard Jungle, the beats and now the hippies and the young radicals—these are figures, essentially, of our interior landscape. They reflect and stand for some otherwise silent currents in American fantasy. They are the passive and gentle—Holden, Franny and now the flower children—who react to the hard circumstances of modern life by withdrawal and quiescence; or else they are the active and angry—the delinquents and now the radicals—who respond by an assault upon the system.

In these images, and in our tendency to identify ourselves with them, we can discover the alienation within all of us, old and young. We use the young to represent our despair, our violence, our often forlorn hopes for a better world. Thus, these images of adolescence tell us something, something true and something false, about the young; they may tell us even more about ourselves.

A Psychoanalyst Looks at Student Revolutionaries

HERBERT HENDIN

The fervor of revolutionary students describing the violence they experience and expect has shocked even those who take refuge in agreeing with their aims but not their methods. Yet these students, however fervid, however forceful, have remained essentially anonymous.

Radical students have told us they believe that America is too unjust to reform or to be worth reforming, that it exploits many in the interests of few, that it cares for nothing but power and money. They have told us that they wish to bring about the end of American life as we know it, and that the revolution they desire will be achieved only through violence. Their commitment to the violent implementation of their beliefs distinguishes the revolutionary students I am discussing from other young people who share their feelings about society. And we have seen that the translation of their beliefs into action leads them into ever fiercer encounters with their colleges, municipal police and Federal authorities. We have listened to their speeches, seen their actions, argued their politics. But have we any idea of what these revolutionary students are like?

So exclusively have we responded to their political activity and political violence that the people behind the politics have remained hidden. Even distinguished psychologists, psychiatrists and social scientists have so concerned themselves with the politics of these students that they have done little more than reflect sophisticated ways of disapproving or approving. For example, in one view, articulately advocated by Bruno Bettelheim, radical students are the product of overpermissive families: the students are violent because they have never had sufficient control exerted over them and consequently have never learned how to control themselves.

An opposing view, most identified with Kenneth Keniston, holds that radical students tend to be "healthier" than nonradicals. They have come from close, supportive families who have encouraged their individuality, and with whom they are not in conflict. Their radical action is the outgrowth of what is best in them, and their outrage is the product of a sound awareness of the American social, cultural and political wrongs of today.

But to understand student revolutionaries it is necessary to move beyond sympathy or antipathy for their politics to explore their inner lives and those internal forces which give their protest its distinctive shape.

From *The New York Times Magazine* (January 17, 1971), 16, 17, 19, 22, 24, 26, 28, 30.

Using psychoanalytic interviewing techniques involving free associations, dreams and fantasies, I am interviewing radical undergraduates at Columbia and Barnard[1] as part of an over-all study of the problems of college students. This particular part of the study grew out of a remark by a student friend who was active in the radical movement. He said that I would never in the course of my over-all study get to know the revolutionary students, because this group avoided the formal university channels on those occasions when they sought help. I asked if there was any way that I could interest radical students in being interviewed, and he replied: "They're hard up for money."

Since I had experience using psychoanalytic interviewing techniques with paid subjects, and was satisfied with the results, I felt it was worthwhile to try it in this case. The first students approached were suspicious and guarded, but after I had talked with them a few times they relaxed and reported back to their friends that I was not interested in judging them but in getting to know them as people and not just as revolutionaries. Actually, most of these students seemed to like the opportunity to explore their own feelings. Only one of the radical students approached refused to be interviewed.

The radical students I have seen are in many ways the successors at Columbia of Mark Rudd–often they are leaders in Students for a Democratic Society, the December 4th Movement (named after the date of the shooting by police of Fred Hampton, Black Panther leader, in 1969) and the Revolutionary Youth Movement (Weathermen). These students are paid $50 for completing a series of five interviews and a battery of psychological tests. Interviews with 15 such students have now been completed. They are white, from middle-class or affluent families and have a variety of religious backgrounds. They all believe in the necessity for a violent revolution and they work actively to radicalize groups ranging from high-school students to soldiers at Army bases.

On campus they have been involved in the use of physical intimidation and actual force against individuals who oppose them, in seizures of buildings and in the destruction of property. Both on and off campus they have been involved in fights with the police. Although none had yet participated in bombings or assaults that might destroy life as well as property, many advocated and all defended such acts as necessary to the cause. Some appeared likely to join a revolutionary underground committed to guerrilla warfare.

I gradually got a picture of the inner lives of these revolutionary students, of the relation between their inner feelings and their outer revolt. Their actual lives were strikingly different from widespread conceptions about them, particularly the ideas that they are the products either of overpermissive families, or of healthy "superior" families with whom they are not in conflict.

James (all names have been changed), an intense and articulate young man, spoke animatedly of the revolution he feels will come to America through violence. He is sure it is inevitable but is uncertain whether it will take the form of a race war

[1] More of the clinical material on which this article is based will appear in the Archives of General Psychiatry.

or of a broad-based battle between all the oppressed and all of those in power. He spent his first year at Columbia organizing in high schools, at the college, at Army bases, and becoming involved in the violent disruption of university life—all of which he sees as preparation for the revolution to come.

When I first saw him, James was depressed and discouraged about the lack of progress of the revolutionary movement during this, his second, year at college. Political activity had been minimal on campus and S.D.S. had found organizing difficult and interest almost impossible to arouse in the majority of students. He wistfully described the mixture of fear and exhilaration he felt in past confrontations with the police. As the interviews progressed, the Panther trial in New York and the conspiracy trial in Chicago had revived the movement on campus and he became part of a group that disrupted a meeting of the faculty senate and took over the platform to demand that Columbia provide bail for the Panthers. The success of the takeover made him outwardly more optimistic about the movement and also seemed to make him come alive.

But James has far more conflict over the use of violent tactics than he realizes. He dreamed that he was leading some dangerous and violent political maneuver that he had managed to pull off successfully. He began to run. He was caught in a barbed-wire fence and badly cut. Blood flowed. He was captured and put in a preventive-detention camp. James called this a "political dream" and enjoyed talking about it in political terms. He spoke of the possibility of going to prison for his radical activity and predicted a right-wing reaction in which revolutionary students throughout the country would be placed in "preventive-detention camps." He believes that would be the only way to stop left-wing violence. He almost seems to need and want some forceful outside reaction to control his behavior.

In talking of his "political dream," James came close to the personal origins of the anguish he feels when there is no preventive-detention camp to stop him from doing what he says he wants to do. He recalled an incident that occurred when he was home visiting his parents over Christmas vacation. Both his parents were anxious about his taking the car out after a blizzard, but his father said nothing and let him have it, although he knew driving was next to impossible. "Fifteen times," James said furiously, "I nearly killed myself or someone else." After he returned home he criticized his father for letting him use the car, knowing the conditions as he did. His father said that he had not wanted him to take it, but that he felt James would think he was overprotective if he refused and would get angry.

James is certainly indicating here that he needs outside control from his father to prevent him from becoming involved in destructive or self-destructive activity. But emotional withdrawal, not permissiveness, would be a more accurate description of his father's behavior. In this instance, his father wants to avoid having to deal with James's anger. James not only is furious at his father's withdrawal but he has learned how to use his father's difficulty in expressing his feelings as a weapon against him. While James began our sessions claiming that his parents supported his aims if not all of his tactics, he eventually admitted with a satisfied smile that he sensed his father was inwardly seething at the things he was doing, but was unable to say anything about them.

These students generally had parents with little ability or desire to see their children as they are, or to confront their actual feelings. This kind of emotional abandonment is anything but "permissive."

Amy, a bright, militant and successful radical leader, was, like most of the radical students, more at ease discussing politics than her personal life. She tried to see her personal feelings in political terms—for example, attributing the loneliness she felt in high school to the fact that all the other kids had more middle-class values than she.

She came to Barnard hoping that it would reflect the diversity of social classes in New York. But she soon came to feel that Barnard was insulated from city life. Although politically sympathetic to S.D.S., she attended only one meeting in her first year. She tended to be cynical and skeptical about what could be accomplished by radical action.

All this changed when the building occupation and strike of 1968 made her feel she had to take some stand. On the second day of the strike, she went into a building and stayed there until the "bust," when she was arrested. This was a crucial point in her political life; she became increasingly active. At first she was shy and held back at meetings, but she gradually got to be known and liked and she became part of the hard-core leadership of both S.D.S. and the December 4th Movement.

Amy in our first sessions emphasized the closeness of her family, claiming that she discussed her political activities with her parents, even though they were "only creeping Socialists" and she is a "violent revolutionary." As our talks progressed, she began to suggest that although it was possible to discuss politics with her family, nonpolitical, personal matters were avoided. But both politically and personally her parents withdrew from her whenever she needed them most. When she called her father for advice before participating in her first occupation of a campus building, he refused to give an opinion other than to say he was sure she would do the right thing.

But whenever they disapproved of what she did, her parents would say that it was not really Amy who occupied a building or got arrested. They implied that she was led or influenced by others and would say that if she thought about it, or was really "herself," she would see things their way.

Commenting that they had always behaved like this, she told of buying a bedspread for her room when she lived with her parents. Her mother said she didn't think it was good for her room and insisted that when Amy thought about it, she would see that it was not really her taste.

Amy's parents repeatedly tried to avoid direct conflict with her by insisting that it was not really Amy who was seeing or feeling or behaving whenever she saw, felt or did anything they did not like. The means they chose for avoiding conflict with her maintained the illusion of closeness without much of the content; they preserved the outward form of discussion without any acceptance of Amy's tastes or character. The only Amy who existed for them was the non-Amy they wished to see.

Nonrecognition or intolerance of her feelings enabled Amy's family to create an illusion of harmony, but left Amy with the problem of coping with the very tastes, feelings and character her parents denied she had. She has partly adopted her parents' way of dealing with her and is not now in touch with her feelings, particularly toward them. She speaks of them in a detached, objective way as being well-meaning but as having a life style that she would not choose for herself.

Kenneth Keniston writes that radical students have achieved a detached, objective view of their parents. But the use of psychoanalytic interviewing techniques makes clear that such detachment, as in Amy's case, usually conceals pain too difficult for the students to face. Their acute ability to see and feel the flaws of society is in striking contrast to their need not to see or know the often devastating effects their family life has had on them.

If Amy is pained by not being seen, Carl's experience with an even more painful family situation has made him want to be invisible. At 22 he has been "busted" six times and convicted twice for his political activity and he is increasingly attracted to the revolutionary underground. He came to his first interview last fall in shorts and sneakers and wore large, dark sunglasses throughout the session. He sank so deeply into his chair that he seemed to be lying rather than sitting. He spoke in a soft, almost faint voice and seemed generally quite depressed. He began the hour by talking about a conflict he feels over leaving the political group he's involved with, a conflict that illustrates the degree to which he conceals his feelings from others.

Carl lives in a commune of radical students who share several Manhattan apartments. He has had the urge to leave them to join a group of activists who are not college-educated and who live and work in a working-class neighborhood where he grew up. He feels they have taught him about people and life and that he is more comfortable with them than with the affluent kids in his commune whom he envies and resents. His bitterest complaints center on Kenny, whom he calls his closest friend. He's been hurt by Kenny's possessiveness toward Ellie, a girl in the commune, and by how intensely he resents any interest she shows in him.

The situation has become worse since Arlene, a girl Carl fell in love with some time ago, has returned from Cuba and joined their group. She told Carl she did not want a serious sexual involvement with anyone and he consequently tried to control or hide his sexual feeling for her. Kenny, however, did become sexually involved with Arlene. He comes to Carl for sympathy, help and advice because he feels "caught" between the two women. When Carl, suppressing his anger, merely replies that he does not want to be bothered with his problem, Kenny acts hurt and has even cried. Carl tries to hide his rage from him much as he tries to conceal his sexual desire for Arlene.

Carl finds it far easier to express his anger with the Establishment than with Kenny. The night of his most intense frustration and rage with Kenny, he dreamed of having a gun battle with the police. His passivity with Kenny and Arlene goes hand in hand with his extreme political activism, a commitment that includes becoming skillful with firearms in preparation for guerrilla warfare. He says he is "very turned on by Weathermen" and he believes he will become part of the revolutionary underground. When I asked whether he felt he'd be able to kill anyone, he answered, "Yes." He thought it might be difficult for him at first, but he expected that some of his friends would be killed and that their deaths would make it easier for him to kill.

Carl's retreat from competition and his need to hide his anger have operated to give him a peculiar role in his political life. While not himself a leader (his old friends jokingly ask him why he hasn't made the big time, like Mark Rudd or Bernadine Dohrn), he is often a catalyst for more violent political protest than the actual leaders have planned. When a friend who had become prominent in S.D.S. was leading an outdoor protest (permitted by college rules) against recruiting on campus by a company involved in military production, Carl took over the group, succeeded in getting it to enter and forcibly occupy the building and physically disrupt the recruiting. Once inside, however, he turned to his friend and said, "It's your group. Now it's your baby."

Carl linked his difficulties in competition and his retreat from the limelight to a lifelong reluctance to show his emotions. "If you show your feelings, you get your legs cut off," was his way of putting it. He was one of the few radicals interviewed who came from families in which there was an actual breakup: his mother and father were divorced when he was 8. His father, whom he saw occasionally through the years, belittled any feelings Carl expressed. Forced to support the family, his mother was bitter about her situation and exhausted from work. Carl describes her as withdrawn and unaffectionate.

Carl learned to keep his feelings to himself and to stay out of his mother's sight. That he somehow knew the degree to which he was supposed to be neither seen nor heard is rather movingly suggested by his behavior as a child: he slept under his bed. He recalls a recurring nightmare during this period in which he came home from school and rang the bell to his house. He was told by his mother that she didn't know him and that he didn't belong there. He went to his cousin's house and they told him the same thing. Finally, he walked across the country to his father's house in California and was told by his father that he didn't know him and that he didn't belong there. The dream ended with him disappearing into the Pacific Ocean.

If Carl is able to conceal his feelings in silence, Nancy, an attractive, witty radical leader, conceals them in vivacity. "I was a nice girl from a nice family and everything in my life moved a certain way until a year and a half ago [the time she entered college] when everything changed," she said. Her current life, which is a series of encounters with the authorities, would seem to have changed from her outwardly tranquil high-school life in her home town.

While she was away during Easter recess at Barnard, the F.B.I. came twice to search her room and she was really "freaked out" about it. She describes being in trouble with the "pigs" almost every day because she won't pay her subway fare (in protest against a fare increase), which results in her being chased through subway stations. She has been in trouble for taking food from the larger chain stores. She feels there is nothing wrong in taking food from the large, impersonal supermarkets since her stealing is less of a crime than she believes the stores are committing against society.

When she came to Barnard, Nancy explained, she realized that there was nothing worthwhile in this society to be part of and the only worthwhile thing was to be opposed to everything in the society. She is active in S.D.S., was one of the organizers of the December 4th Movement, and when I saw her she was under indictment and awaiting trial for her political activities.

Nancy believes that people "aren't interested in your feelings," and that "really, you should take care of these things yourself." "These things" seemed to refer to some inner turmoil. Her accounts of her childhood suggest how she came to think that people aren't interested in what she feels.

Nancy's parents are both professional people with active careers. As the oldest of the children, she had to care for her two younger siblings. She seems to have been disturbed not so much by her duties as by the feeling that she was forced to be independent at too early an age and was deprived of a childhood. She describes her parents as "nice, pleasure-loving people" who are "sort of like camp counselors." She added that she "sort of liked" some of her counselors even though she was miserable at camp. She says, "My parents aren't the sort who feel the family has to do something on a Sunday, so if they are together they get along fine because they are doing things that independently they want to do. If it happens that two of them want to do something at the same time, then it's O.K. If they all had to go to the zoo together, they'd probably kill each other. They're better than families who feel they have to be together. My parents aren't the type who sacrifice themselves for their children. I don't think parents should."

Nancy defends her family's lack of contact by contrasting it with a constricting, self-sacrificing "straw" family in which everyone is bound together through some overwhelming sense of obligation. She talks as though these are the only possible alternatives. She adopts a tragicomic, humorous tone in describing her frustrations with her parents. For example, while she has dropped out of college, is devoting all her time to her political activities, and is scheduled for trial in a few weeks, her last letter from her mother suggests that she take a course in marine biology which her mother enjoyed 20 years ago. Needless to say, Nancy has no interest in marine biology. In a light ironic way, which does not conceal the sadness in her eyes, she told me that her parents were persuaded that her brother stays home from school to study with his friends when actually he spent his time with them "tripping on acid."

Although she alternates between irony and defensiveness in describing her parents' lack of contact with her, it is clear she has experienced this as a profound rejection. That "lack of contact" was her euphemism for emotional abandonment was most movingly suggested in an event she related that occurred after a tonsillectomy when she was 11. She was left alone in the house. She developed a severe hemorrhage and became panicky. Her mother had gone out for several hours and told her to call a neighbor if something like that happened. But she knew that the neighbor was a hysterical woman who would be of no help. Nancy recalls standing by a window for two hours choking on the blood in her throat, waiting for her mother to come home, feeling that her mother had no right to expect her to take care of herself in that kind of situation. She is still figuratively drowning in her own juices and unable to trust anyone enough to ask for help.

James, Nancy, Carl and Amy were typical of the revolutionary students in describing parents who withdrew from them when they needed them most, or were simply unavailable. Obviously many other students have had similar experiences without becoming revolutionaries. But it is striking how pervasive the impact of emotional abandonment was on the lives of all these revolutionary students.

Although most of the students interviewed did have parents with a left-wing or at least liberal background, their ideology proved to be less important than the fact that political discussions were the closest thing to personal exchanges that took place in the family—a circumstance that may have some bearing on the use of politics to express feelings that are personal. An atmosphere of polite estrangement seemed to prevail between these parents who got along well with each other on the surface but who were not deeply involved with each other.

All the students felt their parents had not been physically affectionate toward them or each other, and described their fathers as especially repressed and emotionally tight. Most saw their fathers as successful at work, but as failures as fathers and husbands. Although they felt their parents were capable of compassion and pity for the weak, the oppressed or the handicapped, they did not see them as able to experience genuine passion.

Most of them felt that they too would have difficulty in sustaining personal passion in the intense and powerful way they can experience their political commitment. Their feelings of abandonment and parental withdrawal have left them with a pervasive depression and a diminished self-confidence. Considering their vulnerability and despair, it is not surprising that they feared both closeness and loneliness. They have an unusually great fear of losing out to other men or women in competition for the opposite sex, and in competition for various kinds of achievement. One student described how insecure he felt in high school competing with the ambitious, aggressive, athletic boys who were popular. Although they accepted him, he felt comfortable only when he left them to join the school's "counterculture"—i.e., a group that made fun of the "jocks" and was active in drug-taking and politics.

The idea that student revolutionaries are able to go the straight and affluent way but choose to do otherwise, turned out not to be true. Although they are all intelligent and articulate men and women, most will not finish college. Their frustration, their anger and their increasingly exclusive interest in violent political action deprive them of the necessary patience to finish—even though they realize that education, such as in law, would enable them to contribute more to the radical cause.

Some of the students said they took part in their first serious radical action at college "to see how it felt." They discovered that it "felt" better than almost anything they had felt before, that the exhilaration and excitement of a building-occupation or a confrontation with the police elevated them to a pitch of emotion they did not normally experience. They came to need the exhilaration of a violent political action to such an extent that far from choosing radical politics freely out of a wealth of possible choices, it became the only possible life for them.

The radical involvement, however, does more for these students than give them the thrill of becoming "action freaks." In the revolutionary culture many have found a "family" which understands their emotional needs better than their real families ever did. Since the radical movement discourages exclusive monogamous relationships, it does much to soften these students' anxiety over not being able to form deep attachments. The same young men who complain of passivity in their personal relations find that they can be forceful and aggressive in behalf of the radical cause. Many who suffer from a lack of direction find that the radical involvement brings them to life and focuses their energies. The prospect of each new violent protest provides an outlet for their anger and gives some relief to their depression.

Danger from outside—from college, police and Federal authorities—cements the closeness that comes from shared values and beliefs and tightens the bonds within the revolutionary "family." While their own parents, like Amy's or Nancy's, refuse to realize that their daughters are young revolutionaries—not marine biologists, "nice" girls or moderate Socialists—these students find in the reaction of the authorities some adequate response to themselves. They have a need for enemies that transcends their realistic suspicion that their phones have been tapped, their ranks infiltrated, or their rooms searched by Federal authorities.

But the culture that can give you relief can also lock you in. The radical life is not without its pressure and demands. Considering the emotional background of these students, it is more than ironic that the culture they create is so intolerant of individual expression not oriented toward group aims. One young man who wanted to spend the summer studying music felt too guilty to do so because the movement frowned on it. Several radical students expressed the feeling that to pursue their own interests or personal development was somehow selfish. One young woman radical had been denounced by Weathermen friends for being too monogamous. Another student has fantasies of a campus without a radical culture where he would feel free to chase girls and go for walks in the woods. Still another, totally committed to the life of a revoltuionary student, is glad his brother went to a more tranquil school and escaped the atmosphere that he himself is helping to create.

Revolutionary students admit frankly that their group is not free of some of the vices they deplore in society at large. The competitiveness that they find so distasteful creeps into their lives as well—whether it be competition for the opposite sex or for positions of leadership in the movement. Several criticized their own possessive tendencies toward things and people.

The women complained that "male chauvinism" was unfortunately all too much a part of the movement. They said the men thought they existed to do the duller paperwork. Many felt that the men wished to treat them as revolutionary women in a sexual sense—expecting them to be available sexually without regard for them as people. One girl said she had broken off with a radical leader she had lived with for almost a year because she felt that he really wanted her to stay in the background politically and that she could never find her identity as a radical with him. She subsequently became prominent in an organization of radical women.

Perhaps the greatest pressure exerted by the radical community is on students to prove their commitment to the cause through their willingness to commit violence or be arrested. Since, like James, these students are often inwardly ambivalent or frightened by their own violent tendencies, this demand produces great inner tension. At times these students complain that their way of life is "sick." But they quickly add that it is not as sick as that of the rest of society.

To attempt to understand the politics of radical students without first gaining an understanding of their inner lives is to invite confusion or bewilderment. The fervor with which these students attack property, the intensity with which they scorn America's concern for money, and the force they bring to their agreement with the most militant blacks must be seen in the context of their backgrounds. These young radicals have suffered in families which more than provided for their material needs but which ignored and frustrated their personal needs and continue to be blind to them as people. In rejecting the life style of their parents as too involved with property, wealth and economic security, they are saying that their parents were never concerned in any meaningful way with them.

Identification with the poor and the oppressed permits these radical students to react to poverty and oppression without having to face how personally impoverished, victimized and enraged they feel. Their acute sense of injustice derives from their personal, if often unrecognized, experience as victims. To insist that these students are products of overprivilege, the spoiled sons and daughters of the affluent, is to insist that the only hunger is for food and the only deprivation is material and economic.

Through the college years these students and their parents usually stick together to present a surface picture of harmony. Yet the students have learned their parents' weapons. It is now they who (like James, who knows his father is inwardly seething at his activities) never acknowledge their parents' true feelings at all. They lock their parents into precisely that silence in which they were locked as children, using their parents' fear of emotional confrontation as a powerful weapon. It is now the parents who feel obliged to go along with a situation they hate but cannot control. Inwardly furious, they often continue to support the radicals in or out of college. The students seldom hesitate to accept this support and at times seem pleased at so effectively coercing it from their parents.

Whether or not these students directly attack their parents, they do say they are "irrelevant." But it is the pain that can be inflicted by treating someone as irrelevant, by seeing their needs and character as haveing no *raison d'être*, that these students have learned so effectively at the feet of their parents. There could be no more satisfying revenge.

Student revolutionaries are accused of not providing any alternative plan for a future society. But these students are hardly interested in their own future, let alone in the future of the rest of us. The future will "take care of itself" or "the future as an idea is vastly overrated" are typical of their comments. They predict they will die young either in the revolution or in some nuclear or ecological disaster that will end the world. The prediction of cataclysm for the world must be seen partly as a projection of their inner world, since the inner revolution that may consume them is already under way, their personal environment has already been poisoned, and the bomb that may destroy them may well be of their own making.

(Of course, not all student violence can be attributed to student revolutionaries. Angry, "turned-off" students with no more political goals than the disruption of classes and the cancellation of final exams appear to have been responsible for the bombing of Columbia's Alma Mater statue last spring. Such students at times participate in violent actions initiated by radical students, but their role in the revolutionary group which I am discussing is only peripheral.)

In dealing with radical students, college administrators have tended to see the problem as one of permissiveness vs. discipline. If in the past college administrators have acted toward students with a kind of rigid aloofness, they have now under student pressure adopted a more permissive aloofness. Rigidity and permissiveness, however, are often opposite sides of the same coin. They are designed to enable adult authorities, be they parents or administrators, to avoid confronting the students as people—not merely to avoid student anger but to avoid facing the students' feelings in any significant way.

Student demands are often specifically designed to provoke rejection and subsequent confrontation. When college administrators accede to them, radical students often rightly feel they have yielded through fear. But to be yielded to through fear is as dehumanizing and infuriating to them as having their demands ignored. By treating these students as non-people, as an impersonal force to be managed through ignoring them when possible, through placation when afraid of them, or through force when all else fails, administrators touch some very sensitive chords in many students, arousing feelings of outrage that make it possible for revolutionary students to gain wide support.

The existence of inner turmoil in these students does not invalidate their critique of society. Such turmoil may even suggest a deeper and more subtle indictment of American life. Nor can psychological forces alone explain why students become revolutionaries at a particular time and place in history. But to discuss the historical and social forces that produce revolutionaries without knowing who student revolutionaries are or what they feel is misguided. However, even analysts and social scientists have ignored this inner dimension because of their involvement in the politics of the students. Agreeing with many of the students' criticisms of society, many psychoanalysts and social scientists try to become the students' advocates and allies. They desire to show through compassion that they are not out of touch with the aspirations of the radical young (and, perhaps, not growing old and "irrelevant").

But the students see through a sympathy based on lack of understanding and a compassion that has its source in fear or sentimentality. All this arouses only their benign contempt and further estranges them. As one student said of a judge who gave a sympathetic talk on the problems of students today before suspending sentence: "He means well, but with fools like that running the system, how can the revolution help but succeed?"

Reconciling Youth and the Establishment

JOHN D. ROCKEFELLER 3RD

More than two years ago I began a brief excursion into the world of the young. While preparing for a speech, I decided to try to find out, to my own satisfaction at least, what the youth revolution was all about. The experience turned out to be rewarding, but by the time I delivered the talk, I knew my excursion had become a journey, one that is still going on with no end in sight. In many ways the problem has become more complex and difficult. Our society appears to be more divided and polarized than before. And yet, my thesis then—and now—is that this need not be so, that we are wasting our best chance for constructive action.

I said in my remarks two years ago that the ferment of youth is potentially a powerful and constructive force in dealing with the problems our society faces. If that is true, then the crucial issue is not the youth revolution but the nature of the older generation's response to it.

I believed then, as I do now, that a basis exists for cooperation between youth and the Establishment. I said in the speech: "A unique opportunity is before us to bring together our age and experience and money and organization with the energy and idealism and social consciousness of the young." Ever since I have been trying to find specific ways to combine the resources of young and old. I have discussed this question with many young people—present and former Peace Corps and VISTA volunteers, federal employees, central-city and suburban high school students, leaders of youth organizations, college students, young professionals. I also have talked with members of the Establishment—businessmen, lawyers, government officials, university professors.

An idea quickly emerged that offered promise of fulfilling the need with one major stroke: a "national service" program, launched and sponsored by the federal government, in which young men and women would devote one to two years in non-military service to their country. In recent years this basic concept has been advanced by a number of national leaders. Although the proposed plans vary in

From *Saturday Review* (January 23, 1971), 27–29, 92.

details, the central theme is the same: a large-scale program to employ the restless energies of young people in areas where subprofessional manpower is needed, such as environment, tutoring, and delivery of health services.

In many ways, this approach has great appeal, but I concluded that it is not the answer. Cost and implementation obviously would present formidable challenges. But there is a more fundamental difficulty. A formal national service program, organized and funded by the federal government, is not in tune with the mood and temper of youth today. Most concerned young people do not want to be cogs in a national program. By and large, they are very skeptical about working for the federal government. They much prefer a loose and free form of organization that can move flexibly to targets of opportunity at local and regional levels. And they want to have some influence over any activity to which they make a commitment.

Many young people desire action that is directed toward basic social change, recognizing that change is essential if we are to cope with society's problems. They are not so concerned that government programs cannot generate social innovation, but that these efforts are often indirect, slow-moving, and bureaucratic. Moreover, government's attempts to initiate change are always politically sensitive, all the more so when the young are involved. The former Peace Corps and VISTA volunteers I talked with agreed that on balance their service had been worthwhile. They also agreed that as long as the volunteer engaged in straightforward service activities, everything was fine. But if he pressed for social change he became controversial and therefore a threat.

It is of course disappointing to come across what appears to be a grand solution to a major need and find out that it is no solution at all. While I favor increased government support for programs involving the young, it must be recognized that such efforts inevitably will be mainly in service and training areas rather than in those involving social change. If young people are to work directly on the massive problems confronting our society and if fundamental social change is to be possible where necessary, then I believe it will be the private sector that will have to develop and support the required programs. Is it realistic to envision this happening on a big enough scale to be significant?

One essential condition is youth's readiness to participate. I believe the evidence of the past two years illustrates that young people continue to be actively involved—in political action, in pressing for institutional reform, in scores of new organizations dealing with the environment and other issues. The scale of this involvement justifies saying that the beginnings of a national service program do exist in this country, scattered and sporadic to be sure, but an effort that goes from the bottom up rather than from the top down. It consists of tens of thousands of individual and group efforts by young people all over this nation.

This involvement is all the more impressive because it is voluntary. The young have other options, but they act out of genuine conviction. Far from being some radical frenzy, this commitment is in the best American tradition of private initiative and voluntary action.

At the same time, however, violence and militancy have also increased. A sense of perspective on this issue is badly needed. Every activist movement will contain its destructive elements, and so it is with the young. The small fringe that throws rocks and manufactures bombs receives attention out of proportion to its numbers. The great majority wants to improve this society, to solve the problems we have lived with too long, to help build a decent and just life for all. The chief danger is that these responsible young people will become frustrated through lack of success in their efforts.

The fundamental issue still is the relative lack of response by the Establishment to the constructive potential of the young. We may have a national service effort in the country in terms of the motivation and energy and commitment of tens of thousands of young people. But we do not have it in terms of organization and money and expertise. This is what the Establishment could supply. However, it has not done so to any significant degree. In the past two years, I have not seen a response by the Establishment comparable to the buildup of projects and activities on the part of the young.

Thus we play into the hands of the extremists by frustrating the efforts of the large number of dedicated and positive young people who want to be constructive. By our failure to respond positively to youthful activism, we are throwing away what is potentially our best asset for needed social change; indeed, we may well be converting it from an opportunity to a major problem.

And so we arrive at the underlying questions: Is it possible for youth and the Establishment to come together, to break through the misunderstandings, the anger and hostility, which now divide them? What are the obstacles to cooperation, and can they be overcome? How would both groups react to specific projects in which they work together?

Answers are beginning to emerge from the work and research of a small task force that I have sponsored. The approach was first to develop a number of specific ideas for joint action by young people and Establishment members, and then to test the more promising in a scientific survey of both groups. The survey also was designed to diagnose the mood and temper of the two groups on a wider range of issues and to try to find out what they think of each other.

In the course of the research, 872 students and 408 Establishment leaders (mainly business executives) were interviewed. If these interviews could be summarized in one sentence, it would be this: While there are formidable obstacles to be faced—and they should not be underestimated for a moment—there does exist a solid basis for cooperative effort between young people and the Establishment. Cooperation is wanted by both groups. Both believe that it is urgently needed.

There is substantial agreement among college students and business executives on the issues that must be dealt with on a collaborative basis: poverty, racism, pollution, overpopulation, drug addiction. Ending the Vietnam War remains a vital concern for the students, but when asked about problems to which they will devote their personal time, they rank the war fourth, behind poverty, pollution, and racism. This seems to indicate a pragmatic shift that can be summed up in a comment by one respondent: "Let's stop talking and start doing."

Furthermore, the two groups expressed a willingness to work with each other. In spite of their misgivings, young people are ready to give cooperation a try. By an almost 3-to-1 margin, they say they would rather work with the Establishment in coping with social issues than with protest groups. At the same time, there is a very strong and frustrated wish on the part of business leaders to establish dialogue with the young. Three out of four want active cooperation. Their prevailing view is summed up by the comments of one businessman:

> Whatever the causes of the rebellion, we had better get together with these young people, for the issues they are raising are our issues, the problems facing us as a nation. We need their ideas; we need their help. They are frustrated; we are frustrated. They are angry; we are angry. Neither generation can afford merely anger or frustration. Instead we must work together.

Among businessmen there is less backlash against students than is the case in the general population. The accent is not on writing off or further isolating the college rebels, but rather on talking and working together. For their part, the great majority of students surveyed believe that the American system is flexible enough to allow them to solve problems and overcome flaws without resort to radical change. They overwhelmingly prefer reason to violence.

Most encouraging is the fact that both the students and businessmen endorse all four of the sample project ideas in the survey. One of them deals with a number of ways to encourage and support the involvement of the young in the political life of this country. Another has to do with setting up public interest study and action groups in the Ralph Nader manner, but at the local level. A third, called "Dialogue Week," is a method of bringing young people and business executives together for a substantial period of time. This would be done in a setting designed to help stimulate genuine communication and the planning of an ongoing project.

Ranked highest by both students and businessmen is the fourth project idea, which calls for a two-year environmental program in a major river valley. It would involve creating a student corporation, based in a consortium of universities in the area. The students would draw on faculty expertise as needed and work to enlist the know-how and support of the Establishment in the area, especially business and civic leaders.

So much for the encouraging factors. As I have already indicated, the survey also highlights many formidable obstacles to cooperation. They involve a strange and difficult combination of problems, ranging all the way from the rational and practical to the emotional.

One major factor is the continuing frustration of students over the Vietnam War. Another is the growing number of students who now make a radical diagnosis of society. Between young people and the Establishment generally, there is a mutual display of surface anger and hostility and a deeper kind of mistrust. The students do not trust businessmen to stay with any project in which business interests become affected. The percentage of student activists who regard businessmen as overly concerned with profits as against social responsibility has increased sharply in just one year. For their part, the businessmen are wary of student immaturity and radicalism, and few see any reason why they should subject themselves to harangues and abuse.

There also are the new values held by a great many young people that often conflict with those held by most businessmen. These students do not doubt their ability to make a living, to be successful in the conventional sense if they so choose. Taking these benefits for granted, they discount them and emphasize the importance of the individual, the desirability of social change, the search for meaningful personal relationships and work. They question authority on almost every count and hold up virtually every institution of our society for re-examination. For the most part, they find them wanting.

Another barrier to cooperation is a growing feeling of isolation and alienation on the part of many students as they react to the public's anger with campus unrest. The students are drawing back and intensifying their identification with other minority groups that are seen as fellow victims.

These are the obstacles that have tended to immobilize the situation, to dampen initiatives between two groups for whom mechanisms for coming together do not normally exist in our society. Ironically, they can be surmounted only by coming together, by working in contact with one another, in genuine dialogue.

The forces operating in favor of collaboration between youth and the Establishment and the obstructions standing in the way are fairly evenly balanced. Whether this balance will be tipped positively or negatively will depend very largely on the nature and extent of the leadership exercised by Establishment groups. The main responsibility for a movement toward reconciliation and joint action now rests with the Establishment. Young people have been involved and committed for some time; it is our turn now. The situation cries out for reconciliation, for directing energies toward cooperation rather than conflict, for acting jointly on the awesome problems we face. We must be generative rather than reactive.

A process of reconciliation can succeed if we do not undertake it with naive expectations. The realistic hope is for mutual understanding to the degree that we can work together despite differences in values and attitudes.

The task force will continue its work and is now helping to put several project ideas into operation. But none of us sees these projects as anything more than points of entry, an opening wedge into some of our complex and difficult problems. The hope is to help start a process of reconciliation, of collaboration, and thereby serve to stimulate and encourage many more joint-action projects.

There are almost infinite possibilities for youth-Establishment cooperation, but initiative and ingenuity and commitment will be required to develop and launch them on a meaningful scale. It might be as simple an idea as having businesses and law firms go to campuses not only to recruit students but also to find out how they can help the students to use their developing professional tools in the search for social progress. It might be a state's or major city's developing an intern program that really works. It might be providing logistical support—a meeting place, telephones, transportation—for a local group working on the environment. It might be a genuine effort within a large organization to open up communication with its younger members.

If 100 corporate presidents each undertook to develop or respond to one such idea for youth-Establishment collaboration, what a difference it would make. If they were joined by 100 university presidents, by ten or twenty governors, the heads of our ten largest unions, the leadership of half a dozen of our religious denominations, the presidents of twenty foundations, the leadership of a dozen professional societies—if each of these leaders developed one good project for youth-Establishment collaboration on the pressing social problems of our time, what a massive impact it would have.

I am talking now about new projects based on responsiveness to young people, not merely listing the activities in which we are now engaged. If we can do this on a meaningful scale, it will begin to complete the picture of a national service program generated in the private sector, matching the motivation and drive of the young with a comparable response by the Establishment.

If this could happen, faith in the American system would be redeemed among young activists. It would go a long way toward meeting their urge to be relevant and constructive, to be part of the decision-making process. The best impulses of the Establishment would be maximized, including the desire for reconciliation with the young and readiness to use skills and resources for purposes larger than private success. And perhaps most important, we would make progress on the tough issues that face our society today.

I believe these goals are possible. Whether they are attained will depend on the efforts of each one of us. I have confidence that we will rise to the challenge. And this is the prospect which makes me feel these are exciting times to be alive.

Whose Country Is America?

ERIC HOFFER

The conspicuous role played by the young in our society at present has prompted a widely held assumption that the young constitute a higher percentage of the population than they did in the past. Actually, in this country, the percentage of

From *The New York Times Magazine* (November 22, 1970), 30, 31, 117, 118, 119, 120, 121, 122, 124. Adapted from Chaps. 5 and 6 of *First Things, Last Things* by Eric Hoffer. (Originally appeared in *The New York Times Magazine,* Nov. 1970, under the title, "Whose Country Is America?")

the under-25 age group has remained fairly constant through several decades—it hovers around 47 per cent. The high-school and college age group—14 to 24—has remained close to 15 per cent. The nation as a whole has not been getting younger. The median age of all Americans in 1910 was 24. Today it is 27, and it is likely to go up since the birth rate right now is very low.

The conspicuousness of the young is due to their greater visibility and audibility. They have become more flamboyant, more demanding, more violent, more knowledgeable and more experienced. The general impression is that nowadays the young act like the spoiled children of the rich. We are discovering that there is such a thing as an "ordeal of affluence," that diffused affluence subjects the social order to greater strain and threatens social stability more than does diffused poverty. Order and discipline have up to now been attributes generated in the battle against want. Society itself originated in the vital need for a joint effort to wrest a livelihood from grudging nature. Not only our material but our moral and spiritual values are predicated on the immemorial curse: "In the sweat of thy face shalt thou eat bread." Thus diffused affluence unavoidably creates a climate of disintegrating values with its fallout of anarchy.

In the past, breakdowns of value affected mainly the older segment of the population. This was true of the breakdown of the Graeco-Roman civilization, of the crisis that gave birth to the Reformation, and of the periods of social disintegration that preceded the French, the Russian and the Nazi revolutions. That our present crisis particularly affects the young is due partly to the fact that widespread affluence is robbing a modern society of whatever it has left of puberty rites to routinize the attainment of manhood. Never before has the passage from boyhood to manhood been so difficult and explosive. Both the children of the well-to-do and of families on welfare are prevented from having a share in the world's work and of proving their manhood by doing a man's work and getting a man's pay. Crime in the streets and insolence on the campus are sick forms of adolescent self-assertion. The young account for an ever-increasing percentage of crimes against persons and property. The peak years for crimes of violence are 18 to 20, followed by the 21 to 24 age group.

Even under ideal conditions the integration of the young into the adult world is beset with strains and difficulties. We feel ill at ease when we have to adjust ourselves to fit in. The impulse is to change the world to fit us rather than the other way around. Only where there are, as in primitive societies, long-established rites of passage, or where the opportunities for individual self-assertion are fabulous, does growing up proceed without excessive growing pains.

Can a modern affluent society institute some form of puberty rites to ease the passage from boyhood to manhood? It is of interest in this connection that among the Bantu tribes in South Africa work is replacing the ritual related to puberty. It used to be that a young man had to kill a lion or an enemy to prove his manhood. Today many young natives do not feel they have become full-fledged adults until they have put in a stint in the mines. Could not a ritual of work be introduced in this country? Every boy and girl on reaching 17, or on graduating from high school, would be given an opportunity to spend two years earning a living at good pay.

There is an enormous backlog of work to be done both inside and outside the cities. Federal, state and city governments, and also business and labor would pool their resources to supply the necessary jobs and training.

The routinization of the passage from boyhood to manhood would contribute to the solution of many of our pressing problems. I cannot think of any other undertaking that would dovetail so many of our present difficulties into opportunities for growth.

Though the percentage of the young, as pointed out, has remained constant through several decades, there has been a spectacular increase in the percentage of adolescents. At present, adolescence comprises a wider age range than it did in the past. Affluence is keeping persons in their late 20's in a state of delayed manhood, while television has lowered the threshold of adolescence. Nowadays, 10-year-olds have the style of life and the bearing of adolescents. Even children under 10 have an astounding familiarity with the intricacies and the mechanics of the adult world. By the time a child enters kindergarten, he has spent more hours learning about his world from television than the hours he will spend later in classrooms earning a college degree. It is a paradox that at a time when youths rioting in Chicago are called "mere kids," there are actually few genuine kids any more.

The contemporary blurring of childhood is not unprecedented. During the Middle Ages, children were viewed and treated as miniature adults. Nothing in medieval dress distinguished the child from the adult. The moment children could walk and talk they entered the adult world, and took part in the world's work. In subsequent centuries, the concept of childhood became more clearly defined. Yet even as late as 1835 schoolbooks in this country made no concession to childhood in vocabulary or sophistication. Child labor, so widely practiced in the first half of the 19th century, and which we find abhorrent, was not totally anomalous in a society that did not have a vivid view of childhood as a sheltered, privileged age.

To counteract an old man's tendency to snort at the self-important young, I keep reminding myself that until the middle of the 19th century the young acted effectively as members of political parties, creators of business enterprises, advocates of new philosophical doctrines and leaders of armies. Most of the wars that figure in our history books were fought by teen-agers. There were 14-year-old lieutenants in Louis XIV's armies. In one of his armies the oldest soldier was under 18. The middle-aged came to the fore with the Industrial Revolution. The experience and capital necessary to make an industrialist required a long apprenticeship. One might say that from the middle of the 19th to the middle of the 20th century the world was run by and for the middle-aged. The postindustrial age seems to be groping its way back to an immemorial situation interrupted by the Industrial Revolution.

The middle-aged came to the fore with the Industrial Revolution. Another way of putting it is that the middle-aged came into their own with the full entrance of the middle class onto the stage of history. The present discomfiture of the middle-aged is a symptom of a downturn in the fortunes of the middle class.

Adolescence as a clearly marked phase in the life of the individual, and the practice of keeping physically mature males in a state of delayed manhood are middle-class phenomena. The young of the working class and of the aristocracy come early in touch with the realities of life, and are not kept waiting in the wings. In neither the working class nor the aristocracy does age have the vital meaning it has in the middle class.

Industrialization was the creation of the middle class. It is questionable whether the spectacular "mastery of things," the taming of nature on a global scale, could have been achieved by other human types. No other ruling class succeeded so well in energizing the masses, and infusing them with an automatic readiness to work. Aristocrats and intellectuals know how to generate in a population a readiness to fight and die, but they cannot induce an uncoerced, wholehearted participation of the masses in the world's work.

Indeed, it is doubtful whether a nonmiddle-class society can be modern. Domination by aristocrats, intellectuals, workers or soldiers results in a return to the past—to feudalism, the Middle Ages, or even the ancient river-valley civilizations. It is not as yet certain whether it is possible to have a free-wheeling science, literature and art, or even a genuine machine age, without a middle class.

Yet, despite its unprecedented achievements, the middle class is just now on the defensive, unsure of its footing. With the consummation of the Industrial Revolution and the approach of affluence the middle class seems to have nowhere to go. It no longer feels itself in possession of the true and only view possible for sensible people. One begins to wonder whether the unglamorous, hard-working middle class, so essential to the process of production in a climate of scarcity, is becoming anachronistic in an age of plenty where distribution is the chief problem. Middle-class society is being strained to the breaking point not, as Marx predicted, by ever-increasing misery but by ever-increasing affluence. The coming of affluence has found the middle class unequipped and unprepared for a return to Eden.

Early in the 19th century, Saint-Simon characterized the coming of the industrial age as the passage "from the management of men to the administration of things." He did not foresee that once the industrial revolution had run its course there would have to come a reversion from the administration of things to the management of men. Up to quite recently, the middle class did not have to bother overmuch with the management of men since scarcity (unfulfilled needs), the factory, long working hours, etc. tamed and disciplined people automatically. Now, with affluence and leisure, people are no longer kept in line by circumstances. Discipline has to be implanted and order enforced from without. It is at this point that "men of words" and charismatic leaders—people who deal with magic—come into their own. The middle class, lacking magic, is bungling the job.

Thus, as the postindustrial age unfolds, we begin to suspect that what is waiting for us around the corner is not a novel future but an immemorial past. It begins to look as if the fabulous century of the middle class and the middle-aged has been a detour, a wild loop that turns upon itself, and ends where it began. We are returning to the rutted highway of history, which we left 100 years ago in a mad rush to tame a savage continent and turn it into a cornucopia of plenty. We see all around us the lineaments of a pre-industrial pattern emerging in the postindustrial age. We are rejoining the ancient caravan, a caravan dominated by the myths and magic of élites, and powered by the young.

In this country, the coming of the postindustrial age may mean the loss of all that made America new—the only new thing in the world. America will no longer be the common man's continent. The common people of Europe eloped with history to America and have lived in common-law marriage with it, unhallowed by the incantations of "men of words." But the élites are finally catching up with us. We can hear the swish of leather as saddles are heaved on our backs. The intellectuals and the young, booted and spurred, feel themselves born to ride us.

The phenomenal increase of the student population is shaping the attitudes and aspirations of the young. There are now more students in America than farmers. For the first time in America, there is a chance that alienated intellectuals, who see our way of life as an instrument of debasement and dehumanization, might shape a new generation in their own image. The young's sympathy for the Negro and the poor goes hand in hand with an élitist conceit that pits them against the egalitarian masses. They will fight for the Negro and the poor, but they have no use for common folk who work and moonlight to take care of their own. They see a free-wheeling democracy as a society stupefied by "the narcotic of mass culture." They reserve their wrath for the institutions in which common people are most represented: unions, Congress, the police and the Army. Professor Edgar Z. Friedenberg thinks that "élitism is the great and distinctive contribution students are making to American society." Democracy is for the dropouts; for the élite, an aristocratic brotherhood.

Yet one cannot help but wonder how inevitable is the future that seemingly is waiting for us around the corner. Might not the common people, so cowed and silent at this moment, eventually kick up their heels, and trample would-be élitists in the dirt? There is no earthly reason why the common people who for more than a century have been doing things here that in other countries are reserved for élites, should not be capable of overcoming the present crisis.

Whose Country?

Nowhere at present is there such a measureless loathing of educated people for their country as in America. An excellent historian thinks Americans are "the most frightening people in the world," and our foremost philologist sees America as "the most aggressive power in the world, the greatest threat to peace and to international cooperation." Others call America a "pig heaven," "a monster with 200 million heads," "a cancer on the body of mankind."

Novelists, playwrights, poets, essayists and philosophers depict America as the land of the dead—a country where sensitive souls are starved and flayed, where nothing nourishes and everything hurts. Nowhere, they say, is there such a boring monotony: monotony of talk, monotony of ideas, monotony of aim, monotony of outlook on the world. One American writer says: "America is no place for an artist. A corn-fed hog enjoys a better life than a creative artist." One she-intellectual maintains that "the quality of American life is an insult to the possibilities of human growth."

It is hard to believe that this savage revulsion derives from specific experiences with persons and places. What is there in America that prevents an educated person from shaping his life, from making the most of his inborn endowments? With all its faults and blemishes, this country gives a man elbowroom to do what is nearest to his heart. It is incredible how easy it is here to cut oneself off from vulgarity, conformity, speciousness, and other corrupting influences and infections. For those who want to be left alone to realize their capacities and talents, this is an ideal country.

The trouble is, of course, that the alienated intellectual does not want to be left alone. He wants to be listened to and be taken seriously. He wants to influence affairs, have a hand in making history, and feel important. He is free to speak and write as he pleases, and can probably make himself heard and read more easily than one who would defend America. But he can neither sway elections nor shape policy. Even when his excellence as a writer, artist, scholar, scientist or educator is generally recognized and rewarded he does not feel himself part of the power structure. In no other country has there been so little liaison between men of words and the men of action who exercise power. The body of intellectuals in America has never been integrated with or congenial to the politicians and businessmen who make things happen. Indeed, the uniqueness of modern America derives in no small part from the fact that America has kept intellectuals away from power and paid little attention to their political views.

The nineteen-sixties have made it patent that much of the intellectual's dissent is fueled by a hunger for power. The appearance of potent allies—militant blacks and students—has emboldened the intellectual to come out into the open. He still feels homeless in America, but the spectacle of proud authority, in cities and on campuses, always surrendering before threats of violence, is to him a clear indication that middle-class society is about to fall apart, and he is all set to pick up the pieces.

There is no doubt that in our permissive society the intellectual has far more liberty than he can use; and the more his liberty and the less his capacity to make use of it, the louder his clamor for power—power to deprive other people of liberty.

The intellectual's allergy to America shows itself with particular clarity in what has happened to many foreign intellectuals who found asylum here during the Hitler decade. It is legitimate to assume that they had no anti-American preconceptions when they arrived. They were, on the contrary, predisposed to see what was best in their host country. Though no one has recorded what Herbert Marcuse said when he landed in New York in 1934, it is safe to assume that he did not see Americans as one-dimensional men, and did not equate our tolerance with oppression, our freedom with slavery, and our good nature with simple-mindedness.

We have a record of what some other foreign intellectuals said when they arrived in the nineteen-thirties. It is worth quoting in full the words of Olga Schnitzler, the widow of Arthur Schnitzler: "So much is here to learn and to see. Everyone has been given an opportunity. Everyone who has not been completely worn out experiences here a kind of rebirth. Everyone feels what a grandiose, complex and broad-minded country America is, how well and free one can live among these people without perfidy and malice. Yes, we have lost a homeland, but we have found a world."

Once they had settled down and found their place, many of these intellectuals began to feel constrained and stifled by the forwardness and the mores of the plebeian masses. They missed the aristocratic climate of the Old World. Inevitably, too, they became disdainful of our lowbrow, practical intelligence. They began to doubt whether Americans had the high-caliber intelligence to solve the problems of a complex, difficult age. Hardly one of them bethought himself that in Europe, when intellectuals of their kind had a hand in shaping and managing affairs, things had not gone too well. There was something that prevented them from sensing the unprecedented nature of the American experiment; that the rejected of Europe have come here together, tamed a savage continent in an incredibly short time and, unguided by intellectuals, fashioned the finest society on a large scale the world has so far seen.

Scratch an intellectual and you find a would-be aristocrat who loathes the sight, the sound and the smell of common folk. Professor Marcuse has lived among us for more than 30 years and now, in old age, his disenchantment with this country is spilling over into book after book. He is offended by the intrusion of the vulgar, by the failure of egalitarian America to keep common people in their place. He is frightened by "the degree to which the population is allowed to break the peace where there is still peace and silence, to be ugly and uglify things, to ooze familiarity and to offend against good form." The vulgar invade "the small reserved sphere of existence" and compel exquisite Marcusian souls to partake of their sounds, sights and smells.

To a shabby would-be aristocrat like Professor Marcuse there is something fundamentally wrong with a society in which the master and the worker, the typist and the boss's daughter do not live totally disparate lives. Everything good in America seems to him a sham and a fraud.

An interesting peculiarity of present-day dissenting intellectuals is their lack of animus toward the rich. They are against the Government, the Congress, the Army and the police, and against corporations and unions, but hardly anything is being said or written against "the money changers in the temple," "the economic royalists," "the malefactors of great wealth" and "the maniacs wild for gold" who were the butt of vituperation in the past. Indeed, there is nowadays a certain rapport between the rich and the would-be revolutionaries. The outlandish role the rich are playing in the affluent society is one of the surprises of our time. Though the logic of it seems now fairly evident, I doubt whether anyone had foreseen that affluence would radicalize the upper rich and the lowest poor and nudge them toward an alliance against those in the middle. Whatever we have of revolution just now is financed largely by the rich.

In order to feel rich, you have to have poor people around you. In an affluent society, riches lose their uniqueness—people no longer find fulfillment in being rich. And when the rich cannot feel rich they begin to have misgivings about success—not enough to give up the fruits of success, but enough to feel guilty, and emote soulfully about the grievances of the disadvantaged, and the sins of the status quo. It seems that every time a millionaire opens his mouth nowadays he confesses the sins of our society in public.

Now, it so happens that the rich do indeed have a lot to feel guilty about. They live in exclusive neighborhoods, send their children to private schools, and use every loophole to avoid paying taxes. But what they confess in public are not their private sins, but the sins of society, the sins of the rest of us, and it is our breasts they are beating into a pulp. They feel guilty and ashamed, they say, because the mass of people, who do most of the work and pay much of the taxes, are against integrated schools and housing, and do not tax themselves to the utmost to fight the evils that beset our cities. We are discovering that in an affluent society the rich have a monopoly of righteousness.

Moreover, the radicalized rich have radical children. There is no generation gap here. The most violent cliques of the New Left are made up of the children of the rich. The Weathermen, to whom workingmen are "honky bastards," have not a member with a workingman's background. The behavior of the extremist young makes sense when seen as the behavior of spoiled brats used to instant fulfillment who expect the solutions to life's problems to be there on demand. And just as in former days aristocratic sprigs horsewhipped peasants, so at present the children of the rich are riding roughshod over community sensibilities. The rich parents applaud and subsidize their revolutionary children, and probably brag about them at dinner parties.

As I said, the alienated rich are one of the surprises of our time. It is not surprising to be told that America is a country where intellectuals are least at home. But it is startling to realize that the rich are not, and probably never have been, wholly at ease in this country. The fact that it is easy to get rich in America has not made it a rich man's country. The rich have always had it better elsewhere—better service, more deference, and more leisure and fun. In America, the rich have not known how to savor their riches, and many of them have not known how to behave and have come to a bad end.

There is a story about a British intellectual who traveled through this country toward the end of the last century. He was appalled by the monotony and unimaginativeness of the names of the towns he saw through the train window: Thomasville, Richardsville, Harrysville, Marysville and so on. He had not an inkling of the import of what he was seeing: namely, that for the first time in history common people—any Tom, Dick and Harry—could build a town and name it after his own or his wife's name. At one station, an old Irishwoman got on the train and sat next to him. When she heard his muttering and hissing she said: "This is a blessed country, sir. I think God made it for the poor." Crèvecoeur, in the 18th century, saw America as an asylum where "the poor of Europe have by some means met together." The poor everywhere have looked on America as their El Dorado. They voted for it with their legs by coming over in their millions.

Yet during the nineteen-sixties, poverty became one of the chief problems that plague this country: one of several nagging problems—like race relations, violence, drugs, inflation—which defy solution. From being a land of opportunity for the poor, America has become a dead-end street for some 15 million unemployables—80 per cent of them white, and most of them trapped in the cores of big cities. Money, better housing, and special schooling have little effect. Our society is showing itself unduly awkward in the attempt to turn the chronically poor into productive, useful citizens. Whereas, in the not too distant past, it was axiomatic that society lived at the expense of the poor, the present-day poor, like the Roman proletariat, live at the expense of society.

We have been transferred by affluence to a psychological age. Impersonal factors, including money, no longer play a decisive role in human affairs. It seems that, by mastering things, we have drained things of their potency to shape men's lives. It is remarkable that common people are aware of this fact. They know that at present money cannot cure crime, poverty, etc., whereas the social doctors go on prescribing an injection of so many billions for every social ailment.

In the earliest cities, suburbs made their appearance as a refuge for dropouts who could not make the grade in the city. When eventually the cities decayed, the suburbs continued as the earliest villages. In our cities, the process has been reversed. The dropouts are stagnating in the cores of the cities, while people who are ideally suited for city life seek refuge in the suburbs. The indications are that we shall not have viable cities until we lure the chronically poor out of the cities and induce the exiled urbanites to return.

The diffusion of affluence has accelerated the absorption of the majority of workingmen into the middle class. The unemployable poor, left behind, feel isolated and exposed, and it is becoming evident that a middle-class society, which hugs the conviction that everyone can take care of himself, is singularly inept in helping those who cannot help themselves. If the rich cannot feel rich in an affluent society, the poor have never felt poorer.

Whose country, then, is America? It is the country of the common—the common men and women, a good 70 per cent of the population—who do most of the work, pay much of the taxes, crave neither power nor importance, and want to be left alone to live pleasurable humdrum lives. "The founders of the United States," said Lord Charnwood, "did deliberately aspire to found a commonwealth in which common men and women should count for more than elsewhere."

Again and again, you come up against the mystery of what happens to common folk when they land on our shores. It is like a homecoming. They find here their natural habitat, their ideal milieu that brings their energies and capacities into full play.

Tasks that in other countries are reserved for a select minority, for a specially trained élite, are in this country performed by every Tom, Dick and Harry. Not only did common Americans build and name towns, but they also founded states, propagated new faiths, commanded armies, wrote books, and ran for the highest office. It is this that has made America unprecedentedly new.

It tickled me no end that the astronauts who landed on the moon were not élite-conscious intellectuals but lowbrow ordinary Americans.[1] It has been the genius of common Americans to achieve the momentous in an unmomentous matter-of-fact way. If space exploration remains in their keeping, they will soon make of it an everyday routine accessible to all.

The intellectuals call this giving access to the vulgar—vulgarization. The intellectuals' inclination is to complicate things, to make them so abstruse and difficult that they are accessible only to the initiated few. Where the intellectuals are in power, prosaic tasks become Promethean undertakings. I have yet to meet an intellectual who truly believes that common people can govern themselves and run things without outstanding leaders. In the longshoremen's union the intellectuals have a nervous breakdown anytime a common, barely literate longshoreman runs for office and gets elected.

To me it seems axiomatic that the common people everywhere are our natural allies, and that our chief contribution to the advancement of mankind should be the energizing and activation of common folk. We must learn how to impart to common people everywhere the technological, political and social skills that would enable them to dispense with the tutorship of the upper classes and the intellectuals. We must deflate the pretensions of self-appointed élites. These élites will hate us no matter what we do, and it is legitimate for us to help dump them into the dustbin of history.

Our foreign aid to backward countries in Asia, Africa and Latin America should be tailored to the needs of common people rather than of the élites. The élites hanker for the trappings of the 20th century. They want steel mills, airlines, skyscrapers, etc. Let them get these trappings from élitist Russia. Our gift to the people in backward countries should be the capacity for self-help. We must show them how to get bread, human dignity and strength by their own efforts. We must know how to stiffen their backbone so that they will insist on getting their full share of the good life and not allow themselves to be sacrificed to the Moloch of a mythical future.

There is an American hidden in the soil of every country and in the soul of every people. It is our task to help common people everywhere discover their America at home.

[1] Prof. Victor C. Ferkiss, author of "Technological Man," sees the astronauts as "thoroughly conventional and middle-class and essentially dull people who would make such nice neighbors and such unlikely friends." Could these, he wonders, "be the supermen whom the race had struggled for a million years to produce?"

PART

IV The Profession and the Teacher: Complacency and Confusion

The Articles in Part IV fall basically into six major areas of conflict and controversy:

1. *The growing conflicts between the profession and the consumers of education, plus various factions in the community.*
2. *The alarming polarization among educators over basic principles and practices.*
3. *The continuing problems of ghetto schools and black educators.*
4. *The explosive nature of the relationships between many local school boards and city, state, and federal governments.*
5. *The changing relationship of religion to public education.*
6. *The conflicting opinions about teacher education among professional educators and teacher trainees.*

The first two of these areas–conflict within the profession and conflict between it and other groups–have established histories, though the issues and problems of today are quite different from those of a few short years ago. Charles Frankel once observed that though most of us "disagree of many things [we] nevertheless want to go on disagreeing within a framework of toleration and mutual respect."[1] *Today there seems to be a widespread breakdown of respect and tolerance. Why has it occurred? What is involved? A recent editorial in* The New York Times *probably summarized the difficulties as succinctly as any one can. The Times observed that "the causes of disorder are varied, and they defy simple answers. Overcrowded schools, racial tensions, the callous use of students as pawns in the political and professional battles of militant adults including parents, teachers, and administrators themselves–all have contributed to the current chaos in the school system."*[2]

[1] Charles Frankel, "The Silenced Majority," *Saturday Review* (December 13, 1969), 22.
[2] "To End the School Strife," *The New York Times* (March 2, 1971), 34.

Perhaps the most difficult part of this conflict is that communications have practically been cut off between the various groups, thus making it virtually impossible for one group to understand the discontent of another, let alone deal with it. With this communications gap even over routine problems, how can educators begin to attack issues like educational "accountability," one of the most widely debated problems to face the profession in many years?

The problems of ghetto education, the difficulties of the black teacher and the black community, have been discussed, debated, and rehashed to a degree that one wonders if the main issues involved aren't often being obscured. Several authors offer advice on these problems in the following pages. In reviewing their suggestions the reader should also keep in mind the recommendations of various study groups like the Carnegie Commission on Higher Education, whose recent report, "From Isolation to Mainstream," recommended, among other things, that "black colleges should remain black, upgrade their courses, and double their enrolment, perhaps as soon as 1980."[3]

Extremely important to all areas of education is the federal government. Just where does its role begin and end? To attempt an answer to this question the reader must first examine the various positions within the profession as well as those offered by government officials and interested parents and students. More and more educators and laymen believe that education is too important a matter in today's world to be left to states and local districts. They argue that, ultimately, our national welfare is at stake because education is the means of developing the potential of our greatest resource, the youth of the nation. This argument runs counter to the traditional view, which supports decentralization in all educational concerns, on grounds that greater federal participation will bring federal "thought control." The current wave of objection to defense contracting by the universities has called much public attention to the extent to which federal funds are already being used in ways which may lessen academic independence.

The recent Supreme Court decision upholding the "constitutionality of busing as a means to 'dismantle the dual school systems' of the South"[4] *is further fuel for the fires of both sides of the federal "involvement" question. It has provoked new controversy in both the North and South and will undoubtedly continue as a hot spot in education for years to come. You will find several excellent articles in the Selected References section on recent developments on this subject.*

"Revenue sharing," another phrase currently in the news, calls further attention to the separation question. Would revenue sharing truly be an aid to education or merely another means for the federal government to involve itself? A number of articles in the Selected References discuss pros and cons. An "open admissions" program like that of the City University of New York creates yet another gap between the friends and foes of increased federal aid. Adequate financial support is one of the important factors for success in open admissions.

[3] "Education: Separate but Better," *Time* (March 1, 1971), 56.

[4] Fred P. Graham. "Supreme Court, 9–0, Backs Busing to Combat South's Dual Schools, Rejecting Administration Stand," *The New York Times* (April 21, 1971), 1.

Critics of the move have been watching and warning of the eventualities of involvement by Uncle Sam if adequate funds are not provided by the city and state governments. In reviewing the CUNY program, Fred M. Hechinger warns us that the real danger of "open admissions, particularly as it spreads to other cities," may lie in the "serious problems [it creates] for the private colleges and universities."[5]

Hardly a week goes by without new debate over the public school–private school question. In the forefront of these discussions is the question of financial support for those institutions with religious ties. Those opposed to such aid concede that public schools probably could not accommodate the large church-school population if its members were "forced" upon them. However, they are unwilling to advocate financial support so long as religion and education are tied together; they insist upon complete separation of church and state. Those in favor of financial support for schools with religious ties argue that these schools render absolutely essential and vital services to the community and are entitled to financial aid. Even among these people, however, there is ambivalence; they want the money but are fearful of interference. The controversy continues; and for the moment, at least, no simple solution appears to be in sight.

Though not as widely discussed by the mass media as the question of government control, the curriculum for teacher education is being criticized both internally and by interested outsiders. Is it relevant? Is it providing new teachers with the tools they need for educating our youth? There is genuine belief by all concerned that the subject is in need of critical airing. Tenure is also under attack by student activists, untenured educators, politicians, and other parties; there are indications that some form of compromise arrangement may be made even though it is generally believed to be a most "powerful lure, even more important than a raise in pay,"[6] *when universities are seeking professional talent. The training program for beginning teachers is also under fire. Educators and teacher trainees in growing numbers wonder how well much of the course work and actual teacher training prepare students for the real teaching world.*

These subjects are only a few of the important ones covered in the following pages by a list of distinguished authors. The editor hopes his selection of material will provoke healthy debate among educators and laymen alike.

In dealing with problems and conflicts, we must first determine what they are and where, exactly, the differences lie. Robert J. Schaefer, Dean of Teachers College, Columbia University, begins with this fundamental but important truth in his review of the current travails of education. After questioning the precise nature of the turmoil, Schaefer calls on the profession to continue study and action and to renew its "commitment to teaching effectiveness."

Much controversy has been aroused in recent years over the United States Supreme Court's decisions regarding prayers and Bible readings in public schools.

[5] Fred M. Hechinger, "Open Admissions: Prophets of Doom Seem to Have Been Wrong," *The New York Times* (March 28, 1971), E 11.

[6] Fred M. Hechinger, "Tenure Under Attack by Right and Left," *The New York Times* (April 4, 1971), E 9.

Churchmen as well as laymen are divided in their reactions to these decisions, and even the court itself has not made its stand absolutely clear, although its decisions point to the outlawing of all official participation in religious acts and functions. The article by Rolfe Lanier Hunt provides excellent background for further study.

Jack Starr deals with the problems of Roman Catholic education. Losses of students to public schools, a lack of adequate financial support, competition for students and teachers from public and from other private schools, and a growing concern over adequate preparation for life are some of the questions discussed by Starr.

If education in general is surrounded by strife and conflict, educators and students in ghetto areas must go to the head of the class as those most adversely affected by these travails. Kenneth Clark discusses the problems of the lower-status minority group children and rejects the public schools "convenient" explanations for their "unwillingness" or "inability" to provide quality education for all.

Thomas Sowell believes the problems of ghetto education are being further complicated by colleges that "skip over" competent blacks to admit "authentic" ghetto types. Writing in The New York Times Magazine, Sowell outlines a social theology of "myths" underlying current policies and practices of colleges regarding black students.

"If all it took were black teachers and administrators to change a school system, we would obviously have the best school system in the world . . . which is not the case." These are the words of William H. Simons, president of the Washington Teachers Union in a conversation with Susan Jacoby, education reporter for the Washington Post. Miss Jacoby reviews the changing role of the black teacher from a broad vantage point and concludes that the most important impact he may be making as an educator and administrator is the "image of success" he portrays for black students in ghetto schools.

The public's image of the teacher, developed in a rural America, as a shy, retiring individual who attends dutifully to his classroom but seldom ventures into public life and who meekly submits to rules, regulations, and decisions regarding salaries and working conditions has been changed radically in recent years. Militant teachers in many sections of the country have been boycotting schools, waging well-organized campaigns in state legislatures, blacklisting whole state school systems where desirable conditions were not maintained, and using labor's effective weapon, the strike. An evaluation of this action–its sources and its prospects for the future–is presented by Ronald G. Corwin.

In asking "Will Teacher Be the New Drop-Out?" political scientist, Arnold Beichman predicts that the very structure of higher education cannot "survive in its present form." At the same time, he accuses the profession of "accepting–or ignoring–any kind of political lie so long as its purveyor is young, progressive, a would-be Marxist."

The next seven articles deal with the immediate problems facing the profession and the long-term effects that today's education will have, particularly on the individuals who one day will be educating tomorrow's citizens.

Can we define good teaching? That's the question posed by H. S. Broudy, editor of Education Forum. He discusses the difficulties of definition and concludes that educators have to "lure" enough people into the schools to do a kind of teaching which cannot be finally defined.

Maxine Greene reviews ways in which teachers may regain their "legitimacy" in an era in which the term has lost its meaning. Robert Bush redefines the teacher's role and insists that positive attitudes are called for to offset the pressures on the profession. Dwight W. Allen believes the "current model of teacher-use" must be re-examined in today's world. Allen presents a differentiated teaching staff as one possible solution and a means to improve professionalism in education.

Teacher education is probed in depth in articles by Richard H. Brown, John I. Goodlad, and Margaret Gill. The newer concepts of teaching, the conventional resistance to them, and the question of what will happen to teachers and teaching in the seventies are only a few of the matters discussed.

The concluding articles in Part IV call for understanding and love. Gerhard Hirshfeld points out the reasons why single actions are not adequate to solve universal problems. He believes a "mankind framework and mankind perspective" and a "mankind education" to be essential for survival.

Jack R. Frymier believes educators talk about feelings, emotions, and attitudes but do little about them in class. He leaves us with the argument that finding a way to live together peacefully is not enough—love must be taught as the very "way of life." Probably, the Hirshfeld and Frymier articles should be re-read by all, students and educators alike.

Questions for Discussion and Further Study

1. Is education a discipline? This, perhaps more than any other single question, can probably start the greatest intellectual adventure for professors and laymen alike. It is debatable. It is controversial. Dr. Marc Belth of Queens College of the City University of New York, in his book Education as a Discipline, *examines this question in detail. Another valuable reference is* The Discipline of Education. *Both books are listed in Selected References.*

2. No study of the profession would be complete without a review of the various teachers' organizations. The Selected References contain three excellent articles on this subject: (1) an essay by Michael H. Moskow entitled "Teacher Organizations: An Analysis of the Issues"; (2) one by Carl Megel, representing the American Federation of Teachers; and (3) one by Marion Steet, presenting the view of the National Education Association. In what respects do these two organizations (AFT and NEA) share a common concern? In what respects do their views differ? Are these views mutually exclusive? In what desirable directions do you expect both organizations to move in the future?

3. The issues of greater federal participation in education and of religion in public education continue to cause much discussion. In both areas, students can find more published material than can be read. Care should be taken to select intelligently from the wealth of resources. A particularly fine guide to periodicals is the Social Science and Humanities Index in which excellent scholarly material may be located from fields other than education. With topics such as these, where so many points of view are represented, it is important to identify carefully what you regard as the major issues, and then to concentrate on the varying shades of opinion surrounding each issue.

Selected References

Bell, Daniel. "Quo Warranto?–Notes on the Governance of Universities in the 1970's." *The Public Interest* (Spring 1970), 53–68.

Biddle, Bruce J., and William J. Ellena (eds.). *Contemporary Research on Teacher Effectiveness.* New York: Holt, Rinehart, and Winston, 1964.

Binzen, Peter. "How to Pick a School Board." *Saturday Review* (April 17, 1965), 72–73, 83–84.

Blumenthal, David, and Chester Finn. "Education and the New Breed." *HGSEA Bulletin* (Spring 1969), 7–11.

Calisch, Richard W. "Do You Want to Be a Teacher?" *Today's Education* (November 1969), 49–51.

"Can You Afford College?" *U.S. News & World Report* (February 22, 1971), 25–28.

Cloak, F.T. Jr. "Reach Out or Die Out." *Educational Leadership* (April 1969), 661–665.

Commager, Henry Steele. "Tuition Charges Are a Mistake." *The New York Times* (February 25, 1971), 37.

Conant, James B. "The Comprehensive High School: The Challenge of an Ideal." *The Bulletin of the National Association of Secondary School Principals* (December 1968), 13–23.

Diederich, Paul B. "Progressive Education Should Continue." *Today's Education* (March 1969), 12, 14–19.

Ebel, Robert L. "Prospects for Evaluation of Learning." *The Bulletin of the National Association of Secondary School Principals* (December 1968), 32–42.

"Education's Revenue Share." *The New York Times* (March 7, 1971), 12.

Evans, Rupert N. "The Secondary School and Occupational Preparation." *The Bulletin of the National Association of Secondary School Principals.* (February 1969), 23–40.

"Excerpts from the Supreme Court Ruling Upholding Busing to End Segregation." *The New York Times* (April 21, 1971), 28.

"Furor over Race and 'I.Q.'–Here's the Latest Chapter." *U.S. News and World Report* (June 2, 1969), 54–56.

Goodu, Roland, and Edward R. Ducharne. "A Responsive Teacher-Education Program." *Teachers College Record* (February 1971), 431–441.

Greene, Maxine. "The Philosopher and the Rebel." *Perspectives on Education* (Winter 1968), 7–11, 13–16.

Gross, Leonard. "A High School Fights for It's Life . . . and a Principal for His." *Look Magazine* (March 9, 1971), 21–22, 25–29.

Herbers, John, and Fred P. Graham. "Supreme Court, 9–0, Backs Busing to Combat South's Dual Schools Rejecting Administration Stand." *The New York Times* (April 21, 1971), 1, 28, 29.

Hitchcock, James. "A Short Course in the Three Types of Radical Professors." *The New York Times* (February 21, 1971), 30, 34, 36, 38, 40–41, 44, 46.

Holt, John, "Why We Need New Schooling." *Look* (January 13, 1970), 52.

Hooper, Bayard. "The Task Is to Learn What Teaching Is For." *Life* (May 16, 1969), 34, 38–39.

Horn, Gunnar. "Some Thoughts About Teaching and Teachers." *Today's Education* (February 1970), 13–15.

Hyer, Anna L. "The School and Technology." *The Bulletin of the National Association of Secondary School Principals* (December 1968), 123–130.

"Joyful Classrooms." *Newsweek* (April 5, 1971), 86, 89–90.

Koob, C. Albert. "The Contribution of Non-public Schools." *The Bulletin of the National Association of Secondary School Principals* (December 1968), 74–82.

Levin, Henry M. "Why Ghetto Schools Fail." *Saturday Review* (March 21, 1970), 68–69, 81.

Mead, Margaret. "Establishment's Rank Infiltrated by Dissent." *The New York Times* (January 12, 1970), C51.

Megel, Carl J. "Teacher Conscription–Basis of Association Membership?" *Teachers College Record* (October 1964), 7–17.

Metcalf, Lawrence E. "Poverty, Government, and the Schools." *Educational Leadership* (May 1965), 543–546.

Metzger, Walter P. "The Crisis of Academic Authority." *Daedalus* (Summer 1970), 568–608.

Moskow, Michael H. "Teacher Organizations: An Analysis of the Issues." *Teachers College Record* (February 1965), 453–463.

"Religion and Public Education" (Special Issue). *Theory into Practice* (February 1965).

Resnik, Solomon, and Barbara Kaplan. "Report Card on Open Admissions: Remedial Work Recommended." *The New York Times Magazine* (May 9, 1971), 26–28, 32, 34, 37, 39, 42, 44, 46.

Robinson, Donald W. "How Sinister Is the Education Establishment?" *Saturday Review* (January 16, 1965), 56–57, 75.

Roche, John P. "On Being an Unfashionable Professor." *The New York Times Magazine* (October 18, 1970), 30–31, 80, 82, 84, 92.

Shedd, Mark R. "The Federal Colossus in Education–Curriculum Planning." *Educational Leadership* (October 1965), 15–19.

"Small Share for Education." *The New York Times* (April 12, 1971), 36.

"Special Report: The Elementary and Secondary Education Act of 1965." *American Education* (April 1965).

Stanley, William. "Freedom of Conscience, Religion, and the Public Schools." *The Educational Forum* (May 1965), 407–415.

Steet, Marion L. "Professional Associations–More than Unions." *Teachers College Record* (December 1964), 204–218.

Stevens, William K. "Grade Tests· Flunking Marks for a Widely Used System." *The New York Times* (March 28, 1971), E 9.

______. "A School's Responsibility for Results: Debate Grows." *The New York Times* (March 28, 1971), 47.

Stimbert, E. C., and A. R. Dykes. "Decentralization of Administration." *Phi Delta Kappan* (December 1964), 174–177.

Tyler, Ralph W. "Purposes for Our Schools." *The Bulletin of the National Association of Secondary School Principals* (December 1968), 1–12.

Vecsey, George. "Catholic Schools Today: Challenged and Changing." *The New York Times* (March 1, 1971), 33.

Walton, John, and James L. Kuethe (eds.). *The Discipline of Education.* Madison: University of Wisconsin Press, 1963.

Warshaw, Thayer S. "Teaching About Religion in the Public School: Eight Questions." *Phi Delta Kappan* (November 1967), 127–133.

"What's Wrong with the High Schools?" *Newsweek* (February 16, 1970), 65–66, 68–69.

"When College Is Open to All–The Experiment in Britain." *U.S. News & World Report* (March 1, 1971), 63–64.

Danger: Proceed at the Risk of Rationality

ROBERT J. SCHAEFER

In our educational institutions today, faculty members and students are restless, questioning, plainly skittish. Administrators are apprehensive, resigned or resigning, and exhausted. In innumerable situations, latent animosities and frustrations flare into open confrontations: buildings are seized; classes are disrupted; injunctions are filed; and manifestos are posted. But the precise nature of our educational travail is still unclear. Will our unrest and dissension lead to more humane and rational institutions or must we endure an educational reign of terror?

Whether our common turmoil stems from revolutionary or merely modish forces, there is much that is constructive and positive in the current educational mood. Given the massive failures of leadership in the larger social world, the pervasive sense that the older generation has botched it seems at least tenable. Given the absurdities perpetuated by many of us in authority roles, it is natural that authority structures should themselves be challenged. It is not easy to defend establishment wisdom amidst the chaos that has been wrought. There is the agonizing irony of poverty and deprivation set against our willingness to sink billions of dollars in supersonic aircraft and in unsinkable trainloads of lethal chemicals. There is the blatant ugliness of racism that seems to mock classroom rhetoric and seminar conversation about human unity and human dignity. And everywhere, at least as it appears to the young, there is fraud and phoniness. In a real sense, not be somewhat dubious about the infallibility of hierarchical authority in today's world (including the university) would seem to require either moral indifference or questionable intelligence.

Partly because of the skepticism about authority and partly because of the psychological need to identify with goals outside the self, there is a real push for greater participatory democracy in our educational society. With the basic principle of expanding the sources of wisdom used in reaching policy decisions, there can be little quarrel. And much of the unrest among both students and faculty in schools and colleges everywhere is simply an impatient desire to have a greater voice in controlling their own destinies.

Equally positive in fundamental motivation is the drive towards combining study and action. There is an increasing disenchantment with wholly verbal analyses of social and professional problems and an ebullient faith in the possibilities of learning through immersion in the full complexities of the real world. At best, this

From *Perspectives on Education* (Fall 1969), 1–4. Reprinted by permission of *Perspectives on Education*, Teachers College, Columbia University.

rejection of the merely academic need not be anti-intellectual nor even a-theoretical; abstractions can indeed be illuminated through concrete instances and viable theory cannot afford a permanent separation from live data. Field study and experience can certainly be wholly legitimate forms of the current insistence upon educational relevance.

Closely allied to this concern for leavening analysis with action is renewed commitment to teaching effectiveness. Students no longer endure an indifferent lecture or an ill-planned and meandering discussion with good grace. Neither do they listen docilely, and with feigned adulation, to learned disquisitions on obscure and trivial matters. Department chairmen and committees search diligently for new means of appraising instructional skill and for new forms of recognition for those who excel in teaching, and all of us are reminded in the process that the *prime* purpose of an elegant faculty and a prestigious library is the social and intellectual development of students.

And, although it is perhaps more difficult to assess, there seems to be a heightened moral fervor in the present turmoil. There is a great zest and an exhilarating sense of social purpose, if not in every individual, at least among all elements of the academic community. There is a general if imprecise assurance that things could be put straight if only there were sufficient will and sufficient action. Exalted notions are abroad and people feel themselves equal to great things. To the degree an expanded belief in the attainability of elusive goals actually exists, it can indeed contribute to the common effort to strengthen our educational institutions.

But no revolution is without its terror and no turmoil without its incongruities. Each of the positive factors alluded to has its negative side. What is sometimes deeply frightening and always disturbingly incongruous is the anti-intellectual and irrational aspects of the present educational mood. I refer not to the peripheral aberrations of the radical minority, nor to the more widespread excesses that have occurred during the panic of a police bust or in immediate response to haranguing oratory, but rather to more pervasive and persistent elements of the current scene. What seems threatened is the core value of the university—respect for disciplined inquiry and acceptance of the "authority" of intellectual processes.

It is all very well to be suspicious of the particular individuals who happen to occupy authority positions in the educational structure. Given the degree of ordinary dullness and ineptitude which prevails, it is impossible to defend the rightness of every bureaucratic decree or the soundness of every administrative pronouncement. But when skepticism about persons extends to a loss of faith in the possibility of rational decision making, we face real trouble. If reasoned discourse, the patient search for evidence, and the disciplined pursuit of approximate truth have no authenticity or no authority, why a university at all?

I am, of course, referring to processes and not to any set of absolutes. There is—and it is one of the greatest strengths of the university—no area of scholarship and no set of practices which cannot be subjected to fresh analysis or seen through new conceptual frames of reference. But such attacks on "authoritative" positions have ordinarily been made on intellectual rather than on political grounds. In the current period there is live danger that the understandable rejection of authority figures may degenerate into an unwarranted dismissal of the entire process of rational decision making. There is a real movement to politicize the institutions of education, to substitute a conscious conflict among competing constituencies for the more traditional effort to articulate institutional policies through collegial employment of agreed upon intellectual processes. The various parties to the conflict over policy begin to doubt that there are any norms of judgment or valid means of attaining them beyond the interests and ideologies of the people and groups involved.

In its most pernicious form the otherwise constructive effort to broaden faculty and student participation in university governance takes the form, not simply of expanded intellectual resources and perspectives with which to build responsible policy, but rather of greater specificity of political position in order to articulate the presumed power struggle. A permanent and pervasive state of conflict rather than a carefully nurtured community of interest is seen as inevitable. Obviously, there is conflict of interest in the university, for example, between the faculty member's aspirations for tenure and the institution's standards of excellence, or between student concern for modest tuition rates and faculty regard for adequate salaries. Obviously, too, violence and confrontation have, in extremity, sometimes forced a hearing of previously inadmissable issues. But if the tactics leading to such successes were to be institutionalized into a permanent contention for power, there could only be anarchy. Violence may have its temporary uses in enlarging the effective educational community and in expanding the agenda for shared policy decisions, but certainly not to enshrine power struggle as the single mechanism for governing academic life. We must protect our tradition of resolving educational questions not simply through raw power plays but rather by force of reason and persuasion. Broadened responsibility for institutional governance promises to enhance the quality of educational decisions, but not, I fear, if we substitute the rigidity of interest-bound political stance for the fluidity of reasoned debate.

There is danger, too, that the natural lack of trust in the integrity of those outside one's political constituency will encourage a debilitating and eventually unmanageable system for committee monitoring of administrative detail. It requires patience enough to reach policy decisions through committee deliberation; it is beyond belief that groups could work out and supervise policy implementation. One can easily imagine that all teaching and research would be permanently suspended while we occupy ourselves with the more fundamental tasks of circulating memoranda, preparing political releases, and spying on the registrar. If all of us in the academic world are not to grow completely mad, we must somehow curb our current capacity for mistrust and our exaggerated proclivity for creating committees. Politics can be a full-time job.

Even our current enthusiasm for taking education out of the classroom into the real world has its neurotic tendencies. To some students and faculty members, involvement in social action situations is itself fully educative and requires no concurrent effort to organize such experience intellectually and to relate it to what disciplinary studies can potentially or have already revealed. While we may decry the overly cognitive emphasis of traditional education, there seems little sanity in dismissing analysis and conceptualization as irrelevant vestiges of an evil past. Certainly understanding and the capacity for effective action can be enhanced by field experience, but only if students are helped to impose meaning upon what they observe and feel. If advocacy of intellectual structure becomes merely one among many competing political positions in the educational world there can be no university. We might just as well send students into the streets and after suitable exposure to experiential learning encourage them to mimeograph their own degrees.

There is terror, also, in some of the current rhetoric about effective teaching. With frightening frequency these days, one hears pronouncements about a presumed dichotomy between research and teaching. Certainly there have been fine teachers who have never conducted an empirical investigation nor published a reasoned monograph. It is comparably easy to identify skilled researchers who have been woefully inadequate as teachers. But since the same qualities of mind—a lively curiosity, an ability to deal with abstractions, a passion for intellectual order, and a creative imagination—are essential to both endeavors, it seems absurd to posit an inevitable conflict. The present concern for more responsible teaching, to the degree it ignores the unity of disciplined inquiry in both research and teaching, risks a lowering of teaching standards below even those which currently prevail. What is needed is not punitive action against those who are recognized inquirers, but a more determined effort to identify and reward those whose inquiry in the classroom has not yet become visible to the wider world. While agreeing that much of what is published should perish, along with those who perpetrate it, I cannot comprehend why speaking to the public in print as well as to students in the classroom should disqualify one as a teacher.

I find it particularly disturbing and ironic that the current turmoil, which has been associated primarily with liberal arts colleges within universities, should spill over to professional schools. In the field of education particularly, our commitment to research is as yet so tenuous, our grappling seriously with the reciprocal relations of theory and practice as yet so tentative, our faith in the authority of the processes of inquiry as yet so fragile, and our resistance to the appeal of political positions as yet so incomplete that even a minor revolution could lead to a reign of terror. One could hope, I fear vainly, that the dissension we now experience expresses only superficial anger and threatens no permanent damage. Or one can hope that the energy inherent in the current turmoil can be so skillfully directed as to make a permanent contribution to strengthening and humanizing our educational institutions. Despite the special vulnerability of schools of education to many of the present dangers, I personally feel confident that we have sufficient stability and sufficient resilience to withstand the onslaught whether it be modish or revolutionary in character. It may even be that we will be able to help the larger university to analyze its plight and to undertake the necessary redirection. Where, after all, are there greater concentrations of those fitted by training and professional commitment to do the job? I believe we have both the intellect and the will.

Teaching About Religion in the Public School

ROLFE LANIER HUNT

John stood watching from the street. Members of a group leaving the restaurant were laughing, shouting to each other as they parted, "Happy New Year!" And here it was, weeks from the New Year. Those crazy people must be drunk, he told himself.

At school next morning, when he told his teacher about the incident, she explained that Eastern Orthodox Christians and Jews observe their New Year at seasons set by the calendars of their respective traditions.

Thus John found help at school in understanding some of his neighbors, people with whom he would have to learn to live in this great land.

Children of many traditions come to the public schools: Protestants of more than 250 varieties; Catholics, Roman and Orthodox; Jews, Orthodox, Conservative, Reformed, and "Free"; Hindus; Moslems; Buddhists; Marxist materialists; and others. All of them and their families have been guaranteed freedom of conscience and freedom of religion by the Constitution of the United States, for there is no freedom to believe unless there is also freedom to disbelieve. The needs of our pluralistic society are well served by Constitutional interpretations calling for government "neutrality." Both religion and religious freedom are rooted in our history.

By one definition, religion is the relation of man to the supernatural being called God; by another definition, religion is the loyalty of man to his ultimate values, to his convictions that control his conduct. The Supreme Court of the United States has accepted the latter definition in cases dealing with tax exemption for humanist centers, with whether atheists are entitled to public office, and with the status of conscientious objectors in the matter of compulsory military service. In a 1961 decision *(Torcaso v. Watkins.* 367 U.S. 488) the Court said, "Neither [a State nor the Federal Government] can constitutionally pass laws or impose requirements which aid all religions as against non-believers, and neither can aid those religions based on a belief in the existence of God as against those religions founded on different beliefs." And said the court, "Buddhism, Taoism, Ethical Culture, Secular Humanism, and others are among the religions in this country that do not teach what would generally be considered a belief in the existence of God."

The many faiths that children bring to a public school can be an invitation to distractions and disputes. If, however, the difference and varieties of insights are

From *Today's Education* (NEA Journal) (December 1969), 24–26. Reprinted by permission.

treated as normal and in no way shameful, they may spark learnings and provide occasions for growth in knowledge and in sympathies.

As examples, let us take what every public school has to teach: the Bill of Rights and the Declaration of Independence.

Freedom of speech, freedom of assembly, freedom of the press, freedom of religion—these and other precious rights are spelled out in the first ten amendments to the Constitution, our Bill of Rights. What is a teacher to do when asked in the classroom, "Doesn't the government give these rights?" "Why can't the government take them away?" "Why shouldn't the government jail anybody who speaks up against a policy adopted by the government, like sending soldiers to Vietnam?" "Does a man exist to serve governments, or do governments exist to serve him?" You are close, now, you see, to the first line of defense of democracy against totalitarianism, whether fascist or communist. For historical answers, the teacher sends the questioner back to the Declaration of Independence:

> When in the Course of human events, it becomes necessary for one people to dissolve the political bands which have connected them with another, and to assume among the Powers of the earth, the separate and equal station to which the Laws of Nature and of Nature's God entitle them, a decent respect to the opinions of mankind requires that they should declare the causes which impel them to the separation.
>
> We hold these truths to be self-evident, that all men are created equal, that they are endowed by their Creator with certain unalienable rights, that among these are Life, Liberty and the pursuit of Happiness. That to secure these rights, Governments are instituted among Men, deriving their just powers from the consent of the governed. That whenever any form of Government becomes destructive of these ends, it is the Right of the People to alter or to abolish it, and to institute new Government . . . .
>
> We therefore . . . appealing to the Supreme Judge of the world for the rectitude of our intentions . . . .
>
> And for the support of this Declaration, with a firm reliance on the Protection of Divine Providence, we mutually pledge to each other our Lives, our Fortunes and our sacred Honor.

Such is the answer of history; these things the Founding Fathers believed. Words on the wall of the Jefferson Memorial in Washington echo the thoughts of the writer of the first draft of the Declaration:

"God who gave us life gave us liberty. Can the liberties of a nation be secure when we have removed the conviction that these liberties are the gift of God?"

And in his Farewell Address, George Washington warned us to "with caution indulge the supposition that morality can be maintained without religion."

Because the Founding Fathers so believed, shall the school say to the young questioner, "This you must believe"?

No. The school has to teach the Bill of Rights and the Declaration of

Independence, their texts and contexts, with integrity. Then, given the facts, the youth in the classroom has freedom to believe as he chooses, to follow truth as he sees it.

If there are other answers to the searching questions a student asks, he has a right to meet them. For example, one answer to the basic question, "What is a man?" comes from religion. Jews say he is made in the image of God and is therefore to be respected. Christians agree, adding that a man is one for whom God was willing to pay a great price by sacrificing his Son. Another answer is that man is an animal, a member of the human race, and as such entitled to human rights. For many humanists, that is enough.

When you get into areas like those given thus far, are you teaching religion? Is this not forbidden by the Constitution of the United States?

By the legal definition cited, each answer above is religious, because each involves values that guide conduct. Any prohibitions of the Constitution must apply equally to all of them. What further guidance have we from the Supreme Court of the United States?

In 1963, the Court decreed that public school rules requiring worship that involves use of prayer and Bible readings violate constitutional rights. Newspapers gave their stories headlines like "Bible Thrown out of Public Schools," and even "God Thrown out of Public Schools," so it is no wonder that many well-read persons did not hear these words from the Court:

> . . . The test may be stated as follows: what are the purpose and the primary effect of the enactment? If either is the advancement or inhibition of religion then the enactment exceeds the scope of legislative power as circumscribed by the Constitution. That is to say that to withstand the strictures of the Establishment Clause there must be a secular legislative purpose and a primary effect that neither advances nor inhibits religion . . . .
>
> The conclusion follows that in both cases the laws require religious exercises and such exercises are being conducted in direct violation of the rights of the appellees and petitioners . . . .
>
> It is insisted that unless these religious exercises are permitted a "religion of secularism" is established in the schools. We agree of course that the State may not establish a "religion of secularism" in the sense of affirmatively opposing or showing hostility to religion, thus "preferring those who believe in no religion over those who do believe." . . . We do not agree, however, that this decision in any sense has that effect. In addition, it might well be said that one's education is not complete without a study of comparative religion or the history of religion and its relationship to the advancement of civilizaiton. It certainly may be said that the Bible is worthy of study for its literary and historic qualities. Nothing we have said here indicates that such study of the Bible or of religion, when presented objectively as part of a secular program of education, may not be effected consistent with the First Amendment.

Note the clear authorization for study of the Bible in public schools, so long as such study is for the purpose of general education rather than to persuade and indoctrinate. Whether you believe the separate study of the Bible is preferable to its use when relevant to the regular school subjects is a matter of individual preference, but I tend toward the latter.

Concurring, Mr. Justice Goldberg and Mr. Justice Harlan cited words from the Court's decision in *Engel v. Vitale:*

> There is of course nothing in the decision reached here that is inconsistent with the fact that school children and others are officially encouraged to express love for our country by reciting historical documents such as the Declaration of Independence which contain references to the Deity or by singing officially espoused anthems which include the composer's professions of faith in a Supreme Being, or with the fact that there are many manifestations in our public life of belief in God. Such patriotic or ceremonial occasions bear no true resemblance to the unquestioned religious exercise that the State . . . has sponsored in this instance.

The teacher, then, is quite in order when he teaches history for the secular purposes of the state. But if his tax-paid time is used to tell a student what he must believe in religious faith, that teacher wrongly uses tax funds to push a personal point of view.

Because teachers are human beings, there can be abuses. The religious enthusiast could imply that all good Americans believe as did the Founding Fathers. The materialist could say, "Of course they believed that *then,*" implying that we know better now.

Tolerance, too, has dangers. Used as a creed to guide conduct, professed neutrality can teach that it matters little what you believe, that all creeds are equal. The relativist, affirming the relativity of his own and every other religion, makes a statement not in the least relative by claiming his belief to be universal truth. The middle way has more to offer our mixed society than any other, but we must remember that civil liberties are safe only with people who really believe something: Look for a "crank" to defend your civil rights, one who can say with Patrick Henry, "Give me liberty, or give me death"!

The constitutional phrases forbidding passage of laws "respecting an establishment of religion, or prohibiting the free exercise thereof," do not forbid a teacher in a public school classroom to explain the ritual of the Mass or to have students read its text if the purpose is that of knowing more about our neighbors. A teacher may tell his students that many people believe Jesus is divine, but if he omits the words "many people believe" and says, "Jesus is divine," as if with the authority of the state, he moves from a statement of fact to an expression of faith and transgresses the Constitution.

Facts take on meaning by the way they are arranged, structured, and patterned. If you say that Jews deny the divinity of Jesus, without some attention also to what they affirm, the teaching is less than objective neutrality. If I say, "Our chairman was sober last night," I may tell truth, but I suggest what may be a complete lie.

Let the teacher be a person, freely acknowledging his own interest and hobbies and faith while leaving room for like freedom for others.

The youth in the public school who asks "Why?" is entitled to his question and to the help of the school in meeting the full range of answers to his question, when appropriate to the unit of subject matter and the maturity of the student.

Both Judaism and Christianity are historical religions, with substantial bodies of data that can be taught at an intellectual level. Such teaching will not preclude the need for other efforts by those who wish to teach religion. Beyond facts are feelings, habits, worship and ritual, ethics, theology. Homes and churches and synagogues have much to teach children in their earliest years as well as later. Each agency can improve its program by taking into account the experiences of the child elsewhere.

The public schools can neither bring religion to America nor take it away. They can only reflect the decisions of the community of which they are a part. Since the public school is only one of the educational agencies of our society, and can't do everything, it helps itself by cooperation with other agencies working with the children attending its classrooms for parts of their lives.

The Commission on Religion in the Public Schools of the American Association of School Administrators echoed a consensus long held in the educational profession when it said in 1964, "The desirable policy in the schools . . . is to deal directly and objectively with religion whenever and wherever it is intrinsic to learning experience in the various fields of study." This, said the Commission, "requires topic-by-topic analysis of the separate courses and cooperative efforts by the teachers." The process is going forward: Publishers and producers are developing useful texts and audio-visual aids. Teachers are at work in many states and in national organizations, such as the National Council for the Social Studies and the National Council of Teachers of English.

Every generation has to secure its own freedom. Freedom is bought with a price, of which constant vigilance is a part. Part of the normal life of the citizen of the United States is to work on the question of how public schools deal with religion, part of the never-finished business of a democracy. Our common schools can continue to help us learn to live together in peace under law.

Are the Catholic Schools Dying?

JACK STARR

Catholic schools this year, for the third consecutive year, will lose a quarter of a million pupils, mostly in the elementary grades. From all indications, the drop in these enrollments will continue. Next year, in fact, it may be even more.

"In the next five and a half years, Catholic elementary schools will lose almost 2,000,000 pupils, half their enrollment, unless Catholics vastly increase support of their school system," predicts Msgr. James C. Donohue. He is director of the Division of Elementary and Secondary Education of the United States Catholic Conference.

Monsignor Donohue's powerful organization stands in the center of the crisis threatening America's parochial schools. The Conference consists of all the 265 Catholic bishops from 30 U.S. archdioceses and 126 dioceses. It is this group, says Monsignor Donohue, that is now faced with the decision of what to do with the Catholic schools.

"I don't want to sound trite," he says, "but we're at a crossroads. The bishops of the Church have to decide what the teaching mission of the Church should be in the next few decades, and then reapportion the resources it has to meet that goal."

The feeling comes through that Monsignor Donohue thinks the Church has been unrealistic about both resources and goals. He notes that in 1884, when the bishops met for the Third Plenary Council of Baltimore, they called for " . . . a Catholic school in every parish and every Catholic child in a Catholic school. . . ." More than 10,500 grade schools and 2,400 high schools were ultimately established, but they never served even half of the 11,000,000 Catholic schoolchildren. Since there was no other place for them, the others had to go to public schools. This was allowed to happen, Monsignor Donohue says wryly, despite the firm belief that "public schools were faith-destroyers and Catholic schools were faith-preservers."

The Catholic schools might have muddled along for years to come, however, if it hadn't been for the explosive birthrate after World War II.

"Our schools grew tremendously," Monsignor Donohue says, "much faster than public schools. I don't think we realized what was happening . . . .Maybe we should have asked: 'Are we building too many schools?' We were way over-extended."

The next blow came when the Russians launched Sputnik in 1957, causing a national wave of self-doubt and forcing a crisis on the public schools. Monsignor Donohue recounts: "They had to put in new courses that cost much more money, and they had to upgrade the quality of their teaching. Suddenly we were caught up

From *Look* Magazine (October 21, 1969), 105–106, 108, 112. Reprinted by permission.

in the same crisis, because we had to compete. It was no longer just a matter of building a school and putting a warm body in the teacher's chair. Now, we had to put in expensive science laboratories; and there were so many children that we couldn't rely mainly on nuns [who cost only $1,200 a year], but we had to go out into the marketplace and compete with the public schools for their expensive lay teachers.

Vatican II really hammered us. The keystone of our low school cost is the contributed service of religious—nuns and priests. With the post-Vatican II revolution in the Church, vocations are falling off in ever-increasing numbers. Why? The young are holding back their commitment to the Church because they don't see what the Church is all about. They see rich Rome with its treasures, and, at the same time, see poor societies and struggling people. For years, they haven't heard the Church say much about the Negro question, the urban problem. Meanwhile, many religious are leaving, because this isn't the church they entered. They can't match the old view of authority with the new view of authority."

It distresses Monsignor Donohue, a former superintendent of Catholic schools in Baltimore, with a Ph.D. in psychology, that professionalism is not universal in the Catholic schools. He feels that the pastors, who too often actually run the schools, jealously guard their authority even though they are amateurs in the field of education.

In Patchogue, N.Y., he says, a pastor refused to let a school principal take charge of admissions but delegated the job to his secretary, "a woman who didn't know a thing about education." In Baltimore, when Monsignor Donohue was superintendent there, he introduced the new math into his schools. One of his principals went to her pastor to ask for new textbooks that would deal with the subjects. "What's wrong with the old ones?" asked the pastor, insisting on keeping 20-year-old books.

It is incomprehensible to Monsignor Donohue that superintendents of Catholic schools are not allowed to have their say about quality of instruction, teacher accreditation, curriculum, textbooks or school organization. "In the public schools," he says, "the superintendent, through the school board, controls the purse strings and therefore has his say. In the Catholic schools, it is the pastor, who is quick to remind the educators that it is *he* who is paying the bills. If the pastor doesn't like something, he countermands an order."

Faced with the current fierce inflation and the sharp reduction in the numbers of teaching sisters, some bishops are panicking. "They're closing schools that we should be keeping open," says Monsignor Donohue. "Take some conservative bishop who thinks life will go on as it always has. A mother superior comes in and says, 'Bishop, we'll have 20 fewer nuns next year.' Fifteen or 20 other mother superiors may tell him the same thing. Maybe he'll have 350 fewer nuns when school opens, and he figures he can't afford to hire lay teachers. After all, costs are up 20 percent and collections aren't keeping up. At this point, he's likely to come up with a Band-Aid approach, like: 'Let's close the first grade; our children can go to the public schools; who needs first grade?'

"Cincinnati dropped its first grades five years ago, and I'm still waiting for an intelligent explanation as to why they picked on first grade. Why wouldn't you experiment with different solutions? In 25 percent of the schools, for example, why not try dropping grades seven and eight? This would be a logical time in a child's life for him to enter the public school setup after giving him a start with a Catholic education."

Another tempting area for bishops trying to save money, says Monsignor Donohue, is the "uneconomic" school serving, say, 60 ghetto youngsters in a shabby city slum: "They rationalize, 'It's not paying its own way; besides, if we close it, we won't be affecting the collection box too much.' "

Monsignor Donohue stunned listeners at the 1968 convention of the National Catholic Educational Association when he advocated spending much of the Church resources on inner-city schools. "I haven't changed my mind one iota," he says. "In fact, I've developed my thinking a little further. The problem we're facing is a paralysis of leadership on the part of some bishops and some superintendents of schools. They're so involved in the mechanics of survival, they're wedded to the status quo. They should be saying: 'Some of my resources are shrinking, but what can I do as a service to the world?' Instead, they're panicking. They want to hold on to what they've got."

It is Monsignor Donohue's opinion that the Church schools will be hurt by this attitude. "Unless we change," he says, "we'll wither away, we'll die. We're losing the kids anyway, and the teachers too. We might as well experiment."

A handful of states now permit modest financial aid to Catholic schools, and Church lobbyists have been pumping for Federal aid. Monsignor Donohue says, however, that money alone is not the answer to the problems of Church schools; "If you gave a bishop a blank check to pay for his schools, I'm not sure he'd know how to spend the money because I don't think he knows clearly what he wants the future of Catholic education to be. Is it to build more schools and more schools and more schools? I don't think he'd say yes."

Before any money is allocated, says the priest, "we have to determine what the teaching mission of the Church is for the decades ahead." He believes the Catholic schools, if they are to be any good, "must offer a choice to the public schools. Instead, they have become a carbon copy."

Monsignor Donohue envisions the development of radically different Catholic schools, and would reject Federal aid if it prevented experimentation. "What price the Federal buck," he asks, "if in accepting Federal aid we have to dilute our concept of what a religious-oriented school is? If we do, then I say we ought to get out of the business."

Some of Monsignor Donohue's experimental notions are sure to offend traditionalists. He would "like to see the Catholic classroom become a Christian community . . . . I would trust the school would be ecumenical, run maybe by a number of religious groups, Lutherans, Methodists, maybe even Jewish people. The teachers would be truly free."

Just as offensive to conservatives is Monsignor Donohue's insistence that the

Church must bear Christian witness by serving the ghetto poor. It may seem to the conservatives that the Church currently doesn't even have the money to serve the suburban affluent. Monsignor Donohue suggests that such conservatives take the time to reread the landmark papal encyclicals of recent years: Pope John XXIII's *Pacem in Terris* (Peace on Earth) and *Mater et Magistra* (Christianity and Social Progress) and Pope Paul VI's *Populorum Progressio* (On the Development of Peoples). "In these three encyclicals," he says, "the Church is offering the world the best of its treasury of good concepts."

He believes it is in keeping with these concepts for the Church to help America's urban crisis "by the teaching of the poor—as we are doing in such places as Baltimore and Pittsburgh. And with no proselytizing, since a majority of the kids in city ghettos are not Catholics. We could take the poorest readers and bring them up by putting our best teachers there. In one city, the public-school system might call on us to run a remedial-reading center; in another, a guidance-counseling center; and in another, a special school to teach office skills to girls."

Monsignor Donohue is critical of what Catholic schools are doing to further the faith through religious education. He says: "We've neglected the greatest possibility of all, and that's *adult* religious education. The level of religious sophistication of 80 percent of American Catholics is that of a high school religion course."

To remedy this, he recommends that the Church concentrate more resources on educating adults rather than children. "For the past 50 years," he says, "the Church has been too child-oriented, with 70 to 85 per cent of parish funds going for elementary schools, and a big part of diocesan funds going to diocesan high schools. I would suspect that the largest percentage of devout Catholics are devout because of the training they got from parents. The Catholic schools can put the icing on the cake, but they can't take the place of parents." The future shape of Church schools, he says, will be decided as it becomes more and more apparent that Catholic education needs to concentrate on the very young and young adults, as well as grown-ups. If Monsignor Donohue had his way, he would start Catholic children in prekindergarten classes and concentrate on the early primary grades. He would do away with grades three through eight, but would resume Catholic education in a four-year high school. "If we have to make a choice," he says, "we should keep the high school. These are important years."

Monsignor Donohue is critical of Church secrecy that has withheld from Catholic parents the facts about the parochial-school crisis. "Up to now," he says, "I don't think we've really candidly told Catholics how we're spending the money they give us for education. If we did, if we opened our books completely and the parents saw our problems, I think they'd be moved—that is, if they really want Catholic schools in their communities."

The priest regards it "as just blackmail" to threaten the public schools with closing down Catholic schools and dumping their pupils into the public system unless the Government comes up with financial aid. "If parents really mean this," he says, "what value does the Catholic child have for them? You would have to doubt they want religious schools."

Instead of threatening, he thinks Catholics should point out how public schools benefit from the competition of good private-school systems. It would be in the public interest, says Monsignor Donohue, for the Government to give private-school pupils tuition grants. He points to the success of the GI Bill of Rights which, after three wars, enabled veterans getting Government money to attend Catholic schools without raising any church-state conflicts.

"The biggest question is not money," Monsignor Donohue repeats. "It is the need to determine the direction of the Church schools." Looking ahead ten years, he foresees a much smaller Catholic school system "that is, hopefully, the leading edge in experimentation and quality, and that offers a real alternative to public education." This system, he adds, would continue to have "a major commitment to the educationally disadvantaged."

The changes that are coming don't dismay Monsignor Donohue a great deal. He says: "If we lose just numbers, I don't think we've lost too much. The numbers are not as important as the quality of what we're doing in bearing witness to the education of the poor and disadvantaged. They are not as important as quality education that is distinctly different from the public product."

Answer for "Disadvantaged" Is Effective Teaching

KENNETH B. CLARK

The term "the disadvantaged" has appeared with the frequency of a cliché in the literature on poverty, civil rights, and urban education during the past decade. Like the term "culturally deprived," it has become a euphemism for Negro and other lower-status minority-group children.

The terms are not only useful as a means of categorizing minority-group youngsters, but are convenient explanations for the unwillingness or the inability of the public schools to provide these children with the quality of education necessary for them to be educationally competitive with more privileged children.

It is significant that the discussion of the "disadvantaged" or "deprived" developed in the wake of the thrust for the desegregation of the schools. In fact, it is one of the more subtle forms of white resistance to the movement toward nonsegregated schools.

The concept of the "culturally disadvantaged" is part of the total thesis that

From *The New York Times* (Special Education Supplement) January 12, 1970, C50.

minority-group children suffer from economic, cultural, and political disadvantage and, therefore, cannot be expected to learn as white children do. This argument, like the theory of racial inferiority of these children, assumes that since educational disadvantage reflects more basic disadvantage, one cannot expect the schools to succeed until the fundamental economic or biological disadvantage has been removed.

This thesis I reject categorically. I reject it first on the basis of the abundant evidence that when normal children are taught effectively without regard to economic disadvantage or social or racial status, they learn. The record of public education in the United States historically demonstrates that despite previous conditions of economic or cultural deprivation, human beings have been able to use education as a means of overcoming economic disadvantage.

This has been true of every wave of European and Asiatic immigrants. There is even evidence that this is equally true for Negro youngsters. When they are adequately taught, they also learn.

When one examines the various compensatory or enrichment programs that have been successful in raising the academic achievement of minority-group students, one finds that the significant new ingredient invariably is more effective teaching. It follows that the answer to the question of the best way to teach "the disadvantaged" is embarrassingly simple—namely, to teach them with the same acceptance of their humanity and their educability and, therefore, with the same effectiveness as one would teach the more privileged child.

If, on the other hand, one approaches minority-group children with elaborate theories whose rationale is that they cannot or will not learn, the results will be negative. Children are sensitive to all such condescension, and they will seek to escape the inherent humiliation of the school experience by various devices—by refusing to learn, by apathy, by aggressive acts, or by unconscious forms of retaliation.

Supporting the expectations of poor performance from minority-group children are a complex of psychological or progressive education theories that justify the setting of lower standards for these children on the grounds that it would be cruel and unrealistic to hold them to standards they cannot meet.

On the surface, these explanations are seen as signs not of rejection but, indeed, as reflecting understanding and compassion for the limitations of the culturally deprived child or the inherently inferior child.

Under the guise of compassion and understanding, educational disadvantage is reinforced. This apparent acceptance of these children has precisely the same effect as racial rejection. Such "acceptance" is based on categorizing or stereotyping whole groups of children as inferior; it denies each child, so stereotyped, his individuality and his potential, thus perpetuating the self-fulfilling prophecy of massive educational underachievement for all these children.

So far, the efforts to raise the educational achievement of minority-group youngsters have been minimal. Despite endless conferences and meetings to discuss the problem, not a single urban public school system has addressed itself to a massive educational program to achieve this result. In fact, there is strong evidence to suggest that the average academic achievement of minority-group students has been regressing from year to year in our urban public schools, even as the budget for these schools has been increasing at an alarming rate.

It is my considered judgment that it is possible to raise children in urban elementary public schools to their grade norm within two or three years. It is possible to do this through insisting that every school in the system mobilize its teaching and supervisory personnel to develop a serious program designed to bring each normal child up to grade norm in reading and arithmetic.

Such an educational program can be successful if the following conditions are built in and insisted upon:

1. A system of accountability must be maintained to insure that each teacher is responsible to his principal or assistant principal for the reading achievement of the children in his class. The principal in turn must be responsible to the assistant superintendent or some other supervisor for the efficient performance of his teachers, as reflected in the academic performance of their students.

2. Teachers and principals must be evaluated and rewarded differentially, by promotions and salary increases, in terms of the academic performance of their students. There could be a system of ranks for elementary and secondary school teachers which would be roughly equivalent to the ranks of college teachers. The highest rank should be the master teacher, who would be equal in rank and salary to the principal or assistant superintendent.

It is clear that only with a new system for rewarding teaching will it be possible to change the perspective and practices of teachers of today's educationally disadvantaged children. Such a new approach might also undercut the present elaborate system of rationalization, excuses, and alibis that perpetuate the stagnant or regressive underachievement of minority-group students.

Educational disadvantage is remediable; but unless it is remedied, it will perpetuate all other forms of social disadvantage. Those who are economically or socially disadvantaged are not inherently or inevitably educationally disadvantaged. Schools tend to make it so by assuming and acting as if it were. [Editor's Note: The following tables appeared with Dr. Clark's article in its original presentation in the January 12, 1970 issue of *The New York Times.* The first table from the Bureau of Census indicates the total number and per cent of whites and nonwhites enrolled in schools in 1968. Note the close relationship between both groups. The second table from the 1966 U.S. Office of Education report "Equality of Educational Opportunity" displays the median test scores for various racial and ethnic groups. There is a significantly higher performance by the white group in almost all categories. Is Dr. Clark correct? Is the answer more effective teaching?]

TABLE 1

Enrollment Status of Whites and Nonwhites, Age 3 to 34, in U.S.: Oct., 1968 (in thousands)

Whites	Population	Enrolled in School Number	Enrolled in School Per Cent	Nonwhites	Population	Enrolled in School Number	Enrolled in School Per Cent
3 and 4 years	6,527	977	15.0	3 and 4 years	1,284	250	19.5
5 and 6 years	6,952	6,149	88.5	5 and 6 years	1,311	1,091	83.3
7 to 9 years	10,687	10,595	99.1	7 to 9 years	1,900	1,882	99.1
10 to 13 years	13,960	13,840	99.1	10 to 13 years	2,327	2,303	98.9
14 and 15 years	6,651	6,524	98.1	14 and 15 years	1,068	1,040	97.4
16 and 17 years	6,282	5,702	90.8	16 and 17 years	983	852	86.7
18 and 19 years	5,692	2,898	50.9	18 and 19 years	895	418	46.7
20 and 21 years	5,310	1,742	32.8	20 and 21 years	753	151	20.1
22 to 24 years	6,949	1,006	14.5	22 to 24 years	963	89	9.2
25 to 29 years	10,958	806	7.4	25 to 29 years	1,433	58	4.0
30 to 34 years	9,478	368	3.9	30 to 34 years	1,248	49	3.9
Total, 3 to 34 years	89,446	50,608	56.6	Total, 3 to 34 years	14,164	8,184	57.8

Source: U.S. Dept. of Commerce, Bureau of the Census.

TABLE 2

Estimated Median Test Scores for 1st- and 12th-Grade Pupils: U.S., Fall 1965*

	Racial or Ethnic Group					
	Puerto Ricans	Indian Americans	Mexican Americans	Oriental Americans	Negro	White
First Grade						
Nonverbal	45.8	53.0	50.1	56.6	43.4	54.1
Verbal	44.9	47.8	46.5	51.6	45.4	53.2
Twelfth Grade						
Nonverbal	43.3	47.1	45.0	51.6	40.9	52.0
Verbal	43.1	43.7	43.8	49.6	40.9	52.1
Reading	42.6	44.3	44.2	48.8	42.2	51.9
Mathematics	43.7	45.9	45.5	51.3	41.8	51.8
General Information	41.7	44.7	43.3	49.0	40.6	52.2
Average of the 5 tests	43.1	45.1	44.4	50.1	41.1	52.0

*Note: All scores were standardized to give an overall average, for the population as a whole at each grade level, of 50.

Source: U.S. Office of Education, Commissioner's report on "Equality of Educational Opportunity," July 2, 1966.

Colleges Are Skipping over Competent Blacks to Admit "Authentic" Ghetto Types

THOMAS SOWELL

Campuses across the country are full of optimistic official reports and demoralizing private discussions about programs for black students. As a black faculty member, I encounter more than my share of both. The private discussions revolve around underprepared black students who are in over their heads academically and those white faculty members who fudge their grades out of guilt, compassion or a desire to avoid trouble. Few faculty members are as blunt as the Cornell professor who said, "I give them all A's and B's, to hell with'em." At least he understood the consequences of what he was doing. Others think they are doing a favor to the students, or to black people in general.

While it is uncertain what proportion of black students need, want or get special consideration of this sort, it happens often enough to throw a cloud of doubt over the performances of able black students and to risk the devaluation of their degrees and respect. The effect may be even more disastrous for those black students who are neither fully prepared nor incompetent, but who could make the painful transition to demanding educational standards if they had to, in an environment without easy or "understanding" professors.

The basic myths underlying current policies and practices regarding black college students have been elaborated into a whole system of social theology, interpreted by the anointed and defended against heretics and skeptics. These basic beliefs include the following:

(1) Inadequately prepared black students must be recruited, even for the most demanding colleges and universities, because those are essentially the only kind of black students available in substantial numbers.

(2) The major efforts in admissions, financial aid and counseling must be concentrated on the academically deprived, because the good black students "will make it anyway."

(3) Standardized tests contain too much white, middle-class material to be used in predicting the academic success of black students, relative either to white students or to each other.

(4) Black college students require very special handling, including an education centering on black studies and courses taught by black faculty members.

(5) Flunking black students in a course or putting them out of college for academic deficiencies deprives black people of potential leadership.

From *The New York Times Magazine* (December 13, 1970), 36, 37, 39, 40, 42, 44, 46, 49, 50, 52.

(6) There can be no honest or substantial reason for criticizing these ideas: whites who criticize them are insensitive or racist and blacks who criticize them must be middle-class snobs and certainly not "really" black. (This leaves a loophole for Orientals, but no theology is perfect.)

The consistency of these ideas with each other and with a certain vision of the social process is striking. What is even more striking is how little evidence can be produced to support them, and how much evidence there is against them.

It is a fact—the basic, overwhelming fact—that the public-school education offered in Negro neighborhoods, or in low-income neighborhoods generally, is inferior to that offered in middle-class or upper-income neighborhoods. This is true, with the rarest exceptions, in all parts of the country and in communities of all sorts, including communities populated by liberal faculty members. Only a pathetically small percentage of the students from such inferior schools score well on standardized tests or otherwise show strong academic capability. However, colleges do not admit *percentages;* they admit *absolute numbers.* And in absolute numbers, there are tens of thousands of black students in this country who score above the national average on standardized tests—far too many for the leading colleges and universities to be *forced* to have as many unqualified black students as they do. The real reason for their current mix of black students is in the institutions themselves, their philosophy and approach, and in the kind of people who tend to predominate in the running of programs involving black students.

One of the few real studies done in this area, where assertions abound, indicates that there are more than 50,000 black students who score above the national average on various standardized tests. A team of Columbia University researchers found that, among Southern Negro high-school seniors planning on college, 38 per cent of those who intended to go to integrated colleges scored above the national average, as did 21 per cent of those who intended to go to predominantly black colleges.[1] At the time of the study, there were about 200,000 black students in college, split about equally between the two kinds of colleges. If the percentages among Southern Negro students also applied to their Northern counterparts, this would mean a total of 59,000 black students who scored above the national average.

But the real total of qualified black students is likely to be still higher than this for a number of reasons. Northern black students may have somewhat better academic performances than Southern Negroes, as some other studies indicate. There are also black students who have abilities not shown by standardized tests, and who simply do not take standardized tests, which many black colleges do not require for admission. Moreover, the total number of black students in college has increased enormously since the Columbia study was done in the mid-nineteen-sixties.

While no one knows exactly what happens to Negro students who belong in the

[1] These data are from a study by A. J. Jaffee, Walter Adams and Sandra G. Myers, published in an article in College Board Review, Winter 1967–68, and in a book, "Negro Higher Education in the 1960's," as well as from an explanatory letter from one of the authors.

top colleges and universities but who do not get there, what is known is disturbing. About 10,000 to 12,000 of the black students who score in the top half on standard tests attend the *lowest level* of Southern Negro colleges—nondescript and often unaccredited institutions—while many other black students without the necessary academic skills are being maneuvered through top-level colleges at a cost to the integrity of the educational process which is exceeded only by the psychic costs borne by the students themselves.

How can such a situation exist?

Judging from all the current sound and fury—always a poor basis for judgment—it may be hard to understand how there can still be untapped reservoirs of qualified black students when so many good colleges and universities have recruited so many obviously unqualified ones. The answer is that many of the special programs for black students do *not* seek to fill whatever number of places exist for black students with the best black students available. Some officials will openly state this, others will be evasive before admitting it, and still others will continue to deny it after the evidence has piled up.

One argument for taking less qualified black students over more qualified black students is that social conscience requires that help be concentrated on those who need help most. Sometimes this is accompanied by assertions that academically able black students come from "middle-class" backgrounds and "will make it anyway" without special attention—crucial assumptions of the social theology, not subjected to any factual test. Often intellectually oriented black students are *defined* as middle class in outlook, whatever their actual social origins, and may be passed over by programs seeking "authentic" ghetto types.

The comfortable belief that able black students require no special attention ignores the gaps and weaknesses common in their education (especially in mathematics) and the equally damaging gaps in their knowledge of colleges and universities. Many of those summarily labeled middle class are in fact the first members of their families to go to college, and have no real basis for or guidance in distinguishing colleges, courses or careers.

The basic goal of helping those who need help most, rather than those who can use it best, is not confined to the campus, but pervades many programs sponsored by Government agencies and private foundations as well. The aim is not to cultivate the most fertile soil but to make the desert bloom. This is a more romantic achievement, but there is a serious question whether (1) black or white society can afford such romanticism at this point, and whether (2) it is not a misappropriation of funds designed to produce concrete results for black people if such funds are used to produce a glow of nobility in whites administering such programs.

Illustrations of these attitudes abound. A young black woman with an I.Q. of 142, and grades and recommendations to match, was told by a national organization which finances black law students that she would be eligible for financial aid in law school if her scores were *low* enough! Her scores were, of course, not low enough, so she is now going $2,000 into debt to finance her first year of law school.

A black young man with a brilliant academic record in difficult college courses was turned down by a leading foundation which provides a well-publicized doctoral fellowship for black students, after an interview centering on his sociopolitical orientation (not militant enough) rather than his intellectual abilities or interests. A black high-school girl with impressive credentials was offered inadequate financial aid by an Ivy League university, which she could have attended with the help of a National Merit award she won—except that the university reduced its offer when she got the additional award (she ended up attending a much lower quality college). The same university pours much larger sums than she needed into many inept black students, and even into bongo drums to celebrate Malcolm X's birthday.

Another student with an excellent record (College Board scores in the 700's) was opposed for admission by members of the special black admissions committee because his record looked "middle class" to them. It turned out that his father was an alcoholic and his mother was a maid, but the committee member who brought this out was still unsuccessful in getting the others to vote favorably—and was herself later fired from her post as assistant dean for being out of step with the times.

How do the general attitudes and policies behind these particular cases develop? Probably no one knows fully, not even those who have such attitudes and shape such policies. However, several ingredients are usually present: (1) vague humanitarians who have never thought through whether their purpose is to be charitable directly to those individuals helped or to make such individuals the vehicles of intellectual skills to help the larger black community; (2) sociopolitical doctrinaires, seeking to implement their special vision and/or mitigate their own guilt feelings; (3) practical administrators much more concerned with the immediate problem of appeasing the most vocal blacks (and their white allies) than with any long-run consequences for the black community or the larger society; and (4) ignorance or apathy on the part of those outside the tight circle of decision-makers in such programs.

An additional factor at some institutions is the emergence of opportunists who consciously seek control of the admissions of black students, so as to have the kind of black student body that can be used for personal or political advantage. Here the bias is clearly against the academically able and academically oriented black student, who might not take as many black studies courses, might not need (or want) the special assistant dean for black students, and might be skeptical about the rhetoric designed to make him cannon fodder in various causes and movements.

What is remarkable about the current tragedy is how unchallenged its basic elements are. Most whites simply do not have the knowledge to challenge those individuals (black or white) who step forward boldly as the only true interpreters of black people and their needs. In an era of instant labels, the expression of doubts about or criticism of current policies could bring immediate charges of "racism." Blacks who do not go along with current practices are of course called "Uncle Toms," "Oreos" (black on the outside; white on the inside), and other such terms. But a glance through history shows that telling the truth—in any field—has never been easy or free of cost or dangers. Progress depends on the fact that there have been people who would do it anyway.

The current myths flourish because those who do oppose them are so readily dismissed—the whites for not being black, and the blacks for not being "really" black, in some ideological sense. However, the bulk of the black people in this country are not "really" black by such standards. Many black people who are very militant about their rights as human beings do not automatically buy the rhetoric or program of those who claim exclusive rights to the "militant" label. This makes things inconvenient for those white people who think of black people not as individuals but as some amorphous mass represented by "leaders" or "spokesmen."

Inconvenient as the truth may be, it will have to be faced if there is to be any hope of rational discussion. Stereotypes will not merely have to be changed but abandoned, for the bulk of the black people do not represent anybody's stereotype. Most Negroes are not on welfare (most people on welfare are white), most black families are not fatherless, most Negroes are not anti-Semites, and most black people are not going to forgive anybody for enslaving their ancestors because of some insulting "reparations" or because guilty whites select some hoodlums or incompetents to be "representatives" of "the black community," in college or elsewhere.

There is an undeniable need for more highly educated black professionals and black leaders generally, but this need is not going to be met by handing out more embossed pieces of paper to black students as they leave college. What is needed is precisely what those papers are supposed to represent, together with some measure of confidence that credentials can be used as a rough guide to help sort out the competent from the incompetent. There has never been a shortage of half-baked people, in any race or community. Such people are an additional problem in themselves, partly because they force competent people to take time out from urgent work to oppose them or to undo the damage they cause. White faculty members who pass black students because they are black should at least distinguish generosity from irresponsibility.

Although standardized test results have been used as a handy device for estimating the number of black college students above the national average, such tests are neither perfect in themselves nor the only possible basis for judging ability. Some so-called "intelligence" tests, for example, contain items which really test an individual's knowledge of middle-class culture rather than his reasoning ability. However, such tests are neither valid nor invalid *absolutely*, but only so relative to a particular purpose. For example, if the purpose is to determine whether one class or race is biologically "superior" or "inferior" to another, then clearly this cannot be determined by tests which feature the cultural patterns of one of the two groups being compared.

The invalid uses of standardized tests have enabled some people to claim that those tests are completely invalid, not only for comparing black students with white students but for comparing black students with each other in terms of their relative prospects of doing good academic work. The "irrelevance" of standardized tests (and other academic criteria) for judging the relative academic prospects of black students has become a central article of faith in the current social theology.

What various studies show in fact is that (1) black students in the 600–700

College Board score range do significantly better academic work than black students in the 400–500 range, but (2) that, within the latter group, the rank order of scores has little correlation with the rank order of academic performance *at colleges geared for students with much higher scores.* At other colleges, geared for students in the 400–500 range, test scores for students in that range *do* correlate with performance, for black students as well as for white.[2] What all this means is that students who are in over their heads academically will sink or swim according to motivational factors rather than according to small score differences of only 60 points on a College Board scale that goes up to 800 points.[3] Other studies dealing with much larger ranges have shown the tests to be as predictive for black students as for white students.[4]

The test score "irrelevance" argument is part of a more general attempt to make black students something very mysterious, to be interpreted only by the believers in current social fashions. Such interpreters imagine themselves to be very advanced in their thinking, but they are in fact following a very old tradition, particularly strong in the South, of accepting any degree of incompetence or irresponsibility from the "right" kind of black person. The other side of the coin is suspicion or even hostility toward competent and hard-working blacks who do not exhibit the expected stereotype.

What constitutes the "right" kind of black person has varied greatly with the emotional needs of white people, but the great tragic fact of the black man's history in the United States is that his own ability has always been far less important than his satisfaction of white emotional needs. These emotional needs now include the discharge of guilt feelings, and special care for the incompetent and the abusive black student obviously discharges more guilt than the normal application of academic standards to competent and thoughtful black students.

One of the great untold stories of the academic world concerns the way academically able and intellectually oriented black students are often treated as expendable by "practical" administrators preoccupied with day-to-day problems. Not only do such able black students fail to elicit the zeal that goes into the recruitment and financing of more fashionable types, their interests are often directly sacrificed to appease organized and politicized elements.

Intimidation and physical assaults on nonpoliticized black students by their "brothers" with messianic (or simply hoodlum) instincts are resolutely ignored by

[2] Journal of Educational Measurement, 1967, 1968, and Harvard Educational Review, 1967.

[3] The evidence is even weaker than this might suggest. One sub-group of black students did better academic work than another sub-group of black students who scored about 60 points higher on *one* portion of the College Board exam, but this better-performing group scored about 60 points higher than the others on *another* portion of the same exam. Both groups put together added up to less than 300 students and many of them were at colleges whose average student scores were 100 or more points above theirs. This is the straw of inconclusive evidence which is used to support a mountain of social policy. The study in question is by Kenneth B. Clark and Lawrence Plotkin, "The Negro Student at Integrated Colleges," 1963.

[4] Journal of Educational Measurement, 1967, cites numerous other studies indicating this, as well as presenting its own evidence confirming those findings.

college administrators. To white activist faculty members, it is either something to be blotted out of the mind or an incidental unhappy eddy in the backwash of the wave of the future. Compulsory indoctrination programs for entering Negro freshmen have been a demand of black militants on some campuses, and while it has not been formally granted in most cases, arrangements have been made which amount to the same thing *de facto*. Recruitment, prescreening for admission, and even control of financial-aid funds have been put into the hands of the politicized minority on many campuses, including some of the highest prestige insitutions in the country—Harvard, Yale, Cornell, etc. Some of these things occur in every major educational institution I know of, and in some institutions all of these things occur.

Even where the intellectually oriented black student makes his way into and through college without being directly harmed by all this, he cannot be unaffected by the double standard which makes his degree look cheap in the market and his grades suspect to those concerned with academic standards. Worst of all, he cannot even have the full confidence within himself that he really earned them.

The developing backlash, on college campuses as well as in the larger community, makes it clear that current trends cannot continue indefinitely. The only real question is whether policies and practices can be changed to accomplish the real goal of improving the education of black people, or whether current irrationality and expediency will be allowed to discredit the whole effort. When the failures of many programs become too great to disguise, or to hide under euphemisms and apologetics, the conclusion that will be drawn in many quarters will not be that these were half-baked schemes, but that black people just don't have it. This is what is galling to me as a black man, and what should be disturbing to everyone.

What can be done? Certainly nothing constructive is likely to be initiated by those college administrators who are so preoccupied with their immediate crises that they have no time for wider considerations or for thinking of the long run—the "long run" to them often meaning any time after next week. There are, however, many things that can be done, with the initiative and sustained pressure of the public, the faculty or the trustees. Such interest will undoubtedly be resented by those for whom "academic freedom" includes the right to spend other people's money without being held accountable for the results. But colleges and universities have long since forfeited any claim to a blank check.

Probably the No. 1 priority is to *bring out the facts* as to what is currently happening at each campus, in the recruitment, admission and performance of black students and the standards being applied in programs for them. In some cases, the facts will squelch ugly rumors that are being whispered around campus, and gain additional support for efforts that need and deserve it. In other cases, the facts will show sickening nests of opportunists and bush-league messiahs who are simply using the great educational and social problems of black people for their own ends. In still other cases, the facts will support the efforts of dedicated educators (of both races) who are currently struggling with the charlatans and the doctrinaires (also of both races).

Anyone at all familiar with educational programs—whether for blacks or whites—must know that such programs must be evaluated by someone *not* connected with the programs, if the evaluations are to have any shred of validity or credibility. Most educational programs are in fact, however, evaluated by those who run them, or by other individuals with similarly high stakes in the outcome. Anything as emotionally supercharged as programs for black students can only be evaluated by off-campus investigators, preferably by statisticians chosen for their professional integrity rather than their socio-political views.

Black studies programs are a significant part of the total educational picture for black students on many campuses and also deserve study. Such programs are neither good nor bad *a priori*, but only in terms of what they are actually doing. The field of human knowledge can be entered from any point, including black studies. For those students whose driving interest is in the problems of black people, this can be the best gateway. But whether it is in fact an avenue to wider knowledge or a detour into a blind alley of rhetoric and slogans depends upon the facts of the individual case. Some dedicated people are struggling to make black studies an enrichment of the mind rather than an exercise in glorified parochialism. The facts can only strengthen such people while exposing the frauds.

Black students, by and large, are very pragmatic about black studies programs and stay away from them in droves when they don't measure up, however much the local white faculty members may glorify or apologize for such programs. These students tend also to take or not take courses taught by Negro professors on the same pragmatic basis. Black people in general have had enough experience with inferior education not to want any more of it.

There are many sorts of educational reforms which might be instituted once the facts are known. In some cases, recruitment of black students by a consortium of colleges would avoid the painful human consequences of mismatching students and institutions. In some places, pre-college training centers could beef up underprepared students and match them with schools where they could keep up with the pace. (In certain schools the sheer speed with which topics are covered leaves the underprepared student lost, even though he may be perfectly capable of learning the same things at a pace geared to the level of his academic preparation.) In other cases, the crucial changes that need to be made would be personnel rather than institutional changes. But more important than any particular reforms or innovations is the fundamental need to know the facts and to face them without euphemisms, catchwords or apologetics.

Any honest re-evaluation of programs for black students is bound to bring indignant outcries from predictable quarters, and attempts from other quarters to use such evaluations to eliminate or cut back efforts to educate black students. But the number of able black students available and the desperate need for their talents are both too great for us to allow fear of either of these reactions to interfere with doing what must be done and is long overdue.

Black Teachers: New Power in the Schools

SUSAN JACOBY

Black teachers and administrators are beginning to emerge as a power in the nation's city school systems at a time when the bitterness of black parents toward these schools is overflowing. They are being hired and promoted in growing numbers everwhere, except in the oldest, most rigid bureaucracies such as Boston. Like their white counterparts, black teachers are a part of these systems and have an interest in their preservation. But they also have a stake in the black community that is not shared by most of the white teachers. The new black teacher is more militant in pursuing his interests than Negro teachers of the past, partly because of the revolution in "black consciousness" and partly because the teaching profession is no longer the only option, other than the clergy, for Negroes seeking to enter the white-collar world.

The opening of school this fall proved beyond doubt—if any further proof were needed after the last few years—that schools in the inner cities are focal points for some of the most bitter and potentially destructive racial tensions in our divided society. New York's school strike, which pitted the overwhelmingly white teachers' union and supervisors' association against black groups demanding power to hire and fire teachers and principals, was a disaster both for the schools and for the community as a whole. Whites came to use "mob rule" as a synonym for control of schools by local Negro governing boards. Many blacks regarded the union's rallying cry, "due process for teachers," as a simple expression of union determination not to give ghetto residents a say in what goes on in their schools. Between 90 and 95 per cent of New York's 57,000 teachers are white. Inevitably, the strike divided the teachers along racial lines. Although some Negro teachers supported the strike and some whites opposed it, sources in the schools said a large percentage of the several thousand teachers who reported for work despite the strike were Negro.

If New York had the most serious conflict surrounding the opening of school, its problems were far from unique. In Boston, police outside the Christopher Gibson Elementary School barred the entry of a black principal "elected" by neighborhood groups and guarded the school system's regularly appointed white principal. A Negro assistant principal—also regularly appointed by the school system—supported the community groups at considerable risk to his job. In Newark, ten white teachers filed suit to prevent the school system from appointing several new black principals, claiming regular promotion procedures had been bypassed.

From *Saturday Review* (February 20, 1971), 59–60, 70–72.

Amid all of the racial conflict surrounding the schools, black teachers are in a peculiarly sensitive and sometimes painful position. They have "made it" into the middle class; their students, for the most part, come from families that have not made it. "You look at those black children in front of you and you know that this is where you come from," says one black teacher from Detroit. "Those kids are either what you used to be, or what you might have been."

The phenomenon of black self-hatred, documented most perceptively by black writers and social scientists, is still evident in some Negro teachers who express contempt for "lower class" slum children. But the black teacher has been deeply affected by the identity crisis the black power movement has posed for the entire Negro middle class. As a result, he identifies far more readily with black children in slum schools than did the Negro teachers of the past. That identification is one reason most black teachers work in urban school systems. "If the black teacher does not recognize a special responsibility for the progress and achievement of black children, who will?" asks Zeline Richard, a teacher from Detroit who campaigned unsuccessfully for the presidency of the AFL-CIO American Federation of Teachers (AFT) this year. "I think many black teachers are coming to realize we must be the guardians of the education of all the children in the inner city."

There are other less idealistic explanations for the concentration of black teachers in the city schools. Unlike their white counterparts, most black teachers live in the cities—housing discrimination gives them little choice—and tend to work where they live. It is still difficult for a black teacher to get a job in a suburban school; racial discrimination in hiring is a common practice in many all-white suburban school systems. At the annual AFT convention in Cleveland, it was reported that fewer than fifty Negro teachers were employed by the predominantly white suburban school systems surrounding Cleveland.

Progressive city school officials across the country are aware that one of the main irritants, if not a causal factor, in the bitter New York situation is the fact that more than 90 per cent of the teachers are white, while more than half of the students are black or Puerto Rican. Officials are eager to hire more black teachers and administrators, hopeful that such action will help avert similar confrontations in their cities.

Detroit, which has a school system only one-fourth the size of New York's, has nearly three times as many Negro administrators. When Detroit's school superintendent, Norman Drachler, took over the job two years ago, he regarded the task of bringing more black (and young) administrators into the schools as "one of the really critical initial problems that had to be dealt with." In the past eighteen months the number of Negroes on one Detroit teaching staff has risen from 30 per cent to 40 per cent. More than a third of the teachers in Chicago, three-fourths in Washington, D.C., and half in Baltimore are black. Although the superintendent of schools in Washington is white, most of the other top-level administrators are black.

Black educators are just becoming aware of their growing numerical power and how it might be used to affect the policies of public school systems. On issues not related to race, most black teachers think and behave exactly like most white teachers. Even the most militant black teachers ruefully admit this. William H. Simons, president of the Washington Teachers Union, says, "The tendency to rely on doing things as they have been done in the past is a characteristic that has nothing to do with the color of one's skin. If all it took were black teachers and administrators to change a school system, we would obviously have the best school system in the world here in Washington. Which of course is not the case."

But many of the most important controversies swirling around the schools are related to race, and here the black teacher, joined by some of the younger white teachers, does depart from the average white teacher.

Community control of the schools, as demonstrated by the conflict in New York, is a major issue that tends to separate black and white teachers, although it would be an oversimplification to assert that all black teachers support community control and that whites automatically oppose it. Many black teachers are just as fearful of what they regard as "parent interference" in the classroom as the average white teacher, although younger teachers of both races tend to be less rigid on this issue. Nevertheless, the evidence from cities with large numbers of Negro teachers indicates that if black teachers are not wholeheartedly in favor of more community control, they are at least less hostile toward it than their white counterparts. Says Keith Baird, a curriculum consultant to the embattled Ocean Hill-Brownsville school district in New York: "Community control simply means that blacks and Puerto Ricans will have the same say in running their schools that whites have always had. Naturally, that prospect doesn't frighten black teachers."

In general, black teachers are not as fearful as white teachers that their hard-won due process rights will be destroyed if neighborhood school boards have some control over hiring and firing. Many of the white teachers automatically assume that their jobs will be in serious jeopardy if they are subject to the control of a black school board. All of the teachers fired by the governing board of the Ocean Hill-Brownsville district were white, but the fact that more than two-thirds of the new teachers hired by the board were also white was generally ignored. Says Mr. Simons: "I'm sure it's quite clear to everyone in Washington that we have no intention of letting any local governing board throw out our due process rights. But we see no reason why this should happen. At the heart of the really violent opposition to community control, there is the assumption that a black neighborhood governing board must be by nature irrational and extremist. If you start with this assumption, then naturally there is no potential for negotiation."

In New York, there are not enough black teachers to exert a countervailing influence to the strong anti-community control stand taken by Albert Shanker and his United Federation of Teachers. The picture is quite different in several other cities and within the teacher union movement.

Historically, Negro teachers in the North, fearful of being "the last hired and the first fired," have been strong union members. At least some of the security younger black teachers feel when they display their militancy is attributable to the protection provided by union contracts against being fired for expressing opinions on political and social issues. The AFT's record on race is a progressive one; the struggling union expelled Southern locals that refused to desegregate in 1956, while the powerful, firmly entrenched National Education Association shilly-shallied on the question well into the 1960s.

Understandably, many black delegates to the AFT convention in August were deeply disturbed by a strong statement from newly elected AFT President David Selden that he would push for a merger with the NEA. (The NEA has since rebuffed Selden's overtures regarding a merger.) But the most controversial issue at the union convention was school decentralization and increased involvement by representatives of ghetto neighborhoods in running their schools. "The labor movement has forgotten from whence it came," charged Mrs. Richard, referring to the UFT's position in New York. "The fight of black people today is the fight of the labor movement of yesteryear."

The New Caucus, a dissident group of black and young white teachers within the union, had sought to gain a strong endorsement of community control. New York's UFT, anticipating a strike over the Ocean Hill-Brownsville situation when school opened, succeeded in having the words "community control" stricken from the New Caucus resolution. Said Roy Stell, a delegate from Chicago: "As a black union teacher, you have asked me in voting against this [the New Caucus resolution] to vote against myself. I don't ever want to see the day when my union asks me to go on the picket lines in a strike against my community."

The dispute was papered over by a compromise resolution putting the union on record as recognizing the need for "effective community responsibility and involvement through elected representation in the black, Puerto Rican, and other minority communities of America." The community control issue is a threat to the solidarity of the union, and neither the union leaders nor the dissidents want to see an outright split between black and white union teachers.

The Detroit Federation of Teachers has carefully avoided taking a hard-line stand against community control as the UFT has done. Black teachers account for a third of the Detroit union's membership, and the power of the union—unlike the UFT's position in New York—would be substantially weakened if blacks broke away.

Significantly, the Washington Teachers Union is the only AFT local in the nation that has taken a forthright position in favor of community school boards having a share of power over hiring and firing teachers. Washington and Baltimore are the only large cities in the North where black teachers are in a majority or near-majority. "We teachers have put ourselves on the defensive instead of taking the initiative in regard to community control," says WTU President Simons. "Decentralization and community control could improve education in the large cities, and anything that has even the seeds of improving schooling for children should have the support of teachers. We can protect the rights of teachers through contractual agreements with local boards. And we can work with people if we are only willing to treat them as human beings, regardless of how much formal education they have."

The Washington union supported the city school system's first experiment in community control in an area known as Adams-Morgan, about a mile north of the White House. The Morgan Community School, despite sharp controversy over the project, was one of the few schools in Washington last year where reading scores on standardized tests improved significantly, despite a general decline throughout the system. This fall, the central Board of Education agreed that Morgan's elected neighborhood school board should have expanded powers over staffing, and the union is beginning work on the plan with neighborhood representatives.

Curriculum is another area where the black teacher is beginning to exert an influence in the city school systems. The willingness of large school systems to deal with black history and culture in their curricula seems, regrettably, to have far more to do with the number of black teachers and administrators in the system than with the number of black students. Washington's public school enrollment—now more than 90 per cent black—has been more than three-quarters Negro for the past decade. Yet the history of the black man in Africa and America did not receive any particular emphasis and, in some instances, was actively de-emphasized, until the emergence of a strong, militant teachers' union two years ago coupled with a sharp increase in the number of high-level black administrators.

Despite the fact that school appropriations in the nation's capital are controlled by Southern-dominated Congressional committees, some remarkably candid discussions about racial matters are going on in Washington classrooms. The most skilled teachers use the children's interest in racial topics to spur their interest in the conventional subjects the school attempts to teach.

The weekend after the riots triggered by the Rev. Martin Luther King's death, Washington teachers encouraged the youngsters to express their feelings about the riots in compositions and class discussions, and they did not attempt to elicit the moralistic responses schools usually press their students for. "How did you feel about the looting and the burning?" one teacher asked her sixth-grade class.

"I thought it was all right to loot the white people's stores but not to burn them," replied one girl emphatically.

"Why do you think that?" asked the teacher.

"Because colored people lived over the stores and they got burnt out too."

Another sixth-grader disagreed sharply. "The good stores got looted and burned just like the bad ones," he said. "You can't say that all of the store-owners cheated people. A man on the corner who was always fair to everybody got burned out just like the guys who trick you. It's not right."

The compositions and art work of the children were eventually compiled into a book titled *Tell It Like It Is,* which has been widely quoted and reproduced. "You just don't know," one teacher commented, "how proud these kids were that something they wrote was considered good enough to be printed in a book. Since then we've noticed a greatly increased interest in writing and reading in many of the children, which is an example of how you can take advantage of a pressing current topic to spark their interest in learning. We wouldn't have been allowed to do it ten years ago."

The more conservative teachers in the system are aghast that such activities should be allowed in the classroom. The fact that they are allowed is an indication of a significant change in the school system in recent years—a change that is allowing many teachers to use experiences that are meaningful to the children as a way of interesting them in schoolwork. Black teachers are not responsible for all of the curriculum changes in Washington; some white teachers have been most active in working for curriculum reform that stresses black history and culture as well as the life of the inner-city child. Rather, the presence and pressure of black teachers and administrators have created a climate where such changes are possible. A teaching staff that is 95 per cent white is simply not likely to be excited by the absence of Frederick Douglass from an American History book.

In the long run, the most important impact of the black teacher in the classroom may not be in promoting community control or specific curriculum changes, but simply in serving as an image of success for black students in ghetto schools. The same is true for black administrators, especially black male administrators.

The fact that many black youngsters of elementary school age never come in contact with black adults in positions of power and authority is a genuine tragedy in terms of the child's self-esteem—one that few whites can even comprehend. Assume, for a moment, that Scarsdale, New York, were a community of destitute whites and not a wealthy suburb. Suppose the white Scarsdale child saw only three kinds of black people in his neighborhood—welfare workers—who doled out the family's livelihood—policemen, and teachers. Assume that the white Scarsdale child went to school every day and was taught by black teachers and black principals, with never a white face in sight except among the youngsters. It is not difficult to figure out what conclusions the child would reach about which skin color was the source of knowledge and money and power in his world. This is precisely the situation that confronts many black children in the teeming city slums, with only the colors reversed. The question of whether a school that perpetuates such a system can effectively teach black children is an inherently valid one.

Detroit's Superintendent Drachler is deeply concerned about the need to place qualified blacks in positions of authority in the ghetto schools. "If I have a qualified black principal and two openings—one in a white school and one in a Negro school, I'd probably assign the man to the predominantly Negro school," Drachler says. "I think it's absolutely vital that a child in the ghetto see people of his own race who have achieved, and not think that everyone in authority is white. This is not to say that it isn't important to have Negro administrators in white schools, but that, with a limited number of such people, I think they should be used first where the need is greatest."

The idea that only black teachers can effectively teach black children is nonsense. But the chief characteristic of inner-city schools across the nation is they tend to make deprived youngsters feel like failures at the age of six or seven. The real importance of the black teacher may lie in his unique opportunity to bolster his students' self-image. One first-grader in a Washington school informed his teacher, as she passed out reading readiness workbooks, "Reading is hard. My brother can't read nuthin'. And he's ten." The teacher looked at the boy and said, "I learned to read when I was your age, and I grew up just a block from your house."

Teacher Militancy in the United States: Reflections on its Sources and Prospects

RONALD G. CORWIN

Everyone knows that teaching is a troubled occupation. But few people are probably fully aware of just how widespread are its problems—certainly they are more pervasive than the recent rash of well-publicized strikes, walkouts, and sanctions would indicate. These visible and covert indications of unrest have been bred within a much broader context of discontent that has swept this country in recent years. Existentialism, with its doctrine of personal commitment and decisive action has finally come of age; this generation blames most of its problems on a self-conscious sense of alienation rooted in the failure of existing social arrangements—large segments of the population complain of feeling a loss of a sense of meaningful control over their destiny. Group militancy represents an alternative for people not content with this fate.

With the assistance of mass media, the problems of urban America, especially the voices of the Negro and the alienated adolescent, have finally broken through; other partially disenfranchised groups are following suit. Militancy has become a common response to pervasive sociological tensions and a generic symptom of the failure of existing social institutions. Teacher militancy must be understood in this context.

Sources of Conflict

While the aggressiveness of teachers may be stimulated in the context described, the context in itself is not a sufficient explanation for this aggressiveness. The plain fact is that, in many respects, educational bureaucracies are not working very effectively. People will not feel constrained to accept the authority of a system that fails to come to grips with the pressing problems of the day, nor obliged to administrators who are no more able than they to cope with the ailments of their

From *Theory into Practice* (April 1968), 96–102. Reprinted by permission.

occupation—inadequate financing, competing objectives and cross pressures, educational failures, dropouts, and student discipline problems. School systems have become so complex and have had to adapt to such a wide range of situations that administrators no longer can maintain centralized control over educational practice—although in view of their legal responsibility, many administrators have vainly attempted to preserve the fiction of doing so. This persistent effort, on the part of both administrators and teachers, to maintain customary routines and traditional evaluation standards in a climate of failure, has only aggravated the tension. As teachers have specialized and systems have become larger, teachers have been thrust into positions from which they can exert considerable influence over day-to-day policy. The problem is that most existing systems do not give adequate recognition to the increased influence of teachers and offer few viable ways by which they can resolve their grievances within the existing authority structure. As a consequence, the domains of teachers and administrators have become blurred. Positions of authority in school systems at best have become precarious. We are now witnessing the precipitant shift in this power structure.

This general situation helps to explain some of the findings from a study of staff conflicts in the public schools.[1] The single most frequent type of conflict identified (one in every four) concerned authority problems between teachers and administrators. Much of this tension was associated with a school's professional climate and some of it with the characteristics of the school itself. Professional responsibility requires that some of the traditional administrative decisions be delegated to teachers, and, by and large, administrators have not relinquished their authority willingly. The instability of the authority structure seemed to increase in relationship to a school's size, number of levels of authority, degree of specialization, and its overall complexity. The rates of many types of disputes increased with the amount of authority a faculty member exercised over routine classroom decisions, probably because those teachers with some authority have more to fight about and have more occasions for doing so. Even in these situations, however, there was a lower rate of the more severe, "major incidents" (in which several parties were eventually drawn into heated discussions about an issue).

Much of the conflict is a by-product of the fact that schools are reorienting themselves from sheer obedience to routines to more problem-centered approaches to education. This shift is requiring greater delegation in recognition of the fact that no one group has a full grasp of the existing problems. Although innovation and experimentation have become watchwords in education, little fundamental change has occurred in the wake of scores of new programs—a fact which merely calls further attention to the crisis. Paradoxically, this climate of innovation has generated an atmosphere of defensive conservatism on the part of both administrators and teachers anxious about imminent status changes. Since the offical position of administrators has given them the upper hand in controlling the direction of change at the local level, most of the proposed changes are aimed at improving classroom

[1] Corwin, Ronald G. *Staff Conflicts in the Public Schools.* (USOE Cooperative Research Project No. 2637, 1966.) This report will be published soon by Appleton-Century-Crofts.

teaching through inservice programs for teachers and modified teaching procedures and curricula, rather than involving fundamental alterations in the system itself. The proposals being suggested seem to imply that teachers are responsible for many of the existing problems, and the teachers are understandably apprehensive about accepting the blame. At the same time, of course, opportunities have arisen for new positions of leadership and realignments of groups. People who have long been in positions of subordinate status are becoming sophisticated about organizations, learning to manipulate the existing system and creating organizations of their own to facilitate their purposes. New leaders in time of change do not feel bound by traditional authority nor peaceful means of settling disputes—indeed, the very moral order itself is being disputed.

Some teachers can be expected to capitalize on these opportunities to improve their position. There are several factors in their favor. One of the most apparent examples is the disproportionate number of lower-class people who seem to be attracted to teaching as a way of improving their status.[2] In a society where a person's status is closely linked with his occupational status, his own position rises and falls with the fortunes of his occupation. Also, the lack of opportunity for individual mobility in teaching encourages the efforts of teachers to achieve collective mobility. And, at the same time, they are gaining strength, both in number and in concentration. Given the projected growth of teachers in the work force and the trend toward urban concentration, their absolute power is bound to increase whether or not the proportion of militants grows.

The power of teachers is further enhanced by their responsibility for evaluating the achievement of children, which, in this society, is tantamount to determining their life chances. This power brings teachers into direct confrontation with parents of all social class levels.

Probably the most important basis of teachers' new sense of power is the growing specialization within teaching. Because of specialization, teachers' level of education is likely to increase in the long run; although, until recently, their rate of increase in education has barely kept pace with that of the general population. Of more immediate importance are the educational gains of a small segment of teachers, a marked increase in the specialization in the use of teaching techniques for distinct populations, and the beginnings of separate career lines for teachers of various classes and types of students. Skill at teaching the new math, i.t.a., working with the handicapped, and successful experience in slum schools can not only provide the basis for challenging the conventional authority of laymen, but also ultimately place teachers in positions of superior information compared to the administrators who hire and evaluate them. The traditional role which line administrators have played as "curriculum leaders" has already become unfeasible, and even the effectiveness of the curriculum specialists is limited by pressures on them to achieve system-wide uniformity.

Professionalization represents one very effective means by which members of an occupation can utilize their special knowledge as a leverage for improving the

[2] Davis, James. *Undergraduate Career Decisions.* Chicago: Aldine Press, 1965.

relative position of their occupation, while, at the same time, protecting themselves from the attacks of their adversaries. Hence, professionalization represents both a defense of, and a quest for, status. Without denying the economic interest and material gain undoubtedly involved in the incentive behind some forms of militancy, the distinctive significance of militant professionalism is the shift that it represents from interest politics to the politics of status.[3] In fact, a correlation could not be found between teachers' salaries and their conflict rates in the study of staff conflicts—the only economic variable related to conflict was a positive association between a system's total financial receipts and the rate at which major incidents occurred in high schools. Conflict is probably more closely related to the way existing economic resources are allocated (i.e., the relative deprivation) than to the absolute level of income of a system. It is precisely the satisfactions omitted from material rewards, namely decision-making power, which seem to underlie much of the discontent in teaching.

However, professionalization, itself, is the source of additional tensions, for teachers do not agree among themselves on appropriate standards, and professional principles are incompatible with bureaucratic principles of school organization in many crucial respects. In particular, according to professional principles, teachers would be granted more decision-making authority over the classroom, especially over curriculum content, than they have received within most school systems. To become more professional, teachers will have to gain more power, which will mean challenging the existing system of administration. Hence, in the study of staff conflicts, the incidence of most types of conflict (with an important exception to be noted) in a school increased with the faculty's average level of professionalism. The significant point is that this association was more prominent in the more bureaucratic schools compared to the less bureaucratic ones. In other words, it is in the most bureaucratized schools that a strong commitment to the professional orientation is most likely to lead to conflict. On the other hand, conflict did seem to diminish when the less professionally oriented faculties were bureaucratized.

Alternative Interpretations

In reviewing closely related alternative interpretations, most people would probably be inclined to start with the assumption that conflict simply represents another phase of the Hobbesian war of "all against all," especially among certain belligerent types of people having *deviant personality traits,* i.e., abnormal degrees of vanity, drive for recognition, inability to adjust to others, emotional instability, etc. Without denying the relevance of such factors, it seems more important to recognize that certain *situations* apparently produce tensions which are easily kindled largely independently of the particular people who are part of the situations. For example, in nearly every school interviewed in the study of staff

[3] Hofstadter, Richard. "The Pseudo-Conservative Revolt," in *The Radical Right,* Daniel Bell, editor. New York: Doubleday and Co., Inc., 1964, pp. 75–96.

conflicts, teachers of academic subjects had some complaint against teachers in the extracurricular programs because of the class disruptions created by activity practices and special events. Similarly, vocational teachers often expressed antagonism toward academic teachers and counselors who monopolized the good students and sent them the castoffs. And, schools with high rates of faculty turnover were simply more conflict-prone than more stable schools. Moreover, so important a characteristic as a person's age did not completely account for his conflict rate; the correlation between professional orientation and conflict rate held for all age categories tested.

The most belligerent professionally oriented teachers, far from being marginally "deviant" people, were better integrated into their peer groups, better educated, and more respected and had more group support from their colleagues. While teachers who were both professional and militant did represent only a small proportion of all teachers, it was a group with backing from a broad base of teachers.[4] Yet, it is important to note that while administrative personnel policies have traditionally been based on assumptions about individual psychology, in fact personnel problems in the public schools today seem to be basically sociological in nature.

The personality deviance hypothesis underlies several variants on the *frustration-aggression* theme. In this case, however, conflict is portrayed as a generic human response to social constraints rather than the product of unique personality traits. From this perspective, it appears that teachers have become belligerent because they have been prevented from obtaining their objectives. This may be true, but such an interpretation is rather mechanistic, since in itself it accounts for neither the origin of the objectives frustrated nor the sources of frustration. The *alienation* thesis, which has become so popular, in some respects amounts to a more elaborate frustration-aggression hypothesis. But, in this case, the sources of frustration usually have been traced to social roots, such as disenfranchisement, marginality, and powerlessness, and the objective usually has been more explicitly identified as the search for identity and control over one's destiny or more meaningful participation in life. It is possible that engaging in conflict provides some people with a sense of meaningful participation in their society. This could help to explain our finding that both the personal job satisfaction of teachers and the overall faculty morale increased with individual and faculty conflict rates.

The alienation theme suggests that the militant leadership in teaching is coming from its youngest members who are closest to the current generation of alienated youth. However, the backgrounds of the most belligerent professional teachers indicated that, while it was true that the young males do not seem to be among the most loyal of employees, the middle-aged men most frequently became involved in conflict; apparently it takes time for even the militantly inclined to develop the

[4] Our analysis also suggests that the debate over whether militancy and professionalism are more characteristic of the NEA or AFT affiliates may be misplaced. The differences which were found do not easily lead to a clear-cut answer, and the informal leaders seem to have more influence than the officers of either organization.

respect, the group support, and the margin of security necessary to nurture the capacity for militant leadership.

The alienation theme, however, seems to focus on only the negative side of a larger equation, for while alienated people are in some sense in a state of rebellion against something, at least some of them also seem to be positively identifying with alternative standards, including in some cases, professional standards. It is difficult to believe that teachers who are well integrated into their professional groups are entirely alienated or that these teachers are simply opposed to "the system." It seems more accurate to say that they are caught between competing parts of the system and forced to choose between divergent standards.

Once the dynamics of the interplay among competing alternatives has been introduced, the full complexity of the situation comes into better focus, and some of this complexity is faintly captured in the notions of *relative deprivation and reference group theory.* Relative deprivation alludes to the differences between a person's present situation and some outside standard, often either a former state of his own being or the achievements of his contemporaries. Reference group theory capitalizes exclusively on the social basis of standards by which one compares himself, indicating that they are usually advocated by, or are exemplified in, some social group to which he may or may not belong. Teachers, then, can be expected to compare their station in life with that of persons of equivalent education, income, or work. They are likely to expect rewards at least equivalent to those obtained by people with similar levels of education. Moreover, even when they are making progress, they may become discontented if they are not progressing as rapidly as the groups with which they compare themselves. Hence, although in recent years teachers' average income has increased faster than that of industrial workers (over a 20 per cent increase during the last five years alone), they still lag behind other professional groups. Similarly, more than half of today's high school teachers have over five years of education, but even with this educational progress they have barely kept pace with the general society and still lag far behind other professional groups. Also, the proportion of all teachers with an M.A. has not increased during the past decade (perhaps partly because of the influx of new teachers).[5]

Although not explicit in any of the foregoing concepts, *status congruency* is still another comparative dimension of status which is essential for understanding the complex set of forces behind teacher incentive. It is important to recognize that there are several dimensions of teacher status, each of which may change at variable rates—the status congruency framework explicity focuses on this element of convergence and divergence among a person's present statuses. Incongruence among statuses has become a critical feature of our society. Where there is no longer a close connection between various dimensions of status, such as salary, authority, and level of education, winning salary increments, for example, does not in itself provide access to power. It can be assumed, then, that a group compares its achievements in one area not only with the achievements of other people, but with

[5] *NEA Research Bulletin,* October 1967, 45, 87.

its own achievements in other areas. Hence, teachers are likely to consider their standing in education relative to their salary, occupational prestige, and authority. The consistency of expectations which others have of them, and the demands which can in turn be made, depend upon the consistency of their ranking on the various dimensions of status. Congruent statuses mutually reinforce their position, whereas incongruent ones are likely to lead to confusion and precariousness of status, their lower statuses detracting from their achievements. Therefore, we can expect that people with incongruent statuses will be prompted to increase their respectability in those areas in which they have not yet become respectable enough. A significant advance in one form of status merely illuminates the disparities in the overall status pattern. Consequently, progress in one respect, far from satiating the status quest, can in itself encourage a group to increase its efforts to improve in other respects as well.

Increases which teachers may have made in their authority do not seem to have kept pace with their advances in salary and education in recent years. Such a discrepancy could be an important incentive behind their recent efforts to achieve new levels of authority. Significant in this connection is Goffman's finding that, for people occupying middle- and upper middle-class positions, there was an inverse relationship between the consistency of their statuses and their preference for extensive change in the distribution of power in the society.[6]

The *equilibration* of a *total system* is a product of the mutual congruencies among interdependent positions. Looking at the total system, advances in any one position may threaten counterpositions. In public education, for example, the changing relationship of teachers to administrators, to parents, and to students has played a part in producing the current state of tension. Administrators, for example, have good reason to feel defensive toward teachers. The subordination of teachers developed during an era when they were poorly trained and when administrators had already taken significant steps toward professionalization. But, since that time, teachers have become better trained, and the supply-demand ratio for trained teachers has become more favorable. At the same time, consolidation has reduced the demand for administrators at the highest levels, and the larger role of technical decision and the increasing magnitude of public school systems have inevitably made administrators more dependent upon the judgments of teachers.

Teachers, too, have reason to be defensive about the recent efforts of laymen from all strata to reassert their authority in the wake of the crisis in education. For a time it seemed that, in the big cities especially, administrators had gained the upper hand and communities were content to let the professional administrators run things. However, middle-class parents appear to be more anxious than ever before about the education of their children and the civil rights movement has mobilized previously lethargic lower-class parents, who are also demanding a greater voice in the schooling of their children. Plans to decentralize inner city schools, such as those proposed for New York City, will bypass teachers and increase the

[6] Goffman, Irwin W. "Status Consistency and Preference for Change in Power Distribution," *American Sociological Review,* June 1957, 22, 275–81.

authority of laymen at precisely a time when teachers want more authority for themselves.

Finally, the adolescent revolt, reflecting a new level of power for children, poses another threat to teachers. Children have gained leverage through a variety of devices ranging from innocuous forms of intimidation *via* their parents to slow-downs and outright violence against teachers. In most schools teachers complain about discipline problems, often casting some of the blame on what they believe to be feeble administration.

Given the quest of teachers for power and the mutual defensiveness of teachers, students, and administrators, their relationship assumes more of the character of naked bargaining than of clear-cut subordination. *Exchange theory* provides one way to analyze bargaining relationships systematically. From this perspective, it would appear that as an occupational group comes within sight of the upper occupational bracket, it develops a margin of security which, in turn, alters its ratio of investment to reward. The extended period of training of teachers and the current affluence of this country increases the teachers' career alternatives and reduces the cost of losing. As teachers achieve their own leverage, they can afford to rely less on administrators to do their bargaining for them—especially since administrators are likely to bargain low, operating as they do under different constraints.

Administrators probably are accustomed to thinking in terms of the bargaining model. Therefore, it is important to note that the exchange and congruence models provide different answers to a crucial question. For example, from a strictly bargaining point of view, one might have expected that the recent salary increments compensate teachers for their low authority and prestige; however, we have seen that within the congruence framework, a salary increase may simply encourage employees to achieve other forms of advancement. The shortcoming of the bargaining model is that, in itself, it does not indicate what a group will and will not be willing to bargain away. Less well-educated groups seem more willing to settle for salary as a compensation for their lack of authority, while better educated groups appear to be less willing to tolerate extreme discrepancies between income and authority. The bargaining model, then, must be interpreted against the background of status congruency.

Consequences of Militancy

Turning from the sources of teacher militancy to its consequences introduces several other considerations. First, in order to think clearly about the probable consequences, it is necessary to distinguish the element of militant professionalism from the broader development of teacher militancy. Militancy has many sources, and professionalism is only one. While the most professional schools in our sample had the highest conflict rates, there were some schools with higher conflict rates which were not very professional. Unlike some forms of militancy, militant professionalsim represents more than a negative reaction to the existing system. For example, we found that the most professionally oriented militants in our sample were more concerned about student welfare than their adversaries.

The distinction between militancy and militant professionalism can suggest some very practical points of departure. For one thing, the incidence of "major incidents" diminished rather than increased with professional orientation, even though other types of conflict generally increased with the latter orientation. The one exception was in the most bureaucratic schools, where all types of conflict increased with the faculty's professional orientation. Indeed, conflict seemed to be most prevalent where professional faculties were also highly bureaucratized; bureaucratic controls seemed to be much more effective in the less professional schools. This means that administrative principles which are effective in one situation can backfire in another. The important point it suggests is that administrators may have to put up with some friction if they want to maintain professionally oriented faculties; supporting professionally oriented teachers may be a more effective way to control major forms of conflict than attempting to suppress them by imposing more bureaucratic control. But, it is precisely where militant professionalism is strongest that administrators are probably most tempted to impose additional control. If instead, administrators were to support teachers, teacher militancy could provide them with an effective leverage against community pressures.

Second, when we refer to the militancy of "teachers," we are in fact speaking of a small minority of all teachers. However, their numbers are less important than their potential influence. Opposing professional militancy in effect means opposing the most respected teachers with strong backing from their peers.

Third, the clash between the teaching profession and the bureaucracy is only part of the story. More tension between teachers and lay communities interested in reasserting their control also can be anticipated. Teacher militancy seems to be on a collision course with the civil rights movement in the big cities as lower-class parents begin to assert their authority. It is possible that this latter development will entail more radical modifications in the system than those ever contemplated by middle-class parents. It may be prophetic that the teachers union in New York City has not supported desegregation plans and has been resisting experimental projects leading to greater community control. This defensiveness is probably partly a reaction to the fact that teachers are bearing the brunt of criticism for poor quality education in inner city schools, even though the problem goes far beyond the factors that teachers are able to manipulate from within their classrooms. In any event, the defensiveness probably will persist, until big-city teachers have gained a greater measure of control and status security. Yet, looking further into the future, we can expect that even people who otherwise steadfastly oppose change will be prepared to initiate it if they are sufficiently in charge to control some of its effects and are rewarded for their efforts.

Generally speaking, social conflict reflects the fact that there already have been changes in societal needs and demands which have not as yet been incorporated into the social structure. The concessions that are likely to be made as a result of teacher militancy are therefore likely to involve some basic changes in the structure of public school systems. One need not romanticize the motives of teachers to admit that the problems of education and the interests of American people are so varied and intricate that no one group will be permitted to dominate the system for long without being subject to attack. We are well beyond the point where school policy can be equated to the proclamations of administrators, but this is the myth we have inherited and by which we continue to live.

The only apparent basis for stability is to recognize the growing power of teachers and include them more centrally in the decision-making process. Given the severity of problems under the existing system, it will be difficult to defend any other course. Historically, in this country we have had to learn either to include the excluded or live with strife. Until teachers create a more central place within the system for themselves they will continue to go around it.

Ultimately, the direction which teacher militancy takes will depend upon the answers to two fundamental theoretical and practical questions: First, how quickly will educational bureaucracies be able to accommodate the professional roles of employees? The answer to this question will determine whether the militant professionals or the more extreme, less-professional militants will eventually hold the balance of power, and this can have dire implications for the severity of conflict, as well as for the welfare of students. Alternatives are needed to the industrial-military models of organization, with their chain of command, system-wide uniformity, and universal evaluation standards and incentive systems. We are only beginning to learn that bureaucratization is not equivalent to centralized control, but, rather, promotes subgroup autonomy. The immediate problem is not how to preserve central control but how to harness the potential of this autonomy.

Second, is *power* a limited quantity, or is it possible for teachers to increase their power without diminishing the power of administrators and laymen? It is possible that distinct domains of decision-making authority can be developed for administrators, teachers, and the public in such a way that the total power of any one group will not be sacrificed. This in turn will require that administrators, in particular, find new roles as teachers assume some of their traditional functions. One option open to them is to leave most of the internal matters to teachers, while administrators become more skillful at managing the sociological problems inherent in their relationships with the community and all levels of government. Clearly, the present crisis faced by the public schools has occurred because the external sociological problems have been neglected too long.

However, regardless of the answers to these questions, perhaps we need not be too alarmed about the prospects of militancy. Militancy sows the seeds of its own demise. The fact that teachers are segmentalized (by the very specialization that is the source of their strength) is a constant source of constraint. And as teachers gain concessions they will become more incorporated into the system. Eventually, the existing disparities among the various statuses of teachers will diminish with these gains. We can take some consolation in the practice which history has of converting the value-laden ideological issues of one era into the institutions of the next.

Will Teacher Be the New Drop-Out?

ARNOLD BEICHMAN

All happy universities resemble each other, every unhappy university is unhappy in its own way. Not so long ago, America was the land of happy universities. Each resembled the other—ever-changing curricula; competition for Big Name faculty; large private endowments or generous legislatures; beautiful, big buildings and laboratories; hardworking, career-oriented students; superb scholarly output in many fields; internationally famed institutes for specialization in various studies; burgeoning numbers of Ph.D. candidates; an overall mandarinism, and, above all, freedom from outside interference and inside challenge.

Most universities are today unhappy each its own way—the Ivy Leaguers, the Catholic institutions, the bankrupt black colleges and universities, the regional universities in the South and Middle West, the free municipal universities, the onetime acropolises of California now an Ozymandian nightmare. One institution is unhappy because too many of its new students have low secondary-school ranking and won't be able to keep up and what will the school do with them; that one because it is too close, geographically, to Harlem; another because it is not close enough, spiritually, to the poor of Cambridge, Mass., and contributing to the solution of their social problems; this one because the students are too radical, too revolutionary; that one because the faculty will-to-survive has collapsed; this one because the faculty will not surrender its independence to student defiance or because a state legislature is making threatening noises, because alumni have stopped giving, because faculty are resigning, because, because—as in the Oblonskys' house, everything is in confusion.

The unhappiness mounts as universities, goaded by demands for progress, change, "relevance," modernization, social usefulness, participatory democracy; shamed by their powerlessness and properly fearful of arson, bombings, sabotage and attacks on personnel, introduce reforms. These chiefly relate to student representation on policy-making university bodies or the introduction of the latest manifestation of neocolonialism, Black Studies.[1] These reforms do not really

From *The New York Times Magazine* (December 7, 1969), 48, 49, 181, 184, 185, 190, 191.

[1] I once discussed education in Africa with the late Tom Mboya, back when Kenya was still part of Britain. He told me that the colonial powers encouraged smart Africans to study law, political science or even pedagogy but never engineering, chemistry, medicine, geology, drafting, machine design.

In Algiers in 1962, I looked out of my hotel window overlooking the great railroad yards and said to an Algerian friend, "Well, at least the French left you all their equipment." The Algerian replied, "Yes, they did, but in their years in Algeria, they never taught one of us to be an engine-driver or a fireman or how to repair a locomotive." To recruit thousands of young blacks into hitherto restricted American universities and to fill their heads full of something called Black Studies is to prepare them for nothing. The favorable response by universities to the demand for such curricula should make blacks suspicious. The Black Panthers have denounced Black Studies as "a new trick bag."

satisfy the revolutionary urge and they surely cannot stabilize the inherently unstable process of higher education. For something at once magical and essential to the learning process is disappearing from the American university and, perhaps even from the secondary or high school. I refer to the psychological distance which must exist between teacher and student.

Perhaps this phrase is a synonym for deference, the student's concession that he has something to learn and that the teacher has something to teach him. Psychological distance means that a teacher is an object of awe and respect (even, unhappily, when he may deserve neither) to a student, that the classroom is sacred and the university an object of reverence. Egalitarianism may be a useful political slogan, it is not an efficient teaching technique except possibly for correspondence courses on how to write a novel.

The narrowing of psychological distance between student and teacher simply means that higher education in America can no longer be—except for some of the natural and medical sciences or law—the free-moving object in space it was a few years ago. What it will become is hard to foresee because the campus civil war is far from over.

Clearly our educational structure and intra-university relationships are today exposed to such stress that they cannot survive in their present form. When, in April 1969, a Columbia student blackened the eye of a professor during a building seizure, the balance of psychological forces no longer existed, and not all the court writs or jailings of students can restore what once was a "seamless web." And less visible than the deteriorating student-faculty relationship is the hostility, the mistrust and suspicion among members of the same faculty for each other. One meaning of social order is what has been called "the element of predictability in social life: men can act socially only if they know what to expect of one another" ("Modern Social Theory," by Percy S. Cohen). This predictability among faculty members is gone.

Erosion of the collegial spirit occurred at Berkeley in 1964, arena of the first major university disaster of the decade; at Columbia in 1968; at Harvard and Cornell in 1969, and at other major universities. This absence of collegial spirit is particularly in evidence at annual conferences of the learned societies where student experts in the art of confrontationism have found apt pupils in some of their professors of social science and the humanities.

In describing the American university crisis in such black despairing language, I do not suggest that it was all *douceur de vivre* before the crisis. I am suggesting that the agonies which torture our system of higher education today are utterly different from yesterday's problems. For example, we may be coming to a two-tier grading system, one for whites and one for blacks. I know personally a college teacher who told me that he will not flunk a Negro student no matter how badly he or she does on the final examination or term paper. Last May he faced that problem by passing everybody, regardless of race, color, creed or previous condition of servitude.

This instructor is not the only one who refuses to have trouble by flunking black students. Confronted by an inundation of nonwhite students whose conventional preparation for college is questionable, teachers are simply not going to risk charges of racial prejudice by applying normal grading standards.[2]

Of course, once this kind of nonsense starts, the whole system of grading comes into question. A right-wing student, say, who takes a course with a Marxist professor and receives a well-deserved "C" may argue that he was penalized for his anti-Marxist political opinions.[3]

None of this would matter too much (after all, for years blockhead football stars were given passing grades when they should have been flunked out) if it weren't that we are witnessing a metastasizing atmosphere of intimidation of faculty and administration at American universities, an atmosphere created from within by radicalized professors and students, not by right-wingers or reactionaries.

It is this atmosphere which has made it so difficult to recruit university presidents, deans and lower-echelon administrators as well as faculty. Yet university enrollments are increasing at a rapid rate each year.[4] If the campus civil war escalates or if it merely continues at its present muted level, I would predict withdrawal by faculty members from universities to nonteaching research institutes or into other occupations.

I know an excellent teacher who has left Columbia. I was watching a building take-over on Morningside Heights last spring when this teacher, a friend of mine, came out of his office in a nearby building. He looked at the milling throng on the lawn outside the building, listened to the S.D.S. speakers blaring through the bullhorns, stared at the "Che Lives" banners, the blockaded entrances to the classroom building. "Okay, I've had it," he muttered and walked off to a research institute in order, as he wrote me in July, "to get back to some writing of my own." He had planned and arranged to leave after the 1968 Columbia disaster; what he saw now persuaded him that he had made the right decision. He is not the first; he will not be the last.[5]

(A few weeks ago I stopped in at the office of a faculty friend at Columbia. He waved a letter at me, "Look at this, now I'm on three more committees—

[2] Only about half of black high-school graduates are fully capable of handling a college curriculum, according to Fred E. Crossland, a Ford Foundation education expert (The Wall Street Journal, July 28, 1969).

[3] In *The Province* of July 23, 1969 (a newspaper published in Vancouver, B. C.), I found the report of a speech by John Cherrington, president of the University of British Columbia Debating Society, in which he charged that "teaching radicals" at Simon Fraser University "give low grades to students who do not follow the Marxist revolutionary line." He considered it "deplorable when I have to wait half an hour in my philosophy class for my professor, while he participates in a sit-in, and then to have to listen to him tell students for the rest of the hour of his life history of conflict with the police."

[4] In 1963, total student enrollment in all institutions of higher learning was 4,766,000. In 1968, it was 7,513,000, an increase of 60 per cent in five years. Current expenditure of these institutions is estimated at $17-billion, compared with $8.8-billion five years ago. Teaching staffs are 604,000 compared with 422,000 five years ago (*The Economist*, May 10, 1969).

[5] "Since I have had my present job, we have lost five tenured people, and four of them went to nonteaching institutes . . . . They left because they did not want to participate in all of the things one presumably has to participate in these days. They did not want to do so much teaching as we thought they ought to do, even though this was not very great. The flight from the university is disturbing . . . ." (Robert S. Morison, director, Division of Biological Sciences, Cornell University, in the quarterly magazine *Daedalus*, Fall 1969).

fellowships, library, travel—in addition to taking Professor ____________'s lectures because he's away this semester. Plus negotiations with students about curriculum changes which nobody understands and which has confused the first-year students. Meetings, meetings, meetings! I'm a teacher and I don't want to be an administrator.")

I am even more concerned about another issue which Students for a Democratic Society has raised and one which has found favor with non- and even anti-S.D.S. students, particularly in the graduate schools. I refer to the insistence on a loud student voice in the hiring and firing of teachers and granting of tenure. Speaking as a graduate student, I must in all conscience say that I have seen some pretty poor teachers, whose contempt for students was unconcealed, men who should have been fired, not granted tenure, men who probably were not worthy objects of awe and respect despite my earlier metaphysical statement. However, what S.D.S. students have set as their hire-fire standard is the question of a teacher's politics—not his competence.

However harsh and unprecedented these demands may seem to outsiders, there is so powerful a current of self-examination among faculties and administrators that this undeniable debasement of academic freedom—from within—will almost surely be accepted, in some skillfully disguised manner, particularly by those at our more distinguished private institutions. After all it is becoming a commonplace for Black Studies to be taught by black teachers approved by black students who also decide what is relevant. An American teacher once feared intrusion of outsiders into the university classroom. Those were the days of the American Legion's "Americanism" committees, the uncontrolled power of the public utility or other industrial lobbies, the anti-intellectual, fundamentalist legislators and preachers. The autonomy of the teacher was at stake. He fought back and, by and large, established his autonomy so that the university became off-limits to political demagogues or right-wing industrialists. Even more significantly, he won autonomy from administration and trustees, so that departments of study passed into control of professors.

Today the intruder is the "insider"—the S.D.S. member who marches into a classroom and demands the right to be heard or to prevent a teacher from speaking on the grounds of his alleged racism. And the professor seems as helpless as the university in defending his academic freedoms. Not even at the height of Stalinist penetration of the learned professions in the thirties did campus radicals dare intrude into classrooms to expose a teacher's political beliefs. The administration, the university president, the trustees were the enemy—not the teacher. Teachers in the social sciences at our more distinguished universities are today under surveillance by S.D.S. Red-Guardist organizers. The privacy of the classroom is disappearing and university teachers may well be driven to teach what will placate the S.D.S.[6] To put it bluntly, what alternative do they have?

[6] At the fall meeting of the American Political Science Association in New York I was privy to a conversation among several professors about campus conflict. One of them said, as his auditors nodded agreement: "I'll tell you what's happened to me. This fall when a student gets up and asks me some sticky question, I'm going to look at him and ask myself, is he S.D.S., why is he asking me this question, will my answer be used against me, should I duck it? Starting now, I'm going to be suspicious as hell about questions and discussions."

The rules of the game are that the left-wing student is an idealist with the right to express his idealism however he wishes and, because he is an idealist and young, he must not be treated as a responsible adult but rather must be granted amnesty whatever his offense, short of planting time bombs or some other form of "romantic" violence. The student revolutionary can speak and act with some impunity and when asked what is his program, he can reply:

"We refuse to give proposals for what comes after the revolution. We'll discuss that then. In 1789 the Third Estate in France didn't have any proposals. They just said: 'We are nothing. We want to be everything.' "[7]

Similar nonsense, expressed by S.D.S., receives the approbation of such journalist-thinkers as Henry Brandon who wrote in *The Sunday Times* of London, May 11, 1969, that "the S.D.S. efforts to enlist support among industrial workers have failed so far. They are too fat and conservative." Why industrial workers should support S.D.S. Mr. Brandon failed to make clear.

Earlier I had suggested that the structure of American higher education cannot survive in its present form. So apocalyptic a statement needs some definition. It is not too widely realized, even in America, that admission procedures have been drastically amended by our universities and, in particular, by the most prestigious, so as to enable greater percentages of young people from racial or cultural minorities to be admitted regardless of high-school grades. Admission procedures—the *numerus clausus* for geographical, religious or even political reasons—are among the most closely guarded secrets of our universities.[8]

There is no way of knowing how entrance requirements are being changed so that ascription—for example, color or low economic status—will be the *sine qua non* for admission rather than achievement. Can there be a learning process under these circumstances?

The panic is on. Yet this is only part of the crisis of American higher education. I have dealt very little with the responsibility of the faculty itself for the crisis. While it is easy to blame the teachers, it is difficult to see what really they can do now. Something might have been accomplished years ago had those faculties concerned themselves with those of their number who had become contemptuous of their chosen profession and of their students, of those who spent whatever time they had as off-campus consultants to anyone willing to pay the freight, of those of their number who had demonstrated their incompetence as teachers, both psychic and intellectual.

And even if they had I am unsure it would have helped stem what has become a revolutionary tide of violence against the university, this most feeble reed. For I

[7] "Student Confrontation at Alghero," by Steven Kelman in *The New Leader*, June 9, 1969. The speaker quoted is Marc Kravetz, a French associate of Daniel Cohn-Bendit. He is described as "a longtime activist in the Communist-controlled French National Student Federation."

[8] I know of one important (not Ivy League) Eastern university which has revamped its admissions committee to include what a faculty member told me could be called "hard-liners." He told me that the committee's assessment of an applicant would be primarily directed towards white students—not blacks. The reason for this discrimination was that it could be assumed that black students would be highly radicalized, but that there was no reason why radicalized white students should be admitted in large numbers.

think it is now obvious that no university can long survive if its right to exist is tested each spring or fall.[9]

A university's attempt to exercise power is a demonstration of its faded legitimacy and the transfer of some of its legitimacy to those who questioned it in the first place. In other words, the university cannot successfully protect itself against student "groupuscules" because (1) too often faculties and administrations are reluctant to allow the outside world to interfere, the outside world being public opinion or government, although they are becoming less reluctant to do so; (2) it is easier to surrender bit by bit, position by position than to see a campus dramatically torn apart; (3) we have not yet seen the real climax of the racial struggle at the large urban American universities; that problem has merely been swept under the rug, and (4) the American university has become for radicalized students and faculty the battleground for revolutionary impulses which can find no outlet elsewhere off-campus. In reality what some university administrations and faculties have been saying tacitly is that their legitimacy is negotiable.

What makes all this so critical is that large numbers of faculty members have adapted themselves to the vague yet tangible pressures that the university must become politically *engagé*. Prof. Richard Lichtman, a philosopher, recently stated that "a free and human community of scholars can only flourish when the multitudinous communities of the exploited, the wretched, and the brutalized peoples of the earth have broken the bonds of their subservience and established themselves as men of full stature."[10]

It is this sort of rhetoric which finds approving echoes (and almost no publicly voiced disagreement) in the academy. Along with this goes a demand for what has been called "action Ph.D.'s" by S.D.S. members. When I first heard this mentioned at a student strike meeting in 1968 at Columbia, I thought it must be a joke. Later I asked a fellow student what an "action Ph.D." meant. He replied:

"A lot of this stuff we take in political science, sociology or anthropology is so much junk. Let's face it. You memorize a lot of bull, take an exam or do a paper and the dissertation is even worse junk. What we mean by an 'action Ph.D.' is that a graduate student, after he passes all his requirements, is going to get out, say, to neighborhoods of the poor, the underprivileged and work with them on their problems. For example, he could organize rent strikes in the Puerto Rican neighborhoods or a march on the welfare office or City Hall or against high-priced food stores that exploit them.

[9] "Of all the institutions in our society, the university is most nearly defenseless. It has to be .... The free flow of ideas cannot take place in an atmosphere of physical confrontation .... Once force crosses the threshold, the university is diminished," (M.I.T. president Howard W. Johnson in *The New York Times,* Nov. 4, 1969).

[10] From "The University: Mask for Privilege?" (*The Center Magazine,* January 1968). In the same article, Professor Lichtman wrote: "It is too late now to fall back on the platitudes of academic freedom: no biochemist can be sure that in pursuing the structure of an enzyme he is not perfecting a lethal form of warfare. This government will have to be disarmed before the clear and present danger now subverting thought can be dissolved. Until men of knowledge act to change the world, they cannot claim the unrestricted right to understand it." For a philosopher's reply to this philosopher, see Sidney Hook, "Barbarism, Virtue and the University" in *The Public Interest,* No. 15, Spring 1969.

"All this would be as much a part of the Ph.D. program as passing the orals. In fact, the action would be the equivalent of the dissertation. What about teachers to act as sponsors? Obviously most faculty members wouldn't be suited to supervise such a program, so the university would have to hire professors with our approval who have the kind of political background and interest that this kind of program needs."

I interrupted to ask why a graduate student who was interested in helping the poor through political activity needed or wanted a Ph.D. (and from an "Establishment" university like Columbia!). The answer was quite plausible:

"Look, American society still looks upon a Ph.D. as important. After all that's why I came here as a graduate student. I want a job teaching when I finish and it's hard to get good jobs without a Ph.D. I want to tap the foundations and you need a Ph.D. for that. What I object to are the outmoded requirements, see?"

I saw.

Let me be quite clear: I am not suggesting that the Ph.D. is going to become overnight any less or more meaningful than it is now. There are 281 graduate schools (and 400,000 graduate students) in America and some of their Ph.D.'s are the equivalent of degrees from a barber college. But the pressure for drastic change is on in those graduate schools where it matters, the bellwethers.

It is quite possible that just as universities have found it difficult to resist the insistence on Black Studies, so they will find it difficult to resist white radical student groups able to hold a university for the ransom price of "action Ph.D.'s." And, after all, there will always be at least one professor who, when confronted by this demand, will support it with the statement that young people's interests in curriculum should be encouraged, not rejected, and, besides, it's time we had another look at Ph.D. requirements or else, "these kids are trying to tell us something," etc., etc.

All very plausible, intelligent but, to use a favorite S.D.S. word, "irrelevant" to the issue of higher education. This "at-least-one-professor" is not mythical; he exists and flourishes. For example, there is a belief among some faculty members that S.D.S. is a socially useful organization. So wrote Prof. Robert Lekachman, the economist-historian, in a recent article:

> I cannot conclude even so hasty a set of reflections as this one without some word of appreciation of S.D.S. Fair is fair. On university campus after university campus, it has been S.D.S. which has called visible attention to the brutality of the local police, the obtuseness if not worse of university behavior in surrounding communities, the selfishness of university real estate operations, and the questionable character of some of the universities' entanglements with Pentagon projects. To say this is to point out the considerable weakness of moderates and mild radicals.
>
> S.D.S. has played the role of the farmer who clubbed his balky mule over the head with a two-by-four. When reproved by a humanitarian bystander, he replied that the first necessity of the case was to get the animal's attention. Although I care as little for the illegal occupation of

buildings as I do for the clubbing of mules, I must also note the obvious: Both techniques do genuinely attract the attention of their targets—mules or university administrators."[11]

The violence at our universities is no worse than hitting a mule with a stick; in fact, the violence is progressive because—like Stalin's Five-Year Plans—it leads to good things for future generations.

One reason for the idiotic behavior by faculty members is that they have accustomed themselves to accepting—or ignoring—any kind of political lie so long as its purveyor is young, progressive, a would-be Marxist, a "socialist," a man of the left. The most intelligent scholars I know will never argue the lie that America, as the S.D.S. cant goes, is "sick, inhumane, corrupt"—or ask: compared to whom or what? France, China, Cuba, Greece, Russia, South Africa, Rhodesia, Canada? The most irrational statement can be spoken or published by S.D.S. or other revolutionary groups, utter lies can be circulated about administrators, teachers or students; rarely is there any attempt at refutation. (The S.D.S. had a field day last winter with the published canard that Columbia president Andrew Cordier was responsible, as a onetime U.N. official in the Congo, for the "murder" of Patrice Lumumba. The Columbia faculty silence was deafening.)

A second reason for this sort of behavior is that a growing number of faculty members, particularly in the social sciences, have dropped any pretense that a university is a place for objective scholarship. Last spring I heard one well-known professor, when challenged about whether he still maintained his onetime relationship with the State Department, tell an S.D.S. street audience, "Ridiculous! Why, I came to this university because I wanted a platform from which to oppose the Johnson-Rusk policies on Vietnam."

This statement was published in the student newspaper the next morning. Imagine the faculty reaction had a professor publicly declared he had come to a university for a platform from which to rehabilitate Joe McCarthy's reputation or to attack the Federal Government for being soft on Communism.

Somewhat in the future, I see shaping up the American version of Disraeli's "Two Nations"—left intellectuals, that is, radicalized faculty and students on one side and the rest of us—not necessarily President Nixon's "silent majority"—on the other side of the barricades. The left intellectuals will fancy themselves as the revolutionary class, capable of instigating a revolution. It will all remain fantasy because they haven't studied sufficiently the master of revolution and insurrection, V. I. Lenin, who wrote:

> In order to be entirely victorious, insurrection must depend not on a

[11] From "The Brighter Side," (*The New Leader,* April 28, 1969). Brian MacArthur wrote in an editorial in *The Times* of London, June 17, 1969, that "the brief spasm of student revolt . . . has won significant advances for students, throughout the system of higher education. It has shown that when moderate demands are ignored and negotiations denied to students, the sit-in works . . . " I'd like to see Mr. MacArthur prove his metaphysical statement.

conspiracy or a party, but on a revolutionary class. That is the first point. Insurrection must depend on the revolutionary pressure of all the people. That is the second point. Insurrection must break out at the apogee of the rising revolution, that is, at the moment when activity of the vanguard of the people is greater, when fluctuations among the enemy and among the weak and indecisive friends of the revolution are strongest. That is the third point. It is in bridging these three conditions to the consideration of the question of insurrection that Marxism differs from Blanquism . . . No great revolution has happened, or can happen, without the disorganization of the army.[12]

The attempt at revolution is creating wide fissures between the American people and the intellectual classes. Herbert Marcuse's blueprint for nihilism doesn't trouble me particularly. I am far more troubled by Dr. John Kenneth Galbraith and his view of the future, something I will return to in a moment.

Left intellectuals in the United States have a favorite quotation which they enjoy using whenever they wish to discuss their present discontents. It is a particular favorite because it was uttered by President Eisenhower in his 1960 "farewell address." Thus they can begin the quotation with the phrase, "*Even* President Eisenhower warned that 'we must guard against the acquisition of unwarranted influence, whether sought or unsought, by the military-industrial complex.' " Such is the level of intellectual debate in America that virtually nobody knows the further warning in the same speech:

> We must also be alert to the equal and opposite danger that public policy could itself become the captive of a scientific-technological élite."[13]

I was reminded of this latter Eisenhower statement by some sentiments expressed by Dr. Galbraith in *The New Industrial State*: "As the trade unions retreat, more or less permanently, into the shadows, a rapidly growing body of educators and research scientists emerge . . . . It is possible that the educational and scientific estate requires only a strongly creative political hand to become a decisive instrument of political power."

It is no coincidence that for the intellectuals of the left, center and, curiously enough, the right (like William F. Buckley Jr.) the trade unions have become the enemy. For Dr. Galbraith, the American labor movement has lost its meaning

[12] Cited by Harold J. Laski in his book, "Democracy in Crisis." Perhaps more to the point for the "Weatherman" S.D.S. faction is Engels's statement that "the time of surprise attacks, of revolutions carried through by small conscious minorities at the head of the unconscious masses, is past. When it is a question of the complete transformation of the social organization, the masses themselves must be in it, must themselves already have grasped what is at stake. What they are going in for body and soul. The history of the last fifty years has taught us that." (From Engels's introduction to the 1895 edition of Marx's "Class Struggles in France.")

[13] Another Eisenhower statement in the same speech which is never mentioned: "A vital element in keeping the peace is our military establishment. Our arms must be mighty, ready for instant action, so that no potential aggressor may be tempted to risk his own destruction."

because "they are under no particular compulsion to question the goals of the industrial system."

I offer the trade-union issue as an example of the frustration which is spreading among American academic intellectuals. It is this kind of frustration and a self-validating élitism which leads normally sane academicians to defend the most outrageous S.D.S. campus practices or, at the very least, to ignore them.

The clear and present danger to the American university is that academic opinion is very nearly controlled by a minority of intellectuals who threaten the foundations of the American university as no other single force in American life ever has in our history, even at the height of anti-intellectual crusades.[14]

They, with their student allies, threaten every aspect of intellectual life—what is to be taught, researched, published, who is to be hired or fired—while they seek amnesty for young gangsters and bombers who, mouthing what Norman Macrae, deputy editor of The Economist, has called "the dreariest old Nazism," have committed unprecedented depredations against universities, against scholarship and against culture.

Perhaps this, and more, is the reason why one of the most distinguished and normally equable historians I know recently wrote me: "One thing I would have to say right now is that things look worse and worse, and we may both live to see the eclipse of American liberal democracy."

Can We Define Good Teaching?

H. S. BROUDY

Everybody would like to get his hands on a good definition of good teaching. Despite the efforts of some educational entrepreneurs to produce teacher-proof materials, the teacher is still the key to schooling; with good teaching, almost any curriculum, school organization, and administrative invention seems to succeed. But if good teaching is needed to make an educational scheme go, it is even more necessary to have poor teaching around on which to place the blame for the failure of any and all educational ventures.

Among those who thirst after a definition of good teaching are administrators who would like to rate their teachers on merit and need some sort of objective support for doing so; teacher training institutions, accrediting and certification

[14] "The power of any minority is irresistible as against each single individual in the majority, who stands alone before the totality of the organized minority," wrote Gaetano Mosca in *The Ruling Class.*

From *Teachers College Record* (April 1969), 583–592. Reprinted by permission.

agencies, and, of course, teachers of teachers and various supervisors who have to make judgments about the quality of teaching. Nor should we omit the teacher himself, who both as a student and practitioner would like to know how well he is doing.

Why is a definition of good teaching so elusive? In one sense it is not elusive at all. You can define good teaching any way you like. Simply take any outcome, process, or quality that seems desirable, and then define good teaching as whatever something called a teacher does to bring it about efficiently. Even a cursory fishing in the literature will net such definitions by the dozen. Good teaching has been defined as what the "teacher" does to produce inspired pupils, excited pupils, interested pupils, creative pupils; pupils who are good citizens, who can read, do arithmetic problems and write grammatical English essays. Among other desiderata used to define good teaching are critical thinking, subject matter mastery, ideals, love of freedom, respect for law and order, universal brotherhood, various attributes of character, a love of learning, and a devotion to the arts. I am sure one can add another hatful of items to this list.

Why are such definitions unsatisfactory? For one thing, they tell us nothing about the factors which produce these results. And among the reasons for their not telling us what we would like so much to know is that (a) these fine products are not the result of teaching alone, so that it is virtually impossible to disentangle what the teacher has done from what parents, movies, television, habit, and climate have contributed. (b) Even when we have a fairly strong suspicion that teaching has achieved them, the variety of styles, personalities, and other characteristics of the successful teacher defies reduction to a formula or rule. (c) For some reason or other many teachers produce one type of outcome better than another.

The Search for Criteria

Is the task hopeless? Before answering this question, it might be useful to name a few blind alleys down which researchers for the criteria of good teaching have been led. The first of these is the search for a set of personality or behavioral traits that uniquely determine the good teacher. Despite the hundreds of variables that have been researched, we do not know how many more may be operating. Moreover, we have no way of knowing which variables are relevant until we have a notion of good teaching. The criteria that have been used have been derived from administrators' and supervisors' notions of good teaching, and so the question is begged rather than answered.

Another blind alley is the search for a process or strategy common to all good teaching. Unfortunately, the process picked as essential is also determined by the type of outcome regarded as important, and so the question is begged once more.

Some conceive of the key process as a set of interactions between a teacher and one or more pupils. Some interactions are interpreted psychologically as ways of controlling responses; some are broken down into types of discourse between pupil and teacher. Some regard the teaching act as an encounter between persons in which a drama is played out between forces of dominance and submission, strong and weak selves. Some regard teaching as analogous to an artistic performance, to be judged as a critic would judge a work of art; and some think of teaching as an input-output flow of information.

Still another confusing factor is the level at which the teacher is expected to function. If a teacher is expected to operate as a technician according to prescribed rules for the various operations she or he is to perform; if the teacher has no responsibility for choosing materials, methods, and strategies, then good teaching can be defined in one way. If, however, the teacher is to be granted such responsibilities, then technical efficiency, albeit a necessary condition for good teaching, will not be a sufficient one.

Strange Analogies

This difference in operational level not only confuses the judgment of teaching, but is responsible for many of our troubles in teacher preparation. To put it in a crude and perhaps unkind metaphor: the public, teacher training institutions, and many teachers think—or talk as if they think—that they have received the analogue of a medical education at a medical school. But the truth of the matter—by any standards of comparison—is that the vast majority of our classroom teachers have undergone something more like the training given to a nurse and perhaps closer to that of a secretary than that of a doctor. At most they are white collar craftsmen with somewhat more general education, but far less technical training, than their blue collar counterparts.

Consequently, when people set about defining good teaching, their models may not coincide—criteria for a good doctor, for example, are not the same as for a good nurse. This is simply another way of stating the point previously made about the level of occupational expectation.

Lest I be suspected of snobbishness toward craftsmen in general or nurses in particular, let it be clear that the social usefulness of the craftsman is beyond question. Indeed, it may turn out that craftsmen are what we need in teaching, and a case could be made for believing that craftsmanship is all that school administrators want. In witness whereof I note what all of us know so well, namely, that student teaching or some sort of apprenticeship is regarded in most quarters as the sum and substance of the "professional" part of teacher preparation. In this, teaching differs from plumbing only in the amount of time required for the apprenticeship.

Still another, and perhaps the most confusing, blind alley is the notion that one can set down in verbal form a definition or description of good teaching, such that a layman could use to identify and judge teaching performance.

Many of our difficulties with evaluation, I believe, lie with our inveterate faith that observational schedules can take the place of expertise. It is as if vintage wines were to be judged by a jury of citizens armed with a handbook on viticulture. But we know that this is somehow wrong; the wine expert does not need the book, although he may have written it; and it does the neophyte little good.

So perhaps the case is not hopeless if we think of a definition that could be used by experts.

Achieving Expertise

Can there be experts in so amorphous and complex an enterprise? I submit that expertise here comes about as it does in any field. First, one specializes within a limited domain; second, he and his peers arrive in time at certain agreed-upon distinctions within the domain; third, they build up models of "good" within each domain; fourth, they are familiar with virtually the whole range of samples within the domain; fifth, they know the rules for applying their criteria; and finally, they often share with their peers a theory or theories as to why the rules are applicable. Please consider that complete agreement among experts is not a necessary condition for expertise, but the possibility of distinguishing an expert from the layman is.

Even naive observers can, I believe, grasp directly the meaning of what is going on and distinguish the pervasive qualities in such diverse classrooms as the following:

1. The efficient classroom, in which the most noticeable feature is order: the action moves along smoothly on a predetermined pattern; the teacher is flexible but has genuine and unmistakable authority at all times; children know what is expected of them.

2. The creative classroom in which permissiveness, excitement, improvisation, creativity are the most prominent features. Teacher and pupils act like players in a game or participants in an adventure. There is little predetermined routine. Originality, liveliness, and freedom pervade the situation.

3. The cooperative classroom, in which the pupils attack all learning tasks together; there is a group planning, a group participation, group evaluation. With respect to predetermined structure, it lies somewhere between the other two. The teacher is a committee chairman.

These naive judgments are gross, yet they are the raw experiences out of which more refined judgments emerge. That a teacher knows what she or he is about; that the activity is regulated by method; that the teacher is not a robot; that she is in control of the situation—these are the basic bone-felt qualities that can be perceived even by naive observers as features of the total classroom atmosphere. However, this kind of intuitive report just about exhausts the evaluational potential of the average naive observer.

The refinement of these global judgments by the expert comes about, or can come about, by making significant distinctions within the holistic judgments.[1]

I have indicated that one of the approaches to defining good teaching is in terms of some process that is thought to be a necessary and sufficient condition of

[1] For a more detailed discussion, see my "The Continuing Search for Criteria," AACTE, *Evaluative Criteria Reference Paper No. 3*, 1967.

it. For example, one might think of teaching on the model of therapy with its diagnosis, prescription, and test. Or one might regard communications as the essential process, so that if pupil and teacher really understand each other, by virtue of input, output, feedback, etc., teaching will be successful. Thus far, no single model seems to cover all phases of a teacher's role in instruction, classroom management, and personal relations, not even the model of the teacher as a guide for a group engaged in solving a group problem.

In recent years two developments in education have made it advisable to look at our problem from a somewhat different point of view; not a new point of view, but rather an old one with which the times seem to have caught up. I refer first to the development of educational technology, especially in computer-based programmed instruction, and second to the emphasis on the affective or noncognitive factors in teaching the disadvantaged child. The disaffection of college students with some of their courses also underlines this latter development. These turns of events make it clear that we have to distinguish more sharply than we have between didactic and encounter teaching.

Didactic teaching

One type of teaching is associated with those products of instruction that can be made explicit: psychomotor skills (such as handwriting and reading), conceptual skills (such as using language in thought and expression according to rules of rhetoric and logic), knowledge of subject matter (such as chemistry, history, etc.). In these areas the means and goals of instruction can be specified and the results more or less objectively tested. So far as these outcomes are concerned, the sole criterion in efficiency, viz , the ratio of results to time and effort invested. As B. F. Skinner aptly remarked, most of the customary signs of good teaching–discussion, handwaving, discovery, excitement–are less criteria of efficient teaching than short-term gratifications to the teacher who interprets them as signs of her success. But success in teaching or learning arithmetic or reading or history is not to be equated with the amount of discussion, discovery, or excitement in the classroom. It is rather the amount of arithmetic or history learned. For this kind of learning Skinner would seem to be right when he says that prime method is selective reinforcement.[2]

Further, for this kind of teaching and learning, it may be predicted, programmed, computer-based instruction will be the decisive model. It can do the reinforcing more systematically and more efficiently and with more constant concern for the individual pupil's abilities than can any live teacher. In other words, good teaching for this type of product–and it includes everything that can be formalized into items of information, rules, principles, and problems–is measured by how closely the teacher approximates the methods and efficiency of the most

[2] "Teaching Science in the High School–What Is Wrong?" *Science*, 159, February, 1968, 704–10.

sophisticated computer-based instruction on the market. This type of outcome we may call for convenience and because of customary usage "didactics," or if one can forgive a bit of tautology, didactic teaching.

For this type of teaching it is quite possible to devise steps or stages; indeed, programmed instruction necessarily does so. The following steps are typical of many such sets and the scheme is certainly no younger than the Sophists:

1. Preparation or motivation or setting the stage for instruction. There are dozens of ways of doing this, but the crucial point is whether what Herbart called the apperceptive mass of the pupils is marshalled for instruction.

2. Proposing the learning task. This means that the teacher asks the class to do something and makes clear just what this is with appropriate cues as to how it is to be done, when, etc. This may be accomplished by telling, but there are other ways. The important criterion here is whether or not the learner has a sufficient awareness of what is expected so that he can go ahead with some confidence.

3. Eliciting a trial response. At some time during the teaching act, one samples the efforts of the learner to make sure that all is going well or to find out what is going wrong. This means that the pupil must have done something as a response. Otherwise there is nothing to reinforce or to correct.

4. Correction of the trial response. This needs no emphasis save to note once more that the techniques for doing it are numerous, and that the machines will probably do it very well once they are fully developed. It is at this stage that the teacher makes a guess as to what is wrong, if there is anything wrong, and adjusts the task to what is thought to be the cause of the difficulty.

5. The test response. This is like tasting the stew to be sure it is done properly.

6. Fixing the response for the kind of retention desired.[3]

This schema with suitable adaptations will fit any instance of didactic teaching: imparting knowledge, developing a skill, learning and applying rules and principles, doing problems that involve manipulation of existing and identified elements.

Encounter teaching[4]

However, not all the desirable outcomes of schooling are of this didactic sort. Being creative, being critical, being intelligent, being uninhibited, being friendly, being socially acceptable are not outcomes that can be defined behaviorally or explicitly in any really useful way. They are dispositions and attitudes that involve the total self of the pupil as he interacts with other selves, including the self of the teacher. In the nature of the case, the differences among these persons have to be accepted and respected, and the course of their development cannot be made an explicit goal toward which the teacher systematically undertakes this or that course of instruction. I realize that some educational literature talks as if they could and should, but not even trained psychiatrists would be so bold.

[3] See also the last chapter in my *Building a Philosophy of Education*, 2nd edition. Englewood Cliffs, N.J.: Prentice-Hall, 1961.

[4] Cf. Maxine Greene, Ed. *Existential Encounters for Teachers*. New York: Random House, 1967.

Inescapably the teacher has to play the role of a person, and insofar as this does something to or for the personality of the pupil, we might call it encounter-teaching. I am sure that some of the work on interaction analysis will throw light on encounter teaching, and perhaps we can derive from them some definition of good encounter teaching.

Obviously, one would wish a given teacher to get high scores on both types of teaching, but unfortunately they do not necessarily coalesce in a seamless web. For example, the moment the teacher grades a pupil the relationship changes from person-to-person to judge-to-judged. It must be traumatic for a young child to learn that a loving friend has inflicted the punishment of a poor grade. Even college students cannot always be objective about these matters. Indeed, if I had to nominate the arch villainy of education in would be assigning instruction and evaluation to the same person.

It is difficult to overvalue the importance of encounter teaching. At the early stages of schooling, it is the key to motivation and discipline. Later it is the intangible component of wisdom and intellectual stimulation that under favorable circumstances are generated by teacher in the pupil. It is what Socrates called *maieutic* or the midwifery by which the teacher helps the pupil bring forth his own conceptual creations. It is what college students seek in the teach-ins, the free university, and in a wide variety of bull sessions to which now and then young professors are lured. But while history has celebrated with justice Socrates, Jesus, and other great inspirational teachers, the schools were manned by the descendants of the Sophists who developed the methods that to this day are the methods of didactic teaching. The former created wisdom; the latter preserved and transmitted knowledge and knowledge about wisdom.

So long as the body of knowledge to be taught remained fairly small and tightly organized, so long as a culture was of one mind about values, and so long as personality was developed outside rather than inside the school, the classroom teacher could do both didactics formally and do the other informally. Today's conditions of crowded classrooms, the knowledge explosion, the plurality of values that compete for attention and priority, the diversity of background of the pupils make it virtually impossible for one teacher to do both types of teaching at the same time in the same classroom, or even alternately in the same classroom. A friendly divorce now seems not only advisable but feasible.

The Advisability of Divorce

This divorce is especially advisable now when it has become clear that the psychosocial factors are dominant both in the teaching of the disadvantaged child and of his overadvantaged counterpart in college. It is feasible because at all levels the potential of educational technology for didactic teaching is impressive.

If the divorce should come to pass, we can anticipate a class of teachers devoted to didactics. These would be instructional technicians who operate the machines that feed the programs to the pupil, direct his learning, grade his achievement, and unerringly and without delay record his progress. Their training would approximate that of an X-ray technician in a hospital, about two years beyond high school. At a higher level, program developers and researchers would work either at the universities or at the educational industries. Supervising the choice of programs and making appropriate educational decisions would be instructional managers not unlike the school principal or curriculum director.[5]

What will be the characteristics of the encounter teacher and what will constitute good encounter teaching? Aristotle, Plato, Socrates, Jesus and Moses were all great encounter teachers. So was my sophomore high school English teacher on one occasion. But I would be at a loss to find any personality or teaching style common to all of them. A wide, an extraordinarily wide, variety of social workers, therapists, mental hygienists, counselors, Peace Corps and Vista members, not to speak of socially sensitive members of the League of Women Voters and the PTA, might be competent to do encounter teaching—if one wishes to confine it to personal interactions. One can think of so many possible combinations of traits and styles and backgrounds that the mind boggles at any attempt at generalization.

I suppose a strong interest in the personality and the growth of others is a good prognosis. Being a developing person oneself is another; good encounter teachers grow through teaching; they are greedy takers as well as generous givers. A certain plasticity—even to the point of delayed maturity—is another favorable sign, because it provides for tolerance of divergence and postpones the formation of stereotypes of thought and feeling. However, these are all promising signs but no guarantee of success. Since it is the total personality that operates in encounter teaching, it is the total pattern of traits that counts, and not even the most sophisticated computer can figure out all the possible benign combinations of traits that constitute the good encounter teacher.

Exhibitions of Encounters

Although the arts and the humanities in general can be taught didactically, they are primarily exhibitions in vivid form of the human encounter. One might wish that the school could utilize these forms of feeling in encounter teaching, i.e., establish encounters between the pupil and the personalities created by the arts. If this should be a requirement of encounter teaching, and I am not sure that there is agreement on this point, then the preparation of the encounter teacher would probably have to go well beyond the level of a craftsman applying rules.

Relieved of the need to do didactical work, the encounter teacher could: (1) teach the arts as modes of experience rather than as bodies of subject matter; (2)

[5] Cf. "Some Hazards and Potentials of Educational Technology," in E. L. Morphet and D. L. Jesser, Eds. *Planning for Effective Utilization of Technology in Education.* Denver: Designing Education for the Future Project, 1968.

foster creative work by the pupil in a wide variety of fields; (3) diagnose the emotional and social blocks to learning; (4) participate in the kind of community activities needed to play the role of an encounter teacher; and (5) be the kind of person the mental hygiene experts say he or she ought to be.

However, in this realm the outcomes and the means are not explicit; they cannot unambiguously be translated into behavioral objectives, and the criteria for learning and teaching are therefore neither explicit nor objective.

One may wonder whether the efficiency made possible in didactic teaching by technology will be used to release resources for more and better encounter teaching. There is no reason to believe that it necessarily would; on the contrary, it will take some educational statesmanship to prevent it from being ousted from the school altogether in the name of economy. The unwillingness to pay the price for training teachers to a professional level, and the belief among teacher trainers themselves that technical apprenticeship is all that is really necessary do not provide a hopeful prognosis. The virtual impossibility of defining good encounter teaching will not help either.

On the hopeful side is the fact that America in the next 25 years will not be able to afford shoddy schooling for even a considerable minority of its members. Economic, political, and military health and the sanity of the social order will depend increasingly on a population whose thought and feeling are shaped by the categories of both the sciences and the humanities. As we all know, the hearts of the American people are in the right place, and their minds, for the most part, dwell among noble ideals. All it takes to galvanize these into action is the fear of a decline in the Gross National Product and the prospect of profit. Education has both of these motivations working for it. It promises to be the great growth industry of the future and the indispensable ingredient to growth in every other sector of our economy.

Good teaching can be defined well enough for experts to use in evaluation, but our chances of reaching agreement is far greater in didactic than in encounter teaching. The machine is the norm for didactic efficiency; the high-grade, humanely cultivated person is the model for the latter. However, there is an endless variation of this model, and the problem for the schools is to lure enough of them to do the necessary encounter teaching, a task that is more important than defining our preferred variety of it.

The Fictions of Legitimacy

MAXINE GREENE

Charles V. Hamilton entitled a recent article in the *Harvard Educational Review* [1] "Race and Education: A Search for Legitimacy." He proposes a "Family-Community-School Plan" as an alternative to the existing educational system which, he says, is perceived as illegitimate by the black community. He is not alone in his use of the term 'legitimacy'; in the past year it has become part of the common coinage of controversy. The radical students at Columbia University based their demands for amnesty on the claim that the administration had lost its legitimacy; the Third World Liberation Front at San Francisco State College is similarly convinced of the illegitimacy of those who make the rules. The implications are manifold—perhaps especially for teachers, who have taken for granted the legitimacy—if not the nobility—of what they do for the young.

They tend to think of legitimacy as a function of certain contractual or legal relationships; they conceive it as conformity to rule, principle, law. But this, as Professor Hamilton makes clear, is not at all what the protesters have in mind. He quotes from Seymour Martin Lipset[2] to make his point: "Legitimacy involves the capacity of the system to engender and maintain the belief that the existing political institutions are the most appropriate ones for society." 'Legitimacy,' it appears, is an evaluative term: "Groups regard a political system as legitimate or illegitimate according to the way in which its values fit with theirs." In the view of the protesters in the communities and the colleges, the same may be said about an educational system. A school board's, an administration's, an "establishment's" claims to legitimacy are rejected on the grounds that they are not providing what their constituencies want and need. Hamilton explains that black people have withdrawn their allegiance from existing school systems because those systems are dysfunctional where they are concerned. They have, in so doing, denied the systems' legitimacy. College students who demand separate institutes for black or ethnic studies (and who say their demands are "non-negotiable") are functioning in the same way.

Legitimacy, then, becomes contingent on the response of those presumed to be the beneficiaries of whatever system is involved. On the one hand, the traditional democratic principle is evoked: those affected by a policy should participate in shaping it. On the other hand, traditional notions of professional expertise and authority are challenged. The impact on professionals has been considerable; and teachers everywhere are experiencing strain. There is an implied (not always polite)

From *Teachers College Record* (April 1969), 643–648. Reprinted by permission.

[1] Volume 38, Number 4, Fall, 1968, 669–684.

[2] *Political Man: The Social Bases of Politics.* New York: Doubleday, 1963.

demand that they restructure not only their institutions but their professional self-images, their world-pictures, and the fictions by which they make sense of things.

The term 'fictions' in this context does not refer to illusions or untruths. We are using the term in Frank Kermode's sense:[3] fictions are modes of ordering experience, modes which ought to "change as the needs of sense-making change." Fictions are ways of imposing form upon the inchoateness of experience, of creating a human order in an intrinsically formless world. Without them, history would be merely an affair of successions; schooling would "mean" not more than training young people in particular kinds of behavior. Teachers—who, after all, are charged with the responsibility for "transmitting the culture"—make sense of things with the aid of a number of fictions. Without them, they would find it nearly impossible to interpret and justify what they do.

Continuity may be one of these fictions. Sensitized to change though they may be, teachers often think of themselves as guardians of a continuing human order that is "given" and that possesses unquestioned worth. They see themselves initiating the young into certain public traditions (a permanent structure of values, beliefs, and attitudes) which presumably foster individual fulfillment, and which are as "natural" as the rights with which, according to our Declaration, Americans are endowed. They sustain themselves, too, with the belief that there exists a common "culture" which can be identified with an enduring body of commitments and embodied in curriculum. They assume that mastery of the culture's fundamental precepts is bound to make each individual "better" than he was before he learned them and set him free to be.

One hundred and thirty years ago, when the common schools were new, and when the process of Americanization was a prime educational aim, such fictions made obvious sense. They accorded with the social realities confronted by the schools; they permitted teachers to find things out about themselves and the work they were asked to do; they functioned as agents of change. Because many immigrant children *were* inducted into what was thought to be the American "way of life," because many of them appeared to be willing to comply with the official "morality," because the common school was said to reflect the "public philosophy," public education gained a legitimacy which many thought self-evident. This legitimacy, however, was so identified with the fictions developed as "sense-making" devices, that the fictions became in many ways resistant to change.

One reason for this is that educators tended to forget that they were fictions, human orders imposed upon life. They degenerated, for numerous individuals, into myths. Myth, writes Kermode, "pre-supposes total and adequate explanations of things as they are and were." It is an agent of stability, calling for absolute assent; while a fiction, making sense of "the here and now," calls only for conditional assent.

The persistence—and the degeneration—of old fictions seem to us to account

[3] *The Sense of an Ending: Studies in the Theory of Fiction.* New York: Oxford University Press, 1967.

for much of the shock being experienced when legitimacy is challenged today. The educational scene afflicts many observers as a kind of absurdist play, some phenomenon of the Theatre of the Absurd, which deliberately sets out to defy ordinary expectations and break with traditional conventions which no longer accord with life as lived. Such events as those occurring in the Ocean Hill-Brownsville school district in New York, at San Francisco State, at the University of Wisconsin, are simply not accounted for by the conventions—or the fictions—by means of which educators normally see. Just as we would like Beckett's *Waiting for Godot* to end (as a well-made play should) with the arrival of Godot, or Pinter's *The Caretaker* with the redemption of the derelict, so we want the local school board in Ocean Hill-Brownsville to come to see the advantages of centralized control, and the "insurrection" at San Francisco State to end with an administration once more *in loco parentis* and everyone contentedly back at work.

One function of the Theatre of the Absurd, it happens, is to make audiences conscious of the arbitrariness of old conventions, of such fictions as beginnings, middles, and ends. It is human expectation which makes the lack of plot in *Godot* seem so appalling; it is ancient habit which makes audiences rebel against the unpleasant arrogance of Davies in *The Caretaker.* But both plays, when effective, function to make people aware of the *process* of sense-making and, more thoughtful than they were about the kind of fictions required for dealing with the here and now.

Educators, unlike such audiences, are loath to become self-conscious in this fashion, perhaps partly because their very legitimacy will become questionable if they confront the old fictions as fictions—simply modes of *thinking about* some aspects of reality.

The "needs of sense-making" are changing on all sides, however, and so must educators' fictions change. Professor Hamilton talks about the wide-ranging challenge to "the idea of a common secular political culture," about the historical perspective peculiar to black Americans, and about the "new concern" and the "new tension" which must be reflected by the public school. Fictions having to do with "common-ness," with a "social balance wheel," with "integration," even with beneficence, no longer explain.

Julie Paynter, writing in *Journal,* [4] identifies what she believes are some of the "illusions" permeating what Americans call their history. She attributes some of this to innocence, and some to the simplicity of "the American creed":

> The understanding which Americans have of themselves has tended to exaggerate these aspects of simplicity to the point of distortion. Biography has often seemed a substitute for history, and American citizens have been too easily seduced into assuming an identity based on the individual success story and the *American* experience—that "log cabin to the White House" theme. . . . The past has typically been seen as an unbroken

[4] "An End to Innocence," *Journal,* January 1969, 3–7.

> upward line of continuity and progress, attributed to "the genius of the American people," while conditions favoring that success have been allowed to fade into the background.

She describes generalizations about our national character made possible only "in effect, by reading black people out of the past." She would want to see "the transmission of black culture with its differences intact," a kind of transmission not encompassed by fictions having to do with the common.

In *Black Rage*, the revealing book by William H. Grier and Price M. Cobbs,[5] there is a chapter called "The 'Promise' of Education" which presents the terrible predicament of the black child who comes to perceive "the formal learning process as different, strange, unnatural, not meant for (him) and not really relevant for (him)." The authors state:

> In spite of the yammering of naive observers, education has never offered a significant solution to the black man's dilemma in America. . . . Although education may in the long run be an important instrument for black people, children may have clearer vision when they see the classroom as immediately irrelevant. Their vision is clearer than that of men who plead for black people to become educated in a land which views all blacks as bondsmen temporarily out of bondage.

Julian Bond, the young Georgia legislator, says:[6] "A great many people seem to think that education is the answer to the problems of race in this country, but education as a means of breaking down racial barriers dies as an effective means of social change every day that black ghetto children are taught that whiteness is rightness." How are the "American Dream," the conventional visions of continuity, the notion of "melting-pot" to encompass this? On what grounds can teachers justify legitimacy?

As we have said, it is not only black rage and protest which make the traditional fictions look so questionable. There is also the unrest on the campuses, dramatically exemplified by the events at San Francisco State. Mervin B. Freedman (author of *The College Experience*) describes some of what has taken place in an article for *The Nation.*[7] "Only the theatre of the absurd," he says, "can do justice to some of the scenes. . . ." He sees (and this challenges all customary expectations) "no solution in the present focus." San Francisco, nonetheless, is facing problems which are the problems of all urban colleges and "of American urban society generally."

> The financing of higher education for lower-class blacks and other American minority groups is receiving considerable attention at this time. An

[5] New York: Bantam Books, 1968.

[6] "A New Vision, A Better Tomorrow," *The Humanist,* January/February 1969, 11–12.

[7] *The Nation,* January 13, 1969, 38–42.

even more critical issue than finances is the question of what to do with such students once they arrive on campus. . . . Militant blacks and their allies have thrown light on the hypocritical underpinnings of the "Land of the free and the home of the brave"—the slaughter of Indians, the unjust wars, slavery. They have helped to arrest the march of technology and scientism that a decade ago seemed destined to kill the humanistic spirit. They have greatly contributed to the realization that white, middle class America does not necessarily walk hand in hand with God. And now they are taking on meritocracy, as exemplified by grades and degrees. They demand that colleges contribute to the development of students rather than that students be tailored to the abstract demands of professions, industry, and the like.

The authority of faculty members and their "right" to evaluate are being challenged. Effectiveness, for many students, is being judged in terms of the contribution education makes to *their* individual growth. If, they are saying, any university subordinates individual needs to the needs of the society (or the corporation, or the Federal government), that university promptly sacrifices legitimacy. The only response—the only reasonable response—say the rebellious students, lies in confrontations and demonstrations. These, too, have been excluded by the fictions used by educators to order their experience. Yet Professor Amitai Etzioni, Columbia sociologist, in a paper submitted to the National Commission on the Causes and Prevention of Violence, asserts that "demonstrations are becoming part of the daily routine of our democracy and its most distinctive mark."[8] He speaks of the "textbook model" of democracy which depends on ballot boxes and persuasion—and which does not function properly. The "demonstration democracy" which is alternative to that model is one more example of a challenge to traditional fictions. To make sense of the world described by Etzioni, new fictions will have to be devised; and only when they are, it seems to us, will viable claims to legitimacy once again be made.

We are not asking that educators become Don Quixotes—or Sancho Panzas either. We are simply asking that they abandon absoluteness and the tendency to link legitimacy to degenerated fictions. The educational scene, like the world of the arts, is in crisis. It is alive with innovation, brashness, self-assertion—and a search for new forms. Just as certain audiences see formlessness and obscenity when they venture into the modern theatre, so do certain educators see chaos and barbarism when they contemplate the universities or the schools. Just as certain critics refuse to categorize *avant garde* works as works of art, so do certain educators find it impossible to accept what is happening around them as relevant to education. In both cases, the new is being judged by inapplicable standards. In consequence, audiences, critics, and educators (unable to turn back the tide) can only stand helplessly, watching something they do not understand.

[8] *The New York Times,* February 16, 1969, 60.

The way to surmount strain and shock is by making sense—as best as the individual knows how. The old, degenerated fictions become blinders for too many educators; they cannot give credence to what is occurring; they cannot listen, and they cannot see. They are in no position, then, to conceptualize the challenges to meritocracy, the persistence of "demonstration democracy," student demands for involvement, community demands for control. But they have the capacity to remake their fictions as "the needs of sense-making change." Only as they remake and recreate, it seems to us, will they be in a position to influence what is happening, to direct—in accord with others—the course of change.

This does not mean that they invent new fictions *de novo*, without reference to the paradigms and models of the past. As in the domain of art, there is a shared language where education is concerned; there are memories of significant values, of ideals. Every enraged demand raised in the ghetto is raised against a background of such memories. Every confrontation on the campus is undertaken with the traditional promises, the traditional hopes in mind. Without such a sense of the past, the wants and needs purportedly being frustrated could not have been defined. The very concept of legitimacy, depending as it presently does on the response of communities and student bodies, depends upon a consciousness of what *ought* to be—and this consciousness derives from an awareness of some encompassing human order, transcending the fictions of the now.

It is in the name of such an order that teachers must try to make sense of what is happening at this moment; it is in the name of their own commitments that they must strive to form and try to see. Albert Camus, concerned with justice and with order, would say that this is a moment for teachers to rebel—on behalf of moderation and mastery. "Real mastery," he wrote, "consists of creating justice out of the prejudices of the time. . . ."[9] "Moderation," he wrote, "born of rebellion, can only live by rebellion. It is a perpetual conflict, continually created and mastered by the intelligence. It does not triumph either in the impossible or in the abyss. It finds its equilibrium through them. . . . Rebellion, the secular will not to surrender . . . is still, today, at the basis of the struggle. Origin of form, source of real life, it keeps us always erect in the savage formless movement of history."

And this is how teachers may regain their legitimacy: by creating fictions which make sense, and to which they give conditional assent. Sense-making is what can keep them erect. Sense-making can be their rebellion against "savage formless movement"; new fictions can create new form.

[9] *The Rebel.* New York: Alfred A. Knopf, 1954.

Redefining the Role of the Teacher

ROBERT BUSH

The necessity for a redefinition of the role of the teacher is upon us and may well shape the content and procedures of teacher education for decades to come. As big business and the Federal Government, with their formidable battery of modern technology crashes in upon our schools, classrooms, and teaching with rising crescendo, a permeating sense of disquietude stirs within us.

The public is uneasy, all the way from the parent and the citizen in the local community to the highest echelons of power in Washington. We in the profession are uneasy, too. New and higher than ever demands are being made upon the schools. At the same time, we are confronted with serious shortages of teachers and dollars. With the "knowledge explosion," curriculums are almost out of date before the ink on them is dry. Yet, we are expected to work miracles. These and other factors have conspired to produce a genuine educational crisis and, unless we have a vigorous and creative response to this crisis, the quality of our schools and, indeed, of our whole life will deteriorate.

The Federal Government has entered the arena because our leaders are convinced that the national welfare is at stake—education has moved from the sidelines to become a major productive force, an investment rather than a consumer item in the economy. One of the critical questions is: "Can the computer, automation, and modern technology help solve some of the critical problems in education?"

Big business, mass media, and the Federal Government are all converging to move into a sphere which, traditionally, has been one for local option and in which individual teachers have been relatively free to cope with their own problems. Nevertheless, in the face of teacher shortages and financial crises, school boards and taxpayers are intrigued with the economies that might be achieved if modern technology could be moved into the schools. Employers in all fields have always wanted to use machines when they could, despite the fact that employees have always been suspicious of them and have even tried to destroy them. There is great beauty in the machine: the machine has no temper; it does what it is told with no argument; it has endless energy and never gets tired; it will endlessly repeat dull routine tasks without becoming bored and dissatisfied; it has no prejudice; it will treat equally the slum child in the central city and the affluent child. Most important, it can be junked, thrown away when it's worn out or when it becomes obsolete. These are an attractive set of propositions for the school administrator, the board of education, and the public.

Interesting experiments with the machines are being conducted here and

From *Theory Into Practice* (December 1967), 246–251. Reprinted by permission.

abroad. For example, in American Samoa where education has been shamefully neglected for so long, we are testing whether or not a handful of excellent teachers can, through the use of television programs, radically improve the entire educational system. In Colombia, Alfonso Ocampo, the Rector of the University de Valle in Cali, recently pointed out:

> we are falling behind. With all of the additional monies that are being poured into this country, we are literally falling behind in education. Unless there is some radical application of technology to overcome the snail-like pace at which we are producing teachers and manning our schools, the result is going to be disastrous. If it's disastrous for us, it is going to be disastrous for you. [American educational system]. [1]

We are further troubled because of radical changes taking place in our society in general. New and troublesome concepts are already beginning to affect the way in which we have organized our society. Margaret Mead points to the fact, not yet considered seriously, that we are no longer confronted mainly with a production problem, that distribution is more crucial today. The cost of preserving an affluent society is to get over the outworn idea of an industrializing society, i.e., that in order to share in society's wealth, one must do productive work. The idea that one must work in order to be able to live and to share in the wealth produced is an idea which Mead avers we must change if we are to preserve affluence. This means that a smaller and smaller percentage of highly skilled people will do more and more of the productive work of the world and that larger and larger numbers will stay in school longer, have a shorter work life, retire earlier, do less productive work, and still share fully in the fruits of society. These are bothersome concepts. We have been taught that you not only must but *should* work hard in order to share in the fruits of society. But, now, with automation lifting heavy production off our backs, we may at long last have enough people freed to care for other people—personal service for everyone. Automation can, however, be dehumanizing unless it is managed sensibly. The radical nature of technology is such that there will be fewer jobs and less work for human beings, not more as has been claimed. Further, adjustment must also be made to the obsolete idea that once trained, we are trained for life. Many, perhaps most, occupations will require retraining two or three times. We shall have to rid ourselves of the idea that it is impossible to re-learn. This applies forcibly to what I wish to say about teachers: we need to establish the habit of going to school, of learning new roles and new ways of teaching things.

The Role of the Teacher Today

To contrast the role of the teacher today with what I think it may become, I

[1] From notes taken during a personal interview with Dr. Ocampo in Cali, Colombia, March 1967.

will draw on findings of some studies made over the last decade. Classrooms in public schools were studied with an interdisciplinary team to delineate the teacher's role as perceived by the teacher, by the administrator, and by selected persons in the community, and the role of the administrator was studied as perceived by the teacher, the administrator himself, and by selected laymen in the community.

According to the research, the teacher perceives his main role to be that of purveying knowledge to students, directing their learning—important work, which he felt was often disrupted by many irrelevant things imposed by administrators and laymen and parents. He also perceives that he should keep youngsters under direct control at all times—so does society, for we pass laws to ensure that no pupil shall be out from under the eye of a fully qualified teacher at any time during the day.

The teacher is taught to, and tends to believe, that he should do the whole job by himself, i.e., make the tests, grade the tests, return the results, interpret them, mark all the English themes, and teach all of the subjects. While he will accord others some say in the selection of what is to be taught, how it is to be taught is strictly his own affair, not subject to scrutiny by anyone else. The classroom is his castle. The administrator tends to accept most of this view held by the teacher, but he adds one important proviso: it is important for the teacher to teach youngsters, to teach them well, and to teach them something that is important, but, he should do it in such a way that *everybody is happy about it.* In this, he transfers his own role function as a harmonizer to that of the teacher. The administrator does not seem to care so much what the teacher teaches or how he teaches it as long as all teachers do it in approximately the same way. It is much easier to coordinate, another administrative function, if this is so.

The teacher also believes, and administrators and the community instruct him thus, that he should motivate and discipline the pupils. He should be a model of good behavior and conduct, thereby helping to shape the character and the moral structure of the individual pupil. It is furthermore conceived, particularly in the primary school, that the teacher will teach all the subjects for a whole year, with students moving the following year to another teacher who will teach all of the subjects. In the high school, the teacher is to teach one subject at a time, in a fairly standard period of fifty minutes, to be repeated five days a week for a semester or a year.

There is much wisdom bound up in all of this, and it should not be discarded lightly. But, I submit that it is conventional, and it is culture bound. For example, high schools abroad are not organized as American high schools, and, in elementary schools in some parts of the world, teachers stay with pupils for several years.

The established roles which I have delineated are now being challenged. A new order seems to be in the offing. We hear reports of teachers harmoniously dividing up the labor in wall-less carpeted rooms which are filled with accoustical perfume. What is going to happen? What should happen? What genuine possibilities exist in the new technologies and resources now available and appearing just over the horizon? What new attitudes should be adopted and what demands ought to be made on these developments?

The attitude we take toward the new technology may substantially affect what can be achieved. It is my conviction, not too strong as yet, that we may, at long last, be able to teach and to organize schools as we have really wanted and known how to for a long time. Consider for a moment the computers. At least three ways may be noted in which computers are beginning to be used:

The Field of Data Processing. Computers are being used to make report cards, registration, class lists, test scoring and reporting, processing of pupil personnel data, copying, record keeping, clerical work, attendance, etc. All of these matters have been a heavy burden, all must be well done, and all can be done much better by the computer and other data processing machines. We would be well rid of these tasks. These machines are still not being used widely, but they can and should be.

Building the School Schedule. Work on this problem has been under way for several years at Stanford. As we began study a half dozen years ago to see how well some of the new curriculums were being adopted, almost everywhere we encountered the reaction: "Yes, this is a great idea, but it can't be scheduled." We asked our industrial engineers, "Can the computer help us?" Now, five years and a half million dollars later, we can report that the problem has been licked in the sense that we can now get the schedule off the backs of the school personnel. In our first operational year, we demonstrated modular scheduling in four schools; this has steadily gone up each year until 1967—we shall schedule over one hundred schools. We could have five hundred, but we are still working on different kinds of problems. It is now possible to divide pupils into a variety of groups, have them meet for shorter or longer periods of time, in larger groups and smaller groups, for once a week, or three times a day, in as many combinations as desired. It is now possible to unlock the school. But, the computer will not tell us a single thing about what to do with this unleased potential. It has been interesting to note that in some schools where the computer schedule has been introduced, even though the computer schedule allows for more flexible scheduling, the schools are following precisely what they have for years. However, it is possible, with this potential, to realize Davies' idea of giving students responsibility for their own learning, putting them on their own for a substantial part of time so that they have time to read, write, think, and perform many other tasks handled better without teacher supervision. At the same time we also provide relief for the unbearable load of the classroom teacher and give him some time to read, think, plan, and do many other things, handled more effectively when relieved of the task of supervising the pupil.

Computer Assisted Instruction. On the front page of its August 1966 issue, *Fortune* magazine carried a picture of the school of the future—a handsome young boy, a typewriter keyboard, a television monitor, but look as you will, no teacher. The Ravenswood Schools, in a suburb of Palo Alto, began teaching beginning arithmetic and beginning reading to first graders by computer and with no teacher present. Each pupil has an individual station. The lessons are individually paced and the pupils receive immediate feedback. Learning difficulties can be diagnosed, errors corrected, and extensive research on learning never before possible is taking place. At this time, the process is frightfully expensive and still frightfully frightening to many.

I have cited examples of things that are here now. With teachers freed from the bulk of the routine and with pupils spending substantial time each day on the machines, what will be left? What will teachers do? Much of what the teacher has formerly spent his time doing and what he has been expected to spend his time doing, namely the purveying of knowledge, may be better done with the new technology. The teacher's new and emerging role is going to lie elsewhere, mostly in the realm of interpersonal relationships.

What Will Teachers Do?

If the teacher's role emerges as it should and can, the teacher will be able to view the process of education as a whole and to understand each individual child in his setting. The teacher will have an opportunity to confer and work closely with parents, something never really accomplished. Teachers have been a little more successful in working with parents in the elementary school than in the secondary school, but even in the elementary school the prevailing attitude is one of "toleration." Teachers will be free to work with pupils in small groups and to teach in small groups, e.g., in groups of five, eight, and ten, where I, predict, some of our most important redefinitions of the teacher's role may take place.

Another important change is that the teacher, instead of doing everything for everyone—feeling he must succeed with everyone and feeling guilty if he does not—is going to become the captain of a team rather than a lone operator and the sole arbiter and judge of everything that goes on. He will have machines, tools, materials, and other kinds of assistance available at his call and direction. He will be at the top of the educational pyramid rather than at its bottom, where he has remained for these many years. There will be greater specialization and use of assistance. With greater specialization at all levels, we shall need to guard against mechanization, to keep the process human and flexible. To self-guard against this, a central role of the teacher will be to work with youngsters in small groups.

Some troublesome questions arise concerning the ways in which teachers have been trained. My point of view is that much, if not most, of the current training of teachers is antithetical to effective teaching in small groups. Most of what trainees are taught to do, and most of what they are learning to do is exactly what they should not be doing if they are conducting small group teaching as it should be carried out. In the first place, we have assumed that teacher and student behavior is different from that which occurs in other contexts when the small group is genuinely operating for the correct purposes. Video tape recordings in classrooms where teachers now are teaching in small groups have been made. As anticipated, the teaching is almost identical with that which takes place in regular sized groups and in large groups. The main role is as purveyor of knowledge, lecturer. It is mostly teacher talk. What is the appropriate purpose of teaching in small groups if the assumption that it is different from that which goes on in large groups is accepted? As a beginning, in our study of teaching in small groups at Stanford, we have identified two unique purposes: (1) to open up wide the channels of communication among the members of the group, on an emotional and social as well as intellectual level between pupil and pupil as well as between teacher and pupil; and (2) to provide an opportunity for individuals to apply knowledge and experience gained elsewhere to new situations, the old problem of transfer: to increase the ability to apply knowledge and experience to new problems.

With this as a beginning, we have been attempting to identify the kinds of pupil behavior which we want to foster in these small groups and that are uniquely appropriate for the small group. The next step is to identify the kind of teacher behavior which might reasonably be expected to produce the kind of pupil behavior desired and, then, to determine the kind of training programs which may be capable of producing teachers who can behave in the appropriate manner.

Pupil Behaviors. We want pupils to become genuinely involved in the activity. We want the individual pupil to be willing to put his ideas on the table, to be able to listen to what other pupils and teachers say about his contributions, both positively and negatively, and not react defensively when his ideas are criticized. It is important to be able and willing to put your ideas on the table and to listen to what others say and, then, to be able and willing to speak responsibly about another's ideas, to probe, approve, argue, and disagree.

We want to have the pupil behave not just for the teacher. According to almost all of the records we collected, this seems to be most of what goes on in school—we call it "playing school." The pupils are trying to find out what the teacher wants and generally to give it to him or in some cases to cause him difficulty in getting it. We have lucid examples. In one recording, we were trying to model the behavior of the teacher who was trying to get pupils genuinely involved and reacting because of the relevancy of the situation. The situation was defined as: "We are going to select what we want to study in social studies. And, after we have selected what we want to study, we'll then select one of the topics and go ahead and study it." The group leader stopped after this brief definition. It was quiet for fifteen or thirty seconds. The video tape records show the students beginning to squirm. The teacher sits quietly. After about forty-five seconds, one compulsive person who could no longer keep quiet says, "Well, uh, what about studying the origin of ancient civilizations?"

The teacher replies, "Well?"

Another fifteen or twenty second period of silence and another compulsive student responds, "Well, what about studying the origins of American civilization in Europe?"

Is more necessary? They tried repeatedly to find out what the teacher wanted. Only very skillful teacher behavior finally brought them to the point where they were discussing drugs, the war in Vietnam, and other matters that were uppermost in their minds.

The example illustrates that most of the behavior observed in small groups, and in all others, represents kids "playing school" rather than being genuinely involved, in listening thoughtfully to one another. They hide. They do not feel free to express their ideas. They want to dominate or be dominated. Thus, a further behavior we aim for is to help the pupil to perceive himself accurately—who he is. We aim to help him to learn to feel comfortable in the face of uncertainty, ambiguity, and change and, in the face of such circumstances, to act constructively.

If these are the kinds of pupil behavior desired, then what are the teacher behaviors that are most likely to produce the desired pupil behaviors?

Teacher Behaviors. For the pupil behaviors we have been discussing, the teacher behaviors needed appear to be almost exactly the opposite of most of what we are trying even with our experimental programs in teacher training at Stanford, where the aim in developing the technical skills of teaching is to teach teachers to reinforce specific kinds of student behavior in the Skinnerian model. Instead of giving positive reinforcement for every "proper" behavior, the teacher takes a nonevaluative stance toward pupils' comments. In other ways, he also tries to bring about an open environment for the group to operate in. In an appropriate small group setting, the teacher needs to react sensitively to the ideas, the feelings, and the actions of group members and to convey to each member of the group and to the group, itself, the worthwhileness of all contributions. It is also important in small group interaction for the teacher to alter his behavior appropriately for each phase in the development of the life history of the group. In the beginning, the teacher behaves in one way; as he reaches a certain point, he behaves in another fashion; and, as he comes to the end, he reacts in still another manner. This is not solely "group dynamics" or "sensitivity training," where a small group is thrown together to work out its problems. Here the emphasis is upon responsible professional teachers in small groups. The mode varies. It may at one point be necessary to get out of the way in order to get back in. Some teachers, for example, mistakenly aver that, if they talk too much they must move over to the side and let pupils take over. This is not the responsible role of which we speak. At this point, we are grasping for ways to train teachers to behave differently. We are groping in the dark in new territory, for the most part.

I have illustrated some of the directions we are now considering, but one troublesome problem is: Who sets the task in the small group? How do you modify it? Still another problem is: How do you evaluate work in the small group? The chief characteristic activity in a small group is discussion—not reading, not writing, not lecturing, not memorizing, not taking examinations.

There are certain things which should not be expected to appear in small groups, even though they often do: for example, we shouldn't assume that what has happened in a previous large group meeting will be immediately transferred into the small group. Another expectation is not to find discipline problems in small groups. When small groups are well run discipline problems simply do not appear. One of the most difficult lessons to learn is that everything that happens in a small group is relevant. If the topic gets off what you think is the main track, why did it get off? Who brings it back, why, and in what form? The *modus operandi* of teaching in small groups is more like that of modern jazz improvization than a Mozart concerto. Unfortunately, too many teachers try to conduct small groups in a style of a Mozart concerto. For large group instruction this is appropriate, but small group teaching properly proceeds from the nature of the group and the problems and the ideas that emerge from the group.

Conclusion

We could end this and the next decade with little or no change in the teacher's role. Those who believe this reflect the old proverb: this old anvil laughs at many broken hammers. I am inclined otherwise—if we are cooperative, helpful, and positive in our attitude and seize the opportunity, some exciting achievements are bound to occur. Recently, a national leader, speaking of the situation in the Far East, suggested that we must take a *positive* approach to our position on international affairs. He asserted, "You cannot bomb communism to death, you must feed it to death and clothe it to death and heal it to death. Where there is ignorance you must bring knowledge and where there is poverty you must bring relief. Most important, where there is oppression you must bring justice." Our attitude must be positive, for, if we continue to pursue our traditional pathways, we are like lemmings on our way to the sea.

A Differentiated Teaching Staff

DWIGHT W. ALLEN

Central to the study of the organization of educational programs is the consideration of the role of the teacher in a professional staff. The current model of teacher-use is a model that was originated in the nineteenth century, and needs considerable re-examination, as we consider the problems faced by education today.

The present concept of help for the teacher dates back to a nineteenth century Normal School model, where the teacher typically had completed a ninth grade education and one year of normal school. There was a valid assumption that the teacher was probably not able to cope with educational problems confronting him—or her, so we had to build help for the teacher, a hierarchy of professional staff who were available to teachers as consultants to backstop their inadequacies.

The training of teachers today is not even remotely similar to that of a century ago. Teachers have four or five years of college education and are better able to deal with both their teaching subjects and their students. No longer is even the beginning teacher in danger of being run out of the classroom by his or her students. Yet help for the teacher remains the same: supervisors and consultants and curriculum coordinators and administrators.

We need a new concept of help for the teacher: clerks and proctors and

From *New York State Education* (December 1969), 16–18, Reprinted by permission.

technical assistants and teaching assistants and research assistants. The objective is not to eliminate curriculum coordinators and consultants and other kinds of specialized help, but the emphasis should be on the teacher as a professional, with various kinds of technical assistants to help the teacher with his professional responsibilities. Presently we fail to differentiate between instructional responsibilities which need five years of college experience, and the competence needed to run a ditto machine. The teacher today is cranking his own ditto machine and typing his own stencils, and proctoring, and acting in the capacity of technical assistant as well as instructional leader. We have an undifferentiated staff, reminiscent of the medical profession at the turn of the century when the family doctor was responsible for the full range of medical services without nurses, laboratory technicians, or other assistants.

The current role of teacher is typified by no differentiation in staff responsibilities. A teacher is a teacher is a teacher. Teachers are interchangeable. Promotions are away from students. If a teacher becomes a department head, he teaches fewer students. If he becomes a counselor or administrator, it is likely that he does not teach students at all. It is a rather strange kind of profession where all promotions are away from the clients that we are attempting to serve.

The only way to get promoted as a teacher is either to grow older on the job, or go back to school and take more courses. These criteria do not emphasize the professional aspects of teaching, or the professional responsibilities of teachers. Consider the example of a fairly large high school where three teachers teach identical classes, say ninth grade English. The first teacher has been recognized as the outstanding teacher of the county so we assign thirty students to each of her classes. The next teacher has been on tenure for years but is mediocre almost to the point of being incompetent, so we assign thirty students to her. The third teacher is a first year teacher, untried, possibly outstanding, possibly incompetent, we just do not know, so we assign thirty students to her. We place students into these classes and pretend to them, to their parents, and to ourselves, that they are all getting something called ninth grade English, which is manifest nonsense. Parents would rather have their children in a large class with an outstanding teacher, than in a small class with a marginally competent teacher. Class size is not the prime issue. No matter how few students are in a class, if the teacher is not competent, the instructional situation cannot be good. We need to find some way to differentiate the responsibility of the outstanding teachers and use other teachers in supporting roles. The outstanding teacher should be responsible for the education of more students.

This is not a merit pay proposal. Under merit pay, teachers have the same responsibility but get different compensation. A board of experts monitors teaching competence and differentiates merit categories with special status and compensation. This does not help the students who are not in these favored classrooms. We need instead a differentiated teaching staff where not only do teachers have different compensation, but also have differentiated responsibilities.

For purposes of examining the idea we can identify four categories of teachers, four differential teaching staff responsibilities. Based on a mean salary of $7,800, not atypical in California school districts today, a proposed salary range of $5,000–18,000 would be compatible with present staff expenditures. Additional funds would not necessarily be needed to differentiate staff in accordance with the present example.

The first category would be Associate Teacher, with a range in compensation of $5,000-7,000, perhaps in ten steps (the detail is not important). This teacher would typically have at least an A.B. degree. The staff category should not be tied specifically to preparation or course units, although we can think of median levels of preparation associated with the differential staff ranks.

The second level would be Staff Teacher, with a salary range of $7,000-9,000. Advancement might be more accelerated within this staff category perhaps five annual increments. Typical preparation would be a fifth year of college.

The third category would be Senior Teacher, with a salary of $9,000-12,000, with probably an M.A. degree.

The highest level might be designated a Professor. The title is not so important, but there should be a way to identify instructional responsibilities in the elementary and secondary schools that have commensurate professional responsibility and recognition with instructional positions in higher education. Compensation for the fourth staff category would range from $12,000-18,000 and similar to category three, would have perhaps four steps. This staff level would typically be associated with the doctorate and would enable a person who was interested in classroom teaching to have a full professional career in the classroom.

In the Secondary Teacher Education program at Stanford University approximately 140 candidates are trained each year. These students would compete favorably in any group of professionals. It is a very select group. One of our interns, four years ago at the end of his internship year, was voted the outstanding teacher at the high school in which he was interning, a fine school on the San Francisco Peninsula. The quality of the entire staff is consistently very high, but this intern was voted by the senior class as the outstanding teacher of the year at this high school. Where is this man four years later? He is completing his doctorate in Political Science and is a finalist in one of the outstanding postdoctoral fellowship programs nationally. He is an outstanding person. Could we recommend, in good conscience, that this person stay in the high school classroom? In the high school classroom, he would have to wait ten to twelve years before he could rise to the top level of teacher compensation and recognition, with little opportunity to exercise either his initiative or his enthusiasm in the process.

One of the inequities of teacher salary scales at present is the fact that if one examines the range of teacher competence and the range of teacher compensation, there is probably more concentrated competence in the middle range of the salary schedule than at the top ranges of the salary schedule. Teachers who have outstanding ability and initiative eventually promote themselves away from the classroom and monolithic salary schedules into counseling, administrative and higher education positions. Those who have less initiative and drive, although there are notable exceptions, remain in the high school and the elementary classrooms and eventually rise to the top of the salary schedule. There is no way under present staffing policies, to recognize unusual talent, or to extend its influence to benefit more students.

Consider the first and second staff levels as tenured positions and the third and fourth levels as contract positions. This would not require any modification in tenure laws; a person could be hired as an Associate Teacher and reach tenure as an Associate Teacher. He could be hired as an Associate Teacher or Staff Teacher, and receive tenure as a Staff Teacher. Teachers teaching in contract positions, at levels three and four, could still be tenured at level two, in much the same way that administrators now are not tenured as administrators, although they may hold tenure as teachers in the district in which they are serving as administrators. Typically levels three and four on the staff would be on twelve-month contracts, rather than nine-month contracts, moving in a desirable direction of professionalism. This proposal initially provides for two-thirds of the staff at levels one and two, and about one-third of the staff at levels three and four.

A district would have to think through specific differentiated staff responsibilities and promote teachers to fulfill a particular responsibility. When teachers are promoted by longevity, districts have no control over the proportion of staff dollars in relation to staff positions. Some districts in California anticipate that their median salary level will raise by some $500 over the next five years, on the present salary schedule, simply because of longevity and tenure of staff.

Advantages of a Differentiated Staff

What are the advantages of a differentiated teaching staff? Automatic promotion regardless of competence is eliminated, a real key to improving professionalism in education. There may be five people in a particular school that have the capability to operate at the highest level with only one position available, in the same way that there may be five people that could competently serve as administrators with only one position open. However, once a person is promoted, he undertakes a responsibility which is different than the responsibility he had previously discharged. We may not be able to promote and recognize all of the talent that resides in the teaching staff, but at least there is the potential for the use of talent in differential service. Secondly, if we develop a differential staff we will identify specific responsiblities at each level. The serious identification and development of these responsibilities will take considerable time and effort. A first approximation might be to think of the Associate Teacher as the *Doer* who carries out curriculum developed by more senior members of the staff. The Staff Teacher may be the *Illustrator* who works with the curriculum as it has been developed in general, but illuminates it with different illustrations and enriches it in many ways. The Senior Teacher will probably have some say in the shaping of the *concepts* of the curriculum, and the person who is operating at the top staff level should have a primary role in anticipating directions of curriculum development. This person could be looking ahead ten and twenty years, rather than placing the eduational enterprise in the position of having to respond to developments in the total society after the fact. We need to organize schools and staff to *anticipate* the changes that will be needed in the educational enterprise.

A third advantage is that the higher salary levels would be reserved for persons performing at levels commensurate with the salary level. This would encourage younger, talented staff members. There is a way to recognize talent early and reserve it for the high school or elementary classroom rather than lose it either to other professions or to other leadership positions in education.

A differentiated staff can make effective use of persons who do not wish to accept full professional responsibility. Under the present system, once a teacher is employed, his compensation and responsibility proceed independently of his professional interest or competence. There are a large number of teachers, primarily housewives, who do not wish to accept full professional responsibility and would be delighted to accept a more modest responsibility and compensation. There are many talented people who are unwilling to accept employment in the schools at all, at present, because employment implies this undifferentiated responsibility. We have to think much more imaginatively about the use of the total personnel resources available to the schools, full or part time, and at all levels of competence and responsibility.

The elimination of labor-management connotations in staff negotiations is another important consideration. We are in a decade of decision in terms of how teachers are going to negotiate for professional status. There is a real danger that we will sharpen the dichotomy between the teacher-professional and the administrator-professional, which is most undesirable in the development of more effective education. It is not appropriate to adopt a model in education that is relevant to other circumstances, but not to the development of a profession. By making it possible for classroom teachers to be compensated better and have more substantive responsiblity than some administrators, we will recognize the fact that teaching performance and teaching competence is the heart of the education enterprise.

A differentiated staff will facilitate innovation. If a staff is prepared to undertake differentiated responsibilities, then we will not continue to find ourselves in a position where innovation is painful, traumatic, and difficult. We have to realize that we live in a world of change. We must learn to respond so that we do not have to make a disproportionate effort to institute minor changes.

There is a substantial organizational benefit from a differentiated staff. At present, organizational alternatives are severely limited by constant staffing formulas and monolithic requirements of staff use. The educational organization can become much more flexible—more alternatives can be considered. By identifying staff responsibilities more precisely, we can train staff to accept specific responsibilities. No longer will we be tied to the limitation of retraining the entire staff whenever change is desired.

Finally, there are advantages in the identification and use of differential staff talents. Unsuccessful teachers might be used effectively if they did not have to perform the full range of teaching competencies. Some teachers who are excellent in terms of their creative ability have the fatal flaw of lack of classroom control. If we could differentiate staff responsibilities, to minimize the necessity for such teachers to exercise class control, they could be constructive members of a teaching staff.

Problems of a Differentiated Staff

A discussion of a differentiated teaching staff would not be complete without identifying problems associated with its implementation. First of all, it is difficult to identify differentiated staff responsibilities. We have not thought about the use of staff in such a manner and it would be a major undertaking to differentiate teaching staff responsibilities. Secondly, it would be difficult to establish working relationships among a differentiated staff. Thirdly, a differentiated staff implies modification of the total school program. This may mean that we have to consider different ways of instructing pupils other than thirty at a time with a single teacher, daily, for an hour. The notion of a differentiated teaching staff goes hand in hand with other organizational and program modifications, some of which become possible and others of which become necessary if a differential staff is to be developed. Fourth, there is a lack of precedence of educational decisions in systems in employing diffential staff, and we would have to examine the way in which decisions would appropriately be made. Fifth, we need to develop new concepts of staff training. Teacher education programs would have to be modified substantially, recognizing which of the tasks of teacher education would be pre-service and what portion of teacher education would be in-service training. Some formal training elements might be mid-career elements. A sixth problem is the rejection of differential teaching ranks by current staff threatened by performance criteria. There are now teachers who are enjoying the benefits of an undifferentiated staff without commensurate responsibilities, who are likely to complain. A "grandfather clause" would take some of the pressure off the present incumbents. And finally, there is the need for over-compensation in lower staff ranks during transition periods. We now have teachers on salaries of $10,000-12,000 who would be assigned at the lowest level of differentiated staff. There will have to be provisions for the extra finances necessary initially, to implement a program of differential staffing.

As we look forward to the next decades, unless we face the notion of a differentiated professionalism in the teaching staff, we will limit the quality of American education. Approximately three out of every ten college graduates presently go into teaching. It is likely that we can attract some more top candidates and it is likely that we can eliminate some at the lowest level. But, by and large, we will have a 'body politic' teaching staff much on the order of competence that we now have. We must use them more effectively.

Notes on Teacher Education

RICHARD H. BROWN

Teaching is becoming an unnerving experience. Teachers are unsure of themselves and uncertain of their roles. Many are dreadfully disoriented. The more conservative take recourse in caricaturing the forces of change, defying the bricks coming through the window, growing steadily more unhappy. Others despair or take recourse in an abdication of responsibility, deluding themselves with the thought that they are heeding the popular message and contributing, somehow, to an education that by some mysterious means will be "better." All find themselves badly equipped by programs of teacher education in which substantive changes have been few and far between and which have been confined, with rare exceptions, to alterations in who teaches what to whom, in requirements narrowly defined, and in administrative procedures. For teachers at the collegiate level there are no programs at all.

Nowhere is it more true than in teacher education that even new ways of doing things are obsolete before they are effected. Nowhere is the need greater to go beyond tinkering, to look at the assumptions that are built into our thinking, and to heed a procedural version of the idea that, after all, the medium *is* the message.

The comments that follow rest on certain convictions. Chief of these is that the problems of American education are a product of our efforts, unwitting for the most part, to perpetuate basically authoritarian institutions in an increasingly democratic society in which the clamor for freedom grows steadily more strident. Second is the conviction that learning proceeds essentially from an act of the individual learner, whether it takes place in the context of a classroom or outside; that it takes place at different rates and times for each individual and can be expressed only in terms of his own change as a human being; and that it results from some form of inquiry which begins where the individual learner is and grows out of his desire to know something, as well as his feeling that he is free to learn. A corollary to this conviction is that the chief aim of education is not the transmission of an abstract body of knowledge but the growth of individual learners as they confront new experiences, including knowledge, and in turn transform those experiences.

These hypotheses about learning, in one way or another, link together modern curriculum work and pressures for change in the government of institutions; movements for flexible scheduling, nongraded classes and achievement or competence as a measure of progress; the outcry for independent work and for "relevance." They are equally applicable to schools and to colleges and they are being

From *Change*–the magazine of higher education (March/April 1970), 44–47. Reprinted by permission.

asserted loudly, if not always clearly, both from within the ranks of the academy and from outside.

At times we hear the message too narrowly, as though it had to do only with methods, and at times we hear it too portentously, as though it sounded the doom of all formal education. It does in fact explode the classroom. It challenges all of us to re-think not only what we do but who we are. And yet it has within it the potential to make formal education an infinitely richer and personally more rewarding experience for all who are involved. It calls for teachers to be different kinds of human beings, for new attitudes more than for new skills, for new assumptions more than for new knowledge. It calls for teachers who are able to view themsleves and their role differently from the way most view them at present, for teachers who see knowledge and learning differently, and for teachers who will see differently the relationship of schools and colleges to the outside world. It calls for teachers who are able to do a good deal more than take refuge in telling students something, and able at the same time to do a good deal more than merely providing "comfortable" classrooms.

We need teachers who are capable of being leaders in inquiry, who have an urgent sense of the processes and the possibilities of human growth, and a realistic sense of and respect for the mutuality of the teaching/learning process. Above all, we need teachers with a higher and clearer sense of purpose as teachers than many now have; a confident awareness of what they themselves have to offer in terms of maturity, experience, knowledge and skills; an awareness that students can avail themselves of what the teachers offer only if they—the students—sense and feel and understand what is available, and that they will do none of this unless they respect both the teacher and the situation in which they encounter him.

If we are to get this kind of teacher with any regularity and in any significant number, we shall need to provide not new courses based on and inculcating the same old assumptions but new experiences designed specifically to challenge those assumptions, enabling teachers to be as a consequence both freer and more flexible people.

We need to free teachers from the assumption that prevails in so much of our education that knowledge exists independently of the knower, and that the disciplines constitute bodies of knowledge that can be "covered" rather than ways of inquiring into reality. To do this, we need to give them a good deal of working experience with the relationship between knowledge and process. In the discipline of history, to take an example, they will need enough experience to perceive, not only in their minds but in their very being, the sublime significance of the fact that all we have of the past is inert data to which we go with organizing questions that grow out of our own experience, and that enable us to see some things and not others. They will need to see, not only intellectually but as a fact of life, that because of this, history is always changing, always being rewritten, and thus, in the largest sense, every man is his own historian.

We come closest to giving students this kind of experience when we ask them to do creative scholarly research in a discipline. But seldom do we give such opportunities to teachers going into the schools, and even when we do, rarely do we connect it with their preparation for teaching. Nor is it enough by itself; the task, to be effective, must repeatedly go beyond the doing of the discipline to a consideration of the implications of the "doing" for human beings. The point is not alone to use the skills of the scholar as a way of training the mind, but to enable students to perceive that knowledge cannot be separated from the processes by which it was acquired or the uses to which it is put; that its character is instrumental and dynamic rather than abstract or static; and that it is something that each man constantly works on, however well or badly.

We need to afford teachers new kinds of experiences that challenge them to reflect analytically and intuitively on how they themselves learn, perceiving the relationship of learning to their total experience, to everything they do, and to everyone with whom they come into significant contact. To cite a simple example, how does one explain the phenomenon of returning to a book one has read and underlined five years before, and finding totally inexplicable why certain passages were underlined and not others? What has changed, obviously, is not the book, but the experience and questions one has brought to the book. Again, how does one explain the phenomenon of "learning from kids"—the sudden new insight in the middle of an expository lecture, or in watching one's own three-year-old? Is the learning in such situations self-generated, or is it the result of a quizzical look on a face in the lecture hall, or the fact that the three-year-old's presence altered our experience? Who is the teacher and who the learner? Is the three-year-old less a teacher than the college professor lecturing on the Peloponnesian War, who was also altering our experience? Is it not true that the only significant consideration insofar as learning is concerned is what the learner was doing with the new data or experience in his own mind, and that this in turn was as much a function of the questions he brought to the experience as it was of the experience itself?

To an educational culture determined by word and deed to separate content from process, such phenomena are at worst trivial riddles fit only for methods courses, or at best philosophical questions beyond the ken of educators. But to a culture conscious of the relationship of content to process, they are significant. If we find ways to build consideration of them continually into the experience of teachers, we shall make the question of how people learn intensely human and personal rather than abstract, sensitize teachers to the mutuality of the learning process, and foster their consciousness of the ongoing nature of the teaching/learning relationship both in their own lives and beyond the walls of the classroom.

We need to challenge teachers in fundamental ways to come to grips with the purposes and goals of teaching in contexts in which they deal with and are challenged by students, and in which they have none of the traditional thought-evading armor of established requirements. Perhaps we shall do this best by allowing them extensive opportunity to plan and organize formal and continuing learning situations with students: in short, creative opportunities to design curricula, develop materials, and practice teach. But such programs must go beyond all of these as we now see them if they are to be effective. They must give the teacher both more responsibility and more experience in learning from students than the A to B relationship (with C watching) of most practice teaching. Prospective teachers must be removed from the procrustean bed of teaching six weeks in someone else's course, or the equally procrustean bed of teaching even one's own course in "history" or "English" or "chemistry." They must go beyond the task of consuming a given amount of time in a given curriculum in a given school.

It is important in these experiences that teachers be given both the responsibility and the freedom to plan and work out with students the "ideal" learning experience, without any of the props of the established order. (Postman and Weingartner in their challenging book, *Teaching as a Subversive Activity*, have described a version of this.) If they would teach history, they must be challenged continually as to *why* history, and *why* they do what they do with it, in a situation in which they are afforded no easy outs, either through established authority or through students rendered disinterested through having no responsiblity. They must be challenged to match purpose to materials and to classroom methods—if they opt for a classroom—and to learn in the process to create learning situations mutually with their students.

Teachers need experiences that enable them more effectively to relate what they do in schools and colleges to what goes on outside those institutions, both in their own lives and in those of their students. The evidence is plain for all to see that the days of the self-enclosed school and college are gone. New curricula, whether "modern" in style or not, will partake more of the world around us than the old curricula they supersede. The once little-observed maxim that the best teachers will be those who best know that the world outside the school grows more important than ever. Nor will it be enough merely to know that world in a static sense. For if we are to have open classrooms from which students are free to go to the evidence in their own lives and to which they bring that evidence, we shall need teachers who themselves have lives to which they go.

The only counter to the "relevance" argument is to make our schools and colleges relevant. We shall not be doing this responsibly if we merely jettison the academy, turning our institutions into forums for the discussion of current affairs or into political societies. If we would preserve the values of the academy we must find ways of asking in it the questions that are important to us and to our students in our own lives. If our teachers are to be effective leaders in inquiry they must be able to move easily and comfortably between their classrooms and the outside world, and to make the two one. They will not do this without significant experiences in the outside world, and without encouragement to view those experiences as part and parcel of their growth as teachers.

If it is true in any sense that the medium is the message, we shall have to provide all these experiences in ways that themselves broaden the perspectives of teachers and free them from the unquestioned assumptions of the past. We shall not prepare teachers adequately for an age that challenges caste and class by teaching them in a caste and class system. We shall not prepare them for an age that is beginning to question the ultimate logic of the course system and of the regularly scheduled class period by teaching them everywhere in courses and in class periods. And we shall not prepare them for an age that questions the logic of separating content and method in institutions and through experiences that themselves preserve that distinction.

Ultimately, the search for the experiences teachers need in the modern world is likely to lead us to new views of our own institutions, of their relationships to each other, and of their relationships to the outer world. It is likely to raise among us questions of purpose, values and style, and to bring us face to face with assumptions about the way we do things and the way we live that have been too long unexamined. It will not hurt us if it does.

The Reconstruction of Teacher Education

JOHN I. GOODLAD

This paper begins with identification of some problems pertaining to educational change, with special reference to the education of teachers. Then it briefly presents the thesis with which the paper concludes: namely, that nothing short of a simultaneous reconstruction of preservice teacher education, in-service teacher education, and schooling itself will suffice if the change process is to be adequate. The paper then sets forth some observations on the state of the field with respect to both teacher education and schooling. It concludes with a series of recommendations for improvement which, taken together, are designed to constitute a comprehensive strategy for getting to the jugular vein of the educational system.

At the outset, let me emphasize that what follows is incomplete in several significant ways. For example, I give little attention to the critical matter of what shall constitute process and substance in the basic sequence for the preparation of future teachers. It is difficult to avoid even as glaring an omission as this in an effort designed to deal, in a somewhat balanced way, with major components of the educational structure. Further, there are some exemplar programs pertaining to various parts of this whole. But to my knowledge, no existing model represents total reconstruction of the kind argued for here. However, some of the models currently being fostered and developed under the sponsorship of the Bureau of Educational Personnel Development of the United States Office of Education (Triple T programs) perhaps come closest in design to what is proposed.

From *Teachers College Record* (September 1970), 61–72. Reprinted by permission.

Educational Change and Improvement: A Point of View

The most striking feature of any effort to improve education is its piecemeal character. The curriculum reform movement of the 1950's began auspiciously with both the production of new materials for elementary and secondary schools and the re-education of teachers to deal with new content and method. Within a very few years, unfortunately, the teacher education component was falling by the wayside. As a consequence, much of the intended thrust of what might have been a comprehensive effort at curriculum reform was lost in the classroom. Similarly, there have been significant recent efforts to restructure the school both vertically and horizontally so that pupil progress will be more continuous and so that teams of teachers will work with students as individuals and in groups of various sizes. Regrettably, however, these efforts at school reorganization have not been accompanied by the kinds of curricular and pedagogical changes needed to effect them fully. In general, teachers have not been prepared for nor educated in these redesigned schools and classrooms, but rather are trained in and for yesterday's classrooms. Forward-looking administrators have difficulty finding the innovative teachers needed to redesign schools. Forward-looking teacher educators, on the other hand, experience comparable difficulty in seeking to identify innovative schools in which to prepare new personnel. More often than not, efforts to improve the schools and efforts to improve teacher education proceed with very little mutual awareness. The interlocking character of the system serves to keep it clanking along but provides neither for effective communication nor for reconstruction.

Ironically, within this system of extreme complexity, specific proposals for change are conveyed in the rhetoric of complete solutions. The classic panacea is the teaching of more "liberal arts" courses to end the assumed proliferation of "methods" courses—and sometimes this panacea is offered when there are no methods courses at all. A sad consequence of this folly is that teachers are turned out for the elementary school who have little idea, for example, of how to teach reading. Many of the same people who blindly recommended more liberal arts courses now condemn the teachers for their inability to teach children to read. A favorite set of recommendations pertains to student teaching. There should be more of it, or it should be placed earlier or later, or it should occur at several times in the teacher education sequence. There has been a lot of debate, too, as to whether the introductory course for teachers should be historical, philosphical, or sociological in orientation or whether it should combine all of these into something called cultural foundations. The debate includes whether the course should be at the beginning or at the end of the sequence or whether it should be before or after student teaching. Imbedded in all of these proposals are significant issues which must be resolved and resolved more effectively than in the past. It is the preoccupation with them, however, at the expense of all else, that gives one pause. Teacher educators must get above this myopic dialogue to face the fact that the solution to any one of these issues, no matter how sound or profound, is minuscule in the face of the gargantuan problems of educational improvement now facing us.

Nothing short of total reconstruction will suffice: of the courses in education, of the relationships between courses and practice, of the "mix" of faculty conducting the program, of the school setting for practice, of in-service education of teachers, of the school year, and of all the rest. We must develop comprehensive change strategies which take account of the fact that preservice teacher education, in-service teacher education, and the schools themselves are dependent, interrelated, and interacting components of one social system, albeit a malfunctioning one.

State of the Field: Some Observations

After long participation in and scrutiny of the so-called professional education sequence for teachers,[1] I conclude that most of the courses in it have developed out of accretions of knowledge presumed to be relevant to education rather than out of fresh observations and interpretations of teaching and schooling as naturalistic processes. The courses in education, with a few notable exceptions, are very much like the courses in most other departments of the university in that they are *about* something–in this case, about education. As such, they probably are no better or no worse than these other courses. There is a place for them even in teacher education, just as there is a place for courses about things in surgery, business management, and law. But the subject matter must be as relevant as possible to teaching and the promotion of learning. There must be courses devoted directly to this practice, courses which involve the student in it and which are "about something" only to the degree that they seek to improve and develop understanding of what he is doing right now as a beginning teacher. In effect, then, the teacher education program must be both academic and clinical in character. The future teacher must teach individuals in groups; he must manage a class; he must become a participating member of a faculty group, seeking to change a segment of school practice; and he must, simultaneously, inquire into all of these as he experiences them. The courses about education, in turn, must place all of this in perspective without losing either figure or ground.

But this is not how teacher education courses have been constructed and taught. One result is the substantial disillusionment of the student who comes into them. He expects to get his hands dirty and his feet wet in real classrooms with real children or youth. At least this is what literally thousands of young men and women told us when we interviewed them during James B. Conant's study of the education of American teachers. Instead, they find themselves to be largely passive

[1] The observations in this section are based primarily on direction of or participation in the following studies: the organization of schooling (1963) for the Center for the Study of Instruction of the NEA; James B. Conant's study of the education of American teachers (1963); two studies of the curriculum reform movement (1964 and 1966); a study of school and classroom practices in sixty-seven elementary schools (in press); and a study of the process of change in eighteen elementary schools (in process).

recipients of learning fare not too unlike that in psychology, philosophy, history, or whatever. Consequently, they condemn their education courses, not so much for their intellectual impoverishment as for their failure to bring them into the nitty-gritty of teaching itself.

A glaring aspect of this irrelevance has come sharply into view in recent years. Until very recently, most teacher education programs were conducted as though urban blight and human inequities did not exist. Except in a few urban universities, future teachers were protected from harsh environments and the problems pertaining to them by being placed in safe, homogenized city or suburban schools for their student teaching assignments. All of this is now changing, but the reconstruction required to make the courses relevant to social realities is formidable, indeed.

Another area of neglect is in "pedagogy." Students study principles of learning in their educational psychology courses. Rarely, however, are they provided an opportunity to carry these learnings directly into teaching situations where they may test and receive constructive feedback regarding their efforts to apply. The problem is partly—but only partly—one of numbers. Classes in educational psychology and methods of teaching usually are large. At the very time the future teacher needs a truly clinical orientation, he finds himself in a large lecture class with very little opportunity to see and analyze let alone participate in teaching processes employing the principles being studied. It must be admitted, also, that educational psychologists frequently are far removed from the classroom in their own work and interests and not well equipped to spell out the practical implications of what they teach.

Another set of problems in the teacher education sequence arises out of the several differing sets of values with which the future teacher must cope as he moves through his introductory courses into student teaching in neighboring schools. No consistent, agreed-upon set of values or approaches to valuing pervade the preparation program. In chameleon-like fashion, the student adjusts to one set of values pertaining to the use of theory, research, and inquiry within the university context and then to another, pertaining to survival and the perpetuation of existing practices during his apprenticeship. Since he hopes and expects to be employed by the school system in which this apprenticeship is obtained, the values of the school and classroom where he is placed are powerful and pervasive. In general, then, he is directed not toward what schools could be but toward what they are.

In contrast to the professions of medicine, law, and dentistry, professional attitudes in teaching—and, in fact, professional skills—are left in large measure to chance. In the majority of teacher-preparing institutions, the future teacher takes a few scattered courses in education as an undergraduate while pursuing his degree. The education courses are regarded by many simply as necessary requirements to be met. For vast numbers of students, teaching is not yet a firm goal, but is rather a kind of insurance, especially for young women who anticipate marriage at or soon after graduation. Securing the degree is the major goal, and teaching—at least until the student enters into the student-teaching part of his program—is secondary, at best.

We know that it is exceedingly difficult to change the behavior of young children. It is many times more difficult to change the behavior of young adults. Nonetheless, we proceed on the implicit assumption that significant change will and does occur through a process of osmosis involving lectures, textbooks, and independent study. These techniques are reasonably effective in promoting low-level cognitive changes. It is exceedingly doubtful that they make any profound differences in attitude formation. A student motivated toward the attainment of the degree, dividing his time between this pursuit and scattered courses in education, will develop only by happy chance the commitment necessary for effective teaching in modern society.

Certain conditions built into the conduct of teacher education programs and into the professorship also work against the development of professional attitudes and skills. In major universities there is a high premium on inquiry designed to advance knowledge. This probably is as it should be, since there are few other institutions in our society assuming such a role. Conscientious professors are troubled by a schizophrenic situation in which they see little possibility for research productivity if they give to future teachers the attention professional development deserves. To move beyond anything other than lecturing in seeking to individualize instruction is to take on an exceedingly difficult role and no certain recognition. Assistant professors learn from older colleagues the fate of idealistic young teachers who chose to go the individualized instruction route in teacher education programs. Others are insightful enough to realize that their academic preparation to be students of the educational process is not adequate preparation for the clinical role of guiding neophytes in pedagogy. This latter situation, which many professors caught in the dilemma will quickly recognize, is not likely to be dissipated simply by placing more stress on and giving greater recognition to teaching in universities. Improvement will come only when we recognize that teacher preparation is not something to be done on a mass basis but is akin to other professions in its demands for individualized instruction. To educate teachers properly will require financial outlays for academic and clinical personnel of a kind not yet contemplated in educational planning.

In-service Teacher Education

Turning to in-service education of teachers, we find little to reassure us that constructive educational change is likely to occur as a result of it. Large numbers of teachers on the job are preparing themselves not to become better teachers but to leave the classroom. In one of the studies referred to in footnote 1, we found that large numbers of teachers enrolled in graduate programs were preparing to be administrators. It is questionable that preparing to become an administrator, when no prospect of employment is in the offing, constitutes a sound basis for teacher morale or professional improvement. It is worth noting, also, that securing a degree in educational administration usually serves just as well as a degree emphasizing teaching in gaining salary advancements.

Our study of sixty-seven elementary schools in the United States (footnote 1) revealed a formidable gap between the in-service educational pursuits of teachers and the critical problems of the schools as identified in interviews with principals and teachers. A substantial number was engaged in some kind of extra-school activity, such as an evening class in a neighboring university, a research project with a professor, or some kind of district committee seeking to make recommendations for curricular improvement. But we found few instances of planned faculty attack on the vast array of problems identified by the staff as critical. In only four of sixty-seven schools was there anything resembling a critical mass of personnel engaged in systematic planned attack on these problems. It would appear then that relatively few school faculties are actively engaged in reconstruction. Given this fact, we cannot expect our schools to do a more effective job in their communities simply by doubling and redoubling the kind of in-service education currently under way. A more carefully designed strategy focused directly on the problems of the schools themselves is called for.

Conduct of Schooling

In the same way that certain conditions surrounding the professorship and the education of teachers in universities are not conducive to change, certain conditions surrounding the conduct of schooling contribute more to maintaining the *status quo* than to facilitating effective change. Education probably is the largest enterprise in the United States that does not provide for the systematic updating of its personnel. After basic requirements for certification are met, further study often is optional and at one's own expense. Forward-looking industries, by contrast, make certain that their employees are updated in the latest ideas and techniques, on company time and at company cost. Employees who do not take advantage of these opportunities find themselves unemployed or stalled on the advancement ladder.

Schooling is geared to self-maintenance and not to change. Tackling the problems facing schools today demands team work. But the principal and his staff are engaged in essentially individualistic activities which keep them occupied and separate from morning until late afternoon. It is unrealistic to expect a staff, with tag ends of energy left over, to enter enthusiastically and vigorously into the business of changing schools after school is out. Keeping school is, in itself, exceedingly demanding. It is not at all surprising, then, that the efforts of school staffs, under present conditions of limited time and energy, result in peripheral but not basic changes.

Studies suggest that principals are chosen, not because of their recognized leadership abilities, but with the expectation that they will maintain the system. A nationwide prejudice against women as administrators—changing very slowly—results in the selection of men over women regardless of qualifications. Many elementary school principals have had little or no experience in the classroom and simply are lacking in ability to help teachers with their pedagogical problems. In general, the training of school principals has not been directed toward the development of leadership skills needed for unleashing the creative talents of teachers. Consequently, the principal often tends to routine matters of keeping school while teachers work largely independent of each other in classroom cells. The time, setting, leadership, and resources for reconstructing the school too seldom come together in such a way as to produce the fundamental changes our times and problems demand.

Because only a few school faculties are systematically engaged in improving the school environment for learning, we have in this country surprisingly few models of what redesigned schools could and should be like. The thrust of significant changes recommended for American schooling during the past decade or two has been blunted on school and classroom door.

When one brings into perspective all of these conditions—pertaining to pre-service teacher education, in-service education, and school improvement—one sees that the total system is designed for self-maintenance, not self-renewal. Teachers for schools of today and tomorrow are trained in settings encrusted in the mold of yesterday. Shaking free of this mold necessitates the injection of change into each component part of the system. Because envisioning and dealing with this system as a whole is so essential, each of us must make the effort to rise above myopic concentration on minuscule portions of immediate but relatively minor importance.

A Strategy for Improvement

It is obvious that no single change or innovation is adequate to cope with this complex array of problems. Although no single change will suffice, we must proceed on the assumption that an interrelated series of proposals, if effected, might bring about significant improvement. Most of the proposals enumerated below have been set forth, at one time or another, for the improvement of teacher education. It is not the virtue of any one of them that is significant here. Rather, significance rises out of the potentiality for manipulating simultaneously all or most of the major components of an interacting system.

The first recommendation calls for admission of future teachers into a program requiring full-time commitment. The student accepts the fact that he is entering, full time, upon a professional program designed to prepare him to teach in schools. In the process of engaging in such preparation, he may complete a bachelor's degree in the arts or sciences. But this is now a secondary rather than a primary goal. Whether taking a course in education or in a subject field such as mathematics, the goal is to learn to teach and to become a functioning member of a faculty responsible for the education of young people. This is different from the kind of commitment that usually characterizes participation in a teacher education program today.

Having been admitted, the future teacher immediately joins a teaching team in a teacher education center—a collaborating school—affiliated with the college or university in which he is enrolled. At the outset, participation is limited but specific with respect to authority and responsibility. He receives a small but ascending stipend as a teacher aide. With increase in responsibility, he moves to the role of intern, and ultimately, resident teacher, with the stipend steadily increasing at each level of preparation and responsibility. Even as a resident teacher, however, his salary is substantially lower than that of a beginning teacher today. The concept being implemented here is that passage from the status of college student to school teacher is accompanied throughout by responsible involvement and financial recognition, with both advancing commensurately.

Just as beginning teachers in training are apprentice teachers, collaborating personnel in the schools are apprentice *teachers of teachers.* In the preceding analysis of the current teacher education scene, the point is made that professors of education often are ill-prepared to provide the clinical component which is so critical in the education of future teachers. The best potential source of such personnel is the schools. Consequently, schools of education must recruit from the schools those persons who appear to offer promise for becoming clinical members of the faculty. Clinical faculty members so recruited would retain their basic appointments in the schools while affiliated with colleges or universities. It is characteristic of many good teachers that they simply lack the capability of transmitting their skills or the reasons underlying them to those in training. It would seem appropriate, therefore, that schools of education seek to bring out these talents by assisting outstanding teachers in interpreting their procedures to beginning teachers on the job. Those experienced teachers in the schools who prove to be most competent in this process should be selected as short-term or part-time clinical faculty to work with the academic faculty of teacher-preparing institutions. We see then the emergence of a teacher education effort shared appropriately by persons trained in research and inquiry and persons possessing unusual skills in teaching and, ultimately, ability to transmit these skills to beginners.

It is proposed next that the academic and clinical faculty join in the development and conduct of seminars organized around problems encountered by beginning teachers in the schools. The substance of teacher education courses must emerge, not from the analysis of subject matter assumed to be relevant and selected from appropriate disciplines, but from continuing analyses of the real world of teaching. Although problems of the beginning teacher constitute the initial focal point for bringing to bear relevant knowledge, such problems consitute only the beginning and not the end. It will be the responsibility of the joint faculty to bring into juxtaposition both the theoretical knowledge and the clinical skills needed to cope with the specific problem at hand and related problems likely to emerge in the future. Thus on the surface the curriculum is organized around pressing problems of teaching. Looking deeper, however, one discovers that these problems are merely departure points. Beginning with them, the student is brought into knowledge from many disciplines increasingly seen as relevant to teaching.

To develop a required sequence of courses out of such a process, however, is to return us, ultimately, to the sterility and irrelevance now prevailing. Beginning teachers do not encounter problems in orderly sequences. It is unrealistic to believe that any sequence of courses, however carefully prepared, will suffice for all students. Therefore, it is recommended that the faculty prepare a number of interchangeable modules on teaching designed to provide specific knowledge and skills pertaining to the needs of beginning teachers, needs identified through a feedback system. These modules might include instruction in the specification of educational objectives, evaluation, application of learning theory, use of audio-visual aids, teaching of specific aspects of various subjects, and so on. Stored on videotape, filmstrip, microfiche, and programmed lesson, such modules would serve to satisfy specific needs of individual students arising out of their guided teaching experience.

Next it is recommended that students participate regularly in critiques of teaching taking place daily in their schools. Each day, one or more lessons taught by academic or clinical faculty, teachers, aides, or interns would be subjected to critical analysis by some member of the total team. This activity is missing from the conduct of schooling today. Because it is likely to be threatening to experienced teachers, it is suggested that initial critiques be conducted on the lessons of volunteers. Subsequently, more and more teachers would be willing, experience suggests, to permit their teaching to be used for critical analysis. In time, the teacher education center becomes a place of inquiry into teaching.

A major responsibility of the academic faculty, in the reconstruction proposed here, would be to join the staffs of teacher education centers in the business of school improvement. Specialists in the teaching of reading, the preparation of curricula, the organization of schools, and the role of values in making decisions would regard the teacher education centers as laboratories for extending their academic interests to the schools. The prime in-service activity of each staff member in the teacher education centers would be the identification and resolution of the central problems residing in their schools. The goal would be to engender a process of self-renewing change in which college professors, experienced school teachers, and beginners at several different stages of preparation would play their respective roles.

For such a proposal to become functional, it is necessary that considerable responsibility for decision-making now centralized in school districts be decentralized to individual schools. I have long believed that a single school with its principal, teachers, students, and parents is the largest organic unit for change in our educational system. If individual schools are caught up in dynamic self-renewal, then the school system as a whole is potent. If the school is to be the key unit for change, then the principal must become the key agent for change, since he occupies a position through which he can effectively block or facilitate the process.

If the principal is to provide constructive leadership for change, he must be trained in what is required. It is unrealistic, however, to expect the principal to possess those pedagogical skills required for assisting the staff to teach. In the structure proposed here, this is quite unnecessary. But it is essential that the principal understand the interacting social system of which he is a part and the dynamics of effecting planned change. Instruction in these matters should be at the heart of leadership training.

As stated earlier, the structure of schooling effectively restricts the kind of staff planning required for educational improvement. There simply is not time both to maintain the ship and to redesign it. Consequently, it is proposed that teachers be employed on a twelve-month basis, with at least two months of the year devoted to both personal improvement and total school planning. There are many ways of implementing such a proposal. Under one scheme, teachers teach for six weeks, have a planning week with children out of school, teach for an additional six-week period, engage in a period of planning, and so on throughout the twelve-month year. With teachers employed for twelve months (with a month's vacation) and with children attending school only nine months, approximately two months of nonteaching time are available for the planning activities essential to the self-renewing school.

If teachers are to make effective use of this period of nonteaching, however, they must be part of a team-teaching structure. By teaching in teams, it is possible for members of each group to devote a considerable proportion of their time to planning, preparing instructional materials, evaluating, and replanning. Whatever other arguments there may be for team teaching, a critical one is to provide the kind of flexibility necessary for effective planning to proceed. Also it is difficult to see how beginning teachers can be introduced into responsibility for teaching on a limited basis unless they are members of teaching teams.

Clearly, the commitment and involvement of teachers-in-training called for here requires a substantial period of full-time preparation. It is recommended that the total time span from entry to graduation as a full-fledged teacher be from two to three years and culminate in a terminal professional degree. One possible alternative is to begin the teacher education program with the senior year in college. Students would receive the baccalaureate after one year in the program but would continue into an additional year of post-baccalaureate work. Another alternative is to begin such a program at the post-baccalaureate level with the candidate pursuing two years of work leading to the master of arts in teaching. To repeat, it is essential that students enter into a full-time commitment at the outset and that all other goals become secondary. It is essential, also, that the degree awarded be regarded as terminal. From this point on, the educational system should provide for professional updating at the cost to the enterprise. Persons desiring to move into some other aspect of education would leave teaching in order to pursue advanced, specialized professional education.

It is recommended, also, that there be moderate salaries throughout the training period. Initial stipends would be increased gradually to a level of perhaps $2,000 below present first-year salaries. With completion of the program, however, and admission to the teaching profession, truly professional salaries would prevail. It is proposed that such salaries begin at $10,000 per year and move upward to more than $20,000 over a period of from ten to twelve years. The net effect would be to attract committed persons into a profession of lifelong reward and appeal.

The reader is reminded that the reconstruction proposed here results in reducing the ratio of full-fledged professional teachers to children. The proportion of adults in the pupil-teacher mix is more than made up, however, through the inclusion in each team of aides, interns, and residents, all assuming some responsibility for instruction. Cost estimates reveal that such staffing patterns cost little or no more than conventional arrangements.

A program of the kind outlined here necessitates nonspecification of courses for certification. Approval of individuals for teaching by a state agency would be replaced by approval of teacher-preparing consortia involving colleges and public schools. The decision to award teaching certificates to individuals would belong to the collaborating faculty, after careful observation and evaluation of candidates. Reliability in such appraisals could be improved through periodic use of outside evaluation teams.

Finally, at the heart of the whole, there should be a research center committed to the study of the entire enterprise. Such a center would engage in studies of pedagogy, the effects of experimental programs, the efficacy of various self-renewing strategies in the schools, and so on. Instead of there being a monolithic program, there would be several experimental ones, each with differing entrance requirements, course arrangements, balance of academic and clinical work, and so on. Every component part of the teacher education enterprise would be conducted as an hypothesis to be tested rather than as established assurance of what is effective education of the future teacher.

Conclusion

No part of what is proposed here is startling or unusual. Every element has been proposed; many have been tried. What is unique and unusual, however, is the proposition that all of these ingredients be put together simultaneously in a single collaborative enterprise designed for the inservice and preservice education of teachers and the improvement of schooling.

Clearly, the tasks proposed, taken together, are enormous—perhaps overwhelming. There are two ways to cut down the size of any problem. One is to eliminate some of the component parts in focusing on a few. The other is to focus on the whole by reducing the order of magnitude with regard to each component part. The second alternative is proposed here. The first has been tried and found wanting.

This means then that the arena in which the component parts are to develop, interact, and be studied must be kept as small as possible. Instead of many teacher education centers at the outset, there should be only a few. Instead of spreading the resources of the academic faculty across dozens of schools in an *ad hoc* process of school improvement, energy and talent should be focused on the few schools selected to serve as teacher education centers. Instead of endeavoring to move the entire teacher education program on an even front, existing programs should be allowed to phase out while new programs of a controlled and experimental sort are phased in. Instead of endeavoring to serve many individuals at varying stages in their preparation to teach, teacher-preparing institutions should focus on precise delineation of the group to be served, admitted at a specific time in the college or university hierarchy, with provision for individualization taking place within a defined structure. The principle of unity of structure and diversity of programs thus emerges.

There is no way of knowing at the outset whether a commitment to the kind of attack suggested here will correct the current deficiencies in teacher education and schooling. Nor is there experimental evidence to commend the directions proposed. But until one has created alternatives, there is no way of comparing alternatives. The problems which the strategy proposed here is designed to correct are formidable and of long standing. Redoubling our efforts to deal with them along present lines of endeavor will not suffice. The time is come to break out of old molds, to get beyond immediate preoccupations, in a comprehensive effort to deal with the whole.

Individualizing the Teaching of Teachers

MARGARET GILL

For the past decade or more, theoreticians and practitioners in every field of knowledge have written and spoken extensively about the changes taking place in every aspect of American society. During this same period visible changes of the kind foreseen, as well as some unforeseen, have become increasingly evident. Concurrently other changes, invisible and quite subtle, have been wielding their powerful influences: human values and traditional roles and responsibilities for people and institutions have altered drastically.

Each change, either visible or invisible, has had an impact on education and also on the increased expectations Americans hold for their schools. While expectations have been increasing, it has become very clear that teaching also is changing, or must begin to change, in those classrooms where the education of children and youth has managed to continue as usual.

Roles given to teachers (or *taken* by teachers in an increasing number of school systems) are changing. So are the responsibilities, either given to teachers or demanded and subsequently taken by them. In some areas—urban, inner-city communities especially—there is an impatience with teachers and a growing hostility toward schools on the part of adolescents and their parents. Already there is the suggestion in some places that teachers in the near future may face court action

From *Bulletin of National Association of Secondary School Principals* (December 1968), 131–140. Reprinted by permission.

where parents think poor teaching has prevented the pupil learning and growth they had expected.

Thus, while changes are occurring outside the teaching profession, changes are taking place within the ranks of educators. Once subservient, quiet teachers now are raising a collective voice, angry and demanding. The voice speaks for power. The expression of this kind of teacher power is a recently recognized reality in American life. There is no general agreement between teachers and other segments of American society on what teacher power is. Is it detrimental or beneficial? To whom? Teacher power, representing teachers' present desire for autonomy, is now synonymous with teacher militancy which most often appears in the form of demands for improved working conditions, demands that are increasingly being interpreted by the public as demands for salary increases. This kind of autonomy sought by teachers for their working conditions, completely separate from administrators and instructional specialists, is segmenting the profession and requiring a redefinition of roles, of superior and subordinate responsibilities, and of power and authority.

Real Teacher Power

For the first time, teachers are enjoying a new power. Yet teacher power has always been considerable, because the real teacher power exists only in terms of what teaching is all about–teaching and learning. Here is where power is crucial. Granted this is only one kind of power; however, teachers are expected to use this power that has always been theirs to provide the best possible teaching-learning. Little evidence exists to support the frequently quoted hypothesis that teachers autonomous from other educators are more competent or even more ethical in providing provocative teaching-learning situations. Whether or not teachers help students to learn is a sound base for determining the appropriateness of teacher power.

It is clear that more demands will be made by the public on schools and their total staffs–administrators and instructional specialists, as well as teachers. What do these trends require of teachers? How can teacher education help to meet the requirements? How must teacher education change in view of what is now known about teaching?

What Is Teaching?

Up to the present time, the education of teachers has been carried on in ways suggesting that a pre-packaged set of college courses and supervised experiences with children or youth (all carried out within a specified time, usually four years, under the direction of college or university personnel) prepared a teacher for his first and, all too often, his subsequent teaching assignments. During preparation the focus was on the mastery of predetermined and duly prescribed knowledge, skills, and techniques, appropriate for either the elementary or secondary school level, whichever the would-be teacher selected. In fact, about the only choice available to a prospective teacher in his preparation was the level at which he wished to teach!

This rigid, inflexible program has existed in practically all teacher education institutions with slight variations; it has been required of all prospective teachers; and it has been blessed by state certification laws. Such a program served a real purpose, questionable as we may now think that purpose was, for the first quarter of this century, when the general objectives of schooling were stated as the same for all students. Focus was placed on the teacher rather than on the learners; therefore teaching could too casually be described in terms of imparting knowledge to a particular group of students or in terms of the isolated teacher's predominant role in carrying out this function. All too readily teachers and their teaching behavior with respect to a group of students could be described by parents and administrators as "good" or "bad."

Shift in Emphasis

Then came the shift in emphasis from the dominance of the teacher to the vital and active role of the learner and his own learning process. Increased knowledge about the learning process, further understanding of learners of various age levels, increased amounts and improved quality of printed materials for learning, and technological advances in the kinds and quality of audio-visual materials available removed the focus from the teacher as the imparter of knowledge. As a result, the way a teacher spent his time with a class had to change. That is, the teaching performance had to change.

The teacher could no longer be evaluated apart from his class, apart from the total teaching-learning situation for which he was responsible. Accordingly, any definition of teaching without attention to the learners involved and how they were learning as individuals became harder to justify. In fact, a study of teaching requires an analysis of teaching behavior in a given teaching-learning situation, rather than an effort to determine categories of generally desirable teaching traits. Increasingly in the past decade, researchers who have examined teaching have been proceeding with the analysis of specific aspects of teaching behavior. Up to this point almost no feedback from their studies has influenced teacher education programs.

In spite of the considerable amount of preparation and dedication of teachers, what has been is no longer adequate. Teaching is different! A teacher need no longer be isolated with the same group all day or for the same amount of time for each of five class periods a day. For example, a teacher may spend 20 minutes one day with a given group and 90 minutes with the same group the next day. A teacher may in the same day spend some time with a large group (60-100), with a small group (10-15), and some time with individual students. He may share teaching responsibilities with two, three, or more people as a member of a team where the special skills or training of each individual teacher is used most effectively. Each has a different role with different responsibilities. These roles and responsibilities may shift several times within a given week. At one time one of the people is a leader occupying a superior role; shortly afterwards this same person may fill a subordinate role within the same team. Furthermore, today a teacher has instructional tools and materials available that were not even a gleam in some creative eye at the time he entered his teacher education.

Therefore, the changes in the way a teacher works—changes in teaching—suggest alternative uses of teachers' time and alternative roles and responsibilities that may shift several times for one teacher during a teaching day. Needless to say, preparation which is rigid, predetermined, and carried out apart from the environment in which the teacher is to work does not adequately meet the needs of a prospective teacher. For this prospective teacher will be expected to know how to diagnose a specific teaching-learning situation, then to plan an appropriate learning environment, and finally to choose and exhibit the appropriate behavior required for that particular situation. A multitude of planning decisions must be made by this teacher prior to going into the classroom, not to mention the vast number and kinds of decisions that must be made off the top of his head while he is involved in the specific teaching-learning activity.

What Is Adequate Teacher Preparation?

No matter what the initial, formal preparation of teachers is, it can be termed adequate only if it is based on the premise that preparation is a continuing process during the entire career of each educator—teacher, administrator, and instructional specialist alike. The prevalent distinction between *pre-* and *in-*service preparation, generally applied as it is only to teachers' preparation, has served no clear-cut educational purpose except to evoke negative reactions from serious career teachers who have resented the degrading tone of the "in-service" appellation, almost as much as they have resented the activities all too often meaninglessly planned for them by some administrator or central office curriculum consultant who failed to find out what really was bothering the teachers.

Career-long preparation must become commonplace, available, and required for all educators, but it must be planned individually to assure that each teacher or administrator or instrucional specialist can function effectively in the educational role he may be filling at any given time in his career. Emphasis in this continuing preparation will shift easily as responsibilites shift throughout a career. This requires more time, more people, more effort, more money; but nothing short of such continuing, planned, organized and implemented programs of re-education will suffice to meet the changing and increasing demands on the schools.

What Is the Role of the College?

In the past, colleges and universities working apart from the schools and within the limits of B. A. and teacher credential requirements have been totally responsible for all the pre-service preparation of teachers. This preparation consisted primarily of transmitting knowledge in the various disciplines with mastery in major and minor subject fields achieved by completion of a pre-determined and required number of semester hours with the same requirement for all students. During a prospective teacher's preparation the transmittal of knowledge was the responsibility of the college. Some professional education courses were interspersed throughout the four years of college, but these were generally restricted to the third or fourth year and in a few places withheld until a fifth year following the bachelor's degree.

In addition, all too often it has been the colleges and universities that have provided the major portion of the in-service preparation available to teachers simply through the courses that were offered for teachers in the summer or late afternoon during the school year. These courses that attracted teachers were frequently in the field of professional education and too often in educational administration, instead of academic disciplines. No constructive purpose can be served by assigning blame for the failure of professors in the academic disciplines to recognize their responsibilities for helping teachers keep up-to-date in their disciplines. Neither can we assign blame for their failure to foresee the need to involve themselves in the current curriculum movement which is characterized by changing structures of the disciplines, even those disciplines least expected to change, such as English and mathematics. There is ample documentation of the entry of academicians into the in-service education of teachers. This happened as soon as federal and foundation funds became available for developing new structures of the disciplines, for preparing new instruction materials consistent with the new structures, and then subsequently for re-educating teachers.

Gone forever was the feeling teachers had of security that came from preparation in a discipline, that is, from mastery of the content of a field that had been selected as a major. In some fields, notably in the social sciences, alternative and competing structures have been developed, each alternative having its avid proponents. Even now there is much disagreement over the merits of the various alternative "new" structures of content. Yet how many four-year college programs, leading to a major in one discipline, prepare would-be teachers to discriminate among the competing structures within his major discipline? How is the structure of a discipline evaluated? Who is the final authority in determining structure? Which structure is best?

Implementing New Structures

Moving from decisions about a discipline per se into the school itself, an educator immediately sees many other kinds of decisions that must be made. For example, which, *if any*, of the new structures in a given discipline (including new instructional materials and the required new teaching procedures) should be implemented? One specific illustration is the group of problems relating to grammar now facing many elementary and secondary teachers: Why should transformational grammar be taught rather than the traditional grammar? Who should teach it? A regular teacher in a self-contained elementary classroom or a specialist in a departmentalized organization? Can it be taught best via instructional television or by a "live" teacher? What happens to English at the junior high level following the introduction of transformational grammar at the elementary level? What changes will secondary teachers have to make? And—who should answer these and other questions that arise?

Answers to a few of the questions related to this one example (which will come largely from decisions made outside the classroom and little influenced by teachers) will change the behavior required of teachers within the classroom. New kinds of decisions will have to be made by each teacher involved in the "new" approach to grammar, beginning with how he is to learn this approach and how he must change his teaching accordingly. Immediately another question arises: What *is* the teacher's role in decision-making? How does the teacher's role in instructional matters differ from that of the curriculum specialist?

The Decision-Making Process

In his teacher preparation program, where does a teacher learn the decision-making process? Obviously decisions have to be made often and as situations demand; therefore, college must at least *begin* to develop some skills in the decision-making process and some understanding of what the various fields—such as psychology, sociology, and political science—contribute to the process. As a basis for a teacher's career-long involvement in decision-making within and without the classroom, colleges *can begin* to help develop understanding of ways to analyze a variety of teaching-learning situations, can begin to develop skills in studying teaching behavior in a variety of teaching-learning situations, and can begin to assess the effectiveness of teaching behavior in a given situation. With some understanding of the *processes* teachers need (*not the finished products* of specific skills, techniques and knowledge), a beginning teacher will have a keen awareness of what he may expect in his teaching career. Colleges can begin to develop some understanding of roles and responsibilities, including the shifting superior and subordinate roles within the social organization. Colleges can begin to develop understanding of the continual shift in distribution of power and authority within the school organization and within the larger society.

However, colleges can only begin the process. Initial awareness and understanding are only a beginning and far from adequate for a career. What must follow?

The Role of the School?

Accompanying the new, beginning teacher into his first assignment in a public or private school, a college can have a vital part in his initial on-the-job adjustment and then move on with him into the preparation that continues after the intern period of at least a year and preferably longer. Colleges and schools should jointly provide the supervisory and counseling personnel required for this continuing education, with specific responsibilities designated for the appropriate personnel from either the college or the school. Colleges and schools would make joint appointments of personnel and share the costs, including salaries and other instructional services and materials.

It follows naturally that personnel from the school would be involved in the learning experiences of a prospective teacher prior to his first assignment. Supervisors, administrators, and outstanding teachers from the schools could share teaching responsibilities with college personnel. Joint appointments would involve school personnel on the college staff and college personnel on the school staff. New working arrangements would be required. New responsibilities for the principal would result.

Another measure schools should take in assisting the beginning, first-year teacher is to arrange his schedule more realistically and considerately. He should have a reduced teaching load that would allow him time to work with ample resources—both material and human. Time is needed also to analyze his own teaching performances in a variety of teaching-learning situations with a variety of students who differ in such aspects as socioeconomic backgrounds, intellectual potential, and degree of motivation. In the security of a situation where he is not threatened by what might well be unfavorable feedback from his initial efforts, with the security provided by support from school and college personnel in his efforts to study and improve, and with time to work toward improvement, a beginning teacher can start his professional life with the knowledge that he will be judged, not for tenure purposes, but in order that he can progress according to his own strengths with special attention to his special needs. Too often the beginning teacher has the same teaching loads, including problem classes, as do his veteran colleagues. Unfortunately, a beginning teacher is expected to perform teaching tasks in ways and at levels comparable to his colleagues with years of successful experience. No wonder a beginning teacher faced with this kind of competition finds his justifiable frustration too overwhelming and makes an early decision to leave the classroom.

What Will Happen to Teachers and Teaching?

Simply stated, the process of educating teachers, according to this proposal, should be a learning experience in several stages. The individual teacher is at first described as "prospective" then "intern," and finally "career." The learning process begins with a program cooperatively developed by the college and school that continues throughout a career with the same kind of institutional cooperation. This process of continuous learning, based on teaching performance in a variety of shifting roles and with varied responsibilities, is based on the understanding that teaching performance must change as roles change possibly several times within any one teacher's career.

What will be the results of this continuous, cooperative, and individualized approach to the education of teachers? Teachers will be able to adjust successfully and confidently to the demands for change.

Teachers will have

1. Heightened sensitivity to teaching-learning situations within a school.
2. Increased skills in analyzing teaching-learning situations.
3. Increased understanding of influences within and without the school.
4. Increased understanding of the process of decision-making and the teacher's powerful role in the process.
5. Heightened sensitivity to and acceptance of the distribution of power and authority and the ways each of these shifts within the school organization.

In other words, when emphasis in teacher preparation actually moves to the individual teacher and to an individualized plan for his learning, continuous but changing as it must be throughout his career, teaching can then without question take its place as one of the professions in the estimation of those people outside the ranks of professional educators who continue to question the professional status of teaching.

The planned diversity and flexibility will result from

1. Emphasis on actual performance on-the-job, not something visualized from the unreality of a college classroom.
2. Emphasis on the shared responsibilities of the school and college.
3. Emphasis on organized learning that a teacher must expect to continue throughout his career (included as a part of his job description).

When emphasis in preparation actually moves *from college domination*, a domination supported by state credential requirements, *to joint responsibility* where the college and school share the development and implementation of programs and the recommendation of individual teachers for roles appropriate to their level of competence, then the often-stated goals of diversity, flexibility, and individualization can become as real in teacher education as we hold them to be for education of children and youth.

Only when teaching is accepted in its proper teaching *and* learning environment will individual teachers reach recognized levels of professional competence which will provide the security of real teacher power—that which comes from a teacher's ability to help students learn. Only when this level of teaching performance becomes a goal which each teacher feels confident he can attain, will teacher power be beneficial for teachers and learners alike in terms of what teaching is all about—teaching *and* learning.

Teachers Should Understand Mankind

GERHARD HIRSCHFELD

Why should teachers understand mankind? Why should anybody understand mankind? There are not a few who believe we should not try to understand mankind. They have their reasons. They say people have enough problems that are more urgent and more important than a mankind which is hiding somewhere in the distant and nebulous future. They say mankind is so vast and complex and really unknown, it is a hopeless task, anyway. They say that mankind has existed thousands of years, and no one has been able to find out exactly what it is or means. Life has gone on happily, nevertheless. Why bother now?

Of all the reasons I would accept only one as valid. The idea of mankind is very old. It goes back to ancient Rome, to the Stoics, to Cicero and the younger Scipio. It goes farther back—to ancient Greece, to the group around Socrates. Still farther back to ancient Jerusalem and the Prophets of the Bible. And still farther to the ancient Egyptians, to Akhnaton. And farther back beyond that. What I mean by "mankind," I should add, comprises all nations, all religions, all disciplines and institutions, all cultures and civilizations, and, of course, all individual persons. And if that is not enough, one may add the reality of the past and the potential of the future. All this is mankind. So one can understand why some people want to have nothing to do with it.

But others say: Yes, we should try to understand mankind. Religious orders, since time immemorial, have taught people to be tolerant and understanding toward all men. Intelligent men and women have always held that it behooves enlightened people to try to understand their age as it affects their life, their community, their nation as well as the rest of the world. Their underlying thought was and is that we really cannot understand ourselves unless we understand others.

Today, I submit, we have a far more compelling reason why we should understand mankind than any of those mentioned. The impact of scientific and technological advance has created unrivaled opportunities; it has also created problems of such scope and depth that no single agency can solve them. Among many others, the threat of nuclear war, population, food, automation, the loss of identity, the fading sense of values—are not parochial or segmental but universal or mankind problems. No single nation or bloc of nations can abolish war. No single bank or syndicate of banks can underwrite the economic liberalization of the underdeveloped countries in Africa, Asia, Latin America, involving an investment of perhaps fifty billion dollars annually. No single industry or industrial cartel can solve the world problem of automation. No single educational organization, no

From *Teachers College Record* (March 1969), 541–548. Reprinted by permission.

matter how large, can solve the world problem of illiteracy. And so with population and food, with communication and water resources, geriatrics and medical care.

A Mankind Framework

The implication is clear. The eventual solution of these and related problems requires the mankind framework and mankind perspective. No segmental or parochial approach will suffice. The mankind framework and perspective require mankind understanding. Mankind understanding requires mankind education, i.e., education which gives due and deliberate attention to the mankind dimension and perspective. Here is where the teacher comes in. Only broader education can lead to the mankind plateau. But only the teacher can give us broader education.

In past ages, man had a choice. If he wanted to understand mankind, no one would stop him. If he was indifferent toward mankind, no one would care. Today, there is no choice. The understanding of mankind is a must if survival is what we want. This does not mean that scholars and scientists can provide that understanding tomorrow, and educators can apply it on all levels of education the following week. Involving so much on so vast a scale over so long a period of time, the understanding of mankind is the result of a long and tedious process alternating between research and experimentation. One researches mankind history, applies the findings to experimental classroom teaching, discovers weaknesses and errors, resumes research and starts the process all over.

Why is present understanding of world affairs and world problems inadequate, no matter how many foreign countries and cultures we may cover in our studies? The simple answer is: Because we try to understand them in the segmental, not the universal perspective. Because things look different seen from the viewpoint of the nation and from that of mankind. Because we do not seem to be aware (or if we are aware, we pay little attention) that the change in perspective also changes the nature of the problem and therefore, the most promising approach and indicated solution.

Common Foundations

Take education. Seen from the perspective of the nation's interest, these problems are among the most important: desegregation; federal subsidies to public and private schools; the alarming drop-out rate of high-school students. Seen from the perspective of mankind's interest, some of the most important problems among the majority of the world's population are: the enormous extent of illiteracy; the great scarcity of schools and teaching personnel; the lack of communication and transportation; the scarcity of funds for any kind of organized education, let alone for teacher training and similar programs. This means that the measures which are effective in dealing with educational problems in the United States and other highly developed countries, are not likely to be effective in the underdeveloped countries of Africa, Asia, Latin America, and other areas. Comprehensive knowledge of the workings of an American urban middle-class high school obviously is not the best preparation for the development of a secondary school program in the Congo. The correct evaluation of the educational problem in the less developed areas of the world requires new perspectives, new insights, new ideas. It requires above all an understanding of the idea of mankind as it relates to the educational situation in different parts of the world. Every situation is different, and should be; but all bear some relation to the idea of mankind as a common foundation at the bottom and an overarching concept at the top.

Take medical science. Looking at the great achievements of medical science in the highly developed countries, one is apt to see the miraculous way in which one disease after another is brought under medical control. But looking at medical science from the mankind point of view, one speaks accusingly of the incessant flow of infants being born in ignorance and social indifference; of ever more persons reaching a ripe old age which, however, lacks many of life's necessities. One speaks of the survival not only of the fittest but of the least fit. In the segmental perspective, the problem is largely medical; in the universal perspective, it is largely social, complicated by economic, cultural and political factors. The remedies which fit one diagnosis, do not fit the other.

Take automation. In the United States, the poorly designed and controlled (in the broad social sense) application of principles, devices and methods has helped create massive unemployment, estranged men from their jobs, undermined and confused personal values—all of which may and often does cause serious dislocations in the attitude of and personal relationships within the family. In the newly developing countries, the problems are of a different order: how to protect native traditions, beliefs and values against the powerful impact of highly automated technological devices; how to balance largely undeveloped resources against the rising expectations of the people; how to finance and build an automated industry (if that is what is wanted) on top of a poor semi-agricultural economy. The techniques which are designed for and work well in the framework of the American economy, do not work at all when transferred to basically different conditions in less developed countries.

New Lights on History

In a similar sense, the shift in perspective changes the meaning of freedom. In the perspective of the Russian people, the meaning of freedom is different than in the perspective of the American people; the interpretation of the Indians is different from that of the Latin-Americans. Looking at freedom from the mankind point of view, we find that mankind freedom differs from all of these in that it includes all kinds of freedom. Conversely, none of the national freedoms can qualify as true mankind freedom. In a pluralistic society, which a mankind system by its very nature would have to be, there would be more than one interpretation of loyalties, of commitments, of human rights and obligations.

These examples are cited, not to minimize the importance of the nation but to emphasize the vast difference which the mankind perspective makes in the evaluation of any major problem. However, unless we have the correct evaluation, we can hardly expect to find the right solution or any solution. Incorrect evaluations lead to substantial omissions, even errors, for example, in the teaching of world history. There are not a few high schools where the teaching of Indian history starts with the conquest by Clive, and the teaching of Japanese history with the arrival of Commander Perry in the Bay of Yedo in 1854—as if the true history and rich traditions of these and other Asian countries did not go back several thousand years.

This kind of historical misinterpretation would not be possible if world history were taught from a mankind perspective. It is likely that, seen from this perspective, world history would appear in an altogether different light. We may find Ghengis Khan emerging as a more important world figure than Henry VIII., Simon Bolivar may loom a greater man than Charles V., and Akhbar, ruler of the Mogul Empire, greater than Elizabeth I.

Transcending Limitations

What, then, must be done to make education a major factor in the affairs of mankind? Among basic requirements I would suggest:

1. The need to transcend national, cultural, racial, political and social limitations.

2. The need to learn to think in terms of mankind and to evaluate issues and problems in the framework of mankind.

3. The need to refine educational programs to a point where special emphasis is placed upon the teaching of responsibility to society, and of commitment, first, to the awareness, then, to the understanding, finally, to the interests of mankind as a whole.

The need to transcend national, cultural and other limitations is accentuated by the fact that all individuals grow up in a limited environment, the effect of which, in the process of maturing, is tantamount to indoctrination. The latter is most effective when the balancing factors, which operate outside the limited environment, are weak or absent. The effort to transcend must then concentrate upon broadening the original environment by including the balancing factors. In the case of the teaching of world history, this would mean the broadening of teaching what is largely Western and, to a considerable extent, American history by including a proportionate share of the realities of true world or universal history. By doing this, teachers would be reinterpreting the approach to, as well as the perspective and the framework of, the history course. The same rule would apply to any other social science or, for that matter if in different degree, natural science course. The mankind approach and perspective should not be strangers to any teaching course.

Obviously, the ability to transcend depends upon the ability to think in mankind terms. I find that the process of transcending consists of three steps:

1. The awareness of the need for transcending national and other limitations.
2. The understanding of the reasons why, which will suggest:
3. The course of action, i.e., the dissatisfaction with parochial and segmental explanations, coupled with the determination to concentrate upon evaluating the relevant subject from the point of view of mankind as a whole. My experience indicates that transcending the segmental may be more difficult (often being a habit of long standing—therefore, children may be exempt from this experience) than the application of the mankind point of view which also may turn into a habit. If one manages to think consistently of mankind in relation to a given major topic, it becomes second nature. It would be logical to conclude that the mankind interpretation would serve as the balancing factor in the current teaching of world history.

Mastery and Formation

The learning of mankind thinking would seem to be mostly a matter of thought control combined with self-education, the latter involving the vast literature on world events found in books, paperbacks, magazines, the daily and weekly press, radio, television, films. While they are not ready-made for the purpose of gauging the mankind dimension, they contain the material out of which the mankind interpretation and meaning is stamped and molded. One must master this material before one can work on the formative process. Indeed, one is apt to find that the two merge in a mighty stream of lava erupting from the same crater. But they have different names. Seen through national binoculars, they are, say, the race issue involving in the United States: equal rights, black power, job opportunity, decent housing and related issues. Seen through mankind binoculars, they involve one single issue: the dignity of man. And it is not primarily a principle of equality or opportunity, recognition, job, housing or power—it is a deep and abiding moral right, the right of a human being. It does not involve one nation or one race or one color. It involves all of them.

That is why teachers should understand mankind. If they are to be successful as teachers in this broader sense, they must be prepared to blend the literature on world events with the formative process of the mankind interpretation for the teaching of (a) responsibility of the future citizens regarding their obligations to family and community, and (b) the meaning of commitment regarding the nation and mankind as a whole. Only in this way can their potential as individuals be maximized, can they obtain an education which will help them in meeting the profound problems and issues they are bound to be confronted with as mature persons. The noted educator, Professor Robert Ulich, expressed the need this way:

> All the great teachers of mankind aimed at something more profound than mere instruction, acquisition of knowledge, usefulness and efficiency. Rather, they believed that education, through widening man's intellectual

> horizon, should at the same time lead him deeper into his own self, and this not merely for the purpose of developing his individuality but for the purpose of helping him to discover the unity of his own striving with the hopes and ideals, also the loneliness, the sins, the sufferings and the aggressive tendencies of all mankind. . . .[1]

Professor Mark M. Krug says:

> Adhering to the rules of historical evidence, the teacher ought to balance the story of man's inhumanity to man, of wars, and of the relentless struggle for the survival of the fittest with the equally strong manifestation of striving toward a universally better world. He might find more than enough evidence for the thesis that cultures and civilizations in all ages of history tended to intermingle, assimilate, and diffuse, and that this diffusion has often contributed to the advancement and enrichment of the entire human race.[2]

Professor Elliot W. Eisner puts it this way:

> If students are to think with clarity about the concept of mankind, the value questions with which they cope should be related, as far as possible, to those issues that touch their lives. More meaningful ethical theory, sociology, and psychology can be taught in analysis of James Meredith's entrance into the University of Mississippi than in any long-range series of obtuse discussions on the nature of the good. . . . It is through a concern with human problems as they relate to mankind at large that it may be possible to create the type of understanding that will enable man to use with wisdom those tools which have made this century the most promising and the most perilous he has ever known.[3]

Difficulties in the Way

The goal of enlightened teaching is clear for all to see. But so are the difficulties which the progressive teacher is likely to encounter. Two major difficulties may be mentioned. One is the lack of persistent and methodical thought on mankind as an indivisible entity. Few teachers, comparatively speaking, have familiarized themselves with the concept of mankind, and are thus prepared to discuss in broad outline the meaning and the relationship of nations, religions, institutions, disciplines, cultures, civilizations as well as individuals to mankind as a whole. Some teachers, by an ingenious way of adaptation, have succeeded to add a

[1] Robert Ulich, Ed. *Education and the Idea of Mankind.* New York: Harcourt, Brace and World, 1964, p. xvi.

[2] Council for the Study of Mankind, "Teaching the Concept of Mankind in World History," pp. 34–35.

[3] Council for the Study of Mankind, "Education and the Idea of Mankind."

mankind dimension to their teaching. Others have tried without success, lacking the necessary background and preparation. It is perhaps correct to say that most high school teachers require special preparation and guidance in communicating the idea of mankind as related to the human society if they are to make a significant contribution to the broader and better understanding of the meaning of our age.

The other difficulty is the lack of material for both teachers and students. To be sure, books dealing with mankind as a whole have been written by Teilhard de Chardin, H. G. Wells, Arnold Toynbee, Pitirim Sorokin, Alfred Korzybski and others. However, these and similar books are not (and are not meant to be) consistent and methodical efforts to explore the idea of mankind as an organized system in relation to the parts which compose it. They do not tell the story in depth, on a comprehensive scale, and in unbroken sequence. Toynbee deals with the parts rather than with the whole of mankind. As a result, there is not now adequate material available which will enable teachers to apply the idea of mankind to their courses, and enable students to obtain an understanding of the impact of that idea upon and its meaning to our civilization and our age. Two more recent volumes on world history might be mentioned, one by Leften Stavrianos, the other by William H. McNeill. The latter's *Rise of the West* is a history of the human community in terms of a variety of cultures and civilizations rather than a history of the concept of mankind.

The Council

Obviously, adequate mankind material can hardly be gathered by a single author or presented in a single book. The UNESCO History of Mankind attempted to avoid these difficulties by organizing its project on a worldwide scale. Recognizing the urgent need for and the present lack of material dealing with the idea of mankind as a whole, the organization with which I am associated, the "Council for the Study of Mankind," located in Santa Monica, California, has made a small beginning to fill the gap.

The history of the Council goes back to the spring of 1952, when a few noted scholars at the University of Chicago, among them Herbert Blumer (Sociology), Richard P. McKeon and Charles Morris (Philosophy), Quincy Wright (Political Science), the late Robert Redfield (Anthropology), also Adolf A. Berle (Law, Columbia University), began to hold informal sessions on the subject of mankind. They did not quite know what they meant by "mankind," nor were they able to define the term. Nor did they even seek a concept of mankind in the sense of ideological agreement in a doctrine or philosophy. They rather thought of the concept in the sense of a framework within which to discuss common actions, associations, attitudes, and values.

Like many others, the scholars were disturbed by the grave and urgent problems facing all humanity regardless of race, creed, color, nationality. But when they looked at the proposed solutions, they found that they were American, French or Chinese solutions, democratic or communist, management or labor,

Christian, Jewish or Buddhist, white or Negro—but never mankind solutions. The question arose: "Can we expect to solve universal problems by segmental solutions?" The answer was self-evident and in the negative. In order to understand, let alone, to solve, the problems of mankind, we must learn to understand the meaning of mankind, i.e., its relationship to the parts which make up mankind.

With this decision under its belt, the group set out to arrange a number of conferences dealing with various disciplines as related to the idea of mankind. Fifteen conferences, lasting from two to six days, have so far been held. They included Philosophy, Education, Science, Economics, History, Technology, Law, Nationalism, Mental Health, and others. The attendance averaged 20 to 25, half of whom were specialists in the respective discipline while the other half represented a blending of other disciplines.

The conferences were followed by the preparation and publication of books. The first volume, *Education and the Idea of Mankind,* was edited by Professor of Education Robert Ulich, Emeritus, Harvard University, and published by Harcourt, Brace and World (1964). The second volume, *Economics and the Idea of Mankind,* was edited by Professor of Economics Bert Hoselitz, The University of Chicago, and published by Columbia University Press (1965). The third volume, *The Unity of Mankind in World History*, is now being completed and is scheduled for publication in 1969. Future volumes are to deal with Law, Technology, Population, the Humanities, Communications, and other subjects.

Hand in hand with the preparation of these materials goes their application to educational programs. Panel sessions on the idea of mankind have been held under the auspices of the National Council for the Social Studies. Workship meetings have been held at Wingspread, Conference Center of The Johnson Foundation in Racine, Wisconsin, with high school and elementary school teachers attending; also smaller group discussions in New York, Chicago, Los Angeles, San Francisco, and other cities. A series of monographs on the idea of mankind, specially prepared for high school teachers, has been completed on World History, Education, Science, Philosophy, Technology and Anthropology—with monographs on the Humanities, The Idea of Mankind, Economics, Law and Government still awaiting completion. It is hoped that all of the monographs may be published eventually in a volume *Social Studies and the Idea of Mankind*—A Series of Monographs.

To make the idea of mankind a new and powerful instrument in the effort to give our youth a better education and a broader understanding, i.e., better preparation to deal effectively with the problems of the future, it may be helpful to remember:

1. The process of education (in mankind thinking) should not begin with the students but with ourselves or, in this case, the teachers.

2. It should develop hand in hand with the selection and processing of the required materials.

3. The student may find it easier than the teacher to think in the mankind perspective; he is a product of the mankind age; mankind as a whole is his natural environment unless it is broken up by artificial interference.

The student may not be a friend of abstract ideas. But neither may he have to be sold on the idea that scientific technology has made the world one and that it belongs to mankind, and to no one with better right than to himself.

Teaching the Young to Love

JACK R. FRYMIER

It is time that those who work in schools teach children something about love.

Despite protests to the contrary, most schools in the United States teach about hate. Look at the diagrams on a social studies classroom bulletin board. Study the charts and pictures hanging on the wall. They usually relate to war. Books on desks, maps on walls, and projects assigned to children all add up to the indefensible fact that schools are unwitting participants in teaching young people about the negative aspects of human existence—about how to hate and how to kill.

Educators talk about attitudes, feelings, and emotions and their role in teaching and learning, yet they do little about them in schools. The widespread violence in our society the last four or five years and the continuing involvement of our country in war are real, tangible evidence talk is not enough.

Not only must men find a way to learn to live together in peaceful, loving, accepting ways, this must be taught as a way of life. It literally is.

It shouldn't be necessary to argue, this point of view is so obvious. But, when it comes to organizing educational effort with the objective of helping young people develop positive feelings and positive behaviors toward others, educators do not act as if it is.

Instead, large sums of money and great amounts of energy are spent on substantive aspects. In the many national curriculum reform efforts, for example, the emphasis has been on improving the nature of subject matter by sequencing information differently, idenfifying the conceptual bases, and building upon the structure of the disciplines. The problem of such efforts, however, is that when schoolmen start with subject matter to build goals and objectives, as they have in these reform attempts, then subject matter is where they must ultimately end up.

Man is the end. Objectives and purposes must be stated in human terms. Not in substantive terms, not in social terms, but in individual, personal, human terms. The means to achieve this goes far beyond helping people learn to read and write and to add and subtract—far beyond most of the substantive aspects of schools today. The need to teach the young to love transcends everything else.

From *Theory into Practice* (April 1969), 42–44. Reprinted by permission.

There was a time when there was no great urgency, when it did not make so much difference. That was a time, though, when only a few people would possibly be hurt or killed. That time is gone. We all know that. The young people of this world know that. They are the first generation to grow up within the pale of our awesome destructive power. Concerned and aroused, they are taking drastic measures. Their mood and their methods may be questionable, but their message is not. Their message is real—subject matter, disciplines, rationality is not enough.

It was intelligent and rational thought that the Germans used so methodically to destroy human life in World War II. Nazi Germany's extermination of the Jews was one of the most highly rational activities ever accomplished by man up to that point. The men who were in charge of killing the Jews in the extermination camps were so proficient that they were able to devise schemes to make the Jews literally run to their deaths. They made the Jews run because they had carefully studied the problem of extermination and had found that a winded Jew died faster.

At one death camp, Treblinka, the Germans were so efficient that it took no more than forty-five minutes from the time Jews arrived there by train until their dead bodies were being removed from the gas ovens. In just 6 hours and 15 minutes, Treblinka could process twelve trains of twenty cars each. 24,000 human beings.

That was 25 years ago. Today, rational efforts have brought men to a new pinnacle. The truth of this age is that we possess the power to destroy all life entirely. Plant and animal. This is an impossible reality to comprehend, let alone deal with. Yet, this reality must be faced and it must be faced in ways that will make a difference.

It dare not be assumed that if people know that they will, therefore, behave in kind and humane ways—that children will automatically learn to think and behave positively rather than negatively. They have to be taught.

There are no packaged programs, no teacher's manuals, and no texts on teaching love as a unit. We are our best resource. Each of us. It is by what we are, our attitudes and the behaviors that reflect them, that we teach about love. Or teach about hate.

Speaking out against other people or saying negative things about them is the mildest example of unloving behavior. Allport, in an exploration of human prejudice, identified this manifestation of hate as antilocution. It is the first of five steps that become successively more negative. Avoidance is the second level. It is staying away from other people, not having contact with or approaching them. The middle level is discrimination, subjecting another person to an unpleasant or undesirable experience you are unwilling to impose upon yourself. Striking out against another person or physical attack is the fourth level. Extermination, killing or destroying life, is the final, ultimate, and irreversible level.

These five levels of rejective behavior show how we relate in negative, unloving ways to other people. But they are only one half of human potential. The other half projects positive attitudes and loving behaviors.

Speaking out in favor of another person, saying good things about other people which cause them to be better, is the first level of accepting or loving behavior. The counterpart for avoidance is seeking out other people, deliberately approaching and moving toward other persons and interacting positively with them. The next level of loving behavior is altruism, the unselfish doing of good things, the giving of yourself. Physically touching, caressing, embracing or positive loving behavior is the fourth level; it is showing other people in physical ways that they are good and worthwhile. The fifth level of loving behavior would theoretically be the creation of life. Obviously, the sexual act is this. It is the ultimate intimate relationship between man and woman and, in its potential for the creation of life, it represents the epitome of loving behavior.

It is the positive side of this continuum of behaviors that can be emphasized in teaching. Some people, though, maintain that if feelings are to become personal, they have to be caught not taught. While there is some truth in this, learning cannot be left to chance. Schoolmen have to work at it. They need to arrange circumstances, provide information, and most of all, generate human relationships to make catching these understandings possible. The place to begin in schools is with teachers. For, whether a child becomes negative or positive will depend upon the development of his concept of himself and teachers play a powerful part in its formation.

A child is born with neither a negative concept of himself nor a positive concept. His view of himself is what he sees reflected in others' actions and reactions. Teachers provide this kind of feedback every day. Some of it in the form of such things as grade cards or student conferences is formal. Most, however, is informal—it is what teachers say and do.

Teachers react to children hundreds and hundreds of times during the course of a given day. Almost all of their reactions are immediate, spontaneous, and momentary. Most teachers don't plan it this way. Their intentions are usually the opposite. They mean to be deliberate, thoughtful, and purposeful. Some of the time they manage this—before school when they organize lessons and learning experiences for the day and after school when they mull over their own and the children's successes.

All day long in the classroom, though, teachers simply "bounce" off the children—"What do you want Johnny?" "Everybody open your books to page 73." "Billy be quiet." "John, Helen, and Mary go to the board and do problems twelve, thirteen, and fourteen." There isn't time to be deliberate, thoughtful, and purposeful under the pressures of the teaching situation. The kind of human being a teacher is is what counts.

Some teachers are generally positive. "Atta boy." "Good work." "Keep it up." They feed back data hundreds and hundreds of times a day that tell students they are worthwhile, they are good, they are important, and they count. Other teachers have a basic style of bouncing which is negative. They scowl, they frown, they are discouraging. These teachers feed data back hundreds of times a day, thousands of times a week, and millions and billions of times during the school year with negative results for children.

Teachers have many serious, unconscious biases at work. Teachers, for example, unconsciously favor students in their class according to sex. One study showed that boys attempted to participate in classroom discussions eight times more often than girls (held up their hands, volunteered), but teachers called on girls ten times more often. Teachers differentiate negatively in other ways, too. Studies clearly indicate that youngsters from lower class homes receive less physical attention and less eye to eye contact than children from middle to upper middle class income families.

An in-depth study of 3,000 teachers in a major urban school district contains some of the most alarming data of all. These teachers considered their children below average, their children's motivation below average, and their children's aspirations below average. The tragedy is that children would have little chance to be anything but below average in the classrooms of teachers with views like these.

People become what they perceive—what they experience and psychologically consume. Just as the food we eat and the air we breathe become a part of us physically, so do the sights we see and the sounds we hear, the things and people we experience become a part of us psychologically.

If we degrade another person, then a degraded person becomes the substance of our perceptions. We become what we perceive—we degrade ourselves. The person who destroys another person thus actually destroys himself. It's as if you were to take an apple, sprinkle poison on it, and then eat it.

But when a person behaves positively, when he does things which make other people feel good and worthwhile and important and valuable, he feeds psychologically on good perceptual stuff and also becomes better. This obviously is the golden rule, and the best empirical data that we have today says that it is right. Anthropology, sociology, and social psychology show us that what we do toward our fellow man is what we tend to become.

This applies the same to children. Children tend to become like the people they perceive, like the people they experience and psychologically consume—the people their teachers are. These teachers may be their parents, their friends, or their school teachers. If their various teachers behave in positive ways, they will grow to become positive people.

Schools obviously cannot control all that a child encounters, but one thing can be controlled. Whatever role we play, the one variable over which we can exert the greatest control is ourselves and our own behavior. We have to learn to use ourselves in positive, creative, responsive ways to provide the kind of stimuli, the kind of image, and the kind of feedback to help younger and older children become the positive, loving human beings they can become.

The thing that counts is us. Subject matter, organization, and evaluative techniques are all important, but the major perceptual stuff for a child is other people. In education, the other people are the adults who work in schools.

A child is not born loving or hateful. Love and hate are learned. We have to learn to use ourselves to teach young people to learn to love.

Allport, Gordon W. *The Nature of Prejudice.* Cambridge: Addison-Wesley Publishing Co., Inc., 1954.

Commager, Henry Steele. *Freedom and Order.* Cleveland: The World Publishing Co., 1966.

Fromm, Erich. *The Revolution of Hope.* New York: Harper and Row, 1968.

Glasser, William. *Schools Without Failures.* New York: Harper and Row, 1969.

Jackson, Philip W. *Life in Cl assrooms.* New York: Holt, Rinehart and Winston, 1968.

Kelley, Earl C. and Rasey, Marie I. *Education and the Nature of Man.* New York: Harper and Brothers, 1952.

Lamont, Corliss. *Freedom of Choice Affirmed.* New York: Horizon Press, 1967.

MacLeish, Archibald. *A Continuing Journey.* Boston: Houghton Mifflin Co., 1967.

McNamara, Robert S. *The Essence of Security.* New York: Harper and Row, 1968.

Mydans, Carl and Mydans, Shelley. *The Violent Peace.* New York: Atheneum, 1968.

Rasey, Marie I., editor. *The Nature of Being Human.* Detroit: Wayne State University Press, 1959.

Schwab, Joseph J. *College Curriculum and Student Protest.* Chicago: University of Chicago Press, 1969.

Steiner, Jean-Francois. *Treblinka.* New York: Simon and Schuster, 1967.

PART

V The Outside Influences: Pressures and Constraints

The specific reasons for including a section on outside influences in an anthology dealing with the controversies in education are three: (1) students, educators, and laymen have always evinced a great deal of interest in the indirect forces that influence education, yet the present concern seems to be in becoming more genuinely informed about these vital forces in contrast with what was obviously a "casual" interest just a few short years ago; (2) rapid changes resulting directly from these outsiders are affecting all of us, and with these changes have come important educational reforms–reforms basically designed to provide greater educational opportunities for more youth and for longer periods of time; and (3) accompanying these changes have been an intensity of criticism and conflicting opinions that education must thoroughly understand if it is to survive. Implicit in these reasons is a desire to have the reader take a closer look at American education from a different perspective, where the issues may be viewed in a new context.

Obviously, the indirect influences on education could provide adequate material for an entire course of study. It is too broad a category to be thoroughly covered in one section of an anthology. This section, then, is intended to be nothing more than a brief introduction to a few of the current outside influences, with particular emphasis on three that seem to warrant further study at this time: day care centers, media in general (and television specifically), and industry. It is hoped, however, that brief as this section is, an enthusiastic interest will be developed that will lead to further study; the reading of any of the articles and publications listed in the Selected References would be an appropriate way to begin.

In the lead-off article in this section, Fred M. Hechinger explores the problems that structured routines impose upon people who want to earn college degrees but cannot participate in regular on-campus course work. Hechinger reviews several "accommodations" proposed by some leading professionals, including the idea of "remote control" supervision and increased numbers of community colleges and university learning centers. He warns of the dangers of "second-rate degrees" if these external programs are not properly organized and executed.

In a very short time, "day care" has become a household term across the country, earning its legitimacy with educators and social service workers and with the general public. In order to suggest its current influence, several selections are included. Bettye M. Caldwell, director of the Center for Early Development and Education, University of Arkansas, traces the history of day care and outlines the major reasons for the recent acceptance of this outside service. Jonathan Black provides additional dimension to the drama of parent control of education in a black community in "Oasis in East Harlem." Black compares the day-care centers in a cluster of schools in the Harlem community with others in New York. Since the East Harlem Block Schools are run and controlled entirely by parents, we are shown some rather dramatic contrasts between these day-care centers and others through the eyes of this talented author.

Mass media in the United States are commercial enterprises. In every respect they are important outside influences on the students and educational community alike. But, because they are "commercial" many educators at all levels dismiss them as not being worthy of serious thought and attention. Yet, their students look, listen, and read, and are being educated (for good or ill) by the mass media. Charles S. Steinberg believes that the "mass media can serve as sources of emancipation and liberation from both extremism and ignorance." The reader may find this statement extreme but will be stimulated to examine more carefully the desirable potential of these powerful instruments.

An associate editor of Newsweek, John Culhane, issues a "Report Card on Sesame Street," an article on the visual medium which first appeared in The New York Times Magazine. Culhane reports on the success of the program through a series of interviews with leading educators, NET and commercial network television programing executives and producers, government officials, and members of the Sesame Street staff.

The problems of education, once viewed only from a distance by industry, are now shared jointly by many large corporations and educators. Avco, Ford, P&G, General Electric, and dozens of other corporate giants have already plunged into the education field. Many more are exploring entry. Many entered only to sell equipment. Others are interested in selling entire education programs. Still others "adopted" schools or entered into "partnership" arrangements involving an exchange of commitments by the school and the company. Elliot Carson presents an objective review of these ventures paying particular attention to the MIND program of CPC International, Inc. He underlines the difficulties faced by innovations but calls for further cooperation by education and industry if a more informed and productive manpower resource is to be developed in the years ahead.

Questions for Discussion and Further Study

1. Fred Hechinger suggests that only highly motivated, self-disciplined students can successfully pursue off-campus academic study. He believes most of us

need the day-to-day structure of on-campus classes to learn and mature. Do you agree? Have you personally experienced the interchange of ideas with your peers and with the faculty that Hechinger believes comes only when you work on-campus? If you have had difficulty in establishing these relationships, is it due to class size or work load for you and your instructors? What alternatives do you see that will offer the student population more opportunities for personal contact with the teacher?

2. An increasing number of college students are interrupting their schooling for "leaves." Some are taking a break between high school and their freshman year. The Carnegie Commission on Higher Education has reported that leaves are helpful to many students in gaining a better sense of direction. Yale's president, Kingman Brewster, Jr., suggests a similar approach to higher education with his "volunteer campus" in which the "excessive lock-step continuity of learning from age 5 to 25" would be eliminated. Do you see the benefits of such a program? Should it become part of the regular education process? Should there be a break between high school and college? Would a "sabbatical" midway through college make education more relevant to you?

3. Despite its daily audience of more than eight million children, "Sesame Street" is now under fire. Critics have charged that the programs may not be providing meaningful learning experiences. John Holt, in the Atlantic Monthly, has been prominent among the recent critics, raising specific questions about the value of teaching through adult explanations versus child participation. Do you share Holt's views? Can television match the experience of child–other children–teacher interaction? Is it possible to teach and entertain at the same time? Do you believe that the education profession has failed to keep pace with the television medium as a potential teaching tool? How would you employ television in your own classroom to supplement regular study techniques?

4. Industry and education seem to have much in common these days, and increased cooperation by the two in the years ahead seems certain. Is there a danger in such a move? Will the current drive toward consumerism be aborted or clouded over if the two are too closely linked? Will a cooperative effort make industry and the consumer more aware of the problems each faces? Will it increase the public's knowledge of the financial burdens the public must ultimately assume if we are to have clean air and clean water? Will the public be ready to accept it? Is this the real purpose behind industry's "courting" role as charged by several leading conservationists? What are your views on the steps which industry and education must take if they are to truly aid one another in the years ahead?

Selected References

Ardley, Robert. "Control of Population." *Life* (February 20, 1970), 48–58, 61.

"Banneker at Bay." *Newsweek* (March 15, 1971), 93, 95.

Bender, Marylin. "Universities' Corporate Voice." *The New York Times* (April 4, 1971), F1, F14.

Burger, Robert E. "Who Cares for the Aged?" *Saturday Review* (January 25, 1969), 14–17.
Cass, James. "The Board Room and the Campus." *Saturday Review* (March 20, 1971), 46–47.
Clurman, Michael. "How Shall We Finance Higher Education?" *The Public Interest* (Spring 1970), 98–110
Doan, Richard K. "Pop-ups." *TV Guide* (March 27, 1971), 36–37.
"Education: A Man's Touch." *Newsweek* (March 8, 1971), 76–77.
"Education: New Readings on Reading." *Time* (March 29, 1971), 59–60.
"Education: Recession Hits the Colleges." *Newsweek* (March 22, 1971), 63–64.
Epstein, Leon D. "State Authority and State Universities." *Daedalus* (Summer 1970), 700–712.
Farber, M. A. "The Child Is at the Center of Informal British Schools." *The New York Times* (April 2, 1971), 41–78.
Galbraith, John Kenneth. *The New Industrial State.* Boston: Houghton Mifflin Company, 1967.
Green, Thomas F. *Work, Leisure, and the American Schools.* New York: Random House, 1968.
"Growing Protest Against School Costs." *U.S. News & World Report* (October 20, 1969), 36–37.
Hammel, Lisa. "When a Poet Is in Charge of a Day Care Center." *The New York Times* (March 2, 1971), 26.
Handler, M S. "Program Like 'Sesame Street' Planned for College Freshman." *The New York Times* (March 18, 1971), 79.
Hechinger, Fred M. "Education: A TV Program to Help the Slow Readers." *The New York Times* (February 28, 1971), E9.
Hunter, Charlayne. "Division and Unrest on Rise in Harlem School Complex." *The New York Times* (March 23, 1971), 39, 41.
Klein, Frederick C., and Richard D. James. "School Squeeze: Many U.S. Cities Begin Laying Off Teachers Due to Money Pinch." *The Wall Street Journal* (March 8, 1971), 1, 7.
Kozol, Jonathan. "Look, This System Is Not Working." *The New York Times* (April 1, 1971), 41.
McLuhan, Marshall. *Understanding Media: The Extensions of Man.* New York: McGraw-Hill, 1964.
Pharis Jr., William L., John C. Walden and Lloyd E. Robinson. "Educational Decision Making." *Today's Education* (October 1969), 52–54.
Read, Herbert. "The Necessity of Art." *Saturday Review* (December 6, 1969), 24–27.
"Recession Hits the Campus: Fewer Jobs for Graduates." *U.S. News & World Report* (March 15, 1971), 22–23.
Rosenbaum, David E. "Financial Problems Plague Schools Across the Nation." *The New York Times* (March 15, 1971), 31.
Samuels, Gertrude. "How School Busing Works in One Town," *The New York Times Magazine* (September 27, 1970), 38–39, 44, 46, 48, 50, 52, 55, 58, 60, 62, 65.
"The Troubled American—A Special Report on the White Majority." *Newsweek* (October 6, 1969), 29–36, 45–52, 57–60, 65–68.
Weiss, Paul A. "Living Nature and the Knowledge Gap." *Saturday Review* (November 29, 1969), 19–22, 56.

Making Colleges Fit the Needs of the People

FRED M. HECHINGER

For better or for worse, America has become a credentials-minded society which often shuts out capable people from important and creative employment simply because they lack college degrees. This has led reform-minded educators to call for a new kind of schooling that would eliminate some of the artificial barriers to higher education.

One reason that thousands of Americans have not completed college is that, because of various circumstances, they have been unable or unwilling to follow a structured campus routine. They have seen the traditional requirements of class attendance and course schedules as serious obstacles. Some random examples:

1. A mother of two small children, whose college career was interrupted by marriage, wants to get a degree but her daily routine makes it difficult to cope with any regular schedule of courses.

2. A salesman, who passed up college for a job after high school, would like to "go back" for a degree but cannot afford to give up his job for the campus.

3. A young high school graduate would like more education but senses that campus life at this point would be frustrating and confining.

Two New Programs

In an attempt to accommodate such people, New York last week became the first state to promise two new avenues toward college graduation without attendance. With the joint support of the Carnegie Corporation and the Ford Foundation, the off-campus degree programs would: (1) offer a "Regents' degree" based on a student's knowledge, and (2) establish a nonresidential undergraduate college to administer independent study programs.

Regents' Degree Program. State Education Commissioner Ewald B. Nyquist announced that, with an $800,000 subsidy from the two foundations, New York will henceforth offer a degree based on an individual's demonstrated mastery of the work required for the equivalent of either a two-year (Associate degree) or four-year (Bachelor's degree) undergraduate education.

Under this concept, long accepted for high-school equivalency tests, the question would be what the student knows, rather than where and how he has learned it. Some candidates for the Regents' degree would, on their own, follow the traditional syllabus; others might learn through a combination of reading and practical experience.

The Board of Regents has always had the power to grant degrees. Shortly after World War II, when millions of veterans were looking for space on campuses, Vassar College told state education authorities that it would enroll some of the ex-G.I.'s but that its charter did not permit the granting of degrees to men. The commissioner told the women's college to educate the men and promised that the Regents would provide the degrees.

The expansion of the new external degree program is limited only by the speed with which academic leaders can agree on the content of the equivalency tests, and the ability of the College Entrance Examination Board and the Educational Testing Service, in Princeton, N.J., to design the tests for a full variety of majors. Initial plans call for tests leading to a bachelor of business administration and an associate of arts (general education) degree. The first Regents degrees are expected to be conferred by 1972.

Commissioner Nyquist said: "Some formal and official means must be found to assess and to recognize the attainments of people who are either wholly or partly self-educated."

Students may apply for information to the State Education Department in Albany, N.Y. Degree candidates will be aided by the Home Study Clearinghouse of the state's College Proficiency Examination Program which will suggest independent study materials. The candidates will be tested at designated centers, in written and oral examinations to be developed by faculty committees from existing universities.

Nonresidential Undergraduate College. Dr. Ernest L. Boyer, chancellor of the State University, announced that, with a grant of $1-million from the foundations, the new institution will be created to begin operations in the 1971-72 academic year. The college—it is reported to be planned near Saratoga and is likely to be named Empire State College—will have a president and a resident faculty, but no resident students. It will supervise its students by remote control—by helping them pursue individual programs through correspondence work, televised instruction, tapes and assigned reading.

Students will not, however, be without personal contact with academia. For an initial enrollment of between 500 and 1,000 students, two to four learning centers will be established. These are to be increased to 20 by the time the enrollment reaches 10,000. Before the end of the decade, it is estimated up to 40,000 students may be enrolled.

The centers will offer counseling and tutoring, will adminster tests, keep records and run the admissions program. But eventually all the State University's 70 university, college and community college campuses will cooperate so that there will be a base of contact within commuting distance from every potential student's home.

Tuition is expected to be relatively low since the capital expenditure will be minimal. Potential candidates may learn more about their eligibility by writing to Non-residential College, Box 6096, Albany, N.Y. 12206.

Reform-minded educators see the new programs as the ideal opportunity to question and discard many old assumptions.

Harold Howe 2nd, vice president of the Ford Foundation and former United States Commissioner of Education, said last week: "In the past, we have always asked the students to adjust to the institutions. Now, we will be able to adjust the institution so that it will fit the needs of the people."

Although new to the United States, the two programs follow patterns already tried abroad. External degrees have been administered on a worldwide basis by the University of London since 1836. They are vital to the dispersed population of Australia. University degrees via correspondence courses are big business in Russia. And last month, Britain launched its version of the nonresidential college, known as the Open University, near London. Indeed, a few American universities are also offering limited off-campus programs for credit.

Obstacles

The new roads toward graduation are not without their risks. While it is important that many of the old academic shibboleths be scuttled, the danger is that quality controls may go by the board at the same time. If that happens, the result is a flood of second-rate degrees.

College education, moreover, must do different things for different people. For the majority of college-aged youths, the intangible benefits of campus life—particularly the interchange of ideas with their peers and with the faculty—remain a vital part of their education and the process of maturing.

Only a highly motivated and self-disciplined student is able to pursue the goals of academic study entirely or largely on his own, without the help of the day-to-day requirements as a structure or crutch.

Despite these limitations, the exterial degree and the nonresidential college will be educational lifesavers for a substantial minority of all ages for whom the attendance requirement is an obstacle, often an insuperable one, rather than an aid. This is the first step toward the dream of many progressive educators—to make higher education more than an isolation ward for youth and to measure learning with more sophisticated yardsticks than credit units and hours of attendance.

A Timid Giant Grows Bolder

BETTYE M. CALDWELL

In recent months "day care"—an awkward and somewhat insulting term that few people used in either professional or personal vocabularies as recently as five years ago—has become a household term. Widely heralded by its advocates as a near panacea for many public ills, demanded by women as a civil right, offered as an employment lure by companies hiring large numbers of women, requested by city planners and boards of anti-poverty organizations, and recommended as an essential first step in reducing the large numbers of persons receiving welfare—how could the field have more status? But this pleasurable situation is very new.

Until recently, day care was but a poor relation of both social service and education. Neither field seemed disposed to embrace it fully or to recognize its legitimacy. But, historically speaking, day care has been much closer to the field of social welfare than to education. In fact, it is from the field of social service (child welfare, in particular) that day care received its definition as *care and protection* for children from *families with some type of social pathology*.

Early literature on day care generally took special pains to differentiate day care from education. For example, in the 1960 edition of the Child Welfare League of America's *Standards for Day Care Service* (which sets the standards for all agencies in the field), one finds day care delimited as follows:

> Day-care service has to be differentiated from the nursery school or kindergarten, and from extended school services and other programs for school-age children offered as part of elementary school systems. These have education of young children as their main purpose. The primary purpose of a day-care service is the care and protection of children. This purpose, the reasons for which a child and family may need it, and the responsibility shared with parents distinguish a day-care service from education programs.

At the time the day-care movement gained adherents and momentum in America we wanted to protect young children from such hazards as inadequate supervision, insufficient food, lack of shelter, and physical abuse. As today's knowledge about the importance of early experience for child development was only faintly limned in our consciousness at that time, it is not surprising that the prevailing concept of quality day care failed to recognize education as an integral part of "care and protection."

From *Saturday Review* (February 20, 1971), 47–49.

A second factor that undoubtedly kept the day-care field slightly outside the bounds of general respectability was the designation of the family with problems as the primary group for whom the service was appropriate. To quote once again from the Child Welfare League's influential *Standards:*

> Day care, as a child welfare service, is an expression of the community's concern for the welfare and protection of *children whose parents need help* in providing the care, protection, and experiences essential for their healthy development. [Emphasis added.]

The pamphlet goes on to identify such children as those whose mothers work, whose fathers might not be in the home, who are ill or have emotional problems, or who live in poor housing conditions. Certainly if families must see themselves as exemplifying social pathology in order to use day-care services, the field is not likely to be embraced by those who could give it status in the larger society.

Suddenly, however, day care is "in," and the groups that once neglected it now claim it as their own. Money that cannot be obtained for "early childhood education" may possibly be found for day care. Fundamental child welfare programs that cannot be launched independently can possibly be made available as riders on day-care appropriations. How do we explain the sudden popularity?

One reason that the number of day-care centers did not increase substantially for many years was the implicit fear that, if more such facilities were available, more mothers would be tempted to work outside the home. Yet more mothers *have* gone to work outside the home, including mothers with children younger than six. And these are generally conscientious mothers who want good child care during their working hours. Although relatives and neighbors still constitute by far the most frequently used child-care resources, more and more women have learned about day care, especially educational day care, and have come to request or demand such facilites for their own children. Furthermore, whereas national social policy formerly endorsed financial subsidies to keep mothers with young children at home (the Aid to Families with Dependent Children program), this policy is currently being re-examined. Training and employment of mothers are being urged, and quality day care is recognized as essential to this policy.

Employers also are turning to day-care programs as a way of attracting female workers and reducing absenteeism from the job. The best-known modern program exemplifying this is the day-care program operated in conjunction with the KLH factory in Cambridge, Massachusetts. Similar programs were funded under the Lanham Act during World War II, only to be discontinued at the end of the war when returning veterans dramatically changed the employment picture and displaced large numbers of women from their jobs.

Today, that pattern is being reversed by advocates of civil and personal rights for women. It has taken this group to strip day care of its social-pathology orientation. Stressing that personal fulfillment is a right to be shared by men and women alike and that child care is not the only valid avenue through which women may gain fulfillment, proponents of the Women's Liberation movement have demanded quality day care as a means to that personal fulfillment. At the 1970 White House Conference on Children last December, delegates representing various women's groups were among the most vocal in their demands that child care be made available around the clock throughout the year for all who want it, not just for indigent or minority groups. Such delegates also vehemently urged that federally supported day care be completely divorced from public assistance—thus officially removing the taint of social pathology from day-care services.

Despite the importance of these developments, however, the most fundamental influence has been the steady flow of information about the importance of the early childhood years. Evidence has gradually accumulated that certain kinds of experiences during the early years greatly influence how a child grows up in this society. Although the data are based on only about five years of research, the results have filtered out from scientific laboratories to popular magazines and thence to parents of all social classes, and the result is that parents are clamoring for more such programs for their children. As many of these same parents need child care, the request is generally for day care rather than "early education" per se.

The professionals who give semantic shape to social trends have not been indifferent to the new demands and conceptual changes. In 1969, the Child Welfare League's *Standards* was revised:

> At present, a wide range of resources and facilities, including informal arrangements and organized programs under various auspices, is used for the care of children outside of their homes during some part of the day. These resources and facilities have been established to serve many different purposes. They place differing emphases, reflected in their programs and the children whom they serve, on the responsibility for *care, protection, child development, education, or treatment.*

This new statement recognizes that care and protection involve an inherent developmental and educational component. Day care can no more be separated from education than it can from welfare or health. In breaking away from the earlier narrow concept that artificially tried to separate the two patterns of service, the day-care movement in this current definition has now given itself a new charter.

In a second radical departure from the earlier concept, the new *Standards* suggests that day-care services may be offered more as a service to the mother than to the child. The pamphlet states:

> Day-care programs are promoted and used for purposes in which the interests of the child may be a secondary consideration. Day care is provided to allow mothers, particularly those who are unmarried, to complete their schooling or to train for new careers: to help financially dependent mothers attain self-support and to reduce public assistance expenditures; and to recruit women for, and retain them in, the labor force.

The league is not an organization that can lightly take the subordination of the needs of children, however, and the report goes on to caution:

> Under these circumstances, it is necessary to ensure that day care is in the best interests of the individual children, and that the daily experiences are of benefit to them, or at least not detrimental.

In a subsequent section of the new *Standards*, a third subtle but major conceptual shift is encountered. While the old *Standards* declared, "The primary purpose of a day-care service is the care and protection of children," the new version states, "The primary purpose of a day-care service is to *supplement* the care and protection that the child receives *from his parents* [emphasis added]." It seems as if the field were more willing to share the responsibility at this time, or else were more aware that care and protection for the young child attempted *in loco parentis* has little chance of providing much of either. The implication is that the family carries the major burden and the day-care service only supplements the family's endeavors.

The varied purposes of day care are reflected in a healthy diversity of programs. They include care provided by family members or baby-sitters, day-care centers operated as demonstration and research agencies, centers controlled by parents or offered as a public service by a church or secular organization or provided as a lure by industry, and centers run for profit by a private operator or as a franchise unit of a national corporation. Still relatively scarce are programs that involve a complete blending of day care with education.

The subtle changes in the day-care concept reflect a shift in orientation that is at once both honest and refreshing and yet just a little alarming. The new *Standards* has the audacity to suggest that day care is more than a noble service to the next generation, being in addition an important service and convenience for the present generation. The league is to be credited with recognizing the validity of that orientation. Day-care people *do* tend to get just a bit sugar-coated in talking about what the experience will do for the children—all the social, affective, and cognitive gains that will accrue as a result—that we tend to forget about the families of the children. And often, when we remember them, it has been in terms of concern with modifying their behavior in order to facilitate *our* goals for *their* children.

One of the reasons many persons have resisted day care on a large scale has been the fear that, no matter which generation it focused on, it would weaken the bonds between children and their families. This fear has been more presumptive than factual and has been built upon an irrational equation of day care with institutional care. Day care—daily separation followed by nightly reunion in the context of social relationships that permit a sense of identity to be formed—appears to have none of the socially toxic effects of prolonged institutional care, or even of temporary separations (such as hospitalization) during which family contacts might be terminated for a given time. My colleagues and I in Syracuse recently published data that demonstrated rather persuasively that two-and-a-half-year-olds who had been in day care since around one year of age were as attached to their mothers as were comparable control children who had never had such a day-care experience.

Whatever the source of the fear, it appears to be a strong one. And some of the parent groups advocating more day-care facilites are also reminding the professionals that they, the parents, have a right to share in the planning and decision-making. During the summer of 1970, a workshop was held in Airlie House, Virginia, to prepare a number of pamphlets that could be used as guides by inexperienced groups wishing to initiate and operate day-care programs. A set of principles was prepared that went considerably beyond the league's position in recognizing that day care could sometimes be structured to meet the needs of the parents. Although the document is not now in its final version, the early draft proposed that the primary focus of any day-care program should be the *individual child and his family*—not the child alone or the parents alone. Furthermore, day care was described as a program that could either bring parents and children together or else drive a wedge between them. The statement of principles supported the former goal and stressed that quality day care should never do anything to reduce the family's commitment and responsibility. One suggestion was to supply parents with the information needed to make informed judgments and then to have them participate fully in decisions about what would be desirable for their children in day care as well as in the home.

Thus day care, formerly an advocate for the child, then for the parent (especially the mother), seems now to speak for the family. The policy implications of these different orientations are profound and far-reaching.

Because of its importance in the lives of children, one can imagine day care becoming a bold instrument of social policy. In fact, day care has not made policy; it has followed along when policy has been made. It has grown somewhat haphazardly, changing its own definition every ten years or so. At present it does not know whether it should serve the child, the parent, or the family. It cannot make up its mind whether it is a service for families with social pathology or for all families, whether it should be limited to children from economically underprivileged families or be offered to all children, whether it wants to change children or preserve cultural styles from one generation to the next. It does not know where to obtain its official identity. This confusion can be seen in state licensing patterns. The welfare department handles licensing in thirty-six states, the health department in five, and some different agency or combination of agencies in the remainder. The department of education is the licensing body in only one state, although it shares the task with welfare in one other and makes recommendations in many.

Thus, it is precisely in this area of planning for our children, except in the grossest sense, that we are most timid in this country. With our tradition of valuing rugged individualism, we have been reluctant to say much about the kinds of children we want. Do we want obedient children? Happy children? Adaptive children? Children who remain faithful to the values of their families? Militant children? Bright children? Group-oriented children? Woodstock and Maypole youth or Peace Corps youth? Eventual adults who can slip from one type to another?

Professor Urie Bronfenbrenner has commented on the extent to which child rearing in the U.S.S.R. has a clear objective to train children as responsible citizens of the Soviet state, in contrast to the lack of objectives and belief in autonomy in the U.S. In our concern for individuality we occasionally find license for evasion of the responsibility for guidance.

What the day-care field needs in order to be a powerful instrument of social policy is a forum from which to advertise its potential and a willingness to proclaim its importance. To this author that forum ought to be public education—albeit education defined more flexibly and comprehensively than it is today. Actually there is little justification for a conceptual separation between public education and public day care, for most schools are "day schools" and represent "day education" with or without the supportive family services generally offered under the rubric of day care. The significant difference, however, is that day care generally enters the lives of chidren at an earlier age, and, as infant day care becomes more respectable, the age of entry will become even lower. Any experience that enters the lives of children at a time when they are impressionable, when basic patterns of expressing, thinking, feeling, and problem-solving are being developed and value systems are being assimilated, has no need to feel apologetic.

The suggestion that day care find a forum in education may sound like a partisan recommendation. But I am talking more about a conceptual model for program design than about professional auspices for program operation. This orientation need not close out any of the diverse models now being tried. Essentially the same suggestion has been made by others, including Florence Ruderman in her book *Child Care and Working Mothers:*

> Day care, regardless of the auspices under which it is offered, should be developed as a child-care program: a program directed to optimum social and psychological health of the young child whose mother cannot care for him for some part of the day. . . . But a given family's need for social casework or other forms of help should no more define day care, nor determine eligibility for it, than the existence of social service departments in schools and hospitals now defines these facilities as social work services. For organized child-care service in this country to develop and meet adequately a growing social need, it must be recognized as a positive social institution and enabled to stand in its own right as an essential child-care program.

The challenge becomes one of having comprehensive child care embraced as a legitimate endeavor of that behemoth of public policy, public education, without having it consumed in the fire of an encrusted bureaucracy and without any loss of concern for "care and protection." Public education would do well to stop and reflect occasionally that one of its concerns should be with the care and protection of the children and youth who come within its sphere of influence!

At this moment in history, when we are on the threshold of embarking on a nationwide program of social intervention offered through comprehensive child care, we let ourselves prattle about such things as cost per child, physical facilities, or even community control. And when we begin to think big about what kinds of children we want to have in the next generation, about which human characteristics will stand them in good stead in a world changing so rapidly, we fall back on generalities such as care and protection. Yet any social institution that can shape behavior and help instill values and competencies and life-styles should also shape policy. Early child care is a powerful instrument for influencing patterns of development and the quality of life for children and adults. Because of its power, those who give it direction must not think or act with timidity.

Oasis in East Harlem

JONATHAN BLACK

In the basement of the East Harlem storefront, a dozen four-year-olds are squirming through tunnels, crawling up bunk ladders, and swinging merrily from a suspended automobile tire. There is a delighted squeal, and two children crash down an inclined plane and plop onto a waiting car seat. More giggles and squeals as two more children disappear into a tree-house construction a few feet off the floor.

Roslyn Weiner, director of the nursery, leans against one of the inviting architectural shapes. "We built all this for six hundred dollars' worth of lumber," she beams. "But wait till the Division of Day Care gets a look at it. They'll have a fit. There's no item for lumber in their budget. There's no provision for building stuff like this. They'll tell us it's a health hazard, children get splinters, and we'll have to watch our funding."

A face pokes in the door and announces that upstairs a group of fourth-graders from the neighboring elementary school are about to put on a play about Martin Luther King. Little bodies spill out of the woodwork, and there is a swarm of clapping four-year-olds trooping up the stairs, dropping into a semicircle of chairs around a small platform.

"Tomorrow is Martin Luther King's birthday," one of the fourth-graders explains, "so we're doing a play. First Yvette will show a picture." Yvette climbs up on the platform and holds up a picture of Dr. King. All eyes are glued on the picture. There isn't a peep. "Now Larry will read a little story about Martin Luther King." Larry reads the story to an enthralled silence. "Now here are some paintings our class did." No one is wondering what happened to lunch or his dump truck. "And now we'll all sing 'We Shall Overcome.' " And when it's all over, there is giddy applause, applause that might have greeted Artur Rubinstein at Carnegie Hall.

As the fourth-graders put on their coats to leave, the nursery children are pouncing toward lunch tables, although no one has checked to see if it is "lunch time." Some time later, someone turns out the lights, and the kids begin to crumple up on mats and cots scattered around the long room. In the classroom next door, the lights are on because the teacher has decided his children are not really that tired.

"At most schools and day-care centers," says Miss Weiner, "rest time means 'Relax or I'll kill you!' You're a good teacher if all your children rest. You're a very good teacher if they sleep. Then the teacher gets a break. But here we work when the lights are out. You can't divorce the office from the kids."

Yes, there is some magic afoot here, a most unlikely place, too—a day-care center in East Harlem. A place where mothers are supposed to deposit their kids for half the day while they run off to work. A place where children are trained to be quiet, clean, and orderly.

Some of that magic is undoubtedly due to Roslyn Weiner. She is one of those teachers who wail and rail against the Establishment and institutions and bureaucracies, but she spends most of her energy in creating an eye-opening alternative. How does she survive? She survives because she is part of the East Harlem Block School Day Care Center, which is part of the East Harlem Block Schools (EHBS), a cluster of schools run and controlled entirely by parents.

"I can say anything I want here," says one mother, chatting with Weiner. "I ask questions, make suggestions. I feel free. A nursery should be like your own home. I feel like these children are all my own children. I'm a mother or a sister or a friend, not a 'professional.' These kids aren't afraid to come and sit in my lap. They feel comfortable, and I feel comfortable."

Parent control of education is a topic of trauma in New York City. It conjures up bitter memories. The calamitous failure of community control of schools, even on a limited experimental basis, left a raw wound in this city's public school system. The 1968 teachers strike pitted teachers against parents, children against teachers, and pro-UFT teachers against anti-UFT teachers. The scars of that strike remain. The hope for an education that could bridge the gap between a community and its schools was killed. The hope that schools might grow into something new and exciting, might transcend the suffocating bureaucracies and the deadly polarities of militance, seemingly had been quashed.

But now there are signs that community control of education is neither forgotten nor dead. There are signs that a small number of day-care centers are opening a new frontier, a frontier in which parents can join in the education and destinies of their children. The EHBS centers are such a frontier.

The struggle out of the wilderness will not be easy. The first obstacles have been the inhibiting history of day care itself, and an aged perspective that continues to view day care as glorified baby-sitting, as a custodial service. A mother must work. A mother drops off her child. The child is cared for. The child is kept out of trouble for eight hours. The mother returns, and the child returns to the home. Even as early-childhood professionals have begun to explore the learning potential of those eight hours, they have tended to view them *in vacuo* and have ignored the umbilical ties connecting both school and home. "There can be no real education of children without the family," says Dorothy Pittman, who heads the West 80th Street Day Care Center, another of New York's parent-run centers. "Day care means *caring*, not custody. And caring means home and family."

In poor neighborhoods, in communities of the ghetto, such disregard is all the more tragic and all the more pernicious. "Day care in the traditional sense means separating children from parents," says Weiner. "It means helping and learning in spite of parents. It forces the child into a choice between home and school."

The preschool years are crucial, and the responsibility of day care great: "We fail to recognize the impact of the day-care centers themselves," says another critic, "their impact in reinforcing or even creating destructuve attitudes in poor children. We also do not see that the centers, by ignoring or disdaining the children's culture, family, and community, fail to utilize the most appropriate source in intellectual stimulation in the children's lives."

There is another obstacle to be faced: the Division of Day Care of New York City's Department of Social Services (DOSS), which has had the task of overseeing most city-funded day-care services. DOSS drives progressive-minded people crazy. Over the years, it has become a warehouse of sluggish bureaucrats, close-minded traditionalists, and all those persons committed to day care as a baby-sitting charity service, run by respectable churches and settlement houses for the welfare of the poor and less fortunate. A memorandum from the West 80th Street Center (which was running five years before it finally received funding from DOSS) is not atypical: "In addition to its dictatorial bent and its profound dullness, the division can count as liabilities its incompetence and unresponsiveness. It lacks the number and kind of personnel needed to deal with the rising demands for early-childhood services. Its very style and tradition prevent it from working with the many community organizations that now want to run creative and educational day-care centers."

The day-care Establishment has always been enthusiastic over embracing its own kind, but squeamish at the prospect of day care initiated by unsanctioned parent-community groups. That middle-class, paternalist bias was not crucial in the early years of day care, but with the recent ground swell of community activism the situation has begun to border on the untenable. Day-care centers, set up and run by a variety of small community groups, have enormous difficulty in catching the eye of DOSS, and the community people responsible for the centers turn increasingly bitter.

"There's such a fear of parent involvement," says Weiner. And no wonder. When things aren't going well, angry parents have a nasty habit of showing up in the office of Jule Sugarman, head of New York's Human Resources Administration, sitting down, asking embarrassing, impatient questions, and demanding immediate answers. Parents may have very little insight into the ordeals and intricacies of city bureaucracy, but they know when their children are getting a lousy education. Recently, they've been discovering that a lousy education can begin in the preschool years—it doesn't have to wait until first grade. In fact, by first grade, some children are already irretrievably lost. Consequently, there has been mounting concern among parents that day care be more relevant to their children's lives, and there has been mounting apprehension within the day-care Establishment that parents are becoming a bit too intrusive.

In fact, the conflict is not drawn along such simple lines. Dissatisfaction with New York's day-care programing has come from all quarters, from outraged parents as well as frustrated professionals. Until recently the administration of early-childhood programs was divided among half a dozen agencies and organizations in New York, making for hopeless confusion and overlapping services. The division between funding and licensing created more chaos. The Division of Social Services, for instance, is responsible for the funding of all its centers, but each center must first be licensed by the Department of Health. Twenty-five years ago, such a dichotomy made some sense; today, it is simply another barrier to beginning a day-care center. Not only are the health standards—regarding everything from facilities to staffing qualifications—rigid and antiquated, but they often lead into an absurd circle. You have an unqualified staff, so you can't get licensed, so you can't get funded; and you can't get a qualified staff because you can't afford to pay without funding.

Even such Lewis Carroll logic might have been tolerated as long as day care remained a relatively small phenomenon. But day care is beginning to expand at breakneck speed, and the potential for its expansion is enormous. Out of a total of 825,000 children under the age of six in New York City, something fewer than 10,000 are actually in day-care center programs. DOSS waiting lists alone include 8,000 children. (The figure for all early-childhood-type programs is closer to 50,000 enrollment, still only 7 per cent of all preschool children.)

In March 1970, a beginning was made. Mayor John V. Lindsay appointed a twenty-one-member task force to examine early-childhood services in the city, and hopefully to create some machinery for incorporating the burgeoning day-care movement. Four months later, the task force released its report, *The Children Are Waiting.* The general thrust of the report was to cut away bureaucracy, to consolidate existing agencies under one roof (the Department of Early Childhood Services), to facilitate licensing, to facilitate funding (an "interim" funding program was created to help new centers get on their feet), to loosen up staff qualifications, and to involve a broader spectrum of persons in the work of day care. Among its ten major goals, the task force recommended "strong parent involvement in all early-childhood centers."

It is too early to evaluate the impact of the report. It is too early to tell if some of the report's progressive reforms will mean a real shake-up in the operation of day-care programs or whether it is just another juggling of power on paper. Already, however, members of the community day-care centers, encouraged by the report, have stormed the Human Resources Administration, demanding that the city recognize their existence and provide funding.

As parents and community become more and more intimately involved in the running of day-care centers, there is sure to be opposition. The older, traditionally oriented day-care paternalists fear the possibility of a new uniformed tyranny, a tyranny of parents without knowledge, expertise, or qualifications. There is always talk of qualifications, of *certain things* you have to know, no matter how much you *care.* There is argument that parents have no broad perspective, that they have no experience in day care, that their involvement is limited to the preschool span of their children. And there are counter-arguments—that parents have the *best* knowledge, that day care is *family* education, that a parent's interest is more permanent and does not exclude professional help and expertise. Nancy Stewart, president of the Day Care Council, a private federation of day-care groups in New York City, hopes the debate does not become polarized. She emphasizes "cooperation" and a "team approach."

"Up to two years ago," explains Stewart, "no parents could serve on the board of directors of day-care centers. The East Harlem Block Schools became the first exception, but the door is not yet open. We very much hope we can combine professional expertise with the darling little neighborhood mothers."

But all the nice talk and all the visions of cooperation and all the task force reports have yet to transform the attitude of the Division of Day Care toward EHBS or similar centers. Dorothy Stoneman, executive director of EHBS, bursts into the nursery after a downtown meeting. "I absolutely give up!" she cries. "There is no talking with those people. We just have to go our separate ways."

In a recent letter to Sugarman, Stoneman again underlined her exasperation with the rigidity of the city's day-care guidelines. "Now while everyone in the city is talking about the 'educational component' and the 'social services component' and the 'health component' and the 'community liaison component,' in our [EHBS] centers all of these components continue to depend on the sheer stamina and determination of overworked staff and parents. . . . The patience of the people here has run out. We no longer trust that our participation in committees designed to create changes through discussion and compromise is sufficient to bring about the necessary changes." Included in her letter are requests for thirteen specific budget items, such as equipment, a professional health coordinator, and money for family workers. Twelve of those items are included in the task force's recommendations.

It is a slow business. At EHBS, it is a fight to survive. In numberless other communities, it is a fight to be born. The fate of EHBS may well chart the future of New York's day-care programing. There are exciting things going on at EHBS. There are new ideas flying around. There are new people. There is a light and a glow. And there is that extraordinary phenomenon of parents joining in the education of their children, pushing that education forward, and beginning to dissolve the senseless barriers that divide a community from its schools.

Such innovation will never be absorbed smoothly into the creaking order of things. But if there is struggle ahead, there is also new room for hope. In the middle of a New York ghetto, a bunch of parents are running a day-care center, and it is an oasis of smiles and learning. It is some kind of a frontier.

Mass Media and the Educator

CHARLES S. STEINBERG

The development of such powerful mass media as the press, radio and television by which millions of persons can receive communications content simultaneously and over widely dispersed areas has resulted in a social and educational revolution as far-reaching as the Industrial Revolution of the Nineteenth Century. The reach and potential of mass media pose critical questions and alternatives for education from the elementary level through the graduate school and into broad areas of adult education.

The revolution created by mass media is not exclusively educational. It is ecomonic in that it involves millions of dollars in advertising and consumer spending. It is political, since candidates for public office have largely by-passed the whistle-stop campaign in favor of mass press conferences and televised confrontations that bring issues before the voter with visual directness and immediacy.

But, since the ultimate effect of the media of mass communication is educational, cultural historians are likely to assess the significance of mass media in terms of their educational values. The historian, however, will encounter formidable difficulties in finding proper perspectives for such an assessment. Cultural historians seek information largely in the behavior and attitudes of the educated stratum of society, and the educators, in large measure, have tended to slough off the presence of such a mass medium as television in the hope that, by denigration or neglect, it will cease to be as popular as it is. The educated groups—particularly the growing number of holders of graduate degrees and the university teachers—have developed a curiously myopic and distorted view of the educational and social effects of the media of communication. Despite the fact that a major part of our society is virtually inundated by the flow of mass communication, far too many educators choose to demean and ignore it as unworthy of serious attention or thought. And this attitude persists, despite the fact that educational surveys indicate that students

From *The Educational Forum,* (May 1965), 29:393–398. Copyright: Kappa Delta Pi, An Honor Society in Education. Reprinted by permission.

spend perhaps as much time watching television as they devote to their studies.

Mass media have been the subject of abysmal neglect or misunderstanding by the educator. Studies on the uses of television or radio in elementary and secondary education have not truly come to grips either with the potential or the limitations of these media, and have not gone beyond their superficial uses as audio-visual aids. There has been no genuinely comprehensive study, for example, of the effects of mass communication in the area of the social studies. Yet it is the social studies expert who is frequently called upon to render judgment about the social effect of mass media before this committee or that convention.

These judgments are curiously ambivalent. Too many educators feel constrained to discuss mass media without seeking an actual confrontation with them. Unfortunately, since mass media are not physical sciences but social phenomena, questions involving their meaning and influence cannot be discussed abstractly. Only by trial and error of exposure can one discover their assets and their liabilities. And, by trial and error, one can determine what useful purposes they may serve in a mass society. In order to appraise mass media, educators must "suffer" exposure to them, however outrageous their slings and arrows may be.

For some curiously perverse reason, the learned society—particularly sociologists, whose domain would seem to include a proprietary interest in mass communication—have chosen largely either to ignore mass media or to deliver uncritical judgments about them. Because of this neglect, critical evaluations of mass media by educators cannot be taken seriously, because there is too little evidence that such analysis stems from direct experience. A large percentage of educators attending a convention of the New Jersey State Federation of District Boards of Education were asked about their television viewing habits and choices. The vast majority of those who deplored the paucity of "good" programs admitted ignorance when asked whether they were aware of any of the following presentations: Leonard Bernstein and the New York Philharmonic, Hamlet, Robert Frost reading his poetry, the Boston Symphony, reports on integration, on the population explosion, on birth control and other programs with a social or cultural orientation.

This ignorance of the content of mass media is echoed at other educational conclaves. For the plain fact is that those who are most articulately critical of the effects of mass media are least exposed to these influences, or simply not exposed at all. Those educators who score the mass communicators for dereliction of responsibility either pay scant attention to the mass media, or do not behave as their public pronouncements indicate. Surveys have shown that people simply do not read what they say they would like to read, nor do they watch what they say they would like to watch. The difference in television viewing habits between those who have had a college education and those who have not gone beyond the high school is only about one percent! Even those who have gone to graduate schools devote more than 50% of their viewing time to entertainment programs, yet in response to surveys they indicate that television does not offer sufficient public affairs or news.

The pattern is much the same among teachers of courses in the mass media who devote more time to abstract research based on secondary sources than to direct exposure to the daily experience of mass communication over the airwaves or in the press or magazines.

The curiously inverted intellectual snobbery toward mass media is not only evident at the academic meeting. It is equally prevalent among teachers of the humanities who deliver devastating manifestos before the P.T.A. and other such similar organizations. Indeed, the National Parent Teacher publication has illustrated how slipshod this attitude can be by reviewing television programs which were either no longer on the air or by attributing them to the wrong channel. To educators who do not watch them, mass media are responsible for a variety of social ills from juvenile delinquency to lack of reading readiness.

If mass media are remote phenomena to educators, they are close to the people. The invention of the printing press, as far reaching as its consequences have been, did not exert immediate influence on its society, since few could read or write. But television and the movies are within arm's reach of the wise and the ignorant, the learned and the illiterate. The effects of the mass media are too far-reaching to be ignored. It is high time the learned society recognized this fact and undertook a realistic appraisal of the enormous significance of mass communication in the daily existence of almost everyone within reach of a radio, a television set, a theater magazine or a newspaper. This cannot be accomplished by reading someone else's research. It can only come from exposure.

Fortunately, there are stirrings of discontent with blanket pronouncements on the effects of mass media. Margaret Mead, the distinguished anthropologist, points out that "television, with the strongest immediate appeal to the child and adolescent viewer becomes–because more potent–more likely to be blamed for anything that is wrong in children's and adolescents' adjustment to contemporary society." And some other writers and researchers have concluded that there are other influences and other voices in society which have some relevance to people's behavior patterns–the family situation being a significant one. Mrs. Clifford M. Jenkins, former president of the National Congress of Parents and Teachers, told the United Press International that "parents have a strong responsibility in the control of what children are seeing on their home screens . . . television can't be a baby sitter." Further evidence that conclusions not based on exposure are meaningless is offered by a study of over four thousand British school children. The research by Hilde T. Himmelweit, A.N. Oppenheim, and Pamela Vince indicates that "television is used by different children in different ways." In other words, no conclusion on the effect of mass media is justified without paying heed to such determining factors as age, home, environment, and individual personality differences. Dr. Benjamin Spock, a medical authority widely accepted by parents, admonishes that parents need to keep track of what their children are viewing or reading. "They shouldn't be hesitant in forbidding programs or books which they consider definitely incompatible with the family's needs."

Mass media need the appraisal and criticism of educators. But criticism in the abstract cannot be taken seriously unless it is based on particular experience. The educator who refuses to expose himself to the infinite variety of mass media is like the scholar who refuses to read a best-seller because everyone is reading it. He is hard-pressed to reconcile popularity and mass approval with quality. Carried to its ultimate consequences, such an attitude would not only prove abortive to the developing potential of mass media, but would also restrict popular education to a select few. It would insist that the content of mass media meets only the needs of the minority, while depriving the vast majority of the broad spectrum of education, entertainment, and information which a mass medium like television offers the public.

In a society where scientific method has assumed a quasi-religious significance, even for humanists and social scientists, such an unscientific viewpoint is deplorable. In his failure to confront mass media with the same scientific curiousity as he brings to other disciplines, the educator provides a striking illustration of the other-directed man of David Riesman's "The Lonely Crowd." Riesman's other-directed individual was happier to accept the judgments and values of the peer group, rather than to wrestle with opinions of his own. By abdicating independence of thought and action, the other-directed man achieves acceptance by the peer group without struggle or tension. Hence, the educator finds it easier to fall into the trap of unsubstantiated criticism of the effects of mass media, without a genuine effort to document criticism by experience.

In academic life, too, approbation from the peer group frequently provides a more satisfactory adjustment to life's stresses and strains than the hard search for scientific evidence through the crucible of direct experience. As a result, educators tend to accept uncritically the assumption that the welter of words and pictures emitted by mass media accounts for a flat, inert, stereotyped mass society. The flaw in this hypothesis is that it is false. The truth is that mass media tend to reflect society far more than they influence it. John Dewey's conviction that there was a constant interaction between the organism and its environment is no better illustrated than in the interaction between mass media and mass society. Each counterbalances the other. The public influences media content at least as much, and probably more, than it is subject to the influence of mass media. And it is strikingly evident that other factors, particularly the school, make a formidable contribution to public preference and taste. Not a sociologist, but a physician and a psychologist have turned up evidence that "TV is no bogeyman after all." Doctors Frances Ilg and Louise Ames, of the famed Gesell Institute, confirm a study by Josette Frank, of the Child Study Association of America, indicating that "there was not the expected retardation of school work or reading, damage to eyesight, or serious interference with sleep." Indeed, TV gets many pre-schoolers off to a fast start.

Scholars are in a unique position to evaluate the effects of mass media. They have the training and the technique. What they must do is to devote to mass media the same quality of research which they devote to other disciplines. But the temptation to reject all popular mass entertainment as shoddy is irresistible to the scholar. It is easier to hold mass media culpable for juvenile delinquency than to weigh the effects of such media against the effects of such basic institutions as the home, the school, and the religious institution in the community.

The consequences of this studied disengagement from mass media adds up to a distinct loss to the rest of society. The vast majority is deprived of any serious body of opinion, thought out and arrived at on the basis of experiment, of the limitations and the true potential of mass communication. Teachers who refuse to recognize the influence of mass media in the lives of their students turn away from a confrontation with reality. How much wiser would the educator be if, like the Medieval scholar, he recognized that education is a community matter, not a private affair. By careful study of programs on the air and selection of those newspapers and magazines which have relevance both to school and to society, the educator can provide a criterion of value for students, for mass communicators, and for the whole of society. What is desperately needed is involvement, not neglect, of mass media by the educator and others of the intellectual minority. The great problem resulting from the invention of the printing press was not that it provided literacy for the majority, but that it reached only the very select few who could read and write. The situation is precisely different today. Mass media reach the many, but are neglected by the few.

A balanced appraisal of mass media, rendered by interested educators, would recognize that media content ranges in quality from excellent, to fair, to inferior. Like the publishers' booklists, there is a variety of choice. The newspaper and magazine offer similar gradations in quality, ranging from the pundit on the editorial page to the creator of the daily cartoon narrative. The magazine world ranges from relatively low circulation semi-scholarly publications, designed for the scholar, all the way down the scale to the tawdriest of action-sex-adventure publications. Yet, publishers of books and magazines recognize that audience tastes and needs vary.

For those educators who will evaluate them with taste and discrimination, the mass media have much to offer and leave much to be desired. Certainly, they serve a vital function in the educational process of a democracy. By bringing the world of reality into the home and the school, through exposure of vital social and political issues, mass communication becomes a stimulus to the development of intelligent opinions and attitudes on these very issues. Through the presentation of drama and music, television and radio contribute to the main stream of our contemporary culture. Through coverage of current events, newspapers, radio and television contribute significantly to the information of our citizenry.

What can the educator do to bring about a more discerning attitude toward mass media? It is clear that educators who are exposed to mass media are in a unique position to make valid value judgments. The most constructive step toward an improvement in mass communication content is encouragement based upon involvement. The educator must abandon the dual bandwagon of uncritical acceptance and critical ignorance and render praise for what in his own judgment and from his own experience is meritorious. Let him discover that, in the area of mass media, there is more demand for good books, great music and fine plays than at any other time in our history. There is also much that can stand improvement. And distinctions based on quality can result only from direct experience, not from secondary sources.

Let the educated man be less sensitized to the verdict of his peers and more courageous in his own opinions based on direct experience. And let the educated man act less in a climate of ignorance and more out of a knowledge of the many positive contributions which mass media make to a mass society.

Given proper encouragement, mass media can serve as sources of emancipation and liberation from both extremism and ignorance. They can become energizing sources toward the development of independent judgment and responsibility. And the educator can provide the dual stimulus of greater public discernment in the choice of communication content and greater responsibility for that content on the part of the communicator. In this way, the educator contributes significantly toward responsible mass communication which, in the long run, will provide a better press and a superior television service to the American people.

Report Card on Sesame Street

JOHN CULHANE

From Watts to Westchester County, one recent Monday morning, preschoolers were watching a "Batman" cartoon on television. Batman and Robin were *up* in a tall building watching a crook over in the next building *through* open windows in their room and his. The problem perplexing the dynamic duo was how to get *around* the thugs who were guarding the crook's hideout. Readers of *The Gotham City Times Magazine* can presumably picture this scene because of our familiarity with the relational concepts "up," "through" and "around." But preschoolers often do not understand these terms unless they can see them demonstrated—which is exactly what the Caped Crusader and Boy Wonder did next:

> Robin: Gee, Batman—if we could only get that guy without having to go through the guard.
>
> Batman (*producing a bat boomerang from beneath his cape*): I believe this will assist us in apprehending that arch criminal, Robin. I'll tie this rope around the bat boomerang—like this. . . . Up in the air it goes and

From *The New York Times Magazine* (May 24, 1970), 34, 35, 50, 52, 54, 57, 60, 62, 65, 67, 70, 71.

through that open window. *(The bat boomerang sails from one building to the other, makes a midair turn inside the crook's hideout and hooks the archcriminal so that Batman can haul him in.)*

Robin: Holy vocabulary, Batman! You got him!

Batman: Understanding the meaning of "up," "through," and "around" always leads us in the right direction, Robin.

That 33-second bit of "Batman" animation is part of "Sesame Street," the experimental educational series for preschoolers that ends its first season on May 29. Specifically designed to improve the language, numerical and reasoning skills of children between the ages of 3 and 5, this offering of the Children's Television Workshop of National Educational Television (NET) has proved to be such rollicking entertainment that commercial stations are running it, too. In New York, the hour-long show is seen on five channels, six times a day in all, and the latest Nielsen ratings estimate that almost half of the 12 million preschoolers in the nation watch it on 200 public and commercial stations from coast to coast. In Chicago, showing on a public TV station, it topped such formidable competition for daytime viewing as the "Beverly Hillbillies," "Concentration," a movie and an exercise show—as Variety said: "Probably the first time anywhere that an educational television station has topped the commercial competition."

So well known are the residents of Sesame Street that when lanky, beaky Peter Janssen resigned as Newsweek's education editor recently to join NET, almost everyone at his farewell party got the joke when it was announced that he had been signed to play Big Bird. And on Alcatraz Island out in San Francisco Bay, where 42 Indian preschoolers watch the show on a set donated by the community utilization representative of the Children's Television Workshop, the rocky road to their nursery school bears the sign: "Pathway to Sesame Street." In short, nearly everyone likes the show. Still, if this educational experiment were to get a report card at the end of its first season what academic grades would it deserve?

Obviously, it gets high marks from the Government and the private foundations that jointly provided $8-million for its groundwork and first season, because they have recently pledged a fresh $6-million to cover the cost of producing and broadcasting a second season of 130 new shows. And clearly, the funding agencies have confidence in "Sesame Street's" ability to work on its own: the Children's Television Workshop will sever its ties with NET next season to become an independent corporation, with Mrs. Joan Ganz Cooney, this season's executive director, as president.

Also in the works is a second "Sesame"-type program, this one for grade-school children, aged 7 to 10, which should make its debut in the fall of 1971. "If these fresh attempts are as successful as 'Sesame Street' in capturing the attention and enthusiasm of the young people of America," said James E. Allen, United States Commissioner of Education, "our national campaign to assure by the end of the nineteen-seventies that no boy or girl will leave school without the skill and the desire to read to the utmost of his capacity will be off to a great start." What teacher ever wrote anything more laudatory on a report card?

And what prize pupil ever did better on Awards Day than "Sesame Street," which received television's coveted George Foster Peabody Award last month for "meritorious service to broadcasting"? The citation from the Henry W. Grady School of Journalism of the University of Georgia, which administers the awards, praises the series for demonstrating "what thoughtful, creative educators are doing for tomorrow's leadership."

Mrs. Cooney grades her own show A for appeal and entertainment value and A for teaching letters—but B for teaching numbers. "We set our sights too low," she explained. "We taught children to count from 1 to 10—we could at least have taught them to count from 1 to 20. Next year, we're going to do that and sets and simple addition and subtraction besides." In teaching reasoning skills, she gives the show a low B. "Buddy and Jim [the Laurel and Hardy of the show: adults functioning the way 3-year-olds do] are about the only thing we had that tried to get at reasoning and problem solving, and yet that was one of our principal goals."

But the final test has not yet been mentioned: the disadvantaged child. While the agencies that funded "Sesame Street" wanted to find out how television could give some advance help to all children not yet old enough for school, they particularly wanted to reach those children in the big city ghettos, Indian reservations and Appalachian enclaves who start school not knowing their letters and numbers like middle-class kids, and who get discouraged and lag farther and farther behind as they are shunted from one grade to the next. Have these children been reached? To answer that, one must first see "Sesame Street" as a child sees it.

An adult watching the entire show the day that Batman threw the concept-teaching boomerang would have seen "Sesame Street" as a series of little lessons in symbolic representation, cognitive organization, reasoning, problem solving, and various aspects of the child's world. Yet, if the show was to be successful, the child would see the same bits as a bunch of quick, funny and entertaining moments—like a collection of the catchy commercials that most young children chant around the house. Even the show's theme song is part of the experiment:

> Sunny day, keeping the clouds away
> On my way to where the air is sweet,
> Can you tell me how to get,
> How to get to Sesame Street? . . .

Joe Raposo's melody is bouncy by design, because tests have shown that this kind of beat best attracts the attention of preschoolers. The words of the song are accompanied by quick shots of things preschoolers are interested in—shots of kids their age swinging on a jungle gym and following - the - leader through a field of grain; of a white girl riding a tricycle and a black boy sitting on a tractor; a big brother helping his sister down a slide; kids roller-skating, kids running; a seal wiggling his whiskers . . .

"Every element in 'Sesame Street' must say to every preschooler, 'This is for you,' " said Dr. Edward L. Palmer, the Workshop's 36-year-old research director.

Before joining the Workshop, he was involved in pioneering research in children's TV-watching habits as associate professor of research with the Oregon State System of Higher Education.

How does a 3-year-old child, wrestling with his first phrases, let Dr. Palmer know whether a segment of the show is for him? "The answers we're looking for come from what they indicate by their behavior while watching a segment," he explained. "We watch the children as they watch." For example, during "Sesame Street's" five preseason test shows, Dr. Palmer relied on a device he called a distractor. It was, in fact, a small screen set up next to a television set on which color slides were projected from time to time. If the child watching "Sesame Street" was easily distracted, it was a tip-off that the material being shown was not sufficiently absorbing.

"The children we used for our appeal studies were all poor children in day-care centers," said Mrs. Cooney, "but it turned out that all preschoolers have pretty much the same concerns—and they're all conditioned by the same television shows: 'Batman,' 'Get Smart,' 'Laugh-In.' "

On the television, the theme song fades away, and Sesame Street itself fades in. It is actually a set on a television soundstage on Manhattan's West Side, but it could be any street in East Harlem. ("It looks real, except there's no litter," said one young visitor to the set—and the fact that his attention was immediately attracted by the ideal is the reason the litter is absent.) The viewer sees an aged brownstone, No. 123. If he's a regular viewer, he knows that Gordon and Susan and Bob live there. Gordon (Matt Robinson) and Susan (Loretta Long) are married and they are black. Gordon is a high-school science teacher. Bob (Bob McGrath) is also a high-school teacher and he is white. There is a front stoop from which they greet their friends and neighbors, who are integrated not only by race but—if you count live animals and even fantasy figures like Big Bird—by species. Big Bird is actually a man named Carroll Spinney wearing a bird costume with gorgeous yellow plumage.

On one side of the street are the famous Sesame Street garbage cans, lids tightly shut, including the can that is the home of Oscar the Grouch, one of Jim Henson's band of hand puppets, called Muppets. (Oscar is operated by Spinney when Spinney isn't being Big Bird.) A vacant lot separates 123 Sesame Street from the candy store owned by Mr. Hooper (Will Lee), an elderly white man. The folks on Sesame Street relate even to senior citizens.

Each show starts on this street, and is loosely tied together by a little running story about the people and creatures in the neighborhood. Today, Gordon is host: he'll introduce the various segments of the program's so-called "magazine format." Other days, Bob or Mr. Hooper will do the honors, or Susan will act as hostess. Each segment has a specific educational goal. These goals were set by research groups made up of educators, psychologists, advertising people, film makers and children's authors who met at five three-day seminars in the summer of 1968. For example, the Batman segment was actually called "Relational Concepts—Around/Up/Through" in the outline given the show's writers.

The show begins: the camera pans to the vacant lot, where the viewer sees

Gordon, sitting on a lawn chair, reading a newspaper. We see the headline: NURSE SHORTAGE CRITICAL." Today's running story has been introduced.

"Oh, hi," says Gordon, putting down the newspaper and looking into the camera. ". . . Today, the entire hour of 'Sesame Street' is coming to you through the courtesy of the letter L, the letter U, and the numbers 4 and 5, but most especially by this letter. . ." Gordon holds up a plastic letter Y and the camera zooms in on it. "You know what letter that is? The letter Y."

Each show is "sponsored" by different letters and numbers that the Workshop wants to teach, and, in the time-honored television tradition, must frequently pause for "messages" from its various sponsors. Naturally, repetition of the messages will cause the child to remember the letter M, for instance, just as it causes him to remember M&M, the chocolate-covered candies ("No Mess!").

Now the camera cuts to a commercial for the letter Y called "Yellow Yahoo"—listed in the script as a 1-minute 10-second film essay in symbolic representation. The screen shows a Y-shaped tree: "This is a letter, the letter Y," says a perky narrator. "You know how I know? It looks like the trunk of the tree where the Yellow Yahoos go—listen . . ."

"Yahoo," yells a voice.

"There's the Yahoo now," says the narrator, and he tells of the beautiful yellow bird in many words that begin with Y—which immediately appear on the screen: "When You ask him if his lunch was good, he says, 'Yes, quite Yummy' and then he Yawns . . ."

Fade-in: a frog Muppet named Kermit. "Today," says Kermit, "we are fortunate to have with us Professor Hastings, who is going to lecture on the letter Y. Professor."

Professor Hastings is also a Muppet, with a white walrus mustache and heavy-lidded Ping-Pong-ball eyes. He and the frog engage in a kind of "Who's on First?" bit to teach the letter Y. "Young man, what am I here to talk about?" asks the professor. "Y," says Kermit. "Because I forgot," answers Hastings.

Cut to Sesame Street again. Susan goes next door to Mr. Hooper's candy store to buy a magazine. But Mr. Hooper is closing early.

"Is something wrong?" Susan asks. (The outline told the writer to prepare a minute-and-a-half "Reasoning and Problem Solving" segment to illustrate "Problem Sensitivity—What's Wrong Here?" This is his illustration.)

"My sister Emily is sick again," answers Mr. Hooper. "We tried to get a nurse but they're all so busy, so I'm going to say with her for a while. She lives alone."

"Well, I could stay for you," offers Susan, "because, you know, I was a nurse before I got married to Gordon."

"Thank you, Susan, but she's expecting me," Mr. Hooper says. "I don't think it's too serious. . . ."

"Well, listen, if there's anything I can do, be sure and let me know. I'd be happy to go stay with her."

In addition to "Reasoning and Problem Solving," this brief vignette is intended to dramatize not only the concern of the good neighbor, but the idea that a woman's place is not necessarily in the home.

Next comes a counting film. This one teaches the number 4, so it shows four of many objects in syncopated rhythm—while little boys wait for the inevitable counting-film climax in which a waiter appears at the top of a flight of stairs carrying a tray holding four (or whatever) coconut-cream pies—then falls head-over-heels down the stairs.

"I don't like it," Mrs. Cooney says flatly of the pratfall finale. "Banana-peel humor is male and it's from age 4 on. Younger children—2-year-olds, say—think he's hurt." Then why does the guy stay? "The show, said Mrs. Cooney, "is definitely male-oriented."

"Sesame Street" is male-oriented for the same reason that the character of Gordon dominates the series. "This was done in order to upgrade the black male," said Mrs. Cooney. "We felt very strongly that it would be a good thing to show a black male who works and is strong and who is the force in the Sesame Street community, because the father is missing in so many slum homes."

Yet Gordon as *the* force in the Sesame Street community does not necessarily reflect the views of Mrs. Cooney. "I am a feminist, myself," said the executive director, who, though married, is childless. "Our society doesn't need more babies, we need more doctors." So she pushed for Susan, who is portrayed as also married but childless, to get a job outside the home. "We felt we had put her down a little in making Gordon so important," Mrs. Cooney said. "Susan was just the little woman in the kitchen. We talked about making her a doctor, but it didn't seem real, with them living where they live."

So the next scene in the continuing story of the people of Sesame Street has Susan discuss with her husband whether she should go back into nursing. "The reason we chose public-health nurse," said Mrs. Cooney, "was that the medical services in this country are going to need more and more people. Then, too, we wanted a job with a uniform that little girls could identify."

In the script, Susan wants Gordon to approve her intention to go down to the Public Health Department and renew her license, and Gordon approves. However, the dialogue is partly improvised; like many of "Sesame Street's" improvisational scenes, it is partly clumsy; and for that very reason, it is rather revealing. Susan tells Gordon that she wants to discuss whether or not she should go back to work, but no discussion actually takes place. "After all," she begins, "I'm a trained nurse and I just think they could use my services, and I was wondering what—how you felt about it, what you thought about it?" To this awkwardly phrased question, Gordon replies that he had spoken to her when she came back from Mr. Hooper's store, but she walked right by him without answering. Susan apologizes, explaining that the critical nursing shortage was on her mind. "If it bugs you that much, I'll tell you what," Gordon grumpily concludes: "Try it and see how it works out."

Neil Smith, who has been directing the first season but is now leaving to return to soap operas, says that he would have liked more time to rehearse the improvisational material. "The show has a soft underbelly," said Smith. "It's on five hours a week, so we have to turn out a lot of tape. Some things have to go in the can, not because they are the way I want to see them, but because we've got to produce a certain amount of tape each week." This scene is clearly a case in point: what chiefly comes through is the ambivalence of actor Matt Robinson as a person toward the situation on which he is being asked to improvise. Off screen, Robinson says he realizes that feminists want to use "Sesame Street" to upgrade the female; still, he says, many black Americans consider that the most important role black women can play at present is as ego supports for their husbands. The problem with the scene as played is that it gives the impression that Gordon is acquiescing to Susan's desire to go back to work ("If it bugs you that much . . ."), but doesn't really approve. The effect is hardly a contribution to building a strong male image. I felt that this scene, at least, should not have gone into the can until there was agreement on the effect "Sesame Street" wanted it to achieve.

The transition from this segment to the next is accomplished by Gordon as he watches Susan go off to the nurse's registry. "Well, she's happy now," he rather moodily tells a black child named Kwame and a white child named Ann. "And, speaking of happy people, take a look down there. . . ."

Down the street, Bob McGrath sings "Happiness Is" to another group of children in that gentle, quiet-voiced, nonthreatening Misterogers manner that is the staple of most television for middle-class preschoolers.

But immediately afterward, Oscar the Grouch raises the lid of his garbage can to sing his antihero's version ("Happiness is . . . sand in your sandwich, rocks in your sneakers . . .") and this acerbic touch, to a rock beat, is the kind of thing that keeps "Sesame Street" from getting too bland for the kid who loves "Laugh-In."

Since the relational concepts being taught this particular day include "up," there is now a film of the Muppets singing "Up, Up and Away" while doing a comedy turn in a beautiful balloon.

When the filmed musical number is finished, the camera focuses on the street again. Gordon gives a coffee can with both ends removed to a black boy named Chet and an Oriental girl named Mia and lets them demonstrate the meaning of "through" with their hands—which leads into the Batman film on "up," "through" and "around."

And so the show progresses, from street to segment and back again. Just before Susan returns to Sesame Street in her visiting nurse's uniform, bringing the internal story to a conclusion, the "Yellow Yahoo" cartoon and another Y commercial are repeated. Why? Watching in Chicago, Sarah Biggins, who was a Head Start teacher before she began to teach remedial reading in inner-city schools, knew immediately. "I can see that 'Sesame Street' is definitely geared to preschool because of its repetition," she said. "My nephew, who is 2 and a half, knows most of the numbers 1 to 10, and points them out. But the older kids can get a lot out of it because of the goldmine of creativity involved in the production. Man! Those guys sure know how to get to the young minds."

It is a talent they exercise cautiously. To teach the concept of roundness for example, a script called for the camera to show such round objects as a button, a coin, a pop-bottle top—"and the writer had written in the peace symbol," said Lutrello Horne, the studio producer. "I deleted the peace symbol and substituted something else." Horne touched the peace symbol on his own coat: "I wear that button, but it's not for this show. I couldn't see it as part of 'Sesame Street.' "

"Can you tell me how to get to Sesame Street?" ask the bright yellow buttons that have sprouted all over the land on preschoolers and graduate students alike. The story of how the creators of Sesame Street got there starts in February, 1966, at a dinner party that Joan Cooney gave in her Manhattan apartment. Among the guests were Lewis Freedman, director of programing at Channel 13 and Mrs. Cooney's boss at the time, and Lloyd Morrisett, then vice president of the Carnegie Corporation and now chairman of the newly independent Children's Television Workshop.

"Channel 13 had been having a sensational season," Mrs. Cooney recalled. (Indeed: she won an Emmy in 1966 for a three-hour documentary on the Federal poverty program.) "Lew was saying, 'Television is the new educational tool, whether it's educating now formally or not.' Since Carnegie was in preschool research, something clicked in Lloyd's mind: Why not marry television to preschool education? Within a few weeks he called me and said, 'How would you like to do a study for us on the potential of television in preschool education?'

"I'd never seen a children's show," Mrs. Cooney confessed. "I knew what I knew from McLuhan: kids were watching shows like 'Batman' and 'Get Smart' and they were watching a lot of commercials. I was in television and I'd majored in education at the University of Arizona, but I wasn't in commercial television and I wasn't an educator. But that was what Lloyd wanted: someone in television who could figure it all out for them without any axes to grind on what kind of preschool theory triumphed."

By November, 1966, her report was ready. "Spend a lot of money on this," she recommended. And while Morrisett went after financing, Mrs. Cooney began to look for a staff.

The way to Sesame Street was eventually paved by a two-year grant of $8 million jointly from the Carnegie, Ford and Markle Foundations, Operation Head Start, the Corporation for Public Broadcasting and the U.S. Office of Education. "When the project was announced, I was the only staff," said Joan Cooney. "I had been appointed by the heads of the funding organizations to be the executive director. Within a day or two after the story broke in *The Times*, I got a letter from Michael Dann, senior vice president of C.B.S., whom I had never met. 'You are faced with a very serious problem—whom are you going to select as your executive producer?' he said. 'You are going to make a terrible mistake if you don't go for a guy who has had some experience in volume producing.' "

Dann recommended David D. Connell, who had been executive producer of Robert Keeshan Associates, which produces "Captain Kangaroo." "Kangaroo" is the commercial networks' only daily children's show. While it and "Sesame Street" are both basically entertainment with an informational content, the Captain's quiet conversation and gentle fantasy are oriented toward middle-class kids. Besides, he isn't watched in the slums, because ghetto kids go to bed late and get up after the early-morning "Kangaroo" is over.

"Bob Keeshan deserves all kinds of credit for 'Sesame Street,' " said Mrs. Cooney of the man who is the Captain. "He built extraordinary talent, and although his turnover rate is not high at all, most of the guys who have been very interested in high-quality children's television have passed through his show."

The problem for such men was: "After 'Kangaroo,' what?" As Connell said: "I left 'Kangaroo' because I'd been with the show for 12 years and producing it for 9, and I was at an age and a stage where I thought that if I was going to do something else, I'd better move. But I was discouraged enough about the direction of children's television that I didn't care if I ever did it again."

To produce "Sesame Street," Connell left a vice presidency at Ken Snyder Enterprises, producers of TV, industrial and documentary films, where he did *not* work on children's shows. Then, as the first of a series of reunions of "Kangaroo" veterans, he lured back a writer named Jon Stone who had fled TV for a freelancer's hideout in Vermont.

"Jon Stone has really been the creative spark," said Mrs. Cooney. "He thought through the format, wrote the pilot, and is the head writer now. We were always talking about short segments in various production styles. Jon came up with the idea: 'Why not an inner-city street where these people live and they're neighbors?' "

"It seemed to me that a street in an urban run-down area would give the children we were most interested in reaching a neighborhood to identify with," said Stone, a brown-bearded man with a sense of comedy, an awareness of the possibilities and limitations of the electronic medium and a 38-year-old mind that digs the 3-to-5-year-old mind. "It would be depressing in color scheme, as these streets are, but totally and happily integrated—a street in which the people who live take tremendous pride."

"Initially," said Connell, "we felt we should keep the street very realistic. Initially, it was not a place where fantasy would happen. But we found that when we cut away from the street to a piece of animation, for example, the child's interest went up. Conclusion: we've got to make the street more exciting. So it turned into a street where Oscar can come out of a trash can or Big Bird can come wandering by."

Matt Robinson, for example, who plays Gordon, had been a staff writer, producer and performer for WCAV-TV in Philadelphia. Connell originally hired him as a producer to supervise the making of the live-action films that are dropped into "Sesame Street" as part of the carefully calculated package. Robinson was not to remain a producer long, for Connell was having trouble casting the key role of Gordon. "One day, we asked Matt to read. About two minutes into the first audition, we knew he was the right guy," Connell recalled.

About one minute into any installment of "Sesame Street," viewers know that Connell has the right guy: a big, self-confident man who wears an Afro, a mustache and bushy sideburns, and speaks to children of all colors in a tone that exudes color-blindness. Still, he thinks of himself as a black performer: "Somewhere around 4 or 5," he said, "a black kid is going to learn he's black. He's going to learn that that's positive or negative. What I want to project is a positive image."

"One of our biggest problems," said Joan Cooney, "was naming this street. We had suggestions as square as 'Fun Street' to as hip as '123 Avenue B.' A writer submitted 'Sesame Street.' We got some flack on it. Some people thought the kids would pronounce it 'See Same Street.' But that's because they were linear types thinking of children only reading rather than reading *and hearing.*"

In grading "Sesame Street," which does not, after all, have the captive audience of even the most uninspiring nursery-school teacher, the first yardstick must be: is it being watched by its target audience of preschoolers—from the inner city and rural poverty areas?

A. C. Nielsen has no problem in measuring middle-class viewing: During one week in December, he found 2.2 million homes watching at least part of the show each day. Using rater's formulas for numbers of viewers per set and adding an estimate for the large numbers of group viewers in nursery schools and elsewhere, the Workshop projected a daily viewing audience of between five and six million children. That is still short of the 6.6 million in the age group who watch the major network shows on Saturday morning—designed to teach children to recognize products, rather than letters and numbers.

The viewing habits of the poor, however, are seldom market-researched, though 90 per cent of America's families with incomes under $5,000 have television sets. So, to learn if the poor child was watching, an in-depth study of 500 families in New York's low-income Bedford-Stuyvesant area was conducted for the Workshop last March by the Daniel Yankelovich public-opinion polling firm. Their findings: 90 per cent of the children between the ages of 2 and 5 who spend their days at home rather than in day-care centers or nursery schools watch "Sesame Street." Even more promising, half of the children tune in the set themselves each day without waiting for prompting or help from their elders. The audience in rural poverty areas still hasn't been measured.

Next year, the Workshop will increase its efforts to reach more poor children by waging the kind of promotion and utilization campaigns that it carried out this season in Bedford-Stuyvesant and among the Indians of Alcatraz in 15 or 20 larger cities. The Workshop will be helped, of course, by the self-help of various communities. In New Orleans, this past season, for example, block parties for "Sesame"-watching have been held, with mothers taking turns supervising the children, and the Housing Authority of New Orleans has used its resources to encourage tenants to get preschoolers to take in the show.

But in an area of few expectations in Detroit, a first-grade teacher commented that "Sesame Street" seems irrelevant to the disadvantaged ghetto children. "They have no motivation to watch it, especially at home. Whereas, the black and white, middle-class mothers encourage their children to watch it, the lower-class mother isn't around to encourage it. We tried looking at it in our classroom, but the kids were uninterested. They did enjoy the numbers because they were so fast, but they just didn't want to watch the rest."

Still, the first studies suggest that "Sesame Street" is achieving its limited but quite specific goals. Dr. Palmer gave an example: "When we defined our goals in the seminars, one of them was: 'If a child is shown a rectangle, he can supply its name.' Nothing ambiguous about that. But nothing easy about it, either, if you're 3. I have a nephew who got 'circle,' 'square' and 'triangle'—but instead of 'rectangle,' he said 'refrigerator.' He knew it was some big word that started with an R."

The first impact studies focused on 130 poor children in day-care centers in Tennessee, Long Island and Maine. Half were viewers, half nonviewers; both groups were divided about equally racially. Children who watched "Sesame Street" regularly in its first six weeks made gains two-and-one-half times as great as the gains made by those who did not watch it. One result that Dr. Palmer found dramatic was the learning gains made in letter recognition. The letter W was featured regularly on the early shows through frequent repetition of the 1-minute cartoon spot about Wanda the Witch,[1] Who Walked to the Well one Wednesday in Winter to get Water to Wash her Wig. (If you must know, the Wig was Whipped aWay by a Wild Wind. Moral: Witches Who Wash their Wigs on Windy Winter Wednesdays are Wacky.) Before Wanda and the series got started, one out of four in the viewing group could name the letter. Six weeks later, their numbers had doubled. Yet there was virtually no gain in recognition among the control group of nonviewers. Substantial increases were also noted in the experimental group's ability to solve simple logic, sorting, classification and enumeration problems.

But it is the goals themselves that are challenged by Frank Garfunkel, professor of education at Boston University, who contemptuously refers to "Sesame Street" as "the great palliative."

"If what people want is for children to memorize numbers and letters without regard to their meaning or use . . . without regard to the differences between children, then 'Sesame Street' is truly responsive," Professor Garfunkel wrote to The Boston Globe.

"To give a child 30 seconds of one thing and then to switch it and give him 30 seconds of another," he says, "is to nurture irrelevance and to give reinforcement to a type of intellectual process that can never engage in sustained and developed thought."

Professor Garfunkel's objections were challenged, in turn, by Dr. Gerald S. Lesser, professor of education and developmental psychology at Harvard University, and an adviser to the producers. "Different children learn in different ways and profit from different experiences," Dr. Lesser wrote to the Globe, "and 'Sesame Street' is an effort to provide one option, one alternative that may be useful to some children. We do not intend that this one television series . . . will substitute for all other forms of educational experiences young children need, 'personalized' experiences included. We are providing one small component of what ultimately must become a full range of educational opportunities for all young children."

The use of television techniques to teach continues to gnaw at educators. Carl

[1] Perhaps the best-known of all the "Sesame Street" alphabet "commercials," it was designed and animated by Tee Collins, a native of Harlem and one of the few black animated-cartoonists.

Bereiter, a professor at the Ontario Institute for Studies in Education and an authority on preschool learning, complains that what he has seen of 'Sesame Street' has been too far removed from "structured" teaching. He says that the show has been "based entirely on audience appeal and is not really teaching anything in particular."

Probably the principal objection to the use of television for preschool education, however, is that while the middle-class child will learn the things TV can teach anyway, from a rich environment of books and records and vacations and parental conversations overheard, the ghetto child needs much more than its smattering of cognitive learning. "Mainly to meet the demands of minority group parents," wrote critic Robert Lewis Shayon is the *Saturday Review*, " 'Sesame Street' stressed cognitive learning—the teaching of numbers and letters of the alphabet." Shayon conceded that "early results suggest that minority children do learn from the programs"; still, he is one of those who feel that preschoolers most need the kind of affective learning—learning related to feelings and emotions—that calls for a teacher. "The acquisition of cognitive skills is important," wrote Shayon, "but they are hardly the answer to our society's social and personal ills."

Indeed, it is the fear that "Sesame Street" will become a substitute for "personalized experiences," rather than a supplement to them, that worries educators with long experience in preschool education in the ghetto. "If 'Sesame Street' is the only thing ghetto kids have, I don't think it's going to do much good," said Sister Mary Mel O'Dowd, who drew up the curriculum for Chicago's Archdiocesan Head Start program and now directs the curriculum of Capitol Head Start in Washington, D.C. "It never hurts a child to be able to count to 10 or recognize the letters of the alphabet, but without the guidance of a teacher, he'll be like one of our preschoolers who was able to write 'CAUTION' on the blackboard after seeing it on the back of so many buses, and told me 'That says 'STOP.' "

Significantly, Joan Ganz Cooney is in agreement. "Television is a very poor substitute for a comprehensive preschool development," she said. "All the affective and certain cognitive things are better done by a teacher."

In our racially polarized society, however, one *affective* thing "Sesame Street" can do that many teachers are prevented by circumstances from doing is to show blacks and whites living together in harmony. "Racial equality is being instilled by showing no distinction between races," as Cheri Chamberlain, a fifth-grade teacher in Buffalo Grove, Ill., observed. Or as one mother in New Jersey observed: "When my 4-year-old first started watching 'Sesame Street,' she thought Susan and Gordon were bad people. When asked why, she said, 'They are different from us. Their hair and skin are all funny.' After watching the show for some time, one day she said, 'Mommy, Susan and Gordon are not really funny or bad people. They still have different skin and hair, but now I know them. . . .' "

"The black and white being together—that means a lot," a black Bedford-Stuyvesant mother told a black interviewer. On the other hand, a white, middle-class liberal who has spent a lifetime in television calls the show "a white, middle-class cop-out."

Well, if the show gives in to the temptation to capitalize on its great appeal to the middle class at the expense of the disadvantaged, then it will be a cop-out. But "Sesame Street's" plans for the future don't look that way. For next season, Mrs. Cooney has already promised "new material designed to better reach key ethnic groups, specifically the teaching of English vocabulary to Spanish-speaking children."

A more likely cop-out is that the Federal Government—which provides half of "Sesame Street's" funds, will decide to make the television show a money-saving substitute for Head Start. Mrs. Cooney has anticipated this reaction: "I think the project is going to be attractive to Government officials and Congress because it seems to be cost-effective and an answer to preschool education," she said, "whereas, in my view, it is a project that could help make effective—and enrich—preschool programs. I see its great importance to the inner-city child as a supplement."

President Nixon has written Mrs. Cooney that "the Children's Television Workshop certainly deserves the high praise it has been getting from young and old alike in every corner of the nation. This Administration is enthusiastically commited to opening up opportunities for every youngster, particularly during his first five years of life, and is pleased to be among the sponsors of your distinguished program."

"Sesame Street" alone, of course, will not open up those opportunities. An illustration of why it cannot was in a recent Head Start newsletter in which Oralie McAfee of the New Nursery School at Colorado State College discussed "Using 'Sesame Street' in the Early Childhood Classroom."

"Some things," she wrote, "can really be learned only by doing. . . On television, a concept such as 'round' can be presented only in two dimensions, which really is inadequate. So we would supplement . . . with actual round objects. Eat oranges, grapefruit, and wieners; notice that the clay balls and snakes the children make are round; blow bubbles. . . ."

Making "Sesame Street" a substitute for Head Start would not only be a pennywise cop out, but would bode ill for "Sesame's" future. Head Start was a does-no-wrong darling of the middle-class when it had *its* fad five years ago, and now it is being faulted for failing to outweigh all the defects of life in the ghetto. How much more vulnerable will a television show be to that criticism. Poor kids, like affluent kids, must live in a three-dimensional world, relating to people, not images, and the opportunities that a society offers can't all be on a screen.

Perhaps the best way to evaluate "Sesame Street" at its first season is to consider what it has taught the commercial networks. Before "Sesame Street," the same vice president of daytime programming who worried about whether soap operas were selling soap also worried about whether kids' shows were selling toys and cereal. "The concensus among agencies and executives then was that quality programming for Saturday TV was not commercial," said Jon Stone. "They believed that the kids would tune out. We hope that, what we've proved with this show is that this isn't the case—that kids will watch quality shows and will choose them over sleazy competition. The real gain is that our ratings have shown the networks that quality television is commercially viable."

So now, the eyes of parents who have seen "Sesame Street" are on George Heinemann, vice president of children's programs for NBC; on Allen Ducovny, supervisor of the children's line-up at CBS; on Charles (Chuck) Jones, executive director of children's programing for ABC. If the next commercial season is as wasteful of children's time as this one was, at least there'll be high-salaried executives to blame.

In "The Medium is the Message," Marshall McLuhan reproduced a *New Yorker* cartoon from 1965. It showed a boob watching the tube and commenting to his wife: "When you consider television's awesome power to educate, aren't you thankful that it doesn't?" The kids watched it anyway, of course, and anyway, it does. Just before the first "Sesame Street" program was shown to Head Start children in the Abraham Lincoln Community Center in Harlem, one mother mentioned what TV had already taught her 3-year-old: "He learn the cigarette commercial, the one about you come a long way, baby."

Now we have "Sesame Street," and in New Jersey, recently, a regular viewer—also 3 years old—burst into his parents' bedroom in the middle of the night, shouting and clutching his pillow. His parents woke with a start, thinking: An accident! But the child was shouting: "Mommy, Daddy! My pillow—it's a rectangle!"

We've come a long way, baby.

Education and Industry: Troubled Partnership

ELLIOT CARLSON

After a wave of student violence, the Illinois Bell Telephone Company removed all its personnel from Chicago's Crane High School. The Continental Can Company last fall phased out a much-publicized education course in Harlem after Harlemites, apparently bored by the project, became harder to recruit. And the Insurance Company of North America this school year found itself with no takers when it offered a course on insurance to students in an experimental Philadelphia high school.

These are but a few of the woes afflicting companies that have pitted themselves against the tough problems of urban education. After the summer riots of 1967, many large concerns decided they could no longer stay outside the educa-

From *Saturday Review* (August 15, 1970), 45–47, 58–60.

tional world and participate at a distance—through making financial contributions or hawking educational wares. Instead, they decided to enter the educational arena actively and, at least to some extent, apply the problem-solving techniques of business to vexations that have long plagued educators.

In a little more than two years, some thirty companies "adopted" high schools in about twenty cities; in one case, several companies—including Avco, Ford, Procter and Gamble, and General Electric—adopted the entire school system of Lincoln Heights, Ohio, a predominantly black suburb of Cincinnati. The "partnerships"—a word some executives prefer to avoid the paternalism suggested by "adoption"—usually involve an exchange of commitments between the school and the firm. For the most part, companies agree to provide resources and organize projects that they hope will benefit financially hard-pressed school systems.

Also, dozens of firms have forged programs that go beyond relationships with particular schools. A number of companies have fashioned work-study programs in which students from ghetto high schools spend half their day at school and the other half at jobs, while others have developed work-release policies that permit key employees to work with possible school dropouts in hopes of keeping them in school. A few industrial and commercial concerns have established schools outside the public school system that provide training in basic skills for dropouts and potential dropouts.

There's no doubt that a good many of these partnerships—and/or adoptions—are working out well. General Electric has provided two high schools in Cincinnati with modern washing machines and other equipment, enabling the school for the first time in years to fashion a realistic "appliance technology" course. Michagan Bell Telephone and Chrysler have established more than a dozen programs in two Detroit high schools, ranging from part-time jobs and special vocational courses to remedial tutoring and professional counseling.

For educators traditionally wary of outsiders, such efforts represent a significant departure from the age-old classroom practice. Predictably, some critics have denounced these ventures as public relations gambits; other argue the ventures constitute a new form of white paternalism. And some observers see many of the programs as simply unimpressive in content. They note that the efforts have produced few innovative activities in schools, and that, in some cases, the very notion of partnership has been overestimated.

"Several of the partnerships now a year old report that they have not developed past the announcement stage," a 1969 study of the Institute for Educational Development, a New York-based research group, pointed out. "The act of reaching an agreement to cooperate did not solve the problem of what to do next. For them and for everyone the burden of inventing efficient ways to bring on bona fide improvements in urban institutions will remain heavy and will not be moved easily."

To a considerable degree, woes plaguing companies that tried to develop educational projects in the ghetto resemble those afflicting firms that recently entered the educational arena to make money. In both cases, there were blissful expectations of immediate results. And in both cases, corporate hopes frequently were shattered when the complexities of the educational world proved more baffling than foreseen.

In the mid-1960s, such corporate giants as IBM, Xerox, RCA, CBS, Time, and General Electric plunged into the so-called knowledge industry with a great deal of fanfare. Executives spoke of mobilizing industrial resources and brain power to solve the age-old problems of overloaded and understaffed schoolrooms, and, at the same time, to exploit what was believed to be a $50-billion-a-year education market. But it hasn't worked out that way. Indeed, these ventures have been plagued by management shakeups, scuttled plans, skimpy profits, and, in some cases, prolonged losses.

Critics charge these big companies entered the educational field without knowing what products to sell or how to sell them. Most industry sources now believe these concerns, among other things, misjudged the size of the market. Also, they are said to have overestimated the readiness of schools to adopt new educational techniques and install expensive new machines. Finally, it has been theorized that the big firms simply misjudged the extent to which their national reputations would open educational doors.

Just how badly a company can miscalculate was demonstrated by Raytheon, the big defense contractor that in 1965 acquired a number of education-related firms. Among them were a closed circuit television and language lab manufacturer, a teaching machine outfit, a maker of science equipment, and, finally, D. C. Heath, an old textbook house that was added in 1966. Behind these acquisitions was something called the "systems approach" to the educational market. In effect, the company sought to merge educational materials (software) and fancy educational systems (hardware) into a "fully integrated" marketing approach.

It didn't work. Right off, Raytheon erred by failing to take into account the importance of tradition in the education market. The company took the Heath name off the textbooks, and the upshot was nearly disastrous. The new Raytheon label impressed far fewer educators, and, as a result, the original name was restored. Despite such troubles many industry observers nonetheless were shocked late last year when the firm announced a major retreat from earlier staked-out territory: Raytheon's education subsidiary said it planned to sell its electronic learning systems business and stick exclusively to publishing.

A number of other corporations now readily admit making errors. "The theory was that the future of education is a marriage of software and hardware. The theory is still right, in my estimation, but it's going to be a long time coming," James A. Linen, Time president, last year told *The Wall Street Journal.* Trade sources note that the General Learning Corporation, a Time-General Electric joint enterprise formed in 1965, lost $5-million during its first three years and, in fact, lost money again in 1969 (the venture, however, is expected to show its first profit in 1970). General Learning officials concede that many of the original ideas behind the marriage of GE and Time were wrong. Among them: misconceptions about the level of federal funding and the pace at which the education market would change.

Underpinning many of these ventures has been the assumption that educational problem-solving was somehow compatible with the profit motive. Nowhere was this view more pervasive than at MIND, Inc., a small learning company that CPC International, Inc. (then Corn Products), set up as a wholly owned subsidiary in 1967. Formed to help companies upgrade the skills of low-level employees and to train the hard-core unemployed, MIND seemed to have a bright future. Indeed, for a time it appeared as though the new firm would have no trouble developing and selling innovative education programs, while at the same time returning profits to Corn.

"I think it is significant that MIND is a profit-making business owned by one of our nation's blue-chip corporations. After all, where does one find better problem-solvers than in business," Charles F. Adams, founder and until last year president of MIND, enthused in early 1968. By that time the learning concern already had 130 companies as clients and was negotiating with 200 others. To serve these customers—and find new ones—MIND's staff grew to 150 in seven branch offices scattered across the country. In mid-1968, Adams confidently predicted that the firm's revenues that year would multiply fivefold to $1.5-million from $300,000 in 1967, and would more than triple to about $5-million in 1969.

For its part, Corn seemed enthusiastic about the prospects of its fledgling subsidiary. "Dissemination of knowledge will soon be the largest single effort in our economy, and if a company wants to hook on to the future it has to get out of traditional businesses. One day, Corn Products will have a bigger position in education than in foods," Bennett E. Kline, a Corn vice president, intoned in 1968. This was a staggering prediction for a company whose revenues that year topped $1.1-billion.

But in April of 1969 the balloon burst. Adams suddenly resigned as president of MIND and took with him a number of the firm's key executives, programmers, and salesmen. In fact, the only people left on the job were about a dozen secretaries and bookkeepers. The split-up followed a bitter wrangle between Adams and officers of Corn over how far and how fast MIND was to develop. In the early months of 1969, Adams says his eyes were opened as to the real nature of MIND's relationship with the parent company.

One thing is sure: The MIND experience reveals just how difficult it is for profit-minded giants and education-oriented subsidiaries to prosper under the same corporate umbrella.

"We found that Corn had no plans to make a major financial commitment to develop MIND," growls the thirty-four-year-old Adams, a thinly thatched dynamo who glares owlishly from behind thick-rimmed eyeglasses. "In point of fact, Corn had done no planning on how we might be integrated into their overall marketing strategy and corporate structure."

According to Adams, Corn had neither objectives for MIND nor the willingness to support the subsidiary's officers in their goals (Adams had hopes of turning MIND into a $167-million firm by 1975).

For its part, Corn seems to have become disenchanted with MIND—or at least with its outspoken president. Even though MIND's 1968 sales—just about as predicted—soared 474 per cent to $1.4-million, the company nevertheless continued to lose money. After earlier having projected a profit of $151,000 for 1968, the new firm ended up losing $139,000. Arguing that MIND's operations actually were profitable, Adams says the loss was the result of last-minute expenditures required to expand the sales staff, and thus guarantee even greater growth in 1969. Two other factors apparently conspired against MIND's—or Adams's—ambitions inside Corn. First, Corn's profits had leveled off in the first quarter of 1969, which, according to Adams, reduced its willingness to take risks with capital. Also, Corn named a new chief executive officer, who, reputedly, was less sympathetic to innovative ventures such as MIND.

Whatever the reasons, Adams and Corn parted company with a great deal of bitterness on both sides. The question is raised as to what CPC International's interest was—and continues to be—in maintaining MIND as a subsidiary. Not surprisingly, some "knowledge industry" critics belittle MIND as little more than a gesture that permits Corn to say, "We're doing our part in solving tough social problems." Says Adams: "Corn unquestionably got millions of dollars' worth of publicity out of MIND."

Corn officials reject this view as "absolutely false." Vice President Kline observes simply: "The size of the market didn't warrant the tremendous overhead that had been built up. There were a lot of people on the MIND payroll that just shouldn't have been there." Thus, in the wake of Adams's departure, it was necessary to trim the 150-man staff down to about thirty-five and to reduce branch offices from seven to one, he says. Denying that MIND's woes have alienated clients, Kline notes that the firm now has contracts with about 100 businesses and, at the same time, is solidly in the black. Still, MIND's growth has slowed considerably. According to Kline, MIND's 1969 sales rose no more than 50 per cent, which would have placed them slightly above $2-million—well below the $5-million forecast by Adams in 1968.

How does the MIND program actually work? Put simply, MIND does away with both the classroom and the teacher as educational instruments. In their place are conference tables (around which trainees sit informally) and monitors (nonprofessionals who serve as classroom helpers, but do not provide information). Students learn by hunching over fat basic-education workbooks, and by listening to tapes on earphones plugged into tape machines. Lessons frequently are accompanied by soft music to lull students into a relaxed mood. Theoretically, students are supposed to work at their own speed.

MIND's courses are designed to raise a trainee's math and literacy skills from three to five grade levels to as high as the tenth-grade level in about 160 hours of instruction. Typing courses are designed to train beginners to type forty-five to sixty words a minute after fourteen hours of instruction, and MIND's stenography course is supposed to enable a secretary who can take fifty words of dictation a minute at the start to triple her speed after sixty lessons of fifteen minutes each.

The cost of MIND's basic education course ranges anywhere from $94 per trainee for a class size of seventy students to $562 per trainee for a class size of twelve. Either way, MIND officials maintain their program costs less than the expense of searching for prospective employees who already possess the skills that MIND teaches.

Many big outfits, such as IBM, American Express, Consolidated Edison, Continental Can, and Xerox, have used MIND materials, although with a variety of results. Indeed, the experiences of some of these firms suggest just how hard it is to hit upon the right educational formula for the disadvantaged groups. Generally, companies have been most successful when they haven't felt bound to any particular system.

Beginning its education efforts with a heavy emphasis on the MIND program in 1968, Consolidated Edison dropped this approach early last year, and since that time has turned to more conventional methods. "MIND did some good, but we ended up being unhappy with it," says Bruce Wittmer, Con Ed's director of personnel. The trouble, he notes, was that the tape-recorded materials raised trainees' educational standing only about three-fourths of a grade level after 150 hours—instead of the three to five levels claimed by MIND. "This simply wasn't good enough. They wouldn't have been promotable," he adds.

The problem, according to this executive, lies with both the premises on which MIND is based and some of its newfangled techniques. For one thing, he notes, MIND presupposed that dropouts are in revolt against society and the formal educational system—attitudes that presumably would require a novel kind of educational response. In fact, they are nothing of the kind, according to an extensive Con Ed survey of its trainees. "Most dropouts leave school for personal reasons, such as pregnancy or the need to support their families," says Wittmer. Thus, he observes, conventional methods are perfectly appropriate.

"We found nothing replaces the teacher," says Wittmer. "The MIND people said my secretary could be a monitor. It didn't work."

Consequently, Con Ed hired eight professional teachers who now are teaching more than 300 trainees—"dropouts" from seventeen to twenty-three years of age, and men and women over thirty-five—in basic mathematics and English. These courses are part of a twenty-six-week program consisting of one week of orientation and four weeks of "pre-job" training, nine weeks of educational courses (four hours daily of classes and four hours of skills training), and twelve additional weeks of full-time skills training. At the end of the twenty-six weeks, the trainees will become regular employees of Con Ed.

The New York utility says the program—now in its third year—is working, but not always as smoothly as it would like. One trouble is that normally about 40 per cent of all trainees drop out of the program for one reason or another. Con Ed officials say a 60 per cent retention rate is not all that bad and attribute this modest success to the prospect of employment that spurs most trainees to continue. "The trainee needs something at the end of the rainbow to keep him going," observes Wittmer.

Continental Can, also of New York, learned this lesson the hard way last year when it phased out its highly touted educational course begun in Harlem in 1968. Billed as the first company-sponsored school for basic educational skills in the heart of a city, the venture sought to upgrade the English and arithmetic skills of Harlemites whose educational levels were so low they had little or no chance of finding a decent job. In fact, most of those recruited for the first twelve-week cycle in early 1968 tested at about the fourth-grade level.

At first, the effort seemed to work; forty-five Harlem residents graduated after the first cycle amid a great deal of fanfare. But later the program—administered by MIND, Inc.—faltered and, last fall, was terminated (although Continental says it might resume the effort some time in the future). From the beginning, the venture was plagued by dropouts and recruitment difficulties, which, eventually, became the main headache. MIND monitors would recruit on street corners, in bars, and where people congregated, but fewer and fewer Harlemites seemed interested.

Company spokesmen concede the chief reason for this was that the education course wasn't plugged in to Continental Can's—or any other company's—hiring program. Of 200 graduates from at least one of the four cycles MIND conducted during the two-year period, only twenty-two secured jobs with Continental. The others received neither the guarantee of a job nor job counseling. To be sure, many education course grads by themselves found jobs that normally would have been beyond their reach. Others, however, were disgruntled.

One Harlemite complained: "I thought for sure that if I couldn't get a job with anybody else I could at least get a job with Continental Can. The program didn't even give me that much. I need a job." This young lady also was unhappy that the program didn't give her a chance to take a high school diploma equivalency test, which, she added, "would have helped me with something I need and want."

Just the same, Continental Can officials insist the program was far from worthless. They note that the MIND materials helped trainees raise their academic achievement in arithmetic almost three grade levels and in word meaning almost two grade levels. Nonetheless, Continental Can is, as one official put it, "taking a breather" from its Harlem project. At the same time, the firm is trying to isolate the various factors that contributed to their woes. Spokesmen observe, for example, that trainee motivation was lowered by factors other than the absence of a firm job commitment.

"No stipend was offered trainees, and many of them didn't like meeting in hot buildings that weren't air conditioned," says one unhappy company official.

Occasionally, corporate efforts are beset by woes over which they have little control. A case in point is provided by Illinois Bell, which in 1968 offered its personnel, equipment, and facilities to three Chicago high schools. Under the program, the big utility was to provide teacher aides and substitute typists, bookkeepers, mechanics, and engineers to help fill emergency vacancies at the schools. The venture was slowed several months at the start by a strike that greatly limited Illinois Bell operations. While the program gradually got under way in two schools, it folded early this year at Crane High School in a predominantly black neighborhood. The reason: a wave of student violence. Windows were smashed, fires were set, and, finally, several students tried to carry the principal, James P. Maloney, from the building. While the school's regular teachers were demanding more guards, Illinois Bell decided to pull its staff out of Crane altogether. "Our overriding concern was the fear for the safety of our personnel," said Fred Felton, the company's coordinator for the program. "We haven't given up on Crane. We're just looking for ways to establish a relationship with the place."

Another Illinois Bell official added: "We were in a losing situation from the start. The educational environment was so far gone there that we couldn't contribute a thing. The school was not functioning as a school in the traditional sense. It was just a place where kids gathered."

But even before the disorders some Illinois Bell officials frankly doubted whether their program was correctly shaped to be effective. "Actually, we didn't get much beyond the physical fix-it-up stage. We repaired a few shower heads and mended a couple of broken movie projectors. And we provided a bus for field trips and even gave an award luncheon for the school's athletes. But these were small, meaningless things," admits a spokesman. "We had hoped we might reach a point where we could make a contribution to curriculum—and help ghetto youngsters close the reading gap."

According to Donald E. Barnes, vice president of the Institute for Educational Development, programs often run into trouble when companies are motivated primarily by guilt and a vague desire to do "something for the poor." "The motives and attitudes that go with charity must be avoided," says Barnes. "The result frequently is that executives end up offering something pretty silly and then congratulate themselves for their Christian spirit." Equally dangerous, he notes, is the tendency of some companies to impose programs of their own making on schools, which, he added, resemble organisms that can't easily be tampered with.

For programs to succeed, Barnes suggests observance of a few basic maxims:

1. Executives in charge of programs should have enough authority to make their decisions felt on all corporate levels, even the lowest, where projects often are stymied through lack of follow-up efforts by the men at the top.

2. Executives must develop a tolerance for risk and ambiguity. Frequently, they lapse into a mechanistic view of social change, and think that developing a good educational program is like manufacturing something automatically on an assembly line.

3. Accordingly, officials must reconcile themselves to a certain amount of formlessness that is inherent in schools, and, at the same time, attempt to aid programs that grow naturally out of the school community.

4. Finally, businessmen must get physically inside the school building—and stay there a full school day. "If business is to make a contribution, its men must eat with the faculty and mingle with the students," says Barnes. "This is the only way they can learn the school's problems."

When these maxims are followed, he claims, the results can be impressive. He cites as an example the Economic Development Council of New York City, a group of about eighty-five companies that recently "adopted" two of the city's ghetto high schools: Monroe and Brandeis.

He recalls that recently a Bell Labs systems analyst stationed at Monroe found that excessive manpower and time were devoted to preparing post cards for parents of absent students. But with so many youngsters normally absent (sometimes as many as a third of the student body a day) and with a highly antiquated filing system that kept information dispersed in various cubbyholes, this was slow and tedious work for the handful of people assigned to the task. Indeed, only a fraction of the parents whose children were absent were ever notified of the fact. The Bell Labs expert made a simple suggestion: Install an addressograph machine. This done, Monroe was able to do the job more quickly and efficiently, since with the new machine the school no longer needed a large staff to handle post cards. Thus, Monroe expects to save annually about $18,000–money that now can be diverted to substantive educational programs.

Generally, companies find they're most successful when they emphasize jobs–and job training–over academic content. For instance, Chase Manhattan Bank, in its widely respected training program for the hard-core unemployed, last year found it was meeting some resistance from trainees because of an excessive concern with academic subjects. The program–known as JOB–was formed in late 1967 to train workers who normally wouldn't qualify for employment. Most of the JOB trainees are young, black dropouts who read at the fifth-grade level. The program is open to any young man or woman who can meet the bank's bonding requirements (which exclude felons and narcotics addicts, but not purse-snatchers or former addicts).

Bank officials say the effort to make these individuals into reliable employees is working. But, at the same time, they concede many zigs and zags and blind alleys were followed before the bank hit upon a workable program. At present, JOB trainees get four weeks of full-time study and then spend five months working and studying on alternate weeks. During the program–for which trainees are paid $1.60 an hour–lessons cover mathematics, business fundamentals, reading, and other language skills. Trainees completing the six-month program automatically become full-time Chase employees; at the end of last year, JOB had graduated 255 workers, 128 of whom were still with the bank.

Despite JOB's seeming success, Chase drastically revised the program in mid-1969, because "we found we just weren't doing it right," says Art Humphrey, Jr., JOB's white director. Until that time, JOB was force feeding its trainees heavy doss of black and Spanish culture and other highly abstract offerings. In fact, trainees frequently found themselves sent to museums, Afro-American exhibits, and–to acquire a little white, middle-class culture–plays such as *Hello, Dolly!* A central idea of the effort was to prepare trainees for the high school equivalency test. "This turned out to be impossible," says Humphrey, noting that only about 20 per cent of JOB graduates were found sufficiently prepared to take the test. Also, many trainees became bored and dropped out.

Then Chase finally got around to surveying the trainees themselves. "They told us all this cultural stuff was a waste of time," the official recalls. "Instead, they said they wanted to know about the bank." Not long thereafter Chase shortened the overall program from a year to six months, eliminated many of the "cultural awareness" programs, and even did away with such old academic stand-bys as algebra and English grammar. The program now emphasizes material needed for success inside the bank rather than for passage of a high school equivalency test. "You'll never use algebra in a banking career," explains Humphrey.

And while trainees still grapple with academic material, they do so in a way that is constantly related to a prospective job inside the bank. For example, trainees learn world geography for use in the bank's international department. "We don't teach geography with maps," notes Humphrey. "We teach it by having students think of the world in terms of zones where the bank does business. This way they learn, say, that Cairo is in the Middle East." Also, trainees still must learn communication skills, although no longer must they wrestle with conjugations and other technicalities of grammar. Instead, they learn bank terminology; for instance, they learn that a "platform" isn't a raised area, but simply a designated space for certain bank officials.

Humphrey vigorously denies the charge some critics have made that JOB's orientation makes trainees useful only for Chase Manhattan Bank, thereby limiting their job mobility. For one thing, he notes that JOB's dropout rate has declined to 20 per cent from 35 per cent as a result of the change. "You don't improve a person's position in the job market by giving him six months of book learning," claims the official. "What makes him mobile is the experience he acquires. We think we help him by giving him what he immediately needs for success."

Other firms have made similar discoveries. In Detroit, both Chrysler and Michigan Bell Telephone have established at two different high schools mock employment centers that test, interview, and tell students where they are weak. In the sessions, youngsters study application forms and learn certain techniques of job interviewing, grooming, employment testing, deportment, and other factors essential to entrance into the job world.

Unhappily, companies have made much less progress reshaping curriculums and developing education innovations. To be sure, some modest contributions have been made. Detroit's Northwestern High beefed up its shorthand program after a number of its graduates did poorly on Chrysler's entry-level tests. Michigan Bell each summer sponsors a six-week remedial program for underachieving students from Northern High that, among other things, uses games, painting, photography, and moviemaking to teach math, English, and science courses.

Companies most often are successful when they stick to their own areas of expertise. A notable case in point is General Electric's appliance technology curriculum, developed for use in Cincinnati public schools. Begun in Courter Technical and Withrow high schools, the program includes a closed-circuit television system, instructional material, and appliances supplied at a substantial discount by GE. The company also provided an initial $10,000 grant in 1968 to get the program going.

Now in its third year, the venture seeks to train appliance repairmen for placement at graduation in GE and other corporate service centers across the country. Aim of the effort is twofold: develop competent repairmen, and change the image of the appliance repair profession. To do this, GE shaped the program in a way that would have been impossible without its presence. First, it encouraged students at the two schools to wear ties "so they would resemble what technicians look like after employment," says Warren G. Rhodes, a GE educational consultant.

More important, GE yanked out of the two schools all the obsolete equipment—such as twenty-year-old Bendix washing machines mounted on concrete blocks—on which students previously tried to learn this technical craft. In place of the old machines, GE installed sparkling new washers complete with solid-state wiring and transistorized controls. "The old appliances were unrepairable," recalls Rhodes. "It was like trying to train auto mechanics for today's cars on Model Ts."

With the gleaming new equipment, youngsters are flocking to the course and the dropout rate has dipped (GE doesn't guarantee employment to students, but it does have first crack at the brighter ones). In fact, GE feels this particular curriculum is working so well it may attempt to have it installed elsewhere.

Granted, companies aren't always successful when they seek to base educational efforts on their own products or business activities. One failure occurred last fall when the Insurance Company of North America offered a course in insurance to high school students in Philadelphia's new experimental Parkway Program. The program is unique in that students do not attend set classes in a regular school building but, instead, show up for courses held in a variety of downtown institutions. The students wander around town on their way to courses of their choice (selected from a catalogue similar to the type college students use).

Competing with courses on protest literature, adolescent psychology, and various off-beat subjects, INA offered a course on the workings of the insurance industry. But on opening day not a single student showed up for it. "Most teen-agers just don't give a damn about insurance," one official plaintively put it.

But from such experiences executives are gradually learning what makes for a workable program: commitment at the top that makes itself felt throughout the company, appointment to the school of full-time company representatives who can learn the school's problems from the inside, willingness to tolerate experiments and programs that may seem formless to the executive eye, and, perhaps most important of all, a disposition to link educational efforts with job opportunities or job counseling.

At this point, it is too early to tell whether businessmen will overcome the difficulties they have encountered and make a permanent contribution to the nation's school systems. Equally uncertain is whether executives will be any more successful developing education as a lush market for new and fancy products. Some are frankly doubtful. "Big business seems unable to change old habits of mind," snorts Charles Adams, founder of MIND. "They insist on looking at the education market the same way as they would look at, say, the peanut butter market. They're trying to force feed the schools the things they know how to produce. You can neither solve human problems nor develop this particular market in this way."

Meantime, even some big outfits remain unflinching in the face of troubles that have plagued other concerns in the educational arena. The other day, RCA was hired by the Camden, New Jersey, Board of Education as the prime contractor in a joint effort to reform Camden's entire public school system.

Whatever the outcome of this and other ventures, it is clear that the traditional relationship between businessmen and schools is changing. No longer do executives think it is sufficient merely to provide jobs for students; they're beginning to realize they must take an active role in working with schools to help develop this manpower resource. Yet, it is also clear this is turning out to be a much tougher task than expected.